The House of Gordon

Aberdeen University
Studies : No. 8

The House of Gordon

UNIVERSITY OF ABERDEEN.

COMMITTEE ON PUBLICATIONS.

Convener. Professor JAMES W. H. TRAIL, M.A, M D, F.R S, Curator of the University Library

UNIVERSITY STUDIES.

General Editor PETER JOHN ANDERSON, M A, LL.B., Librarian to the University

No 1.—*Roll of Alumni in Arts of the University and King's College of Aberdeen*, 1596-1860. Edited by P. J. Anderson. 1900

No 2.—*The Records of Old Aberdeen*, 1157-1891 Edited by Alexander Macdonald Munro, F.S A. Scot. Vol. I. 1900.

No. 3 —*Place Names of West Aberdeenshire* By the late James Macdonald, F S.A. Scot. 1900.

No 4 —*The Family of Burnett of Leys*. By the late George Burnett, LL D, Lyon King of Arms 1901.

No. 5.—*The Records of Invercauld*, 1547-1828. Edited by the Rev John Grant Michie, M.A. 1901.

No 6 —*Rectorial Addresses delivered in the Universities of Aberdeen*, 1835-1900 Edited by P. J. Anderson. 1902

No. 7.—*The Albemarle Papers*, 1746-48 Edited by Charles Sanford Terry, M.A., Professor of History in the University 1902

No 8 —*The House of Gordon*. Edited by John Malcolm Bulloch, M A Vol I. 1903

No. 9.—*The Records of Elgin* Compiled by William Cramond, LL.D Vol. I 1903.

No. 10.—*The Records of the Sheriff Court of Aberdeenshire*. Edited by David Littlejohn, LL.D. Vol. I (*In the press.*)

Photogravure by T & R Annan & Sons Glasgow.

Abergeldie Castle from the North.

The House of Gordon

Edited by
John Malcolm Bulloch, M.A.

Volume I

Aberdeen
Printed for the University
1903

The House of Gordon

Edited by

John Malcolm Bulloch, M.A.

Volume I.

Aberdeen

Printed for the University

1903

THE ABERDEEN UNIVERSITY PRESS LIMITED

CONTENTS.

b

BALLADE OF THE GAY GORDONS

In distant days of Border Raid,
    Ere Scot was Scot, and foe was foe,
'Twas hard to tell the hostile blade,
    And harder still it was to know
    For whom to strike the battle blow—
The kindly keep, the adverse moat,
    Yet, even then, in weal or woe
The Gordons had the guidin' o't.

They fought and fell in sun and shade;
    The battle sometimes brought them low,
Yet never were their sons afraid
    To face the risks of overthrow
    The slogan rang from hearts aglow
With courage 'neath the mailéd coat
    With "Bydand!" cry and bended bow
The Gordons had the guidin' o't

The March was mastered by their aid,
    And proudly did the king bestow
The mighty track of glen and glade
    Athwart the Grampians' line of snow.
    And since the days of Long-Ago,
Where'er they've stood, where'er they've smote,
    The stories of their prowess show
The Gordons had the guidin' o't.

Envoy.

Cock of the North! To you we owe
    The hearts which, at your slogan note,
Are fain to prove, by veldt and voe,
    The Gordons hae the guidin' o't.

        —J M B.

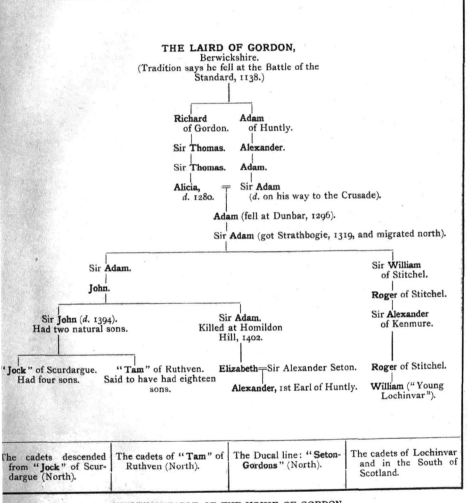

SKELETON TABLE OF THE HOUSE OF GORDON.

John Gordon, grandson of Sir

Sir John (*d.* 1394), had two natural sons.

"**Jock**" of Scurdargue (Rhynie).

Alexander, *Hence*	John, *Hence*		William, *Hence*		James, *Hence*
Ardbroylach.	Achanachie.	Farskane.	Ardmeallie.	Darley.	Auchleuchries.
Arradoul.	Artloch.	Fechil.	Auchintoul.	Dilspro.	Balmuir.
Auchenhuif.	Auchmull.	Glenbucket.	Auchline.	Dorlaithers.	Bonnyton (Ayr).
Buckie.	Auchoynany.	Gollachie.	Auchmenzie.	Drumbulg.	Braco.
Cairnfield.	Avochie.	Hilton.	Badinscoth.	Drymes.	Fetterletter.
Cracullie.	Bad.	Invermarkie.	Balmad.	Fernachty.	Haddo.
Deskie.	Balbithan.	Kindrocht.	Banchory.	Fulziemont.	Earl of Aberdeen. }
Drumin.	Botarie.	Kinmundy.	Barnes.	Johnsleys.	Lord Stanmore. }
Glengarrock.	Cairnburrow.	Lungar.	Birkenburn.	Kincraigie.	Methlick.
Inverharrach.	Cairnwhelp.	Park.	Blelack.	Kinnoir.	Nethermuir.
Knawen.	Carnousie.	Pitlurg.	Bogardie.	Knock.	Savoch.
Knockespock.	Drumhead.	Rothiemay.	Bourtie.	Law.	Scotstown }
Minmore.	Drumwhindle.	Soccoth.	Buthlaw.	Leicheston.	(in Renfrew). }
Netherbuckie.	Edinglassie.	Straloch.	Cairness.	Lesmoir.	Sheelagreen.
Prony.		Techmuirie.	Coclarachie.	Manar.	Tillytelt.
Tulloch.			Coldstone.	Merdrum.	
Wellheads.			Collithie.	Newton.	
			Coynachie.	Oxhill.	
			Cracullie.	Terpersie.	
			Craig.	Tilliechowdie.	
			Crichie.	Tillyangus.	
			Culdrain.	Wardhouse.	

The cadets of "**Jock**" of Scurdargue.

TENTATIVE TABLE SHOWING THE CHIEF BRANCHES

The descendants of the brothers "Jock" and "Tam" and of their

Adam, who got Strathbogie.

Sir Adam (killed 1402).

Elizabeth=Alexander Seton.

Alexander, 1st Earl of Huntly.

"Tam," of Ruthven,
Hence

Ardmillan.
Auchinreath.
Auchinstink.
Balveny.
Bochrom.
Braickley.
Clunymore.
Contlie.
Daach.
Hallhead.
Kennertie.
Kethocksmills.
Kinernie.
Noth.
Pethnick.
Pitglassie.
Sauchen.

George, 2nd Earl.

Alexander, 3rd Earl,
Hence
Marquis of Huntly.
Duke of Richmond.
Earl of Sutherland.
Auchindown.
Auchdregny.
Birsemoir.
Cluny.
Cotton.
Croughly.
Delmore.
Dunkinty.
Gartay.
Gordonstoun.
Pittendreich.
Ruthven.
Tombae.

William,
Hence
Ardlogie.
Gight.

Lord Byron.

James,
Hence
Chappelton.
Coffurach.
Cromellat.
Corridoun.
Letterfurie.
Myrieton.
Orkney.

Alexander,
Hence
Abergeldie.
Birkhall.
Craibstone.
Grandholm.
Haffield.

Adam,
Hence
Backies.
Beldornie.
Drummoy.
Golspitur.
Sidderay.
Wardhouse.

"Tam's" cadets.

The Seton-Gordons.

OF THE GORDONS IN THE NORTH OF SCOTLAND.

(legitimate) cousin, Elizabeth, who married Alexander Seton.

Sir **Adam Gordon**, got the lands of Strathbogie, 1319.

Sir **Adam**,
Ancestor of the Gordons in the
North of Scotland.

Sir **William**,
Ancestor of the Gordons in the
South of Scotland.

Roger of Stitchel.

Alexander of Stitchel.

Roger of Stitchel.

William of Stitchel and Lochinvar.
(The famous "Young Lochinvar".)

Sir John, *Hence*	Alexander, *Hence*	George, *Hence*	Roger, *Hence*
Balmaghie.	Airds.	Troquhain.	Crogo.
Barnbarroch.	Auchendolly.		
Buittle.	Auchenreoch.		
Craichlaw.	Bar.		
Culvennan.	Barharrow.		
Gelston.	Barnhead.		
Glenluce.	Bristol.		
Grange.	Burnshaw.		
Greenlaw.	Campbellton.		
Holm.	Carleton.		
Kenmure.	Colquha.		
Lochinvar.	Cullindoch.		
Muirford.	Earlston.		
Penynghame.	Hallheath.		
	Kilsture.		
	Kirkconnel.		
	Whytpark.		
	Wincombe Park.		

TENTATIVE TABLE OF THE GORDONS IN THE SOUTH OF SCOTLAND, NOTABLY THOSE OF
LOCHINVAR.

This table has been compiled chiefly from the Earlston MS. Most of the Gordons in Ireland and (*via* Ireland)
in America are descended from the various branches of the family in the South of Scotland.

THE PURPOSE AND THE METHODS OF THIS BOOK.

You may remember the tragedy—common-place enough, no doubt, and yet so true—of Mr. Henry James's poignant little story, *The Madonna of the Future*. It tells of an artist who became possessed of a great desire to paint a picture of the Virgin which should be an epitome of the representations of all the ages and all the schools of thought and of art. For years he accumulated materials by ransacking the galleries of the world. He knew the Raphaels and the Rubenses by heart. He had sketches of Giotto and Titian: memories of Moroni and Murillo: notes on Dürer and the Dutchmen. But he never painted his Madonna: and when he died posterity discovered that his great canvas was nothing but a paralysed daub. The moral of that story is the inspiration of this book.

The endeavour to paint the picture of the House of Gordon has been extremely disappointing. It began in the middle of the sixteenth century when the Piedmontese monk, John Ferrerius, confronted the task. He was followed by a long line of patient workers; but the sum total of their labour bears no sort of proportion to the time spent upon it. Delay has increased the difficulty of the subject · the difficulty has made the desideratum seem all the greater: and the desideratum has set up a standard of definitiveness, which has resulted, to use Olive Schreiner's phrase, in " a striving and striving and ending in nothing ". The desire to compass the task, however it has arisen, has always been strong : and makes it unnecessary for me to apologise for the present attempt to trace the history of the House throughout its numerous branches. I could become as cynical as anybody on the "waste" of labour involved in such an endeavour : and I could show cause why it need not be undertaken But such a criticism would be wholly superficial, for the "waste" of labour is not inherent in the desideratum ; it is merely incident to the methods by which realisation has been pursued for more than four centuries. In short, if any apology were necessary, it would be not for the work undertaken, but for the work not undertaken, or rather not published ; for therein lies the crux of the whole matter.

Premising then for the moment the immense fascination of the subject, we have to attribute the failure to do anything worthy of the name of a survey to the bogey of definitiveness, which by its very desirability has by a curious irony defeated itself, and resulted in a perpetual (and pathetic) pother. In speaking thus, I am far from belittling the industry of the many workers who have devoted so much time to the subject : but I can find no other phrase to describe the endless going over of the same ground, which manuscript after manuscript demonstrates in a melancholy way. Let me explain how the enthusiasm of the worker and the timidity of the publisher have operated against the progress of the task

Few men have had the temerity to propose a survey of the whole House, as their starting point The worker has almost invariably begun on a particular branch of the family , and, even at that, each enthusiast has had to begin, in the absence of the printed results of his predecessors' labours, not where they left off, but almost exactly where they started. Fascinated by the interesting side issues of his quest, he has hesitated on the brink of the completed monograph, and has gone on accumulating material, first on the environs of the particular sept on which he began, then on the wider issues of a leading line, and lastly he has become possessed of the desire to tackle the whole subject. An examination of the manuscript collections of several workers has borne out this theory of the elusiveness of the subject, and I may be permitted to support it by my own experience, which is quite typical.

Always fascinated by the Gordons—as a mere boy I helped my father to accumulate much material for his *Historic Scenes in Aberdeenshire* at a time when greater attention to " versions" might have been more to the point—I became thoroughly interested in the subject again in the summer of 1897 when the Byron revival began to attract notice. This resulted in the compilation of a rough (and incorrect) chart of the " Ennobled Gordons and Lord Byron" (*Scottish Notes and Queries*, Oct., 1897), prepared with the view of tracing the poet's wayward- ness. The necessity of having to summarise the history of the Duke of Fife's fortunate family and the achievements of the Gordon Highlanders (*apropos* of their famous exploit at Dargai) led me further afield ; and before I knew where I was I found myself in possession of a great mass of collateral informa- tion, much of which had never been co-ordinated into readable form. The picturesque possibilities of the subject very soon became apparent, and, though many of these had been exploited, a great number had not been touched upon. There was, for example, the alliance of Lady Catherine Gordon with the Polish statesman and poet, Count Andreas Morsztyn, by whom she became the ancestor of Stanislas Poniatowski, the last King of Poland　There were the achievements of Colonel John Gordon of the Gight family, who was partly responsible for the assassina- tion of Wallenstein in 1634. the Jacobite intrigues with Admiral Thomas Gordon, governor of Kronstadt · the escapade of young

Gordon of Wardhouse, who lost his head as a spy at Brest in 1769; the crazy abduction of Mrs. Lee, De Quincey's "female infidel," by the two young Aboyne Gordons; the elopement of Lord William Gordon, brother of the Rioter, with the charming Lady Sarah Lennox; and so on. My point is this, that but for the inducement of being able to publish (in newspaper form) the result of my inquiries, I might have gone on, like so many of my predecessors, accumulating material for years, in the hope of one day being able to write a history of the House more or less definitive; until I should have been too tired, or too paralysed by the vastness of the subject, to put anything on printed record at all.

This is precisely what has occurred to so many workers in the same field. They have been immensely industrious · some of them have even been methodical · and most of them have collected much material, which would have been of great service to their successors if it had been printed. But how was that to be done, when the desire for a definitive work always loomed large before them, and when there was no fair chance of publishing the piecemeal effort; for the commercial publisher has offered no inducement, and the antiquarian clubs have either tabooed the partial contribution or fought shy of a project which seemed to have no beginning and less of an end? What has happened? The enthusiast has passed away without being able to publish the results of his labour, without giving the next worker the chance of knowing what has been done, what might be taken as finished, and what line he might pursue to most advantage. Sometimes the very existence of the enthusiast has been forgotten and the benefit of his labour lost. His papers have been carefully guarded by his representatives for sentimental—and sometimes dog-in-the manger—reasons; or else they have been ignorantly consigned to the paper mill by executors who knew nothing, and cared less, about the matter.   In very few cases have collections such as these found their way into libraries available to the public.   Even if they had, it will be found all too frequently that the material so laboriously gathered is in such a state of confusion that none but the original compiler could provide a key to it, for the worker with the best intentions in the world who has no hope of publishing his discoveries ceases to have a care for their manipulation by posterity.

One of the most remarkable cases in proof of the point is the so-called *Balbithan MS.*, which forms the first item in the present volume.   Here is a document of unique interest ; a guide of first-rate value and validity, which covers ground traversed by no other work.   And yet, notwithstanding the fact that it has been in existence for possibly two hundred years, the student has had to wait until now for the opportunity of seeing it in print. Meantime, the MS. has been copied by several workers ; these copies, in turn, have been re-copied ; and in the process endless errors have crept in, vitiating more than one printed deduction. The extraordinary neglect of the materials for a history of the House is further illustrated in the case of Sir Robert Gordon's *Genealogical History of the Earldom of Sutherland*   Written in 1630, it was not put into type until 1813, and then less as a genealogical venture than as a matter of personal pride on the part of the Marchioness of Stafford, the last of the long line of Gordons who had borne the name of Sutherland.   Sir William Fraser justly contrasted the attention which had been paid to Hume's *History of the Douglases*, written about the same time (1644) and published in 1743.

It might be argued with some show of reason that the earlier publication of material on the House of Douglas has been the cause of the more thorough investigation of the history of that family.   Accepting this explanation, one is confronted with the

fact that the published accounts of the House of Gordon are very
inadequate and disappointing.   I do not forget that seventeen
years before Hume's book on the Douglases there had appeared
the *History of the Antient and Illustrious Family of Gordon* by
William Gordon ; but it is really a history of Scotland told in
terms of the ennobled Gordons   Even at that, however, it might
have been followed up by further inquiries.   Yet how was this
done?   In 1754 a Charles Gordon (whose origin is uncertain)
issued a *Concise History* of the House, which is more or less
a condensation of William Gordon's two volumes, and even the
reprint of 1890 contained little more than can be found in a good
modern peerage.   In fact, the first real contribution to the history
of the House was the publication of Sir Robert Gordon's great
work in 1813.   Excepting Sir William Fraser's *Sutherland Book*
(1892), which was an expansion, based on charter chests, of Sir
Robert's monograph, nothing of first-rate quality was done until
1894, when the *Records of Aboyne*, edited by the present Marquis
of Huntly, was issued by the New Spalding Club
     In the intervening eighty years we had various efforts to ex-
tend our knowledge of the subject, but nearly all of them were
spasmodic and incidental.   The publications of the old Spalding
Club (1841-71) form an invaluable quarry of facts ; but the Club,
with all its enthusiasm, shirked the task of compiling a special work
on the subject   It discussed the matter at its initial meeting in the
year 1839, and Mr. Murray Rose informs me that he has seen a
letter in which Cosmo Innes referred to an elaborate history of the
cadets of the House upon which a friend was engaged.   Transcripts were made of all available Gordon charters; but the scheme,
if ever formulated, fell through, and the material seems to have
been used up in various issues of the Club.   With such a start,
however, as the publications of the Club afforded, some one, it
might have been supposed, would have taken up at least one line

of cadets.   What has been the result?   Just three monographs
—two on the Gordons of Lesmoir and Terpersie by Captain
Wimberley, and a pamphlet on the Gordons of Croughly by the
late Captain Huntly Blair Gordon   It is somewhat remarkable
that both these compilers were partly of English parentage.
Each of these books, however, is mainly sectional, and even
at that is by no means exhaustive.   In any case, they form
no part of a scheme to deal with the whole family, root and
branch, and therefore they represent a vast mass of duplicated
labour.   Some of that labour might have been profitably ex-
pended on other branches of the family, for it has to be noted
that none of the printed histories touches that important branch
of the Gordons who elected to remain on the Borders when the
great exodus to the north took place.   Not only so, but
most of the printed histories deal with the main line represented by the Marquis of Huntly and the Duke of Richmond
and their cadets. The other branches which spring from "Jock"
and "Tam" Gordon have been so much neglected that even
Lord Aberdeen's family has gone without a chronicler.

Disappointing as the direct work on the House of Gordon
has been since the year when William Gordon issued his verbose
history, there has been an increasing interest in topography
and genealogy in general.   We have had histories of nearly all
the great Aberdeenshire families—the Frasers, the Farquharsons,
the Forbeses (very incompletely), the Skenes, the Bairds, the
Burnetts, the Leslies, the Lumsdens, the Cadenheads, and so on
The contributions to topographical literature have even been
greater, and have reached the general reader in a popular
County Series (Blackwoods')   Kirk Session, Municipal and University records have been ransacked, and though there has been
a strong disinclination to co-ordinate the matter thus unearthed,
there is scarcely a parish that has not had its chronicler   Most

important of all is the splendid series of records, such as the Registers of the Privy Council, and of the Great Seal, published officially during the last twenty years, which make it unnecessary for the worker to spend money on having the Register House ransacked for his special benefit. True, there are sources of information, notably the treasures in the Aberdeen Town House and Sheriff Court House, which have been imperfectly tapped : but if we are to wait until that is done thoroughly, we shall be as far from tackling the subject as ever.

A cursory glance at the materials I have enumerated will soon convince the student that the ground to be covered is enormous. For instance, a searching inquiry into the history of one branch alone, the Gordons of Lesmoir, who were descended from " Jock" Gordon of Scurdargue, discloses the fact that they produced some thirty distinct branches, holding different estates in as many parishes scattered over five counties. In the entire survey of land-owning families bearing the name of Gordon, we have hundreds of families, the cadets descending from " Jock " of Scurdargue alone running into a hundred families.

It ought to be noted here that in making this calculation I have not attempted to trace the family further back than their appearance in Scotland : and even then, their beginnings are very doubtful. For instance, the most recent critic of the origin of the Gordons, Mr. George S. C. Swinton, suggests (*Genealogist*, New Series, vol. xv.) that they were originally Swintons, and he places the traditional brothers, Richard and Adam, thus :—

Ernald or Hernulf of Swinton and of Aldcambus.

Cospatrick de Swinton	Richard de Swinton	Adam
(master of the Swinton family)	(afterwards de Gordon ?)	(de Gordon ?)

Writing in *Notes and Queries* (March 29, 1902) he asks :—

Can any human being named Gordon or de Gordun be dated in Scotland before 1200 ? That is the approximate date which, by comparing the witnesses with other dated charters, I give to charter cxvii. in Raine's *North Durham* in which Richard de Gordun and Adam de Gordun, the traditional brothers, made what is, I believe, their first appearance. Any way, this charter cannot be earlier than 1182, in which year its grantor, Patrick Earl of Dunbar, great-grandson of the above-mentioned Cospatrick, succeeded.

Putting all other questions aside, we come to the solid fact that a Sir Adam Gordon got Strathbogie in 1319, and migrated from the Borders northwards   Thus the family split into two great halves.   Sir Adam's eldest son, Adam, got the estates in the north; and his descendants, mostly located in the counties of Aberdeen, Banff, Moray and Sutherland, represent the senior line.   Adam's second son, William, retained the family holdings in the south of Scotland.

Another great division then occurred among the Gordons in the north.   Sir Adam (of 1319) had two great-grandsons, John and Adam.   John had two natural sons, the traditional " Jock " of Scurdargue and " Tam " of Ruthven.   Adam, their uncle, had an only daughter, Elizabeth, who went to the south for a husband, Alexander Seton, and thus reinforced the northern strain with the old Border blood.   She founded the so-called " Seton-Gordons," represented mainly by the ducal line.   But the great majority of the cadets in the north are descended from " Jock " and " Tam," who represent the senior line in its genealogical purity.

The Gordons in the south of Scotland are believed to be descended from William, second son of Adam of 1319.   Their history, as I have pointed out, has been followed with much less minuteness than that of the family in the north ; but enough is known to show that the southern cadets number many hundreds. They are particularly interesting as the ancestors of the Gordons in Ireland and of most of the old Gordon families in America (notably Virginia), who come of Scoto-Irish stock

The wide distribution and the fascination of the House of
Gordon is not a mere theory put forward by the enthusiastic
genealogist.   A very curious example of the belief in the
ubiquity of the race is afforded by Mr. Stead's never-ending
story, " To be Continued in our Next," which was begun in the
Review of Reviews, January, 1903.   The story is a statement of
the news of the day told in terms of fiction .—

> We take the chief events of the month and use them as
> the central incident of a series of short stories, each of
> which . is linked on to all its predecessors and
> those which will come after it by its bearing upon the
> fortunes of the *Gordon family, whose widely scattered
> members are at the heart of most human affairs in all
> parts of the world.*

If this journalistic exaggeration is not quite valid, the
task of tracing the fortunes of the House is so great that the
individual worker, trammelled by the desire for definitiveness,
can make no progress   For this reason the New Spalding Club
has resolved to tackle the subject in a piecemeal way by issuing
monographs on different cadets without reference, for the present, to a general scheme for a history of the family   This book,
while aiming ultimately at definitiveness, starts primarily in the
interests of the monograph   The issue of several of these monographs under one cover, as in the present instance, is mainly
accidental.   The collected form has been adopted here as an
earnest, an advertisement if you will, of the desire of the New
Spalding Club to undertake a task which is so great a desideratum for all genealogists and topographical students   But the
essential characteristics of the monograph are preserved, most
notably in the separate pagination of the account of each family,
so that those who wish to bind them up in their ultimate sequence
may be able to do so.   Indeed, it was the original intention to issue

the monographs separately from time to time as occasion offered;
and once the old manuscript accounts of the family, hitherto unpub-
lished, are printed off this will be done, for it is of the utmost
importance to put into type as much matter as has been prepared.
The idea of the Club has been to make a start, to do something to
place ascertained facts on record ; and to this end the monographs
that were actually ready have been printed.   There has been no
attempt to begin with any branch on the ground of its seniority.
But it may be said that the Gordons of the direct line have been
purposely passed over for the present, for they have been done
over and over again ; not exhaustively, it is true, but with
sufficient clearness to offer an accurate idea of their development.   What has hitherto been neglected are the descendants
of the other great line of the Gordons in the north, the descendants of " Jock " and " Tam ", while the smaller cadets on both
sides have been scamped, although the mere fact that their
poverty made men of them by driving them abroad—as, for
instance, the Russian General, Patrick Gordon of Auchleuchries
—gives them an interest reaching far beyond the confines of
their paternal acres.

But if the selection of the families to be dealt with has been
to this extent haphazard, the method of dealing with them will
be found to be more or less on a definite plan.   The method employed is that of the undisguised chronological compilation of
actual facts, set forth without comment.   Each entry opens with
the year, the month and the day, and closes with the citation of
the authority.   For the most part there has been no attempt
to "run on" the matter thus brought together, for nothing
is so irritating in genealogical books as the method of
"setting" them as if they were connected narratives, whereas
in the great majority of cases they are merely chronological
compilations, with unavoidable *lacunae*, which make a narra-

tive almost impossible. In a few cases, such as that of Colonel
John Gordon, of Wallenstein notoriety, it has been possible
to cast the known facts into something like the shape of a
story, but the general method is chronological. It need hardly
be said that if, in the present state of our knowledge, we cannot
write a story, the construction of a history, in any sense worth
speaking of, is still more remote, because it is essentially a definitive process; and definitiveness, as I have argued, cannot be
aimed at in the present state of our knowledge In any case,
the book suitable for the man who runs and reads—and several
such could be written about the sensational adventures of the
Gordons—is quite beyond the scope of an organisation like the
New Spalding Club, the duty of which, I take it, is to supply a
quarry rather than create a structure.

The plan, then, has been to take the laird, or at any rate
the senior representative (for the time being) of each cadet, as a
unit. After a very brief introduction and summary of his position, his career is built up in a series of extracts (chronologically
arranged), compiled from all sorts of sources. Furthermore,
these extracts have been printed in smaller type, as an indication
that the busy reader may conveniently skip them if he so choose.
By means of the chronological introduction of each paragraph
the reader can discover at a glance whether certain facts which
he may have come across are stated. At the close of these
extracts, the facts about the "unit's" marriage are given, and
these are followed by an account of his children and their descendants set out in the orthodox genealogical manner. His
children are indicated by Arabic figures and one indent. his
grandchildren by Arabics - within - brackets and two indents .
his great-grandchildren by Roman figures · and so · on as
follows .—

1.
2. } the Children of the unit.
3.

(1)
(2) } the Grandchildren of the unit
(3)

i.
ii. } the Great-grandchildren of the unit
iii.

(i)
(ii) } the Great-great-grandchildren of the unit.
(iii)

The surname of descendants has not been given except in cases where it is something other than " Gordon ".

The families treated in this volume illustrate some of the leading characteristics that have made the name of Gordon famous all over the world   The House of Abergeldie, always strong territorially, and still powerful in the regions of its ancestors of four centuries ago, gave the world an intrepid soldier in the person of Sir Charles Gordon, who, in his thirst for adventure, showed the Prussians how to beat the Dutch at Amstelveen, in 1787 : while his brother, William, distinguished himself at the capture of Martinique and endeared himself to the people of Barbadoes.   The Gordons of Coclarachie were the ancestors of Major-General Alexander Gordon of Auchintoul, who began his career in the army of Peter the Great, and put his experience to such use as a Jacobite leader.   The Gordons of Gight, the most unruly family that ever reigned in Aberdeenshire, produced the man who checkmated Wallenstein, and gave us the brilliant Colonel Nathaniel Gordon, of anti-Covenanting fame . while they are known universally as the maternal ancestors of Byron, who displayed so many of their lawless characteristics throughout his life.

In addition to these monographs, the volume contains some very valuable repositories of facts in general about the Gordons. First and foremost is the unique *Balbithan MS.*, which is printed for the first time. It affords the most minute account of the descendants of " Jock " and " Tam " Gordon, and forms a most appropriate set off to a volume which starts with cadets and not with main lines   The index to Gordons in the Retours and the Services of Heirs supplies another want, for though the volumes are to be found in most public libraries they are indexed in a very puzzling way, and are not always available to the genealogist who is beyond the reach of libraries.   Then there is an index to the invaluable *Poll Book of Aberdeenshire*, which was compiled in 1696 and printed, with a most inadequate index, in 1844.   The other indexes tap various sources of information, and should prove of assistance in identifying members of the House.

This opening volume is far from exhausting the material which has already been brought together.   The present writer alone has ready for the printer monographs on the Gordons of Pitlurg, Cairnburrow, Park, Glenbucket, Auchleuchries, Knockespock, Rothiemay and the minor septs attaching to the same.   He has compiled an alphabetically arranged list of Gordons who distinguished themselves in every conceivable activity, in every part of the world, but whom he is at present unable to assign to the particular families to which they belong.   Over and above that, he has notes, gathered from time to time in conducting systematic researches, on no fewer than 369 families who possessed lands ; and of those ninety belong to one great branch, the Gordons of Lochinvar.   Captain Wimberley, the historian of the Gordons of Lesmoir and Terpersie, has placed his material, greatly enlarged since the publication of his monographs, at the disposal of the Club, and this will be printed in the second volume.

The justification of the piecemeal method here adopted and deliberately advocated has been proved by the fact that the announcement that the Club was to deal with the House led Rev. Stephen Ree to place at its disposal his admirable deduction of the Gordons of Coclarachie. Again, the knowledge that I was interested in the subject led the late Father William Gordon, Superior of the Brompton Oratory, to give me the elaborate notes which he had been compiling for years on his family, the Gordons of Kethocksmill, near Aberdeen. These I was able to print in *Scottish Notes and Queries* the very month in which he died   But for that publication his work might have been lost sight of altogether. The intense interest in the whole subject is evidenced by the many communications I have received from all parts of the English-speaking world. The most recent came from an American, Mr. John Gordon late of Buenos Ayres, who belongs to the Gordons of Holm, cadets of the Lochinvars. For years he has been making elaborate (and expensive) researches into the history of his line, and he has placed all his material at the disposal of the Club. American genealogists, always keen on origins, have been particularly enthusiastic. I am especially indebted to the Hon. Armistead C. Gordon, Staunton, Virginia, whose work has disentangled the history of the Gordons in Ireland. Mr. Henderson Smith, Edinburgh, has come forward with his knowledge of bookplates belonging to the family, while scores of other correspondents have plied me with letters of inquiry on doubtful points in their pedigree.

A glance at the skeleton tables of the cadets of the Gordons prefixed to the volume will show the wide extent of ground to be covered. Indeed the work is so vast that one can well understand how it could never be attempted on a definitive basis, nor even by preconceived co-operative methods. But there is no doubt whatever that it can be ultimately overtaken in a piecemeal way · and, if not completed, much may be done, with enthusiasm and industry, to realise the desideratum of centuries.

The accompanying bibliography, incomplete in itself, indicates what has already been achieved   The scheme of the Club is to focus those spasmodic and tentative efforts, and produce a work more or less worthy of the great family, which, under the most varied conditions, has distinguished itself all over the world.

I have to thank many helpers for suggestions, assistance and encouragement   In particular, I am indebted to Mr. P. J. Anderson, the secretary of the Club; to the Rev. Stephen Ree, who has thrown himself with immense enthusiasm into the whole scheme; to Captain Douglas Wimberley, and to Mr. Murray. Rose, whose vast knowledge has always been placed at my disposal.   Special thanks are due to Mrs. Skelton, who undertook the very laborious task of indexing the Poll Book and the Services of Heirs, besides making tedious transcriptions with rare accuracy for other parts of this volume

In conclusion, let me say that the Club will be only too glad to hear of any research that has been made, with a view to its incorporation in the present scheme   The great difficulty involved in devising a plan of operation must be held responsible for the blunders and omissions in this opening volume.

J M. BULLOCH.

118 PALL MALL, LONDON,
    15th October, 1903.

APPENDIX TO PREFACE.

A SKETCH BIBLIOGRAPHY OF GORDON GENEALOGY.

THE following list does not pretend to be a complete bibliography of the genealogy of the Gordons   Anything approaching definitiveness would cause endless delay: and even then the list would be incomplete.   So this bibliography is the merest skeleton of the data which I have gathered for years, and only the shadow of the material that is available   but it deals with all the leading lines both in the north and south of Scotland.   The literature of the Gordons in the north of Scotland is familiar.   The great store-houses of information to the north-east of Scotland are the *Antiquities of the Shires of Aberdeen and Banff* (Spalding Club, 5 vols , 1843-69) and Lord Huntly's *Records of Aboyne* (New Spalding Club, 1894)   The history of the Gordons who remained in the south has, as I have noticed in my preface, been more neglected, but the prominence of the family may be gauged from the fact that in P. H. McKerlie's *Lands and Owners in Galloway*, 1870-79, there are 164 entries dealing with Gordons possessing land, and fifty-nine other entries giving only Christian names.

This list has been prepared chiefly on the principle of citing monographs on different branches, and of noting books where they are mentioned, but where one might not naturally search for them   No attempt has been made to include any of the printed public records, for the searcher instinctively turns to them for information, which their elaborate indexes readily supply.   These records are ·—

> *Scots Acts of Parliament* (1124-1707).
> *Services of Heirs* (1545-1799)
> *Registrum Magni Sigilli* (1306-1651)
> *Register of Privy Council* (1545-1630)
> *Exchequer Rolls* (1264-1588)
> *Accounts of Lord High Treasurer* (1473-1513)
> *Calendar of Documents relating to Scotland* (1108-1435).

Calendar of State Papers, Scotland (1509-1603).
Calendar of Scottish Papers (1547-1569).
Documents illustrative of the history of Scotland (1286-1303).
Laing Charters (854-1837).
Scots Testaments (1514-1800).
Historical MSS. Commission Reports.

As an example of the richness of these records, I may cite minor families of Gordon noted in the *Scots Acts of Parliament* alone —

Aberdour (1787-93); Achomachy (1698), Adiwell (1581), Aikenhead, Airtloch (1662-1703); Ardlogie (1639-56); Ardoch (1748-57), Aroquhain (1674); Arradoull (1663-92); Auchinachie (1643-1782), Auchinangzie (1573), Auchincairne (1662), Auchindore (1591-1633); Auchindoun (1587-1600); Auchinhalrigg (1724); Auchinhannok (1655-1710), Auchinhove (1678), Auchinreith (1647-65); Auchlean (1652), Auchlyne (1714-34), Auchmull (1744); Auchmunziel (1745); Auchridie (1702); Auchtirairne (1574); Baccharowe (1690), Balcomy (1686-1703); Balcraig (1608), Balery (1607), Balgown (1786); Ballegorno (1743); Ballone (1649); Balmade (1673-74), Balmeg (1648-1794); Balmuir (1790), Banchory (1740-51), Bandane (1607); Bandloch (1645); Barharrow (1662); Barannine (1595-1654); Barnfalzie (1662); Barnharnie (1690); Barns (1698-1740); Barrelmad (1661), Barroch (1662); Bellieturey (1649); Beoche (1607-16); Bermart (1662); Birkenbush (1754-70); Birkinburn (1647); Birness (1751-56); Blackford (1645); Blaikat (1548-1634); Blairmad (1728), Boddam (1685-89); Boghall (1661); Boigs of Darley (1681); Boytath (1720); Braichlie (1663-1704); Branelane (1669), Brora (1649), Buitle (1645-58); Cairstown (Kerston) (1750-99), Camdell (1685-96); Carrell (1643-1766); Carron (1797), Castraman (1610); Chirmers (1656-62); Clerkseat (1740); Clone (1596); Cloinyard (1687), Cloves (1718), Coldwells (1766-83); Colholstane (1559); Coliston (1690-1719); Combrie (1665), Corachrie (1622); Cowbairdy (1773-82), Coyanach (1704-99), Crabstoun (1735); Crago (1620); Craigellie (1704); Craigieheid (1682), Craigmyle (1763); Cranach (1689-90); Crathienaird (1767); Creiche (1553-1663), Crimonmogate (1685-89), Cringlay (1663), Culreoch (1646); Cumry (1779); Cults (1662), Cuffurroch (1724); Dallochie (1685-1770); Dendeuch (1737); Deskfurd (1556); Doil (or Doll) (1648-85), Dorlathers (1753), Drumjoy (1648); Drumrash (1773); Drumwhyndle (1693-1735); Dungeuch (1695); Dundeauch (1682-90), Eaynbo (1648); Edintore (1742-63); Enrick (1649); Farnachtie (1737); Fetterangus (1768), Fidderey (1649); Forskan (1713); Gaitley (Gaithy) (1700-02); Gallachie (1647); Gararie (1672-1704); Gartie (Garve) (1678-1704); Gedgill (1662); Glascoforrest (1574), Glasnick (1649), Glass (1645-46),

Glassauch (1643-49); Gleanicht (   ); Glencatt (1744); Glendaveny (1774); Glenderrick (1734); Glenlady (1662); Glenluce (1610-49), Gordons-milne (1639-50), Govell (1704); Greencastle (1776), Grievshop (1778), Hallcraig (1706); Hallhead (1685-1704); Hillhead (1712), Hilton (1735-44), Hospidell (1704), Humetoun (1686); Innermarkie (1628-33), Invergordon (1766); Invernaver (1667); Kegnith (1702); Kilgour (1723), Killileoch (1697), Killielour (1657-62), Kinaldie (1740); Kinbo (1664), Kincaldrum (1659); Kingoodie (1697), Kingsgrange (1774-77); Kinmundy (1704-41); Kinnedour (1718); Kirkdaill (1628); Kirketilbreke (1644), Kirkhill (1694-1708), Kirkland (1617-1731); Knarie (1605); Knockgrant (1645); Knockgray (1643-90), Knockreoch (1610); Langdale (1661-63), Langwell (1704); Largmoir (1648-1704); Laussie (1741); Law (1645-96); Little Cocklaw (1766-74); Littleknox (1788), Littlemylne (1647); Logie (1704-52); Lumsdeall (1661-62); Makait-nay (Mercartney) (1607-62); Midgarthie (1663-67); Midmar (1621), Migstrath (1690); Mill of Esslemont (1744); Mill of Kincardine (1744-70); Minidow (1759); Minybowie (1662); Moy (1649); Mundork (1626), Mureick (1645-46); Nether Boddom (1698); Newbigging (1704); Newcoundaw (1647), Newhall (1764-87); Newmilne (1649); Newtoun (1644), Newtyle (1681-85), Over-barr (1690-1708); Overhall (1647-1704); Oxhill (1647), Pennyghame (1648), Pinkaitland (1690), Pittendreich (1645-63), Rainieshill (1731); Rany (1645); Rathleif (1678); Robertoun (1646-62), Rogart (1667-85), Rothiemurkus (   ), Rovie (1663-85), Sallach (1649), Sands (1732), Seaton (1690-1704); Shives (1546-65); Skibo (1678), Spedoch (1687); Strangaslyle (1650); Strathdoun (1567-1606); Swellend (1669), Techmuir (1648-1747); Thornbank (1661-85); Tilliangus (1567-1663); Tillisoules (1696), Tillythroskie (1639), Towie (1712); Tulloch (1637-56); Uppat (1649), Waterside (1662), Wet-crage (1598); Whiteley (1783); Whitepark (1612-28); Woodhall (1704-46); Zeochrie (1694).

In this bibliography I begin with the MS genealogies, and go on to a classified list, arranged alphabetically according to the lands held by them. I am deeply indebted to Rev. Stephen Ree for his invaluable help in examining several of the MSS.

I.—MANUSCRIPT SOURCES (a) ARRANGED CHRONOLOGICALLY.

Ferrerius MS.—*Historiae compendium de origine et incremento Gor-doniae familiae, Joanne Ferrerio Pedemontano authore, apud Kinlos, 1545, fideliter collectum.*

Ferrerius, who was an Italian from Piedmont, was brought in 1528 to Scotland from Paris by Robert Reid, afterwards Abbot of Kinloss and Bishop of Orkney, and for some time taught the monks of Kinloss in Morayshire A notice of him will be found in Stuart's *Records of Kinloss* (p xiii -xxii) The preface to his history of the Gordon family is addressed to George, fourth Earl of Huntly, and is dated at Kinloss, March 30, 1545, and in it he says that the history was written at the request of the Earl's kinsman and secretary, Mr William Gordon, who had supplied him with an outline in Scots (*idiomate vestro*) of the family history He further states that he had read the histories and annals of Scottish affairs, except those that were written in the vernacular, and that his history is based upon what he found in the public chronicles (*in publicis historiarum monumentis*). William Gordon, the historian of the house, who made use of a copy of Ferrerius, says " That History is very short and superficial, and comes no further down than the Year 1545, it may be printed in less than two Sheets of Paper, and so must be very defective, as indeed it is " There are several transcripts of the MS.—two in the Advocates Library, Edinburgh, two in Gordon Castle The laird of Parkhill owns a fifth

Macquair MS.—*Vera narratio ingentis et miraculi plenae victoriae, partae apud Avinum in Scotiae borealibus partibus a Georgio Gordonio Huntlaeo et Francisco Haijo Errolio Catholicis principibus contra Archimbaldum Cambellum Argadorum imperatorem 5 Nonas Octobris anno domini 1594.*

This MS , consisting of twenty folio pages, is now in the Advocates Library, Edinburgh (MS 33 2.36). The writer was a priest who accompanied Huntly's forces, and is said to have been Alexander Macquair, S.J An English translation, slightly abridged in some parts, is given (vol 1, pp 136-52) in Sir John Graham Dalyell's *Scottish Poems of the Sixteenth Century* (Edinb, 1801) In vol 1., pp 255-70, of the *Spottiswoode Miscellany* (Edinb., 1844), there is printed " Account of the Battle of Balrinnes 3d of October, 1594 ". This account is " from a MS formerly belonging to the Rev. Robert Wodrow, now in the Library of the Faculty of Advocates," and is founded on the *Vera Narratio*, though containing some additional information. The MS. of the *Narratio* was probably written previous to 1629, as the cover of the volume in which it occurs bears that it was presented to Camden in that year by Sir Robert Cotton. The hand is early seventeenth century. The volume contains the Battle of Balrinnes (ballad) in a different hand.

Domus Gordon Comes Huntley.

A genealogical table in the same volume in the Advocates Library as contains the Vera Narratio (MS. 33. 2. 36) The descent terminates with the sixth earl, and is accompanied by two coats of arms the Earl of Huntley and the Lord Seaton.

MS. of circa 1600.

A MS of nineteen folio pages, without title or date, is in the possession of Mrs. Elphinstone Dalrymple, of Kinellar Lodge. It is called " a Gordon Pedigree of 1580 " in *Records of Aboyne*, p. vii , but that date is clearly erroneous, as the Battle of Glenlivet is unmistakably referred to on page 16 The MS deals with the Houses of Petlurge, Carnburrow, Haddoch, Auchmeinzie, Tillemnnatt and Lesmoir.

MS. of circa 1610.

A MS of sixteen pages folio, without title, is in the Advocates Library, Edinburgh (MS. 35 5 5a) It begins—"This George Gordone first Marquis of Huntley succeeded his father George the yeir off God   ," and ends abruptly with the account of the battle between the Macleans and the Macdonalds in 1597 It was written in the lifetime of the Marquis, after 1607 and before 1620.

Alexander Ross's MS.—*Sutherlandiae Comitum Annales · in quibus eorum origo et incrementa, vitae et res bello paceque gestae dilucide explicantur: multa quoque notatu digna in regionibus Scotiae vltra Caledonios, a Scriptoribus nostris vel breviter tacta, vel penitus omissa, fusius proponuntur Authore Alexandro Rossaeo Aberdonense Scoto, 1631*

The original is in Dunrobin A quarto MS ("penes Dom Robertum Sibbald") is mentioned in Nicholson's *Scottish Historical Library*, 1702 (p 245 †) The "dedication bears date from Ross's study at Southampton, August 1, 1627 He begins with a description of the county, and largely proceeds with the Annals of the Earls to 1625." In the Advocates Library, Edinburgh, there is a small quarto MS. (34, 6, 18) with the title . *Gordoniorum et Southirlandorum historia duobus libris descripta · quorum prior Huntileae familiae res gestas a Joanne Ferrerio Pedemontano conscriptas complectitur ; posterior vero Southirlandiae comitum originem et incrementa, vitas et res bello paceque gestas, in quo multa notatu digna in regionibus Scotiae ultra Caledonios, a scriptoribus nostris vel breviter tacta vel penitus,omissa, fusius explicantur. Authore Alexandro Rossaeo Aberdonense Scoto* The portion containing the *Southirlandiae comitum Annales*, etc , extends to eighty-one pages, of which four are blank. The dedication begins· Viro stemmatis splendore et virtutibus eximio, D Roberto Gordonio, equiti aurato, Britanniarum regi ex interioris cubiculi familiaribus, Alexandri Southirlandiae comitis filio secundo-genito, jam Southirlandiae Tutori, et primo Scotiae (ut vocant) Baronetto, Alexander Rossaeus S P D , and ends Ex musaeo nostro Southamptoniae primo die Januarii anno millesimo sexcentesimo vigesimo sexto. A different but contemporary hand has corrected *Januarii* into *Augusti* and *sexto* into *septimo*, and the same hand (apparently the author's) has made frequent corrections throughout the volume In the dedication Ross states that he had the "Annales" ready for publication several years before, but the volume had been lost ; that he had now prepared them anew at the request of Sir Robert Gordon, and had dedicated them to him for various reasons, but chiefly because Sir Robert had not only incited him to write the history, but had also supplied him with his own observations and collections. Sir William Fraser, in the Preface to his *Sutherland Book*, describes Ross's "Annales" as only an abstract in Latin of Sir Robert Gordon's work. It would probably have been better to say that Sir Robert Gordon, recognising that Ross had worked up only the material he had supplied, had so freely used Ross's MS in writing his own history, that Ross's "Annales," though written first, serves as an abstract in Latin of Sir Robert's work. Sir William Fraser deals not only with the Dunrobin copy of the MS , but also with two in the possession of Mr. Gordon of Halmyre (descended from the Gordons of Gordonstoun),

Funeral procession of the first Marquis of Huntly, 1636.

An apparently contemporary representation in the possession of the Society of Antiquaries of Scotland. The painting is on a roll of paper measuring 16 ft. 9 in in length, by 8 in in breadth The dresses and armorial bearings are of great interest

Records of the Regality of Huntly (1640-1744).

These are preserved in H M. General Register House, Edinburgh, and the following description has been kindly furnished by Dr. Maitland Thomson.—

" 1 Deeds, 1 vol , 20 Oct , 1686—5 Jan , 1734.
2. Hornings and Inhibitions, vol. 1., 15 Oct., 1687—14 Apr., 1710
3 — vol 11 , 11 Nov , 1717—11 Jan , 1748. (This volume, though not used till 1717, was issued by a Clerk of Session on 11 July, 1710)
4 Court Book, 7 Oct , 1697—30 Mar , 1711 (Huntly)
5 — 10 July, 1724—2 Feb., 1739 (Huntly)
6. — 24 Nov 1721—10 Aug , 1733 (Fochabers and Gordon Castle).
7 — 30 Apr , 1698—25 Aug., 1736 (Badenoch and Lochaber)
8. Volume of original papers, 19 Mar , 1700—27 Aug , 1744, with a few earlier documents (1640 onwards) added at end (Badenoch and Lochaber) "

Prony MS.

It will be seen from the *Balbithan MS.* (59, 60), that there was a " manuscript that goes under Proneys name ". The Gordons of Proney were cadets of the Buckie family William Gordon in his *History* (1 , 5) says, " I have an old MS before me written by one, John Gordon, son to George Gordon of Prony ". What has become of the Prony MS. nobody knows It was used by Theodore Gordon in his MS. history of the Gordons, and there are copies of fragments of it in the Lyon Office

MS. of circa 1644.

The University Library, Aberdeen, possesses a fragment of a quarto MS. account of the Gordons It begins at page 31 and ends abruptly at page 46 This MS must have been used as the basis of some of the Balbithan MS. and is possibly part of the Prony MS

Delmore MS.—*A Genealogical Account of the Family of Gordon and their Cadets, with a note of their Lives and Fortunes.*

William Gordon of Delmore (fl 1553-1604), son of Alexander (who was the second son of the third Earl of Huntly), is said to have spent his leisure hours in writing a history of the Gordons, which about the middle of the eighteenth century was in the possession of James Man, a historian resident in Aberdeen. The history, of which no trace has since been discovered, is thus described by Man (Gordon's *Scots Affairs*, 1 , p xxxii) " There is little in it but mere genealogy till we come to 1630; and the rest of it has been engrossed, almost word for word, by Spalding in his Memoirs So there needs nothing more to be said of it, only it goes a little further than Spalding into the year 1645." " The whole of it could not have been written by William as he did not live so long " (*The Croughly Book*, by Capt. G H. B. Gordon, 1895, pp. 59, 60). He was the ancestor of the Gordons of Croughly.

Sir Robert Gordon's Tables, *compyled and collected together by the* *great paines and industrie of Sir Robert Gordon, Knight baronett of Gordon-stoun, sone of Alexander Earl of Southerland, copied out of his papers and continued be maister Robert Gordone his sone,* 1659

> A folio MS in Dunrobin Castle containing Genealogical Tables of Huntly, Suther-land, Gordonstoun, Ferack, Garty, Lochinvar, Drummoy, Sideray, Enbo, Backies, Craighton and Overskibo, apparently framed by Sir Robert to accompany his *Earl-dom* (*cf.* p 104, l. 7 from foot). A transcript for the use of the Club has been kindly supplied by the Rev J M Joass, LL D, Golspie

Straloch MS.—*Origo et progressus familiae Gordoniorum de Huntly in Scotia.*

> The author was Robert Gordon of Straloch, the mapmaker, who died 1661 It was written in his old age, and William Gordon (*History of Gordons,* i, p xxiv) says that Straloch's "old Age and the Situation of his Dwelling hindred him from searching into the Registers and publick Records, so that it is in many Things very defective But what we have of it is very well done, and deserves the greatest Credit, for he was a Gentleman of the strictest Veracity" The original is now in Gordon Castle, having been presented to the Duke of Gordon in 1773 by John Gordon of Craig, and consists of forty-one pages folio, with forty-nine or fifty lines on the page. On blank pages at the end are pasted two small sheets, the one having notes by Mr Robert Burnett of Crimond. the other having notes by Dr George Middleton, Prin-cipal of King's College (1684-1717) James Man (Gordon's *Scots Affairs,* i, p viii) says Straloch's "History of the illustrious Family of the Gordons, which is carried down only to the year 1595, is writ in a clear and concise Latin style and very exact as to the geography of places, with which he was so well acquainted I have seen the original MS of this book (which has been composed after 1655, as appears by his mentioning Spotswood's and Johnston's Histories, which were not published till that year) with the Remarks of Mr Robert Burnett of Crimond and Dr George Middleton, Principal of the King's College of Aberdeen, upon it I have likewise seen several copies of it" A transcript is in the Advocates Library, Edinburgh, but the first leaf is wanting. A transcript is in the possession of the laird of Parkhill, this was copied in 1763 for Rev Theodore Gordon, and the copy is now in Gordon Castle A transcript (including Principal Middleton's notes) was in the possession of Rev Dr Woodward, Montrose, and at his death passed into the hands of A W. Macphail, bookseller, Edinburgh, who offered it in December, 1899, for £2 15s. and subsequently sold it.

MS. of circa 1670.—*A genealogie of the name of Gordon with the branches and cadets thereof.*

> This is a quarto MS of 12 pages, and is bound up (with copies of the MSS of Ferrerius and Straloch) in a volume now in the possession of the laird of Parkhill It deals with Huntly (to about 1668) and with "Jock" and "Tam". A copy of the part dealing with "the genealogie of Thomas Gordon of Daach," made on a foolscap sheet about 1760 for (or by) John Gordon of Craig, is now in the Univer-sity Library, Aberdeen

Burnet MS.—*The pourtrait of true loyalty exposed in the Family of Gordon without interruption to this present year 1691, with a relation of the siege of the Castle of Edenbrughe in the year 1689.*

> This MS. is now in Blairs College, near Aberdeen. It is a quarto volume of 303 pages, and has the book plate of the Scots College at Paris. The dedicatory letter, addressed " to the Right Honourable the Earle of Huntly," extends to four pages (not numbered) and concludes " My Lord, your Lo. most humble and most obedient servant, W. R." William Gordon in his *History* (p. xxiv.) says it "was written (as I am told) by one Mr. Burnet, a Priest of the Romish Church, who lived in Scotland in King James VII.'s Time, and I am sorry I can give no further Account of him, only I've been told he was a Mearns Gentleman ". The copy of Gordon's *History* in the University Library, Aberdeen, has the following note in the hand-writing of Professor Thomas Gordon: "This author's name was David [Burnet]. He studied in the Scots College at Rome from the year 1661 to 1669, when he was ordained a priest and came as a missionary to Scotland, where he remained for seven years. From 1676 to 1680 he was Prefect of Studies in the Scots College of Paris. In 1680 he returned to Scotland and died anno 1695. He was for several years Chaplain to the family of Gordon at Gordon Castle, where he was much esteemed. This information from Bishop John Geddes. T. G." William Gordon describes the author as "honest, loyal, and a Man of good Learning"; and says also, "as he continues his History much further than any of the former Authors I have mentioned, so he is more exact and full than any of them ; yet in many Things, even of Moment, he is very defective, and gives but a lame Account of what happened to the Family of Gordon in the Time of the Rebellion against Charles I. and II. It appears he did never see Sir Robert Gordon's MS. History, nor has he at all looked into the Registers or Records, and so behooved to be guilty of many Omissions He seems to have been pretty well acquainted both with the Scots and English Historians ; but being an entire Stranger to our Registers, has with them fallen into a good many chronological Mistakes." Lord Huntly had the use of this MS. in preparing his *Records of Aboyne* (p. vii.). There is a transcript in the Advocates Library, Edinburgh, a small quarto of 62 pages, written about 1750; and on the margin of the title page there is this note : " The most part of this MS. is printed in Gordon's History of the Family of Gordon ".

Mackenzie MS.—*Collections of the most remarkable accounts that relate to the families of Scotland.*

> This MS., which is in the Advocates Library (34. 3. 19), was begun by Sir Patrick Lyon of Carse (d. 1695 ?) and annotated by Mackenzie. It deals with the supposed French origin of the Gordons; the Huntly and the Gordonstoun families.

MS. of circa 1700.—*The abridged history of the antiente and most illustrious family of Huntly and Duke Gordone togither with the genealogie and armes blazoned in abrupt lynes.*

> This is a small quarto volume in Gordon Castle. Its contents are : The names of the authores from which the history is compyled, 1 p. The epistle to the reader, 6 pp. The Armes (pen and ink), 1 p. The Armes of that most noble and antient house of

Huntlie blazoned in som abrupt lynes, 12 pp The genealogy of that noble and illustrious family of Huntlie or the lyne of the ancestores of Duk Gordone according to the best and most exact genealogies and accountes thereofe, 18 pp. The history of the most antient and illustrious family of Huntlie or ane account of the transactiones of the ancestoures of Duk Gordone, 197 pp. A table or index of the most materiale points contained in this traitaise, 15 pp. The history ends with a brief notice of Lewis, the third Marquis. The author's name is not given. This MS. is probably that referred to in the following note by the late Mr. C Elphinstone Dalrymple. "Mr. Spottiswood of Spottiswood (then an old man), writing to William Gordon of Harperfield in 1781, says · 'I was told by my father's clerk, who served him all his life, that he was employed by the old Duke of Gordon, who held out the Castle of Edinburgh against King William, and in this cause he had occasion to give a history of the family, with which his grace was so pleased that he ordered the clerk to make a copy of it to be deposited in his charter kist, which he did, but he had forgot the particulars and the year, which according to my conjecture behoved to have been about the year 1703 or 1704 '."

R. M.'s MS., 1707.—*Genealogie of the familie of Gordon*, collected by R. M. Anno Dom. 1707.

This MS. is referred to by Joseph Robertson in a footnote (p 38) to his edition of the Diary of Patrick Gordon of Auchleuchries (Spalding Club). The MS. was then in the Skene Library. In 1899 when part of that library was sold, the Duke of Fife informed the present writer that he knew nothing of the MS

Balbithan MS.

This unique document is reprinted in the present volume from a copy in the possession of Mrs. Charles Elphinstone-Dalrymple, of Kinellar Lodge It is valuable mainly as a guide to the descendants of " Jock " Gordon of Scurdargue.

Lesmoir MS.—*Genealogy from father to son of the House of Lesmoir, as it was painted on the chimney of the said House, and bears date 1405, transcribed therefrom by Dr. Thos. Gordon of Craigelly.*

It is printed in Captain Wimberley's *Memorials of Lesmoir*, p. 99. The date 1405 is probably a mistake for 1505. The pedigree comes down to the issue of Sir James Gordon, XIII. of Lesmoir, but does not give his son George as baronet As Sir James died about 1743, the pedigree must have been made before that date

Theodore Gordon's MSS.—*A Genealogy of the name of Gordon* " with the branches and cadets thereof agreeable to the preceding histories of Straloch and Ferrerius, and likewise to ane old MS. written by John Gordon son to George Gordon of Proney, and several other unexceptionable authorities ". By Theodore Gordon, minister of Kennethmont.

Rev. Theodore Gordon was the son of William Gordon, Drumbulg, and married Anne Gordon, youngest daughter of Professor George Gordon, professor of Hebrew, King's College, Aberdeen, a member of Kethocksmill family Theodore Gordon died in 1779 A copy of his work (made by the late Dr. Burnett) is in the Lyon

Office, Edinburgh   There is also a copy of the MS. somewhere in Aberdeen, where
it was copied by the late Rev. William Gordon, superior of the Brompton Oratory.
He could not remember, however, who lent him the MS   In Gordon Castle
there is a small quarto volume containing (1) a copy of the Ferrerius MS extending to thirty-one pages , (2) a copy of the Straloch MS extending to 160 pages ;
and (3) continuatio historiae ac series rerum illustrissimae familiae Gordoniorum, extending to forty-three pages and dealing only with the Huntly family to
1760.   There are several marginal notes on (1) and (2), and at the end of (1) there
is this note : Quae etiam ego transcripsi anno 1763 ac stricturas quasdam in margine
adjeci —T G.   The volume is not in the handwriting of Professor Thomas Gordon,
who was the brother-in-law of Theodore, but there is inserted at the beginning of
the volume the following —

" Accot Proft Gordon To James Dalgarno Dr

To copying 31 sheets at 2d per sheet	-	-	-	-	-	£0	5	2
To 2 Quires of 8d paper	-	-	-	-	-	-	0	1	4
						£0	6	6

OLD ABERDN, 19 *Sept.*, 1751.

Received payment of the above Accot and the same's hereby discharged by

                                        JAS. DALGARNO."

From letters in the possession of the late Mr C Elphinstone-Dalrymple, it appears
that Professor Gordon got the above copy made for Rev. Theodore Gordon.   In
Gordon Castle there is another MS copy (24 pp. folio) of (3) Continuatio, etc , with
this inscription . " Presented to His Grace the Duke of Gordon by John Gordon of
Craig, 1781 ".

Harperfield MS., 1784.—*Tables of Pedigree of the Family of Gordon in Scotland . . . 1057-1784, by William Gordon, of Harperfield, 1784.*

A copy of these tables is in the Advocates Library, Edinburgh, and another was sold at
Dowell's, Edinburgh, on December 3, 1878, for £4 17s. 6d.   I have failed to trace
this copy   The compiler (born 1720) was the fifth son of Dr John Gordon, of Hilton,
and brother of Dr James Gordon of Pitlurg   He was a barrister of the Middle
Temple, and bought Harperfield in Lanarkshire.   He died in 1787 and left Harperfield to his nephew, Colonel Thomas Gordon.   Several of his tables are printed in
Wimberley's *Gordons of Lesmoir.*

Tilphoudie MS., 1788.

The family of Tilphoudie is dealt with in a MS of 1788, of which a copy, filling thirty-four folio pages and endorsed by " John Stuart, Gen. Reg Ho ," Edinburgh, is in
possession of the New Spalding Club   It goes into details of genealogy in the
eighteenth century

Brydges MS.

A MS. by Sir Egerton Brydges [1762-1837], bought from the Phillipps collection, is
in the Advocates Library (6. 1. 17)   It deals with the Gordons of Embo.

Deuchar's MSS.—"*Genealogical Collections relative to the Family of Gordon.*"

These are mentioned in an editorial note in *Notes and Queries* for 30th March, 1867. Alexander Deuchar was a seal engraver in Edinburgh.

Sinclair MS.—Memoranda relative to the Families of Gordon and Forbes in Mr. Alexander Sinclair's collections now in Crawford Priory Library.

Alexander Sinclair (1794-1877) was the second son of the Right Hon. Sir John Sinclair of Ulbster, 1st Bart. He was a very learned genealogist and wrote an essay on Heirs Male Col Robert Boyle writes to me "Mr. Sinclair made many notes, but they are not of much use to others, as they are mostly undated, and give no authorities, and one of his notes is frequently contradicted by another, presumably later in date, but there is no means of knowing which of the two is the first and which the revised edition. The notes that I saw were chiefly in the form of fragmentary tables of pedigrees" This is so typical of Gordon genealogy, as I have pointed out in my Preface.

Ronald MS.

A history of the Gordons in the Cabrach was compiled by William Ronald, M A (K C.), 1822, schoolmaster of Cabrach.

I.—MANUSCRIPT SOURCES (*b*) ARRANGED ACCORDING TO OWNERSHIP

Abergeldie MSS.

See Hist. MSS Comm *Report*, VL, 712

Aboyne MSS.

See Hist MSS Comm *Report*, II, 180   To a considerable extent the earlier papers have been printed in Lord Huntly's *Records of Aboyne*, but several old rentals of Mar are still in MS. An inventory (MS) of the muniments is in existence

Blairs College MSS.

The Hist. MSS. Comm *Report*, II, 201, gives the titles of two manuscripts. *The genealogies of the families of Scotland, collected by Sir George Mackenzie* [1636-91], *His Majesty's Advocate*; and *An account of various noble Scottish families with topographical notes, written in 1728*   The college authorities decline, meantime, to permit examination of these MSS. See also *Burnet MS (supra).*

Charleton MS.—*Memoirs of the Origin and Descent of several Branches of the Surname of Gordon*, 1822

Mr. More-Gordon of Charleton, Montrose, tells me that he has "a MS book written by Cosmo Gordon in 1822, containing the history of several families of the name of Gordon". It was given to Mr More-Gordon's grandfather, Harry Gordon, by Cosmo Gordon, Liverpool, who was a cousin. A copy of it is now in possession of Miss Jean Anne Gordon, Elgin, daughter of the late Rev. George Gordon, LL D,

f

minister of Birnie, near Elgin It is a quarto volume of about 318 pages and deals with the ducal Gordons (pages 1-246) and the Beldornie Gordons

Dunrobin MSS.

See Hist. MSS. Comm *Report*, ii., 177, which refers to an inventory of the papers See also *Sir Robert Gordon's Tables* and *Alexander Ross's MS. (supra)*

Earlston MSS —*A Short and Concise Abridgement of the origin of the name and illustrious family of Kenmure, with their no less renowned descendants.*

This manuscript contains the most elaborate account of the Gordons in the south of Scotland that I have come across It is a folio of 101 pages, written by the fourth baronet of Earlston, Sir John Gordon (born 1720: died 1795), and is divided into three main sections The Kenmure family gets thirty-one pages, the families of Airds, Ayton and Earlston thirty-eight, while the author devotes twenty-nine pages to his autobiography, in which he describes at length his experiences as an officer in the Scots Brigade in Holland The manuscript, which is exceedingly interesting, if a little prolix, is now in the possession of Sir William Gordon, Bart., of Earlston, whom I have to thank very much for his courtesy in allowing me to examine it minutely.

Fyvie MSS.

See Hist MSS. Comm *Report*, v , 644 A number of documents dealing with the Fyvie Gordons are in the possession of the Rev Dr. Milne, Fyvie.

Gordon Castle MSS.

See Hist. MSS Comm *Report*, 1 , 114 Selections from these papers were printed in 1846-49 by the Spalding Club *Miscellany*, vols iii. and iv. A detailed MS. inventory in Gordon Castle makes the documents accessible See also *Ferrerius's MS.* and *Straloch MS* and *MS of circa*, 1700 *(supra)*

Gordonstoun MSS.

" The more important part of the papers at Gordonstoun consists of the correspondence of Sir Robert Gordon, of documents which he collected, or which came at a later period into the family archives through connections formed by the marriages of his descendants . . A record of the Barony of Gordonstoun is preserved, beginning in 1663 The collection is very extensive and miscellaneous, and contains many authentic materials for the domestic history of the North of Scotland during the seventeenth century " (Dr John Stuart in Hist MSS Comm. *Report*, vi , 681-88). Sir William Gordon-Cumming has courteously granted permission to Mr Ree to examine the enormous (and uninventoried) collection at Gordonstoun.

Haddo MSS.

See Hist MSS Comm *Report*, v , 608 These papers include many charters of the lands of Haddo, Kellie, Methlick, Auchtercoull, etc A portion of the correspondence was printed in *Letters illustrative of public affairs in Scotland*, 1681-84 (Spalding Club, 1851) The papers are being examined by the Rev. James Brebner, M A , with a view to a deduction being contributed to *The House of Gordon* by the Earl of Aberdeen

Pitfour MS.—*Genealogical Notices of the Gordons of Cairnburrow, Rothiemay, Glenbucket, Park, Farskane and others (ten pages). Compiled by James Mitchell, Factor, Pitfour, circa* 1830.

> Mitchell was a native of Banff, and entered the service of James Ferguson of Pitfour, M P, as a lad. He was factor from 1789 to 1839, and died about 1840, leaving between £3,000 and £4,000 invested at 3½ per cent, the interest being divided yearly among the schools in Fetterangus, Longside, Rora, St Fergus and Banff, and a sum of £1 10s. every second year amongst "old men and women, widows, natives of and residing on the Pitfour estates, who have never been under church censure". There is no date on the MS., but it is written on foolscap, bearing the watermark "Wallyfield, 1815". Mitchell was apparently keenly interested in local history. This volume, which belongs to the Pitfour family, and is now in the hands of the assistant factor, Mr John Fullerton, himself an industrious antiquary, contains an account of the Duff family, running into eleven pages notes of "Tryals" from 1537-1701 (ninety-six pages), copies of documents regarding the liberation of two of the domestic servants of Sir John Gordon of Haddo (eight pages), facsimile of the signatures of the Earls of Huntly (two pages), an account of the Abbey of Deer, with copies of charters (twenty-six pages), copy of tack by William Earl Marischal, 1699, rental of Marischal's lands in Buchan, 1712, sale of the forfeited estates of Marischal, Panmure and others, 1764, remarks on the purchase of Marischal's lands in Buchan by Ferguson of Pitfour (eighteen pages), notes on monuments in the Abbey Church of Deer (two pages), and charters by Fergus, Earl of Buchan (seven pages) Some of the items have been printed in *Scottish Notes and Queries* by Mr. Fullerton. The MS deals with the families of Cairnburrow, Rothiemay, Glenbucket, Park, Edinglassie, Carnousie, Farskane, Artlock, Balbithan and Edinglassie

II.—PRINTED SOURCES (forming also an Index to the "Balbithan MS.")

Aberdeen (Earl of).—See Haddo.

Aberdour.—*Family of Dingwall-Fordyce*, Jervise's *Epitaphs*, 56, 57, Pratt's *Buchan* (1901), 305

Abergeldie.—Burke's *Landed Gentry* (1898), i, 596-97; Macfarlane's *Geneal. Coll*, i, 378, 379; ii, 414, *Records of Aboyne*, 22, 219-26, 227, 275, 278, 386, 521, *Records of Invercauld*, 29, 30, 31, 35, 38, 40, 41, 66, 80, 83, 84, 86, 94, 98, 105, 112, 116, 117, 120, 155, 167, 169, 170, 172, 173, 176, 180, 182, 183, 186, 189, 190, 191, 192, 193, 194, 239, 260, 262, 264, 278, 293, 297, 338, 361, 366, 367, 389, 390, 428, 434, 463, 465, 471, 474. Jervise's *Epitaphs*, ii., 161-62, also *infra* under **Huntly.**

Aberlour.—Forfeited Estates papers in H.M. Register House; Macfarlane's *Geneal. Coll.*, ii, 18; Cramond's *Annals of Banff*, ii, 191

Affleck.—*Spalding Club Misc.*, iii., 127.

Afton.—McKerlie's *Lands and Owners in Galloway*, iii, 416, 421, 424, 426; *Book of Robert Burns*, ii, 351, 352.

Aikenhead.—See *Earlston MS.*

Airds—McKerlie, iii , 67, 110, 160, 164, 190, 204, 313, 389, 390, 408, 412, 414, 416, 418, 423, 424 , iv., 54, 73, 78, 282, 298, 302, 305, 318, 408, 447; v., 11, 52, 121, 202, 301, 361.

Altyre.—Betham's *Baronetage*, v , 547-56 ; Burke's *Peerage*, under Gordon-Cumming Roualeyn George Gordon-Cumming, second son of 2nd bart , is sketched in *Dict. Nat. Biog.* See also **Gordonstoun.**

Ardbroylach.—*Balbithan MS.*, *infra*, 57, 61 ; Macfarlane's *Geneal Coll.*, ii , 489

Ardestie.—Cadet of **Gight.**

Ardlogie.—Cadet of **Gight.**

Ardmachar.—Cadet of **Gight.**

Ardmeallie.—*Balbithan MS.*, 53 , Jervise's *Epitaphs*, i , 232 ; ii , 382.

Ardoch.—Chambers's *Book of Days*, ii., 41, 42 ; *People's Journal*, March 1, 1902.

> These articles deal with the two daughters of Adam Gordon, who married successive Earls of Kellie · and how they rescued a baby from the sea

Ardwell.—McKerlie, iii., 19, 21 ; iv , 261.

Arradoul.—Cramond's *Church of Rathven , Donean Tourist , Balbithan MS* , 64 ; Macfarlane's *Geneal. Coll.*, i , 386

> A MS account of this family in the handwriting of Major-Gen. Gordon on paper watermarked 1861 is in possession of Rev. John Allan, Birch Cottage, Elgin

Artloch.—*Balbithan MS.*, 33, 41, 47.

Ashludie.—*Scottish Notes and Queries*, May, 1902 *Harrow School Register*, 427, 441.

Auchanachie.—*Balbithan MS.*, 40 ; Macfarlane's *Geneal Coll.*, ii., 22, 60, 188, 446 , Buchan's *Ancient Ballads*, ii., 127-9

> Great confusion arises out of old-fashioned spellings It is confused with Auchynachy, Auchanassie and Auchoynany, all of which are different estates

Auchendolly.—Burke's *Landed Gentry* (1898), i., 600, 601.

> A curious fact about this estate is that it was given by Miss Gordon of Auchendolly. to Michael Biddulph, the well-known London banker, because he was connected with the Gordons of Abergeldie (see *infra*, p. 104). ·

Auchenreoch.—McKerlie, iii., 223 ; iv., 54, 73, 79, 82, 470 ; v , 194, 308-10.

Auchinarrow.—*Balbithan MS*, 67, 68.

Auchindoir.—Jervise's *Epitaphs*, i., 286; ii, 208, 209, Macfarlane's *Geneal. Coll.*, ii., 25, 31, 37, 222.

Auchindoun.—*Balbithan MS.*, 22, 23; Macfarlane's *Geneal. Coll.*, ii., 92, 419.

> John and then his brothers, Adam and Patrick, sons of the 4th Earl of Huntly (*Records of Aboyne*, 468-69), were lairds of Auchindoun Adam is supposed to be the " Edom o' Gordon " (of the ballad) who burned Towie Castle

Auchinhuif.—*Balbithan MS.*, 53, 57, 60, 61-63; Macfarlane's *Geneal. Coll.*, ii., 15.

Auchinreath.—*Balbithan MS.*, 66; *Scottish Notes and Queries*, ii., v., 14.

Auchintoul.—*Balbithan MS.*, 52, 65; Jervise's *Epitaphs*, i., 235, Forfeited Estates papers in H M. Register House.

Auchleuchries —

> The interest of this family centres in General Patrick Gordon of Peter the Great's army, who left a very valuable diary, published in German under the title of *Tagebuch des Generals Patrick Gordon* [1655-1669], by Obolenski and Posselt, vol 1, Moscow, 1849; vols. ii. and iii., St. Petersburg, 1851, 1853, 8vo. A summary of this book was published by the Spalding Club in 1859, edited by Joseph Robertson, under the title of *Passages from the Diary of General Patrick Gordon*, 4to, pp. 244. This edition contains an appendix dealing, from the documentary point of view, with the family of Auchleuchries Patrick Gordon, by Alexander Brueckner, St. Petersburg, 1878 (pp 184 in Russian). See also " The Last of a Long Line the Decay of the Gordons of Auchleuchries," by J M Bulloch, *Aberdeen Free Press*, April 6 and 13, 1901. Jervise's *Epitaphs*, i , 313 Temple's *Thanage of Fermartyn*, p. 309 Pratt's *Buchan* (1901), 450. *Notes and Queries*, 2, ii , 344 , iii., 118.

Auchlyne.—*Balbithan MS*, 47, 48. Cadet of **Lesmoir**.

Auchmenzie.—*Theodore Gordon MS.*, *Balbithan MS.*, 50; Macfarlane's *Geneal. Coll.*, ii., 238

Auchmull.—*Balbithan MS.*, 40.

Auchnastink.—*Balbithan MS*, 67.

Auchoynany.—*Balbithan MS*, 36, 39, 47.

Auchterarne.—Cadet of **Lesmoir**.

Auchynachie (or Auchindachy).—*Balbithan MS*, 49

Avochie.—*Balbithan MS.*, 32, 39, 40; Jervise's *Epitaphs*, i., 232; ii., 382, 383; Burke's *Landed Gentry* (1898) i , 597, 598 , and under Forbes-Gordon

Backieleys.—*Balbithan MS.,* 52.

Backies.—See **Sir R. Gordon's MS. Tables** (*supra*).

Bad.—Cadet of **Avochie.**

Badenscoth.—*Balbithan MS.,* 37, 46, 47, 48; Temple's *Fermartyn,* 103-5. Pratt's *Buchan* (1901), 387   See also under **Lesmoir.**

Balbithan.—*Balbithan MS.,* 139; Temple's *Fermartyn,* 350.

Balcomie.—Cadet of **Lesmoir.**

Balmad.—Cramond's *Annals of Banff,* II., 253, 254, 267, 322.

Balmaghie.—Burke's *Landed Gentry,* 2nd, 3rd, 4th and 5th editions; McKerlie, III., 106, 112.   See under **Portugal.**

Balmuir.—Cadet of **Auchleuchries** and **Nethermuir.**

Banchory.—*Balbithan MS.,* 51.

Bar.—McKerlie, III., 191, 313, 408; IV., 14, 19, 27, 59, 75, 263, 282, 293, 302, 303, 322, 327, 345.

Barharrow.—McKerlie, III., 223; V., 173, 309

Barnbarroch.—McKerlie, III., 17, 220, 348, 349, IV., 55, 115.

Barnes.—Cadet of **Lesmoir;** *Balbithan MS,* 47.

Barrack.—Pratt's *Buchan* (1901), 189

Barskeoch.—McKerlie, IV., 78-80, 97, 99, 447; V., 310, 312, 313

Belcherrie.—*Balbithan MS.,* 31, 32, 42, 65.

Beldornie.—*Balbithan MS,* 11, 12, 57, 65; Macfarlane's *Geneal. Coll.,* 1, 237; II., 47, 414   See also **Charleton M.S.** (*supra*)

Bellabeg.—*Balbithan MS.,* 42, 43.

Binhall.—*Scottish Notes and Queries,* Feb., 1901; May, 1902.

Birkenburn.—*Balbithan MS.,* 33, 43, 45, 46, 49; *Pedigree of the Gordons of Birkenburn, Cadets of Lesmoir* (a single sheet folding genealogical table by Captain Wimberley in 1898); Jervise's *Epitaphs,* I., 165, 360.

Birkenbush.—*Add. MSS.,* Brit. Museum, 28, 231 f 176; 28, 235 ff. 187, 193.

Birkhall.—Cadet of **Abergeldie.**

Birsemoir.—*Balbithan MS.,* 21, Macfarlane's *Geneal. Coll.,* i., 246, 248; ii., 69, 83. Patrick Gordon, Governor of Pennsylvania, belonged to this family, Burke's *Commoners,* iv., 9

Blaiket.—McKerlie, iii., 372, 394; iv, 75; v., 300, 301.

Blelack.—*Balbithan MS.,* 42, 43, Michie's *Logie-Coldstone;* Jervise's *Epitaphs,* i., 275.

Bochrom.—*Balbithan MS,* 67

Bogardie.—*Balbithan MS,* 43

Boghole.—*Balbithan MS.,* 45. See also **Crichie.**

Boigs.—*Balbithan MS,* 31, 63, 64

Bonnyton (Ayrshire).—Cadet of **Nethermuir.**

Botarie.—See under **Pitlurg;** *Balbithan MS,* 28, 30

Bountie.—*Balbithan MS.,* 51.

Bovaglie.

This family, farmers on the estate of Abergeldie, are said to be cadets of Hallhead Mr. D S. R. Gordon has a MS. account of this family.

Braco.—*Balbithan MS.,* p. 54, 55; *Scottish Notes and Queries,* 2, i., 28; Macfarlane's *Geneal. Coll.,* ii., 19, 21.

This family was dealt with by J. M Bulloch in two articles, " How the Queen might have had no Birthday," *Aberdeen Free Press,* May 24 and 25, 1899

Braickley.—*Balbithan MS,* 47, 64, Macfarlane's *Geneal. Coll.,* i., 377, 379; iii, 252; Taylor's *Braemar Highlands,* 160-64, Michie's *Deeside Guide,* *Records of Invercauld,* 35-43, 73, 251, 254, 278, 285, 356, 357, 475. " The murder of the Baron of Brackley (1666)," in the *Aberdeen Free Press,* Nov. 19 and 22, 1901; *London Mag.* (1824), ix., 355-6.

The " Ballad of the Baron of Brackley " will be found in nearly all ballad collections, notably Buchan's *Gleanings of Scotch . . . scarce old ballads,* pp. 68-70.

Broadland.—*Balbithan MS,* 44.

Buckie.—*Balbithan MS.,* 28, 56-59, 65; Pitcairn's *Criminal Trials,* i., 175; Jervise's *Epitaphs,* i., 281, 282, 346

Buthlaw.—Temple's *Fermartyn,* 272-75 and 476, 477; Burke's *Landed Gentry* (1898), i., 601, 602.

The most distinguished member of this family was Thomas Gordon of Cairness (1788-1841), major-general in the Greek army, son of Charles VII. of Buthlaw He is dealt with by Mr. Gordon Goodwin in the *Dictionary of National Biography*. Reference may also be made to the general's *History of the Greek Revolution* (published by Blackwood), 2 vols., 8vo, 1832

Cairnbannoch.—*Balbithan MS.*, 15.

Cairnbulg.—Burke's *Landed Gentry*, 2nd, 3rd, 4th and 5th editions; Pratt's *Buchan* (1901), 241, 245, 248, Jervise's *Epitaphs*, ii., 58

Cairnburrow.—Temple's *Thanage*, 220-25, *Balbithan MS.*, 30, 32-38, 45, 57, 58, 59, 62; see **Pitfour MS.**, *supra*, see also under **Park**; Macfarlane's *Geneal. Coll*, ii, 3, 8, 64, 237, 238, 421, 490

Cairness.—Cadet of **Buthlaw**.

Cairnfield.—*Balbithan MS*, 65, Burke, 2nd, 3rd, 4th, 5th, 6th and 9th editions; Jervise's *Epitaphs*, 1, 275

Cairnwhelp.—*Balbithan MS.*, 15, 36, 40.

Campbelton.—McKerlie, iii, 52, 220, 228, 248, 373, 496, iv., 119, 120, 289, v., 202, 205, 209, 278, 279, 304.

Cardoness.—McKerlie, iii, 7, 15, 18 to 24, 57, 209, iv., 448.

Carleton.—McKerlie, iii, 190-95, 210, 314, 408, 417, 423; iv., 76, 100, 291, 303, 322, 480, 481.

Carnousie.—*Balbithan MS.*, 36, 38; **Pitfour MS.** (*supra*).

Carroll.

Anne, the daughter of Joseph Gordon, W.S, of Carroll, married Sir William Siemens, and a good deal about the Carroll family will be found in Pole's *Life of Sir William Siemens*, 1888. The will of Joseph Gordon, sometime of Jamaica and lately of Navidale, and brother of John Gordon of Carroll, is a lengthy document in the *Edinburgh Commissariot Testaments*, cxxxi, part 2.

Chapeltown.—*Balbithan MS.*, 54; Temple's *Fermartyn*, 284, 285; *Family of Leslie*, iii, 317.

Lord Brougham's great-grandmother was a member of this family

Clashtirum—*Scottish Notes and Queries*, May, 1902; Jervise's *Epitaphs*, i, 274, 278

James Gordon, a distinguished prelate of the Roman Catholic Church, who became vicar apostolic of Scotland, belonged to this family. He is dealt with in the *Dictionary of National Biography*.

Clethins.—*Balbithan MS*, 49.

Cloves.—Cadet of **Lesmoir**.

Cluny.—*Balbithan MS.*, 19-22, 62 , *Records of Aboyne,* 229-36 ; G E. C 's *Complete Baronetage,* ii., 297 ; Jervise's *Epitaphs,* ii , 48, 127, 129-32 ; Macfarlane's *Geneal Coll.,* 1 , 258 ; ii., 27, 28, 62, 447.

> Patrick Gordon the author of *Britane's Distemper* (Spalding Club), belonged to the Cluny family. See also Hartpury, Burke's *Landed Gentry,* 4th 5th and 6th editions

Clunymore.—*Balbithan MS.,* 67.

Cobairdy.—*Gen. Acct, of James Young, etc* , p. 139. Cadet of **Park.**

Cochlarachie.—*Balbithan MS.,* 51-53 ; Temple's *Fermartyn,* 276-79 , *Records of Aboyne* 167-70 See Mr. Ree's deduction in the present volume.

Coldwells.—Mair's *Presbytery of Ellon,* 190 , Pratt's *Buchan* (1901), 433, 434

> To this family belonged John Gordon, Bishop of Galloway (1644-1726), described in the *Dict Nat. Biog* , and Col. Fabian Gordon of the Polish Cavalry, fl 1783 (*Services of Heirs*).

Collieston.—Cadet of **Pitlurg**

Collithie.—*Balbithan MS.,* 36, 51.

Comray —Jervise's *Epitaphs,* ii., 258, 259.

Contly—*Balbithan MS ,* 66, 67.

Cormellat.—*Balbithan MS ,* 32, 41, 59.

Corrachree.—*Balbithan MS ,* 50.

Cotton.—*Balbithan MS.,* 20, 21

Captain John Gordon, of the Swedish army, belonged to this family See *Deeds of Montrose,* 283-85

Coynachie.—Cadet of **Birkenburn.**

Cracullie (or Craigtullie).—*Balbithan MS.,* 20, 42, 43, 61, 62, 64

Craibstone.—*Balbithan MS.,* 11, 37.

Craichlaw.—McKerlie, iii., 46, 296, 297, 315 ; iv., 54, 245 ; *Scottish Nation,* ii , 322

Craig.—*Balbithan MS.,* 49-51, 52 , *Harperfield MS* ; Jervise's *Epitaphs,* ii , 208, 209; Macfarlane's *Geneal. Coll.,* ii., 247.

Craigston.—*Balbithan MS.,* 33.

Crichie.—Cadet of **Lesmoir**; *Balbithan MS ,* 43, 45.

James Gordon, Jesuit priest, of this family, is sketched in the *Dict. Nat. Biog*

Crogo.—McKerlie, iii., 82, 95, 96, 303.

Croughly.—*The Croughly Book*, complied by Captain George Huntly Blair Gordon, R E. ; edited by J Percy Gordon, and printed by subscription for private circulation, 1895, 8vo, 103 pp

> The family of Croughly in the parish of Kirkmichael are descended from Alexander, 3rd Earl of Huntly (died 1524) This pamphlet, which opens somewhat cynically in sketching the decay of the power of the Gordons, gives a very complete record of the later members of the Gordons of Croughly, who have been distinguished as a Service family, the most notable active member being General Redmond Gordon of the 15th Hussars, a brilliant cavalry leader in the South African War of 1899-1901 The author of the book, Capt G H. B Gordon, R E. (born 1857), succumbed to pneumonia, Nov. 18, 1897 He was the great-grandson of James Gordon of Croughly (1726-1818) He collected a good deal of matter on other branches of the Gordons It is still in MS. (in the possession of Rev. Andrew Meldrum, Logierait), but is not of great value The editor was his cousin, John Percy Gordon (born 1840), a solicitor in London See also Jervise's *Epitaphs*, 1 , 70

Culdrain.—Cadet of **Birkenburn.**

Cullindoch.—McKerlie, iii., 16, 17 ; iv., 271, 282-90 , v., 205, 278

Cults.—Jervise's *Epitaphs*, ii , 322, 323 ; Macfarlane's *Geneal Coll.*, 1 , 379

Culvennan.—Burke's *Commoners*, iii., 610 , *Landed Gentry*, 2nd, 3rd, 4th, 5th, 6th editions , McKerlie, iii., 276, 365, 367, 395, 396 , iv., 132, 266, 277 ; v., 94, 133, 255 , *Scottish Nation*, ii., 322.

Cushnie.—See **Hallhead.**

Dallachy.—Cramond's *Annals of Banff*, ii., 323

Dalmore.—*Balbithan MS* , 68

Dalpholly.—This family held a baronetcy created 1704 Rev. Sir Adam (died 1817) is biographed in the *Gentleman's Magazine*, vol 87, p 556

Davoch (or Daach) —*Balbithan MS.*, 66-68 , *Scottish Notes and Queries*, May, 1902.

Delamont (Co. Down) —See **Florida.**

Deskie.—*Balbithan MS.*, 65.

Deuchries.—*Balbithan MS.*, 55.

Dilspro.—*Balbithan MS.*, 43

Dorlathers.—*Balbithan MS* , 52.

Drimnin.—Burke's *Landed Gentry* (1898), i., 601.

This family, which has remained Roman Catholic, is a branch of the Minmore line, and that in turn of the Knockespock The present Roman Catholic Bishop of Jamaica is a brother of the present laird of Drimnin See *Medical Directory*, 1903

Drumbulg.—*Balbithan MS.*, 43, 45, 59, 60.

Drumearn.

Edward Strathearn Gordon, a Lord of Appeal, was created Baron Gordon of Drumearn, 1876 The peerage became extinct 1879 (see G E C.'s *Complete Peerage*, iv , 53), but his issue will be found in the peerages since 1897, when a royal decree granted the courtesy title of Honourable to the children, of both present and deceased life peers. Lord Gordon was the son of Major John Gordon, 2nd Queen's Regiment, who was the son of Adam Gordon, of Griamacharry, Kildonan (1750-1831), beyond whom the family cannot be traced. Sir Thomas Edward Gordon (see Debrett's *Knightage*, 1902) is the son of Captain William Gordon, who was a son of this Adam Lord Gordon's daughter Ella married Gen. Sir John James Hood Gordon.

Drumhead.—*Balbithan MS.*, 40.

Drumhill.—*Balbithan MS*, 67.

Drumin.—*Balbithan MS.*, 57, 58, 59.

Drummoy.—*Balbithan MS.*, 12, 13, 32

Drummuir.—Cadet of **Park.**

Drumwhindle.—*Balbithan MS.*, 37, 41.

Drymies.—*Balbithan MS.*, 50.

Dunkinty.—*Balbithan MS.*, 23, 24.

Earlston.—The family, created baronets 1706, is described in all the baronetages, notably Burke and Debrett. See McKerlie, iii , 30, 85, 98, 145, 181, 191*b*, 195, 197, 229, 297, 307, 308, 314, 318, 321, 367, 387, 399, 414*b*, 427, 429, 435, 436, 438, 440, 441, 443 ; iv , 26, 61, 62, 63, 66, 76, 78, 80, 100, 282, 291, 302, 306, 318, 480, 481 ; v , 37, 43, 60, 121, 198, 300, 301 , *Scottish Nation*, ii., 325 , *Records of the Corrie Family*, A D 802-1899, by J[essie] E. Corrie , London Mitchell & Hughes, 1899 , vol. i, 109-129.

Miss Corrie's book includes pictures of Earlston Castle, the arms of the Earlston family , of Sir William Gordon of Afton, brother of Sir Alexander Gordon of Earlston , and of the oak cabinet carved in captivity by John Gordon of Earlston. The connection between the families is clearly stated in a pedigree by Miss Corrie, printed on one sheet (57 inches by 30 inches), entitled *Genealogical Table of the Houses of Gordon, Corrie and Goldie*, published 1897 The Earlston family, who were zealous Protestants, figure very largely in Covenanting literature. In the *Dictionary of National Biography* there will be found good summaries of the line of Alexander Gordon (1587-1654), of his second son, William (1614-1679), and of the latter's son, Sir Alexander (1650-1720), all by Mr Henry Paton.

Edinglassie.—*Balbithan MS.*, 33, 36, 38.

Edintore.—See *Memoir of Dr John Gordon* by Daniel Ellis, F.R S.E.. (Edin. 1823).

Edinvillie.—*Balbithan MS.*, 58.

Ellon.—Burke's *Landed Gentry* (1898), i., 602; Temple's *Fermartyn*, 502, 503; Chambers's *Domestic Annals*, iii , 422 (for the murder of two sons); *Times*, June 9, 1873 (for the declaration of marriage by George John Robert Gordon—a very strange case), *Seven Gardens*, by E. V. B , 1900, Sutherland Edward's *Life of Sir William White*, 75 , *Mary Boyle*, 176, 177; *Aberdeen Free Press*, Feb. 17, 1903; Jervise's *Epitaphs*, ii., 121.

Embo.—The Gordons of Embo, created baronets in 1631, will be found in any baronetage, notably G E. C.'s, ii , 392 ; *Scottish Nation*, ii., 324; Burke's *Royal Descents*, 116. See **Sir R. Gordon's MS. Tables; Brydges M.S.**, *supra*

Enniskillen.—See *Notes and Queries*, 2, x., 90

Essie.—*Balbithan MS* , 57, 63   See also **Scurdargue.**

Esslemont.—See **Hallhead.**

Farskane.—Jervise's *Epitaphs*, i , 274.   Cadet of **Cairnburrow.**

Panmure Gordon, a well-known London stockbroker (died Sept 1, 1902), belonged to this family   J M. Bulloch has in his possession a volume compiled of numerous cuttings about his curious career, and containing catalogues of his extraordinary collections.

Fechil.—Temple's *Fermartyn*, 504-6 ; *Gen. Acct of James Young*, etc., p 226. Cadet of **Pitlurg.**

Ferack.—See **Sir R. Gordon's MS. Tables**, *supra*.

Fernachty.—*Balbithan MS.*, 33.

Fetterangus.—Cadet of **Lesmoir.**

Fetterletter.—*Balbithan MS* , 15, 53, 54

Florida (Co. Down) —Burke's *Commoners*, iv., 376 ; *Landed Gentry*, 9th edition, ii., *supra* 172, 173 . Dartmouth Papers, *Hist. MSS Com*

Sir Lionel Smith, Bart (created 1838), married as his second wife (in 1819), Isabella Curwen, youngest daughter of Eldred Curwen Pottinger of Mount Pottinger by his wife Anne, daughter of Robert Gordon of Florida , and his son Lionel (2nd bart , born 1833) assumed the additional name of Gordon in 1868   James Bentley Gordon (1750-1819), historian, and George Gordon (1806-79), horticultural writer, both of Irish birth, are described in the *Dict Nat Biog*

Fulziemont.—*Balbithan MS*, 42, 50.

Fyvie.—Temple's *Fermartyn*, 28-31, 45, 46, Jervise's *Epitaphs*, ii., 29, 124; Burke's *Visitations*, 2nd series, i., 10-12. See also **Fyvie MSS.** (*supra*); the Gordons, baronets of Halkin, in any Baronetage.

Garie.—*Balbithan MS.*, 44.

Garty.—Macfarlane's *Geneal. Coll.*, ii, 420. See **Sir R. Gordon's MS. Tables**, *supra*.

Gight.—Temple's *Fermartyn* 72-78; *Methlick, Haddo House, Gight and the Valley of the Ythan*, 67-79; Lord Huntly's *Records of Aboyne*, 53-56; also deduction in the present volume.

Glascoforest.—Cadet of **Lesmoir.**

Glassaugh.—Cadet of **Lesmoir.**

Glen.—McKerlie, iii., 5, 33, 34, 74, 89, 159, 179, 219, 313, 334, 348, 382, 437, 488, 501, 502; iv., 54, 55, 92, 253, 281, 285, 290, 291, 302, 434; v., 194, 197; 202, 204, 209, 292, 294, 313.

Glenbucket.—*Balbithan MS.*, 36, 37, 38, Jervise's *Epitaphs*, i., 69, Allardyce's *Historical Papers of the Jacobite Period* (1895-96), 288, 310, 353, 354, 355, 372, 391, 397, 398 and 545. See also **Pitfour MS.** and under **Knockespock.**

> John Gordon, the famous Jacobite leader, held these estates, which have been owned by several branches of the Gordons. The editor has prepared a lengthy deduction

Glencat.

> This family produced a notorious swindler whose career is detailed in two pamphlets entitled *Memoirs of John Gordon of Glencat*, "who was thirteen years in the Scotch College at Paris, wherein the absurdities and delusions of Popery are laid open," 12mo, 1733 *The Masterpiece of Imposture*, "or the adventures of John Gordon and the Countess of Gordon, *alias* Countess Dalco, *alias* Madame Dallas, *alias* Madame Kempster, containing the reality of an history and the amusement of a romance, being an answer to the late *Memoirs* of the said John Gordon of Glencat. Done with authentick account by Elizabeth Harding London, printed for the author," 8vo, 1734

Glendaveny.—Cadet of **Lesmoir.**

Glengarack.—*Balbithan MS.*, 63. *Presbytery Book of Strathbogie*

Glenluce.—C. A Gordon's *Concise History of the Gordons* (1890), pp. 125-30

> Rev Robert Gordon, the last of the Non-juring Bishops, belonged to this family. See Lathbury's *History of the Non-Jurors* and *The Jacobite Lairds of Gask*

Gollachie—*Balbithan MS.*, 33.

Golspitur.—See *Pitcairn's Criminal Trials*, iii., 231, *Balbithan MS.*, 13.

Gordon, Parish of.—See *Old Stat. Acct.*, v., 88, *New Stat. Acct.*, ii, 33; Chalmers's *Caledonia* (ed. of 1888), iii, 385

Gordonbank.—See Nisbet's *System of Heraldry* (1804), vol ii., Appx., p. 220. See under **Portugal.**

Gordonstoun.—See Fraser's *Sutherland Book;* Douglas's *Baronage*, p. 2, G. E C.'s *Complete Baronetage*, ii, p. 277, Foster's *Members of Parliament Scotland;* also **Sir R. Gordon's MS. Tables, Gordonstoun MSS.,** *supra.*

Grange.—McKerlie, iii., 111-277; iv., 236, 237, 299; v., 195, 292, 306, 307.

Greenlaw.—Cadet of **Kenmure.** Also McKerlie, iii., 146, 365-68, 395, 423, 507, iv., 62, 66, 68, 69, 207, 235, 266, v., 61, 119, 232 and 387.

Haddo.—*Balbithan MS.*, 53-56, Jervise's *Epitaphs*, ii., 23-25; Macfarlane's *Geneal. Coll.*, i, 138, ii, 23, 37, 48, 235, 240, 482; Temple's *Fermartyn*, 1-16; *Methlick, Haddo House, Gight and the Valley of the Ythan*, 53-64; the Gordon letters, *Spalding Club Misc.*, vol. iii., G. E. C's *Complete Baronetage*, ii., 451. "A Gordon Vendetta of Last Century how [the 2nd] Lord Aberdeen's son [Hon. Cosmo Gordon] killed an officer in a duel," by J. M. Bulloch, *Aberdeen Free Press*, Feb 27, 1899, "Waterloo Day : the price that the North paid for the victory [by the death of Sir Alexander Gordon, grandson of the 3rd Earl of Aberdeen]," by J M. Bulloch, in the *Aberdeen Free Press*, June 17, 1899. The ennobled Gordons of Haddo, Lord Aberdeen's family, are described in all the peerages of course. *Case on behalf of the Rt. Hon. John Campbell, Earl of Aberdeen in the Peerage of Scotland, claiming a writ of summons to Parliament as Viscount Gordon of Aberdeen, in the Peerage of the United Kingdom*, 1872, 121 pp *Minutes of Evidence Taken before the Committee for Privileges to whom was referred the petition of the Rt Hon John Campbell, etc.*, 1872, 81 pp (The official account of the death of the sailor Earl.) Baron Stanmore (created 1893), son of 4th Earl of Aberdeen, belongs to the Haddo family.

Haffield.—Burke's *Commoners*, ii., 219; *Landed Gentry*, 2nd, 3rd, 4th, 5th and 6th editions. Cadet of **Abergeldie.**

Halkin.—Cadet of **Fyvie.**

Hallhead.—*Balbithan MS*, 17, Temple's *Thanage*, 512-17; *Records of Aboyne*, 27; Burke's *Landed Gentry* (1898), i., 599; *Scottish Notes and Queries*, March and May, 1898, Pratt's *Buchan* (1901); 435, 438. See also Gordon-Gilmour, Burke's *Landed Gentry* (1898) i., 585.

> Adam Lindsay Gordon (1833-70), the Australian poet, belonged to this family. See *Dict Nat Biog* A. Patchett Martin's *Beginnings of an Australian Literature* Walbrook's *Life*, 1891 · Percy F Rowland's *New Nation*, 1903

Hallheaths.—Cadet of **Kenmure.**

Harperfield.—Cadet of **Pitlurg.**

Hartpury.—Family name Gordon-Canning, descended from the Cluny Gordons. See Burke's *Landed Gentry* (9th edition), i., 233, 234

Holm.—McKerlie, iii, 19, 74*b*, 77, 82, 83, 89, 90, 93, 109; iv, 53, 86, 300, 306, 307, 342, 440; v., 195.

> Mr John Gordon, 22 South Audley Street, London, has made large collections on the history of this family and has placed his material at the disposal of the Club

Huntly.

> It is a curious fact that this family, the Gordons of Huntly, both in the main and ducal line, and in the matter of its cadets, should have had more attention paid to them than any other branches of the House of Gordon. This is all the more strange in that they were not of pure Gordon blood They were " Seton Gordons," a term that has been used (one recalls Mrs Byron's reference), and is still sometimes spoken of with a touch of contempt. And yet nearly all the printed histories and most of the manuscripts devote themselves to this line as if it summed up the family I have, therefore, included under the title of " Huntly " those books which really deal with this line, under the guise of histories of the whole race

Genealogie de l'illustre et ancienne maison de haut et puissant prince Mylord Duc de Gourdon, Marquis de Huntly, Comte d'Ainzie, Seigneur de provinces de Badenots et Lokaber, Baron de Stradoun, d'Achindoun, de Strabolgy, etc, Pair d'Escosse, descendant par les Rois d'Escosse, des Rois d'Angleterre, des Rois de France et d'autres Princes Souverains. [Circa 1700]

> A folio volume of six pages printed on parchment and now in Gordon Castle. In the same volume there is a MS translation into English made by Archibald Anderson, library keeper at Gordon Castle, in 1748, followed by a continuation of the genealogy to 1748, and by a "short account of the principal transactions during the time of Alexander, second of that name and fourth Duke of Gordon," beginning in 1758 and ending abruptly in 1765. This volume is referred to on p 61, of C A Gordon's *Concise History.* A MS copy of the genealogy in French is mentioned in Nicholson's *Scottish Historical Library*, 1702, as being then *penes Dom Robertum Sibbald.*

The History of the Ancient, Noble and Illustrious Family of Gordon,

from their first arrival in Scotland in Malcolm III's time to the year 1690 ;
together with the history of the most remarkable transactions in Scotland from
the beginning of Robert I, his reign, to the year 1690, containing the space of
400 years   all faithfully collected from ancient and modern Scots and foreign
historians, manuscripts, records and registers of this nation.   In two volumes.
By Mr. William Gordon, of Old Aberdeen.   Edinburgh · printed by Mr.
Thomas Ruddiman, for the author, 1726-27   8vo   Vol 1, pp xxxi, 440, vol.
ii, pp viii, 624.

> This is an account of the Gordons told in the terms of the general history of Scotland
> In his Preface to the second vol he says "I have already, in the Introduction to
> the First Volume, accounted for the motives that induced me to publish this History,
> and the Authors from whom I collected it   In that Introduction I promised to
> bring down the History of the Nation, with that of the Family of Gordon, to the
> year 1689, but the many and various Accidents that happened during the Rebellion
> in King Charles I's Time having swell'd this Volume to a greater Bulk than is
> proper for an Octavo Book, I was forced to break it off abruptly at the martyrdom of
> that most excellent Prince, and confine myself to the History of the Family of Gordon "
> Next to nothing is known about the author save that he was a student at Marischal
> College, 1694-98.   In his *History* (ii., 405), he says " I shall give an account of
> it [the taking of Kelly in 1644], as I had it from *an uncle of my own, Gilbert Keith*
> of Caldhome, who was there with his chief the Earl Marischal, and other gentlemen
> who were present ".   Scott (*Fasti Eccles Scot.*, iii, 589), says that William Gordon
> —minister of Kintore, 1679 to 1695 (ejected), and died 1697)—married *Janet Keith*,
> and had two sons Alexander and James, and two daughters—Catherine (married
> Mr Rob Keith, min of Ballantrae) and Anna   Munro's *Old Abdn* (i, 280), shows
> that in 1702 "Mr. Wm. Gordon, merchant burgess of Aberdeen, sone to Mr
> Wm G, min at Kintore," was admitted a burgess of Old Aberdeen.   Thus the
> min of Kintore had at least one son more than those mentioned in Scott's *Fasti*
> May not the Mr Wm Gordon, burgess of Old Aberdeen, in 1702, whose mother
> was Janet Keith, be the historian, "Mr William Gordon of Old Aberdeen," whose
> uncle was Gilbert Keith ?   Gordon's book is not very useful, but it is rising in price
> Wodrow in a letter to Dr James Fraser dated Aug 27, 1728 (*Analecta Scotica*, 1, 3, 20-1)
> says —" I am told Mr. Gordon of Aberdeen, who was at Sheriffmuir and who hath
> lately published the *History of the Gordons* designes an answer to my book.   If he
> support what he sayes by no better vouchers, and breath the same bitter and violent
> spirit of slavery, that in my opinion is pretty plain in his *History of the Gordons*, I
> imagine, if I live to see his book, I shall notice it as little as I have done the pelts I
> have got from some Jacobite and high flying writers on the other side "

A concise history of the Antient and Illustrious House of Gordon, from
the origin of the name to the present time: together with an account of the
pedigree of his grace the Duke of Gordon and of the Right Honourable the
Earl of Aboyne, and the Lord Andrew, Count Gordon, nearest collateral
branches of the illustrious family, all faithfully collected from Scotch and

Foreign historians, manuscripts, records and registers.   By C [harles] A. Gordon   Aberdeen   printed for the author, 1754   8vo   Pp xi , 320.   It was reprinted by D. Wyllie & Son in 1890 (8vo , pp xi., 155) , edited by A. M Munro

> Nothing is known of the author of this book (which is mainly a condensation of William Gordon's work) except his own statement that he was "a stranger in this country"

Surgundo   Edinburgh   Thomas G. Stevenson, 1837.

> This metrical history of the Gordons written in some 2000 doggerel couplets is really entitled *The Valiant Christian*, and was edited by Charles Kirkpatrick Sharpe, who printed fifty copies in 1837 as a quarto of 69 pp   The original is in the Advocates Library, Edinburgh.   There is no vestige of the author's name , but at the bottom of the first page is this memorandum   "Lent by Patrick Gordon of Bonhall [Binhall ?] to Glenbucket", and on the blank page at the end   " John Gordon of Glenbucket ".   Its argument runs —
>
> > " The Authores Proheme poyntes at his sadde fate
> > Gordone Duke Raymore [Moray] killes, vhich breids debate.
> > The Gentilles rysse in armes, and him assealles ,
> > Chrystes lawe he doeth professe, and stille preveilles "
>
> The names of persons and places in the poem are written as anagrams.   Thus Abergeldie appears as " Rabidegell ", Avochie as "Chiava ", Knockespok as Paesseneok and so on.   The hero Surgundo [Gordonus] is the first Marquis of Huntly.

The Records of Aboyne, MCCXXX-MDCLXXXI   Edited by Charles XI , Marquis of Huntly, Earl of Aboyne, P.C., LL D.   Aberdeen : printed for the New Spalding Club, 1894, 4to, pp. xliii., 589

> This is a brilliant piece of genealogical work, in which Lord Huntly had the able assistance of Mr D Murray Rose (*cf Notes and Queries*, 8, iv , 287).   It contains an excellent sketch of the rise of the Gordons, and takes the reader down to Charles I , Earl of Aboyne   While primarily dealing with the ennobled Gordons of Huntly, it contains brief deductions of various cadets who crossed their path in the innumerable land transactions recorded in Lord Huntly's charter chest   It is a model of how such a book should be done

A history of the Family of Seton during eight centuries   By George Seton, advocate, M A Oxon. etc.   Edinburgh   privately printed by T & A Constable, printers to her Majesty, 2 vols., 1896

> These volumes, forming probably the most sumptuous of Scottish family histories, treat the Huntly branch as cadets of the great Seton family (pp. 375-459)

Genealogical Collections concerning families in Scotland made by Walter Macfarlane, 1750-51, 2 vols   Edinburgh · printed for the Scottish History Society, 1900.

> " GORDON—from the printed and MS. histories of that name composed, as also observations thereon deduced from original writers."   See vol ii., pp 409-23

Minutes of evidence taken before the Lords Committees to whom was referred the petition of George, Earl of Aboyne, stating his right to the titles, honours and dignities of Marquess of Huntley, Earl of Enzie, and Lord Gordon and Badenoch, 1838, 43 pp.

> The Earl of Aboyne presented a second petition claiming the older title of Earl of Huntly, but this claim was not pressed. *Lords Journals,* lxix , 27 ; lxx , 329, 342, 358, 383, 402, 471

Claim of George, Marquis of Huntley to be added to the Union Roll of the peers of Scotland, 1838, 14 pp. and pedigree.

> When the Union Roll was drawn up the Marquisate was merged in the Dukedom

Memorials of the Troubles in Scotland and England, A D 1624—A D 1645, by John Spalding, 2 vols. 4to   Spalding Club, 1840-1

> This classic contains the best account of Gordons who took part in the religious struggle mentioned.   Among the families more elaborately treated (see index) are the Gordons of Ardlogie and Gight, Haddo, Newton, Birkenburn, Cairnburrow, Park, Glenbucket, Straloch, Buckie and Rothiemay

Inquiry into the Law and Practice in Scottish Peerages. By John Riddell. 2 vols Edinburgh, 1842   Huntly, pp. 341-2, 526, 872-93, 1032-3.

Caledonia. By George Chambers. Paisley, 1888. See ii , 544 , v., 396

Pedigree of Gordon of Huntly and Abergeldie.

> Privately printed by Sir Thomas Phillipps, bart

The Earls of Huntly with regard to filii carnales. By Alexander Sinclair. In *Herald and Genealogist,* vi , 595.

Marquisate of Huntly, in Maidment's *Collectanea Genealogica* (Edinb., 1883), p. 110.

Arms of Dukes of Gordon are dealt with by G. E. C. and illustrated in Howard's *Miscellanea Genealogica,* iii., 133.   •

> The seals of the early members of the Huntly Gordons were described by P J. Anderson (with illustrations) in *Scottish Notes and Queries,* 1 , xi , 65-6.

The Gordon Book, edited by J. M. Bulloch, 1902

> This volume (8vo, pp 84) was published in connection with the Fochabers Reading Room Bazaar. It contains fourteen full-page pictures and articles by the editor on Jane Maxwell, wife of the fourth Duke of Gordon and on her daughter the Duchess of Richmond besides a list of all officers of the name of Gordon, who fought in the South African War, 1899-1901 A good deal of out of way gossip about Jane Maxwell has been contributed by J M Bulloch to *Bon-Accord* (Aberdeen), July 3,

10 and 17, 1902, Oct. 2 and 9, 1902, and July, 16 and 23, 1903   The later volumes
of *Scottish Notes and Queries* contain a great deal of matter about the Duchess

The Gay Gordons, in the *Scottish Review*, xxv., 246-69   April, 1895
Also under same title by J. M. Bulloch, in *Blackwood's Magazine*, Feb. 1898.
The Gay Gordons is also the name of a volume of "Ballads of an ancient
Scottish Clan". Edited by Armistead C Gordon, Staunton, Virginia   1902.

> Mr. Gordon is a lawyer in Staunton, is descended from an Irish branch of the Gordons
> who were probably descended from the Gordons of Craichlaw in Wigtonshire
> The volume (of which 250 only were printed—in black and red, Jensen type) is an
> octavo and contains the ballads of "Edom o' Gordon," "Gordon of Brackley,"
> "Knockespock's Lady," "Kenmure," "Young Lochinvar," "Lewis Gordon," "O
> Where, tell me Where, "The Baron of Brackley," "Kenmure," 1715, "Castle
> Gordon," "Suspense" (by a Virginian Gordon, written upon "Chinese" Gordon at
> Khartoum) the "Gay Gordons" by Henry Newbolt," and "Ivy" by the editor.

Invercharrach.—*Balbithan MS.*, 57, 67

Invergordon.—*The correspondence of Sir John Gordon, baronet, of
Invergordon, on occasion of the Rebellion, Autumn, 1745, containing some
particulars of those Times*   Edited by James Maidment (Edinb., 1835)   See
also Fraser's *Earls of Cromartie.*

Inverlochy.—Cadet of **Croughly.**

Invermarkie.—Macfarlane's *Geneal. Coll*, i., 335; ii., 243, 483.   Cadet
of **Cairnburrow.**

Invernettie.—Temple's *Fermartyn*, 266, 267   Cadet of **Lesmoir.**

Johnsleys.—*Balbithan MS.*, 44.

Kenmure.—Burke's *Landed Gentry* (1898), i., 595, McKerlie, ii, 66,
74, 216, 243, 244, 254, 312, 365, 389, 410, 411, 421; iv., 42, 53-68, 70, 72,
v, 199; G E. C.'s *Complete Peerage*, iv., 344-46, Fergusson's *Laird of Lag*,
38, 50, 51, 90, 91, 126, Hewlett's *Scotch Dignities*, 49, Forfeited Estate papers
in H.M. Register House.   John and William, 1st and 6th viscounts, are dealt
with in the *Dictionary of National Biography*.   A tabular pedigree of the
family written on the opening of a sheet of folio paper was sold at Sotheby's
in the *Phillipps Collection*, on May 1, 1903   It was undated, but the water-
mark was 1802.   The pedigree went as far as Robert, "who but for the attainder
would have been Lord Kenmuir"   *Add MSS* (Brit. Museum), 33, 596, f. 33.

Kennertie.—*Records of Aboyne*, pp 22-29 and 126-31, 226-29.

Kethocksmill.

An attempt to deal with this family was made (pp 615-23), in *Virginia Genealogies*, *a genealogy of the Glassell family of Scotland and Virginia, also of the families of Ball, Brown, Bryan, Conway, Daniel, Ewell, Holladay, Lewis, Littlefrage, Moncure, Peyton, Robinson, Scott, Taylor, Wallace and others, of Virginia and Maryland* By Rev Horace Edwin Hayden, M.A , Wilkes-Barre, Penn , 1891-97 8vo , 759 pp The late Rev Father William Gordon, Superior of the Oratory, Brompton (1827-1901), spent the latter years of his life in investigating the history of his family, and the present writer was greatly indebted to him in compiling the descent of the family in *Scottish Notes and Queries*, July, 1900, and May, 1902

Kincraigie.—*Balbithan MS.*, 47, 51, 67.

Kindroch.—*Balbithan MS* , 31, 32

Kinellar.—Cadet of **Lesmoir.**

Kinernie.—*Balbithan MS* , 67.

Kinmundy.—Temple's *Fermartyn*, 309-14 ; see also under **Pitlurg.**

Kinnoir.—*Balbithan MS.*, 42, 43.

Kirkconnell.—McKerlie, iii , 21, 314 , v., 194, 195, 281.

Knawen.—*Balbithan MS.*, 55, 56, 57, 60, 61

Knock.—*Balbithan MS* , 45 ; Macfarlane's *Geneal. Coll.*, 1 , 252

Knockbrex.—McKerlie, iii., 199, 210, 211 ; iv., 171

Knockespock.—*Balbithan MS* , 17, 43, 48, 57, 63, 64 ; Burke's *Landed Gentry*, 2nd and 3rd editions , *Scottish Nation*, ii., 321 ; Jervise's *Epitaphs*, ii., 87.

Law.—*Balbithan MS* , 47, 48.

Leicheston.—*Balbithan MS.*, 33, 43, 47, 49

Lesmoir.—*Balbithan MS.*, 43-45. The *Genealogy from father to son of the House of Lesmoir*, as it was painted on the *chimney* of the said house, transcribed therefrom by Dr. Thomas Gordon of Craigelly, and printed on pp. 99, 100 of *Memorials of the family of Gordon of Lesmoir, in the County of Aberdeen*, by Captain Douglas Wimberley, late of the 79th, or Cameron Highlanders . printed for the author at the office of the *Northern Chronicle*, Inverness, 1893, 4to, pp. 170. *Printed statement of the claim to the Baronetcy*, by Captain Herbert Spencer Compton Gordon, 1887 , Douglas's *Baronage*, 30 ; Temple's *Fermartyn* (260-71) ; *Records of Aboyne*, 75-86 and 193-99 , G. E C 's *Complete Baronetage*, ii., 299, 300.

Letterfourie.—*Balbithan MS*, 18, 19, 57, Jervise's *Epitaphs*, 1, 277, *Scottish Nation*, 11., 323. See any Baronetage.

Sir Robert Gordon of Gordonstoun, second son of Adam, Earl of Sutherland, was created premier baronet of Nova Scotia, 1625, and on the death of his great-great-grandson in 1795, without issue, this baronetcy passed to James Gordon of Letterfourie, who was descended from James I of Letterfourie, brother of Adam, Earl of Sutherland A branch of this family settled in Holland, and the *Biographisch Woordboek der Neder-landen* states that Solomon Gordon, of the Swiss Regiment in Holland, was the great-grandson of James I. of Letterfourie Solomon's daughter, Gertrude (born 1669), was a poet, and is biographed in the *Woordboek* Another member of this family was Otto Dirck Gordon, Colonel of a Company of the Civil Guards, Utrecht

Lettoch.—*Scottish Notes and Queries*, 2; iv, 141.

Loch Dougan.—*Earlston MS*

Lochinvar.—*Balbithan MS*, 7-9; G E C.'s *Complete Baronetage*, 11, 314, Wood's *Walter Pringle*, 93-6, 103, 107. *Add. MSS.* (Brit Museum), 33, 531, f. 213

Scott's ballad of "Young Lochinvar" refers to this family Another version appears in Buchan's *Gleanings of* . . *old ballads*, 74-5

Logie.—Pratt's *Buchan* (1901), 243; see under **Ardmeallie.**

Lungar.—Temple's *Fermartyn*, 310. See also under **Pitlurg.**

Manar.—Burke's *Landed Gentry* (1898), i, 598, Jervise's *Epitaphs*, 1., 360, *Scot. Notes and Queries*, 2, iv, 141, Dingwall Fordyce, *Family Record*, ii., 24, 25. Gordons as Watchmakers, *Scot. Notes and Queries*, 2, v, 51.

Merdrum.—*Balbithan MS.*, 52

Methlick.—See **Haddo.**

Midmar.—See **Abergeldie,** and Macfarlane's *Geneal. Coll*, 11, 323, 414

Milrig.—Burke's *Landed Gentry*, 1, 233

Minmore.—Jervise's *Epitaphs*, 1., 146; Burke's *Landed Gentry* (1898), 1, 601 Cadet of **Knockespock.**

Monaughty.—Cadet of **Lesmoir.**

Murfad.—McKerlie, 111., 35, 414; iv, 56, 57, 61, 262, 281, 282, 292, v., 59, 292.

Netherbuckie.—*Balbithan MS*, 57, 65.

Nethermuir.—*Balbithan MS.*, 35, 55, 56; Dingwall Fordyce, *Family Record*, 1., 153, 154. Paterson's *History of Ayr*, i, 220, 221 See also under **Auchleuchries** and **Bonnyton.**

Newark-upon-Trent.—Betham's *Baronetage*, iii., 316, 317.

This family was descended from the Gordons of Craichlaw. They were created baronets, 1764 The baronetcy became extinct, 1831. *Add MSS* (Brit. Museum), 32, 718, f. 60, etc.

Newtimber (Sussex)—Burke's *Landed Gentry* (1898), i., 599.

Newton.—Temple's *Fermartyn*, 263, 264; *Balbithan MS*, 44; Jervise's *Epitaphs*, ii., 326; *Scottish Notes and Queries*, 2, iv., 162, Macfarlane's *Geneal Coll*, i., 257, 335; ii., 27, Family Bible at Newton owned by Mr. A. M. Gordon.

Noth.—*Balbithan MS.*, 16, 50, 51, 60.

Overskibo.—See **Sir R. Gordon's MS. Tables,** *supra*

Oxhill.—*Balbithan MS.*, 43.

Park.—*Balbithan MS.*, 36-39; Temple's *Fermartyn*, pp 221-26, 282, 283; Riddell's *Inquiry*, pp. 709-10; Burke's *Landed Gentry* (1898), i., 428, 429, *Notes and Queries*, 6, vii, 415. Forfeited Estates papers in H.M. Register House. Cadet of **Cairnburrow.**

Parkhill.—See **Pitlurg.**

Parkmoir.—*Balbithan MS*, 67, 68.

Pethnick.—*Balbithan MS.*, 66, 67.

Pitglassie.—*Balbithan MS.*, 67.

Pitlurg.—*Balbithan MS.*, 28, 30, 31. Jervise's *Epitaphs*, ii., 30, 31. "The Straloch Papers" in the *Miscellany of the Spalding Club*, vol. i., 3-58. These letters date from 1586 to 1646, and are addressed chiefly to Sir John Gordon of Pitlurg and Robert Gordon of Straloch, the map-maker. See also Temple's *Fermartyn* (pp. 303-17), Burke's *Landed Gentry* (1898), ii., 1356-57; *Scottish Nation*, ii., 321; *John Gordon of Pitlurg and Parkhill*, 1885. See lives of Robert Gordon, founder of Gordon's College, by A. Walker (1876), and R. Anderson (1896).

Pittendreich.—*Balbithan MS.*, 17, 20, 21. Cadet of **Cluny.**

Prony.—*Balbithan MS.*, 32, 41, 42, 55, 58, 59, 60, Macfarlane's *Geneal. Coll*, ii., 410. See **Prony** and **Theodore Gordon MSS.,** *supra.*

Rhynie.—*Balbithan MS.*, 45, 52

Rothiemay.—*Balbithan MS.*, 24, 57, 65; Temple's *Fermartyn*, 144-150

This family were notorious in connection with the bloody vendetta which they carried on with the Crichtons of Frendraught. The first laird of Rothiemay (who belonged to the Cairnburrow family) was killed in a march dispute with Crichton in January,

1630, and his son, the second laird, was burned at Frendraught House in the follow-
ing October, along with John, Viscount Aboyne, son of the first Marquis of Huntly
An enormous amount of literature deals with their feud, notably in the *Privy Council
Register.* Reference may also be drawn to D Shearer's *Notes on the Parish of
Rothiemay* (Huntly, 8vo, 36 pp) and Cramond's *Rothiemay House* (Banff, 1900)

Rothney.—*Scot. Notes and Queries,* 2, iv , 141 , Jervise's *Epitaphs,* 323.

Rusco.—McKerlie, III , 34, 35, 46, 159, 219, 334, 348, 437, 488, 501,
502 ; iv., 27, 262, 281, 282, 322 ; v., 85, 86, 294.

Saphak.—Cadet of **Crichie.**

Sallagh.

Gilbert Gordon of Sallagh continued Gordon's *Earls of Sutherland* from 1630 to 1651.

Sauchin.—*Balbithan MS.,* 66, 67.

Savoch.—*Balbithan MS.,* 54, 55.

Schives.—See **Gight.**

Scotstown.

The Gordon-Oswalds are descendants of Gordon of Balmuir, a descendant of the
Nethermuir family. See Walford's *County Families,* 1902.

Scurdargue.

"Jock" Gordon of Scurdargue was one of the two illegitimate cousins of Elizabeth
Gordon, the heiress who founded the ducal line, and it is his descendants who
occupy the main part of the *Balbithan MS.*

Seaton.—Macfarlane's *Geneal. Coll.,* II., 217.

Sempill.—*Add. MSS.* (Brit. Museum), Catalogue for 1882-7.

Shalloch.—*Earlston MS.*

Sheelagreen.—Temple's *Fermartyn,* 264-66 ; *Balbithan MS.,* 55. See
under **Newton.**

Shirmers.—McKerlie, III., 63, 76, 78-83, 90, 96, 104, 410 , IV., 62 ,
v , 58 A pedigree (MS.) of this family, prepared by the College of Heralds,
is owned by Major Evans-Gordon, M.P.

Sideray.—See **Sir R. Gordon's MS. Tables,** *supra.*

Smithston.—*Balbithan MS ,* 36

Soccoth.—*Balbithan MS.,* 45, 62.

Sorbie.—See Knowles' *Account of the Coultharts,* 1855 Burke's
Visitations, 2nd series, I., 47, 271.

Stanmore (Baron).—See **Haddo**.

Lord Stanmore, youngest son of the 4th Earl of Aberdeen, and created Baron, 1893, was
associated when young with Bentley Priory, Stanmore It is a curious fact that
Bentley Priory is now in the possession of Mr Frederick Gordon, the founder of
the Gordon Hotels of London and elsewhere Mr Gordon was born in Herefordshire,
but he writes that his family came originally from Aboyne His son Vivian is an
officer in the 1st Gordon Highlanders. Lord Stanmore's son is an officer in the
3rd Gordons—so that the two families, totally unrelated, have joined a common
cause

Stitchel.—See **Lochinvar**.

Straloch.—Cadet of **Pitlurg**.

This family, which is descended from the Gordons of Pitlurg, included some notable
men Robert Gordon (1580-1661), of Straloch, together with his son James Gordon
(1615 ?-1686), the famous parson of Rothiemay, contributed greatly to the maps of
Scotland in Bleau's "Atlas" In addition to the Straloch MS , see the Straloch
papers (*Spalding Club Misc* , 1-58) , Scots Affairs (Spalding Club, 1841)

Strathdon.—Macfarlane's *Geneal. Coll.*, 11 , 60, 217, 218, 418, 419, 446.

Sutherland.

After the Huntly Gordons themselves, the history of their cadets who became Earls of
Sutherland—and used the family name of Gordon until the time of John, Earl of
Sutherland (1660-1733), who "quitted" it at a date unknown—has been more
elaborately dealt with than that of any other branch of the family. The published
histories are as follows —

*A Genealogical history of the Earldom of Sutherland, from its origin to
the year* 1630. Written by Sir Robert Gordon of Gordonstoun, Baronet
With a continuation to the year 1651 [by Gilbert Gordon of Sallagh] Pub-
lished from the original manuscript. Edinburgh . printed by George Ramsay
& Co , for Archibald Constable & Company, Edinburgh , and White, Cochrane
& Co , London, 1813 Folio Pp. xvi + 575 + xi

This fine folio is printed from the MS in possession of the Duke of Sutherland The
writer, Sir Robert Gordon of Gordonstoun, who dedicated his work to John Earl of
Sutherland, dating from Dornoch 1630, was the 11th Earl of Sutherland's second
surviving son by Lady Jane Gordon, daughter of the 4th Earl of Huntly He died
1656. The work was continued (pp 447-562) by Gilbert Gordon of Sallagh The
oldest MS. of Sir Robert Gordon is preserved at Dunrobin It is a folio of
228 pages, to which is prefixed (according to the *Sutherland Book*, 1 , x) —

    (1) An elaborate title page, extending over the whole page ,

    (2) Catalogue of the principal authors consulted, including volumes collected by
        the learned William Camden, 2 pp ,

    (3) " The Epistle dedicatorie " to John, 13th Earl of Sutherland (2 pp);

    (4 & 5) Descriptions of the armorial bearings of the Earl of Sutherland and Sir
        Robert Gordon (one page each) ,

(6) " The description of the provvince off Sutherland with the Commodities thereoff " : 7 pp ,

(7) The Preface, one page.

Appended to the *Genealogie* proper there is a short discourse of the Earle of Southirland his precedencee in Parliament of the Earle of Catteyness, wryten the year 1617 by Sir Robert Gordoun, 12 pp   The volume is beautifully bound in russia leather, and on a fly leaf of the modern binding is the following note holograph of the second Duke of Sutherland : " This manuscript of the History of the Family of Sutherland was given to me by Mr Richard Gordon, descendant of Sir Robert Gordon in 1643 —Sutherland." Underneath that note is another—" This volume is altogether in the handwriting of Sir Robert himself " This second note is in pencil by the late Mr Cosmo Innes   Sir William Fraser took a different view   " Throughout the copy there are many additions and alterations in the undoubted handwriting of Sir Robert, extending occasionally to whole pages, while his marginal additions are numerous These certainly show that the finely engrossed copy was made from an earlier draft which had been superseded by the copy on which the author made his additions and emendations from time to time.   In this way the copy of the original draft had come to be considered as the original " Sallagh's continuation extends to sixty-three folios   This and a copy of Sir Robert's manuscript belong to Sir Robert's son, Robert Gordon of Cluny   It was acquired by Lady Jean Wemyss, the Countess of the 14th Earl of Sutherland, and presented by her to her son the 15th Earl in 1705. It is this copy that was printed.   It was entrusted by the Marchioness of Stafford to Archibald Constable in October, 1806, to be printed privately as a presentation quarto, but it did not appear till 1813, and then it came out as a folio in the ordinary way.   It was edited by Henry Weber (1783-1818), the crazy Anglo-Westphalian, who was Scott's amanuensis.   He challenged Scott (see Lockhart's *Life*) in a moment of madness to a mortal duel in the year of the publication of this book. There are three other MSS besides the Dunrobin one in existence and the Duke of Sutherland possesses some interesting supplementary tables by Sir Robert, *supra*, p. xxxv.   While dealing primarily with the noble house of Sutherland, Gordon's work throws a flood of light on other branches.

The Sutherland Book, by Sir William Fraser, K.C B , LL.D   In three volumes [vol. 1, Memoirs, pp. xlvi. + 520 . vol. ii., Correspondence, pp. xxxviii. + 381 : vol. iii., Charters, pp. lix + 357]. Edinburgh, 1892.   Printed by Constable.   4to.

This bulky work forms a dry-as-dust supplement to Sir Robert Gordon's very readable work.   It is very similar to the other family chronicles by Sir William Fraser (1816-1898).

A large amount of valuable genealogical matter appeared in connection with the succession of Lady Elizabeth Sutherland to the Earldom, 1766   The 18th earl (and his wife) died of " putrid " fever at Bath in June, 1766, leaving an only daughter, Elizabeth, then thirteen months old   Her claim to succession was opposed by (1) Sir Robert Gordon of Gordonstoun, as heir male of the body of Adam Gordon, Earl of Sutherland, by his wife *suo jure* Countess   (2) by George Sutherland of Forss, as heir male of the first Earl of Sutherland.   The literature bearing on this subject consists of—

l

Case of Sir Robert Gordon, Bart.: to be heard at the Bar of the House of Lords, March 16, 1769 · 15 pp., 4to

Supplemental Case of Sir Robert Gordon, Bart., in which all facts and arguments in support of his claim are stated, and the inaccuracies in his original case and appendix (which were printed before the proofs arrived from Scotland) are corrected : To be heard at the Bar of the House of Lords before the Committee of Privileges — day of —, 1770   40 pp , 4to

Pedigree of Sir Robert Gordon (in connection with the case): one page.

Brief for the Counsel of Sir Robert Gordon, Bart   To be heard at the Bar of the House of Lords before the Committee of the Privileges on — the — day of March, 1771 : 158 pp., 4to. [" Lady Elizabeth Sutherland's voluminous additional case was not delivered to Sir Robert till Nov. 9 last, and six weeks were employed in examining it, and in detecting the errors with which it abounds.   There remained, therefore, a very short and inadequate space of time for the preparing and the printing of the present brief. On this foundation Sir Robert Gordon rests his apology for the inaccuracies of language and errors of small moment which may appear in it."]

Appendix (32) to the Case of Sir Robert Gordon · 35 pp , 4to.

Pedigree of the claimant, George Sutherland of Forss, Esq., as set forth by himself : one page.

The additional Case of Elizabeth claiming the Title and Dignity of Countess of Sutherland by her guardians · wherein the Facts and Arguments in support of her Claim are more fully stated, and the Errors in the additional cases exhibited for the other claimants are detected   177 pages.

The Sutherland Peerage, 1771, with an appendix of notes on Lord Mansfield's speech, 1771, 30 pp

The House of Lords decided on March 21, 1771, in favour of Lady Elizabeth Sutherland.

Earldom of Sutherland in " Reports of Claims preferred to the House of Lords"   Edited by James Maidment, Edinb , 1840 (pp. 55-83)   See also Riddell's *Inquiry,* p 606

A lost chapter in the History of Mary Queen of Scots Recovered : Notices of James, Earl of Bothwell, and Lady Jane Gordon, and of the dispensation for their marriage, remarks on the law and practice of Scotland relative to marriage dispensations   By John Stuart.   Edinburgh: 1874.   4to, pp 115.

Lady Jane Gordon, daughter of the 4th Earl of Huntly married (1) in June, 1565-66, James Hepburn, Earl of Bothwell   On May 7, 1567, this marriage was annulled as being within the fourth degree of consanguinity, and on May 15, Bothwell married Queen Mary.   Lady Jane married (2) Dec. 13, 1573, 12th Earl of Sutherland

Swiney.—Henderson's *Caithness Family History*, p 336.

Tarmore.—Cadet of **Cluny**.

Techmuiry.—Cadet of **Pitlurg**.

Terpersie Gordons.—*Balbithan MS*, 39, 46-49, 50, Temple's *Fermartyn*, 103 ; *Notes on the family of Gordon of Terpersie*, with a table of their descent. By Captain Wimberley. Inverness printed at the *Northern Chronicle* Office, 1900 8vo, 17 pp

> Captain Wimberley who was born in 1828 is the second son of the Rev. Charles Wimberley, Chaplain H E I.C S, who married in 1825 Mary, daughter of Major General Charles Irvine (son of the 17th laird of Drum), by Diana, second daughter of Sir Alexander Gordon, 6th Bart of Lesmoir. Captain Wimberley, who is to contribute an account of the Lesmoir Gordons to the next volume, has compiled deductions of the families of Irvine of Drum, of Wimberley and of Campbell.

See also *Scottish Notes and Queries*, Nov., 1900 ; Forfeited Estates papers in H.M. Register House.

Threave.—Burke's *Landed Gentry* (1898), i., 661, McKerlie, iii., 118, 127,'481, 482.

Tilielt.—Mair's *Presbytery of Ellon*, 20, 21, 30, 31, 36, 38, 47, 75, 76, 110, 111-14, 122, 123, 130 ; *Balbithan MS.*, 54, 56.

Tillyangus.—*Balbithan MS*, 50, 63

Tillyfour.—*Balbithan MS.*, 48.

Tillyminnat.—*Balbithan MS*, 42.

Tillytermont.—*Balbithan MS*, 30, 41-43, 49-51

Tilphoudie.—*Balbithan MS.*, 51 ; *Records of Aboyne*, 97, 140-44, 208-19, 270-75. See also **Tilphoudie MS.**, *supra*.

Toldu.—Macfarlane's *Geneal Coll.*, i., 252.

Tombea.—*Balbithan MS*, 21 22.

Torrisoul.—See under **Avochie, Beldornie, Wardhouse.**

Troquhain.—McKerlie, iii., 68, 70, 71, 96, 191, 250, 277, 408, 412, 429, iv., 54, 74, 97, 173, 299, 302, 303, 306, 307, 313, 314, 316, 317, 427, 462, v., 36, 280-282, 306, 307, 319.

Tulliegreig.—Temple's *Fermartyn*, 457 ; *Records of Aboyne*, 236-40

Tulloch.—*Balbithan MS*, 62, 63.

Wardhouse.—*Balbithan MS.*, 48, 50 ; Burke's *Landed Gentry* (1898), 1, 598-9, "an Aberdeenshire Dreyfus" (Alexander Gordon) by J M. Bulloch, *Aberdeen Free Press*, Aug. 26, 1898 ; *Scottish Notes and Queries*, Nov, 1898, *Bentley's Miscellany*, Nov. and Dec, 1868, " The Romance of a Waistcoat," by J. M. Bulloch, in *Black and White*, Nov. 19, 1898; *Catalogue of the Wardhouse Silver Plate* (sold in Aberdeen Nov. 3, 1898); Admiral Sir James Alexander Gordon, *Macmillan's Mag.*, Feb, 1868, Laird Clowes' *History of the Navy*, vol. 6, and *Dict. Nat. Biog.* The ballad of "Annie Gordon of Wardhouse and Peter Smith of Auchline" is given in a MS. in the possession of Mr. Compton Smith; see also *Scot. Notes and Queries*, iii., 191; iv., 46, 191

Waterton.—Burke's *Landed Gentry* (1898), i, 601, 602.

Wellheads.—*Balbithan MS.*, 57, 65.

Whiteley.—See under **Pitlurg.**

Wincombe Park (Wilts).—Burke's *Landed Gentry* (1898), i., 101.

GORDONS ON THE CONTINENT OF EUROPE.

Austria.

John Gordon of the Gight (*q.v.*) family assisted at the assassination of Wallenstein at Eger, 1634

France.

Some genealogists, notably Rymer (*Foedera*, 1, 791), maintain that the Gordons originally came from France. The Abbey of Gourdon (department of Lot) was the scene of many "treasure" digging expeditions down till 1842 (*Chambers Journal*, Nov. 20, 1897). Bernard Gordon, a notable physician, wrote a book *De Curandis Morris*, 1305 (see Larousse). M. de Gourdon was Governor of Calais, and owned ships He betrayed Gravelines to the Spaniards in 1578 (*Calendar of State Documents, Foreign Papers*, 1560-78, and Gordon's *Earls of Sutherland*, 137). The "Counts of Gordon" descended from the Glenluce family are dealt with in C. A Gordon's *Concise History of the Gordons* (reprint 1890), pp 125-130. Several soldiers of the name are dealt with in Father Forbes-Leith's *Scots Men at Arms of France*. Angelique Gordon, poet, is biographed in Larousse A Gordon family in Alsace (consisting of Gilbert Gordon, Captain of the Bourbon Regiment, chief surveyor for the town of Lichtenberg, and his brother John, Captain of the Navarre Regiment) were recognised by the Duke of Gordon as kinsmen in 1722 (quoted in *Aberdeen Free Press*, Sept 15, 1887). A Capt Gordon, who invented a flute, who was a member of the Swiss Guards in Paris and threw himself into the Lake of Geneva in 1847, was dealt with by J. M. Bulloch in the Aberdeen Philharmonic Society's Bazaar Book, Feb, 1899 Adjutant Commandant Gordon of the French army, murdered in 1815, is dealt with in *Scottish Notes and Queries*, 2nd series, vol. ii, 31, 79 Arthur Young in his *Travels in France* describes a Gordon who was imprisoned in the Bastile for thirty years. Mirabelle de Gordon, a French engineer, came to Scotland with the Jacobite leaders, 1745 (Chevalier Johnston's *Rebellion*, edited by Winchester, 1, 70, 71, 81, 83) Alexander Gordon of Wardhouse was executed at Brest for espionage, on Nov 24, 1769. In May, 1900, a Colonel Gordon was arrested while sketching from a boat, Fort Taureau, at Finistére A great many Jacobite refugees named Gordon sought sanctuary in France. Members of the family (notably the Hallhead Gordons) landed at Boulogne and Bordeaux, Rouen and Paris. William Gordon, the banker in Paris,

figures frequently in Jacobite literature   see specially " a letter dated March 20, 1723,
directed to Monsieur G[ordon], London, folio 1723 "   For priests of the name see
Records of the English Province of the Society of Jesus, 7 vols., 8vo, London, 1877 ,
also *Dict. Nat. Biog.* for James Gordon (1553-1641) confessor to Louis XIII. Adam
Lawrence Gordon was rector of Douai about 1666 (*Hist. MSS Com.*, v , 654).
Father Gordon was principal of the Scots College at Paris, 1751 (*Oliphants of
Gask*)   Lady Henrietta Gordon (*fl.* 1658), daughter of John, Viscount Melgum,
was maid of honour to Princess Henrietta, Duchess of Orleans (see Blakhal's *Three
Noble Ladies*, 1844).   For the Gordons at Waterloo see Dalton's *Waterloo Roll
Call*, 1890.   See also *Diary of the Scots College at Douai.*

Germany.

A great many Gordons became traders in Germany.   The references are too scattered to
be noted here, but special attention may be called to Mr Th A. Fischer's excellent
books . *The Scot in Germany* (1902), pp. 8, 26, 33, 58, 60, 113, 118, 133, 162, 218
and 255 , and *The Scots in Eastern and Western Prussia* (1903), pp. 37, 105, 199,
203, 205, 223.   Andrew Gordon (1712 1751), professor of natural philosophy at
Erfurt, gained a great reputation as an electrician (*Dict. Nat Biog*).   Gordons at
German universities will be found in various university *Fasti.*

Greece.—See Cairness.

Holland.

Many officers of the name of Gordon are dealt with in Ferguson's *Scots Brigade in
Holland*.   The *Biographisch Woordboek der Nederlanden* deals with Gertrude
Gordon (born 1669), poet: and Otto Dirck Gordon, a soldier, both said to be
descended from the Letterfourie Gordons.   Robert Jacob Gordon, Dutch Com-
mander-in-chief at the Cape, who committed suicide there in 1795, was dealt with
by J. M. Bulloch in the *Anglo-Saxon Review*, Dec., 1900; see also Kaye's *Life of
Sir John Malcolm* (1856)   Presbyterian ministers of the name are dealt with in
Steven's *History of the Scots Church at Rotterdam* , also Scott's *Fasti*, 1 , 154, 182,
543.   For traders see Munro's *Lord Provosts of Aberdeen*, 200 , Cramond's *Banff*,
II , 220 , (English) *Privy Council Acts*, 1 , 235, 416 , Birth Brieves in *Spalding Club
Misc* , vol 5 (see under Abergeldie, *infra*, pp. 98-9)

Italy.

For priests see *Records of the English Province of the Society of Jesus*, 7 vols , 1877.
Francis Gordon, who died in the service of the King of Naples, belonged to the
Craig family (Wimberley's *Gordons of Lesmoir*, 107)

Poland.

In the year 1727 Mr. Finch, "late Envoy from the King of Great Britain to Poland,"
wrote a letter to the Duke of Gordon (probably at His Grace's request) giving the
descent of Lady Catherine Gordon, daughter of the 2nd Marquis of Huntly and wife
of Count Morsztyn.   This document seems to have been highly prized, for I have
seen two copies of it (it fills a sheet and a half of foolscap).   One is in possession of
Rev Dr Milne, of Fyvie, and the other belongs to the New Spalding Club   There is
also a copy in Gordon Castle   Taking this document as a basis, the present writer
has written several articles—" The Last King of Poland," in the *Aberdeen Free*

Press, May 3, 1898, and the Aberdeen *Evening Gazette*, Nov. 17, Dec 15, 1902; and "The Gordons in Poland," in *Scottish Notes and Queries*, May, July, Sept and Dec, 1898, Aug 1902 Col. Fabian Gordon of the Coldwells family was in the Polish service (see *Services of Heirs*) A notorious character, Patrick Gordon, nicknamed "Steelhand," who gave the Covenanters a lot of trouble, went into the Polish cavalry. He is dealt with in the *Diary of Patrick Gordon of Auchleuchries* (Spald. Club), and in articles by J M. Bulloch on "Mercenaries" in the *Aberdeen Free Press*, Jan 24-25, 1901 His origin has not yet been settled For Sir Francis Gordon, H.M. Agent in Poland, see Braco Robert Gordon, founder of Gordon's College, Aberdeen, was a merchant in Dantzig. See biographies of him by Alexander Walker (1876) and Robert Anderson (1896)

Portugal.

Lieut.-Col. John Gordon, died 1785, was in the Portuguese army. He was a brother of George Gordon of Gordonbank (*Edin. Commissariot*, vol 126). Alexander Gordon, of Funchal, Madeira, is described, in 1764, by Lord Adam Gordon as "my relative and kind host" (*Genealogist*, xiv.). The wine firm of Cossart, Gordon & Co, Madeira (so called since 1861), was founded in 1745 In 1758 Thomas Gordon entered into partnership with Francis Newton. He came from Kirkcudbrightshire, and purchased the estate of Balmaghie (*q.v*). John Gordon, of Lisbon, had a son, Edward, who entered Christ Church, Oxford, in 1781 (Foster's *Oxford Graduates*)

Russia.

Owing to the fact that many Russian and Polish Jews have taken the name of Gordon— some say from the town of Grodno—the genealogist of the Scots house encounters great difficulties not only with the Gordons in Russia and ancient Poland, but also in every corner of the world to which the Hebrew, driven from the Pale, has betaken himself The great authority on the subject of the Gordons in Russia is the *Diary of General Patrick Gordon of Auchleuchries* (*q v*), the favourite of Peter the Great See also *The History of Peter the Great* (1755), by General Alexander Gordon of Auchintoul, the son-in-law of the above Patrick. Admiral Thomas Gordon, who was Governor of Kronstadt, was dealt with by J M Bulloch in the *Aberdeen Free Press*, Sept. 3, 19, 1898, and in *Scottish Notes and Queries*, Dec., 1898, and Jan, 1900; also in *The History of the Russian Fleet under Peter the Great*, edited by Admiral Sir Cyprian Bridge (Navy Records Society). Admiral Gordon's ancestry is not known. The famous Jacobite, General John Gordon of Glenbucket, had a son in the Russian Navy.

Spain.

There have been many Gordons in Spain. Captain Juan Gordon was killed on the *San Felipe*, one of the Spanish Armada (*Spanish State Papers*) Godfred Gordon, "a Spanish lord, descended from a noble house," behaved with great gallantry at the siege of Bergen-op-Zoom, 1588 (Gordon's *Earls of Sutherland*, 197) The Gordons of Wardhouse (*q.v.*) have long been in Spain, and the present family is almost Spanish A William Gordon was in the Spanish army, 1719 (*Jacobite Attempt of 1719*) William Gordon, a Scoto-Hispano Jesuit priest, went to convert the North American Indians, and wrote *Historia de las Missiones Jesuitas en la California*

baja desde su establecimento hasta, begun at La Paz, 1734, ended at Santiago, 1737
The MS. (small 4to, 360 pp) is described in Quaritch's great catalogue (vol v) as
, "very charming".. America returned the compliment in the person of Mrs. Alice
Gordon Gulick (died Sept 14, 1903), who was president for thirty years of the
International Institute for Girls in Spain (*Times*, Sept. 15, 1903)   Mrs Gulick
(whose maiden name was Gordon) belonged to an American family.

Sweden and Norway.

The wars of Gustavus Adolphus took several Gordons to Sweden, notably Col. John
Gordon of the Cotton family (see Wishart's *Deeds of Montrose*, edited by Morland
Simpson, 282-6).   Col. Alexander Gordon, grandson of Bishop William Gordon of
Aberdeen, was also in the Swedish army (Gordon's *Earls of Sutherland*, 477-8)
See also Spottiswoode, *Misc.*, ii , 384, and Donner's *Brief Sketch of the Scottish
Families in Sweden and Finland*, Helsingfors, 1884   William Gordon of the
Farskane family was a merchant at Christiansand, *circa* 1758.   William Gordon
was a merchant in Gothenburg in 181.. (*Scots Mag*)   George Gordon, vice-consul
for Sweden at Algiers, belonged to the Lesmoir family (see Wimberley's *Gordons
of Lesmoir*, 71).

GORDONS IN AMERICA.

ϟ Many branches of the family of Gordon are to be found in America.   Several emigrated
from Scotland to Virginia, as in the case of the ancestors of Mr John Gordon, of Rio
de Janeiro, who is now working on the history of the Gordons of Holm.   His
brother, Mr Seton Gordon, of New York, is also a great enthusiast   Another
branch settled in Massachusetts, where Mr. G. A Gordon has compiled a good deal
of material on the family.   As an indication of the prominence of the family in
America it may be noted that in the American *Who's Who*, 1901-2, seventeen Gordons are biographed as against twelve Grants and three Forbeses.   The family figures
in many of the genealogies which Americans are so fond of compiling, and which
unfortunately are so rarely to be found in libraries in this country   There is a good
deal about it in Hanna's *Scotch Irish* (New York, 1902)   Mr Armistead Gordon,
of Staunton, Virginia, has collected a vast amount of matter (still in MS) on the
family in America.   Descended from the Gordons of Sheepbridge House near
Newry, co Down, he has directed his attention specially to the Gordons in Ireland.
He writes to me . "I have lists of all Gordons now [1903] living in New York City,
Chicago, Philadelphia and Toronto, with their street addresses, and in the four
cities they number something over 1,200   Among these, however, are many
Russian and Polish Jews "   Captain Charles Gordon of U S. *Chesapeake* (38
guns), was dealt with by J M. Bulloch in the *Banffshire Journal*, Sept. 9, 1902.
General Patrick Gordon, the first Governor of Pennsylvania (born 1644, died 1736),
belonged to the Birsemoir family (see Appleton's *Encyclopædia*, Dalton's *Blenheim
Roll*, Burke's *Commoners*, iv , 9)   Rev. William Gordon (1728-1807), the historian
of the United States, was a Herts man (*Dict Nat. Biog*)   The following
references to the family of Gordon are given in the index to *American Genealogies*,
5th edition, Albany, N.Y., 1900 (pp. 136, 137) --— -

American Ancestry, iii , 23, 105 , iv , 155 , vii., 50 , viii., 53 ; x., 56,

Bedford, N. H. Centennial, 308-10, Bell's *History of Exeter, N. H.*, 21-24;
Chandler's *History of Shirley, Mass.*, 426; Cochrane's *History of Antrim,
N. H.*, 510-12; Cogswell's *History of Henniker, N. H.*, 590-94; Cothren's
Woodbury, Ct., ii, 1498-1501; Dearborn's *History of Salisbury, N. H*,
170; Goode's *Genealogy*, 122, Green's *Kentucky Families*, *Hall Genealogy*
(1892), 66-72; Hayden's *Virginia Genealogies*, 249-53, Hayward's *History
of Hancock, N. H.*, 610-13; Lincoln's *History of Hingham*, ii., 277; Mor-
rison's *History of Windham, N. H*, 538-42, *Old North-west Genealogical
Quar.*, ii., 49; *Richmond, Va., Standard*, iii, 31-47; Ridton's *Saco Valley,
Me, Families*, 701-5; Robertson's *Pocahontas Descendants*, 236, Slaughter's
Bristol Parish, Va., 203; Smith's *History of Petersborough, N H*, 93-95;
Walworth's *Hyde Genealogy*, 667-69; *Washington, N. H., History*, 448-50;
Whitehead's *Perth Amboy, N.J.*, 60-68. Mr. Armistead Gordon supplies
the following additional references to the Gordons in America, and especially
in Virginia *Ancestry of Benjamin Harrison* (Keith, 1893), 48; *Albemarle
County (Va.), History of* (Woods, 1901), 211, 212, 379, 381, 382, 383, 384,
404, *Debates of the Virginian Constitutional Convention of 1829-1830*,
Journal of a Young Lady of Virginia in 1782 (1871), 7, 8, 9, 10, 14, 15, 20;
Hening's *Statutes at Large of Virginia*, 1619-1800, ii., 370, 378, 557, 583;
vii., 188, 215, 608; viii., 57, 610; xi., 369; xii., 215, 216; xv., 184, xvi., 37,
Historic Homes of the South West Mountains of Virginia (Mead, 1899), 231-
40; *Culpeper County, History of* (Green, 1900), i., 7, 34, 66; ii., 23, 26, 33,
35, 40, 41, 51, 55, 114, 124-26, 145, 158; Appleton's *Cyclopædia of American
Biography*, 685-87, including biographical sketches of fourteen Gordons in
America; *Middlesex (Virginia) Parish Register from 1653 to 1812* (1897),
23, 94, 99, 100, 174, 177, 180, *Memoir and Correspondence of Thomas Jeffer-
son* (Randolph, 1829), iv., 336, 414; *Letters and Times of the Tylers* (Tyler,
1885), i, 343, 399, 476, 508, 527, 584; ii., 48; *Virginia and Virginians*
(Brock, 1888), ii., 828, 829; *Old Churches, Ministers and Families of Virginia*
(Meade), i., 153, 165, 192, 285, 364, 445; ii., 10, 13, 212, 213, 276, 285, 318;
Grigsby's Virginia Convention of 1776 (1855), 190, 206; *Grigsby's Virginia
Convention of 1788*, *Sketches of Virginia*, first series (Foote, 1850), 359-70;
North Carolina Historical Register, i, 546, 547, *The Virginia University
Memorial* (1871), 752, 755; *Proceedings of the 7th Congress, Scotch Irish
Society in America* (1895), 174, 306, 370, 374, *Virginia Historical Magazine*,
vii., 9, 16, 79, 205, 311, 312, 398, 404, 414, 438, ix., 222, 265, 326; x., 96,
106, 210, 279, 291, 308, 309, 315, 324, 432; *William and Mary College
Quarterly*, i., 116, 139, 147, 170; ii., 76, iii, 68, 221; iv., 119, 284; v., 60,
201, 255, vi 22, 82, 155, 168, 186, 188, 260; vii, 181, 190, 198; viii., 29,
48, 49, 91, 189; ix., 32, 33, 41, 49.

GORDONS IN BRITISH COLONIES.

Africa.

For the Gordons who fought in the South African War of 1899-1902 see a list by J. M
Bulloch of " The Gordons as Campaigners in Africa," printed in the *Gordon Book*
(1902), 75-84   See also under *Holland (supra)* for Robert Jacob Gordon, the
Dutch commander-in-chief at the Cape, who christened the Orange river

British Columbia.—The Gordons of Nanaimo and Cemox ; (Burke's
Colonial Gentry (1891), vol I.).

Canada.—*Canadian Men and Women of the Time*, 1st edition, 1898.

The best-known Canadian of the name is the Rev. Charles W Gordon, of Winnipeg,
who has made a great success with some novels written under the name of " Ralph
Connor "   His father, Rev. Daniel Gordon, belonged to Blair Athole, and was at
Marischal College, 1842-6   He emigrated to Canada   This Daniel is not to be
confused with the Rev Daniel Miner Gordon (son of William Gordon, a native of
Sutherland) who made a great tour, in 1879, which he described in *Mountain and
Prairie, a Journey from Victoria to Winnipeg via Peace River Pass* (Montreal,
✝ 1880, pp. 310)   The Rev. Charles Gordon's ancestry was dealt with in the *Aberdeen
Free Press*, Feb 23, 1889, Dec 29, 1900, Jan. 2, 1901   His English publishers
have issued a leaflet entitled *Ralph Connor. an Interpretation.*

Egypt.

The outstanding Gordon in the history of Egypt is Charles George ("Chinese")
Gordon (1833-1885) the hero of Khartum.   An immense literature has been written
about him, the British Museum catalogue containing 90 items, including lives by
M. A. de Bovet, Boulger, Sir W. Butler, Forbes, Haines, Hake, Swaine, Tabarie,
Walch and others.   But his connection with any line of the Scots house is still
untraced   Tentative solutions have been offered by J. M. Bulloch in the *Genealogical Magazine*, Oct., 1898, *Scottish Notes and Queries*, Nov., 1898, Feb., 1901
and Jan., 1903.

India.—The appearance of the Gordons in India has mainly been in the
Army or the Civil Service.   For notices of them reference should be made to
Dodwell and Miles's Alphabetical Lists of (1) *Officers of the Indian Army*
(1760-1837); (2) *Medical Officers of the Indian Army* (1764-1838), (3) *The
Honourable East India Company's Bombay Civil Servants* (1798-1839) ;
(4) *Bengal Civil Servants* (1780-1838); (5) *Madras Civil Servants* (1773-
1839).   For more modern services see the *India List* published annually by
Harrison, the *Indian Army List*, Thacker's *Indian Directory.*

Jamaica.—*Scottish Notes and Queries*, May, 1902.   *The Antiquary*
(ed. Jewitt), IV., 129, 130, has an article by Charles Sotheran on Gordon and
French families.

k

FAMILIES WITH COMPOUND GORDON NAMES.

A considerable number of families have hyphened " Gordon " either before or after other surnames In many cases it is easy to trace the reason of this In others the reason is not so obvious The Army List, the happy home of the hyphen, contains the greatest number of those compound names, showing at least that the Gordons are still animated by their old martial spirit It may be noted as proof of the fighting faculty of the Gordons that in the Monthly Army List of Aug '1903, there were 86 officers of the name (and 18 with the hyphened name) wearing the king's uniform , against 93 supplied by the Burnetts, Forbeses, Farquharsons and Leslies— perhaps the most common Aberdeenshire surnames after Gordon

Gordon-Browne.—See Cambridge *Matriculations*, 1851-1900.

Gordon-Canning.—See **Hartpury.**

Gordon-Cumming.—See **Altyre.**

Gordon-Cumming-Skene.—See **Pitlurg.**

Gordon-Dalrymple.

Mr. Arthur Dalrymple Gordon-Dalrymple of Greenknowe, Gordon, Berwickshire, and Langlee, Roxburghshire, is the son of the late Mr Arthur Forbes-Gordon of Rayne, Aberdeenshire (whose father, born Forbes, assumed the additional name of Gordon under the entail of his cousin, John Gordon of Avochie). His mother, Christina Dalrymple, was co-heiress of the laird of Greenknowe and Langlee. This lady's mother (Catherine Milne) was an Aberdeenshire woman (see Tancred's *Annals of a Border Club*)

Gordon-Dill.

This family claims descent (*via* Ireland) from the Gordons of Glenbucket See Cambridge *Matriculations*, 1851-1900 (under " Dill "); *Medical Directory*, 1903 ; *Army List*, 1903 , *London Directory*, 1903.

Gordon-Duff.—See **Drummuir.**

Gordon-Gilmour.—See **Hallhead.**

Gordon-Hallyburton.

Lord John Frederick Gordon, third son of the ninth Marquis of Huntly, took the additional name of Hallyburton See *Add. MSS.* (British Museum), 35,798, f. 383 , 35,802, ff 56, 556 , 35,800, f 102 , 35,802, f 510 , Foster's *Members of Parliament* (Scotland), 152

Gordon-Hogg.—See *Medical Directory*, 1903.

Gordon-Ives.—Burke's *Landed Gentry* (1898), 1 , 801.

Col. Gordon Maynard Ives of Bentworth Hall and Gaston Grange, Hants, son of John Robert Ives by the Hon Emma, daughter of third and last Viscount Maynard He adopted the additional name of Gordon in 1897.

Gordon-Leith.—See Thacker's *Indian Directory*, 1903

Gordon-Lennox.—Family name of the Duke of Richmond who represents the senior female line of the Dukes of Gordon.

Gordon-Moore.

In 1850 Lord Cecil Gordon, fifth son of the ninth Marquis of Huntly, adopted the additional name of Moore

Gordon-Munn.—See *Medical Directory*, 1903.

Gordon-Oswald.—See **Scotstoun.**

Gordon-Paterson.—See *Navy List*, 1903.

Gordon-Sims.—See Thacker's *Indian Directory*, 1903

Gordon-Smith.—See *London Directory*, 1903; also *Medical Directory*, 1903.

Gordon-Vaudin.—See *Navy List* and Crockford, 1903.

Gordon-Woodhouse.—See Kelly's *Titled Classes*, 1903

Gordon-Wright.—See Kelly's *Clergy List*, 1903

Conway-Gordon.—Burke's *Landed Gentry* (1898), v., 602.

Duff-Gordon.—See **Fyvie** and **Halkin.**

Evans-Gordon.—See **Shirmers.**

⸆ This family is descended from the Gordons of Shirmers. Major W. E. Evans-Gordon, M P, has in his possession a pedigree of the family compiled at the Herald's office. His arms are given in Fox-Davies' *Armorial Families.*

Fellowes-Gordon.—See **Knockespock.**

Forbes-Gordon.—Burke's *Landed Gentry* (1898), 1, 599

Arthur Forbes (died 1873) assumed the additional name of Gordon on succeeding to the estate of Rayne, under the entail and settlement of his late cousin, John Gordon of Avochie (*q v.*)

Forlong-Gordon.—See **Pitlurg.**

William Forlong of Erins, Argyllshire, married Crawford, daughter of the Lieut.-Gen Gordon-Cumming-Skene of Pitlurg, and their son Thomas Alexander George (b 1831) of South Erins, Argyllshire, assumed the name of Gordon on succeeding to his mother's estates (Walford's *County Families*, 1903).

Hamilton-Gordon.—Family name of Lord Aberdeen and Lord Stanmore.

McHaffie-Gordon.—Walford's *County Families* (1903).

Maitland-Gordon.—See **Kenmure**

More-Gordon.—See **Charleton MSS.**, *supra.*

Pirie-Gordon.—See **Buthlaw.**

Smith-Gordon.—See **Florida.**

Wolrige-Gordon.—See **Hallhead.**

ADDITIONS AND CORRECTIONS.

ABERGELDIE.

[NOTE.—*The pagination referred to is that at the bottom of the page*]

Page (72) —RACHEL GORDON, X. OF ABERGELDIE, and not her husband, Charles Gordon, was the issue of Alexander, VIII. of Abergeldie. The brass in the table is placed wrongly at this point

Page (75) —ALEXANDER GORDON OF MIDMAR Instrument of compromitt of the brief of perambulation of the marches between the lands of the barony of Stonywode, belonging to Andrew Frissal, and the lands of the Forest of Cordyce, belonging to Alexander Johnston of that ilk, to William Earl Marischal, and Alexander Gordon of Midmar, dated November 13, 1499 (*Inventory of papers formerly belonging to the family of Johnston of Caskieben, but now in the possession of Lord Saltoun*)

Page (77) —The 3rd Laird. Penuet, February, 1530. James Cheyne, Procurator to the laird of Abirgeldie, " requirit Dauid Andersoun and Maister Androwe Tulydef, bailzeis, to mak ane esy gait and passage betuix the brig of Dee and chapell of the samyn, quhairthrow thai may eselye without impediment, wyrk and lawbour thair watteris, protestand alwayis quhat damnage or skaith thai sustenit thairthrow suld cum on the toune and nocht on thame, and that in name and behalf of his master the lard of Abirgeldy, quhilk send with him seruand to that same effect " (Stuart's *Extracts from Aberdeen Council Register*, vol. 1, p 129).

Page (83).—The 4th Laird. The name of his daughter who married Thomas Menzies, " de Balgony," was Margaret. They had a son Michael who was at Douai as a boy of 14 in 1655 " ad figuras " (*Diary of Scots Coll. at Douai*)

Page (88) —The 6th Laird died in March, 1631, not in 1630 as stated (*Privy Council Reg.*).

Page (89), *line* 13 —Auchmill should be Inchmill. In any case the sentence quoted refers to the 6th laird, not his son William (who is mentioned in the *Balbithan MS.*).

Page (89), *lines* 14 *and* 15.—Thomas Gordon, "Abergeldie filius, annorum 17, pro figuris," was dismissed from the Scots College at Douai in 1633 "propter ineptitudinem in Maio" On the same date (Jan 6, 1633) his brother James, aged 14, "pro trivialibus scholis, dimissus propter ineptitudinem in Sept." (*Diary of Scots Coll at Douai*).

Page (90).—The 7th Laird Alexander Gordon, fiar of Abergeldie, was prosecuted, Jan. 25, 1631, for carrying arms (*Privy Council Reg.*). On Aug 11, 1631, Alexander Gordon of Abergeldie petitioned the Privy Council ·as follows: Some years ago, he was heritably infeft in the lands of Abergeldie under reservation of the liferent of his father, William Gordon of Abergeldie, who died in March last. He shortly afterwards obtained warrant from the Lords of Session for the inventorying of the goods within the place of Abergeldie and his own entering on possession, and his mother Elizabeth Seatoun, widow of William Gordon, left the place and went to Knock of which she was life rentrix. " But on ——— " she came back to Abergeldie and "has taken possession thereof with her family and will not remove". He craved that letters should be issued "charging her to remove" and the Privy Council agreed to this On July 2, 1632, Donald Farquharson of Inchemarrow was cautioned for Abergeldie to appear before the Council to underlie their censure touching his misbehaviour towards his lady under pain of 500 merks, and commanding him not to visit Jesuits and Papists (*Ibid.*) On Sept. 6, 1632, the tack granted to Lady Abergeldie of her conjunct fee was cancelled by the Council (*Ibid.*) Alexander Gordon, VII. of Abergeldie, owed in 1633-4 the following sums: 200 merks to John, son of Alexander Keith, portioner of Duffus; 300 merks to James Irving in Cullairlie; 1,000 merks to James Irwing (second lawful son of John Irwing of Artamphart) and Anna Keith his spouse, lawful daughter of the late Alexander Keith, portioner of Duffus, 1,400 merks to Robert Irwing of Fedderit; 1,000 merks to Arthur Ross of Sterein on the lands of Brasbeig; 9,225 merks to Mr. William Burnet, minister at Kinnernie in a woodset on the lands of Badinleithe and Kinnernie (*Spald. Club Misc.*, iii., pp. 89, 108, 111, 116, 130 and 138)

Page (97).—CHARLES GORDON, 12th Laird, had a book plate described by Mr. J. Henderson Smith, Edinburgh, thus· (Motto over crest "God with us"). Quarterly: 1st, azure, 3 boars heads couped; 2nd, or, 3 lions heads erased gules; 3rd, azure, 3 fraises; 4th, or, 3 crescents within a treasure flory counter-flory gules; all four quarters within a bordure company of 6 pieces or, 8 gules. A rare Chippendale plate of date *c.* 1740-1750 The shield is set in a rococo frame with floral accessories, and the helmet is set affrontee, which it should not be The crest is a greyhound trotting.

Page (105).—COSMO HUNTLY GORDON was at Harrow School, April, 1869 —Dec. 1871. He entered the Buffs 1874, and became a major 1891. He was A.D.C. to the governor of the Straits Settlements, 1880-1, and at the Staff College, 1887-8 (*Harrow School Register*, p 373). He is now (1903) Deputy Assistant Adjutant-General at Barbadoes His half-brother, CHARLES, is now in the 4th East Surrey Regiment. GEORGE HAMILTON GORDON is in the Artillery, not the Engineers as stated on page 105

Page (110).—LEWIS GORDON, 18th Laird, died at Lee, Kent, May 27, 1903. He was in business for 50 years, retiring in 1897. He had a paralytic stroke in July, 1900, and from that time to his death was an invalid. He was succeeded by his son Reginald Hugh Lyall Gordon, 19th Laird of Abergeldie.

GIGHT.

Page (189).—The second Laird's wife The *Balbithan MS* statement that the second laird of Gight married a daughter of Robert Gordon of Fetterletter seems corroborated by a letter in the Morton Charter Chest, for a copy of which I am indebted (since writing about my inability to get it on page 211) to Mr. Murray Rose. The letter is written "to my werray guid my Lord Erll Mortoune" by "Dame Elizabeth Gordoun Lade of Gycht," who dates from Fetterletter, Oct. 21, 1597. The letter runs.—

My Lord eftir my maist hairtlie commendationes of service I haif desyrit the Laird of Bolquhallie [Mowat with whose family the 5th laird of Gight had a vendetta in 1601] to spek your lordship sundrie tymes lyk as I spak your lordship with the Laird Bolquhollie in Aberdein at your lordships last being ther with the King's Maiestie for the Waird landis of Fettirlettir and Lethinthie and will maist ernistlie requeist your lordship to latt me haif eis and eis thairin as your lordship hes done to utheris obefoir And your lordship sall find me as freindlie and thankfull thairin as ony wtheris that hes delt with your lordship And thairfoir I send this Lettir with the young Laird Bolquhollie to your lordship luiking for favor and ressonabill eis herin seing the samyne hes been left and na effect takin therin I will request your lordship for ane favorabill answer with this berar in writt wtherwayis your lordship may appordone me to sek the best reminde I may for my landis as wtheris wassellis to my Lord Buchan hes done afoir, quhilk I will be lothe do except your lordship refus ressone quher of your lordship hes nocht bene in us

Page (263)—The 6th Laird's daughter MARY, wife of ALEXANDER INNES, of Coxton. This lady proved nearly as troublesome as the rest of her kins folk. On Dec 24, 1640, Gilbert Ross, minister of Elgin, is appointed to go to the goodman of Cokstoune and his wife Marie Gordon "that she may quyte her obstinacie in poperies, repair to the kirk, and hear the word and partake of the Sacrament" (Cramond's *Churches of the Parish of St Andrews-Lhanbryd*, p 6) On Feb. 18, 1641, the goodwife of Cokstoune is to reply within eight days. On April 29 she promised to go to church. On Jan. 27, 1642, the minister reported that he had good hopes for her conversion. For the present she is sick unto death, so no process is to be used against her On July 27, 1643, she was to be processed if she be not a constant hearer of the word and "vse conferences, reading to the good meanes whilk may most conduce for her conversione from poprie and superstitione". On Aug 10 she declares herself to be a Protestant and of the reformed religion and promises to be a constant hearer of the word. On Nov 2 she is to be excommunicated if she do not "constantlie heare the word". On Nov. 15 she promises to hear the word "if it should pleas God her health sould serve". On June 18, 1646, the Presbytery ordained that some of the brethren should go and speak with the "goodwyf of Cockstoun" On Aug 6 it was reported that she had gone to Balvenie, "but Cockston did deale with her and be a good instrument to mov her to giv satisfaction to the kirk" On May 7, 1647, it was ordained that if the goodwife of Coxton conform not, the process of excommunication is to go on against her. She died Aug. 20, 1647. In Lhanbryd old churchyard there is a stone tablet on the side wall of the aisle in her memory, erected by her husband Alexander Innes of Coxtoun. "Two shields of arms—Innes without difference, but without Aberchirder, and Gordon—also, I think, without difference" (*Family of Innes*, p 258)

Page (264) —The 7th Laird The *Book of Annualrentaris* shows he was a good deal in debt. In 1633-4 George Gordon "younger of Gicht" owed: 1,000 merks to Alexander Keith, portioner of Duffus; 3,000 merks to Alexander Lyon of Muiresk; 4,000 merks to Patrick Wod in Litill Ardo on the lands of Chapeltoun of Schives, 100 merks to William Watson at the Mill of "Tollie" (*Spalding Club Misc.*, iii, 96, 132).

Pages (270-1, 273).—The 8th Laird's daughter, MARIE. Marie Gordon married Lieut.-Col. John Gordon In a single page manuscript deduction of the Newton family, in the possession of Mr. A. M. Gordon of Newton, it is stated that John Gordon, son of James Gordon of Newton ("who married Auchmacoes daughter"), married "the Ladie Gight". This clearly means the Marie Gordon who puzzled me so much. She and her husband seem to have acted as tutors for her brother "Sir George's" daughter (Mrs Davidson) The Newton deduction further solves the difficulty (stated on page 273) about the two John Gordons

Page (270) —The 9th Laird. "Georgius Gordon, filius Baronis de Gight," entered Douai "ætat 12 ad figuras," on Nov. 9, 1663 (*Diary of Scots Coll. at Douai*).

Pages (280-1) —The 11th Laird's issue. I find from papers in the possession of Mr. A. M. Gordon of Newton that it was only the second son of the 11th laird of Gight who took the name of "Davidson". The rest called themselves Gordon. The second son, Alexander Davidson of Newton, had a son Alexander Davidson alive in 1784 when his grandmother, Mrs. Margaret Duff Gordon, widow of the 11th laird, bequeathed £200 to her son Lieut. Archibald Gordon, failing whom to Alexander Davidson, the son of her second son, and £100 to each of the latter's daughters, Mary and Margaret. She left her daughter Elizabeth her sole executrix Robert Gordon, youngest son of Alexander, XI. of Gight, was alive in 1772, when it is stated that his patrimony, £400, had gone to purchase him an ensigncy in the 44th regiment. I find that Ensign Robert Gordon of the 44th Foot was gazetted a lieutenant in the 35th Foot in July, 1776 (*Gent.'s Mag*)

Page (281).—The 12th Laird. Details about his connection in the estate of Newton, which his father owned, will be given at length in the section dealing with Newton.

THE BALBITHAN MS.

NEW SPALDING CLUB.

PREFATORY NOTE.

THE valuable genealogical account of the family of Gordon, known as the *Balbithan MS.*, is set in type here for the first time. It is printed from a small octavo volume of 159 pages, in a handwriting of the beginning of the eighteenth century. There is no title on the back, and no title page, but the late Mr. Charles Elphinstone-Dalrymple, to whom the manuscript belonged, and whose widow has kindly lent it to the Club, had written on the fly-leaf the legend : " Copy of the Genealogical Account of the Family of Gordon, called the *Balbithan MS.* ".

The origin of the document is far from clear. The Dalrymple volume may or may not be the original, but it is certainly the basis of most, if not all, of the transcripts that have been made during the last quarter of a century. Some idea of the mystery of the manuscript is conveyed by the fact that one genealogist, the Rev. Dr. Temple, Forgue, gives two different accounts of its authorship in four years. In a letter to Mr. A. M. Munro, dated 16th October, 1890, he declares that the manuscript " was compiled about 1730 by one of the Gordons of Craig, and came somehow into possession of Gordon of Balbithan— hence the name ". In his *Thanage of Fermartyn* (Aberdeen, 1894, p. 350), the same writer tells us that " James Gordon, I. of Balbithan, was the author of a MS. history of the Gordons of date about 1730, called the *Balbithan MS.* ". Which of these statements is correct, I cannot say ; nor do we know how Mr. Dalrymple, who was a keen genealogist, and who married one of

the Gordons of Parkhill, came to possess the *Balbithan MS.;*
nor whether his was the original. The number of obvious mis-
spellings of place names suggests that it was only a copy.

One thing, however, is certain. The manuscript of 1730
is identical in parts with an older one of 1644, a fragment of
which, written on quarto sheets of paper and beginning at page
31 and ending abruptly at page 46, is now in the University
Library, Aberdeen. There has, however, been a slight re-
arrangement of the text. Thus the 1644 fragment begins with
the Cluny Gordons (page 19 of this Balbithan reprint) and goes on
to page 24. It then turns back to pp 7-9, and afterwards jumps
to pp. 56-65. Equal obscurity overshadows the authorship of
the 1644 MS.; but the bare fact that both it and the *Balbithan
MS.* deal at greatest length with the descendants of "Jock"
Gordon of Scurdargue, suggests that the compiler, whoever he
was, belonged to one of the many cadets of "Jock's" house. He
only touches on the Lochinvar Gordons—"I leave it to others
to fill up what remains, not being informed thereof". He deals
very briefly with the ducal line; and in the case of the descendants of "Tam" Gordon, the brother of "Jock," he soon finds
himself "run aground for want of further and better information".

It is difficult to say when the *Balbithan MS.* was first used
by genealogists. The manuscript pedigree of the Drummuir
family, made about 1821, and now in the possession of Mr.
Thomas Gordon Duff of Drummuir, was plainly based on it.
Dr. Davidson seems to have made use of it in his *Earldom
of the Garioch*, 1878, while Dr. Temple in the *Thanage of
Fermartyn*, 1894, makes constant use of it, having had a
transcript of Mr. Dalrymple's copy.

Whatever the origin of the *Balbithan MS.*, there can be no
doubt as to its great value to the genealogist, for a reference to
state documents and other historical sources corroborate its

validity. As a whole it is wonderfully correct, especially in its details, coming down to beginning of the eighteenth century. Some cadets are brought down to a later date than others Thus the Gight family is made to stop short at the eighth laird, though the existence of his daughter, the tenth laird (who died in 1740), is just mentioned—without a name. Other families, for instance, Park and Craig, are dealt with much more minutely during the period 1720-30.

The *Balbithan MS.* has been printed exactly as it is written ; it is for the compilers of the pedigrees of the various branches of the house of Gordon, to deal with any emendations or additions that may be necessary. The variants of the 1644 MS. have been noted

In conclusion, it should be stated that the Gordons of Balbithan were cadets of the Gordons of Park, and did not purchase Balbithan until eighty-one years after the 1644 manuscript was written. One of the supposed compilers, James Gordon, I. of Balbithan, was not very fortunate in his own descendants, for his male issue died completely out in the person of his son, General Benjamin Gordon, II. of Balbithan The estate then passed to a Forbes, and then to an Abernethy ; an ironic comment on the point of view which flouted the " Seton Gordons," and reminiscent of Sir Walter Scott's luckless attempt to found a line bearing the magic name of Scott.

J. M. BULLOCH.

7th November, 1901.

THE BALBITHAN MS.

To begin this History I propose this method to myself. First of all, I shall give an account of the Cadents of Huntley their descent, as they happened by prioritie of time, beginning from Sir Alexander Gordon the fourth of that Family of Huntly, who flourished in the Reign of K. Alexander the first Sirnamed the fierce about the year 1107, and so go on till our times.

As for the Families of Jock and Thom two Cadents of Huntly in the Reign of King Robert the Second about the year 1388, tho' I say these two Brothers were the first Cadents of Huntly, after Lochnavarr for any thing we read of, and so might claim a priviledge to be inserted in order of time yet upon the account of their Legittimacie being Contraverted by some I shall here leave their Geneaoligie to be treated of in the last place.

LOCHNAVAR.

The first Cadent I find of the Family of Huntly is Robert Gordon of Stitchel third son to Sᵣ Alexander Gordon of Huntly the fourth of that Family, who lived in the Reign of King Alexander Sirnamed the fierce anno 1107. This Robert Gordon was also the third brother to Sᵣ William Gordon the fifth of Huntly who dyed in Affrica fighting in Support of Lewis the ninth King of France against the Saracens anno 1260. This Sᵣ William dying without issue the Estate of Huntly fell to his Second Brother Sᵣ Adam Gordon, and before the said Sᵣ William left his native Country he left to this Robert Gordon the third Brother the Lands and Barronie of Stitchel. The King gave him the Lands of Ballachlaggan and Kenmoirdy for killing the wild Scot in Galloway. The said Robert married a noble and rich Heiress in Galloway by whom he had the lands called Glen Lochnavar and Kenmuire; upon this lady he begot two sons S[r] John Gordon of Lochnavar and Robert Gordon of Glenturk, of whom the family of Glenturk is descended, he had also a natural son Adam Gordon, whom the great Sir William Wallace made Governour of the Castle of Wigtoun, of whom the Family of Vigtoun is descended. Their Father departed   .

His Son Sir John Gordon of Lochnavar married   ,
who begat three sons S[r] Robert Gordon of Lochnavar, William Gordon of Park of whom the family of Park, his third son Alexander Gordon of Muirfadd of whom the Family of the Haddibeys are descended. Their Father departed   .

His son S[r] Robert Gordon of Lochnavar married Elizabeth Corson Heretrix of Glen, and begat three sons S[r] William Gordon of Lochnavar, and John Gordon of whom the familys of Knockenard and Garry are descended; his third Son Robert Gordon called red-haffet of whom the family of Collithy's come. Their Father departed   .

His son S[r] William Gordon of Lochnavar married my Lord Sachar's Daughter Chrichton and begot two sons, S[r] John Gordon of Lochnavar, and William Gordon of whom the families of Arieck and Crastanount and Killenoch are descended. Their father dyed   .

His Son S[r] John Gordon of Lochnavar married Elizabeth Maxwell daughter to my Lord Haries with whom he begot three Sons, S[r] Robert Gordon of Lochnavar and William Gordon, of whom the families of Denmuckham [Den and Muckham[1]] are descended, his 3d Son Alexander Gordon of whom the family of Burdcross is descended. Their father dyed   .

His Son S[r] Robert Gordon of Lochnavar conquest the Lands of Badenoch [Bannoch[1]] and Boyll in Ireland; he married Elizabeth Ruthven daughter to the Earl of Gaurie and begat four sons, John Gordon Viscount of Kenmore, his second William Gordon of Butole and his family, James Gordon of [Upper[1]] Burdcross and his family, his fourth son Alexander Gordon of Arrick and his family. Their father departed in peace   .

His son John Gordon 2d Viscount of Kenmore married the Earl of Argyle's Daughter Campbell and sister to the M. Argile and begot sons

[1] MS. of 1644.

and daughters who all dyed in their nonage. Sr Robert Gordon of Lochnavar brothers son, son to William Gordon of Butle is now called James Gordon Lord Lochnavar and Viscount of Kenmore who Lived 1664, [Lives in this present year 1644[1]] and here I leave it to others to fill up what remains not being informd thereof.

The next Cadents I read of was Jock and Thom two sons of Lord Adam Gordons Lord of Huntly and Strathbogie and the Eleventh of that noble Family begotten upon Elizabeth Cruickshank, Asswanly's daughter about the year 1376, but for the above reason I pass by them and proceeds to the next Cadents viz.

The Family of Abergeldie.

The Geneologie of Alexander first Earle of Huntlys second son Sir Alexander Gordon of Abergeldie begotten on Chancellour Chrichton's Daughter about the year 1445. Here the Manuscript that goes under Proneys name is guilty of an double error: the first in calling the forsaid Alexander Gordon of Abergeldy the third son of Alexander first Earl of Huntly, whereas indeed he was the second son begotten on Chancellour Crichtons daughter, the second error is in asserting the forsd Alexander Gordon of Abergeldie to be not only the third son of the first Earl of Huntly but also begotten on the Heiress ·of Enzie Ægidia Hay, whereas indeed as above he was the second son of the said first Earl begotten on Chancellour Crichtons daughter. As for the Heiress of Enzie Aegidia Hay she only bore to the said first Earl of Huntly only one son named Alexander, and after that was divorced. Her son Alxr. got from his Father the first Earl the Lands of Tough and Tillabody in Stirlingshire wherewith he rested satisfied retaining the name of Seton to this day.

Having cleared this I return to Sr Alexander Gordon first Laird of Abergeldie who married the Earl of Errols Daughter Hay, upon whom he begot two sons and four daughters. His Eldest son George Gordon, his second son William Gordon Laird of Netherdealls who dwelt in

[1] MS. of 1644.

Ruthven of Cromar; his eldest daughter married my Lord Lovat, the second married the Laird of Craigevarr Mortimer, the third married the Laird of Clova Ogilvy, the fourth married the Laird of Derlaithers Garden (of whom is come the family of Mr Robert Garden of Belliemore) and after his decease she married the laird of Achlossen Ross. Their Father the said Sr Alexander Gordon dyed   .

His eldest Son George married Grizal Stuart the Earl of Buchan's Daughter with whom he begat a son called Alexander Gordon, he had also a Natural son called William Gordon in Logies. Their father the said George Gordon and second Laird of Abergeldie dyed   .

His son the forsaid Alexander third Laird of Abergeldie married the Heiress of Barns Jean Leith Lady Meldrum, with whom he begat three sons viz, Alxr Gordon, the second James Gordon of Lastis, and Mr William Gordon   Their Father dyed   .

His eldest son Alexander Gordon 4th Laird of Abergeldie married the Laird of Drum's daughter Irvine, with whom he begat six sons and six daughters, his eldest son Alexander Gordon, the second Mr. William Gordon of Stering, the third John of Craibstone, the fourth George Gordon who was killed at the Battle of Glenlivet 1594, the fifth son Thomas Gordon of Grandhome, the sixth James Gordon of Eston, his eldest Daughter married Alexander Gordon of Tulloch Chancellor of Murray, his 2d Daughter married Mr. Thomas Menzies Provost of Aberdeen, the 3d Daughter married the Laird of Achenhoove Dugat and after his death she married the Laird of Ballquhain Lesly, the fourth Daughter married Patrick Mortimer, the sixth a natural Daughter married James Farquherson of Inveray. Their father dyed at home.

His eldest son Alexander Gordon fifth Laird of Abergeldie married Margaret Mcintosh, Lady Grant and Lady Pitsligo   He dyed without issue

His brother Mr William Gordon of Stering succeeded being the sixth Laird of Abergeldie, he married the Laird of Peitbroths. Daughter Seton with whom he begat five Sons and two Daughters, his eldest son Alxr Gordon of Abergeldie, 2d John Gordon, 3d William Gordon, 4th Thomas Gordon, the 5th Son James Gordon; his eldest daughter married Donald [Farquharson] son of Monaltrie, the 2d Mary, married the Laird of Sheves Gray   Their

Father the 6th Laird of Abergeldie dyed in the House of Abergeldie
. 1630.

His Eldest son Alexander Gordon 7th Laird of Abergeldie married
Mr Thomas Nicollsons daughter who had succession. [Alexʳ married
Euphemia Graham of Morphie by whom he had an only child Rachel
Gordon, heiress of Abergeldie, who married Captain Charles Gordon,
son of Peter Gordon 2nd son of Minmore from whom the present
family derive.[1]]

THE CADENTS OF ABERGELDIE.

Sir Alexander Gordon first Laird of Abergeldy his second son
Wᵐ Gordon of Netherdeal married and begat a Daughter who married
, and got with her in Tocher the Lands of Netherdale.
The said Mr William Gordon was killed in Ruthven by John Gordon
alias John Geer.

James Gordon of Lestis married Donald Coutts daughter of Kinarnie
with whom he begat three sons, viz. Thomas Gordon, John Gordon in
Letach in the parish of Skene, and James Gordon Burgess in Aberdeen,
and Alexander Gordon.

This forsd. William Gordon married Janet Cairngill and with her
he begot Alexander Gordon Burgess in Aberdeen

John Gordon of Craibston married and had succession.

Thomas Gordon of Grandhome married Alexander Forbes of Miln
of Gellans Daughter and had succession, and after her Death he married
the Laird of Lesmoirs daughter Lady Frendraught.

James Gordon of Eston married Marion Scrimgeour and with her
he begat one Son appearand Heir of Eston.

The forsd William Gordon natural son to George 2d. Laird of
Abergeldie married the Laird of Tullochs daughter Irving with whom
he begat five sons Alexander, Robert, James, and John Gordons of
Coull.

BELDORNIE.

The Cadents of Mr Adam Gordon 3d son of Alexander first Earl of
Huntly begotten on Chancellour Crightons Daughter comprehending
the familys of Beldorny Drummois and Golspeter in Sutherland.

[1] Added by Mr. Dalrymple.

This Mr Adam Gordon Dean of Caithness and Governour of Petty begat three natural sons and a Daughter on a Gentlewoman viz. Mr George Gordon of Beldorney, John Gordon of Drummoyes in Sutherland, and Mr William Gordon Chancellour of Dunkell; his Daughter married the Laird of Findlater Ogilvy and after his death she married John Gordon son to George 5th Earl of Huntly.   The forsaid Laird of Findlater Ogilvy disponed the Lands of Findlater and Achindown to the said John Gordon Laird of Findlater who married his Lady

The said Mr George Gordon of Belldornie married the Barron of Killravocks Daughter Ross, with whom he begot two sons and two Daughters viz. his eldest son Alexander Gordon of Belldornie, the 2d son George Gordon dyed without succession; his Eldest Daughter married John Gordon of Bucky, the 2d married the Goodman of Kinninvie Lesly   Their Father the said George builded the House of Belldorney and dyed   .

His Eldest Son the forsaid Alxr Gordon of Belldorney married the Laird of Grants Daughter with whom he begat four sons and three Daughters viz. his eldest Son George Gordon of Belldorney, 2d Alexander Gordon of Kyllehon in Badenoch, 3d son Adam Gordon Glenrinnes; his Eldest Daughter the Laird of Asswanly, his 2d Daughter married William Gordon of Farnachty, his 3d married Alexander Grant in Tulloch.   Their Father the said Alexander dyed   .

His Eldest Son George Gordon of Belldorney married the Laird of Newtowns Daughter Gordon, with whom he begat Sons and Daughters.   1631 his eldest son Gordon of Belldorney married the Laird of Muirhouse daughter Lyon with whom he begat

DRUMMOYES.

Mr Adam Gordons second Son John Gordon of Drumois married the Vicar of Kilmachlys daughter Sutherland, with whom he begatt four sons viz. Hugh Gordon of Belnatom, Alexr Gordon of Sidera, John Gordon of Golspiter, and little John Gordon of Bakes.   Their father the said John Gordon of Drumoye died   .

His Eldest Son Hugh Gordon of Belnatome married Ossala Tulloch

the Provost of Forres Daughter with whom he begat Oliver Gordon of Drumoye, he had two natural sons viz. John Gordon in Gartly and Thomas Gordon in Helmsdale. Their Father Hugh Gordon dyed .
His son Oliver Gordon married Andrew Minro Miltons daughter with whom he begat three sons viz Hugh Gordon of Bellentome, Mr Gilbert Gordon and John Gordon of Killmalyie mar.; and to his second wife he married the Daughter of James Clunas burgess in Cromartie with whom he begat three Sons and two Daughters.

John Gordon of Drummoy his 2d son Alexander Gordon of Sidera married William Innes of Daughter with whom he begat a daughter who married Charles Peop, and to his 2d wife he married the Parson of Duffus daughter Keith with whom he begat John Gordon fiar of Sidera, who married Jannet Symer daughter to Mr Symer Burgess in Edenburgh who had succession.

John Gordon of Drummoys third son John Gordon of Golspeter married and begat three sons and four daughters viz. John Gordon younger of Golspeter, George Gordon of Rogey, and Hutcheon Gordon, he had also a natural son called Alexander Gordon of Uppat. Their Father the said John Gordon of Golspeter dyed . His son John Gordon younger of Golspeter married the Laird of Findracies daughter Lesly who had Succession. His natural son Alexander Gordon of Uppat married the Laird of Pullrosies daughter who has succession.

John Gordon of Drumoyes 4th son little John Gordon of Babeys married Margaret Innes daughter to with whom he begat three sons, viz. Robert Gordon who dyed unmarried, Adam Gordon of Gillecalmorell, and Alexr Gordon of Savach; he had also two natural sons viz. Gilbert Gordon of Ruging and John Gordon of Brora. Their father the said Little John Gordon dyed . His son Adam Gordon married Mackeys Daughter and has succession; his second son Alexr Gordon of Savach married Hector Monro's Daughter of Pitfower and has succession.

SUTHERLAND.

The Cadents of George 2d Earl of Huntly's second Son Sr Adam Gordon, begotten on Errol's sister; of whom is descended the Family and Earl of Sutherland about the year 1479

Sʳ Adam Gordon Lord Aboyn married the Heirress of Sutherland with whom he begat three sons and one daughter, viz. Alexander Gordon second Earl of Sutherland, Mr Gordon and Mr Adam Gordon; his daughter married George Gordon of Tillachawdy; he had also a natural son Thomas Gordon in Mallades. Their father the forsaid Adam first Earl of Sutherland died   .

His eldest son Alexander 2d Earl of Sutherland married the Earl of Athols daughter Stuart with whom he begat John Gordon 3d Earl of Sutherland. His Father the said Alexander dyed

His son John 3d Earl of Sutherland married the Earl of Argile's Daughter Countess of Murray, she died without succession, he married to his 2d wife the Earl of Lennox's Daughter Countess of Errol, with whom he begat Alexander Gordon 4th Earl of Sutherland His Father dyed   .

His son the forsd. Alexander Gordon fourth Earl of Sutherland married the Earl of Huntly's daughter Margaret Countess of Bothwell with whom he begat three sons and two daughters, viz. his eldest son John Gordon 5th Earl of Sutherland, Robert Gordon Knight Barronet, and Sir Alexʳ Gordon of Newdells; his eldest Daughter married the Laird of Ballnagown Ross, the 2d Daughter married Mackey Laird of Strathnaver   : the 4th Earl of Sutherland dyed   .

His eldest son John 5th E. of Sutherland married my Lord Elphinston's daughter with whom he begat three sons and two daughters viz. John Gordon his eldest son 6th Earl of Sutherland, Adam Gordon, and George Gordon; his eldest daughter married the Laird of Frendraught James Crighton, his second daughter married the Laird of Pitfodells Menzies   Their father dyed   .

His eldest son John 6th E of Sutherland married my Lord Drummond's Daughter and begat sons and daughters, viz. John and George Gordons; after her death he married my Lord Lovat's daughter.

The Cadents of the Family of Sutherland.

The first Earl of Sutherland's 2d son had one Daughter who married John Gordon of Golspiter.

Mr. Adam Gordon of Farar his Brother married the Goodman of

Cairnborrow's daughter Margaret Gordon first spouse to my Lord
Salton's Son Michael Abernethie. This Margaret Gordon, after her
second Husband's death viz. the said Adam Gordon of Farrar, married
to her 3d. Husband the Laird of Lesmoires Second son Alexander
Gordon of Birkenburn.

Adam first E. of Sutherland his Natural son Thomas Gordon
of Meillades married and begat sons.

Sir Robert Gordon Knight Barronet 2d. son of Alexander 4th E.
of Sutherland begotten on the E. of Huntly's daughter Countess of
Bothwell married Mr John Gordon Dean of Salisbury's daughter a near
Relation of George 4th E. of Huntly, of whom is come the Family of
Gordonston. His son   Gordon heir of Mowney married Mr
Robert Farquhar of Mownie his Daughter.

Sir Alexʳ Gordon of Newdale married and

GIGHT.

The Cadents of George 2d. E. of Huntlys third son William
Gordon Laird of Gight and Sheeves, begotten on Errolls Sister, about
the year 1479.

Sir Patrick Maitland Barron of Gight and Sheeves leaving only
three Daughters, Earle George got the gift of the Ward of their
marriage, and his said third son William Gordon not being willing to
marry any of the three daughters, Earl George provided them of other
Husbands, with whom he transacted for the Lands of Gight and
Sheeves, which he gave to his son the said William.

This William Gordon Laird of Gight married Jannet Ogilvy Laird
of Boyn's daughter, wᵗ whom he begat three Sons, and a Daughter.
His eldest son Sir George Gordon of Shives, 2d. James Gordon of
Cairnbanack, and John Gordon of Ardmachar; his Daughter married
John Grant of Bellindalloch. Their father the forsd. William Gordon
first Laird of Gight was killed in the Battle of Flowden 5th Septr. 1513.

His eldest son Sʳ George Gordon of ˉSheeves and 2d. Laird of
Gight married a daughter of Robert Gordon of Fetterletter, who was
brother to the Laird of Haddo. The said Sir George Gordon built the
House of Gight and dyed without issue.

His brother James Gordon of Cairnbannack succeeded, the 3d. Laird of Gight, and married the Laird of Strathloch's daughter Cheyn, with whom he begat two sons, viz. the eldest son Alexander Gordon Laird of Gight, and Mr. William Gordon, who perished in the water of Boggie without succession; he had also a natural son John Gordon in Milltown of Noath. Their father, the forsd. James Gordon of Cairnbannack dyed   .

His eldest son Alexander Gordon 4th Laird of Gight married Agnes Beton daughter to the Cardinal, with whom he begat one daughter who married Sr George Hume Earl of Dunbarr. He was killed on the shoar of Dundee by the M^r of Forbes and the Goodman of Towie Forbes, where the Laird of Gight and the Goodman of Towie killed each other.

His Uncle John Gordon of Ardmather married James Gordon's Daughter who was the first Laird of Lesmore, with whom he begat four sons and daughters: his eldest son succeeded to the Estate of Gight and was called William Gordon, the 2d son Captain John Gordon was killed at Dunniebirsell, the 3d. son Alexander was killed at the wars in. Holland, the 4th son George Gordon was killed by the M^r of Monteith; his eldest Daughter married the Laird of Strichen Chalmers and after his death she married the Laird of Philorth's brother, the 2d. daughter married the Laird of   Hay and after his death she married Patrick Grant of Rothemurcus, his 3d daughter married the Laird of Achynachie Sinclair, the fourth married the Laird of Banchory Garden, the 5th married the Goodman of Clackriach Keith, and one married the Laird of Haddo's brother. Their father the said John Gordon of Ardmather dyed   .

His eldest son the said William Gordon succeeded to the Estate of Gight, being 5th Laird of Gight, he married the Laird of Kellies daughter Achterlownie with whom he begat seven sons and seven daughters; his eldest son George Gordon Laird of Gight, John Gordon of Ardlownie, William Gordon killed in Turreff, the 4th Patrick Gordon, and Adam Gordon killed by Francie Hay, Alex^r Gordon, and Robert Gordon. One daughter married Sr Adam Gordon of Park and Glenbuicket, one married the Laird of Bucholly, another married the Laird of Cults Alexander Innes, one James Cheyne of Pennin, one the Goodman of Harthill Leith, one married Alexander Gordon of Tulloch and after his death she married Thomas Gordon of Pittendreich brother to the Laird of Cluny, and another married George Gordon of Cushney. Their father the forsaid William Gordon dyed

His eldest son George Gordon Sixth Laird of Gight, married the Laird of Bonnytown's Daughter Wood, with whom he begat two sons and three Daughters, his Eldest Son George of Gight, one Daughter married William Hay Broth[r] to the Earl of Errol, one married the Laird of Foverin Turin, one married the Goodman of Coxton Innes; and after the death of the Laird of Bonneton's Daughter he married my Lord Salton's daughter Abernethie with whom he begat one son and a daughter, his Son Geo. Gordon of Ardestie married the Laird of Cars Daughter Monteith   Their father the said George dyed anno 1641

George Gordon 7th Laird of Gight married my Lord Ogilvies Daughter and begat two Sons and a Daughter.

George Gordon 8th Laird of Geight married the Laird of Ludquharn's Daughter Keith, and begat a daughter and dyed

THE CADENTS OR 2D SONS OF GEIGHT

Captain John Gordon married the Laird of Shevthins Daughter Affleck with whom he begat two Daughters and was killed at Dinnibersell without more succession.

John Gordon of Ardmather's son Alexander married a Gentlewoman in Holland and begat with her Captain Alx[r] Gordon in Holland. This Alexander married in Holland and begat a Son who was a Captain anno 1633. Captain George Gordon son to John Gordon of Ardmather married the Lady Skillmaroch and begat one Daugh[r]

John Gordon of Ardlogie married Cap[t] Thomas Keir's Daughter, with whom he begat four sons and two daughters, Captain Adam, John, Collonel Nathaniel Gordon, Captain Gordon , one Daughter married Cap[t]. John Gordon Son to Knockespack.

Patrick Gordon Son to William Laird of Gight married Margaret Ereskin Daug[r]. to the Laird of Ardeslie and has succession.

Adam Gordon Son to William Laird of Gight married
Daughter to   of that Ilk.

Robert, William Laird of Gights Son married Ogilvie Kempkairns daughter. Alexr. Married   daugr. of   Hay

James Gordon of Cairnbannacks natural son in Milltown of Noath married and   .

LETTERFURIE.

The Genealogie of George 2d. Earl of Huntly's youngest and 4th Son James Gordon of Letterfurie.

James Gordon of Letterfurie married the Laird of Germachs daughter Jannet Butter with whom he begat four Sons, viz his eldest Son John Gordon of Curriedown, Patrick Gordon of Letterfurie, Wm. Gordon in Orkney, and Alexander Gordon of Crommellat.

John Gordon of Corriedown married Elizabeth Currour, with whom he begat John Gordon of Curriedown; he married to his 2d. wife the Goodman of Muiraik's Daugr Gordon, and with her he begat John Gordon of Chappelton, he married the Goodman of Achanachies daughter Gordon, with whom he begat Adam Gordon who was killed by one Leslie in Keith 1634, and James Gordon in Dunbanane sometime Baillie in Strathbogie.

Patrick Gordon of Letterfurie married the Goodman of Drainies daughter Innes, with whom he begat five sons and Daughters, his eldest son James Gordon of Letterfurie, John Gordon of Coffurach, Tho. Gordon of Currydown, Robert Gordon Burgess in Elgin, and Mr Patrick Gordon; one Daughter married the Goodman of Tannachy Stuart, one married John Ross of Bellivate, one married Walter Ross of Badyvochell. Their Father the said Patrick Gordon dyed   .

His eldest son James Gordon of Letterfurie married the Goodman of Buckie's Sister Gordon, and dyed without issue.

To him succeeded John Gordon, Thomas Gordon his eldest Son, who married   Gordon of Achintoulls Daughter and with her begat one son called James Gordon of Letterfurie who married Grizell Dunbar daughter to Sir William Dunbar of Durn, with whom he begat four sons and four daughters, viz: his eldest son Pat Gordon, William Gordon, James Gordon, and Alexr Gordon; his eldest daughter Jannet Gordon, his 2d. daughter Anne Gordon married to Logie Ogilvie, his 3d. Jean Gordon who dyed unmarried, and the youngest Mary Gordon;

all these save Jean yet live. The forsaid John Gordon after his wife Gordon of Auchentoull's daughter her death married to his 2ᵈ wife Mary Innes Achluncharts Daughter on whom he begat a son Alexander Gordon present Governour of Port Sᵗ Ferara.

The forsd. Thomas Gordon married the goodman of Buckie's daughter who has succession seven sons and one daughter married on Walter Ogilvie of Ragell.

John Gordon of Coffurach married Jas. Harper's Daughter who has succession.

Robert Gordon married William Lesly's Daughter Burgess in Elgin with whom he had succession, and after her Decease he married the Goodman of Coxton's daughter Innes; his children with the first wife James Gordon of Ardneadlie Baillie of Eurie [Enzie], John Gordon of Achinhallrick, and Thomas Gordon of Myreton, and one Daughter married to Innes of Drainy and after to Hay of Knocken.

William Gordon in Orkney married there and has good succession

Alexander Gordon of Crommellat married a Brother Daughter to Abernethie Lord Salton, and begot with her three sons, his eldest son John Gordon in Littlemill, Alxʳ. Gordon in Craigyhead, and Gordon who married Ritcheson's daughter in Haughs of Grange and got with her the Woodsett of Walkmill of Rothiemey, and after her Decease the said Alexander married the Goodman of Muraicks daughter Gordon with whom he begat sons and daughters, his eldest son Adam Gordon at the Miln of Gartley.

CLUNY.

The Cadents and Geneaologie of Alexander Laird of Strathawen and Cluny, the 3ᵈ son of Alexander 3ᵈ Earl of Huntly.

The manuscript here under Proneys name has fallen into another mistake in calling this Alexander Laird of Strathawen the second son of Alexʳ third Earl of Huntly, whereas indeed he was only his third son · for the said Alexander third Earl of Huntly had only four Sons, viz. George the Eldest who died without succession and of whom there is no memory, John the Second Lord Gordon of whom is come the Family of Huntly, Alexander the third Son who was Laird of Strathawn and thereafter of Cluny of whom is come the Family of Cluny, and the 4th son William Gordon who was Bishop of Aberdeen

The said Alexander first Laird of Strathawen married the Laird of Grants Daughter with whom he begat two sons and four daughters, his eldest son Alexander, heir of Strathawen, and John Gordon. His eldest daughter married the Laird of Altar Cumming, one married the Laird of Pitsligo Forbes, one married Pat. Gordon Goodman of Oxhill, the 4th daughter married Andrew Halyburton of Drummoys. The said Alexander their Father excambed (with his father) the Lands of Strathawen, with the Lands of Cluny in Mar, reserving his own liferent, and the Heritable Right of Blairfindy. He dyed in peace in Drummin. It seems also that the said Alexander first Laird of Strathawen first married my Lord Glames Daughter, by whom he had no children, and after her death he married Grants daughter as above.

His eldest Son Alexander Gordon heir of Strathawen married the Laird of Banff's Daughter Ogilvy with whom he begat a daughter, who married James Gordon of Birkenburn. He died without further succession.

His Brother John Gordon succeeded to the Estate of Cluny. He married Thomas Gordon of Auchenheif and Goodman of Craculhe's daughter Margaret Gordon with whom he begat two sons and five daughters, his eldest son Sir Thomas Gordon, and John Gordon of Bissmoire, his eldest daughter married the Laird of Pitcaple Lesly, one married the Laird of Cubbardy Murray, one the Laird of Craigievarr Mortimer, one married the Laird of Pittodrie Ereskine, and the fifth married John Grant of Carron. Their Father the said John Gordon Laird of Cluny built the Castle of Blairfindy and dyed therein anno 1586.

His eldest son Sr Thomas Gordon Laird of Cluny married the Earl of Angus Sister Dam Elizabeth Dowglass with whom he begat six Sons and a Daughter, his eldest Son Sir Alexander Gordon of Cluny Barronet, Patrick Gordon of Ruthven, William Gordon of Coxton [Cottone[1]], Mr. Thomas Gordon of Pittendreich, Mr George and John Gordons; his Daughter married James Cumming Laird of Alter. Their Father the said Sir Thomas married to his second wife Grizall Stuart

---

[1] MS of 1644.

the Earl of Atholls Sister with whom he begat two Daughters, the one married the Laird of Carnousie Ogilvy, the other the Laird of Birkenbog Abercromby. The said Sr Thomas died in Cluny

His eldest Son Sr Alexr. Gordon Barronet of Cluny married the Laird of Craigstons daughter Urquhart, who was tutor of Cromarty, with whom he begat one son Sir Alexander Gordon heir of Cluny, who married the Laird of Wardhouse daughter who dyed in France without succession. His father the said Sir Alexander Gordon of Cluny married to his second wife the Laird of Newtons daughter Lady Wardess.

THE CADENTS OF THE FAMILY OF CLUNY.

John Gordon of Bissmoire married the Laird of Lesmoirs daughter who was first Lady Auchintowell and after married [afterward[1]] Lady Ballindalloch with whom he begat two sons, his eldest son Patrick Gordon of Bissmoir, his second John Gordon of   .
Their father the said John Gordon of Bissmoir was killed at the ride of Tarnway by ane shott from the House 1591.

His eldest son Patrick Gordon of Bissmoire married Jean Lesly Daug^r to the Provost of Aberdeen and has succession, viz: Alexr'. Gordon of Bissmoir who married Patrick Lesly Provost of Aberdeen's daughter. The Provost Sir Patrick Lesly purchast the Lands of Eden His brother John Gordon [married[1]] and has succession.

Patrick Gordon of Ruthven married the Laird of Cowdies Murray's daughter and has succession.

Wm. Gordon of Cottan married   Gordon and has succession.

Mr Thomas of Pittendreich married the Laird of Gights daughter Gordon, and has succession

George Gordon married the Parson of Kinairnies daughter Burnet.

Sir Thomas youngest son John Gordon married ane Captains daughter in Holland.

This Alexander Gordon who was first Laird of Strathawen had two natural sons, viz: George Gordon of Tombea, and William Gordon in Dellmore This George Gordon of Tombea married Jannet Grant and begat with her two sons and a daughter viz'. Alex^r Gordon in

[1] MS. of 1644.

Tombea, and James Gordon in Achdrigny; his daughter married Alexander Grant in Inverury Their father George Gordon died in Tombea. His son Alexander Gordon in Tombea married Jannet Stuart with whom he begat four Sons, Geo. Gordon in Tombea, Jo., Patrick and William Gordons. Their Father dyed [in peace[1]] James Gordon in Achdrigny begat one son called William Gordon; this forsd. William Gordon in Achmoir [Delmoir[1]] married Issabel Grant with whom he begat four sons viz. Alexander Gordon who dwells [dwelt[1]] in Cruchly, Thomas Gordon in Neve, John in Inverury, and Adam Gordon in Achnascra. Their father was killed by some of the Clanchattan in Dellmore, his fourth son married and had succession in Strathawen.

The Cadents of John Lord Gordon.

Alexander Bishop of Caithness had a son Dean of Sutherland [Salisberry[1]] whose Daughter married Sir Robert Gordon brother to the Earl of Sutherland and James Gordon Chancellour of Murray, who dyed without succession.

The Cadents of William Gordon, Bp. of Aberdeen

fourth son to Alexander 3d Earl of Huntly.

This William Gordon Bishop of Aberdeen had two natural Sons, viz. Mr John Gordon who coft some Houses in the Old town of Aberdeen, and Mr Walter Gordon; the said Mr John Gordon dyed without Succession, his brother Mr Walter succeeded to his Houses and Lands and married and begat a son called Wm Gordon

The Cadents or Second Sons of George 4th Earl of Huntly.

John Gordon 3d Son to George fourth Earl of Huntly married the Lady Findlater, daughter to Sir [Mr[1]] Adam Gordon Dean of Caithness and Governour of Petty; he was execute at Aberdeen after the battle of Corrichie 1563; he had no Children.

Adam Gordon Laird of Achendown the fourth son fought first the battle of Tillyangus against the Forbesses, where my .Lord

---

[1] MS. of 1644.

Forbes Brother [Son[1]] black Arthur was killed, with severall others; and within forty days thereafter fought the Battle att Craibston near Aberdeen, where my Lord Forbes eldest Son was taken prisoner; the Forbesses killed, and quite defeat. Immediately thereafter at the Bourd of Breichen he chased fourteen Earls Lords and Barrons taking many Prisoners; he also took in the Houses of Drumminor, with several other houses belonging to the Forbesses; he banished the Forbesses out of the North to Dundee where they remained three Quarters of a year, he possessed their Houses [with his Captains and friends[1]] and took up their Rents during that time. He dyed in peace in the Town of Perth the second of Decr· 1580.

His Brother Sir Patrick Gordon succeeded to the Lordship of Auchindown and Gartly, he married the Lady Gights Daughter [Gight Dam[1]] Agnes Beton, he was a brave Champion like to his brother Adam, and did good service to his Nephew Geo: first Marquise of Huntly in time of his troubles; he was killed in the Battle of Glenlivat [Oldchonachon in Strathawin[1]] 14th Octr: 1594; he had no succession save only a natural son, Captain in the French Guards.

Mr James was a religious man and dyed in France as did Mr William his brother who was designed for Bishop of Aberdeen.

Mr Thomas Gordon married the Lady Innes, he had a natural daughter married Thomas Hamilton in Caithness.

The youngest Brother Mr Robert Gordon was killed rashly and had no Succession.

THE CADENTS OF GEORGE 5TH EARL OF HUNTLY.

Alexander Gordon Laird of Strathawn Second Son to George fifth Earl of Huntly married the Earl of Caithness daughter Sinclair Countess of Erroll with whom he begat a son Alexr. Gordon Lord of Dunkintie, and three daughters. Their father the said Alexander dyed in peace att Cambell [Camdell[1]].

His Son Alexander Gordon Laird of Dunkinty married the goodman of Ballindalloch's daughter Margaret Grant with whom he begat five sons and three daughters; his eldest son George Gordon, Alexander

[1] MS. of 1644.

and John Gordons   He excambed the Lands of Strathawen for the
Lands of Dunkinty and got a great sum of money.   He and his eldest
son George were killed at the Stalking in the forrest of Glenawen 9 [19 [1]]
August 1633 by some of the [rogues of the [1]] Clachattan lurking there
and were buried in the Gordons Isle in the Chanry Kirk of Elgin.

THE CADENTS OF GEORGE FIRST MARQUISE OF HUNTLY.

Francis Gordon the Second son died young while he was Student
at the Colledge.

Lawrence Gordon his fourth Son died in Strathbogie of Eighteen
[20 [1]] years of age.

His fifth son Lord John Gordon of Melgin [Melgum [1]] and Aboyn
married Sophia Hay daughter to the Earl of Errol with whom he begat
one Daughter Henret Gordon; the said Lord John was burnt in the House
of Frendraght and John Gordon Laird of Rothemay, with four Servants
Gentlemen, upon Fridays night the eight of October 1630 and buried in
the Isle of Gairtly.   It's here remarkable that before this tragical
accident the said Family of Frendraught was in a very flourishing
condition as any of their rank in the North, and tho' they were not to
be reached by the Law after tryal, yet it seems the Secret but Just
Judgment of God so pursued them that their Estate suddenly vanished
away like the morning dew, and their posterity evanished, scarcely
being any now living to represent them, and besides all whoever
matched with that family were liable to signal misfortunes.   Meldrum
of Hatton being put to a legal Tryal for that horrid murder suffered
upon the account of *malum minatum et damnum secutum.*

THE CADENTS OF GEORGE SECOND MARQUISE OF HUNTLY.

His eldest Son George Lord Gordon was killed at the Battle of
Alford.

James Lord Aboyn the second Son dyed in France of sickness
and toil contracted in Montrose Wars

Lord Lewis the third son married the Laird of Grants daughter,
Argile then being in possession of the whole Estate of Huntly, and

[1] MS. of 1644

the other two above Brothrs. dying without children the said Lord Lewis succeeded and was reponed to his Parentall Estate of whom is come the Family of Gordon. The said Lord Lewis begat on Grants Daughter one Son, Lady Anne, Lady Mary, and Lady Jean Gordons; his eldest son George first Duke of Gordon who succeeded his Father and got the gift of his forefaulted Estate from King Charles the Second. The eldest daughter Lady Anne never married, the second daughter Lady Mary first married the Laird of Meldrum Urquhart, and after his Death she married the Earl of Perth Chancellour in King James the 7ths time, and was by him Created Duke and Duchess of Perth. Lady Jean Gordon the 3d daughter married the Earl of Dumfermling Seton who died in France without succession.

Charles Earl of Aboyn Etc. 4th Son to the said George 2d Marquise of Huntly married the Laird of Drum's daughter Margaret Irvine who had no children. The said Earl Charles of Aboyn married to his second wife the Earl of Strathmores daughter Lyon, with whom he begat three sons and daughters, his eldest son   who succeeded to his Father, Mr George and Mr John Gordons. His eldest forsd.   Earl of Aboyn married the Earl of Strathmores daughter Lyon, with whom he begat John Earl of Aboyn now in Life, and three daughters Lady Helen the eldest married to the present Representative of Kinnaird, the second Lady Elizabeth and the 3d Lady Grace Gordons. The said John present Earl of Aboyn married the Lord Carnwaths daughter Lockart.

My Lord Hary Gordon 5th Son to George Second Marquise of Huntly married Madam Rulten but had no succession, he dyed att Drumdellzie in Strathbogie.

George Lord Gordon who was killed att Alford had a Natural Son James Gordon of Achmull, who has a son James Gordon in Loanhead now in life.

I need not here inform my Reader that George first Duke of Gordon having married Elizabeth eldest daughter to the Duke of Norfolk had no more Children but only one Son and a Daughter, his Eldest and only Son Alexander Second Duke of Gordon married the Earl of Peterborrows daughter his Sister Lady Jean Gordon married my Lord Drummond thereafter Earl of Perth and by King James the Seventh Duke of Perth.

Jock and Thom.

The Geneaology of Jock the Heiress Eldest Brother and stock of Pittlurge.

I proceed now to account for the genealogie of Jock and Thom the Heiress two Brothers begotten by Adam Gordon fifth Lord of Huntly on Elizabeth Cruickshank Aswanlies daughter in the Reign of King Robert the Second about the year 1383.

Here indeed occurs no small difficulties raised and objected by the contending Partys pro et con, the Family of Huntlys disputing the Legittimacy of the said two Brothers Jock and Thom their birth; the second difficulty is, allowing their birth to be good and Lawfull, the Cadents of Jock who was undoubtedly the Eldest brother and so owned *nemine contradicente* spleet amonst themselves; some contending Buckies Family was Jocks eldest son, others again contending and that not without Reason that Pitlurge's predecessors was undoubtedly Jocks eldest son begotten in a Lawfull and regular marriage.

In these straights it is hard, yea simply impossible, to satisfy all Parties, as I observed before, only as a Lover of the truth without being attached to either of the contending partys I shall without prejudice or favour plainly set down, what is commonly alledged by each to support their pretensions, and what has been most commonly and universally received about these disputes, from the beginning to this present Age; and Last of all I shall Leave it to the impartial Reader to make a Judgment according to the strength and weight of the Evidences brought and Examined by both sides in sober cold blood.

As to the first, the Legittimacy of Jock and Thom their birth, it's questioned on these Heads. First, that it was inconsistent with the Honour and Prudence of Lord Adam Gordon to have married so meanly and far below his birth, as this Elizabeth Cruickshank was, who at the best must claim no higher than the station of a private and obscure Gentlewoman and a mean Vasalls daughter; and the rather to confirm this, it was never alledged they were formally and Lawfully married, but only hand fasted, and if there was any private promises made twixt the parties *spe matrimonii*, yet the same were not binding in Law, and accordingly the said Lord Adam annulled the same by his entering into a lawfull and regular marriage w^t another the Earl of

Sommerveile's daughter, and *Esto* they had been Lawfully married, yet on second and Just considerations the first marriage might have been annulled by Divorce or non adherence etc.

To this its answered that inequality of Birth does in no ways dissanull marriages, many Instances might be adduced where great and noble persons have married below their birth meerly for fancie and pleasure; and if the marriage was clandestine and not so formall Lawfull and regular as it ought to have been, its to be remembered that Church discipline or Ceremonies of the Church were not then so strictly observed as now they are, especially having to do with a person of Lord Adam's Birth, honour and great Interest and Sway in the North. *Consensus et Copulatio facit matrimonium*, only the Church by the Ceremony, declares the marriage Lawfull, which was real before their declaratory Sentence, and we know that a Justice of Peace in England [Scotland] may Lawfully marry where both parties are willing and Consenters.

2do its answered inequality of Birth in that marriage was the ruin of Jock and Thom, they not being capable by Friends to Copp or debate with the Heiress their Sister, or claim any share in their Father's inheritance save only what he pleased to give them out of his free good will.

Lastly its answered their Legittimacy was owned in so far, as Jock and Thom and their posterity to this hour were allowed to bear and keep in their publique Ensigns and Coats of Arms, upon all publick and private occasions, the bare and simple Arms their father and all the Family of Huntly had used from their first arise in Scotland till then; without any addition or alteration, far less any mark of Bastardie, and to be sure (as was observed formerly) the office of herauldrie and giving out Coats of Arms and bestowing other such honours was the Kings province the fountain of all honour who very well knew how to bestow honours on such as were worthy and deserving of them, and if any should take upon them to assume to themselves such Coats of Arms as they deserved not, they were severely handled by authority for their presumption, and if there was any blot in their birth be sure it was insert in their Scutcheon, and there were narrow Inquiry of this taken by the King and others he employed for that purpose. Now the Lairds of Pittlurge Jocks Representatives being frequently honoured with the dignity of Knighthood by the Kings, and having also att Pinkie and several other publick Battles and appearances still carried in their Banners and Coats of Arms the Antient Arms of the House of Huntly without any mark of Bastardie, could they have done this so avowedly publickly and without challenge had they not been truly thought deserving of the Same as their right and proper heritable due. I shall trouble my Reader with no more on this first objection viz: Jock and Thom's Bastardie.

I proceed to the second difficultie viz: whither Pittlurge or Buckie be the eldest son of Jock both laying claim to it, whose pretensions and reasons shall be impartially examined and weighted. Its beyond Contraversie that Jock and Thom were the two sons begotten by Lord Adam Gordon fifth Lord of Huntly and Strathbogie upon Elizabeth Cruickshank Asswanlie's daughter before the said Adam his second marriage with the Earl of Somervills daughter, and that of these two Brothers Jock was the eldest; in this all parties agree. But then comes the competition who was this Jocks eldest Lawfull son? Buckie and these come of him assert that this Jock was first married to Hanault Mccleud of Heiras daughter, Sister to the Lady Mcintosh at that time, with whom he begat a Son called Alexander Gordon of Essy of whom Bucky is come.

Pittlurge and all come of him absolutely deny this marriage, tho' they own that Jock begot on this McLeod the said Alexander Gordon, who was only a Bastard begotten on a free woman but not of a married Couple.

Pittlurge further advances that his predecessor the said Jock was never Lawfully married save only to the Laird of Gights daughter Maitland with whom he begat three sons viz. John Gordon of Botarie, William Gordon of Tillytarmount, and James Gordon of Haddo. Their Father the said Jock or John Gordon the Heiress brother gave Botarie and the Lands of Langar in the Merns which he conquest, to his eldest Lawfull son John of Botarie and gave the lands of Essy and Scordairg to his Bastard Son the forsd Alexr. Gordon of Essie. For Confirmation of Pittlurge's pretensions its further advanced that both parties Buckie as well as Pittlurg doe own Jocks marriage with the Laird of Gights Daughter Maitland, and the issue proceeding therefrom to be Lawfull, which never any to this

hour made ever the least objection or exception against; whereas all
come of Pittlurg did ever and constantly deny any Lawfull marriage
twixt Jock their sd predecessor and Mackleod of Haris daughter.
Again, the Lairds of Pittlurg as the eldest Sons of Jock were richly
provoided, at first with large provisions of Lands by their Fathers, viz,
the Lands of Pittlurge Boaterie and Langor, were advanced and
dignified with the Kings honours, and on all publick occasions behaved
and were owned by all as the Representatives and Chiefs of Jocks
Family without any opposition Contradiction or Challenge or pretensions
to the contrary; till of Late the last Duke of Gordon coming North
with his Lady to Aberdeen, and being to be publickly entertained by the
Magistrates of that Burgh, the throng of Gentry and others attending
them was very great and pressing up stairs who could first make his
entry, by chance Bucky went up some steps of the stair before the
Laird of Pittlurge, and Pittlurge in the throng takes hold of Buckie's
coat to win up. Buckie not out of any design sets Pittlurge back, only
to keep himself free of the Press. Pittlurge takes this as a design of
Buckies to take place before him, whereas indeed there was no such
thing in Buckies mind: however Pittlurg retires and is highly offended.
The Duke and Dutchess missing Pittlurge call for him again and again,
till the story is told that had passed, the Duke and Dutchess send for
Pittlurg to his Quarters, telling they would not sit down to Dinner till
he came. Upon this Pittlurge comes and is placed at the Head of the
Table on the Dutchess Left hand the Duke being on her right hand, and
the Laird of Buckie had his place below the Duke By this Situation
and preferment of place att Table, both Duke and Dutchess seemed to
give the precedence to Pittlurge, and did all they could for to humour
him and take away the quarrel. Pittlurg not satisfied with all this,
sends Buckie a Challenge to fight, the Duke and Dutchess finding
matters come to that height interpose at Meldrum, and in a publick
company Buckie offers satisfaction to Pittlurge, assuring he had no
such Design against him to strive for Place or Precedence, and in
testimony thereof drank first to Pittlurg his Service, whereupon the
Seeming mistake was comprimised and Pittlurg satisfied. This tedious
but true relation I had from severall good Gentlemen witnesses present
to all had passed. Besides I have known Buckie express himself very
modestly and mannerly on that head without the Least tincture of

pride vanitie or affectation, only the grand Objection they insisted upon was this, that M^{c}leaod of Haris daughter being of such account and following they could not imagine how Jock in point of good manners could or was safe, to get her with child, and not marry her. However this might be answered, I think these nice and frivolous intestine debates amongst friends ought not to be too passionately insisted upon, especially considering both Partys own Jock for their common undoubted parent and therefore let none take it ill that I begin and go on with the Laird of Pittlurge's Genealogie as Representative of Jock, seeing antiquity tradition and uninterrupted possession seems all to concur to give Sentence in his and predecessors favour; reserving all due honour and respect for the Family of Buckie, which all must own is truly antient and honourable.

PITTLURGE.

To return then as I hinted before John Gordon the Heretrix brother married to his Lawfull wife the Laird of Gights daughter Maitland with whom he begat three sons viz. his eldest son John Gordon of Boterrie of whom Pittlurg is come, his 2^d son William Gordon of Tillytermont of whom Blelack Lesmoir and Craig are come, and James Gordon of Meithlick thereafter Laird of Haddo his third Son of whom are come the Earl of Aberdeen. Their father the said John Gordon dyed and was buried in the Kirk of Essy, others say in the Kirk of Botarie.

His eldest son John Gordon of Botarie Langar and Pitlurge married my Lord Pitsligo's daughter Forbes, with whom he begat two sons John Gordon Laird of Pittlurge Botarie and Langar, his second son James Gordon of Cairnborrow. Their father the forsd John Gordon excambed the Lands of Langar with the Barroney of Travechin, he conquest the Lands of Pittlurge. He dyed in peace and was interred in the Burial place of the Kirk of Botarie.

His son John Gordon second Laird of Pitlurge married the Earl of Athols daughter Stuart, with whom he begat a son John Gordon third Laird of Pittlurg; likewise he begat on a Gentlewoman Maitland two natural sons and two daughters viz. William Gordon of

Belchirrie and George Gordon of Kindrught; one daughter married the goodman of New Forbes, another married Menzies Provost of Aberdeen. Their Father the forsaid John Gordon 2^d Laird of Pittlurg was killed at the battle of Pinkie anno 1547. [He married secondly Margaret Drummond. It was his son who fell at Pinkie.[1]]

His son John Gordon 3^d Laird of Pittlurge married Jannet Ogilvie of Cullen's daughter, with whom he begat a Son John Gordon of Pittlurge. Their father died.

His Son John Gordon fourth Laird of Pittlurg married my Lord Forbes daughter with whom he begat two Sons [and a daughter Barbara married Hon. Alex. Elphinstone, 3^d son of fourth Lord Elphinstone[1]] viz John Gordon fifth Laird of Pittlurg and Mr Robert Gordon of Strathlock. Their Father dyed in Kinmundy and interred in their ordinary burial place in Martinkirk anno 1600.

His Son John Gordon sixth Laird of Pittlurg married the Laird of Kinnairds daughter Kinnaird, with whom he begat a daughter married to Thomas Gordon son to John of Bagos sherriff Deput of Aberdeen.

His Brother Mr Robert Gordon seventh Laird of Pittlurg and Strathlock married the Laird of Lenturks daughter Irvine, with whom ne begat Ten sons and six Daughters; viz: the eldest son Robert, John, Mr. William, Alexander Advocate in Edenburgh, Mr James Parson of Rothemey, George, Hugh, Arthur, Patrick and Lodvick Gordons; one daughter married Alexander Urquhart of Craighouse in Ross, Mary was married to the Goodman of Achencreive Richard Maitland, Jean, Barbara, Margaret, and Anne his daughters.

His eldest son Robert Gordon eight Laird of Pittlurge and Strathlock married the Laird of Leyes daughter Burnet.

The Genealogy of the Laird of Pittlurg's natural sons.

William Gordon of Bellchere married Janet Gordon the Goodman of Blelacks daughter with whom he begat two Daughters, one married Thomas Spens in Brunstone the other married William Grant of Blairfindie. His Second natural Son called George Gordon in Fyvie, who married and begat John Gordon Burgess in Aberdeen. His 3rd

---

[1] Added by Mr. Dalrymple.

Natural Son George Gordon of Kindrught was Master-hushold to the first Marquise of Huntly who married   .

CAIRNBORROW.

The Cadents or second Sons of the Laird of Pittlurge viz James Gordon of Cairnborrow gotten upon the Laird of Pitsligo's daughter Forbes.

James Gordon of Cairnborrow was the 1st Laird of Pittlurg's Second Son and first Cadent of that family begotten upon the Laird of Pitsligo's daughter Forbes. The said James Gordon of Cairnborrow married the Laird of Barns daughter with whom he begat three sons, viz his Eldest son George Gordon of Cairnborrow, his second son William Gordon of Abachie, and his third Son Mr James Gordon of Cromellat. Their father the said James Gordon of Cairnborrow dyed and was interred amongst his predecessors in their ordinary Burial place of Martin or Botarie Kirk.

Here again Abachie's people do pretend to be the said James Gordon of Cairnborrows eldest son, but very unjustly; for it does not consist with reason, prudence, or practice, that the Father should leave the greatest and far better part of his Interest, and that by which he and his successors were designed and tituled to his second son George Gordon of Cairnborrow (as Abachies people would have it) and only leave Abachie, which was but a small and inconsiderable part of his Estate to his eldest son by which the father nor his eldest sons were never designed nor took the Title thereof; but on the contrair the said George Gordon the eldest son and Representative of his father retained the paternal Estate and Title, and he and his has been so owned even by Abachie and Achanachie giving Cairnborrow the preference, as their Paternal and heritable due and right, whereof Instance could be adduced were it proper.

So I go on with the Genealogie of this eldest Son George Gordon of Cairnborrow who married Alexander Gordon of Drumoyes Daughter, Sister to Alexr Gordon of Proney, Katharin Gordon who was spouse to Achencrive Maitland, next to the Laird of Ardneidlie Baylie, and thereafter married the said George Gordon of Cairnborrow with whom he begat a Son and two daughters viz: John Gordon of Cairnborrow: his eldest daughter Margaret Gordon married first my Lord Salton's Son Michael Abernethie with whom he begat a Daughter married to John Gordon of Licheston, the said Margaret was second spouse to Mr Adam Gordon son to the Earl of Sutherland and after his death she married Lesmoir's son Alex^r Gordon first Birkenburn; George Gordon of Cairnborrows second Daughter Katharine Gordon married first Drainie Innes and after his death she married the Goodman of Coxton Innes. Their Father the said George was killed in the Battle of Pinkie 1547.

His Son John Gordon of Cairnborrow married Bessy Gordon Buckies daughter with whom he begat Eight Sons and three Daughters, his eldest Son John Gordon Laird of Cairnborrow and Edenglassie, the second George Gordon of Sockach, the third son James Gordon of Farnaughtie, the fourth Son Mr William Gordon who coft Cairnborrow, the fifth Mr Arthur Gordon, the Sixth Son Mr Thomas Gordon of Artloch, 7th Son Robert Gordon of Gollachie, Eight Son Patrick Gordon of Craigston in Sutherland; all these Eight sons with their Father each having a Jackman and a footman went with the Earl of Huntly and Erroll from Cairnborrow to the Battle of Glenlivat, a good Company being twenty Seven well mounted men out of one Family. His eldest daughter married the Laird of Eden Meldrum, and after his death she married the Laird of Craigston Tutor of Cromarty her name was in the Said House of Craigston. His Second daughter Margaret Gordon first maried the Goodman of Craighead Mr John Duff who bore to him Eleven Sons of whom is come Braccho, and all the opulent Sir-name of Duffs; after the Craigheads Death she married the goodman of Milton Ogilvie in the parish of Keith; she built the House of Craighead, which is now reazed, she built the House of Milton, Achoynanie and the Steeple of Keith; her name and Husbands is on the House of Achoynanie dated 1601; she was interred in her Paternall Burial place in the Kirk of Botarie. His third daughter married Mr Alex^r Gordon of Tulloch Chancellour of Murray Glengerack's Predecessor. Their Father the said John Gordon of Cairnborrow dyed in Cairnborrow and was honourably buried in Martin kirk.

His Son John Gordon Laird of Edenglassie and representative of the Family of Cairnborrow married first the Laird of Wattertons daughter Bennerman now Lairds of Elsick, with whom he begat three

Sons and two daughters, his eldest son William Gordon Laird of Rothemey and Stock of Cairnborrow, his second Sir Adam Gordon of Park Glenbuicket Innermarkie Edenglassie and Achinandach, his third son John Gordon Laird of Invermarkie Edenglassie etc.; his eldest daughter married the Laird of Brux Forbes, his second daughter married Robert Coutts Laird of Achterfoull. The said John Gordon Laird of Edenglassie etc. married to his second wife the Lady Benum and Lady Foveran, her name is on the House of Glenbuicket which he built but by that Lady he had no Succession. He coft the Lands of Benum, had also Caffurrach Tynet and Tulloch in the Enzie; he sold the Lands of Benum again and with the money thereof he assisted his two eldest sons to buy the Lands and Estates of Rothemey and Park from the Lord Salton Abernethie, which cost them very dear, not only the price of the Lands but also continual trouble and Law pleas, and the life and blood of two worthy Gentlemen Lairds of Rothemey the father and the Son Successively. Their father dyed in peace in the House of Edenglassie, and was honourably buried in the Kirk of Edenglassie, but should have been in the Kirk of Botarie the Ordinary Burial place of their family and good Ancestors

His Eldest Son William Gordon Laird of Rothemey and Representative of Cairnborrow married first the Barron of Killravock's daughter Ross Lady Foules who had no succession; after her death he married my Lord Forbes daughter Katharin Forbess with whom he begat two sons and five daughters. His Eldest Son John Gordon Laird of Rothemey unmarried was burnt in the House of Frendraught with Lord John Gordon of Aboyn 8th of October 1630. His Second Son James Gordon a Student at the Colledge who succeeded to his father and Brother. The forsaid William Gordon Laird of Rothemey their Father was killed by the Laird of Frendraught and the Laird of Banff Ogilvie, they being five score of men horse and foot and the Laird of Rothemey being but ten Horsemen 2d January 1630, so that if you reckon right you'll find only ten months twixt the killing of the Father and the burning of the Son.

It's credibly reported of this worthy and brave Gentleman that finding Frendraught's Party too strong for him, he was reasonably averse to go out and encounter them (the contraversie being about some Marches and a little parcel of Contraverted ground) till his Lady insinuate if he did not go, it would be a reflexion on his Honour. This if it was true, was but bad Counsell, and unadvisedly offered. Rothemey upon this goes out with only ten of his menial Servants mounted in haste on horse and engages Frendraught and Bamff and being overpowered with numbers his Horse is killed under him and falls to the ground with his Rider. In this fall Rothemeys Helmet went off and ere he could recover himself he received his Death wounds in the Head, notwithstanding of which he gets hold of a firelock and with one`shot he killed one Adam Gordon of Frendraughts Partie and wounded some others fighting Couragiously till he gott another Horse which he mounted and made a honourable retreat and comes home with his Servants to the House of Rothemey, and seeing his Lady tells her he had faced Frendraught, and called for a Drink to his Servants who had behaved themselves as became and desired his Piper to play and with his Servants he Danced round about the Hall and having lost much blood and finding himself faint, he desired his Lady to make his Bed and told her he would never rise again in life

After the death of the said William and John Gordons father and son the said James Gordon a Student then at the Colledge succeeded to the Estate of Rotheymey. He married the Laird of Pittfoddells daughter Menzies, with whom he begat sons and daughters, his eldest son John Gordon Laird of Rothemey and Representative of the family of Cairnborrow.

His eldest son the said John Gordon married Elizabeth Barcley Heiress of Towie and with her got the Lands of Towie. With her he begat two Daughters viz Mrs Anne Gordon who dyed unmarried of a Decay, the second daughter Mrs Beattie Gordon married first Sir George Innes of Coxton who dyed at Scoon after Shirriff-muire; with her the said Sr George begats sons and daughters The said John Gordon of Rothemey begat on his Lady the Heiress of Towie a son called Peter, who being next dore to an Idiot was induced to Dispone the Lands of Towie to the said Sir George Innes his Brother in law who now possesses the Estate of Towie, the right Heir only retaining ane Aliment during life.

James Gordon Laird of Rothemey had Several daughters, one married To Nethermuire Gordon, one married to Wartle Elphinston, one married to David Tyrie of Duniedeer.

PARK.

It's here to be remembered that the Family of Rothemey being terminated and Extinct in the person of the said Idiot, the Right of Representation fell in to Sr John Gordon of Park as Heir to his Grandfather Sr Adam Gordon of Park who was the second brother to the said William Gordon first Laird of Rothemey and representative of the family of Cairnborrow; and therefore I go on with the Genealogie of the said Sr Adam Gordon of Park with Heirs Successors and Cadents.

Sir Adam Gordon of Park was the second son of John Gordon of Edenglassie etc., begotten on the Laird of Watterton's daughter Benerman. He married to his first Lady the Laird of Gight's daughter Gordon, with whom he begat two Sons and a Daughter, viz. Sr John Gordon Second Laird of Park Glenbuicket Edenglassie Invermarkie Auchinhandoch Achoinane and Cabrach, his Second Son Captain Adam Gordon married to Cairnwhelp's daughter; their Sister Issabel Gordon married John Innes of Coldcoats of whom is come the present Laird of Dunkintie. The said Sr Adam Gordon after his first Ladys death married to his second Lady Helen Tyrie the knight of Drumkilbos daughter, with whom he begat three sons, viz, Patrick Gordon Laird of Glenbuicket, his second son Francis Gordon who went to Polland and married a rich match there, he dyed in Polland without succession, His third son   who was Father to the tutor of Glenbuicket; one daughter married John Innes of Codrain Father to Sr Alexander Innes of Coxton of whom the Towie Innesses alias Barcley are come, one Daughter married David Tyrie of Duniedeir, another married Thomas Gordon of Milne of Smithston, another Magdalen married Gordon of Collithie alias Paullie. Their Father the s^d Sir Adam Gordon dyed in Glenbuicket Septr 1629 and was Interred in the Church of Glenbuicket.

His eldest son Sr John Gordon second Laird of Park etc. married Hellen Sibbald daughter to Sr James Sibbald of Ramkiller in Fifeshire with whom he begat three sons and three daughters, viz. his eldest son Sr John Gordon of Park and Cluny, his second son Sr George Gordon of Edenglassie Invermarkie Auchinhandoch Carnousie

and Crannoch, his 3ᵈ son Mr David Gordon of Achoynanie, he had also
a natural son Patrick Gordon of Rhynie; One of his Daughters married
the Laird of Muirhouse Lyon, another married the Laird of Eden
Leslie, the third daughter married the Laird of Tillery Cuthbert.
Their Father the said Sᵣ John Gordon second Laird of Park dyed and
was honourably Interred in his Isle of the Kirk of Park.

The said Sᵣ John's Brother Patrick Gordon of Glenbuicket married
the Lady Leyes Couts with whom he begat a Son   Gordon Laird
of Glenbuicket who married the Laird of Glenbervie's daughter Dowglass, with whom he begat three Sons and a Daughter, viz. his eldest
son Captain Adam Gordon Laird of Glenbuicket who dyed abroad in
Holland of a Decay, his Second Son Lifetennant Robert Gordon who
married and yet lives, his 3ᵈ Son Ensign Alexander Gordon who
yet Lives; their Sister dyed. The said Patrick Gordon Laird of Glenbuicket dyed att Aberdeen and was buried in the Gordons Isle in the
Cathedral Kirk of Oldmacher being Laid down by my Lord Gordon's
side who was killed at Alford being both of them very Intimate in their
life, and brave men as the Age produced, and now no doubt are more
ardent in Love and affection in heaven. The said Patrick Laird of
Glenbuicket had a Brother who was father to John Gordon tutor of
Glenbuicket who married Agnes Gordon Badinscoth's Daughter with
whom he begat three sons and two daughters, viz, George, Alexander,
and little Captain Adam Gordon, One Daughter married John Ogilvy
heir of Kempcairn

The said Sir John Gordon second [sic] Laird of Park and by
Rothemeys death representative of Cairnborrow married four times
honourably. First he married my Lord Dundees Aunt Graham, with
whom he begat one daughter Hellen Gordon married to the Laird of
Achlunchart Innes, who yet lives. After his first Ladys death he
married Mʳˢ Jean Forbes sister to Sᵣ Alexander Forbes of Tallquhon
with whom he begat a Daughter Mrs Beattie married on John Gordon
of Drumwhyndle now of Craibston who yet lives; After his second
Ladys death he married Mrs Katharine Ogilvy of Kempcairns daughter
with whom he begat two daughters Mrs Anne married Arradoull Anderson
who yet lives, another Mrs Margaret who married Innes of Knockorth
she also lives; Lastly after his third Ladys death he married Dame
Helen Ogilvy (who yet lives) the Earl of Airly's daughter with whom

he begat one son (who succeeded his father), Viz Sr James Gordon fourth Laird of Park and representative of Cairnborrow His Father the forsd Sr John Gordon third Laird of Park dyed and was honourably interred in his Isle within the Church of Park.

His Second Brother Sr George Gordon of Edenglassie Carnousie Sherriff-principal of Bamffshire and Captain of the Independent Troop of Horse that belonged to the Earl of Annandale married Mary Abercromby daughter to Sr Alexander Abercromby of Birkenbog, with whom he begat two sons and four daughters, Viz. his eldest son John Gordon Laird of Edenglassie, and George Gordon his second son now Laird of Carnousie and Cranoch who lives ; his eldest daughter married the Laird of Boynlie Forbess to whom she bore one daughter married to the present John Gordon Laird of Glenbuicket, his second daughter married the Laird of Diple Duff to whom she bore this present Laird of Bracoe Duff and severall Sisters, his 3^d daughter Mary died unmarried, the 4th daughter Elizabeth married the Laird of Lewchars Innes, and bore to him the present Laird of Lewchars and daughters. The said Sir George Gordon of Edenglassie and Carnousie dyed att Carnousie and was honourably and splendidly buried in the Isle of Corncairn or Ordewhill his whole Troop in Mourning and a great retinue of his friends accompanying his Interment with all Martial Solemnitie

His eldest Son John Gordon Laird of Edenglassie married Mary Gray Coheiress of Ballegerno with whom he begat a Son George Gordon who married a Gentlewoman of the Sirname of Carnegie, the said George Gordon went abroad and being a sprightly and handsome Gentleman and great Schollar lives very genteel as I am told in Holland.

His second Son George Gordon present Laird of Carnousie and Cranoch married the Laird of Brux daughter Forbes, with whom he begat four sons and four daughters, viz Arthur Gordon young Laird of Carnousie, the Second Roderick Gordon, Charles and Alexander Gordons ; his eldest Daughter married the Laird of Law and Wardhouse, the second married Sir William Gordon of Lessmoir. His eldest son Arthur Gordon of Carnousie married the Lady Lessmoir Mary Duff with whom he begat   . '

Sr John Gordon second Laird of Park his third son Mr David

Gordon Laird of Achoynane married Jannet Gordon daughter to the Laird of Terpersie with whom he begat a son James Gordon of Achoynane now of Balbithan [the Author of this Memoir?] and a daughter Mary Gordon. The forsaid James Gordon of Achoynanie married first Elizabeth Burnet Sister to Sir Alexander Burnet of Craigmyll with whom he begat severall sons and daughters who dyed in their nonage and after the death of his s^d first wife he married Towie Innes daughter Grandchyld to the Laird of Balvenie Innes, with whom he begat one son Benjamin Gordon, and three Daughters viz Isabel, Henret and Hellen Gordons.

The forsaid Sir James Gordon fourth Laird of Park and Representative of the family of Cairnborrow married to his first Lady my Lord Saltons daughter Helen Frazer, with whom he begat two Sons and a daughter, viz, his eldest Son Sr William Gordon of Park the fifth and present Laird, his second son John Gordon; his daughter Mrs Hellen Gordon married to Culben Duff After the death of Saltons daughter the said Sir James married the Lady Ballquhain my Lord Elphinstons Sister with whom he begat one Son Laird of Cobbardie and three daughters viz. Mrs Ann Mrs Beatty and Mrs Mary. The said Sr James their father dyed of ane Apoplexy in his journey to Aberdeen att Pooll Wells and was honourably transported from thence to the Church of Park and interred in his own Isle, his death was very much Lamented by all, being a brave and good Gentleman snatched away in the flower and prime of his years.

ABACHIE.

The Genealogie of William Gordon of Abachie second Son of James Gordon of Cairnborrow begotten on the Laird of Barns Daughter.

The said William Gordon of Abachie married Robert Innes of Drainies daughter with whom he begat a Son and two daughters, his eldest Son James Gordon of Abachie; his eldest daughter married the Laird of Ardneidlie Thomas Baylie, his second daughter married the Laird of Pittcaple Leslie. Their father the said William Gordon dyed

His son James Gordon of Abachie married the Laird of Foverans daughter with whom he begat four Sons, viz: John Gordon of Abachie,

George Gordon in Drumhead, Alexander Gordon in Baid, and William Gordon in Auchmull. Their father the said James Gordon dyed   .

His eldest Son John Gordon of Abachy married the Laird of Netherdales daughter Abernethy with whom he begat three Sons and five daughters; his eldest Son John Gordon of Abachie, Adam Gordon of   in Kaithness, and Patrick Gordon of Cairnwhelp; the eldest daughter married the Laird of Muiresk Dempster, one married James Duff of Tillysoull, one married Andrew M^cpherson of Cluny in Badenoch, one married George Ogilvy of Achairn, one married James Gordon of Davoch in Ruthven. Their father dyed in Achanachie.

His eldest son John Gordon of Abachie married my Lord of Inverachies daughter Sister to the Earl of Athol Stuart, with whom he begat four sons and daughters, his eldest Son John Gordon fiar of Abachie, George Gordon of Achanachie, James and Thomas Gordons

The forsd John Gordon fiar of Abachie married the Laird of Wardhouse daughter Leslie, with whom he begat one Son called John Gordon of Achanachie. The forsaid John fiar of Abachie dyed in the flower of his Age before his father.

His Son John Gordon married the Laird of Talquhons brother daughter Forbes.

The Second Sons of the house of Abachie and Achanachie.

George Gordon of Drumhead married and begat John Alexander and George Gordons and one Daughter who married John Lesly of Haughs thereafter married Tho: Gordon of Artloch.

Alexander Gordon of Baid married and begat Alexander Gordon who married Jannet Slorach. He died in Baid without Succession.

William Gordon of Achmull and Adam Gordon in Kaithness married and begat.

Patrick Gordon of Cairnwhelp married Dunbar with whom he begat Sons and Daughters, his daughter married Captain Adam Gordon Son to the Laird of Park his eldest Son Gordon in Tillysoull married Skipper Anderson's daughter, one daughter married Lachlan Ross of Corriedown.

George Gordon of Achanachie married the Earl of Mortons brother daughter w^t whom he begat four Sons John Gordon.

CROMMELLAT

The Genealogie of Mr James Gordon of Crommellat third son of James Gordon of Cairnborrow begotten on the Laird of Barns Daughter

This Mr James Gordon of Crommellat married Alexander Gordon of Pronies daughter Issabel Gordon with whom he begat two Sons, Viz John Gordon of Crommellat, and Thomas Gordon Constable of Strath bogie. The said Mr James their father was killed by a Gentleman of the Name of Birnie who was execute for the same.

His eldest Son John Gordon married the Laird of Netherdales daughter Jannet Abernethy with whom he begat a Son called John Gordon who went to Pole and married a rich merchants Daughter there and became very rich and has Succession The forsaid John Gordon of Crommellat begat two natural Sons, William Gordon who dwelt in Sutherland, and Mr Thomas Gordon in Overhall Pedagogue to my Lord Gordon second Marquise of Huntly The forsd William married in Sutherland, Mr Thomas Gordon in Overhall married the Goodman of Achanachie's daughter.

Mr James Gordon of Crommellat's second Son Thomas Gordon married and begat two Sons and a daughter, viz: Alexander Gordon married Mrs Dempster and was servitor to my Lord Gordon, and John Gordon servitor also to my Lord Gordon he married Alexander Gardens daughter of   ; Thomas Gordons Daughter married Patrick Gordon in Collithie.

Before I end the Genealogie of Cairnborrow and their Cadents I must tell you that Severalls of their Posterity are extinct, only the family of Artloch is represented by William Gordon of Drumwhyndle and William Gordon of Farsken, two Brothers, sons of William Gordon a Second Son of Artlochs who first coft Farsken.

TILLYTERMONT.

The Genealogy of William Gordon of Tillytermont, Second Son to Jock the Heiress Brother, begotten on the Knight of Gights daughter Maitland his Last Wife.

Here indeed I must own that this William Gordon of Tillytermont being the first Cadent come of Jocks Family should have had the first place, Cairnborrow being only the second Cadent taking place next to Tillytermont or whoever is representative of that Family; this acknowledgment will plead my Excuse and therefore I proceed.

This William Gordon of Tillytermont married Sir John Rutherfords Sister with whom he begat two Sons viz. George Gordon of Fewllmont of whom the house of Blelack and Lessmoir, and Patrick Gordon of whom the Family of Craig are descended.

The forsaid George Gordon of Fewlement married   Innes of Meillers daughter with whom he begat four sons, viz: Alexander Gordon of Tillemmnat, James Gordon first Laird of Lesmoir, William Gordon of Breaklay and Thomas Gordon of Bowmakellach. Their father the said George Gordon dyed in Tillyminnat 1481.

His eldest Son the said Alexander Gordon of Tillyminnat married the Laird of Lessendrums daughter Bisset, with whom he begat James Gordon of Blelack. His Father the said Alexander was killed in the Battle of Flowden 9th Septr 1513.

His Son James Gordon of Blelack married Margaret Calder the Laird of Asslowns daughter, with whom he begat three Sons and two daughters, viz John Gordon of Blelack, George Gordon of Kinnour, and Alexander Gordon of Waternadie; his eldest daughter married George Gordon of Proney, his second daughter married William Gordon of Bellchirie. Their father the said James Gordon of Blelack was killed in the Battle of Corrichie 16. Octr. 1562.

His eldest Son John Gordon of Blelack married Mr Matthew Lumsdells of Tillyangus daughter with whom he begat five sons and.. four daughters, viz; his eldest Son Alexander Gordon of Blelack, John Gordon of Bellabeg, James Gordon Burgess in Aberdeen, George Gordon of Cracullie, and Robert Gordon in Dubbs; his eldest daughter married William Gordon in Dasky, one married James Calder, one married Alexander Midleton of Kincrage, and one married George Lesly of Monelie. Their father the said John Gordon dyed   .

His eldest Son the said Alexander Gordon of Blelack married the goodman of Achmeddens daughter Katharine Baird with whom he had no succession. The said Alexander Gordon bought the Lands of Proney and died in Peace in Culldrain in August 1650 years.

His brother Son John Gordon of Blelack succeeded and married the goodman of Finzeans daughter Elizabeth Farquherson.

The Genealogie of the Second Sons of the Family of Blelack.

George Gordon of Kinour married Robert Middletons of Borlands daughter, with whom he begat two Sons and daughters viz, his eldest Son James Gordon of Bogardie, his second Son Alexander Gordon. Their father the said George died in Kinoure January 1586.

His eldest Son James of Bogardie married the goodman of Kirktons daughter Carnegie with whom he begat Sons and daughters, his eldest son George Gordon   James Gordon of Bogardie married to his second wife the Lady Cubardie Dunbar, and had Succession by her.

James brother Alexander married and has succession.

John Gordon of Ballabeig married the goodman of Pittalochies daughter Forbes with whom he begat three Sons and daughters : His eldest Son John Gordon succeeded to the Lands of Blelack, his second Patrick, and third Son Alexander Gordon.

James Gordon Burgess in Aberdeen married Alexander Calder of Eastermigvies daughter, after her death he married Katharine Forbes with whom he begat Sons, viz, John Gordon etc.

George Gordon of Cracullie married James Gordon of Knockespacks daughter Bessie Gordon with whom he begat three sons and daughters, viz, William, James and Geo: Gordons.

Robert Gordon in Dubbs married Jannet Lesly with whom he begat a Son Mr Alexander Gordon.

LESMOIR.

The Genealogie of George Gordon of Fewlmonts Second Son James Gordon first Laird of Lesmoir.

The forsaid James Gordon first Laird of Lesmoir married two Ladies, his first was a daughter of Patrick Stuart of Lethers Lady Eden, with whom he begat Six Sons and three daughters, viz, his eldest Son George Gordon 2d Laird of Lesmoir, his second Son James Gordon of Crichie, 3d Son Alexander Gordon of Birkenburn, fourth son Mr William Gordon of Terpersie, fifth son Patrick Gordon of Oxhill, and the Sixth Son John Gordon of Licheston.   The said James married to his second Lady the Laird of Findlaters daughter Ogilvy Lady Gartlie, wt whom he begat two Sons, Hary Gordon of Dilespro or Savach, and Thomas Gordon of Drumbuilg.   His eldest daughter of the first marriage married John Gordon of Ardmather, the 2ᵈ married the Laird of Ludquharn Keith, and the third married the Laird of Meldrum. The said James Gordon their father first Laird of Lesmoir died in Lessmore.

His eldest Son George Gordon second Laird of Lessmoir married the Laird of Towies daughter Forbes, with whom he begat three sons and three daughters, viz, his eldest son Alexander Gordon third Laird of Lesmoir, James Gordon of,   and John Gordon of New-town, his eldest daughter married the Laird of Tallquhon Forbes, one married the Laird of Carnousie Ogilvy, one married the goodman of Achintowll Innes, and after his death she married the goodman of Bellendalloch Grant, and after his death she married John Gordon of Birsmoire brother to the Laird of Cluny who was killed at the ride of Tarnway. Their Father the said George died in Lessmoir

His eldest Son Alexander Gordon third Laird of Lesmoir Married the Laird of Pittsligos daughter Margaret Forbes, with whom he begat four sons and three daughters, his eldest son James Gordon fourth Laird of Lesmoir, Mr John Gordon Parson of   , George and Alexander Gordons; his eldest daughter married the Laird of Watterton Bannerman, one married the Laird of Leyes Burnet, the third married the Laird of Frendraught Crighton, he had a natural son called Ja: Gordon in Buchan. Their father the said Alexander dyed in Lessmoir.

His eldest son James Gordon fourth Laird of Lessmoir married the Laird of Inverrugies daughter Keith, with whom he begat three Sons and a Daughter, viz, his eldest Son James Gordon fiar of Lessmoir and fifth Laird, William Gordon Laird of Broadland, Alexander Gordon of Gerry or Johnsleyes; his daughter married the goodman of Cocklairachy younger, and after his death she married the Laird of Craig Gordon.

His Son forsaid James Gordon fiar and fifth Laird of Lessmoir married the Sherriff of Cromarties daughter Urquhart, with whom he begat James Gordon younger of Lessmoir and Sixth Laird. His Father the said James of Lesmoir dyed in France before his father, being cutt of the Stone Septʳ 1633

This forsaid James Gordon younger of Lesmoir and Sixth Laird married the Laird of Pittfoddels daughter Menzies, with whom he begat two sons; and dyed in July 1634 before his Grand father and was honourably interred in the Kirk of Essy 6ᵗʰ of August 1634.

The Cadents or Second Sons of the House of Lessmore

James Gordon of Crichie married the Laird of Gartlys daughter Barcley with whom he begat three sons, George Gordon of Crichie, Mr James Gordon a Jesuit who lived 1634, and John Gordon of Rhynie, their father James Gordon departed .

His eldest Son George Gordon of Crichie married Katharin M^cintosh, with whom he begat Adam Gordon of Boghole   He repudiate the said Katharin M^cintosh and married the Laird of Gights daughter Jean, with whom he begat two sons and daughters, his eldest Son William Collonell Gordon.

The forsd John Gordon of Rhynie married the goodman of Altowrleys daughter, with whom he begat Hary Gordon who dwelt in Tomaclagan in Strathawen, and he married

BIRKENBURN.

The Genealogie of Alexander Gordon of Birkenburn third son of James Gordon first Laird of Lesmoir

The said Alexander Gordon of Birkenburn married the Goodman of Cairnborrows daughter Gordon, with whom he begat James Gordon of Birkenburn Barron of Monaltrie ; after her death he married the Laird of Abergeldies daughter Gordon, with whom he begat Hary Gordon of the Knock, Duncan and James Gordons.   Their Father the said Alexr dyed .

His eldest Son James Gordon of Birkenburn married Alexander Gordons daughter of Strathawen, with whom he begat four Sons, his eldest son Alex^r Gordon of Birkenburn, George William and John Gordons.   Their father was killed att the Hunting by Alaster Calder a Gentleman.

His eldest Son Alexander Gordon of Birkenburn married Thomas Gordon Drumbuilgs daughter Margaret Gordon, with whom he begat sons and daughters, James and Adam Gordons.   His eldest son James Gordon married the goodman of Achencrives daughter Maitland, with whom he begat sons and daughters, viz, Alexander Gordon of Birkenburn, His second Son William Gordon of Sockach married the goodman of Merdrums daughter Elspet Gordon

The Last named Alexander Gordon of Birkenburn married Hellen

Bisset Lessendrum's daughter, with whom he begat three Sons, viz Alx^r Gordon his eldest Son who dyed unmarried, James Gordon the second Son who also dyed unmarried both in the flower of their Age, William Gordon his third Son now present Laird of Birkenburn married Magdalen Duff Provost William Duffs daughter in Inverness with whom he begat   .

Hary Gordon of the Knock married Walter Barcleys, daughter he was killed att the Hership of Glenmuick and Abergeldie 1592.

TERPERSIE.

The Genealogie of Mr William Gordon of Terpersie fourth Son of James Gordon first Laird of Lesmoir.

The forsaid Mr William Gordon of Terpersie married the Laird of Bamffs daughter Ogilvy Relict of Sir Alexander Gordon younger of Strathawen, with whom he begat George Gordon younger of Terpersie commonly called Ho ! ho ! The said Mr William Gordon was att the Battle of Corrichie with his Chief the twenty Eight of October 1563, and ten years thereafter was with Adam Gordon Laird of Auchindown · att the Battle of Tillyangus where he killed Black Arthur Forbes my Lords Brother and the champion of that Sirname and Family He was also with the said Adam Laird of Auchindown att the Battle of Craibstone att Aberdeen, and with him at the Bourd of Brechin, where the sd Adam was still victorious He built the house of Terpersie and · cast a ditch about it hard on the Marches twixt my Lord Forbes and him. The said Mr William Gordon of Terpersie was forefaulted with his chief, as were all the Gentlemen of the name of Gordon and others present with their Chief att Corrichie He dyed in the House of Ranes in the Enzie and was honourably interred in Rannes Isle within the Church of Raphven.

His son the forsd Geo Gordon of Terpersie succeeded, who married the Laird of Inverquharities daughter Ogilvy with whom he begat three sons and a daughter, viz William Gordon of Terpersie his eldest son, John Gordon of   , and Patrick Gordon of Badenscoth ; his daughter married the Laird of Culter Cumming. Their father was a great purchaser of Lands and departed in peace 1634.

His eldest Son William Gordon of Terpersie married the blind Lady Litchestons daughter Gordon, whose mother was a daughter of the Earl of Findlaters Ogilvy, with whom he begat five Sons and two daughters, viz, his eldest Son Alexander who dyed unmarried, the Second James Gordon who succeeded to the Estate, the third John Gordon Laird of Law, the fourth William who dyed unmarried, and the youngest son Hary Laird of Achlyne; one daughter married young Kincragie Gordon, another married Robert Stuart of Newtown. John Gordon of married the Barron of Braichleys daughter with whom he begat sons and daughters. The said William Gordon of Terpersie died at Terpersie and was interred att the church of Tillynessle.

His son the said James Gordon of Terpersie succeeded, he married Anne Gordon the Laird of Craigs Sister who was educate in France with whom he begat a Son George Gordon of Terpersie and two daughters, one married Leith of Threefield, another married Mr David Gordon of Acheynanie. Their father the said James Gordon dyed at Terpersie and was honourably interred in the Church of Tillynessle.

His son the said George Gordon Laird of Terpersie succeeded, who married Anna Burnet Sister to Sir Alex^r Burnet of Craigmyle, with whom he begat two sons and four daughters, viz, Charles Gordon present Laird of Terpersie and Thomas Gordon; one daughter married Patrick Leith who should have been heir of Threefield and Whitehaugh, the 2^d married Mr William Leslie minister at Craigfergus. Their father the said George Gordon dyed and was buried amongst his Ancestors in their burial place within the Church of Tillynessle.

His eldest Son Charles Gordon present Laird of Terpersie succeeded who married Adam Gordon at the Mill of Artlocks daughter, with whom he begat .

The Cadents of the Family of Terpersie.

Patrick Gordon of Badenscoth married the Laird of Blackfoord's daughter Gordon, and after her death married the Laird of Bamffs daughter ·Ogilvy with whom he begat Three sons and two daughters, . viz, Geo: Gordon of Badenscoth, James Gordon of Barns, and John

Gordon Burgess in Aberdeen; one daughter married the Laird of Knockespack Gordon, of whom is come the present Laird of Glenbuicket, another married the Tutor of Glenbuicket John Gordon.

John Gordon of Law Second Son to William Gordon of Terpersie married Issabel Gordon daughter to Leicheston, with whom he begat three sons, viz, John Gordon younger of Law, James Gordon of Darley, and Hary Gordon in Drumhead who yet lives. Their father dyed and was buried in the Church of Kinnethmont.

His Eldest son John Gordon of Law married the Laird of Culters daughter Cumming, with whom he begat John Gordon his eldest Son present Laird of Law and Wardess. His father the said John Gordon of Law fell in an accident of killing a Gentlewoman in Fivy as was alleadged but could not be proven; the brave young Gentleman however dyed of Melancholly in the flower of his Age.

His son John Gordon of Laws and Wardess was three times married, first he married Mr Robert Irvine Minister of Towies Daughter with whom he begat a son Arthur Gordon present Laird of Law and Wardess younger, he married to his second Lady Mary Gordon daughter to Achlyne, and after her death he married Hay Lady Crimon, with both wch. Last named Ladies he had no succession.

The forsaid Hary Gordon of Achline, William Gordon of Terpersies youngest Son, married Innes of Tillbouries daughter with whom he begat three sons and a daughter, viz, his eldest James Gordon of Achlyne and Newbigging, George Gordon of Knockespack, and John Gordon Burgess in Aberdeen; and his daughter married John Gordon Laird of Law. Their father the said Hary Gordon dyed and was interred in the Church of Clat.

His eldest Son James Gordon of Newbigging married Rachel Burnet Craigmyles Sister, with whom he begat two Sons and two daughters, viz; Alexander Gordon his eldest Son who dyed unmarried before his father's death, the second Son James Gordon of Tillyfour who married Craibstons daughter Sandilands with whom he begat a Son James Gordon who succeeded to his Grand father and is now present Laird of Achlyne and Newbigging; the said James his eldest daughter married Mr Robert Leslie second Son to Kininvie who yet Lives, the Second daughter Barbara Gordon married Mr Fairbairn present Minister at Gartly· who yet lives.

Having ended the Genealogie of Terpersie and finding no memory of Patrick Gordon of Oxhill Lesmoirs fifth son, I come now to the Genealogie of John Gordon of Licheston the Sixth and youngest Son of James Gordon first Laird of Lesmoir.

LICHESTON

The forsaid John Gordon of Licheston married my Lord Saltons brothr daughter Abernethie with whom he begat four Sons, James Gordon of Licheston, William Gordon of Clethins, Geo: Gordon of Cowtfield, and John Gordon Goldsmith. The forsaid John Gordon of Licheston married to his second wife the Laird of Findlaters daughter Ogilvy Lady Birkenbog, with whom he begat two Sons and three daughters, viz, Alexander Gordon Laird of Achynachie, and Hary Gordon of Glasshaugh; one daughter married William Gordon of Terpersie, one married the Laird of   and thereafter Archibald Grant in Belnatome, and one married John Gordon of Artloch. Their father the said John Gordon dyed   .

His eldest Son James Gordon of Licheston married the goodman of Tullock's daughter Beatrix Gordon and begat Sons and daughters, viz, Geo: James Alexander and William Gordons; one daughter married James Young Burgess in Elgin, Bessy and Margaret. Their father the said James dyed

George Gordon of Licheston married the goodman of Birkenburns daughter with whom he begat three Sons and two daughters

There are severall others come of the Family of Lesmoir who are now in a manner extinct, others whose Genealogie I am a stranger to, which for the said Reasons I am here forced to pass over in Silence, and therefore shall proceed to William Gordon of Tillytermont his other Sons.

CRAIG.

The Genealogie of Patrick Gordon of Craig Second Son of William Gordon of Tillytarmont.

This Patrick Gordon coft the Lands of Craig and was the first Laird thereof, he married the Laird of Towie Barcley's daughter with whom he begat five sons, viz, his eldest Son William Gordon Laird of Craig, his second Son Patrick Gordon of Achmenzies of whom the family of Tillachowdie, Thomas Gordon, Mr John Gordon Chaplain of Coclairachie, George Gordon of Milltown of Noth forbear of the family of Coclarachie.   Their Father the said Patrick Gordon dyed 1513 killed at the battle of Floudon.

His eldest son William Gordon Second Laird of Craig married the Laird of Laithers daughter Stuart, with whom he begat two Sons and a daughter, viz, Patrick Gordon third Laird of Craig, and James Gordon of Tillyangus; his daughter married the goodman of Corsindea Forbes Their father the said William dyed 1555

His Eldest Son. Said Patrick Gordon third Laird of Craig married the Laird of Wardess daughter Lesly, with whom he begat four sons, and William Gordon fourth Laird of Craig and John Gordon of Drumes.   Their father the said Patrick was killed at the Battle of Pinkie 1547 [and three sons].

His Son William Gordon fourth Laird of Craig married the Laird of Strathlochs daughter Cheyn, with whom he begat two sons, viz, John Gordon 5th Laird of Craig and Patrick Gordon of Foulzement. Their father the said William Gordon dyed 1607

His eldest son said John Gordon 5th Laird of Craig married the Laird of Towies daughter Barclay, with whom he begat two Sons, viz, John Gordon Sixth Laird of Craig, and Patrick Gordon; one daughter married Patrick Murray of Auchmull in France, another married Robert Stuart of Newtown.   Their father said John dyed in April 1634.

His Son said John Gordon Sixth Laird of Craig married the Laird of Lessmoirs daughter relict of Geo Gordon fiar of Coclarachy, with whom he begat a son and a daughter, viz, Francis Gordon Seventh Laird of Craig, his sister Anne Gordon married James Gordon Laird of Terpersie   Their Father the said John Gordon Laird of Craig, went to France with a Company of Soldiers and dyed there anno 1643.

His Son said Francis Gordon Seventh Laird of Craig being also bred in France returned to his native Countrey and Heritage and being Popish he married first the Laird of Pittfoddels daughter Menzies with whom he begat a Son called Francis Eight Laird of Craig, and after her death he married Gordon of Corrachries daughter with whom he begat a son John Gordon who was Page to the first Dutchess of Gordon.

Their Father the said Francis Laird of Craig dyed a Little after the Revolution 1689.

His eldest son Francis eight Laird of Craig married my Lord Bamff Ogilvey his eldest sister, with whom he begat Sons and daughters, his eldest son Francis Gordon ninth Laird of Craig ; one daughter married the Barron of Lesmurdie Stuart, another Mary married Mr George Skine Parson of Kinkell, another Barbara   Their Father the said Francis was taken Prisoner att Sherriffmoor and dyed in Stirling 1716

His Son said Francis Gordon ninth Laird of Craig married first Ballfluig's daughter Forbes, with whom he begat a son John Gordon tenth Laird of Craig ; he married the Lady Towie Barcley to his Second Wife, and after her death he married the Lady Montcoffer with these two last he had no succession [by the last two Sons, Francis and William].[1]   Their Father the said Francis Gordon Laird of Craig dyed in England Anno 1727.

His Son said John Gordon tenth Laird of Craig married the Lady Achlyne with whom he begat three Sons and a daughter   [He dyed anno 1740   His eldest Son John Eleventh Laird of Craig is married to Ann the Eldest Daughter of James Gordon of Banchory, and by her has children Marg^t Ann, James and Francis Gordons   He was married 2dly to Maria Cumine eldest daughter of Charles Cumine of Keninmonth.   Died 1 March 1800 Years   Succeeded by his Eldest Son James, 12th Laird, married Ann Elizabeth daughter of John Johnstone of Alva in Stirlingshire, an advocate at the Scots bar.[1]]

The First Cadents of Craig were the Family of Tullochaudie which indeed was numerous, prolifick and considerable, having by one marriage Nine Sons besides daughters of whom came the Gordons Kingcragie, Bagown, Bunty, Collithie, Drumgask, Pot, Cults   The most of these are now extinct and their descendants not well known by me, for which reason I pass over them and proceed to the next Cadent of Craig which I find to be Coclearachie.

COCKLEARICHY

The Genealogie of George Gordon of Milltown of Noth fifth son to the first Laird of Craig.

---

[1] Added in a later hand.

This George Gordon of Milltown of Noth married the Laird of Berrydales daughter Oliphant Lady Asslown, with whom he begat his son George Gordon of Cockclearachy, his father dyed

His son George Gordon of Cockclearachie married the Earl of Sutherlands brother daughter, with whom he begat George Gordon of Cockclearachie. His father was execute by Queen Mary for his Chiefs Cause the Earl of Huntly after the Battle of Corrichie. His Son Geo Gordon of Cockclearichie married James Duncan of Merdrums daughter with whom he begat four sons and three daughters, viz, George Gordon his eldest Son fiar of Cockclearichy, Alexander Gordon of Merdrum, Hugh Gordon of   , Mr William Gordon Doctor of Physick; his second daughter married Mr Robert Bisset Laird of Lessendrum, one married the goodman of Rhynie George Gordon, one married Seatton of Mymmes. Their father the said George dyed in Cockclearichie 1633.

His Eldest Son George Gordon fiar of Cockclearichie married the Laird of Lessmoirs daughter (who after his death married John Gordon Sixth Laird of Craig) with whom he begat two sons, George Gordon fiar of Cockclearichie, and Mr James Gordon   The said George Gordon fiar of Cockclearichie departed before his father

His Son George Gordon fiar of Cockclearichie married Grizell Setton the Laird of Pittmeddens daughter, with whom he begat sons and daughters, George, Alexander and James Gordons   George dyed young   Alexander married Issabel Gray daughter of   with whom he begat three sons and daughters, viz, his eldest son Alexander Gordon made Major General in the Muscovite Service, George Gordon of Dorlethers his 2d son, and James Gordon of Backieleys his third Son; the said Alexr their father was made one of the Senators of the Colledge of Justice 1687, and dyed sometime thereafter att Achintowll; his eldest Son said Major Generall Gordon married abroad Livetennant Generall Gordons daughter and besides his paternal estate of Achintowl he purchased the Lands of Lethers; the Second Son George Gordon of Dorlethers married Barbara Mackenzie daughter to the Laird of Ardloch, with whom he begat three sons and a daughter all yet alive, their father the said George perished by Sea going to Holland 1716, James Gordon the third son first married Barcley of Cottcairns daughter and after her

death he married Margaret Chalmers daughter to   Chalmers
wrtter in Edinburgh.

James Gordon of Ardmellie Second Son of George Gordon of Cockclearachie married Issabel Meldrum daughter to the Laird of Lethers,
with whom he begat three sons and a daughter, viz, Peter Gordon his
eldest son and Laird of Ardmellie now alive, his Second son Alexander
Gordon Laird of Logie in the parish of Crimon, his third son James
Gordon of Banchry present merchant in Aberdeen; his daughter
Mrs Mary Gordon married Laithentie Skeen and dyed   .

William Gordon Second Laird of Craig had a second son James
Gordon of Tillyangus whose descent is now extinguished save only
James Gordon now of Cairnbrogie who is Representative of the said
Family; their Cadents I know not

HADDO

The Genealogie of James Gordon of Methlick or Haddoe the third
son of Jock begotten on the Knight of Gights daughter Maitland his
Lawfull Wife.

The said James Gordon purchased [His wife was Canea Harper
"half portioner of Methlick" of which her father "Johannes de
Citharista" was the owner; James G or his son acquired the other
half of the barony, and thus arose the Gordons of Haddo[1]] the
Lands of Methlick and thereafter the Lands of Haddo being the
first Laird thereof. He married Anna Harper w^t whom he begat four
sons and four daughters, viz, his eldest son Patrick Gordon Laird of
Haddo, Robert Gordon of Fetterletter, Mr Alexander Gordon first
Chancellor of Murray and Chanery of Ross and thereafter Bishop of
Aberdeen, and George Gordon of Achenniff in Buchan; his eldest
daughter married the Laird of Allardes, the Second married Fraser
Laird of   , the third married Andrew Prott Burgess in Aberdeen, the fourth married George Gray Burgess in Aberdeen   Their
father dyed   .

His eldest son Patrick Gordon second Laird of Haddo married the
Laird of Findlater's Daughter Ogilvy with whom he begat three sons
and three daughters, viz, his eldest Son George Gordon third Laird of
Haddo, Mr James Gordon Parson of Lonmey, and Alexander Gordon

[1] Added by Mr Dalrymple

first Goodman of Bracoe ; his eldest Daughter married the Laird of Towie Forbes, another married the Laird of Altar Cumming, the third married the Goodman of Blairy or Kilravoch Dunbar. Their father the said Patrick dyed

His eldest son George Gordon third Laird of Haddoe married the Laird of Delgaties daughter Hay, with whom he begat his eldest son James Gordon fourth Laird of Haddo His father the said George dyed

His Son said James Gordon fourth Laird of Haddoe married Gilbert Menzies Provost of Aberdeens Daughter, with whom he begat five sons, viz, his eldest son George Gordon fifth Laird of Haddo, Robert Gordon of Savoch, David Gordon of Nethernure, John Gordon of Tillyhilt, and James Gordon ; and a Daughter who married Esslemont Cheyn, their father the said James dyed

His eldest son George Gordon fifth Laird of Haddo married the Laird of Muchels Daughter Fraser, with whom he begat a son James Gordon Sixth Laird of Haddo His father the said George dyed

His Son said James Gordon Sixth Laird of Haddo married the Earl of Marshal's daughter Keith, with whom he begat two sons, his eldest son George Gordon Seventh Laird of Haddo ; their father the said James Gordon Sixth Laird of Haddo married to his second wife the goodman of Tillyhilts daughter Gordon. Their Father the said James dyed

His eldest son George Gordon seventh Laird of Haddo married the Laird of Wattertons daughter Bennarman with whom he begat a son John Gordon eight Laird of Haddo who married the Laird of Talquhons daughter Forbes, and with her he begat sons and daughters, his eldest son Patrick Gordon ninth Laird of Haddo, and Charles Gordon. Their Father the said John Gordon eight Laird of Haddo was execute att Edenburgh by the Covenanters in July 1644.

The Cadents of James first Laird of Haddo.

Robert Gordon of Fetterletter married and begat a daughter who married Sir George Gordon Laird of Gight and Shives ; he had a natural Son Alexander Gordon, who begat William Gordon att the Mill of Idoch in Buchan. Their father departed

George Gordon of Acheniff or Chappellton married Marion Meldrum daughter to the Laird of Fyvie, with whom he begat two sons John and James.

Mr Alexander Gordon Bishop of Aberdeen had many Bastard Children, viz, David Gordon of Savoch, etc.

Alexander Gordon of Braccoe married Issabel Annan Daughter to the Laird of Achterellon with whom he begat sons and daughter; his eldest son Patrick Gordon of Bracoe married Jannet Seton Easter-disblairs daughter. His father said Alexander dyed .

His son Patrick Gordon second of Bracoe married and begat three Sons, viz, John Gordon of Bracoe, Mr. Patrick Gordon who coft Bracoe, and Alexander Gordon of Shellagreen. Their father dyed .

His eldest son John Gordon third of Bracoe begat James Gordon of Bracoe, Alexander, Sir Francis Gordon, and John Gordon of Deuchries

James Gordon forsaid of Bracoe married Sarah Lesly, with whom he begat John Gordon, he sold the Lands of Bracoe to Alexander Lyon The forsaid Mr. Patrick coft the Lands of Bracoe from the said Alexander Lyon; the said Mr Patrick married the Laird of Pittoderies daughter Ereskin with whom he begat sons and daughters; Mr Patrick dyed 1643. The said Family is extinct save only one Charles Gordon who was Ensign to the Towns Company of Edenburgh and Contemporary with Captain Peter Ghrame anno 1686.

Alexander Gordon of Shellagreen married

Sir Francis Gordon was Embassador to the King of Britain in Pole and dyed in Aberdeen 1643.

John Gordon of Deuchries married the Laird of Burlies brother daughter and begat James Gordon.

Robert Gordon of Savoch married the Laird of Shethons Daughter Affleck, with whom he begat three sons, viz, George, James and Gordons, and a daughter who married the goodman of Craigston Forbes, and thereafter married William Gordon of the House of Proney, one Daughter married Edward Crawford of Corbshill, and another George Forbes.

David Gordon of Nethermure married the goodman of Achencrives daughter Maitland, with whom he begat two Sons and Daughters, viz Gordon of Nethermuire and James Gordon of Knawen. Their Father dyed . His Son Gordon of Nethermuire married the Parson of Kinkells daughter with whom he begat five sons, viz,

George Gordon of Nethermuire, Gilbert Gordon now of Knowen. Sir James Gordon of Knowen married Elizabeth Jamieson alias Johnston with whom he begat two sons and daughters, viz, Patrick and Thomas Gordons, and a daughter who married William Gordon fiar of Tilly-angus.

John Gordon of Tillyhilt married the goodman of Achanachies daughter Gordon and begat James Gordon of Tillyhilt.

Having in the former part of this Book treated of the Genealogie of Jocks Posterity begotten on his Lawfull Wife the Knight of Gights daughter Maitland, viz, his eldest son John Gordon of Botarie of whom Pittlurg, and William Gordon of Tillytermont His second Son of whom Blelack Lessmoir and Craig, and his third son James Gordon of Methlick of whom Haddo are come ; my proposed method requires that in this place I should touch the Genealogie of Jocks Posterity begotton on McLeud of Harris Daughter who (tho' the legittemacy of that marriage be Contraverted) was a Gentlewoman of good and honourable Descent and every way suitable to have been his Lawfull wife, upon which consideration their issue deserves all due respect and honour without the Least contempt or unnatural and fruitless contraversies and therefore I proceed to their Genealogie

BUCKIE.

The Genealogie of Jock the Heretrix Brother begotten on McLeud of Harris Daughter.

The said John Gordon as is storied was sent to Mcleod of Harris Family of purpose to care for his Education in the Highland Tongue which was then of no small accont ; and having there contracted an Intimacy with his daughter Hanault [Hamiltone[1]] McLeod being the second daughter and sister to the Lady Mcintosh att that time, on her he begat a Son called Alexander Gordon of Essy of whom Buckie is come. His Father dyed in Essy and was interred in the Kirk of Essy.

The said Alexander Gordon his eldest Son (begotten before his Fathers marriage with the Laird of Gights daughter Maitland) suc-

[1] MS of 1644.

ceeded to his Possession of Essy and married the Laird of Ballquhoins Daughter Lesly; with whom he begat four Sons and two Daughters viz, his eldest son John Gordon of Essy, Alexander Gordon of Drumin Duncan Gordon of Knowen, and James Gordon of Ardbroilach in Badenoch [Badegott[1]]; his eldest Daughter married the Laird of Caskyben Johnston, his Second married Gilbert Hay of Achlochyries in Buchan. Their Father the said Alexander Gordon of Essy Killed the Barronbog of Strath Earle att the hunting in Badenoch for which he sustained great trouble, and dyed in Essy and was buried besides his father in the Kirk of Essy.

His eldest son John Gordon of Essy married the Heretrix of Bodom Spens, with whom he begat four sons, viz, Alx[r] Gordon of Buckie Constable of Bog of Gight, Thomas Gordon of Auchinheives goodman of Craicullie, William Gordon of Knockespock, and David Gordon. Their father the said John of Essy sold the Lands of Boddam and coft the Lands of Buckie; he dyed in peace.

His eldest son Alexander Gordon of Buckie married Jannet Drummond daughter to the Laird of Inchpafra, with whom he begat two Sons and a Daughter, viz, his eldest Son John Gordon of Buckie, and William Gordon of Aradowl; his daughter Bessy married John Gordon of Cairnborrow; also the said Alexander Gordon of Buckie begat on a Gentlewoman Margaret Ellis four natural Sons, viz, Thomas Gordon of Deskie, Alexander Gordon of Netherbuckie, George of Wellheads, and James of Invercharrach. Their father the Said Alx[r] Gordon dyed [in peace[1]]

His eldest son John Gordon of Buckie married Mr George Gordon of Belldornys Daughter, with whom he begat three Sons and two Daughters, viz, his eldest son George Gordon of Buckie, Mr William Gordon of Cairnfield Baillie of Enzie, and Alexander Gordon of Rothmeys; his eldest daughter married James Gordon of Letterfury, the second married Donald Irvine Burgess in Elgin. Their Father was killed in the Battle of Tillyangus 1571 and honourably buried in the Kirk of Dunbennan.

His eldest son George Gordon of Buckie married the Laird of Craigston's daughter Beatrix Urquhart Tutor of Cromarty, with whom

[1] MS. of 1644.

H

he begat two sons and three Daughters, viz, his eldest son John Gordon fiar of Buckie and Laird of Hillton, and William Gordon ; his eldest Daughter married Thomas Gordon of Edenvilly brother to the goodman of Letterfury, his second Daughter married Thomas Stuart of Drumin son to the Barron of Kinmaichly, his third daughter married Alx^r Dunbar of Aslesk

His eldest son John fiar of Buckie Laird of Hillton married the Laird of Glenveichy's daughter Cambell, with whom he begat three Sons, of whom some dyed in their Nonage ; and John Gordon Heir [fiar[1]] of Buckie forsaid married the Laird of Glenurchies daughter, and after her death he married Jean Scott Daughter to Sr John Scott of Scotstarbet he had no Succession by her ; he dyed in Aberdeen before his father anno 1630

The Cadents of the House and Family of Buckie.

Alexander Gordon of Drumin married the Laird of Lochstericks daughter [Christan[1]] Logan with whom he begat four Sons and daughters ; his eldest Son Alx^r Gordon of Proney, David Gordon of Incharny [Lincharne[1]] and Braikleys, William Gordon of Tombreachly, and Mr James a religious man ; his eldest Daughter Katharine married the goodman of Achencrive Maitland and after his death she married the Laird of Lammentons Son Thomas Baillie of Ardmylies and to her third Husband George Gordon of Cairnborrow, his second daughter married the Laird of Achynachie Saintclare, his third daughter married Wm Craig of Craigston, he had a natural Daughter married Wm Middleton of Boreland of whom the Middletons of Glentaner are come, he was Baillie of Badenoch and Strathawn. In his time John Stuart son to Sir Walter Stuart who disponed Strathawn to Alexander third Earl of Huntly made a great uproar assisted by the Grants and Clanallan, moved the Country to shake off Huntly's Authoritie ; upon which the said Alexander Gordon of Drumyn came out of Badenoch with two hundred men in Arms upon Saturdays night to the Wood of Fegan anent Kirkmichaell and understanding that the said John Stuart with his principall Associats the Grants and Clanallan were within the Kirk on the Sabbath day, he caused every man of his

Party cutt a faggott and carry along with him, and coming quietly to the Kirk he filled the Doors and Windows with the said Faggotts, and then called for fire to burn them, whereupon all within were glad to give out pledges to the said Alexander Gordon for their Obedience and good Behaviour in all time coming, which were sent to Strathbogie to the Earl Alexander. The forsd. Alexander Gordon of Drumin dyed in the Castle of Drumyn and was interred in the Kirk of Inverawn 1504.

: : !

PRONEY.

His eldest son Alexander Gordon of Proney who dwelt in Drumbuilg married the Laird of Tallquhons daughter Mary Forbes, with whom he begat four Sons and two daughters, his eldest Son Alx[r], and Second John both killed at the Battle of Pinkie 1547 with their father, James of Eastermigvie killed in the Battle of Corrichie 1563, and his youngest son George of Proney; his eldest daughter married Thomas Baird [of Odrinhuifes[1]] Baillie in Bamff, the second married Mr James Gordon of Crommellat brother to George Gordon of Cairnborrow. This Alexander was Baillie of Strathbogie and Mar, he was M[r] Household to the then Earl of Huntly, he took in the House of Rothemay with the confedrates within the same who Banded against the House of Huntly. He was killed bearing the Earl of Huntly's Standard w[t] his two forsd Sons Alexander and John, and his Brother David Gordon of Inchairne [Sincharny[1]] and Braikleys in the forsd Battle of Pinkie, where the Earl of Huntly was taken Prisoner anno 1547

His youngest son George Gordon of Proney married James Gordon of Blelacks daughter, Elspet Gordon, w[t] whom he begat four sons and a daughter, his eldest son James Gordon of Proney, Alexander Gordon in Drumbuilg killed in the Battle of Glenlivet [Oldchonachen[1]] 1594, William Gordon thunder slain 20th of July 1612, and John in Proney; one Daughter married Alexander Forbes in Keithmore, one married Alexander Cumming in Ruthven. Their Father said George of Proney dyed in Hilltown of Drumbuilg and interred in the Kirk of Gartly 15th of July 1654 [1604[1]].

His eldest son James Gordon of Proney married the Laird of

[1] MS. of 1644

Craignetties daughter Bessy Farquerson, with whom he begatt six Sons and a Daughter, his eldest son Patrick Gordon of Proney, George who dyed of Eighteen years of Age, Thomas who dyed of the Same Age, John Burgess in Stricken, William and Arthur Gordons who both dyed young; his daughter married Hugh Calder brother to the Laird of Asswanlie [Aslonie]. Their father dyed in Hilltown of Drumbuilgh 1614.

His eldest son Patrick Gordon of Proney married the Laird of Balvenies Sister Issabel Innes, with whom he begat a Son and a daughter, his son called George dyed without issue. His father dyed in Drumbuilg 1624

John Gordon Lawfull Son to George Gordon of Proney married Elizabeth Johnston daughter to James Johnston in Bunhill [Brunhill[1]], with whom he begat three sons and daughters, viz, W[m], Thomas, and George. The forsd William in Monthgatlehead [Montgarryhead ?] married Margaret Burnet

Alexander Gordon heir [yor[1]] of Proney had a Natural Son called Alexander, who married Issabel Strachen with whom he begat two sons viz, Alexander Gordon in Noth, and Robert in Scurdarg Their father was killed and his son Alx[r] married   and begat James Gordon a Merchant.

James Gordon of Proney had two natural sons, viz John Gordon who dwelt in Corriedoun [Corstasten[1]] and Alexander in Gairtly; this John married   Innes, with whom he begat John Gordon.

KNOWEN.

Duncan Gordon of Knowen third [fourth[1]] son to Alexander Gordon of Essy married the Goodman of Mellat's daughter Maitland, with whom he begat Eight sons, viz, his eldest son William Gordon of Knowen who dwelt in Kinmundy, the forsd Duncan Gordon had three sons fighting about the Earl of Huntlys standart killed in the Battle of Pinkie 1547.

Duncan Gordon's son Thomas [of Qtbog[1]] married Jean Forbes of the House of Tallquhon, with whom he begat Alexander Gordon of Achenhieff and George Gordon their father [this word not in 1644

[1] MS. of 1644

MS.] married two wives, first Elspet Meldrum Daughter to the goodman of Achenhive, with whom he begat Robert Gordon in Proney, his
second wife was Jannet Maitland with whom he begat Six Sons and
three daughters, viz, John, William, Peter Merchant in Pole, Mr James
Parson in Kinnore etc, married Agnes Barclay daughter to Mr Adam
Barcley Minister att Alford, Alexander his fifth son, and Richard his
sixth son

ARDBROGLACH.

James Gordon in Ardbroglach [Ardbryloch [1]] in Badenoch fourth
[third [1]] son to Alexander Gordon of Essy married   and begat Adam
Gordon of Ardbroglach, and two Daughters ; his eldest Daughter married
Donald Og M^cquherson, who bore to him [four [1]] sons [James [1]] Paul
and William M^cquhersons, Euen M^cpherson of Cluny in Badenoch etc;
his second Daughter married one of the Chiftains of the Clancameron
[special of the Glencameron [1]] called Donald M^cmartin, of whom some
of the Lairds of M^cmartin are come, their father dyed   .

His son Adam Gordon of Ardbroglach married   and begat
Alexander Gordon of Ardbroglach and James Gordon. Their father
the said Adam Gordon was killed att the Battle of Pinkie 1547.

Alexander Gordon Adams son married   Stuart and begat
Alaster Gordon in Ardbroglach who dyed without succession.

[James Gordon of Ardbryllochs second son Alexr. married and
begatt a son called James Gordon in Ardbryloch. This James begatt
Adam and Alexr Gordons in Ardbrylloch   This Adam begatt a son
John Gordon who lives 1631 years [1]]

ACHINHIFF.

The Cadents of John Gordon of Essy begotten on the Laird of
Bodams Daughter Spense, viz, Achinhiff or Cracullie.

Thomas Gordon of Auchinhiff or Cracullie Second Son to John
Gordon of Essy married the Laird of Inchpafra's daughter Drummond,
with whom he begat four sons and a daughter, viz, his eldest son
Alexander [Thomas [1]] Gordon of Cracullie, James Gordon of Achenhiff,

[1] MS. of 1644.

Mr Alexander Gordon of Tulloch, and George who dyed without heirs; his daughter Mary Gordon married John Gordon Laird of Cluny. Their father the said Thomas was killed att the Battle of Corrichie 1563[2 [1]].

His eldest son Alexander [Thomas [1]] Gordon married the Laird of Pittmeddens daughter Panton, with whom he begat one daughter who married James Gordon son to Cairnborrow who dwelt in Finnachty. Her father said Alexander dyed w[t]out more children.

His Brother James Gordon of Achenheiff succeeded, who married Bessy Rutherford with whom he begat two daughters, the Eldest Barbara Gordon married the Laird of Assloon Alexander Calder, the Second married the Goodman of Harthill Leith, and after his first wifes death the forsd James Gordon married my Lord Saltons Daughter Lady Innes, they had no Heirs. The forsaid James of Achinheiff or Cracullie had a Natural Son called Alexander Gordon in Mortloch who married   Anderson with whom he begat two sons and daughters, his eldest Alexander, his second   Gordon. The forsaid James was Baillie in Strathbogie and dyed in Cracullie 1586.

His brother [Mr [1]] Alexander Gordon of Tulloch Chancellor of Murray succeeded to his Brothers Lands, and he married three wives. His first was the goodman of Balfluigs daughter Forbes, with whom he begat a Daughter, who married Geo: Gordon of Sockach brother to Cairnborrow. His Second Wife was the Laird of Abergeldies daughter Gordon with whom he begat three Sons and two daughters, viz, Jas, Thomas, and John Gordons they dyed young; his eldest daughter married Duncan Grant of Belnatome, the second married Adam Duff of Drummoor. His third wife was Bessy Gordon a Daughter of Cairnborrows with whom he begat two sons, viz, Alx[r] Gordon of Achinhiff and Tulloch, and Robert Gordon. [Lykewayes the forsd Mr Alex[r] . . . son Hugh Gordon portioner of Dummoys who m . . . the Laird of Thomastowns daughter Forbes with whom he begat a Son John Gordon in Abercattie. Their father dyed in Tulloch [1]]

The forsaid Alx[r] Gordon of Auchinheiff and Tulloch married the Laird of Gights daughter with whom he begat two sons, his eldest son W[m] Gordon of Achenhiff and Tulloch, and   Gordon.

[1] MS. of 1644.

The forsaid Wm Gordon married the Laird of Cluny's daughter Gordon, with whom he begat two sons and a daughter, his eldest son Alexander Gordon of Glengerrak and Thomas Gordon of Cranoch, the Daughter married Lesly of Bochrome, the said William went to France and was a Captain there and dyed in France.

His eldest Son Alexander Gordon of Glengarrak sold Tulloch and coft the Lands of Newmills in Strath[i]sla, he married Keith, Brodie Lethenties daughter w^t whom he begat a son called Cha: Gordon and four daughters; one daughter married first the Laird of Buckie of whom this Buckie is come and after his death the Laird of   , a Second Daughter married Easter Binns in Murray, the third daughter Mary Married Brodie of Windyhills, the fourth married James M^cky in Newmills. Their Father said Alexander took Patrick Roy M^cgrigour ane catharine and another John Drum who were execute att Edenburgh, he also killed another Associate of Roy's att Keith where they fought valiantly upon Pauls day or rather the Evening anno 1667. He built the New House of Newmills in Strylla and dyed in Killbruiach in Murray.

His Son Charles Gordon of Glengerach married Bracoe Duffs Daughter with whom he begat Sons and daughters.

KNOCKESPOCK.

The Genealogie of William Gordon of Knockespock third son of John Gordon of Essy begotten on Bodoms Daughter Spense

The said William Gordon of Knockespock married the Laird of Achinhives daughter Dowgat with whom he begat two Sons, his eldest son Alex^r Gordon of Knockespock, and Hary Gordon who dyed without Heirs. Their father dyed [in peace [1]].

His son Alexander Gordon of Knockespock married the Laird of Ardneedlies Daughter Bailie, Lady Asswanly, with whom he begat four sons and daughters, his eldest James of Knockespock, Mr Al^xr Burgess in Elgin, Robert in Clat, and John Gordon of Bouges sherriff depute of Aberdeen, his eldest daughter married William Gordon of Tillyangus. Their forsaid father dyed [in peace [1]].

[1] MS. of 1644.

His eldest Son James Gordon of Knockespock married William Gordon of Ardneidlies daughter, with whom he begat three sons and three daughters, viz his eldest son William Gordon of Knockespock, Captain John Gordon, and M[r] Thomas Gordon, the eldest daughter married Donald Farquherson of Inchmarnoch, one [the youngest[1]] the Barron of Braichley, one Mr George Gordon of Cracullie. Their father dyed in Knockespock Sep[tr] 1631 and was buried in the Kirk of Clatt.

His eldest son William Gordon of Knockespock married the Laird of Gairns [David Garden of Garden's] daughter with whom he begat sons and Daughters viz James Gordon and Captain Alexander Gordon.

The s[d] James married the Laird of Lessendrum's Daughter Bisset and begat . . . The said James went to France Captain in a Regiment and dyed there 1643

The Second Sons of the House of Knockespock.

Mr Alexander Gordon Burgess in Elgin married Marjory Grant with whom he begat two Sons James and Hugh Gordons, after his first wifes death he married Anne Gordon the Laird of Strathawns daughter The forsd Alexander Gordon had a Natural son gotten with a Gentlewoman of the Sirname of Stuart called William Gordon of Menmoir, who married Jannet Grant with whom he begat four sons viz, Alx[r], Patrick, [The 2nd son Patrick or Peter married Janet Gordon of Cluny and had a son Charles who married Rachel Gordon, heiress of Abergeldie, and from them come the present family of Abergeldie [2]] Hary and John Gordons, he married to his second wife Grant of Achorochans daughter

John Gordon of Bouges sherriff deput of Aberdeen married Arbuthnet with whom he begat two sons, viz, Thomas and Hary Gordons who was killed in Germany.

William Gordon of Arradowl [or Fochabers [1]] second son of Alexander Gordon of Buckie married the Lady Innes with whom he begat a Daughter married to Jas. Gordon of Knockespok He dyed in peace without further Succession, he had only a Natural Son called William Gordon in Lunan.

---

[1] MS. of 1644.   [2] Added by Mr. Dalrymple

John Gordon of Buckies Second Son Mr William Gordon of Cairn-field begotten on Belldornies daughter married three wives, his first wife was the Laird of Achintowls daughter Forbes with whom he begat a son John Gordon of Cairnfield, his second wife was the goodwife of Skeith, his 3ᵈ wife was the goodwife of Findochty thereafter goodwife of Drainie. He dyed 5ᵗʰ Janry 1632 [in Cairnfield in peace [1]].

John Gordon of Buckies third son Alexander Gordon of Rothmeys married the Laird of Tillymorgens daughter Cruckshank, with whom he begat two sons John Gordon of Rothmeys and . . .

The Genealogie of Alexʳ Gordon of Buckies Natural Sons

Thomas Gordon of Deskie married John Gordon Vicar of Keith's daughter with whom he begat four sons, viz, William Gordon in Daskie, John, Alxr., and James Gordons. Their father dyed . His son William Gordon of Dasky married John Gordon of Blelacks daughter Issabel Gordon, wᵗ whom he begat three Sons, viz, Thomas, John and Alexander Gordons; the forsd Thomas married the Barron of Kenmaichleys brother daughter Stuart.

Alexander of Buckies second Natural Son. Alexander Gordon of Netherbuckie Baillie of Enzie married Christian Duff and begat a Son called William Gordon who married the Parson of Rivens daughter Hay, with whom he begat two sons, viz, William Gordon in Tarnaughty and John Gordon in Nether Bucky. Their father and grand father both dyed in Netherbukie. William Gordon in Tarnaughty married the goodman of Belldorneys daughter Gordon with whom he begat sons. John Gordon in Netherbukie married the goodman of Kininvies Daughter Leslie with whom he begat sons.

Alexr Gordon of Buckies third Natural Son. George Gordon of Wallheads married the Laird of Asswanlies daughter Calder with whom he begat four Sons viz Alexander Gordon in Bellyhill, Thomas Gordon in Fochabers, and John and Peter Gordons. Their father dyed .
His eldest Son Alexr married Achintowls daughter Forbes and begat George Gordon. Tho: Gordon in Fochabers married Robert Gordon of Belcheries daughter, with whom he begat George Gordon of Wallheads; he had a Natural Son Archibald Gordon who begat Robert Gordon who married one called the White Hen of Dundee.

[1] MS. of 1644.

Having now gone through the Genealogie of the Family of Huntly and their Cadents as also having discussed the Genealogy of Jock the Heiress eldest Brother with the Cadents and descendants come of him, Order now requires that in the Last place we treat of the Genealogie of Thomas Gordon of Davoch the Heiress second Brother begot on Elizabeth Cruickshank Laird of Asswanlies daughter.

DAVOCH

The Genealogie of Thomas Gordon of Davoch the Heiress Second Brother

The forsaid Thomas Gordon of Davoch married three wives with whom he begat Sixteen Sons   I find no succession but by five sons The said Thomas married to his first wife Sr Thomas Hay of Enzies Sister, with whom he begat a Son Patrick Gordon of Achinieath Corriedoun and Cotton hill, which he excambed with the Lairdship of Sauchen The said Thomas married to his second wife Sr Walter Innes Daughter of that Ilk, with whom he begat four sons, viz, Wm Gordon of Ballvenie, Mr Adam Gordon chancellor of Murray and Parson of Kinkell whose name is upon several places of the said Kirk in Gilded Letters yet extant with their date, his third son Tho. Gordon of Kenchie or Braikleys, the fourth George Gordon of Cushney or Hallhead.   The forsd James Gordon married to his third wife Chisolm of Straglass Daughter, with whom he begat John Gordon who got the possession of Davoch from his Father.   The said Thomas had other sons, but I have not their Names and find no Succession come of them. Their Father said Thomas dyed in Davoch and was interred in the Church of Ruthven whose monument is there yet extant

His son Patrick Gordon first Laird of Sachen married two wives, with the first he begat Patrick Gordon second Laird of Sachen, he married to his second wife the Laird of Pittmeddens daughter Panton, with whom he begat Alexander Gordon of Pethnick and Contly in Stryla who dwelt thereafter in Parkmore in Balvenie and was forbear of the House of Invercharrach   Their father Patrick Gordon first Laird of Sauchen dyed

His eldest son Patrick Gordon second Laird of Sachen married the Laird of Achlossens daughter Ross, with whom he begat three sons and daughters, his eldest Son Alexander dyed without Succession, the Second William Gordon Laird of Sachen, the third son John Gordon in Brunhill of Cromar. Their father Patrick Gordon Second Laird of Sachen dyed .

His son William Gordon third Laird of Sacken married Forbes with whom he begat Patrick Gordon fourth Laird of Sacken. His Father the said William dyed

His son Patrick Gordon fourth Laird of Sacken married Burnet with whom he begat two Sons, his eldest Son William Gordon fifth Laird of Sachen married the goodman of Kincragies daughter Gordon with whom he begat sons, viz, Alx^r Gordon fiar of Sachen, and John Gordon. Their father the said William Gordon became in such dangers that he passed into Ireland and dyed there 1639.

His eldest son Alexander Gordon fiar of Sachen married Robert Gairn of Tillyfruskies daughter who dyed in England without Succession 1654.

John Gordon of Drumhill first married Jannet Coutts, with whom he begat John Gordon younger of Drumhill Forrester of Cullblean who dyed also without Succession.

The Second Sons of Robert Gordon first Laird of Sachen

Alexander Gordon of Pethnick and Cantly who dwelt in Parkmore married the Laird of Badenoch's daughter Symmer, with whom he begat five Sons, viz, John Gordon of Invercharrach, Duncan Gordon of Clunymoir, Alexander Gordon of Bochrome, James Gordon in Parkbeig, and Alex^r alias Alaster Gordon in Achorlise. Their father the said Alexander dyed in peace and was interred in the Kirk of Mortleach.

His eldest son John Gordon of Invercharrach married the Heretrix of Invercharrach and the Barron of Carrons Sister, with whom he begat Gordon Barron of Achnastink who dyed w^tout Succession. He married to his Second Wife the goodman of Drainies daughter Innes with whom he begat five Sons, viz, William Gordon of Invercharrach, Robert Gordon of Pittglassie, James Gordon of Kinernie, William Gordon of Achinarrow, and Alexander Gordon of Parkmoir, all in the Parish of Mortleack. The forsd John Gordon of Invercharrach had a Natural Son begot on a Gentlewoman called Alastair Gordon att the Mill of Botarie. Their father the said John Gordon of Invercharrach dyed in peace, he was very Hospitable and a good Hunter.

His eldest son John Gordon of Achinstink married, and begat William Gordon of Achnstink, who married and begat Alex^r Gordon of Achinstink, who married Issabel Cumming and begat Sons who dwelt in Mortlach

John of Invercharrach's second Son dyed without Succession

James, Robert, and Alexander of Parkmoir dyed without Succession

John Gordon of Invercharrach's son Wm Gordon of Achinarrow married and begat Alaster Gordon of Achinarrow, John Gordon in Easterkinmaichly, and James Gordon of Craiggon of Delmore. The said William there father dyed in Peace.

And here I find myself run aground for want of further and better Information concerning the Family of Davoch, whose Representative this day is hard to be condescended upon, many of the forsaid Families and also their descendants being now extinct and without Succession, So that my Reader I hope will excuse this rude and imperfect draught of the whole, and if any more versant in antiquity and Genealogy shall make up my defect, I'll reckon it good service done to the truth and Sirname of Gordon.

HOUSE OF GORDON.

ABERGELDIE.

BY

JOHN MALCOLM BULLOCH, M.A.

NEW SPALDING CLUB.

K

·PREFATORY NOTE.

THERE are various sources of information on the family of Abergeldie. There is a pedigree in the *Balbithan MS.* (pp 9-11); in Burke's *Landed Gentry*, 1898 (corrected by the late Hugh Mackay Gordon, XVII. of Abergeldie); by Rev. J. G. Michie in the Crathie Church Bazaar Book *Under Lochnagar*, 1894, and in Lord Huntly's *Records of Aboyne;* while there is a brief account of the contents of the charter chest in the sixth report of the Historical MSS. Commission, appendix (p. 712); and various stories are given in Rev. J. G. Michie's *Deeside Tales.* Many references to the Abergeldie family, more particularly in connection with various land transactions and march disputes, will be found in Mr. Michie's *Records of Invercauld.* Two articles on the Abergeldie Gordons by the present writer appeared in the *Aberdeen Free Press* of 10th and 17th Nov., 1900. He is indebted for special information to the late Mr. Hugh Mackay Gordon, who told him that many family papers were destroyed by a fire in 1812; to Mr. Kenneth Gordon, Lee, Kent; to Dr. Charles Gordon, Pietermaritzburg; to Mr. D. Murray Rose and to others. The picture of Abergeldie Castle which is reproduced in this monograph is from a photograph by Annan of Glasgow, and represents the fine old structure from the north.

J. M. B.

118 PALL MALL, S.W,
February 10, 1902.

THE LAIRDS OF ABERGELDIE.

ALEXANDER GORDON, 1st Earl of Huntly.

SIR ALEXANDER GORDON, I. of Abergeldie.

GEORGE, II. of Abergeldie.

JAMES, III.

ALEXANDER, IV.

ALEXANDER, V.   WILLIAM, VI.

ALEXANDER, VII.

ALEXANDER, VIII.

JOHN, IX.   RACHAEL, X. = CHARLES GORDON.

PETER, XI.

CHARLES, XII.

PETER, XIII.   DAVID, XIV.

MICHAEL FRANCIS, XV.   ROBERT, XVI.   ADAM.

HUGH MACKAY, XVII.   LEWIS, XVIII.

ABERGELDIE.

The lands of Abergeldie lie in the parish of Crathie, Aberdeenshire. The meaning of the name is the " confluence of the Geldie " with the Dee at the west end of the castle. The derivation of " geldie " is very uncertain. (Macdonald's *Place Names of West Aberdeenshire*, p. 2.) The lands have been held by the same family of Gordon, descendants of the 1st Earl of Huntly, practically since 1449, though actual possession did not come until 1482. The interest in the family has been heightened by the fact that Queen Victoria as owner of the neighbouring estate of Balmoral, rented Abergeldie during many years, and that her mother, the Duchess of Kent, and her son, King Edward VII., as Prince of Wales, used to live there. He is still the tenant (until 1922), at a rent of £4500 a year. The Empress Eugenie, who is descended from the old Scots family of Kirkpatrick, has frequently stayed at Abergeldie.

The castle, which stands on the south bank of the Dee about six miles above Ballater and two below Balmoral, has been much altered and added to; but, according to MacGibbon and Ross's *Castellated and Domestic Architecture of Scotland*, which contains a view of the building from the north-east (figure 520), it still retains the original tower which formed the nucleus of the whole, and which with its rounded angles, its crow-stepped gables and its somewhat elaborately corbelled angle turret, is a good and picturesque example of a sixteenth century manor house in Aberdeenshire. The means of access from the north bank of the river was formerly by a picturesque contrivance called a " rope and cradle " bridge, the bridge being really a rope from which the cradle or basket containing the passenger was suspended, and along which it ran.

The arms of the Gordons of Abergeldie as registered 1676, are: Quarterly: 1st, Azure, three boars' heads couped or; 2nd, Or, three lions' heads erased gules, 3rd, Or, three crescents within a double tressure

flory counterflory gules; 4th, Azure, three fraises argent; the whole
within a bordure quarterly argent and gules   Crest: A deerhound
argent collared gules.   Motto: "God for us".

ALEXANDER, 1ST EARL OF HUNTLY.

(Died 1470.)

Abergeldie appears in the hands of the Gordons for the first time in
1449, when it was in possession of Alexander, the first Earl of Huntly,
who got it from the king for his services in suppressing the rebellion
headed by the Earl of Douglas.

Abergeldie was originally part of the vast possessions of the notorious
Earldom of Mar.   Thomas, Earl of Mar, the last of the direct male line
(he died in 1376), granted "Abbirgedly" in 1358 to "Duncan son of
Roger," who was bound to give suit at the Earl's three courts held "apud
lapidem de Mygvethe"—a stone at the Earl's great manor of Migvie in
Cromar.   In 1435 James I. boldly claimed the Earldom for reasons
denounced by all the genealogists.   In 1436 the lands were in the hands
of John Mowat, for in 1438, according to the accounts of the Chamberlain
of Mar, a payment is entered out of the rents of Cambusnakist by the
King's grant of £10 to John Mowat for his right of the lands for the
two previous years.   In 1445 and 1446, the receiver of the king's rents
is ordered to inquire carefully who is in possession of the lands, and
what is their value, and in 1449 he reports them to be in the
hands of Alexander, 1st Earl of Huntly, and in 1451 the Chamberlain
accounts for £10 as the rent of Abergeldie, which is said to be in the
Earl's hands.   But the Roger claim was still recognised so late as 1507
as I shall show.

The Earl of Huntly married Elizabeth, daughter of Lord Crichton,
Chancellor of Scotland, and had (Records of Aboyne) :—

1. GEORGE, 2nd Earl of Huntly, who married the daughter of James I
2. Sir ALEXANDER, I. of Abergeldie
3. ADAM, Dean of Caithness, ancestor of the Gordons of Beldornie, Drummuy,
   and Sidderay
4. JANET.
5. ELIZABETH, mar. (1) the 2nd Earl of Erroll, and (2) John, Lord Kennedy.
6. CHRISTIAN, mar. William, Lord Forbes.

SIR ALEXANDER GORDON, I. OF ABERGELDIE.

(*Son of* 1st *Earl of Huntly . died before* 1504.)

Sir Alexander Gordon clinched the hold that his house had got on Abergeldie. He received various lands in the barony of Midmar. The following dates bear on his annexation of Abergeldie and other estates :—

1482. *Dec.* 26.—By deed of gift, James III. granted the lands of Abergeldie to Alexander Gordon (*Records of Aboyne*, p. 219).

1485.—He had a lease from David, Abbot of Arbroath, of the great tithes of the churches of Coull and Kinernie (*Antiquities of Aberdeen and Banff*, 11 , p 28).

1488. *Nov.* 22.—He got a charter of the lands of Tullitermont from his brother, Lord Huntly (*Aberdeen Burgh Sasines*, vol. i.)

1489. *Jan.* 23.—He got a grant of the lands of Eastoun in Cromar from the King upon the resignation of John Rutherford of Tarland (*Great Seal*)

1501. *Nov.* 1.—His charter on Abergeldie and Eastoun, which were incorporated in one free barony, was confirmed (*Great Seal*).

1503.—He sold Old Midmar to James, Lord Ogilvie of Airlie, who however was to " tak na profit of the said lands " until Gordon's grandsons Alexander or James came of age to complete a marriage either with Janet or Marion, Lord Ogilvie's daughters. If the marriage did not take place, the lands were to remain in the hands of the Ogilvies until the sum of 600 merks was paid (*Abergeldie Charter Chest*, quoted in the *Records of Aboyne*, p. 220).

Sir Alexander, who died before January, 1504, married Beatrice Hay, daughter of the Earl of Erroll. On Oct. 1, 1504, when she was a widow, she was found entitled to her terce of the lands of Carnetralzeane and others in Kinellar, of the davach of Abergeldy and of Easton, and of the lands of the barony of Midmar (*Antiq. of Aberdeen and Banff*, iii., p. 242). The first laird of Abergeldie had, according to the *Balbithan MS.* ·—

1. GEORGE, II. of Abergeldie

2. WILLIAM, of Netherdale, who lived in Ruthven of Cromar. In 1522 he raided the Corryhoul lands of Agnes Grant, the widow of John McAllan, in Inverernan and took away much booty (*Antiq. Aberdeen and Banff*, iv., p. 477). In April, 1530, James Gordon of Abergeldie as surety for William, was ordered to pay to Agnes "sex score of yowis price of the pece v schillingis, lx of wedderis & yeild scheip price of the pece iiij schillinges, & foure score of lambs price of the pece ij schillings. And for the proffictis of the said vj^{xx}. yowis in woll, mylk, & lammis xxvij pundis. The proffictis of the saidis lx wedderis & yeild scheip sen the tyme of the said spulye three pundis. The proffictis of the said lxxx lammis sen the said spulye as saidis iiij pundis " (*Acta Dom*

Conc.)   On March 8, 1532-33, King James V. granted a charter to
Agnes Grant, who had by that time married Thomas Cuming, of six
bovates of the sunny half of the lands of Craibstone, apprised from
James Gordon of Abergeldie for 126 marks due by him as surety for
William Gordon's plunder of 60 rams & barren sheep, 100 wethers
& 80 lambs (*Great Seal*)   His nephew James, the third laird of Abergeldie, became surety for him.   The *Balbithan MS* says he was killed
at Ruthven by John Gordon *alias* John Geer   He married and had—

> MARGARET, who got Netherdale as her tocher (*Sasine*, 26 May,
> 1530)

3 JANET, married before Oct, 1501, at which date she was living, Thomas
Fraser, Lord Lovat, and had a son—

> HUGH FRASER, Lord Lovat, who was slain by the Macdonalds at
> Lochlochy, 1544.   He was the ancestor of the present
> Lord Lovat

4. *Daughter*, married Mortimer, the laird of Craigievar (*Balbithan MS.*).

5. *Daughter*, married ——— Ogilvy of Clova (*Balbithan MS.*).

6 BEATRIX (alive 1555), married (1) Garden of Dorlaithers (" of whom is
come Mr. Robert Garden of Belliemore "). (2) Ross of Auchlossin
(*Balbithan MS.*); she was alive in 1574 (*Records of Aboyne*, p. 222).
In 1487 there was a marriage contract (*Antiq Aberdeen and Banff*, III.,
p. 299) between the heir apparent of Alexander Irvine of Drum and
a daughter of Alexander Gordon of Midmar, but the ceremony never
seems to have been solemnised, and the girl may have been one of the
four daughters mentioned in the *Balbithan MS.*

GEORGE GORDON, II. OF ABERGELDIE.

(*Son of I.: died before* 1523.)

This laird is distinguished by the fact that he got complete and
indisputable possession of the lands of Abergeldie.   Like everything
connected with the Earldom of Mar, his tenure had been, to say the
least of it, shaky.   The Crown still put forward claims and the Roger
family also had a claim   Gordon first cleared off the claim of the
Crown :—

1507.   *Feb.* 25 —The Privy Council decided that George Gordon was " quit fra"
the petition of the Crown, which claimed the lands, "because it was clearly sene
. . that the said lands of Abergeldie war destynct and separate lands fra the
properte of [the Earldom of] Mar, when it was cled with ane Earl, and quhen it
wes uncled with ane Earl, as our soverane Lordis old rollis sene and considered
propertis" (*Records of Aboyne*, pp. 220-1).

Then he got rid of the Rogers' claim :—

1507. *March* 24.—By a notarial instrument (in the Abergeldie Charter Chest) dated March 24, 1507 (a month after the Privy Council decree), wherein it is set forth that in the Court of the King's Justiciar held at Dundee, there appeared Thomas, son of Alexander, asserting himself to be heir of Christina Roger, his great grandmother, in the lands of Abergeldie and others in the Earldom of Mar, and confessing that he had been fully satisfied and paid by George Gordon of Midmar, his rights therein being thereby renounced, and the original charter granted by Thomas, Earl of Mar, to his predecessors being now delivered to the said George (*Hist. MS Com*, 6th Report, Appendix).

The second laird was alive in 1510, but died before 1523. He married Margaret Stewart (the *Balbithan MS*. calls her "Grizal"), daughter of the Earl of Buchan. She died in 1534. They had :—

> 1. ALEXANDER, alive in 1503 (*Abergeldie Charters*), but apparently dead before his father (*Records of Aboyne*, p. 221) though the *Balbithan MS*. gives him as third laird.
> 2. JAMES, III of Abergeldie
> 3. WILLIAM, in Logies (an illegitimate son), who married the daughter of —— Irving of Tulloch, and had five sons The *Balbithan MS.*, however, names only four, namely, Alexander, Robert, James and John Gordon of Coull.

JAMES GORDON, III. OF ABERGELDIE.

(*Son of II. killed at Pinkie, 1547.*)

On April 24, 1523, the young laird, "having arrived at the years of 'discretion and marriage,' petitioned his guardian [Walter Ogilvie in Boyne] that he might be 'coupled' in lawful matrimony. Ogilvie . . offered him his choice of two damsels in every respect equal to himself— Janet Sinclair and Elizabeth Ogilvie" (*Records of Aboyne*, p. 221). But he scorned them both and married Janet Leith, daughter and coheir of George Leith of Barnes, and widow of Alexander Seton of Meldrum. He was returned heir to his father only on October 6, 1534. In 1528 he had confirmation of a charter by John Stewart, Earl of Buchan (his uncle or grandfather), of the lands of Grandoum, Auchmull, Perslie, and others (*Great Seal*)

Abergeldie, as I have shown, had to pay dearly for his uncle William's raid on Agnes Grant. He had to surrender six bovates of the sunny half of the lands of Craibstone. The other part of

Craibstone, in the barony of Grandholm, he sold to James Cheyne, burgess of Aberdeen. Abergeldie was to pay Cheyne "the sovme of sewyntene scoire of merkis in gold of angell nobilis crovnis of weicht unycornis and Leitht crovnis . . . witht ane sufficient lettre of tak . . . of the said landis . . . for all the termes . . . of fyfteyne zeiris . . . followinge the rademynge . . . of the said landis for tene merkis of pennye maill . . monye of Scotland and als one , sufficient lettre of balyerye of the said landis . . for the said 15 zeiris . . . thane . . . I sall ranunce the said landis . . to the said James": witnessed 5th August, 1536 (*Antiquities of Aberdeen and Banff*, iii., p. 222). This transaction gave rise to a feud between the Aberdeen burgh authorities and Forbes of Strathgirnock, who had some claim on the property.

The third laird was killed at Pinkie in 1547 (*Exchequer Rolls*). He had three sons and at least one daughter :—

1. ALEXANDER, IV of Abergeldie

2 JAMES of Lastis. Mr. Michie says he killed Gilbert Knowles and his son at the Calsayend The *Balbithan MS.* says he married (Dec. 1, 1574) the daughter of Donald Coutts of Kinarnie and had :—

    (1) THOMAS

    (2) JOHN, Ledach, Skene.

    (3) JAMES, burgess of Aberdeen.

    (4) ALEXANDER. He may have been the merchant in Aberdeen who wrote very many poems in the Scottish language (Maidment's *Catalogues of Scotish Writers*, p 120).

3 Mr WILLIAM, married Janet Cairngill and had Alexander, burgess in Aberdeen (*Balbithan MS*).

4. BETRIX. She had for liferent the lands of Knock. This is mentioned in the precept of sasine given to her in 1556. It is unusual to sign sasines, and the designation is curious. The sasine, which is in the Abergeldie charter chest, has been summarised by Mr. D Murray Rose as follows: "Alexander Gordon de Perslie dilectis meis Johanni Leyth . . ballivis meis in hac parte Salutem Quia vendidi . . . dilecte mee Beatrice Gordon, sorori honorabilis viri Alexandri Gordon de Abirgeldy, in vitali redditu terras meas de Knock cum suis pertinentiis jacentes in parochia de Glenmyk infra vicecom. de Aberdeen tenandas in capite de me . . . vobis . . . precipio . . . quatenus . . . sasinam dictorum terrarum cum suis pertinentiis dicte Beatrice in vitali redditu . certo attornato . . . per lie thak et raip ut moris est . . tradatis Reservando tamen libere tenementum dictarum terrarum . . . Jacobo Gordon de Leismoir patri meo pro toto tempore

vitae sui. In cujus rei testimonium presentibus mea manuali sub-
scriptione subscriptis sigilum meum proprium est appensum apud
Aberdene decimo tertio die mensis Julii Anno Domini Millesimo
quinquagesimo Sexto Coram huis testibus Thoma Chalmer de Cultis
Alexandro Chalmer ejus filio Willelmo Cristesoun Magistris Gilberto
Murray et Johanne Nicholsoun notariis publicis cum diversis aliis.
Alex. Gordon of Parsle Brynkburn with my hand."   She was the
second wife of Alexander Gordon (3rd son of James Gordon, I. of
Lesmoir), I of Birkenburn. She was the mother of.—

   (1) HARRY, in Knock. He was killed in Nov., 1592, by the raiding
     party of Mackintoshes who also killed the Baron of
     Brackley (*Earls of Sutherland*, p. 217)
   (2) DUNCAN of Perslie
   (3) JAMES.

5. HELEN, "daughter of James Gordon of Midmar and Abergeldie," apparently
  the 3rd laird, married Thomas Fraser of Durris (Macfarlane's *Genealogical Collections*, ii , 323) and became the grandmother of Sir Alexander
  Fraser, the famous physician who trepanned Prince Rupert, and
  whose daughter, Carey Fraser, married (about 1678) the third Earl of
  Peterborough. Sir Alexander's son Charles translated Plutarch (*Dict.
  Nat Biog*)

ALEXANDER GORDON, IV. OF ABERGELDIE

(*Son of III.   died* 1596)

This laird signed a bond against the regent, 27th April, 1560 (*Cal.
Scottish Papers I.*, p. 383), " to expel the French maintained by the Queen
dowager and take plain part with the Queen of England's army, sent by her
for that purpose ".   He was known as " Black Alister," and Mr. Michie
(*Deeside Tales*, p. 140) relates some wild legends about him—notably one
concerning an attack which he made on the Forbeses of Strathgirnock,
who had a bitter feud with the Gordons of Knock.   Abergeldie surrounded
Strathgirnock's house and broke into it.   Forbes was knocked down by
a musket ball, and then hanged, and Abergeldie served himself heir to
the lands of Strathgirnock, and came into the lands of Knock as nearest
of kin.   Certain it is he took part in Huntly's rebellion in 1562, and
was compelled to ward in St. Andrews (on Oct 30) under penalty of
5,000 merks Alexander Irvine of Drum was co-cautioner with him
(*Privy Council Register*).   In 1564 his lands were restored to him by

Queen Mary (*Records of Aboyne*). The following items in his career are interesting :—

1565   *Oct* 12.—Abergeldie was one of the assisors at the trial of Alexander Lyon of Aberdeen and his wife for the murder of John Wood of Colpna (Pitcairn's *Criminal Trials*, i., 471).

1566. *May* 4 —Tack by James, Lord St. John, Preceptor of Torphichen, to Alexander Gordon of Abergeldy and his heirs and assignees "ane or ma being of na hiar degre nor himself," of the teynd schevis of the Kirkis and parochynnis of Tullich and Oboyne, with their pertinents, lying within the diocese and Sheriffdom of Aberdeen for the space of 19 years, which shall begin at the out running of the tacks made by the said Lord St John to Beatrix Gordon, Lady Auchlossin [who was, according to the *Balbithan MS*, the grand aunt of the 4th laird] and Mr Robert Gardyn, hir sone, and to their assignees of the saidis kirkis and teyn sheves for 19 years following the feast of Lammas 1555 : The said Alexander Gordon entering thereto at the feast of Lammas 1574 and paying yearly of teind duty the sum of 75 merks within the burgh of Aberdeen at the feast of St. Bartholomew in August, or at the farthest in a whole yearly sum . . . , within one month next thereafter   At Edinburgh 4 May 1566   Witnesses John Forbes of Brux, Patrick Leyth of Harthill, Robert Abercromby, James Boyd, servant to the said Lord St John (*Records of Aboyne*, p. 222).

1568. *May* 8 —The laird of Abergeldie was one of those (including 9 earls, 9 bishops, 18 lords and others) who signed the bond of adherence to Mary against those who had threatened to " tak hir majesties lyfe maist unjustlie from hir, expres agains all lovable law of God and man" (*Calendar of Scottish Papers II*, p 404).

1574. *Sept* 1.—"The quhilk day in presens [at Aberdeen] of my Lord Regentis Grace and Lordis of Secreit Counsaill, compeirt Alexander Gordon of Abirgeldy and producit ane vallentyne deliverit to him for presenting of Matho Frig befoir the Justice or his deputtis, quhilk he ressavit upon the fourteene day of August last bipast : and that same nycht he send away spyis to se gif he was at the Mylne of Hoill, quhair he remainit with his fader   And the spyis remainit thair quhill the deponaris weir cuming, quhilk wes from the — day of the same moneth.   And efter the resett of this valentyne [Abergeldy] depones that the said Matho come to his faderis hous, and how sone he come the spyis quhom the deponar directit come bak agane and tauld the deponar that he [Frig] wes thair, supponand he sould not haif past away. Notwithstanding befoir the deponaris cuming he wes eschapit " Abergeldie denied that he gave the spies orders to arrest Matho   On the same day James Gordon of Haddo was surety that Alexander Knowis, younger, burgess in Aberdeen, would be "harmless " of Abergeldie whose uncle James had killed Gilbert Knowles and his son in Aberdeen   Penalty £1,000 (*Privy Council Register*).

1578.—He took part in the attempt to decide a dispute between the Forbeses and the Gordons (*Acts of Parliament*)

1588 —He subscribed a bond at Aberdeen in defence of the "trew religion " and his Majesties government (*Privy Council Register*).

1592.—Sir Robert Gordon (*Earls of Sutherland*, p 218) says that Abergeldie as baillie in Badenoch to Lord Huntly was ordered by his master to raid the Mackintoshes in Petty for the slaughter of the Baron of Brackley.

1594. *Oct.* 3.—At the battle of Glenlivat Lord Huntly was supported on the left by "the laird of Abergeldie" (*Earls of Sutherland*, p. 227).

His son Alexander is called "apparent" as late as Oct. 24, 1594, but "of Abergeldie" in 1598.

The fourth laird, who "dyed at home," according to the *Balbithan MS.*, married Janet Irvine, daughter of Alexander Irvine, VII. of Drum (Wimberley's *Family of Irvine*, p. 6), and had six sons and six daughters :—

1. ALEXANDER, V. of Abergeldie.
2. Mr. WILLIAM, VI. of Abergeldie.
3. JOHN of Craibstone : alive 1614 ; he "had succession" (*Balbithan MS.*).
4. GEORGE, killed at the battle of Glenlivat, 1594. Birrell in his diary, as quoted by Pitcairn (*Criminal Trials*, i., 361), says : " The goodman of Dorth and his son were slain at Balrinnes. This Dorth was the brother of Abergeldie." Mr. Michie says he got Knock from his father, who bought the property. There seem, however, to have been two different families of Gordon in possession of Knock.
5. THOMAS of Grandholm.—A charter was granted on July 25, 1604, by William Allan, burgess of Aberdeen, with assent of Andrew Hervie of Alrik, and James Hervie, his eldest son and heir, for their interest in terms of a contract between the granter on the one part and Thomas Gordon of Grandholm for himself and Margaret Forbes his wife on the other, granting to them and their heirs male in feu farm the town and lands of Carnefield (*i.e.* Balgownie) with manor house, etc., also the lands of Danestoun and Corthyburn (St. Machar) : to be held from the granter of the Principal, regents, etc., of King's College (*Laing Charters*, p. 357). On March 4, 1606, Thomas Gordon of Grandoun was admitted a burgess of Aberdeen (*New Spald. Club Misc.*, i., 101). In 1607 Thomas Gordon of Grandholm granted a letter of reversion in favour of George, Marquis of Huntly, over the lands of Auchoilzie in Glen-muick as principal, and the lands of Brodland, Newton of Watter-nady, as in warrandice, which Huntly had sold him redeemably for 2,000 merks (*Records of Aboyne*). In the same year Robert Stewart, burgess in Aberdeen, became bond for Gordon in 1,000 merks that he would not reset or intercommune with Patrick and Thomas Fraser, sons of Thomas Fraser, elder of Durris, who had been put to the horn for the slaughter of William Irvine and Robert Burnet. According to the *Collections on the Shires of Aberdeen and Banff* (p. 231), Grandholm was called Dilspro "while possessed by the Jaffrays". In 1626 Thomas Gordon of Dilspro was caution in £20 (*Privy Council Register*) that Sir James Gordon of Lesmoir (whose sister Thomas Gordon of

Grandholm married) should pay his College of Heralds bill (Sir James was made a baronet in 1625). Dilspro had belonged to the Lesmoir Gordons, for the first Laird of Lesmoir had a son Harry of Dilspro. In Nov, 1638, Thomas Gordon, "late of Dilspro," resigned the shady half of the lands of old Govill in New Machar to John Kintie. Thomas of Grandholm married (1) Margaret Forbes, daughter of Alexander Forbes at the Mill of Gellan, and they had sasine on the lands of Carnfetie, July 2, 1604 He married (2) Janet, daughter of Alexander Gordon, 3rd Laird of Lesmoir, and widow of James Crichton of Frendraught, whose son was the host of Lord Aboyne when the latter was burned at Frendraught in 1630. (A Thomas Gordon appears in 1635 as one of the Gordons called on to give caution for their good behaviour, especially in view of the Frendraught affair.) A Thomas Gordon of Dilspro married Margaret, daughter of John Allardyce of that Ilk. (Information from Mr. D. Murray Rose) Again Thomas Gordon "of Grandhum" was married to Elspet Grant, apparently a widow, for (according to the *Privy Council Register*, x., p. 486) on March 28, 1616, Alexander Watsoun, messenger in Aberdeen, complained that when he went to summon James Murray, brother of the Laird of Cowbardie, and others, to appear before the Council to answer the charge of ravishing Marjorie Fergusoun, daughter of Elspet Grant ("now wife of Thomas Gordoun of Grandum"), and was executing the charge against Arthour Chalmer, in his house in the Kirktoun of Kinnoir, he was attacked by the said Arthur, who "preassit to haif rivene his Majesties blasin of his breist," struck him with "fauldit nevis," and pulled out a long dirk, with which he would have slain pursuer, had he not escaped. Pursuer having gone afterwards to the house of Alex. Mathesoun, messenger, "and efter supper haveing past to his bed for taking the nichtis rest thairintill," the said Arthour, accompanied by Johnne Abircrombie in Sandistoun, and other accomplices, to the number of ten, all armed, came to the house about midnight, surrounded it, "strak in at the windois" with swords and long weapons, forced an entrance at the door, and thereafter most cruelly assaulted pursuer, who "narrowlie eschaipit from thame". The Lords order Chalmer and Johnne Abircrombie to be denounced rebels. The Thomas who married Elspet Grant may have been the son of Thomas of Grandholm, who, according to the *Balbithan MS.*, "had succession" by his first wife It is just possible that these Grandholm Gordons represented different cadets (which may account for the several marriages mentioned). A Thomas Gordon of Grandholm had at any rate a daughter:—

> AGNES, who married Rev. Thomas Forbes, minister of Keig, son
> of the 6th Laird of Corsindae. They had:—

ISOBEL FORBES, who married Robert Lumsden of the Cushnie family (Lumsden's *Forbeses*)

6 JAMES of Easton.—In 1609 (July 13) he brought an action against David Kynnynmonth of Craighall, William Gray of Bandirrane, and George Seton of Parbroth, for remaining unrelaxed from hornings of Feb. 20 and June 23 (1609), for not paying complainer as assignee to his brother (William) 6,000 merks as principal and £1,000 expenses, with 720 merks over and above. He married (according to the *Balbithan MS.*) Marion Scrimgeour, apparently a relation of Sir James Scrimgeour of Dudhope, Constable of Dundee, who frequently was surety for his brother. He had a son by her (*Balbithan MS.*). Sir John Scrimgeour of Dudhope married Margaret Carnegie whose sister was the wife of a Gordon of Cairnburrow Was this James laird of Balmoral ?

7. *Daughter,* married as his second wife Alexander Gordon of Tulloch, Chancellor of Moray, a cadet of the Buckie family (*Balbithan MS.,* p. 62) She bore him three sons who all died young.

8. *Daughter,* married Thomas Menzies, Provost of Aberdeen (*Balbithan MS.*).

9. MARJORIE, married (1) Robert Duguid of Auchenhove; and (2) John Leslie, XI. of Balquhain (died 1638) (*Balbithan MS.*). Duguid was first married to Janet Forbes who divorced him for adultery in 1583. He then contracted a marriage with Marjorie Gordon, "as then held incompetently" (Leslie's *Leslies,* iii, 442): but on account of his extreme youth, King James VI. granted him remission and dispensation, July 29, 1589, as if he had married Marjorie Gordon for his first wife. By Duguid she had a son William, VI. of Auchenhove, and Robert (*Birth Brieve*), who married Marie Forbes and had a son Robert in Poland.

10 *Daughter,* married Patrick Mortimer of Enzie.

11 *Daughter.*

12. CATHERINE (natural), married James Farquharson, I of Inverey (Michie's *Records of Invercauld,* p. 112).

ALEXANDER GORDON, V. OF ABERGELDIE.

(*Son of IV. : died* 1601)

This laird was an ardent Roman Catholic. The following items refer to him :—

1593. *March* 3 —Alexander Gordon apparent of Abergeldie as Principal and Sir James Scrimgeour of Dudhope (probably a relation of his sister-in-law, Marion Scrimgeour, the wife of James Gordon of Easton) as surety gave 2,000 merks assurance not to join the Catholic Earls (*Privy Council Register*).

1593 *May* 26.—Sir John Gordon of Pitlurg was caution in 2,000 merks for Alexander Gordon, apparent of Abergeldie (1) that by June 15 he should return to the Clerk of Council a bond subscribed by Alexander Irving apparent of Drum, (2) that he should keep ward besouth the water of Dee till he return Lord Marischal's letter allowing his liberty. In respect of the surety he is relieved of his present ward in Edinburgh (*Privy Council Register*).

1594. *June* 12.—Alexander Gordon apparent of Abergeldie is charged to appear before the King to answer for his good rule and loyalty (*Privy Council Register*).

1594 *July* 11.—He was denounced (along with John Gordon of Newton, Robert Gordon of Savoch, and George Gordon of Cochlarachy and others) for not appearing to answer the charge of being "treasounable practizaris and conspiratoris agains the true religioun" (*Privy Council Register*).

1594 *Oct.* 24.—The Privy Council ordered the forfeit of the caution given on June 13, 1593, by Gordon as principal and Alexander Irving younger of Drum as surety for him in 2,000 merks to appear before them. On Nov. 4 there is a warrant under the sign manual freeing Irving as surety (*Privy Council Register*)

1598. *Dec.* 9.—Registration by John Halyday as procurator of bond by Sir James Scrymgeour of Dudhope, constable of Dundee, for Alexander Gordon of Abergeldie in 2,000 merks not to harm John, Earl of Mar   Subscribed at Dundee, Nov. 30, 1598 (*Privy Council Register*).

The fifth laird of Abergeldie married before 1586 Margaret Mackintosh, daughter of William of that ilk, who had previously been the wife of Duncan Grant, Laird of Grant, who died in 1581, and of the Laird of Pitsligo.   On April 2, 1604, she had sasine on the lands and barony of Abergeldie (*Aberdeen Sasines*). On Dec. 21, 1604, she married William Sutherland of Duffus (*Great Seal*, Nov. 25, 1608) who died before 1616; she was alive in 1627 (Fraser's *Chiefs of Grant*, vol i.).   The *Balbithan MS.* says he died without issue, but he really left an only daughter :—

> BEATRICE, who had sasine on the lands of Waukindale, Tollibog, Hilloch, Auldtoun, etc , on Jan 20, 1601 (*Aberdeen Sasines*, vol. 11).

He also seems to have had an illegitimate son, for according to the *Privy Council Register* a commission was granted in June 16, 1629, to the lairds of Pittodrie, Glenkindie, Invercauld, Monaltrie, and others to arrest :—

> "ALEXANDER GORDON, the natural son of Alexander Gordon of Abergeldie, Alaster McComeis McFerrucher, his brother on the mother's side, and Robert Smith in Clauch, ane toune in the barony of Abergeldie, who on May 27 were put to the horn at the instance of Marjorie Brebner with Duncan Stewart as son, Robert Stewart in Aberardour

and Arthour and James Stewart as brothers, and the remaining kin and friends of the deceased John Stewart in Aberardour for failing to answer for the slaughter of the said John Stewart. Power is given of fire and sword and there is a clause of immunity."

The fifth laird died in 1601 and was succeeded by his brother,

WILLIAM GORDON, VI. OF ABERGELDIE.

(Younger son of IV   died 1630.)

He was retoured heir to his brother on May 30, 1601. He had originally got Birkhall (formerly Stering) from his father. The most interesting incident in his career was his connection with the Catholic plot usually known as the " Spanish blanks," by which a Spanish invasion of this country was to be manœuvred. The chief figures in the business were a Scots priest William Crichton and Father James Gordon, the son of the Huntly who had fallen after Corrichie. Young Abergeldie's connection with the scheme may be told thus —

1591. *March* 7.—Row says that on this date William Crichton ("quho hes remained in Spaine these two yeares") sent William Gordon, "sonne to Abergeldie, with letteris to Mr James Gordon jesuit to let Papists heir know quhat travel Crichton had taken with the King of Spaine since his arriving thither": and that the King of Spain was to invade England and alter the religion of Scotland by Crichton's advice. Therefore Crichton craved, "be this gentleman," so many blanks and procurations to be sent to him, as could be had of the noblemen here, "for the assureance of his trafficke". Upon the receipt of the blanks, it was proposed to send, at the end of the spring of 1592, an army of 30,000 men, landing either in the Clyde or in Kirkcudbright. The answers were taken by George Ker, but he was apprehended at the Isle of Cumbray He bore many letters. One of them was written in French by Huntly and signed by two other noblemen, regretting "the defeate of the Navall Armie qúhilk the King of Spaine called blasphemouslie *The Invincible Armado* ". Huntly is said to have averred that the Navy had not taken the right time in view of the great winds in harvest—"forgeting," adds Row, that "the Lord of Hosts, who comands winds and seas, did avowedlie fight against him, proving his 'Invincible Armado' verie easilie vincible ".

1593 *March* 5—William Gordon and others were denounced as rebels for having failed to appear before the Privy Council to answer "touching the hearing of mess and resetting of priestis and papistis" (*Privy Council Register*).

1594. *Oct* 3 —He was present at the battle of Glenlivat, for he got remission in 1603 (*Spalding Club Miscellany*, vol iv., p 159) His old friend Father Crichton has left a curious account of the battle (printed by Father Forbes Leith in his *Narratives of the Scottish Catholics*, 1885).

1602. *April* 13—Notwithstanding that Huntly had been ordered to arrest certain Papists, it was announced by the Privy Council that Abergeldie and others had not "purged themselves of the excommunication under which they live, but still remain in this country practising against the true religion" (*Privy Council Register*)

1602   *Nov* 21.—He had sasine of the lands of Ballogie, Mill hole, etc. (*Aberdeen Sasines*, vol. 11.).

1602   *Dec.* 20.—He had sasine of the Barony of Midmar (*Aberdeen Sasines*, vol. 11).

1603.   *July* 20 —William Gordon of Kennertie was caution in 2,000 merks that Abergeldie should not harm John and Harry Stewart of Ballagan, Andrew M'Andow, John Moir M'Allaster, Donald M'Allaster (his brother), John M'Comie, John Ker, John Gordon, and James M'Patrick (the last three in Crathie)   The bond was signed at Abergeldie before James Gordon, Abergeldie's brother, and others (*Privy Council Register*).

1605.   *June* 10.—Alexander Montgomery, citizen of Old Aberdeen, was caution in 300 merks that Abergeldie should enter John Donald, Findlay Dow and Patrick Ewen in Stradie, alleged to be his men, to answer to the Council for going to the house at Craigmonth of Ogle, occupied by William Johnston, tenant of James Fenton of Ogle and breaking up the doors spoilying the goods (*Privy Council Register*)

1605   *July* 18 —Fenton got Abergeldie and his associates denounced as a rebel for robbing and wounding Johnston   In 1608 Abergeldie's brother-in-law Patrick Mortimer of Enzie was surety in £1,000 that Abergeldie should bring his three servants to the Council.   Fenton himself was put to the horn in 1609 for an offence of his own (*Privy Council Register*)

1607.   *Feb.* 21.—John Scrimgeour, apparent of Dudhope, was caution in £1,000 that Abergeldie should not reset his kinsmen Thomas and Patrick Fraser, sons of the laird of Durris, who had been put to the horn on July 22, 1606, for the slaughter of William Irvine of Glassick (Glassel), who married a Margaret Gordon, and Robert Burnet of Cowcardie in June, 1606.   On Jan. 13, 1607, Abergeldie reset the Frasers and was fined 1,000 merks (*Privy Council Register*).

1607.   *Aug* 13.—He had charter under the Great Seal of the lands and barony of Abergeldie.

1608   *Feb.* 5 —Abergeldie was caution in £2,000 for Alexander Irving of Drum (who in turn was caution for his brothers Robert, James, William and John) not to harm the Forbeses, of whom a list is given (*Privy Council Register*)

1608.   *Nov.* 26.—Abergeldie and his old Catholic associate Patrick Butter, son of Patrick, sometime of Marytoun, found caution in 500 merks not to wear hagbuts or pistolets in future (*Privy Council Register*)

1609   *June.*—He was made a Justice of the Peace for Aberdeenshire.

1611   *January* 10.—Two of Abergeldie's tenants on Easton and Loichmaynis, George and James Ross, complained that albeit the reset and intercommuning with that "vnhappie and rebellious race and handful of wicked people callit" the Clan Gregor was strictly discharged, yet on Aug 27, 1610, Nicol Davie, accompanied by ten or twelve armed men went to the market of St. Mary's and felled them (the Rosses) to the ground, and wounded them with drawn swords; and all the people bolted in fear Davie was denounced as a rebel (*Privy Council Register*)

1611. *Jan.* 15.—Abergeldie, Sir Robert Gordon of Lochinvar and James Gordon of Lesmoir were caution for the conduct of Lord Huntly after his present ward in Stirling Castle in the sum of 20,000 merks (*Privy Council Register*)

1611. *Dec.* 3.—Abergeldie was ordered to arrest Coutts of Auchtercoull (*Privy Council Register*).

1612. *Jan.* 23.—He was ordered to arrest several of the Leslies (*Privy Council Register*).

1612. *July* 28.—He was ordered to arrest James Gordon of Auchdryne and other "broken men" (*Privy Council Register*)

1614. *April* 1.—The *Aberdeen Register of Deeds* (as quoted by Mr. Rose) records a contract between Arthur, Lord Forbes, on the one part and William Gordon of Abergeldie on the other; whereby, for 18,000 merks, the said Lord dispones to the said William Gordon heritably without reversion or regres the town and lands of Lairie with the croft thereof, callit Carrieauchtane, town and lands of Strathgirnock, with the pendicles thereof called Tarnagowne, Candacraig, Lynefork, otherwise called Overpleuche of Strathgirnok. the town and lands of Easter and Wester Abirgardynes, Kirktown of Abirgardyne, with woods, boiges, fishings on the water of Dee, and Glengardyne scheilling, commonties, common pasturages, pertaining to the said lands and specially to the lands of Lairie, Strathgirnok and Abirgardyne, with the manor place and stanehous foundit upon Wolt on the said lands of Easter Abirgardyne; all lying in the parish of Glengardyn, barony of Aboyne and shereffdom of Aberdeen. And likewise in security of the said sum the said Lord Forbes has constitut the said William Gordon, his heirs, etc, to be assignees in and to the contents of a reversion given to him by Arthur Forbes of Boigis and Margaret Forbes, his spous, for redeeming from them or their heirs the town and lands of Sonehume (Sonehinnie ?) with the pertinents and teynd sheaves thereof lying in the parish of Midmar, barony of Cluny and Sheriffdom of Aberdeen ; by payment of 300 merks and farther, for security to the said William Gordon of the said lands of Sonehume, the said Lord Forbes has sold the said lands to him : constituting here also the assignee in and to a letter of tack of the teind sheaves of the town and lands of Lairie, etc, above mentioned made to the said Lord Forbes by the Principal, Masters, Regents, and Members of the King's College of Auld Aberdeen for the space of a liferent and two 19 years tack of date at Aberdeen Oct. 13, 1608: And in and to another letter of tack and assedation of the teind sheaves of the said lands, granted to the said Lord Forbes by Mr John Strathauchin, person of Kincardine, with the consent of the patron Bishop, Dean, and Chapter of the Cathedral Kirk of Aberdeen, for the space of two liferents and three 19 years, for the yearly payment of 8 merks teind silver and two bolls meall, of date at Aberdeen, Oct. 11, 1611. Reserving to the said Arthur Forbes of Sonehume and his said spouse, their right and tack of the teind sheaves of the said lands of Sonehume, during the next redemption thereof from them , And seeing that the said Lord Forbes has disponed heritably to Alexander, Master of Forbes, his

Lordship s son, the said whole lands, mills, etc , above specified, with the whole living and lordship of Forbes under revision of an angell of gold ; Therefore the said Lord binds himself to give to the said William Gordon a declarator and decreit of the Lords of Council and Sessions upon the lawful redemption of the said lands in favour of the said Lord Forbes, finding and declaring the same to be lawfully redeemed from the said Alexander, Master of Forbes, his son   At Aberdeen, 1st April, 1614 Witnesses, Mr Thomas Menzies of Balgownie, Thomas Gordon of Grandoum, Mr Robert Forbes, portioner of Fynnersie, etc

1617. *Sept.* 10 —He was one of those who appeared before the Privy Council on behalf of the Gordons when the latter and the Hays "choppit hands" and buried the hatchet that had been sharpened over the extraordinarily barbaric murder of Francis Hay, who had shot (in a duel) Adam Gordon of the Gight family (*Privy Council Register*)

1621   *March* 14 —He was retoured heir to James Gordon, his grandfather, in the lands of Carntralzane, Beldestone and others (*Inquis Spec Aberdeen*).

1621   *Dec.* 6 —He was ordered to arrest certain Macgregors for the murder of William Macpherson (*Privy Council Register*).

1623.   *Nov* 7 —When the Justices of the Peace for Aberdeenshire were ordered to appear in the Tolbooth of Aberdeen all did so except Abergeldie, Gordon of Brackly and another, who, giving no excuse, were each fined £40 (*Privy Council Register*).

1628.   *March* 20 —"Sir" William (he is thus described) was commissioned to arrest several Highland thieves in Braemar and Perthshire (*Privy Council Register*).

1630   *March* 25 —Robert Skene, younger, Burgess in Aberdeen, son of Robert Skene of Slydie and Erdifork, got decreit against William Gordon of Abergeldie on a bond to the late Robert Skene, dated May 29, 1618   There was a similar decreit on July 19, 1634, and again on July 22, 1642 (but these last two must have been against the next laird) (Skene's *Skenes*, p. 76)

The sixth laird of Abergeldie, who died at Abergeldie in 1630, married Elizabeth Seton, the "Laird of Peitbroth's" (Parbroath's ?) daughter (*Balbithan MS*).   Burke (*Landed Gentry*, 1898) says that he married (1) Francisca daughter of Andrew Lord Gray, but I cannot verify the statement: which "has always been handed down in the family".   According to Baird's *Genealogical Memoirs of the Duffs* (pp 137, 138), Catherine Ruthven, daughter of —— Ruthven, provost of Perth and brother of the Earl of Gowrie, married "Gordon of Abergeldie" (William ?) and had a daughter Jean, who married Adam Duff of Drummuir, who died about 1660.   He had five sons and two daughters:—

1 ALEXANDER, VII *of Abergeldie*

2. JOHN   The "Livetennand Colonell Gordon, brother to the Laird [of] Abirzeldie," who in 1642 "schippit" at Aberdeen men for Lord Argyll's regiment in France, as mentioned by Spalding (*Troubles*, II , 187), may

be the John Gordon in Littlemill who had been in perpetual service with the rebels—fighting at Inverlochie, Kilsyth and other battles first as captain, then as major and then as Lieut -Colonel.   He appeared before the General Assembly Commission at Aberdeen in May, 1647, and begged for pardon   There was a John Gordon in Littlemill in Ruthven son of Alexander Gordon of Cromellat and grandson of James Gordon, I. of Letterfourie   A John Gordon in Littlemill was excommunicated as a papist, Nov, 1643   A John Gordon in Littlemill was made a burgess of guild of Aberdeen on March 16, 1663, and similar honour fell to his son Patrick Gordon on Oct. 12, 1664.

3. WILLIAM.   He was served heir to his father in the lands of Grandoun, Auchmill, Pershe and Craibstone, June 17, 1607 (*Inquis. Spec*).

4 THOMAS.

5. JAMES.

6. MARGARET, married Donald Farquharson of Monaltrie (known as Donald Oig)   He was an enthusiastic anti-Covenanter and frequently figures in Spalding and in *Britane's Distemper*.   On March 15, 1645, he was slain "anent the court de guard—a brave gentilman, and ane of the noblest capitans amongis all the hielanders of Scotland" Next morning his body was found in the "calsey stript naikit, for they had tirrit from of his bodie ane ritche stand of apparrell bot put on the samen day.   His corpis ar taken wp the wynd, and put in ane cloiss kist and had wp to the Cheppelhill, thair to ly on the Castelhill "   On the following day, Sunday (March 17), " Donald wes buriet in the Laird [of] Drumis Iyll, with mony wo hairtis and dulefull schottis " (Spalding's *Troubles*, II., 455-7)   *Britane's Distemper* gives Farquharson a fine character   He was "beloued of all sortes of people . . . he gaue proofe of alse much true curraige as any man could hawe. . . . There was no man more humble, no man, saue a prodigal, that cared lesse for to morrow. . . . He was upon a sixe monthes stay at court, so become so weell lyked of, and in so good grace with, his soueraine lord, as he euer after called him his man.   In fine, nether is my judgment nor my experience able to give a true charectore to the lyfe of this gentleman's singular and most commendable parts."

7. MARY, married a Gray of Schivas and thus increased the influence of the Abergeldies in Buchan, for her brother-in-law Farquharson was the constant companion of Nathaniel Gordon of the Gight family, who was ultimately executed   She gave a great deal of trouble to the Ellon Presbytery, which excommunicated her in 1668 (Mair's *Ellon Presbytery Records*).   " A View of the Diocese of Aberdeen" (*Collections for a History of the Shires of Aberdeen and Banff*, p. 334) declares that the Grays of Schivas were "still Roman Catholicks " in 1732.

ALEXANDER GORDON, VII. OF ABERGELDIE

(Son of VI.: died 1655)

Like his father before him he was all for the old order : and neces-
sarily a strong anti-Covenanter   He figures frequently in Spalding,
and suffered for his faith :—

1626. *Sept.* 12.—Alex. Gordone, "fiar of Abirzeldie," was admitted a burgess
of Aberdeen (*New Spald. Club Misc.*, ı., 142).

1635. *Aug.* 7—Alexander Gordon of Abergeldie and other Gordons were
summoned before the Privy Council to find caution for their good behaviour (*Privy
Council Register*).   His rents this year were £1368 13s. 4d. (Michie's *Records of Invercauld*, p. 464)

1639. *May* —Abergeldie was one of the gentry who gathered round Lord
Aboyne at Aberdeen as a counterblast to the meeting of the Covenanters at Turriff
(Spalding's *Troubles*, vol. i., p. 88).

1644. *March* —Abergeldie was one of the lairds who met Lord Huntly in Aberdeen (Spalding's *Troubles*, vol ıı., p. 330)

1644 *July* 6—Thomas Nicolson, advocate, Procurator for the Estates of the
Kingdom, complained to the Parliament that he had " by great chairge and expense
acquyred not only yᵉ heritable right and property of the landis of Aberzeldie, bot
also hes obteint yᵉ gift of yᵉ single escheit and escheit of lyferent of Alexander
Gordon of Aberzeldie from yᵉ Kingis Majestie off all landes haldine be the said
Alexander of the king, be vertew qʳof I [Nicolson] have yᵉ only good and undoubted
right to yᵉ said lands of Aberzeldie and to yᵉ mailles and dewtyes therof which I
have bestowed and imployed yearly for yᵉ mentinance and intertenement of Katherine
Nicolsone my sister, spous to yᵉ said Alexander Gordon and of her sevine childrene.
Till latlie dureing the tyme of thir troubles in yᵉ north there are thrie hundreth
men and above of these [belong to the Laird of Glenorchy's regiment], which wer
leveyed for pacifieing yᵉ saides troubles, who have entered wpoun yᵉ saides landes
of Aberzeldie (since the returne of my Lord Marques of Argyle from yᵉ northe) :
and [they] satt doune wpoun yᵉ poore tennentes, and quartered therewpon full thrie
or four dayes and are as zit ye most pairt of them, wpoun yᵉ saides boundes as I am
informed quherby they have not only impoverished and depeopled yᵉ tennents by
destroyeing and takeing away all ther cattell, sheepe, and horse, bot also have eatine
and distroyed yᵉ haill growand corn wpoun yᵉ saides landes, both of that pairt which
wes labored be yᵉ tennentes, and of yᵉ other pairt thereof, which wes in mainesing,
[*sic*] wherby the tennentes will not only be alluterly [*sic*] wnable to pay me yᵉ fermes
for yᵉ next cropt, but also yᵉ poore tennents, and I my selfe, will otherwayes susteine
great loses throw yᵉ impoverishing and herrying of yᵉ ground in maner foirsaid, and
yoʳ lo[rdshi]ps supplicant will be put to great chairges and expens for yᵉ mentinance of my sister and her childrine without yoʳ lo[rdshi]pis provyd remeid " He

begs for an order for the removal of the soldiers so that his sister and her children—
"who are now dispersed in ye cuntry of Angus in severall strangeres houss attending
till ye Lord provyde remeid"—may return to their home   He asks also that a sum
of money should be granted by the Parliament to his sister and her children " who will
be destitute of interteinment and mentinance this yere to come in respect of ye dis-
troying of ye grounds, goudes and cornes ".   The Parliament remitted the matter to
the Committee of Estates, which declared "that to be publict debt dew" to Nicolson
which the Committee "eftir consideratioune and tryall shall think fitting to be restored" to him (*Acts of Parliament*).   Spalding (*Troubles*, II, 418) says that Argyll
did not leave "ane four futted beaste" in Abergeldie

1644. *Aug.* 9.—Notwithstanding Nicolson's petition and position Abergeldie
was one of the castles that the Covenanters " be the sond of the trumpet " at the
cross of Aberdeen ordered at this date to be razed.   But the castle " standis still "
(Spalding)   In 1732, according to Sir Samuel Forbes, it was "ruinous".

1644   *Sept.* 16.—Abergeldie and Donald Farquharson of Tulligarmont or Monaltrie (his brother-in-law) with several other distressit gentilmen jo \Montrose in
Aberdeen and marched to Inverurie (Spalding's *Troubles*, II., 413).

1644.   *Nov.*—Abergeldie was one of those regarding whom the Estates
ordered the authorities to " mell with the papistis rentis " in order to recompense
Forbes of Echt (Spalding's *Troubles*, II., 433)

1645.   *Feb.*—Abergeldie joined Montrose in his expedition to Lochness
(Spalding's *Troubles*, II., 443).

The seventh laird, who died in 1655, married (contract 8 (12) May,
1624) Katherin, sister of Thomas Nicolson, advocate, Edinburgh, the
ancestor of the Nicolsons of Glenbervie.   They had :—

1. ALEXANDER, VIII. of Abergeldie.
2. JEAN.
3 ANNA, married Cruickshank of Tillymorgan   In 1689 she is described
    as a widow, and at the same date she and her sister Jean are stated
    to have been granted a pension (*Calendar of Domestic State Papers*)
    The dates suggest that they were the daughters of the 7th laird
    Mr Michie (*Records of Invercauld*, pp 239, 260) says that William
    Farquharson of Inverey married as his second wife Ann Gordon,
    "daughter of Abergeldie".   She brought Balmoral to the Farquhar-
    son family.

ALEXANDER GORDON, VIII. OF ABERGELDIE.

(*Son of VII*)

The eighth laird was involved in the feud which arose between John
Gordon of Braickley and the Farquharsons of Inverey in September,

1666 (Macfarlane's *Genealogical Collections*, vol. 1, pp 377-380). In the course of the quarrel Braickley and his brother William and James Gordon of Cults were killed. The affair is recounted in the well-known ballad on the Baron of Braickley.

It seems to have been during the life of the 8th laird that Abergeldie was garrisoned by General Mackay's troops. In 1689 Mackay set out to arrest Viscount Dundee, who escaped to Glen Ogilvie and thence to Braemar, where he was protected by Colonel John Farquharson of Invereye (the notorious "Black Colonel"). As Invereye House was very small, Dundee transferred himself to the stronghold of Abergeldie and from there directed the insurrection   Mackay burned the country for twelve miles round Abergeldie, destroying 1,400 houses   He burned Invereye and then descended on Abergeldie, which was held by 72 of his soldiers in 1689. David Guthrie, of Castletoun, minister of Glenmuick, preached to the garrison on Nov. 3, 1689 (*Gideon Guthrie*, 1900, p. 38).

The record of Privy Seal, as quoted in Amelia MacGregor's *History of the Clan Gregor*, notes under August 13, 1685: " Eschait Liferent of Alexander Gordon of Aberzeldie, James McGregar, in Glencallater, James McGreigar ther Alexander McGrigar ther James McGrigar ther given to Charles, Earl of Marr, —— fferquharsone of Invercald and —— McIntosh, Lady Invercald, his mother ". The *Particular Register of Sasines* for Aberdeenshire notes (vol. xiii., p. 279) that in February 16, 1689, there was recorded " Sasine to Allaster Mcgrigor, sometime in Balnacroft, now in Tornawarran, on heritable bond by Alexander Gordon of Aberzeldie, under reversion of 1,000 merks in the lands of Tornawarran. Witnesses Gregor McGregor in Belno, Robert and John McGregors, sons to John McGregor, Portioner of Wester Micrae." The record of justiciary as noted in Amelia MacGregor's *History of the Clan Gregor* (vol. ii., p. 14) notes that on June 13, 1692, Malcolm McGregor of Ballater and Alexander McGregor, sometime in Clachenturne, now in Tilliechurder, were charged along with Gordon of Abergeldie, at the instance of Robert Steuart of Innerchat with burning his house

The eighth laird married Euphemia Graham, daughter of Robert Graham, the laird of Morphie. She was alive in 1696 (*Poll Book*). They had:—

1. JOHN, IX of Abergeldie
2. RACHEL, X of Abergeldie.

John Gordon, IX. of Abergeldie

(Son of VIII.: died 1698)

He married Elizabeth, daughter of (the late) Hugh Rose, XIV. of Kilravock. The marriage contract, which is dated Dec. 11, 1694, is witnessed at Kilravock by Sir Charles Ramsay of Balmain, Alexander Rose of Clova, Hugh Rose of Broadly, Captain Charles Gordon in Pitchaise, Mr. William Falconer, minister at Dyke; and Mr David Guthrie of Castleton, minister of Glenmuick, Alexander Falconer in Kinstearie, and Henry Rose of Ardersier (*Register of Sasines*, Elgin, vol. v.). In the *Family of Kilravock* (page 385) she signs her "deed of destiny" as Betsy Rose, in what Cosmo Innes calls a "s̃. Roman hand". Her brother, Kilravock, "instantly makes payment of 7,000 merks in name of tocher. She is to be infeft in 1,400 merks of yearly rent out of ye barony of Abergeldie, and to have the manor house of Abergeldie to live in if she becomes a widow during the life of Euphemia, Abergeldie's mother, and after Euphemia's death to have the house of Knock as a dowery house" The house of Knock was described by Mr R. A. Profeit in *Under Lochnagar*. John Gordon died in 1698 without leaving issue and was succeeded by his sister Rachel In 1696 the value of Abergeldie's property in Glenmuick was £430 out of the total of £1,122, and in Kincardine £140 (*Poll Book*).

Rachel Gordon, X of Abergeldie.

(Daughter of VII.)

Rachel succeeded her brother John in 1698 She married (before July 5, 1698) Captain Charles Gordon of the Minmore family, which was a cadet of the Knockespocks and descended from "Jock" Gordon of Scurdargue. Thus, though the direct male line of Gordon of Abergeldie was broken, the name was retained, for Abergeldie is one of the very few estates in Aberdeenshire which have been retained by the same family for so long a period as four centuries The captain's descent runs as follows (*Balbithan MS.*):—

"Jock," of Scurdargue, illegitimate cousin of Elizabeth Gordon, had a son,
　　Alexander, of Essy, who had a son,
　　　　John, I. of Buckie, who had a son,
　　　　　　William, I of Knockespock, who had a son,
　　　　　　　　Alexander, II. of Knockespock, who had a son,
　　　　　　　　　　Alexander, burgess in Elgin, who had a natural son,
　　　　　　　　　　　　William, of Minmore, who had a son,
　　　　　　　　　　　　　　Peter, of Minmore, who married Janet Gordon
　　　　　　　　　　　　　　of Cluny and had a son,
　　　　　　　　　　　　　　　Charles, married Rachel Gordon of Abergeldie.

Charles Gordon who, described as "in Pitchaise," witnessed his
brother-in-law's marriage contract in 1694, signed a bond for the Earl
of Aboyne insuring the peace of the country in 1700 (Allardyce's *Jacobite
Papers*, p. 21), and he was made a Commissioner of Supply in 1704
(*Acts of Parliament*). He built the house of Birkhall in 1715. He had :—

(1) PETER, XI. of Abergeldie.

(2) ALEXANDER. He was at the Grammar School and at Marischal College
　　1706-1710, and was an advocate and merchant in Aberdeen. An
　　Alexander Gordon, who had served his apprenticeship with Alexander
　　Thomson, was admitted a member of the Aberdeen Society of Advo-
　　cates, June 4, 1718 One of his servants, Charles Davidson, was im-
　　prisoned at Aberdeen for taking part in the rebellion of 1745 (Allar-
　　dyce's *Jacobite Papers*, p 237) He acted as tutor and guardian to his
　　nephew Charles, XII. of Abergeldie. He is apparently the Alexander
　　Gordon in Aldihash, Glenmuick, "sometime merchant in Aberdeen,"
　　who died Nov., 1751, Charles Gordon of Abergeldie being his executor
　　dative *qua* creditor Charles had paid £165 13s. 4d. for his grave
　　linen, coffin and funeral expenses, £36 to a physician "for his pains
　　and trouble" in coming about 18 miles and attending the defunct
　　during his sickness whereof he died ; together with other sums paid
　　to John Watt, Charles Stewart, James Glass, James Mackandrew,
　　Thomas Ogilvy and others The inventory contains the sum of £225
　　8s Scots, as the value of the defunct's household furniture, cow, calf,
　　an old horse and other effects, rouped on Dec. 24, 1751, by Samuel
　　Gordon in Miltown of Braickley and Charles Farquharson in Drum-
　　napark, Joseph Gordon in Birkhall being judge of the roup (*Aberdeen
　　Commissariat Testaments*)

(3) JOSEPH, in Birkhall, was cautioner for his brother Peter's widow, as
　　executrix to Peter's will, Nov. 29, 1735 (he was alive Dec., 1751).
　　I think it was his wife who sheltered the Oliphants of Gask when the
　　latter were in hiding after Culloden Old Gask, Laurence, 6th laird,
　　lived in the moors near Birkhall for six months under the name of

"Mr. Whytt," while his son, the 7th laird, took the name of "Mr. Brown," and this disguise they kept up for 20 years. Gask landed at Maisterland, Sweden, on Nov. 10, 1746. His escape was planned by Mrs. (Eliza) Gordon of Birkhall as described here in a letter to Gask's wife as follows (see the *Oliphants of Gask*) :—

> Madam—The bearer, John Glass, tould me you asked him for a mare I should have of Gasks   When I had the honour of seeing him first, he had a big brown mare.   He desired me either to sett her att liberty in the hills, or send her to any place I thought she was safe in.   Andrew Forbes younger of Balfour, came here two days after I gott that mare.   He took her along with him and put her into Parks in the Mearns.   One Baillie Arbuthnott att Edinburgh proved the mare to be hiss   Your nephew the Master of Strawthallan knew all the story and seed the threatening letters I gott about her.   My nephew Abergeldie when he has the honour of seeing your ladyship will inform you likewise.   Andrew Forbes sent me an account from ... e time off Culloden to August for keeping the mare in Parks, which accoun ... have not paid nor do I desire to pay, because I think it reasonable the gentleman who has the nag ought (to) pay that himself.   If you please to inform yourself concerning the mare, you will find all to be Truth I have wrote you   All I have belonging your husband is a silver snuff box, which he oblidged me to take as a memorandum off him   Whenever you please to call for it, I have it ready   No doubt there might have been some small things lost, as I was oblidged to remove them oft times from place to place.   If it pleases God to send Gask to his Native Country, he will do me the justice and honour to acknowledge me one of his friends.   His watch which I caused mend, he sent an express for it two days before he left Glenesk   I seed a letter from a gentleman, written from Gottenborg, who writes me Mr White and Mr Brown is in very good health   I trust in Almighty God you'l have the pleasure off seeing them in triumph soon, and I am with regard and esteem
>
> Your Ladyship's most
humble servt
ELIZA GORDON

PETER GORDON, XI OF ABERGELDIE.

(Son of X. : died 1733.)

He entered Marischal College in 1706.   He was three times married, (1) to Margaret, daughter of Peter Strahan, Edinburgh ; (2) to Elizabeth, daughter of Lord Gray ; (3) to Margaret, daughter of Sir George Foulis of Dunipace, and sister of Sir Archibald Foulis, who assumed the name of Primrose and was executed as a Jacobite at Carlisle at the same time as the laird of Terpersie, Nov. 5, 1746   Peter Gordon died in Sept., 1733, and left his widow as his executrix   According to his will,

(95)

which was confirmed Nov. 29, 1735, with his brother Joseph Gordon in Birkhall as cautioner, there was owing to the laird the following sums:—

£775 3s. 4d Scots, the value of his " sheep, some kine and young store " which were rouped, with Thomas Gordon, portioner of Crathienaird, and John Gordon, his son, as judges.

£475 12s Scots, the estimated value of his riding horses, plough oxen and some young store on the Mains of Abergeldie.

£250 15s Scots, " as the amount of the whole produce of the Mains of Abergeldie in Peter Gordon's own hand, cropt 1733, that cropt being for the most part bad or wrong in the High Country, and to which the sums last mentioned, the said rideing horses, oxen, and grain, etc , were appretiate by John Bowman in Gowindargue and John Gordon in Balmorall ".

The Bond of Caution by Joseph Gordon, dated Abergeldie, Nov. 22, 1735, and written by John Gordon, the eldest son of Thomas Gordon, portioner of Crathienaird, is witnessed by Alexander Gordon, Abergeldie, merchant, Aberdeen. The following entries in the Aberdeen Inventories also refer to the will :—

1737. *March* 24.—Peter's widow, who had by this time married Harry Lumsden of Cushnie, appeared before the Commissary of Aberdeen, and reported that she had added, eiked and conjoined to the sums of money formerly given up the sum of £149 2s. 6d. received by her for wood sold since the last confirmation. David Lumsden, eldest son to the late Charles Lumsden of Harlaw, was her cautioner.

1740. *March* 1 —She accounts for £9 stg. as the price received by her for a " yellow horse," which had belonged to Abergeldie.

As stated, Peter's widow, Margaret Foulis, married Harry Lumsden of Cushnie, as her second husband. Peter Gordon had the following children, by which wife I cannot say —

1. CHARLES, XII. of Abergeldie
2. JANET, died unmarried at Edinburgh, Feb. 14, 1811, aged 87 (*Scots Mag.*).
3. RACHEL, died unmarried.
4. EUPHEMIA, married in or before 1752 James, 5th Viscount Strathallan, whose father had been killed at Culloden Her husband held the peerage for four days, April 14-18, 1746, when it was forfeited He died 1765, and she on July 5, 1796 They had:—
    (1) James Drummond (*de jure*), 6th Viscount Strathallan. He was an officer in the navy, and died unmarried 1775.
    (2) Andrew John Drummond (*de jure*), 7th Viscount Strathallan; a general in the army His petition for the restoration of the peerage honours was rejected by the House of Lords 1790 ; and, as he died unmarried, the Abergeldie strain in the Drummonds died out. The family honours were restored

in 1824, to his cousin, the great-grandfather of the present
Viscount Strathallan, who was born in 1871, and is heir-
presumptive to the Earldom of Perth.

5. JEAN, died unmarried (Burke's *Landed Gentry*, 1898).
6. BARBARA (daughter by the second wife), married David Hunter of
Burnside.

CHARLES GORDON, XII. OF ABERGELDIE.

(*Son of XI. : died* 1796.)

He was born in 1724 (*Scots Mag.*). He was served heir to his
father in 1737 and to his grandfather Charles in 176 He entered
Marischal College in 1739. The principal improvements on Abergeldie
Castle were made by him. He voted in 1786 for Skene of Skene in
the Parliamentary contest against Ferguson of Pitfour.

He married (contract Oct. 6, 1750) his cousin Alison, daughter of
David Hunter of Burnside "and widow of one Paterson". "They
lived together," says their tombstone in Glenmuick churchyard, "nearly
half a century in this part of Deeside, the best of parents, giving a
good example in every way and serving to the utmost of their power all
who stood in need."

The 12th laird died at Birkhall, March 19, 1796, aged 72 (*Scots
Mag.*), and his wife died in March, 1800. He left his eldest son Peter
his executor under date Feb. 8, 1783. From the will (*Aberdeen Inventories*
in the Register House) it appears that he had acquired since his marriage
in 1750 the following lands :—

From James Farquharson of Invercauld.—The Town and Lands of Toldow,
Tombrack, and Altveit, in Glenmuick in excambion for the lands of Dilliefour and
Broghdow and the Glen of Glencallater in Braemar and Glenmuick.

From Charles, Earl of Aboyne.—The Forest of White Mounth and the Haugh of
Achallie, commonly called the Haugh of Dalmullachie, in Glenmuick.

All these lands, together with Abergeldie, he left to his eldest son
Peter. To his other sons, he left 100 merks Scots each, to be paid out
of the sums and subjects conquest and acquired by him during his
marriage. His daughter Margaret (Mrs. Skene) was excluded as she
had already got her marriage portion. There were owing to him at the
time of his death the following sums :—

£14 15s stg. and interest thereof, since due, contained in a bill dated May 20, 1794, drawn by James Gordon, then in Spittal of Glenmuick, now in Tombrack, upon and accepted by John Thow in Haugh and John Donaldson in Lochside.

£1 5s stg. as the expense of raising and executing horning at the defunct's instance against the said John Thow and John Donaldson, on the foresaid bill.

The 12th laird had the following children :—

1. PETER, XIII. of Abergeldie.
2. DAVID (3rd son), XIV. of Abergeldie
3. CHARLES (2nd son), born 1756   He assisted in raising the 71st Fraser Highlanders formed at Glasgow during the early part of the American War by Lt.-Gen the Master of Lovat, and got a lieutenancy in the regiment in April, 1776   He went with it to America and got a company in the 26th Cameronians on Jan. 8, 1778   When the Cameronians arrived home in a skeleton state in February, 1780, he became regi- mental major and obtained a brevet lieut.-colonelcy in April, 1783 In 1787, when French intrigues led to the invasion of Holland by the Prussians under the Duke of Brunswick (for according to the *Gent.'s Mag.* he possessed a "perfect acquaintance with the topography of Holland" and spoke several continental languages), Gordon accom panied the Duke, and planned the capture of Amstelveen, which was the key of the defences of Amsterdam   As an attack in front was impossible the Duke determined to take the enemy in the rear Thomas Bowdler in *Letters written in Holland* says that, to deter- mine if this was possible, Gordon, "who had acted as a volunteer throughout the expedition, was directed to proceed in a boat along the Harlem Meer and make as accurate a survey as possible of the ground behind Amstelveen   This dangerous but important service was executed with courage, ability and success, and our countryman passed several of the enemy's batteries. He proceeded along the Harlem Meer to the further part of it where the lake terminates in a long narrow tongue, which is called the Nieuve Meer. He examined the situation of the ground near the water and returned in safety to the Duke, making his report that the enterprise though difficult was not impracticable   The Duke immediately resolved to undertake it, and a detachment of between 600 and 700 men embarked in float-boats at the valley of Aalsmeer. The troops were ordered to proceed along the Harlem Meer to endeavour to land and gain the high road between Amsterdam and Amstelveen, and then by attacking the post in the rear to make way for the entrance of the Duke's army   As this object was of the greatest importance, the Duke for fear the detachment which crossed the lake should not be successful ordered two companies to endeavour, under cover of the night, to proceed along a footpath

(98)

by the edge of the water, and in like manner to get the road at the
back of Amstelveen. The charge of the embarkation was committed
to the same British officer [Gordon]. Under his direction the whole
was conducted in such a manner that not one boat was overset, nor
one man lost either in embarking or landing the soldiers [at Leile]
After the troops landed they were forwarded under the command of
a Prussian officer" Gordon seems to have been recalled to England
and made lieut -colonel of the 41st Regiment which had till then been
a corps of invalids   "Viator A," who had investigated Gordon's
career, writing to the *Gentleman's Magazine* (vol. lx , p. 1066), speaks of
Gordon's "intrepidity, activity and military knowledge"   He adds :
"Upon the probability of war between the Houses of Austria and
Brandenburg, he joined the Prussian army in Silet in the course of
last spring [1780], and from the great estimation in which he was
held by the chief personages, there it is probable he would have been
conspicuously employed there had a rupture actually taken place.
Sensible of the services rendered in Holland by Colonel Gordon, and
highly pleased with his intelligence and activity, the King of Prussia
not only treated him with every mark of flattering attention, but
invested him with the [Prussian] Order of [Military] Merit [which
like all foreign Orders, until 1814, carried knighthood with it in
England. He got permission to wear it in England, Aug 3, 1790. Up
to 1793 he was the only foreigner on whom this decoration had
ever been conferred.] The King of Prussia also I believe gave him
the strongest letters of recommendation to the Sovereign of this
country. When Colonel Gordon passed through Saxony a short
time since upon his return to England, I heard the highest praise
bestowed on him by the first military characters in the Electoral
service   At Brunswick I heard him mentioned with the greatest
esteem and commendation by the most illustrious personages at the
Court, and the reigning Duke of Brunswick gave him letters for this
country full of approbations and esteem." A letter from Gordon to
the Duke of Leeds, dated Dresden, April 3, 1790, says the Duke of
Brunswick wished him for his A D C , and the *Dictionary of National
Biography* says that Gordon "appears to have gone through the
campaign of 1791-2 as British Military Commissioner" In 1793
a large expedition (4,891 strong) went to the West Indies under
Sir Charles Grey (1st Earl) and Admiral Jervis. Gordon was one
of the three brigadiers (pending the arrival of the Duke of Kent)
who commanded the attack on Cas de Navire, at the attack on Martinique, and was thanked in general orders (see Rev Cooper Willyams'
Account of the campaign, 1796)   He was employed at the capture of
St Lucia and was made governor of the island.   Difficulties and
disputes as to prize rights in property in the captured islands led to

the most unfounded charges of confiscation and extortion against the sea and land commanders of the expedition Against Gordon like accusations proved either better founded or more successful. Formal complaints were made against him, in his capacity of governor of St Lucia, of extortion and taking bribes from disaffected persons to allow them to remain in the island and afterwards breaking faith with them. Gordon was court-martialled and sentenced to refund the money and be cashiered   In consequence of his past services and circumstances disclosed at the court-martial he was allowed to receive the value of his commissions, for the sentence of cashiering was confirmed neither by the authorities in the West Indies or at home   He survived his dismissal more than forty years   He appears to have been in Holland in 1803 and in communication with the home authorities just after the Peace of Amiens   He died in Ely Place, London, 26th March, 1835, aged 79 According to Mr. Hugh Gordon, the 17th laird of Abergeldie, Sir Charles, was constantly employed by the Foreign Office in various capacities on the Continent from 1799 to 1815. " I well recollect him visiting at my father's house at Blackheath, when I was a boy, as a fine, upright old gentleman, and I have a good portrait of him painted some years earlier."

4. ADAM, of Denmark Hill, London, was born in 1758   He and his brother David, who married sisters, were members of the firm of Gordon & Biddulph, iron manufacturers, engineers and shipbuilders. Mr John Biddulph, their partner and brother-in-law, was also a partner in the banking firm at Charing Cross, now Cocks, Biddulph & Co   The Biddulphs are an old family, who settled at Ledbury in Hereford in the 17th century.   One of them was married to the sister of Major-General Shrapnel, the inventor of shrapnel shell (1793)   Adam Gordon married Penelope, the daughter of Michael Biddulph.   He died on the 28th May, 1800, leaving an only son :—

>   WILLIAM, of Haffield, Hereford, born Dec. 8, 1794   He matriculated at Brasenose College, Oxford, in 1812 (*Foster*).   He was High Sheriff in 1829   He married at St George's, Bloomsbury, Dec 21, 1820, Mary, eldest daughter of William Wingfield, a Master in Chancery, by Lady Charlotte Digby (Burke's *Commoners*)   Besides two daughters, Charlotte Florence and Caroline Anne, he had a son :—

>>   REV. EDWARD WILLIAM, born May, 1828.   He was educated at Christ Church, Oxford, 1847-1851 ; M A. 1854 , and was called to the bar at Lincoln's Inn 1860 (*Foster*)   He married, at Florence, on May 5, 1855, Mathilde Henriette Adelaide Heloise,

daughter of Baron de Hagermann, and died April
29, 1879, leaving issue —

    (i.) ARTHUR MICHAEL WINGFIELD, born May 11, 1859
    (ii.) HERBERT EDWARD, born March 4, 1862.
    (iii.) CLARA GEORGINA MARY, born Dec. 26, 1856.
    (iv.) EDITH LUCY, born Oct. 23, 1860.
    (v.) ALICE EMILY, married Arthur Midgley Kettlewell.

5. WILLIAM. He was born in 1765 and was a tertian and magistrand at
Marischal College, 1778-80. Then he entered the 60th Regiment, now
the King's Royal Rifles He was captured (Oct. 19, 1781) at the
siege of Yorktown, Virginia, where he commanded the light infantry
company of the 71st Regiment (Michie's *Records of Invercauld*, p.
184) In recording his death at Dominica on July 6, 1793, in the
28th year of his age, the *Scots Magazine* says: "It was owing to
Major Gordon's gallant conduct at the head of the storming party
composed of a small column of light infantry, who dashed into
the enemy's walls and forced the commandant to surrender at
discretion, that the island of Tobago was captured [The 17th
laird of Abergeldie possesses several letters by him dealing with
Tobago, copies of resolutions in praise of him passed by the Council
of the island. The silver vase, which was presented to his father
in his memory, is still preserved as an heirloom in the family.]
For during the event, Brigadier-General Ayler, who commanded
the main body of the troops, had been obliged to fall back and
knew not that the fort had been taken till the fact was announced
by the firing of the morning gun and the hoisting of the British
colours by Major Gordon When the attack on the island of Martinique
was afterwards determined on, Major Gordon was appointed to the
command of the light infantry companies of all the regiments in the
Leeward Islands, in which important situation he evinced the same
intrepid spirit And at the landing of the troops on that expedition
he pushed forward and penetrated upwards of six miles into the island
under every possible disadvantage, exposed to a heavy fire from the
enemy, almost incessant rain succeeding scorching sun, and during
forty hours under arms, without a morsel to eat or any other cover-
ing but the heavens The House of Assembly at Barbadoes, in which
island Major Gordon had commanded the battalion many months,
voted to him in June last [1793] an elegant sword as a token of their
respect and expression of their approbation of the uniform regularity
and good conduct of his troops. And the inhabitants in general
testified their regard to him by stocking with every kind of refresh-
ment the man-of-war on which he embarked against Martinique,
where his gallant and soldier-like conduct in repulsing an attack of

the enemy was so peculiarly distinguished that the Commander in-Chief returned particular thanks in public orders "

6. ALEXANDER SINCLAIR, *d s p* June 30, 1837, aged 77. He was adjutant to the London and Westminster Volunteers The Abergeldie family possess an oil portrait of him on horseback, with drawn sword, in the uniform of the regiment (*Scottish Notes and Queries*, 2nd series, i., 95).

7. JOHN, died young

8. MARGARET, married Oct 26, 1769, Dr George Skene, physician in Aberdeen, VI of Dumbreck He was made Professor of Natural Philosophy in Marischal College at the age of 19 Mrs Rodger (*Aberdeen Doctors*, p 68) says a portrait of his wife "shows a lady of keen Aberdeenshire features in a mob cap and ribbons" Dr Skene died suddenly March 25, 1803, aged 61 his wife died Jan 16, 1802, aged 51 He had five sons and six daughters (Anderson's *Fasti Academiae Mariscallanae*, ii., 46) His fourth son,

> ANDREW SKENE, became Solicitor-General for Scotland (Skene's *Skenes*, pp. 73-4)

PETER GORDON, XIII. OF ABERGELDIE.

(*Son of XII. died* 1819)

He was born in 1751 and entered Marischal College in 1762. He was one of the assessors to the Lord Rector in 1804 (*Fasti Acad. Marisc.*, vol. ii , p. 19). Mr. Michie (*Under Lochnagar*) says he was captain in the 81st Regiment, which was raised by Colonel William Gordon, brother of the Earl of Aberdeen, and disbanded in 1783. In *Deeside Tales* Mr. Michie says he was a lieutenant in the Gordon Highlanders, and was instructed to get recruits for the new regiment (1794) The Peter Gordon, however, who was a lieutenant of the Gordons at that date is stated in Gardyne's *Gordon Highlanders* (p 20) to have died in 1806.

It was in his time that Keith wrote (*Agriculture of Aberdeenshire*, 1811)—

Abergeldie abounds in so many natural beauties as are seldom to be met with in one place, and it is at least doubtful whether the present venerable mansion would not in this Highland district be preferred by a person of taste and sensibility to a modern house of the most correct architecture

He married (1) Mary, daughter of John Forbes of Blackford (*Landed Gentry*, 1898), and (2) at Glenkindy in April, 1803 (*Scots Mag*), Eliza-beth Ann, second daughter of Alexander Leith of Freefield (by Mary Elizabeth, daughter of James Gordon of Cobairdy). Her brother, Sir

Alexander Leith, the "Knycht of Glenkindie," was a notable soldier. His second wife died without issue at Palmer's Cross, Morayshire, Oct., 1855, and was buried in Elgin Cathedral (*Descendants of James Young*, p. xvi.). It was probably in honour of one of the thirteenth laird's wives that Robert Petrie (1767-1828), the famous Strathardle fiddler, composed the air known as "Mrs. Gordon of Abergeldie," to which Mr. W. M'Combie Smith has written a ballad called "A' for Love". It may be noted that Burns's song, "The Birks of Aberfeldy," was founded on an earlier song in which Abergeldie was the place mentioned.

The thirteenth laird died at Aberdeen on Dec. 6, 1819, aged 68 (*Scots Mag.*), and was buried in Glenmuick Churchyard, and was succeeded by his brother David, for his only daughter (by his first wife),

KATHERINE, died at her uncle's house, Dulwich Hill, Camberwell, January 26, 1802, in her 18th year (*Scots Mag*).

DAVID GORDON, XIV. OF ABERGELDIE.
(*Younger Son of XII. died* 1831)

Born in 1753, he is probably the David Gordon who was at Marischal College 1768-72. He began his career in the army, for he was captured at the siege of Yorktown, Virginia, Oct. 19, 1781, along with his brother William (Michie's *Records of Invercauld*, p. 184) He was back at Birkhall by Aug. 24, 1782 (p. 191). He was, as stated, a member with his brother Adam of the firm of Gordon & Biddulph. He married June 15, 1789, his brother's wife's sister Anne, daughter of Michael Biddulph of Ledbury. Mr Michie says that it was in his time that there arose a complication of march interests between the estates of Abergeldie and Birkhall which was finally settled in the law courts in an action by the late laird Mr. Hugh Mackay Gordon and King Edward VII., then Prince of Wales. The Laird of Abergeldie lost his case. David Gordon was served heir to his brother Peter on Feb 28, 1820 (*Services of Heirs*) He died Oct 22, 1831, aged 78. Mr. A. I. McConnochie states (*The Royal Dee*, p 77) that the last occasion on which we have mention of birch wine being produced at Abergeldie was at the funeral of this laird. In 1810 the author of *The Scenery of the Grampian Mountains* got some of the "excellent birch wine" from the thirteenth laird, and it seemed to him to be "superior to the finest champagne". David Gordon's wife died Feb. 26, 1841 He had four sons and three daughters   I may say that all these later descents are taken from the article in Burke's *Landed Gentry* (1898), which was specially corrected by the late Mr Hugh Mackay Gordon —

1. CHARLES DAVID, born October 30, 1790   He was at Harrow with Lord Byron, with whom he was a great favourite.   Letters from Byron to him (dated Aug 4 and 14, 1805) are printed in Mr. Prothero's *Byron*. In the latter Byron says —

> Believe me, my dearest Charles, no letter from you can ever be unentertaining or dull, at least to me   On the contrary, they will always be productive of the highest pleasure as often as you think proper to gratify.

Byron once visited him at Abergeldie   He married, April 22, 1819, Marian, eldest daughter of Robert Phillips of Longworth, Hereford (by a daughter of Michael Biddulph of Ledbury)   He died Nov. 24, 1826, leaving four daughters —

   (1) ANNA MARIA, married in 1871 Count von Schmising Kerssenbrock, and died May, 1889   She had the superiority rights over Birkhall   They were bought up by the Prince of Wales, now King Edward VII.

   (2) KATHERINE FRANCES, married in 1842 Duncan Davidson of Tillychetly, Aberdeenshire, and died Feb., 1868.   She had an only son —

      Henry Oliver Duncan Davidson of Tillychetly (born 1856), who is an assistant master at Harrow School   He is married and has issue.

   (3) ISABELLA MARGARET, married (1) in 1854 Anthony Gibbs of Merry Hill, Herts, brother of the 1st Baron Aldenham, and (2) in 1866 R H Lee Warner of Tyberton Court, Hereford.   She died March 15, 1895

   (4) EMILIA LUCY

2. MICHAEL FRANCIS, XV. of Abergeldie

3 ROBERT, XVI of Abergeldie.

4. ADAM, born March 30, 1801   He married at Topsham Church, Devon, Nov. 8, 1825, Susan, sixth daughter of Rev John Swete of Oxton House, Devon, and lived at Blackheath near Charlton, Kent   He died Jan. 14, 1839   She died March 21, 1861, leaving seven sons and a daughter

   (1) HUGH MACKAY, XVII of Abergeldie

   (2) LEWIS, XVIII of Abergeldie

   (3) CHARLES VINCENT, Colonel, Madras Corps, born Dec. 2, 1829. He went through the whole of the Mutiny   He married (1) June 15, 1854, Emma Morgan (died 1859), second daughter of Charles Godwin, and (2) in 1866 Frances Edith, eldest daughter of George Olliver of Kingston,

Sussex. He died June 6, 1897, having had two sons by his first wife and the rest of his children by his second ·—

    i. COSMO HUNTLY, born June 13, 1855 Major in the Buffs (East Kent Regiment) He went through the Zulu War. He married, Oct 19, 1892, Ida Mary, daughter of Captain O W. Ford, late Bengal Army

    ii. ROBERT FRANCIS, born Aug. 24, 1856; died May 30, 1861.

    iii. CHARLES GERALD, born Oct 15, 1868, Captain Steinacker's Horse in the South African War, 1900-1

    iv. GEOFFREY SETON, born Nov 2, 1880, Lieut. East Yorkshire Regiment (gazetted May 26, 1900).

    v. JOHN EDMUND, born June 9, 1887.

    vi FLORENCE.

    vii. HELEN BLANCHE.

    viii CONSTANCE EVELYN

(4) REV. ADAM STEPHENSON, was born on Nov. 27, 1831, and was educated at Oriel College, Oxford, 1850-1854; M A 1856. He was curate of Chelsfield, 1855-69 He lives at the Villa Gourdon, Cannes He married Aug 11, 1869, Julia Isabella, daughter of Rev. I W Baugh, rector of Ripple, Worcester She died Feb. 9, 1892

(5) DUNDAS WILLIAM, born March 24, 1833 He entered the Bengal Artillery, and was killed at Lucknow on Jan. 8, 1858

(6) COSMO, born Nov. 2, 1837, Major, Madras Staff Corps, died July 19, 1878.

(7) JAMES HENRY, C.B, D S O, born Jan 25, 1839 He entered the service of the East India Company and was attached to the 46th Madras Native Infantry in 1857, and entered the Madras Staff Corps in 1869 He became Colonel in 1883, and served in the Burmese War, 1885-6 He was granted the D S.O. in 1887 and created C B in 1893. He married, Jan 28, 1869, Arabella, 2nd daughter of the late Charles Hewit Sams of Lee, Kent (his brother Hugh, the late laird of Abergeldie, married her elder sister), and has—

    i. CHARLES CECIL, Captain, Royal Scots, born Sept, 1871 ;' died April, 1899

    ii. GEORGE HAMILTON, Captain, Royal Engineers, born March 29, 1875.

    iii LUCY, married 1889, Lieut -Col Willoughby Verner Constable, R.E.

    iv JULIA MARGARET ARABELLA

(8) ANNE CECILIA GORDON

5. ANNE PENELOPE, died 1868
6. HARRIET MARGARET, died 1865
7. MARY ANNE, married, May 6, 1824, Rev William Swete, brother of the
   wives of her brothers Adam and Michael, and died 1859

MICHAEL FRANCIS GORDON, XV. OF ABERGELDIE.

(Son of XIV · died 1860)

He was born April 21, 1792, and married, at Kenton, Devonshire, on
Aug. 31, 1820, Caroline, fifth daughter of Rev. John Swete of Oxton
House, Devon.   His brother Adam married her younger sister, while
his sister Mary Anne married the latter's brother.   The fifteenth laird
died Dec. 31, 1860, and was succeeded by his brother, Admiral Gordon,
for his sons predeceased him   He had :—

1. FRANCIS DAVID, born July 24, 1821. Was a law student at Edinburgh,
   1839-40   He was killed at Jhansi in 1857 during the Mutiny.
2. JOHN HENRY, born Jan. 7, 1824 , died April 20, 1848.
3. MICHAEL LAWRENCE, born Sept 3, 1833 , died Oct 27, 1850.
4. WILLIAM HERBERT, born May 29, 1840 , died Dec 6, 1850.
5. CAROLINE ANN, married, 1854, E P St Aubyn, Lt -Col. Madras Army,
   and has issue.
6. MARGARET, married Rev F. Cardew and has issue.
7. BERTHA, married at Gittisham, Devon, on October 4, 1855, Charles
   Gordon, a doctor at Pernambuco, Brazil, where she died Dec 4, 1857.
   Dr. Gordon, who is the son of James Gordon, Ballater, was a bajan
   and magistrand at Marischal College, 1846-48.   He took the M D.
   of King's College, 1850   From Pernambuco he went to Pietermaritzburg, Natal, where he and his brother were living in Feb , 1900
   He married again   He had two daughters by his first wife —

   (1) MARGARET ALICE, died at Algiers, March 23, 1883
   (2) BERTHA, died at Bath, Jan , 1872.
   (3) CHARLES AUSTIN, the son by the second wife, was educated
       at Oxford and became a mining engineer.   When the Boer
       War broke out in 1899 he joined the Imperial Light Horse,
       and was present at Elandslaagte, being afterwards be-
       sieged in Ladysmith   On Dec. 17, 1900, he was accidentally
       wounded at Johannesburg, and lost his left leg

ROBERT GORDON, XVI. OF ABERGELDIE.

(*Brother of XV.* · *died* 1869.)

Robert Gordon was born Sept 7, 1796   He entered the Navy, May 24, 1810, as a second class volunteer on board H.M S. *Phœbe* (44 guns)   In this vessel—subsequently to the reduction of the Isle of France—he contributed (May 20, 1811), while cruising off Madagascar in company with H.M.S. *Astrea, Galatea* and *Racehorse,* to the capture, after a long and trying action with the French, of three 40-gun frigates   The *Phœbe* had seven men killed and twenty-four wounded.   On May 25, five days later, he was present at the surrender of the *Néréide* and of the settlement of Tamatave, and in the following summer he co-operated in the conquest of Java.   Becoming a midshipman (Jan , 1813) on H.M S. *Centaur,* he cruised in the North Sea and Channel, and was transferred (Jan , 1814) to H.M S. *Tonnant* bearing the successive flags on the North American and Cork stations of Sir Alexander Cochrane and Sir Benjamin Hallowell, under the former of whom he took part in many operations against the Americans, and was present at the attack on New Orleans   On July, 1816, he was transferred to H.M.S. *Queen Charlotte,* the flagship of Lord Exmouth, who invested him with the rank of Acting Lieutenant, thus enabling Gordon to share in that capacity in the bombardment of Algiers, Aug. 27, 1816.   He subsequently served on H.M S. *Iphigenia* (at Jamaica), *Ontario* and *Confiance, Herald* and *Pearl* (on the West India Station).   This last vessel was put out of commission in Dec , 1834, and by 1849 he had not been employed again.   He attained post rank 1857 (O'Byrne's *Naval Biographical Dictionary*)   He was sometime Deputy Master of the Corporation of Trinity House.   He died *sp* Feb 18, 1869, and was succeeded by his nephew.

HUGH MACKAY GORDON, XVII. OF ABERGELDIE

(*Nephew of XVI.*   *died* 1901)

He was born on Sept. 24, 1826   Col Munro, A D C. in Jersey to General Hugh Mackay Gordon, was his godfather   He was a retired

Lieut.-Col. and Hon. Col. of the 2nd Volunteer battalion of The Queen's
Own (Royal West Kent) Regiment. On May 19, 1859, he married Susan
Amelia, elder daughter of the late Charles Hewit Sams of Lee, Kent,
whose younger daughter married his brother, Colonel J. H. Gordon,
D.S.O., C.B. He died at the Courtyard, Eltham, at 10.30 A.M. on
March 19, 1901, leaving no issue.

Mr. Gordon, who had a house and stayed during the summer months
at Ballater, took a very great interest in the history of his family—he
communicated with the present writer on a point of genealogy only
six days before his death. He had resided in Eltham over thirty years,
and took the keenest interest in the affairs of his parish and its neighbour-
hood. Indeed he was so closely connected with Eltham that the local
paper, the *Eltham Times*, in a long obituary (March 22) made no mention
of his having been laird of Abergeldie. The journal says:—

He was for twenty-five years a member of the Eltham Vestry, retaining his
seat upon that body until its dissolution last year under the new London Local
Government Act. It was an anomaly of the Local Government Act of 1894 that the
formality of appointing a chairman at each meeting had to be respected. But Colonel
Gordon, whenever present—and it was seldom he missed an attendance—was elected
to the chair, and the kindness, courtesy and ability with which he presided over the
deliberations of that sometimes turbulent body can only be properly appreciated by
those who were privileged to sit under his presidency. Colonel Gordon was one of
those who were strongly opposed to Eltham being included in the Woolwich Municipal Borough. He felt that Eltham, having more in common with Lee than with
Woolwich, which comprised the area administered by the Lee Board of Works, should
be itself created a Municipal Borough. But when it came to be officially decided that
Eltham must be annexed to Woolwich, Colonel Gordon threw his whole heart into
securing for the parish such representation upon the Borough Council as should
make the new alliance, so far as Eltham was concerned, a success. Those who
attended the inquiry held by the Commission under the London Government Act for
the purpose of hearing evidence prior to the final adjustment of the proportion of
representatives for the three parishes comprising the Woolwich Borough were struck
with the force and pertinacity with which he, in his capacity as representing the
parish, argued in favour of Eltham's representation being increased. Had his health
permitted, there is no doubt that Colonel Gordon would have been Eltham's first
Alderman upon the new Borough Council.

For many years Colonel Gordon was a churchwarden of the Parish Church, an
office from which he retired in 1898. He was a trustee of all the Eltham charities,
was treasurer of the Eltham National Schools since 1876, and formerly twenty years
treasurer of the Eltham Cottage Hospital, until he resigned the appointments this
(1900-1901) winter in consequence of failing health. To mark their appreciation of

Colonel Gordon's great services to the Cottage Hospital, of which he was one of the founders, and largely instrumental in establishing the new hospital, the subscribers at the annual meeting a fortnight ago gave directions for a resolution of thanks to be engrossed on vellum and presented to him, and, anxious that he should not entirely sever himself from an institution which owed so much to his kindly interest, elected him president for the ensuing year   The managers of the Eltham National School, at their meeting on 6th March, when Colonel Gordon's resignation from the treasurership of the schools was before them, passed a resolution placing on record their great regret that he had found himself obliged to resign the office he had held for so many years . . . Colonel Gordon was also, up to the time of his death, president of the Eltham Rose and Horticultural Society.

But Colonel Gordon did not confine his services entirely to the parish in which he had made his home. He was a Justice of the Peace for the counties of London and Kent, and there was no more regular attendant than he upon the judicial bench at Clerkenwell, he was also a familiar figure upon the magisterial bench at the Blackheath Petty Sessional Court   He was chairman and treasurer of the Greenwich Pier Company, a liveryman of the Goldsmith's Company, and a prominent and ardent freemason, as well as an honorary member of the Oddfellows   Colonel Gordon was a colonel of the West Kent Volunteers, from which he retired, with the long service medal, upon attaining the age limit. He was one of the original volunteers, joining the ranks of that useful arm of the Imperial forces when it was first established. All classes learned to love and respect him and the poor had no truer friend

His estate was valued at £68,746 16s. 7d gross, and £67,669 0s. 11d net. He bequeathed—

To the executors £500 for accumulation until the lease of Abergeldie Castle to trustees for Queen Victoria shall expire, and then to apply this sum to put in order the roads on the Abergeldie estate, many of which in his opinion had not been kept in proper order; and the trustees may also apply this fund in payment of the expenses of contesting the claim of the Duke of Fife to seats in the Parish Church of Crathie He bequeathed also £2,000 in trust for accumulation until the expiration of the lease, and then, if it shall not be renewed, for the purchase of furniture for Abergeldie Castle and Abergeldie Mains or farmhouse, to devolve as heirlooms with Abergeldie, also the sword given to his great-uncle by the Westminster Light Horse Volunteers, and the vase of Dresden China flowers brought over by Sir Charles Gordon as a present for the Prince Regent. To his god-daughter, Arabella Sams, £500, to other children of Mr. J S Sams, £250 each, to his brother James Henry, £500, to his nephew Cosmo Huntly Gordon, £1,500; to his sister Anna Cecilia, £2,000, to his sister-in-law Mrs. Francis Edith Gordon, £100 and cottages at Preston, Sussex; to the children of his late brother Charles Vincent Gordon, other than Cosmo, £1,000, to the children of his brother James Henry, £1,000; to his brother Lewis Gordon, his wife, £1,000, and to the children of his brother Lewis, other than his eldest son, £1,000; to his cousin Margaret Cardew and her children, £200, and to

Margaret Mabel Lennox, daughter of his partner, £100; and to his wife £1,000, the furniture of his house at Eltham, and the income of a sum of £30,000, which, subject to her life interest, is to be in trust—as to one-third for his brother James Henry and his children, as to one-third for his said sister Cecilia during her life, with power of appointment to her of £5,000, and as to the remainder of her share for his brother James Henry and his children, and as to the remaining one-third for his nephew Cosmo Huntly Gordon for life, and subject to his life interest, as to £5,000 as he may appoint and as to the remainder of his share for the other children of the testator's brother Charles Vincent; he devised the house which he had lately built at Ballater in trust for his wife during her life and subject to her life interest, for his brother James Henry during his life and subject to his life interest for his nephew Cosmo Huntly; and the effects at Ballater are to devolve as heirlooms therewith. Mr. Gordon left his residuary estate to his wife.

Lewis Gordon, XVIII. of Abergeldie

(Brother of XVII.)

The present laird was born on Jan. 23, 1828   He married, July 17, 1862, Louisa Isabella, 4th daughter of William Lyall, and has—

1. Reginald Hugh Lyall, born July 14, 1863   He is married and has one daughter, Gertrude Alice Margaret

2 Bertram Fuller, born March 10, 1868, married Florence, 2nd daughter of Charles Lorking Rose ; no issue. He is in business.

3 Lewis Malcolm, born May 13, 1873   He is 2nd officer in the P and O. Company, and a sub-lieut. in the R N R.

4 Kenneth Francis, born Feb 2, 1877   He is *curator bonis* of his father.

5. William Maurice, born 1880   He is in business   He is serving (Nov., 1901) with a section of the London Scottish Volunteers who are attached to the Gordons in South Africa   I am indebted for this information about his brothers and sister to Mr. Kenneth Francis Gordon

6. Emily Flaxman.

Other Gordons in the Abergeldie Country.

Several Gordons in the district of Abergeldie are difficult to
connect Some of these may be connected with the Gordons of Knock
or the house of Braichley I simply print my notes on them for the
use of other investigators

Abergeldie —Maidment in his *Catalogues of Scotish Writers* (p 120) prints a
manuscript (in Wodrow's hand) which states that "Mr Alexander Gordon, a merchant in Aberdeen of the House of Abergeldie, wrote very many poems in the
Scottish tongue which were very elegant and 'learned, for all his letters he wrote
to his wife were poeticall".

Jervise (*Epitaphs*, II , 164) says that a daughter of Abergeldie married a medical
officer in India named Gordon, the son of a notorious poacher "Jamie " Gordon

Mary (?) Gordon married Nathaniel (?) Morren.—Mrs. Harper, Aberdeen, tells the
present writer that her ancestor Nathaniel (?) Morren married a Mary (?) Gordon of the
Abergeldie family about 150 years ago. "This Morren returned from France or Belgium
with one of the Gordons as secretary, valet, barber surgeon or in some other more or
less menial capacity He fell in love with one of the daughters, Mary Gordon The
family opposed the marriage, and the pair went off. together, but were shortly after
forgiven and received back to Abergeldie A farm was bought for them, and they
settled somewhere near Rayne (Barflet may have been the name) My grandmother,
Harriet Morren, was the grand-daughter of this pair, and the Gordon Christian
names remained in his family—George, Hugh, etc " I cannot trace this alliance

Aucholzie —The estate of Aucholzie, pronounced "Achwillie," is dealt with at
length in Michie's *Records of Invercauld* (pp 26-37), Aucholzie The estate was long
held by a family named Stewart, and on July 9, 1714, we have the marriage contract
registered between Anna, daughter of Robert Garden of Corse, and Alexander, son
of William Stewart of Aucholzie (*Records of Invercauld*, p 28). The Earl of Aboyne
ultimately became proprietor of the lands in consequence of the debts due to him by
James Stewart The lands passed in 1766 to the Farquharsons of Invercauld,
and were finally sold to Sir James Mackenzie of Glenmuick. A family of Gordons
occupied Aucholzie from about 1750 to 1875 (with the exception of the years 1815-17
when it was let) In 1875, when Aucholzie was sold to Mackenzie, the grazing was
turned into a deer forest The founder of the family, so far as I have been able to
discover, was—

DONALD, who went to Aucholzie, about 1750, from Bridge of Lee, Glenesk
According to Mr John Gordon, Cullisse, Nigg, he married —— Small,
Altonree, Glenmuick   Her sister Euphemia married Peter Gordon,
in Ardmeanach, Glenmuick, who is now represented by Mr. D. Stewart
Ramsay Gordon, Edinburgh   According to another account Donald
Gordon married (possibly as his second wife) Elspet Taggart, a
widow (she is described on the stone in Glenmuick Churchyard as
Elspet Donald, probably her maiden name)   She and her husband
died in 1810, aged 80 (Jervise's *Epitaphs*, and information from Mr.
William Gordon, Auchallater)   Donald Gordon had—

1. JAMES, born 1757; married (1) about 1786 Ann Leys (died
1791), and (2) Ann Gordon (died 1827)   James had—

(1) WILLIAM (by the first marriage), born 1788, died
1875.   He married (1833) Helen Fletcher, and
had—

i JAMES, died young.

ii WILLIAM, went in 1870 to Auchallater,
where he still resides

iii JOHN, died young.

iv ANNIE, married John Watson, and has
a son and two daughters

v. MARGET, married her cousin, James A.
Gordon, Arabella, and died 1900

(2) DONALD (by first marriage, died young).

(3) ALEXANDER (by second marriage), born Feb. 8,
1794   He married and had issue : now all dead

(4) SAMUEL (by second marriage), born March 24, 1798
He went to Ross-shire in 1854.   He married
Helen Hunter of Polmood, Forfarshire, and had—

i. JAMES A GORDON, of Arabella, Nigg,
Ross-shire   He married his cousin,
Marget Gordon (died 1900), and has
four daughters, Annie, Elizabeth,
Meta and Ada. (Information from
Dr J. Scott Riddell.)

ii. JOHN, at Cullisse   He married Jane
Forbes Paterson. He has—

(i) ALEXANDER PATERSON.

(ii.) SAMUEL HUNTER.

(iii.) ANNIE HUNTER.

(iv) JANE GRINDLEY, married to
Dr. John Scott Riddell,
surgeon, Aberdeen.

(5) JANE, born Feb. 9, 1804

(112)

Ardmeanach —I am indebted to Mr. D Stewart Ramsay Gordon, Edinburgh, for some details of this family A John Gordon was tenant in Ardmeanach, Glenmuick, in 1696 (*Poll Book*) He may have been the father, or grandfather, of—

1. JOHN GORDON, born at Ardmeanach about 1720 Mr D. S R Gordon says that tradition assigns the origin of the Ardmeanach Gordons to the family of Knock, and an old aunt of his, Margaret Stewart, "said *her* mother prided herself on belonging to the Gordons of Braichlie" Mr. Gordon also tells me that his family claims kin with some Gordons in Lethnot, Forfarshire. To return to John, born about 1720, he married in 1752 —— Watt, and had—

    (1) PETER, married Euphemia Small, Altonree, Glenmuick, whose sister married Donald Gordon, Aucholzie. As a marriage present Peter got a punch bowl from the laird of Abergeldie. It is now in the possession of Mr D. S. R Gordon. Euphemia Small lived to be nearly a hundred years of age Peter had—

        1. SAMUEL (the youngest of the family), born at Upper Aucholzie, July, 1797 He married in 1832 Mary Ramsay, of Newbigging, Forfarshire (descended from William Forbes VI of Newe) He went to Bellamore in 1805, and died there at the age of 88. He owned Woodside, near Brechin He had—

            (1) D. STEWART RAMSAY, born at Woodside in 1845 He married Mary Glegg, and has a son—

                a. REGINALD GLEGG, born at Valparaiso, Chili, Sept 26, 1878.

    (2) SAMUEL, tenant of Tombreck, died Dec., 1798, aged 48 (Jervise's *Epitaphs*) He had a daughter—

        1. JANE, who died at Newton of Tullich, May 9, 1874, aged 103 (Jervise's *Epitaphs*).

Balmoral —The first reference I can find to Balmoral occurs in the Exchequer Rolls of Scotland under 1539, when Alexander Gordon and John Gordon appear as tenants of Balmoral, while John Reid Gordon was a tenant of Crathienaird There was a James Gordon of Balmoral in 1633 when the *Book of Annualrentaris* (Spalding Club *Miscellany*, Vol III.) was compiled. He owed money to Alexander Keith, portioner of Duffus, and to George Irvine of Dorvattie (Dornasillie ?). In 1629 the King granted Patrick Gray of Invergowrie and his heirs and assignees the lands of Hayistoun and Scrogiefield in Forfar which James Gordon of Balmoral resigned (*Great Seal*). I suggest that this James—who is described as "of Balmorall," valued at £88, in

1635 (Michie's *Records of Invercauld*, p. 463)—is the James of Easton (son of the 4th laird of Abergeldie) the husband of Marion Scrimgeour, who apparently was a relative of Sir James Scrimgeour of Dudhop, Constable of Dundee In 1696 Charles Farquharson was laird of "Balmurell" (*Poll Book*). He was the second son of William Farquharson of Inverey, by his second wife, Anne Gordon, "daughter of Abergeldie," who brought the estate of Balmoral to the Farquharsons. They held it until it was bought by Earl Fife, from whom it passed, after a tenancy by Sir Robert Gordon, brother of the (premier) Earl of Aberdeen, to Prince Albert

The Aberdeen Inventories in the Register House contain the will of John Gordon in Balmoral, who died 1750. He declared in his will that he "cannot write". The will is dated Oct. 9, 1750, and the executor is James Gordon in Balmoral, the testator's eldest son He left 10 merks Scots for the poor of Crathie. There was owing to him 600 merks contained in a bond dated Nov 22, 1714, granted by him to the now deceased James Farquharson of Balmoral The will was confirmed Feb 4, 1767, James Gordon in Belnacroft being cautioner (bond signed at Abergeldie, Jan 26, and witnessed by Charles Gordon of Abergeldie) John Gordon married Margaret M'Donald and had—

1. JAMES, "eldest son". Executor of his father's will, 1767 He was left the "equal half of the croft" (of the tack held by his father) for the year 1751 ; and the other half to be divided between his wife Margaret M'Donald and his second lawful son,
2 DONALD
3 JEAN, "my youngest daughter," spouse to Robert Mitchell "presently" (1750) in Balmoral got £50 Scots under her father's will.

Crathie.—Thomas Gordon, Crathie, had a son James who was at Marischal College, 1767-71 (Anderson's *Fasti Academiae Mariscallanae*)

Littlemill (*Crathie*) —A broken headstone in Glenmuick Churchyard refers to Alexander Gordon of Littlemill, and his wife Bessie Smith who came from Birse I have an interesting letter from Mr J. Leask, Bombay, bearing on this descent. Alexander Gordon died in 1809, aged 82, and his wife in 1800, aged 59 They had a son—

1 GEORGE, who died at Leith, 1834, aged 64 Like his forbears for genera-tions he was a farmer at Littlemill He married Betty Gauld (died at Littlemill, 1866, aged 80) Betty Gauld was the daughter of a farmer at Migvie who had married Mary Moir Her brother Donald had a daughter who married John Skeen of Tarland and had, among others, Surgeon William Skeen (three of whose sons are doctors) and Surgeon Andrew Skeen, whose widow married in 1887 Sir Henry Thoby Prinsep, High Court Judge at Calcutta. George Gordon and Betty Gauld had a large family Among these:—
(1) GEORGE, died at sea.
(2) JOHN, engineer, London

(114)

(3) WILLIAM, began life as a planter in Ceylon, and then
  farmed at Littlemill   He died in 1897   His
    Daughter married Mr. J. Leask, Bombay.
(4) DUNCAN, died in Ceylon
(5) JAMES, died in Ceylon.
(6) MARY (Mrs Lancaster, London).
(7) AGNES, married —— Simpson, Aberchirder, and is dead

John Gordon, weaver, the brother of Alexander Gordon, who married Bessie
Smith, was the father of—

1. GEORGE,
2 ALEXANDER, } brewers, Caledonian Road, London.

3 JOHN,
4. JAMES, } mechanical engineers, London

5. DOUGLAS.

LIEUTENANT-GENERAL HUGH MACKAY GORDON

There was a lieutenant-general in our army at the beginning of the
19th century who bore the same name as the 17th laird of Abergeldie,
and yet, though he is said to have been "in some way" connected
with that family, the precise relationship is difficult to trace

His father, according to information sent me by the late laird of
Abergeldie, was an Alexander Gordon of Boston (Mass.), a merchant.
His mother was Miss Jean Mackay, "who was said to have been born
at Inverness about 1718, and who was a grand-daughter of Captain
Hugh Mackay of Scoury, Sutherlandshire   She died in Edinburgh,"
on June 29, 1789 (according to the *Scots Magazine*), when she was a
widow. Mr. George H. Gordon of Somerville, Mass , tells me, however, that Gordon was named after Dr Hugh Mackay, a Scots resident
in Boston, who was a friend of his father   He was the fourth son.
His eldest brother, George, was baptised in Boston, Aug. 6, 1755,
Alexander, the second, on Aug. 21, 1757, and a sister Anabella on

April 27, 1758. Mr. G. H. Gordon also notes that Hugh M. Gordon, who was baptised in King's Chapel, Boston, on Sept. 5, 1760, was a pupil at the Boston Latin School 1766-7, at which he had as a school-mate Sir David Ochterlony, a general in the East India Service. Mr. B. F. Stevens, in his *Campaign in Virginia*, and Cannon, in the *Historical Record of the 16th Regiment*, give these particulars about him :—

He served as a volunteer under Sir William Howe in America, 1775-6; was ensign in the 71st Regiment, 1777; lieutenant in the 16th Regiment, 1778, and sailed from New York for the West Indies, joining his regiment at Pensacola in January, 1779 He stayed there until 1780, when he was sent to solicit reinforcements from the Commander-in-Chief, returning to Pensacola in 1781. He was taken prisoner while A D C. to Major Campbell. He got his company in 1788, and went to the East Indies in the following year. He was present at the capture of the Cape of Good Hope in 1795. He became brevet major in 1796. He was Quartermaster-General in Bengal, 1797. He became brevet lieut -col in 1798; and major in 1799 He returned to England in 1801. He was military secretary to the Commander-in-Chief in Ireland in 1805, and Lieutenant-Governor in Guernsey in 1816, in which year he was colonel of the 16th Foot. He was a lieut.-gen in 1821.

He also commanded the British forces in Madeira for a time. The 17th laird of Abergeldie possessed two most interesting views of the town of Funchal dedicated to the general and drawn by one of his A.D.C.'s, a Portuguese officer He also had a large mass of his letters and papers at Eltham, and a portrait of him by Opie. General Gordon died in Dean Street, Mayfair, on March 12, 1823, and was buried in a vault under St. James's Church, Piccadilly.

\

COCLARACHIE.

BY

THE REVEREND STEPHEN REE, B.D.

.

.

NEW SPALDING CLUB.

Q

PREFATORY NOTE.

A GENEALOGICAL deduction of the Gordons of Coclarachie is given in the *Balbithan MS.* (pp. 51-3), and it is singularly accurate as far as it goes. This deduction is reproduced, with additions, in Temple's *Thanage of Fermartyn* (pp. 276-9). The early members are briefly noticed in Lord Huntly's *Records of Aboyne* (pp. 168, 210). The present accounts are drawn up according to the scheme of the general editor, Mr. J. M. Bulloch.

Mr. W. F. D. Steuart of Auchlunkart has kindly granted me free access to his charter chest, and also permission to publish the documents that form the Appendix. For the families of Auchintoul and Ardmeallie I have had the use of all the notes that Mr. Bulloch had collected regarding them, and have also received much aid from Dr. Cramond, Cullen. Assistance has also been readily given in various ways by Rev. James J. Calder, Clerk of Strathbogie Presbytery, Mr. J. G. Fleming, Solicitor, Keith; Mr. R. B. Gordon, Procurator Fiscal, Elgin; Mr. Muirhead, Commissioner for the Duke of Richmond and Gordon, Fochabers; Sir J. Balfour Paul, Lyon King of Arms; and Captain Wimberley, Inverness.

S. R.

BOHARM, *February*, 1902.

THE LAIRDS OF COCLARACHIE.

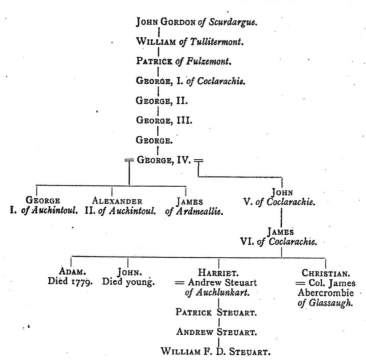

JOHN GORDON *of Scurdargus.*

WILLIAM *of Tullitermont.*

PATRICK *of Fulzemont.*

GEORGE, I. *of Coclarachie.*

GEORGE, II.

GEORGE, III.

GEORGE.

GEORGE, IV.

GEORGE
I. *of Auchintoul.*

ALEXANDER
II. *of Auchintoul.*

JAMES
of Ardmeallie.

JOHN
V. *of Coclarachie.*

JAMES
VI. *of Coclarachie.*

ADAM.
Died 1779.

JOHN.
Died young.

HARRIET.
= Andrew Steuart
of Auchlunkart.

CHRISTIAN.
= Col. James
Abercrombie
of Glassaugh.

PATRICK STEUART.

ANDREW STEUART.

WILLIAM F. D. STEUART.

COCLARACHIE

The lands of Coclarachie lie in the parish of Drumblade, Aberdeen-shire.

On December 6, 1425, Alexander Stewart, Earl of Mar and Garioch, granted the half of the lands of Culclarochy and the sixth part of the lands of Gerry to Alexander Seton, Lord Gordon (*Antiq. Aberd. and Banff*, iii., 517-8). These lands were apparently given to found the chaplaincy of St. Mary of Coclarachie, for on March 20, 1557, Mr David Carnegy, rector of Kinnoul, and possessor of the chaplaincy, feued the lands to Mr Thomas Ker (*Ibid.*) On December 9, 1564, Thomas Ker of Coclarachie granted a letter of reversion of the lands of Begeshill in favour of William Leslie of Balquhain, and renewed it in November, 1566 (Leslie's *Family of Leslie*, iii., 44-5) Afterwards this half came into the possession of the Marquis of Huntly, and in 1617 was acquired by George Gordon.

The other half of Coclarachie was held in 1504 by Alexander Winton of Andat, in the parish of Tarves, for in a Head Court held at Aberdeen on January 9 of that year the Laird of Andat was found in default for his lands of Coclarachie (*Coll. Aberd and Banff*, pp. 111-3). This half passed to his two daughters, Elizabeth and Margaret

Elizabeth Winton was the second wife of George Gordon of Milton of Noth, and her only child, Jonet Gordon, succeeded to a fourth part of Coclarachie. Jonet Gordon married Patrick Forbes of Kinmuck, in the parish of Keithhall, and her son, Alexander Forbes, in 1560 sold his fourth part to his mother's half-brother, George Gordon of Blairdinnie.

Margaret Winton received sasine on a fourth part of Coclarachie in 1518 (*Exchequer Rolls*, xiv., 606). She married William Leslie, eldest son of George Leslie of Aikenway in the parish of Rothes, Morayshire, and grandson of George, first Earl of Rothes; and her son, George

Leslie, was served heir to her in a fourth part of Coclarachie on October 1, 1549 (*Retours*). On July 15, 1557, George Leslie obtained from the Marquis of Huntly the lands of Tocher in the parish of Rayne, Aberdeen-shire, in exchange for his fourth part of Coclarachie (*Reg. Mag. Sig.*, December 12, 1557). This fourth part was acquired by George Gordon in 1587.

Coclarachie remained in possession of this family till 1767. The arms borne by Gordon of Coclarachie, not recorded, appear to have been: Azure, three boars' heads erased within a bordure or.

GEORGE GORDON, I. OF COCLARACHIE.

(*Died before* 1534.)

George Gordon, of Milton of Noth in the parish of Rhynie, also designed "of Coclarachie" in right of his second wife, was a son of Patrick Gordon of Fulzemont. According to the *Balbithan MS.* (p. 51) he was the fifth son, but according to Lord Huntly's *Records of Aboyne* (p. 210) he was the fourth son

"George Gordoun of Coclaraquhy" is one of the sureties nominated in a contract, dated at Elgin, November 9, 1527, between Elizabeth, Countess of Sutherland and her husband, Adam, Earl of Sutherland on one part and their son and apparent heir, Alexander, Master of Suther-land, on the other part ; but he is not among the sureties who took oath, on November 17 following, in accordance with the contract (*Orig. Paroch Scot.*, ii., 664-5). This absence may point to his death at that time he was dead before May 18, 1534, when his daughter had sasine on Coclarachie.

George Gordon of Milton of Noth married (1) a daughter of Oliphant of Berridale, widow of Calder of Asloun, and by her had (*Rec. of Aboyne*, p. 210) :—

1. GEORGE, afterwards of Coclarachie.
2. JAMES.
3. BESSIE. Probably this is the Bessie Gordon who married Laurence Leith of Kirkton of Rayne, from whom descend Leith-Hay of Leith-hall (Burke's *Landed Gentry*—Leith-Hay).

He married (2) about 1512 Elizabeth Winton, daughter of Alexander Winton of Andat, who was heiress of a fourth part of Coclarachie, and who died in 1526. The only child of this marriage was

4. JONET, who as heir to her mother got sasine on a fourth part of Coclarachie, May 18, 1534 (*Appendix* I). She married Patrick Forbes of Kinmuck (brother of Mr. Duncan Forbes of Monymusk), who appears, as portioner of Coclarachie, on a jury of appretiators of Middle Pitfodels, June 6, 1539 (*Reg. Mag. Sig.*, iii., 2133). On June 23, 1554, Alexander Forbes was served heir to Jonet Gordon, portioner of Coclarachie, in a fourth part of Coclarachie, etc. (*Retours*). By a charter, dated at Aberdeen, November 15, 1550, and confirmed under the Great Seal, December 1, 1554, Alexander Forbes son and heir of the late Patrick Forbes of Kynmukkis (with consent of Mr. Robert Lumisden, his curator) sold his fourth part of Coclarachie to his paternal uncle, Mr. Duncan Forbes of Monymusk, with reservation of his liferent of the same. This sale must either have been a formality during his minority, or have been afterwards cancelled, for on February 10, 1560, Alexander Forbes sold the lands to George Gordon of Blairdinnie.

GEORGE GORDON, II. OF COCLARACHIE.

(*Son of I.: executed* 1562.)

George Gordon of Blairdinnie, in the parish of Clatt, was the eldest son of George Gordon of Milton of Noth and Coclarachie   By a charter, dated at Aberdeen, November 16, 1556, and confirmed under the Great Seal, August 13, 1586, William, Bishop of Aberdeen, feued to George Gordoun of Blairdynnie, " the hauch of Bogy " in the parish of Clatt. On February 7, 1560, George Gordon bought the fourth part of Coclarachie that belonged to Alexander Forbes, the son of his half-sister, and he got sasine thereon on February 10 following, being described in the instrument of sasine (*Appendix* II.) as " Georgius Gordoun hereditarius de Blairendenny ". He was taken prisoner at the battle of Corrichie in October, and was executed at Aberdeen on November 2, 1562, at the same time as Sir John Gordon, second son of the Marquis of Huntly (*Balbithan MS*, p. 52 ; Macfarlane's *Genealogical Collections*, i., 237).

He married a daughter of John Gordon of Tilphoudie, who was

second son of Adam Gordon of Aboyne and his wife Elizabeth, Countess of Sutherland, and by her had :—

> 1. GEORGE, his successor (*Rec. of Aboyne*, pp 42, 210).
> 2. BESSIE (Temple's *Fermartyn*, p 277).

GEORGE GORDON, III. OF COCLARACHIE.

(Son of II.: died 1633.)

George Gordon, III. of Coclarachie, was a minor at the time of his father's forfeiture and execution, but was included in the remission for Corrichie, granted February 26, 1567 (*Spalding Club Misc.*, IV., 155). On November 20, 1587, he bought from the Earl of Huntly a fourth part of Coclarachie (*Appendix* III.). Having joined the Earl of Huntly and having been present at the Battle of Glenlivet in October, 1594, he was again forfeited, and did not obtain remission till April 2, 1603 (*Spald Club Misc.*, iv , 159) On March 16, 1615, he obtained confirmation under the Great Seal of the charter of February 7, 1560, by which his father had acquired from Alexander Forbes a fourth part of Coclarachie, it being explained that the delay in obtaining confirmation had been caused by his father's death soon after the purchase and his own minority at the time of his father's death. Having resigned the fourth part purchased in 1587, he received from the Marquis of Huntly on May 21, 1617, a charter on the three fourth parts of Coclarachie, redeemable on payment of 6,000 merks (*Appendix* IV.). He thus obtained the whole of Coclarachie, which remained in possession of his descendants till 1767. This laird also acquired other lands in Aberdeenshire.

1582.—He is said in *Records of Aboyne*, p 168, to have been made a burgess of Aberdeen in May, 1582, along with other followers of Huntly. This is probably founded on the extract in *Spald Club Misc*, v. 52-3, where the entry "Ge. Gordoun of Clockrachy" occurs, but in *New Spald Club Misc.*, i., 77, the entry is given as "Go. Gordoun of Clochrathn"

1590. *August* 8 —He found James Gordoun of Knokespik cautioner for him that James and George Leslies in Tailyeauch shall be harmless of him (*Privy Council Register*).

1591. *July* 23 —Bond of caution of date July 17, for £1,000, by him for John Lumsden of Cuscheny that he will not harm James Robertson in Westir Lochell. John Lumsden of Cuscheny grants a bond of same date and for same amount for

William Strachan of Glenkindie that he will not harm the same James Robertson (*Ibid*)

November 11 —He was witness of a notarial instrument executed at Lesmoir (*Rec. of Aboyne*, p. 170).

1593 *March* 3 —He was surety in 1,000 marks for John Gordoun of Auchannachie that he should do nothing in hurt of his Majesty's government nor take part with George, Earl of Huntly, etc (*Privy Council Register*)

1594. *June* 12.—He was charged to appear before the King and Council to answer concerning "persute and invasioun of his Majesties declairit tratouris, rebellious and unnaturall subjectis, treasonable practizaris and conspiratouris aganis the trew religioun presentlie professit within this realme, his Majesties persone and estate and libertie of this countrey". Failing to appear on July 11, he was then denounced rebel (*Ibid.*).

1600.—He was tenant of Huntly's lands of Learge in Cabrach (*Spald Club Misc.*, iv., 281)

1602 —He and Bessie Duncan, his spouse, had sasine on the third part of lands of Corbanchrie, Overtouris, Cokstoun, Jempsone, Duncanstown and New Merdrum, Balnakellie, etc (*Records of Aboyne*, p. 168) On 17th May there is sasine on the half lands of Merdrum and Balnakellie in favour of him and Bessie Duncan, his spouse, in liferent, and to Alexander and George Gordon, their sons, heritably (*Ibid*, p 168).

1603 —By a charter dated at Huntlie, May 23, 1603, and confirmed under the Great Seal, January 12, 1604, George, Marquis of Huntly, sold to him Birkinhill, Fidlerseat, Bordelseat, and Kirkhill in the parish of Gartly, redeemable on payment of 6,000 merks.

1607 —He and George Gordoun, his son and heir apparent, were witnesses to a charter, dated at Grantulie and Buckie, April 28 and May 13, 1607, and confirmed under the Great Seal, July 4, 1608, by which Alexander Gordoun of Baldornie, George Gordoun, his elder son and heir apparent, and John Gordoun of Buckie for his interest, sold to Abraham Forbes of Blackton the lands of Waster Foullis, Craigmylne and Eister Lochill in the lordship of Monymusk.

To him was directed the precept of sasine in the charter, dated at Aberdeen, May 27, 1607, and confirmed under the Great Seal, February 14, 1609, by which Arthur, Lord Forbes feued to Robert (Forbes), commendator of Monymusk, the lands of Tilliryauche and Tullauchvayneis in the barony of Cluny

He was a witness of mutual bonds of caution, dated at Aberdeen, December 11, 1607, by Robert (Forbes), commendator of Monymusk, and Abraham Forbes of Blacktoun that they would not harm Alexander Irving of Drum (*Privy Council Register*, viii, 636-7).

1608. *December* 10.—He got sasine on Tailzeoche (*Sasines*)

1612 —By a charter dated at Aberdeen, June 4, and confirmed under the Great Seal, July 28, Francis, Earl of Errol sold to him the town and lands of Bomatuithill, the shady half of the Maynis of Slaynis, the town and lands of Auchmabo, the town and lands of Brogane, with the mill of Brogane in the parish of Slains. George Gordoun, apparent of Coclerauchie, was one of the witnesses.

July 28.—He was one of those to whom a commission was granted to apprehend and try according to law certain persons of the names of Gordon and Grant in Upper Banffshire, "brokin men, committing oppin reiffis, privie stouthis, slauchteris, mutilationis, soirningis and utheris insolencyis" upon the good subjects in the adjacent parts (*Privy Council Register*).

1617.—"George Gordone of Blerindinie and Talzeauche" was one of the feuars of the Bishopric of Aberdeen within the parish of Clatt (Munro's *Old Aberdeen*, i., 57).

1619. *May* 13.—He and his sons, Alexander and Mr. William, gave their consent to the sale, by James Ogilvy of Auchleuchries and Marjorie Gordoun, his spouse, of Waster Auchleuchries (Gen. Pat. Gordon's *Diary*, p 205).

1629 *May* 17.—With consent of his sons, Alexander Gordon of Merdrum and Mr. William Gordon, doctor of medicine, he made provision for his grandson, George Gordon, in view of his marriage with Grissell Seton, daughter of Alexander Seton of Pitmedden (*Appendix* VI).

George Gordon, III. of Coclarachie, married Bessie, daughter of James Duncan of Merdrum. Bessie Duncan survived her husband. In a court held at Aberdeen, February 20, 1634, by William Cordoner, sheriff-depute, "Bessie Duncan, relict of umquhill George Gordone of Coclarachie, declarit be Doctor Williame Gordoun, doctor of medicine, her sone, that shoe hes hir lyfrent of the third pairt landis of Coclarachie, wedset of the Merques of Huntlie for the soume of 6,000 merkis Quhairof thair is to be defaisit that the said Bessie is restand to Marjorie Duncan, hir sister, the yeirlie annuelrent of 2,000 merkis, with the quhilk yeirlie annuelrent the wodsett is granted and no uther wayes; and that shoe is restand to Alexander, Mr. Hew and Williame Gordones, hir children, Mr. Robert Bisset of Lesindrum, George Gordoun of Raynie, and Williame Seatoun of Hadow, equallie amongs them, 600 merkis; to George Gordoun of Coclarachie, 500 merkis" (*Spald. Club Misc.*, iii., 123). In 1636 "the guidwyff of Coclarachie" was residing in Old Aberdeen (Munro's *Old Aberdeen*, i., 354); and probably the charter of liferent to Grissell Seton on December 15, 1643 (*Appendix* VII.), was granted shortly after Bessie Duncan's death. This laird had four sons and four daughters.

> 1. GEORGE, the eldest son, died before his father. He is mentioned in notices of his father, 1602, 1607, 1612; and was dead before June 18, 1618, when his widow was wife of John Gordon, younger of Craig

(*Reg. Mag. Stg.*). He married Jean, daughter of James Gordon of
Lesmoir, and by her had.—

    (1) GEORGE, IV. of Coclarachie.

    (2) JAMES (*Balb MS*, p. 52); or ALEXANDER (Wimberley's
       Gordons of Lesmoir (1893), p. 109, from Prony MS.; also
       Theodore Gordon's MS.).

2. ALEXANDER, of Merdrum. On May 17, 1602, he got sasine on the half lands
    of Merdrum and Balnakellie. See notices of his father, 1602, 1619,
    1629 On December 18, 1634, he was one of those who were ordered
    to be summoned as witnesses regarding the disorders that had arisen
    in the north since the burning of the house of Frendraught (Spalding's
    Trubles, 1, 423). On February 22, 1637, he gave evidence regarding
    certain accusations made by George Gordon of Rhynie against Mr.
    Henry Ross, minister of Rhynie On October 20, 1638, he was chosen
    by the Presbytery of Strathbogie ruling elder to the General Assembly,
    and the same presbytery, on April 24, 1644, chose " for Rhynie and
    Essie, Alexander Gordon of Merdrum " as one of a " list of able men
    from euerie parochin for to be insert in a commission for sorcereris and
    charmeris ". On July 26, 1646, he was one of those who were ap-
    pointed to "estimat and appreciat" the manse of Rhynie. He was
    one of the elders of Rhynie who were present at a presbyterial visita-
    tion of that parish on August 13, 1651 (*Presbytery Book of Strathbogie*,
    pp. 13, 19, 53, 67, 207) He married and had, at least, one son and
    two daughters :—

        (1) JAMES, of Merdrum. James Gordon, younger of Merdrum,
        appeared before the Presbytery of Strathbogie on February
        23, 1648, and confessed his accession to the late rebellion,
        and was ordained to "satisfy" in his parish church, but
        on May 17 the minister of Rhynie reported that "James
        Gordon of Merdrum had fled the boundis for the tyme".
        In 1651 the presbytery summoned before them all delin-
        quents who had not then obeyed their injunctions, and on
        October 29 " compeired James Gordon in Merdrum . . . and
        being humbled in sackcloathe was accused of quadrilaps
        in fornicatioune, deserting his repentance, contempt of the
        Session of Rynie, drunkenness, relapsing into rebellion
        with James Grahame, and the setting lightly of his father
        and his admonitiounes. Confessed all . . . was ordained
        to satisfie the discipline of Rynie in sackcloath thrie
        quarters of a yeare, for purgeing away the long continued
        scandell of his former ill spent life in maner abouewritten
        . . . promised obedience therunto in euerie thing according
        to his abilitie" (*Ibid*, pp. 85, 89, 213). He had sasine on

Merdrum in 1654 (*Sasines*). He married and had three
daughters, Margaret, Jean, and Marie, who had sasine on
New Merdrum in January, 1669 (Cadenhead's *Family of
Cadenhead*, p. 36).

(2) BARBARA, who married (1)   Orem, and (2) on December
24, 1663, William Lunan in Dallob, son of the Rev.
Alexander Lunan, minister first of Monymusk and afterwards of Kintore By her second husband she had a son,
William, and a daughter, Anna, both of whom married and
had issue (*Ibid*, pp 32-6).

(3) ELSPET, who married William Gordon of Sockach (*Balb. MS.*,
p 45).

3 HEW. He was witness of a bond of caution dated at Straloch July 16,
1621 (*Privy Council Reg*, July 25, 1621)   By a charter, March 9, 1633,
James Ogilvy of Auchleuchries, proprietor of the lands afternamed,
and Hew Gordon, lawful son to George Gordon of Coclarachie, with
consent of Marjorie Gordon, spouse of the said James Ogilvy, granted
certain parts of Auchleuchries to Marie Ogilvy, daughter of said
James Ogilvy, and future spouse of John Gordon, third son of the
deceased Patrick Gordon of Nethermuir, and to their heirs. By
a charter, August 19, 1633, Sir Alexander Hay of Delgatie, immediate
superior of the lands afternamed, granted to Hew Gordon, lawful
son to the deceased George Gordon of Coclarachie, the lands of
Easter and Wester Auchleuchries (Gen. Pat. Gordon's *Diary*, p 207).
[March, 1645] "as Montross is in Angouss, the Viscount of Fren-
dracht, the Lord Fraser, the Maister of Forbes, thair freindis and
folloueris leaves thair houssis and cumis to the feildis, and beginis to
oppress whome they culd overtak. And first thay mell vpone the
hie way with Hew Gordoun, sone to George Gordoun of Coklarachie"
(Spalding's *Trubles*, ii., 462).

4. WILLIAM, A.M., doctor of medicine   See notices of his father, 1619,
1629, and of his mother. He may have been the William Gordon,
A M., who was Mediciner at King's College, Aberdeen, from 1632
to 1640; but no direct proof has yet been discovered

5 MARJORIE   She married (1604) James Ogilvy, younger of Blerack, and
had a daughter, Marie, who married (1633) John Gordon of Auchleuchries and had issue, of whom the second son, Patrick, became
a General in the Russian army, and had, by his first wife, a daughter,
Katherine Elizabeth, who married Major-General Alexander Gordon
of Auchintoul

6. *Daughter*, who married Mr. Robert Bisset of Lessendrum, and had issue

7. *Daughter*, who married William Seton of Hadow.

8 CHRISTIAN, who married George Gordon of Rhynie and Sheelagreen, and
had issue.

George Gordon, III. of Coclarachie, died in 1633 between March 9 and August 19, as is shown by the charters referred to under notice of his third son, Hew.

GEORGE GORDON, IV. OF COCLARACHIE.

(Grandson of III. : died 1663.)

This laird succeeded his grandfather in 1633, though he and his first wife had received, on the occasion of their marriage in 1629, a charter on Coclarachie and also on Overblairton and Pettens in the parish of Belhelvie, Aberdeenshire (*Appendix* VI.). On October 6, 1643, he sold the lands in Belhelvie to George Davidson, burgess of Aberdeen (*Scottish Notes and Queries*, ii., 102); but he also acquired lands in the parish of Marnoch, Banffshire, including the barony of Auchintoul

1635.—He was one of those to whom a commission was granted on March 19, 1635, to apprehend certain rebels and "brokin men" who were oppressing the Laird of Frendraught and his tenants; and on August 7, 1635, he was one of those who were charged to appear personally before the Lords of Council and to find sufficient caution "for observing his majestie's peace and keeping of good rule and quyetnes in the countrie under paine of rebellion" (Spalding's *Trubles*, i., 426, 429).

1643 —He was one of "the Committee appointed by the Estaitis for the taxatione and loane of moneyes within the shirefdome of Abirdein," which met at Aberdeen on October 3, 1643, and on that day he, Sir Robert Gordone of Straloch and George Gordone of Knockaspock, were appointed a sub-committee for the district of the Presbytery of Strathbogie He was also present at meetings of the Committee on October 4, 1643, and January 6, 1644 (*Spald. Club Misc*, iii , 143-7).

He married (1) in May, 1629, Grissell, daughter of Alexander Seton of Pitmedden, by whom he "begat sons and daughters" (*Balb. MS.*, p. 52) :—

1. GEORGE of Auchintoul. See p. 17.
2. ALEXANDER of Auchintoul. See p. 18
3. JAMES of Ardmeallie. See p. 27.
4. MARIE, who married in March, 1659, John Grant in Lettoch, eldest son of James Grant of Auchernick (*Elgin Commissary MS. Records*, 26th June, 1684)

Grissell Seton died in 1644, and George Gordon, IV. of Coclarachie, married (2) in December, 1645, Elizabeth, daughter of Alexander Fraser of Philorth, and widow of William Meldrum of Haltoun of Auchterless

(*Appendix* VIII.). Elizabeth Fraser had, by her first marriage, an only child, Isabella Meldrum, who married in May, 1664, William, eldest son of John Forbes of Asloun (*Appendix* IX.). The children of the second marriage were :—

    5 JOHN, who succeeded to Coclarachie.

    6. CHARLES.

    7 JANET, who in September, 1696, became the second wife of Alexander Leslie of Little Wartle and had no issue (*Appendix* XI.).

George Gordon, IV. of Coclarachie, died in 1663. On August 5, 1664, a warrant was passed under the Great Seal appointing Elizabeth Fraser tutrix-dative to John, Charles and Jonet Gordon, her lawful children, mention being made therein that a year and a day had elapsed since the death of George Gordon of Coclarachie (*Auchlunkart Charter Chest*).

JOHN GORDON, V. OF COCLARACHIE.

(*Son of IV. : died* 1714.)

John Gordon, V. of Coclarachie, the eldest son by the second marriage of George Gordon, IV. of Coclarachie, was a minor when his father died in 1663, and received sasine on Coclarachie in February, 1670. He was a student at King's College, Aberdeen, in 1668 (*Fasti Aberd.*, p. 487). The valuation of Coclarachie in 1696 was £330 6s. 8d. Scots (*Poll Book*, ii., 271).

He married in December, 1679, Anna, daughter of Sir James Baird of Auchmedden (*Appendix* X.), by whom he had :—

    1. GEORGE,

    2. ALEXANDER, } alive in 1696 (*Poll Book*, ii , 271), but died before their father.

    3. JAMES, who succeeded to Coclarachie.

    4. CHRISTIAN.

    5. ANNA, who married in June, 1712, James Lunan, eldest son of Alexander Lunan, M A., minister of Daviot, Aberdeenshire (*Appendix* XII).

    6. ISOBEL.

John Gordon, V. of Coclarachie, died on July 8, 1714.

JAMES GORDON, VI. OF COCLARACHIE.

(Son of V.; died 1771.)

James Gordon, VI. of Coclarachie, was served heir to his father on July 14, 1721 (*Index of Heirs*), and a Crown precept of sasine on a fourth part of Coclarachie was issued in his favour on July 24, 1721 (*Auchlunkart Charter Chest*). He was elected a burgess of Banff on September 30, 1727 (*Burgess Ticket* in Auchlunkart Charter Chest)

On February 26, 1767, he sold the lands of Coclarachie to Alexander, Duke of Gordon, but sasine was not taken till May 1, 1771 (*Index of Charters* in Gordon Castle).

He married, in 1730, Jane, daughter of Robert Bisset of Lessendrum, by whom he had :—

1. ADAM, who died in 1779, his sisters being served heir to him on August 4, 1779 (*Index of Heirs*).

2. JOHN, who was a student at Marischal College, Aberdeen, 1772-73 (Anderson's *Fasti Acad. Marisc.*, II, 344), and died before his brother

3 HARRIET, who married in December, 1778, Andrew Steuart of Auchlunkart, in the parish of Boharm, Banffshire, second son of George Steuart of Tanachie in the parish of Rathven, Banffshire He was a Writer to the Signet in Edinburgh, being admitted on July 15, 1763, and he was elected a burgess of guild of Aberdeen in 1767 In 1771 he bought the lands of Auchlunkart. Andrew Steuart died at Peterhead on October 10, 1798, and his widow died at Auchlunkart on September 10, 1814. Their children were :—

    (1) PATRICK STEUART, of Auchlunkart, succeeded also to Tanachie on the death of his cousin, George Steuart. At Edinburgh, on June 21, 1800, he was admitted one of H.M Royal Company of Archers (*Auchlunkart Charter Chest*). He married on November 9, 1820, Rachel Missing Duff, daughter of Lachlan Gordon of Park, by whom he had an only son, Andrew Steuart He died at Paris on March 25, 1844, aged 64, and his widow died at Auchlunkart on May 8, 1872, aged 84.

        i ANDREW STEUART, of Auchlunkart and Tanachie, B.A. Cantab, 1844 (First Class in Classical Tripos, and a Senior Optime), M.A, 1848, was M.P. for Cambridge, 1857-62. In 1885 he resigned Auchlunkart and Tanachie in favour of his only

surviving son, William. He married, in 1847,
his cousin, Elizabeth Georgiana Graham, third
daughter of Thomas Duff Gordon of Park, and by
her (who died on March 28, 1888) he had:—

> (i) PATRICK STEUART, died in infancy
>
> (ii) GEORGE ALEXANDER STEUART, scholar
> of Winchester College, died June, 1865.
>
> (iii) THOMAS GORDON STEUART, died young.
>
> (iv) WILLIAM FRANCIS DAY STEUART, now of
> Auchlunkart and Tanachie, married in
> 1899 Florence, daughter of S. Ham-
> mond, Woolwich.
>
> (v) HARRIET ELIZABETH STEUART, married
> in 1871 General William Gordon, C.I.E,
> youngest son of the late Adam Gordon
> of Cairnfield, Banffshire, and has issue.
>
> (vi) RACHEL ELEANOR STEUART, married, in
> 1880, Hastings A. Clarke, Achareidh,
> Nairn, and has issue.
>
> (vii) LOUISA MARY STEUART.
>
> (viii) MABEL STEUART, married, in 1894, C. A.
> Seton, Preston, Linlithgow, and has
> issue

(2) JAMES STEUART, Captain, Royal Scots, killed at St. Sebastian
on September 2, 1813, unmarried. "Captain Steuart's
brilliant but short career was terminated in front of the
castle of St. Sebastian while reconnoitring along with Major-
General Hay, to whom he was aide-de-camp, he received
a musket ball in the head and survived about an hour,
leaving a character most honourable and as an officer most
distinguished " (*Scots Mag*, lxxv, 799).

(3) GEORGE STEUART, Midshipman, R N, died in February, 1820,
unmarried.

(4) MARY STEUART, who married David Monypenny (Lord Pit-
milly), one of the Senators of the College of Justice, and
died on December 2, 1808, without issue

4. CHARLOTTE, who married Col. James Abercrombie, of Glassaugh, Banffshire, son of General James Abercrombie of Glassaugh, but had no
issue.

James Gordon, VI. and last of Coclarachie, died at Aberdeen on
November 29, 1771, in the 77th year of his age (*Aberdeen Journal*).

THE GORDONS OF AUCHINTOUL.

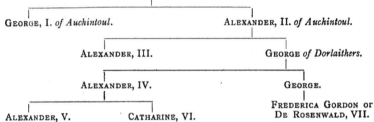

GEORGE GORDON, IV. *of Coclarachie.*

GEORGE, I. *of Auchintoul.*   ALEXANDER, II. *of Auchintoul.*

ALEXANDER, III.   GEORGE *of Dorlaithers.*

ALEXANDER, IV.   GEORGE.

ALEXANDER, V.   CATHARINE, VI.   FREDERICA GORDON or DE ROSENWALD, VII.

The arms of Gordon of Auchintoul as recorded in 1765 are: Azure, a mullet between three boars' heads couped or within a bordure of the last. Crest: a demi-boar proper. Motto: "Bydand".

GEORGE GORDON, I. OF AUCHINTOUL.

(Son of George Gordon, IV. of Coclarachie: died 1661.)

George Gordon, I. of Auchintoul, was the eldest son, by the first marriage, of George Gordon, IV. of Coclarachie.

On July 8, 1646, the King granted the lands and barony of Auchintoul, in the parish of Marnoch, Banffshire, to George Gordon of Coclarachie, in liferent, and to George Gordon, his eldest son, in fee, and to the heirs of the body of George Gordon, junior; whom failing, to Alexander Gordon, second son of George Gordon, senior, and his heirs (*Reg. Mag. Sig.*).

The "noblemen, gentlemen and heretouris" of Aberdeenshire held meetings at Aberdeen on November 11 and December 2, 1659, at the request of General Monk, and elected commissioners to meet him and confer with him on the affairs of the time   Among those present at the first meeting was the " Laird of Auchintoull younger," and at the second meeting " Auchintoull Gordoune" (*Rec. of Aboyne*, pp. 319, 323).

He died before his father in 1661, unmarried, and his next brother, Alexander, was served heir to him on July 24, 1661 (*Retours*).

ALEXANDER GORDON, II. OF AUCHINTOUL, LORD AUCHINTOUL.

(*Brother of I : died* 1710.)

On the death of George Gordon, I. of Auchintoul, his brother german, Alexander Gordon, succeeded to Auchintoul in accordance with the provisions of the charter of July 8, 1646.

1669 —At a meeting of the Synod of Moray in April, 1669, the Presbytery of Strathbogie gave in a report regarding the papists within their bounds, among whom was Alexander Gordon of Auchintoul; and the Synod enjoined the Presbytery to begin a process against him   The same injunction was renewed at next meeting of Synod in October following   In April, 1670, the Presbytery reported to the Synod that Auchintoul was under process. At subsequent meetings of Synod the same report was given in till April, 1672, when the Presbytery reported that he had been called before the Privy Council, and that consequently the process against him was laid aside (*Synod of Moray MS. Records*).

1678. *July* —Infeftment was given in the town and lands of Auchintoul and others to Alexander Gordon of Auchintoul in liferent and to Alexander Gordon, his eldest lawful son, in fee; the liferent of Isobel Gray, spouse of the said Alexander Gordon, elder, being reserved, and the foresaid lands being erected into a barony to be called the barony of Auchintoul (*Geneal Mag.*, 1901, p. 361).

1684. *January* 8.—He was admitted an advocate (Brunton and Haig's *Senators of the College of Justice*, p 431).

1687. *February* 2 —He witnessed a deed executed at Delmanie, in the parish of Boharm, Banffshire (*Auchlunkart Charter Chest*)

1688. *June* 15 —He was admitted an Ordinary Lord of Session (Fountainhall's *Decisions*, 1, 506) As the Revolution took place soon after, he held office only for a few months, but continued to be known as Lord Auchintoul.

1704 *May* 15 —The list of papists given in to the presbytery of Strathbogie by the minister of Marnoch includes "Alexander Gordon of Auchintoul, sometym Senator in the College of Justice, baptized and brought up in the reformed protestant religion which he professed in his youth till he went to France, since which time he has been a professed papist , his children all born and bred in the Romish religion, and forisfamiliat; there are only two daughters with him, viz., Mary and Margaret, unmarried, both papists " (Blakhal's *Narration*, Spalding Club, p. xxxvi).

(134)

1709. *February* 10.—William Duff of Braco on February 21, 1707, sent his servant to the house of Auchintoul, who counted down "on the table in specie current at the time" the amount of the principal and interest of a debt of £1,000 Scots due upon bond by his deceased father to Alexander Gordon of Auchintoul; and upon Auchintoul's declining to accept the money, the servant consigned it in the hands of Grant of Ruddry and protested that Braco was free of interest in time coming. Among other reasons for declining to accept the money at that time, Auchintoul alleged that "there was a rumour, then dispersed and which ultimately fell out, that the money of Scotland was to be called in and made conform to that of England in terms of the Union, and he apprehended that Braco was taking advantage to palm upon him the loss" that would thereby arise, and which he estimated would amount to about 500 merks. The Lords of Session found that Auchintoul should have accepted the money when it was offered and that the loss must fall on him (Fountainhall's *Decisions*, ii., 490).

Lord Auchintoul married Isobel Gray, " daughter of Gray of Braik and niece of Lord Gray" (*Life*, prefixed to Major-Gen. Gordon's *Peter the Great*), "with whom he begat three sons and daughters" (*Balb. MS.*, p. 52).

1. ALEXANDER, succeeded to Auchintoul.
2. GEORGE, was in Monedie in 1704, when he and his wife, Barbara McKenzie, with "but one chyld, on the breast," were returned as among the papists in the parish of Marnoch (Blakhal's *Narration*, p. xxxvi.), was in Monedie in 1709 (*Strathbogie Presb. Rec.*), and was afterwards of Dorlaithers, in the parish of Turriff, Aberdeenshire. He perished at sea in 1716 on his way to Holland (*Balb. MS.*, p. 52). He married Barbara, daughter of Alexander Mackenzie of Ardloch, and niece of Sir George Mackenzie, first Earl of Cromartie (Fraser's *Earls of Cromartie*, ii., 53), and by her (who died on May 26, 1762, aged 80) he had "three sons and a daughter" (*Balb. MS.*, p. 52). The eldest son, Alexander Gordon of Dorlaithers, succeeded his uncle in Auchintoul. The second son, George, who died in July, 1762 (*Marnoch Sess. Rec.*), married, and had two daughters: the elder, Frederica, married Quieten de Rosenwald in the service of the Emperor of Germany, and in 1798 succeeded her cousin, Catharine Gordon, in Auchintoul; the younger, Christine, married Theiner de Retheim, Major in the German army: and both were widows in 1798 (*Auchintoul Titles*).
3. JAMES, "third son to the Laird of Auchintoul, living in the house of Cairnborrow," was included in the list of papists given in to the presbytery of Strathbogie by the minister of Glass on May 11, 1704 (Blakhal's *Narration*, p. xxxvi.). He married (?) a daughter of Barclay of Cottcairn (*Balb. MS.*, p. 52), and she died under circumstances indicated in two letters printed in Fraser's *Earls of Cromartie* (ii., 51-3).

In one of the letters Sir George Mackenzie, first Earl of Cromartie, writing to John, Earl of Mar, on November 30, 1707, says: "This day one James Gordon, a sonne of the quondam Lord Auchintowl, had a persuit against Duff of Braco for comeing with 29 or 30 armed men to seaz the said James on account of a ryot committed by him on Alexander Alexander. Braco defended himself as being oblidged, as a baron, to seaz any committers of ryot, as also he had the shirrefs warrand to search and seaz the said James   The advocats for James alleadge this to be a gross ryot in Braco and ane infringment of our act of Habeas Corpus, &c.   But unhappily, by Bracos clamorous irruption into the hous, his lady who was a while befor brought to bed did from the fright fall into a fever and dyed   Now that which is notable in this process is that Braco did raise a lybell against Gordon for raising so scandalous lybel against him and befor any procedur he pleaded that Gordon, the persuer, should also enter the pannell. . . . The Lords made Gordon also enter the pannel . . . We are next day of court to hear them on the principall cause." The other letter is from Barbara Mackenzie, wife of George Gordon, to her uncle, Sir George Mackenzie, first Earl of Cromartie, and, though not dated, was evidently written a short time before the Earl's own letter

My Lord—I took the freedom to writ in sommer with my husbands brother to your Lordship, who owns himself much bound and oblidged to your favour and civility, and I no less, who flatter myself with the fancy that a share of them were on my account, for which I render your Lordship my cordiall thanks, and intreats your protection and friendship to him in an action he has befor your Lordship wherin he pursues Braco for the death of his wife   I need not enter on the detail of the affair, you'll be sufficiently acquainted with it ; but one thing I must say, the poor gentilman has but too great raison to pursue Braco in this affair, he having occasioned the death of a very good wife, my particular friend, their being no room left to doubt but his affrighting of her was certainly the occasion of her death, who was known befor that, particularly to myself, to be one of the strongest and healthfullest women in the countrey.   My Lord, I must sollicit your favor and beg your justice not only in my brother-in-laws behalf but likewise in my own and all women who are bearing children, for how can we secure ourselves against the being affrighted out of our lives if this go unpunished ?   These people, with whom my brother has to do, boast so much of their wealth that they undervalue and despise men of meaner fortuns and think to do all and secur for themselves against all events with their money.   But I have no fears on that head, being long agoe convinced of your Lordships judgement, integrity and justice.   My

Lord Auchintoulle, who presents you with this, can inform you better than any man, having been witnesse to all the sad tragedie, and I'le assure you, my Lord, that nothing, no not his sons concern, will make him say any thing contrary to truth.

I'm always glaid to hear of your Lordships health, and wishes and prays for the continuance of it My husband kisses your hands and longs to be known to you. My sister Mary do's the same but particularly, my Lord,

Your most obedient neece and humble servant,
BARBARA McKENZIE

James Gordon married (2) Margaret Chalmers, daughter of a solicitor in Edinburgh, who survived him and died at Edinburgh on January 21, 1739, leaving two daughters (*Edinb. Commissariot*, Dec 12, 1740).

> (1) KATHERINE, died abroad, unmarried, in 1768 (*Edinb. Commissariot*, April 11, 1769).
>
> (2) CLEMENTINA, married at Edinburgh in 1751 James Elphinston, and died at London in 1778 Elphinston was a native of Edinburgh, who removed to London in 1753 and set up an academy at Kensington, which he successfully carried on till 1776 He died at London on October 8, 1809, aged 88, being survived by his second wife, a daughter of the Rev. James Falconar and niece of Bishop Falconar. He was a friend of Johnson and other prominent literary men of his time, and was himself the author of several educational works (*Gent.'s Mag*, Nov, 1809)

4. *Daughter*, married John Gordon of Letterfourie (*Balb. MS.*, p 18)

5 MARY, }
6 MARGARET, } unmarried in 1704.

Lord Auchintoul died at Auchintoul in 1710

ALEXANDER GORDON, III OF AUCHINTOUL.

(*Son of II.. died 1751*).

The third laird, the eldest son of Lord Auchintoul, was the most distinguished member of the family. He was born at Auchintoul on December 27, 1669, and at the age of fourteen was sent to Paris to complete his education. During his stay in France he entered the French army and rose to the position of Captain. Returning to Scotland after the Revolution he did not find the position of public affairs to his mind, and accordingly about 1692 he went to the continent and soon found his way to Russia. There he joined the Russian army, then under the command of his kinsman, General Patrick Gordon of Auchleuchries. His first commission was obtained under exceptional circumstances. Not long after his arrival he was present at a marriage, where some young Russians, notwithstanding his remonstrances, persisted in speaking in contemptuous terms of all foreigners, and specially of Scots. The dispute proceeded from words to blows, but ended in Gordon's favour. A complaint having been lodged against Gordon, he was summoned before the Czar himself to answer for his conduct Having heard Gordon's account of the incident, the Czar said—" Well, Sir, your accusers have done you justice in allowing that you beat six men; I also will do you justice"; and thereupon he gave him a Major's commission In the same year Gordon was made a Lieutenant-Colonel, and three years later, in 1696, he had command of a regiment at the siege of Azof. When the Czar in 1700 gave liberty to the slaves on condition that they should become soldiers in his army, Col. Gordon specially distinguished himself by his skill in training the new men in the methods that had been adopted for reforming the army. At the disastrous defeat of the Russians by the Swedes at Narva on November 30, 1700, Col. Gordon became a prisoner of war, and remained in the hands of the Swedes for nearly seven years, having been released by exchange only in September, 1707. Immediately after his release he met the Czar at Pleskow, was ordered to accompany him to St. Petersburg, had frequent conferences with him there, and was raised to the rank of Brigadier. In the following year he was made a Major-General, in reward for the successes he had gained over the Polish troops. While in service in Poland in 1711 he heard of his father's death, and having obtained permission to leave the Russian service he returned to Scotland in the end of that year. He at once began to make several improvements on the house of Auchintoul, and he also enlarged his estate by the purchase, in 1712, of the lands of Laithers in the parish of Turriff, Aberdeenshire. On June 27, 1713, he was served heir general to his father (*Index of Heirs*).

In the rebellion of 1715 he took a prominent part. He attended the Earl of Mar's hunting-match at Braemar on August 27, and was also present at the meeting at Aboyne on September 9, at which it was decided that the time had come to take up arms. Thereafter he was sent into the Highlands to raise the western clans, and soon collected a body of over 4,000 men. An attempt to surprise Fort William proved unsuccessful, and he then marched towards Inverary with a view to giving the Jacobites of Argyleshire an opportunity of joining his standard. After Gordon had been some time before Inverary, thereby preventing the Earl of Islay from taking action, the Earl of Islay in October "appointed Clanronald and Glengary to treat with Sir Duncan Campbell of Lochnell and Lieut.-Col. Campbell of Finab on the part of General Gordon, and it was agreed that Gordon and his people should abandon Argyleshire and compensate the poor people for their losses, and on the other hand that the Hanoverian troops should not molest the clans" (*Townshend MSS.*, Hist. MSS. Com. Reports, p. 164). Thereupon Gordon withdrew his men towards Perthshire, arriving at Drummond Castle about the beginning of November, and on November 10 joined the Earl of Mar's army. At the battle of Sheriffmuir on November 13 the centre of the first line, which proved victorious over the Government troops, was under the command of Gordon. When the Chevalier's army reached Montrose on February 3, 1716, it was placed under General Gordon and he received from the Chevalier a commission "to command the army till dispersed and to act and in all things contribute as much as in him lay to the common safety" of the men. The army reached Aberdeen on February 6, when General Gordon intimated the instructions he had received; and thereafter he conducted the march westwards to Badenoch, where the men who had not already withdrawn quietly dispersed. From the time that he received full command he conducted the march with such prudence and skill that, though closely pursued, he lost few of his men (Browne's *Hist. of the Highlands*, chaps. xii.-xiv.). Thereafter he retired to the Highlands and in 1717 escaped to France. In February, 1719, he was at Bordeaux in consultation with those who were planning the invasion of 1719, which ended in the defeat at Glenshiel on June 10, 1719. When it was reported that the Spanish ships were to sail from Passage on March 8, "General Gordon falling sick a few days after, it was found he could not make the voyage" (Oliphant's *Jacobite Lairds of Gask*, p. 452); but in April he, with forty other officers, left Bordeaux in two Swedish ships (Dickson's *Jacobite Attempt of 1719*, p. 247). He was

included among those attainted for treason, but by being misnamed
Thomas in the Act of Attainder of 1716 he did not lose his estates.

Major-General Gordon did not return to Scotland till 1727, and
thereafter he lived quietly the life of a country gentleman. On June
28, 1729, he received from James Mitchell of Auchanacie in the parish
of Keith a discharge for 10,000 merks which had been borrowed on the
security of the lands of Auchintoul (*Sasines*). He did not take any part
in the rebellion of 1745, though the leaders of the rebel forces were in
communication with him in February, 1746 (Oliphant's *Jacobite Lairds
of Gask*, p. 182). The village of Aberchirder was founded by him in
1746, the first feus being given off in that year (Dr. Cramond in *Aberdeen
Free Press*, September 24, 1901). In his later years he occupied his
time in writing a life of the Emperor of Russia, under whom he had
served, which was published in two octavo volumes at Aberdeen in 1755,
with the title—*The History of Peter the Great, Emperor of Russia, to which
is prefixed a short General History of the Country from the rise of that
monarchy, and an account of the Author's life.*

Major-General Gordon married (1) in 1699 or 1700 Katherine
Elizabeth, elder daughter of General Patrick Gordon of Auchleuchries,
and widow of Colonel Strasburg of the Russian army, and by her (who
died in December, 1739) he had several children who all died in infancy.
He married (2) Margaret, eldest daughter of Sir Thomas Moncrief of
that Ilk, by whom he had no issue. His widow died at Edinburgh on
September 19, 1788 (*Scots Mag.*).

Major-General Gordon died at Auchintoul on July 31, 1751 (*Scots
Mag.*), and was buried in the churchyard of Marnoch. Having no surviving issue he was succeeded in Auchintoul and Laithers by his nephew.

ALEXANDER GORDON, IV. OF AUCHINTOUL.

(*Nephew of III   died* 1763.)

Alexander Gordon of Dorlaithers, eldest son of George Gordon of
Dorlaithers, was served heir general to his uncle, Major-General Alexander Gordon of Auchintoul, on July 24, 1753 (*Index of Heirs*). Alexander Gordon of Dorlaithers joined the rebels as a volunteer in 1745,

and in 1746 the rental of Dorlaithers was said to be £60 sterling, with a mansion house in "pretty good condition" (*List of Rebels*, Scot. Hist. Soc., pp. 30, 312).

He married Helen, second daughter of Alexander Irvine of Drum, and by her (who died on December 6, 1764, aged 64) he had a son, Alexander, and a daughter, Catharine, who both succeeded to Auchintoul.

The fourth laird died on June 2, 1763, aged 58 (Jervise's *Epitaphs*, ii., 224).

ALEXANDER GORDON, V. OF AUCHINTOUL.

(*Son of IV.. died 1768.*)

Alexander Gordon, V of Auchintoul, succeeded his father in 1763. He was an officer in the rebel army of 1745 (*List of Rebels*, Scot. Hist. Soc., p. 30); and was in France in 1748, when he received from the King of France a gratuity of 800 livres (Browne's *Hist. of the Highlands*, Stuart Papers, No. cxxiv.). From John Abernethie he bought the town and lands of Corskie in the parish of Marnoch and had sasine thereon on May 15, 1764 (*Sasines*). He died unmarried on March 30, 1768.

CATHARINE GORDON, VI. OF AUCHINTOUL.

(*Daughter of IV.· died 1797.*)

Catharine Gordon was served heir to her brother, Alexander Gordon of Auchintoul, on August 12, 1768 (*Index of Heirs*). On September 19, 1772, sasine was granted to Lord Adam Gordon of Prestonhall in liferent and Miss Katherine Gordon of Auchintoul in fee upon the barony of Auchintoul; and on September 23, 1772, sasine was granted to James Irvine of Kingcaussie in liferent and Katherine Gordon of Auchintoul in fee upon the lands of Mid Culvie and others in Marnoch (*Sasines*). She died unmarried in June, 1797, and was succeeded by her cousin.

FREDERICA GORDON OR DE ROSENWALD, VII OF AUCHINTOUL.

(*Cousin of VI.*)

Frederica Gordon, widow of Quieten de Rosenwald, was served heir of provision special to her cousin, Catharine Gordon of Auchintoul, in the barony of Auchintoul and the lands of Laithers on July 12, 1798 (*Index of Heirs*), and that year sold the lands to John Morison, afterwards of Bognie On May 10, 1799, Christine Gordon, widow of Theiner de Retheim, Major in the service of the Emperor of Germany, resigned her half of the lands of Corskie in favour of her sister, Frederica Gordon, widow of Quieten de Rosenwald in the service of the Emperor of Germany; and on June 17 Madame de Rosenwald sold the whole lands of Corskie to John Morison of Auchintoul *(Auchintoul Titles)*. According to tradition, the weather of the first winter that Madame de Rosenwald and her sister spent in Scotland after the death of their cousin was so severe that they resolved to return to Germany; but the vessel in which they sailed was never heard of again and was believed to have foundered in a storm (*Banffshire Journal*, July 30, 1889).

THE GORDONS OF ARDMEALLIE.

GEORGE GORDON, IV. *of Coclarachie.*

JAMES, I. *of Ardmeallie.*

PETER, II. *of Ardmeallie.*	ALEXANDER, II. *of Logie.*	JAMES *of Banchory.*
JAMES, III. *of Ardmeallie.*	ROBERT, III. *of Logie.*	THOMAS *of Premnay.*

The arms of Gordon of Ardmeallie as recorded in 1721 are: Quarterly: 1st and 4th, Azure, three boars' heads erased or within a bordure of the last charged with eight crescents (referring to the Seton descent) gules; 2nd and 3rd (for Meldrum), Argent, a demi otter issuing out of a bar wavy sable. Crest: a boar's head erased or. Motto: " Byd bee ".

JAMES GORDON, I. OF ARDMEALLIE.

(Son of George Gordon, IV. of Coclarachie; died 1723.)

James Gordon, I. of Ardmeallie, was the third son, by the first marriage, of George Gordon, IV. of Coclarachie. He obtained possession of the lands of Ardmeallie in the parish of Marnoch, Banffshire, between 1672 and 1674.

The former proprietor was John Gordon. There is recorded in the *Elgin Commissary Records*, on October 24th, 1681, a discharge, " written be Johne Gordone of Ardmellie and subscribed at Patrick Brouns hous in the Raws of Strathbogie the fourth day of July 1672 befor thir witnesses James Innes in Ardmellie and Johne Gordone of Ardmellie," by which James Gordon, merchant in Aberdeen, having received " nyne bolls and thrie firlotts of oats with the fodder," discharged his uncle, Robert Gordon sometime in Ardmellie, of a bond, dated May 17, 1672, for " thrie scoir and seven merks ". James Gordon of Ardmeallie was the husband of Isobel Meldrum on January 16, 1674, when she and her two sisters were served heirs portioner to Mr. John Hay of Logie, their uncle (*Retours*).

Through his wife James Gordon of Ardmeallie became in 1674 portioner of the lands of Logie in Crimond, Aberdeenshire. Mr. John Hay of Logie died 1673 and left these lands to the three daughters of his sister who had married Peter Meldrum of Laithers, and these three sisters were served heirs portioner on January 16, 1674 Mary, the eldest, had married David Stewart of Newton, commissary of Moray; Isobel, the second, had married James Gordon of Ardmeallie; and Elspet, the youngest, had married Mr David Cumming, minister of Edinkillie in Morayshire. Before 1696 David Stewart and James Gordon had acquired Mrs. Cumming's right, as they alone appear as portioners of Logie in the Poll Book (ii., 48) David Stewart died in February, 1705, and his widow died in June, 1708 (*Index of Heirs*); and shortly after James Gordon acquired the whole of Logie.

1679 *December* 15 —He witnessed the marriage contract of his half-brother, John Gordon of Coclarachie (*Appendix* X.)

1696. *May* 5.—He had sasine on an annualrent of 6,600 merks out of Rattanach and Knachland in the parish of Rothiemay (*Sasines*).

September 26 —He gave his consent to the marriage of his half-sister, Janet Gordon (*Appendix* XI.).

1700. *November* 7.—He was chancellor of the jury that condemned James Macpherson, the freebooter (Cramond's *Banff*, i , 101)

1708. *March* 15.—He was made an ensign in Aberdeen on account of the threatened invasion of the French (*Aberdeen Burgh Records*)

July 2.—His wife was served co-heir to her sister, Mary, widow of David Stewart, commissary of Moray (*Index of Heirs*)

James Gordon of Ardmeallie married Isobel, second daughter of Peter Meldrum of Laithers, by whom he had three sons and a daughter:—

    1 PETER, succeeded to Ardmeallie.
    2 ALEXANDER, succeeded to Logie in Crimond before 1721 (*Coll. Aberd and Banff*, p. 426). In 1746 the laird of Logie was said to have a rental of £260 sterling, with "a fine house" (*List of Rebels*, Scot Hist. Soc., p 305). He married, and had a son and two daughters:—
        (1) ROBERT, succeeded to Logie. Robert Gordon, younger of Logie, joined the rebels at Edinburgh in 1745 (*Ibid* , p 91), and was one of those who were excepted by name from the general pardon of June, 1747 (*Gent 's Mag* , June, 1747; Chambers' *Rebellion of* 1745-6, 7th ed , p 482). On October 4, 1752, he was served heir to his father (*Index of Heirs*).

He seems to have sold the lands of Logie. He married and had twin sons and a daughter.

i. JAMES, born at Milton of Drum in the parish of Peterculter, Aberdeenshire, was a farmer at Logie in Crimond and afterwards at Mains of Orrock in the parish of Belhelvie, and was distinguished for improvements in the cultivation of turnips. He died at Aberdeen on November 6, 1841, aged 89 (*Scottish Notes and Queries*, viii., 99; Smith's *Hist. of Aberdeenshire*, p. 428).

ii. ALEXANDER, twin brother of James, was a student in Arts at Marischal College, Aberdeen, 1763-67, and thereafter studied medicine at Aberdeen and Edinburgh Having obtained a certificate from the Corporation of Surgeons, London, he entered the Royal Navy in 1780 as a surgeon's mate, was raised in 1782 to the rank of surgeon, and served on H M.S. *Otter*. In 1785 he was placed on half-pay, and, after spending some time in London in the special study of midwifery, he went to Aberdeen and began general practice there. In 1786 he was appointed physician to Aberdeen Dispensary, and was annually re-elected till he left Aberdeen. While in Aberdeen he gave lectures on midwifery to medical students In 1788 he received the degree of M D. from Marischal College. In January, 1796, he relinquished his practice in Aberdeen, having been called on to resume active duty in the Navy; and in the same year he was admitted a Member of the Corporation of Surgeons, London. In 1799 he was invalided home, and went to Logie, the residence of his brother, where he died on October 19, aged 47. In 1795 he published a *Treatise on the Epidemic Puerperal Fever of Aberdeen*, which was reprinted at Edinburgh in 1822 as an appendix to Dr. William Campbell's *Treatise on the Epidemic Puerperal Fever of Edinburgh*, 1821-22 Dr. Campbell says in his preface (p. xii.)—"To the present work I have added the valuable essay of Dr. Gordon as an appendix, for it is now entirely out of print, although a publication of the first practical utility, and one the possession of which must be desirable to every man in practice, since to its author we are

unquestionably indebted for having been the first
to prove that puerperal fever was not quite so
untractable as the plague, but that it might on
the contrary be successfully encountered". The
value of the treatise was again recognised in 1849,
when it was reprinted by the Sydenham Society
(Anderson's *Fasti Acad Marisc*, ii., 131, 334;
Scottish Notes and Queries, viii., 99; Biog. Note by
his grandson, Dr A Harvey, in reprint of *Treatise
on Fever*, 1849, Rodger's *Aberdeen Doctors*, pp 46,
67). Dr. Gordon married in 1783 Elizabeth
Harvey, and by her (who was born on February
21, 1760, and died on March 10, 1840) he had two
daughters.

> (1.) MARY, born on November 12, 1784,
> married Dr. Robert Harvey of Braco
> near Inverurie, and died on June 14,
> 1818, leaving, with other children, a son
> Alexander Harvey, A.M, M.D, Pro-
> fessor (1860-78) of Materia Medica in
> the University of Aberdeen
>
> (11.) ELIZABETH, died on January 7, 1793,
> aged 6

> iii. *Daughter*, died, unmarried, at Banff on July 29,
> 1824, aged 70 (*Aberdeen Journal*)

> (2) ISOBEL, died, unmarried, at Aberdeen in March, 1780 (*Aberdeen
> Commissariot*, Gen Reg House, July 20, 1780).

> (3) ELIZABETH, died, unmarried, at Aberdeen on August 8, 1790
> (*Aberdeen Journal*)

3 JAMES was a merchant in Aberdeen. He purchased in 1724 the lands
of Banchory in the parish of Banchory-Devenick, Kincardineshire,
but sold them in 1743 to Alexander Thomson, advocate in Aberdeen
(*Coll. Aberd. and Banff*, p. 265, Henderson's *Banchory-Devenick*, p.
20); and in 1741 possessed lands in the parish of Premnay of the
annual value of £766 13s 4d Scots (*Scottish Notes and Queries*, 2nd
series, ii, 120). He died at Aberdeen on February 6, 1751, aged 67.
"He acquired a considerable fortune by merchandize, with an irre-
proachable character, was universally esteemed for many valuable
qualities and distinguished for his benevolent and peaceable disposition" (*Aberdeen Journal*) His brother, Alexander, had from him on
loan £11,200 Scots (*Aberdeen Commissariot*, Gen. Reg. House, June 20,
1753) He married (1) Margaret, daughter of Robert Cumming of
Birness, and had two daughters, who on May 7, 1740, were served

heirs portioner to their aunt, Ann Cumming, daughter of Robert Cumming of Birness (*Index of Heirs*)—

    (1) ANN, who married in 1757 John Gordon of Craig, and died in 1774, leaving issue

    (2) ISOBEL.

He married (2) Mary, daughter of James Buchan of Auchmacoy, and had—

    (3) THOMAS, who was served heir to his father on November 9, 1751 (*Index of Heirs*). He succeeded to his father's lands in the parish of Premnay; and also acquired Sheelagreen in the parish of Culsalmond, and in 1798 Heathcot in the parish of Maryculter (Henderson's *Lower Deeside*, p. 201). He died at Suffolk Street, London, W.C., on July 19, 1819, aged 73 (*Gent.'s Mag.*), and was succeeded by his sister, Mary. He bequeathed to the parish of Premnay £1,000 and to the parish of Culsalmond £600, the interest of which sums is applied for the support of the poor of these parishes (Smith's *Hist. of Aberdeenshire*, pp. 462, 1166)

    (4) MARY, who married on January 21, 1768, Dr. (afterwards Sir) Alexander Bannerman, Professor of Medicine in King's College, Aberdeen, and had issue (Anderson's *Officers, etc., of King's College*, p. 38). She succeeded to her brother's lands, but soon sold them.

4. MARY, married   Skene of Lethintie (*Balb MS*, p. 53).

James Gordon, I. of Ardmeallie, died in 1723; for in June, 1723, it was reported to the Kirk Session of Marnoch that "James Gordon of Ardmeallie, lately deceased," had bequeathed 100 merks for the poor of the parish (*Marnoch Session Rec.*).

PETER GORDON, II. OF ARDMEALLIE.

(*Son of I.. died* 1762.)

Peter Gordon, II. of Ardmeallie, was the eldest son of James Gordon of Ardmeallie.

1709. *April* 24.—Peter Gordon of Ardmeallie was one of the heritors of Marnoch (*Marnoch Session Rec.*)

1726. *August* 10.—He had sasine on part of the moss of Tilliedoun (*Banff Sasines*).

1729. *March* 11.—He had sasine on an annualrent of 200 merks out of Haddo in the parish of Forgue (*Sasines*)

1733.—He bought the lands of Barrie in the parish of Marnoch from William Duff of Crombie (*Antiq. Aberd. and Banff*, ii., 426).

1747   *September* 4.—He and his spouse had sasine on a tenement in Portsoy (*Sasines*).

1748.   *May* 27.—He was one of those qualified to wear arms after the Jacobite rebellion (*Banffshire Journal*, May 30, 1899).

1750   *March* 20.—The presbytery of Strathbogie visited the school of Marnoch and ascertained that, although they had on February 15, 1749, "recommended all schoolmasters to take particular care that the several schoolhouses should not be alienated to any other purpose than the teaching of youth allenarly, and had ordered every schoolmaster to get an extract of this resolution as a sufficient warrand for them not to give up the schoolhouses for to be used for selling of ale and other abuses at mercats or other publick occasions, which the presbytery understood had been frequently practised, particularly at Marnoch," yet Patrick Gordon of Ordmelly, after being shown a copy of the presbytery's resolution, had by letter demanded from the schoolmaster, John Smith, the keys of the schoolhouse for Marnoch fair on March 6, 1750, and "Mr. Smith still refusing to deliver up the keys, James Gordon, younger of Ordmelly, with several others in company, did on the said day in a violent and riotous manner break open the door both of the schoolhouse and school-chamber, breaking and destroying the seats belonging thereto, and making use of the schoolhouse through that day for selling of ale and other purposes   The presbytery looking upon this as a matter of publick concern   . and having discoursed with Ordmelly thereanent," resolved that they would, "if he persisted in claiming any property in the said schoolhouse in time coming, take care to guard against any encroachments of the like nature, and this they intimated to him" (*Strathbogie Presb. Rec.*)

He married (1) in 1706 Ann, daughter of Robert Bisset of Lessendrum (Temple's *Fermartyn*, p. 252), by whom he had three children who died young; and (2) Mary, eldest daughter of James Duff of Crombie (Baird's *Duffs*, p. 46), by whom he had:—

   1. JAMES, who succeeded to Ardmeallie.
   2. ARCHIBALD, who received from his father, on June 30, 1733 (*Sasines*), the lands of Zeuchrie, part of Ardmeallie, but died, unmarried, in September, 1741, before his father. On April 5, 1753, his brother, James, was served heir to him in these lands (*Index of Heirs*), his father having renounced his right in the lands (*Sasines*, September 28, 1753).
   3. MARY, who married John Gordon of Avochie, in the parish of Huntly, and died on April 5, 1785, leaving issue (Jervise's *Epitaphs*, ii. 382).
   4. HELEN, who married John Innes of Muiryfold, in the parish of Grange, and had no issue.

Peter Gordon, II of Ardmeallie, died at Ardmeallie in April, 1762 (*Marnoch Session Rec.*).

JAMES GORDON, III. OF ARDMEALLIE.

(Son of II. : died 1791.)

James Gordon, III. of Ardmeallie, was the eldest son of Peter Gordon of Ardmeallie. In 1757 he had sasine on February 8 on Ardmeallie, on May 5 on Barrie, and on May 6 on Northfield (*Sasines*).

He married on January 25, 1757, Janet, daughter of John Leith of Leith-Hall (*Scots Mag.*).

He died at Ardmeallie on July 31, 1791 (*Scots Mag.*), and after his death the lands were sold to John Morison, afterwards of Bognie.

THE GORDONS OF COCLARACHIE.

APPENDIX OF DOCUMENTS.

I.

In Dei nomine amen per hoc presens publicum instrumentum cunctis pateat evidenter et sit notum quod anno domini millesimo quingentesimo trigesimo quarto mensis vero Maij [die] decimo octauo Indictione septima pontificatus sanctissimi in Christo patris domini et domini nostri Clementis pape diuini anno vndecimo in notarii publici et testium subscriptorum presentia personaliter constitutus honestus vir Patricius Orum de Cardndavit atturnatus et eo nomine honorabilis domine Jonete Gordoun filie quondam Georgij Gordoun de cujus atturnatus mandato michi notario publico subscripto lucide constabat documento sub data apud Edin-brucht decimo die mensis Aprilis anno regnj supremi domini nostri regis vigesimo quiquidem Patricius Orum atturnatus nominatus quo supra quasdem literas papiro scriptas formam sasine et possessionis in se continentes a nobili et potente domino Jacobo murraue comite ac vicecomite principali de Aberdein sigillo suj officij varrantatas et munitas in medium produxit et presentauit fide digno viro Johanni Bessat vni de maris deputatis vicecomitatus de Aberdein vigore quarum literarum ipsarum Johannem Bessat requisivit quatenus sibi Patricio Orum nominato quo supra statum sasinam et possessionem omnium et singularum terrarum quarte partis terrarum de Kovclairochy cum quarta parte molendini et pertinentiis earundem cum dimedia sexte partis terrarum de Garrye et quarta parte terrarum de Drumdurnotht cum pertinentiis daret et deliberaret secundum vim formam et effectum dictarum literarum dicto maro directarum quasquidem literas per prefatum marum cum reverentia qua decuit receptas michique traditas et intellectas subsequente verborum forma perlegi et ad noticiam circumstantium deduxi James erl of murraif leftenand generall of Scotland and scheref principall of Aberdein to George Bessait mair of fee of the said scherefdoum and to his deputs greiting for samikill as we haif resauit ane precept of our souerane lords chappell charging ws to causs possessioun to be giffin to Jonet Gordoun or hir lauchfull attornay of all and haill the fovrt pairt of the lands of Kovclairoquhy with the fovrt pairt of the myll of the samyn and of the half of the sext pairt of Garry and of the fourt pairt of the lands of Drumdurnotht with thair pertinents as in our souerane lords precept derekit to ws thairapoun mair fullely is contenit of the quhilk precept the tenour follouis Jacobus Dei gratia rex Scotorum

vicecomiti et balliuis suis de Aberdene salutem quia per inquisitionem de mandato
nostro per vos factam et ad capellam nostram returnatam compertum est quod
quondam Elizabet Wentoun mater Jonete Gordoun latoris presentium obijt vltimo
vestita et saisita vt de feodo ad pacem et fidem nostram de totis et integris terris
subscriptis cum suis pertinentiis viz. de quarta parte terrarum de Kovclairoquhy
cum quarta parte molendini eiusdem et dimedia sexte partis terrarum de Garrye et
de quarta parte terrarum de Drumdurnotht cum suis pertinentiis jacentibus in
regalitate de Gareacht infra balliuiam westram et quod dicta Joneta est legitima et
propinquior heres eiusdem Elizabet matris sue de dictis terris cum quarta parte
molendini prenotati cum pertinentiis et quod est legitime etatis et quod de nobis
tenetur in capite Vobis precipimus et mandamus quatenus dicte Jonete aut suo certo
atturnato latori presentium sasinam predictarum terrarum cum quarta parte dicti
molendini cum suis pertinentiis juste habere faciatis sine delatione saluo jure cuilibet
capiendo securitatem de lxx libris de fermis dictarum terrarum cum quarta parte
dicti molendini cum suis pertinentiis existentium in manibus nostris per spacium
septem annorum vltra elapsorum ratione varde que ferme extendentes annuatim ad
x libras nobis debite et hoc nullo modo omittatis presentibus post annum minime
valituris teste me ipso apud Edinbrucht octauo die mensis aprilis anno regni nostri
vigesimo primo We charge you therefor that incontinent thir our lettres sein ye
pass with the said Jonet or with hir lachfull attornay to the said fovrt pairt lands of
Kuovclarachy with the fort pairt myll of the samyn and to the half sext pairt lands
of Garry and to the fovrt pairt lands of Drumdurnotht with thair pertinents and gif
till hir or thaim heritabill stait and possessioun of the said lands with thair pertinents
saiffand all vthir mens rychts becauss we haif takin ane honourable man Villiam
Forbes of crossindavy cautionar and souertie for the byrunning malis of the forsaid
lands awand to our souerane lord efter the form of his precept derekit to ws thairapoun and this on na vaas ye leif ondoun as ye vill ansuyr to ws apoun the executioun
of your office the quhilk to do we commyt to you coniunctly and seueraly our full
povers be this our precept deliuering the samyn be you devly indorsait and execouit
againe to the berar giffin vnder our seall of office at Aberdein the xvi day of Maij in
the zer of God ane thousand vᶜ xxxiiij zers Post quarumquidem literarum lecturam
prefatus Johannes Bessait marus antedictus accessit ad dictam quartam partem de Kovclarrachy et ibidem super solum earundem per traditionem terre et
lapidis ut moris est sasinam et possessionem dictarum terrarum quarte partis de
Kovclarachy cum pertinentiis prefato Patricio Orum atturnato nominato quo supra
tradidit et deliberauit ipsum Patricium nominatum quo supra in quodam domo dicte
quarte partis includens igne extincto habitatoribus expulsis investiuit et inclusit
secundario prefatus marus accessit ad quartam partem molendini de Kovclarrochy
et in omnibus fecit, similiter tertio dictus marus accessit ad dimediam sexte partis de
Garry et in omnibus fecit similiter quarto predictus marus accessit ad quartam
partem terrarum de Drumdurnotht cum suis pertinentiis et in omnibus fecit similiter
et in signum dicte sasine et possessionis antedictus marus elegit sibi bouem vnum
nigri coloris cum cornubus albis pertinentem magistro Johanni Smolt tenenti in dicta

quarta parte de Drumdurnotht   Super quibus omnibus et singulis prefatus Patricius
Orum dum ut premittitur investitus atturnatus nominatus quo supra a me notario
publico subscripto sibi fieri petiit instrumentum vnum vel plura publicum vel publica
Acta erant hec apud Kovclarrachy et molendinum eiusdem et Garry horis decima et
vndecima ante meridiem vel eo circa et apud Drumdurnacht hora quarta post
meridiem aut eo circa sub anno die mense indictione et pontificatu quibus supra
Presentibus ibidem discretis et honestis viris magistro Johanne Gordoun Johanne
Maky Johanne Covbayn Georgio Leslie Patricio Dauistoun magistro Johanne Smolt
testibus ad premissa vocatis pariterque rogatis.

> Et ego Willelmus Dauidsoun presbyter Aberdonensis diocesis sancta
> apostolica auctoritate notarius publicus quia etc

ABSTRACT OF I

Instrument of sasine attesting that on May 18, 1534, Patrick Orum of Cardndavit as "attorney for Jonet Gordoun, daughter of the late George Gordoun," produced letters from James, Earl of Moray, Sheriff Principal of Aberdeen, containing
Crown precept of sasine which enjoined sasine to be given to Jonet Gordoun, as
legitimate and nearest heir of Elizabeth Wentoun, her mother, of the fourth part of
Kovclairoquhy with the mill of the same, of the half of the sixth part of Garrye, and
of the fourth part of Drumdurnotht, and stating that William Forbes of Crossindavy
had become security for £70 Scots, feuduties resting for seven years; and that
accordingly John Bessat, one of the mairs of Aberdeen, gave sasine in presence of
Mr. John Gordoun, John Maky, John Covbayn, George Leslie, Patrick Davistoun
and Mr. John Smolt, the notary being William Davidsoun

On the outside of the Instrument is this note:—"23 Junij, 1554 product. et
admiss in assisa," *i.e.*, "23 June, 1554, produced and admitted in an assize"—evidently
the assize at which Alexander Forbes was found heir to his mother, Jonet Gordon

II.

In Dei nomine amen per hoc presens publicum instrumentum cunctis pateat
evidenter et sit notum quod anno incarnationis dominice millesimo quingentesimo
sexagesimo mensis vero Februarij die decimo Indictione quarta pontificatus Pij pape
quarti anno secundo in mei notarii publici et testium subscriptorum presentiis personaliter constitutus honestus vir Georgius Gordoun hereditarius de Blairrendenny
habens et tenens suis in manibus quandam cartam alienationis pergameno scriptam
cum precepto huiusmodi sasine sub sigillo et subscriptione manuali honesti viri
Alexandri Forbes sigillatam et subscriptam sibi Georgio Gordoun suisque heredibus
et assignatis de et super totis et integris quarte partis omnium et singularum terrarum
de Cokclaroquhy quarte partis ville et terrarum de Nevbiging quarte partis crofte de
Futty vnacum duabus bovatis terrarum de Garry ac etiam quarte partis molendini
de Cokclaroquhy nuncupati molendini de Ryalbain cum terris molendinariis et
astrictis multuris omnium et singularum predictarum terrarum cum universis suis

pertinentiis jacentibus in dominio de Drumblait et infra [vicecomitatum de Aberdeen] per prefatum Alexandrum Forbes factam et concessam quamquidem cartam vnacum precepto sasine discreto viro Andrea Makie balliuo in hac parte dicti Allexandri Forbes et in huiusmodi precepto specialiter nominato exhibuit et presentauit quiquidem balliuus dictam cartam cum precepto huiusmodi in manibus suis recepit et mihi notario subscripto deliberauit . . . quodquidem preceptum perlegi et exposui cuius tenor sequitur subsequenti verborum forma Allexander Forbes portionarius de Cokclaroqûhy dilectis meis . . . coniunctim et diuisim balliuis meis in hac parte specialiter et irrevocabiliter constitutis salutem Quia vendidi et alienaui hereditarie . . . Cokclaroquhy suis heredibus et assignatis totam et integram quartam partem meam omnium et singularum terrarum et molendini subscriptarum viz. quartam partem ville et terrarum de Cokclaroquhy . . mando quatenus sasinam et possessionem hereditariam . . . prefato Georgio Gordoun suis heredibus et assignatis . tradatis . . . sigillum meum proprium est appensum apud Aberdeen septimo die . Presentibus ibidem . . . Gordoun in Cokclarroquhy Jacobo . . ibidem Wilhelmo Bisset ibidem et Johanne . . . in Balquharne testibus ad premissa vocatis . . .

    Et ego vero magister Johannes Grey clericus, etc.

ABSTRACT OF II.

    Instrument of sasine attesting that on February 10, 1560, "George Gordoun, hereditary proprietor of Blairrendenny" produced a charter of sale with precept of sasine, dated at Aberdeen February 7, 1560, by "Alexander Forbes, portioner of Cokclaroquhy," and received sasine in "the fourth part of the town and lands of Cokclaroquhy, the fourth part of the town and lands of Newbiging, the fourth part of the croft of Futty, with the two oxgangs of the lands of Garry, as also the fourth part of the Mill of Cokclaroquhy, commonly called the Mill of Ryalbane . . . lying within the barony of Drumblait and county of Aberdeen"; in presence of . . . Gordoun in Cokclaroquhy, James . . . there, William Bisset there, and John . . . in Balquharne ; the notary being John Grey.

    The instrument is to a large extent illegible through damp. The charter of sale of February 7, 1560, was confirmed under the Great Seal on March 16, 1615 (*Reg. Mag. Sig.*).

III.

    In Dei nomine amen. Per hoc presens publicum instrumentum cunctis pateat evidenter et sit notum quod anno incarnationis dominice millesimo quingentesimo octuagesimo septimo mensis vero Decembris die secundo ac regni S D.N. Jacobi sexti Dei gratia Scotorum regis anno. . . . In mei notarii publici et testium subscriptorum presentiis personaliter comparuit Georgius Gordoune de Coclarathie tenens et habens suis in manibus quandam cartam nobilis et potentis domini Georgii Gordoune comitis de Huntlie etc. preceptum sasine in fine eiusdem continentem sigillo et subscriptione manuali dicti domini Georgii Comitis de Huntlie roboratam de data infrascripta per eundem dominum Comitem confectam datam et concessam dicto Georgio Gordoune de Coclerathie heredibus suis et assignatis de et super totis et integris [terris] quarte partis ville et terrarum de Coclerathie quarte partis de Newbiging crofte de Futtie et quarte partis molendini de Coclerathie nuncupati lie Myll de Ryalbane et quarte partis multurarum omnium et singularum predictarum terrarum et quarte partis silue et nemorum et quarte partis lie Cruikhaiches ex boriale partis aque de Bogy jacentis occupate per Joannem Strachin cum universis et singulis suis pertinentiis jacentibus infra dominium de Drumblet et vicecomitatum de Abirden provido viro Jacobo Duncan de Merdrem balliuo dicti domini Georgii Comitis de Huntlie in hac parte virtute dicti precepti specialiter constituto exhibuit et presentauit Quamquidem cartam preceptum sasine in fine eiusdem continentem prefatus balliuus ad manus recepit et mihi notario publico [subscripto] ad perlegendam publicandam et interpretandam contulit quam ego etiam ab eodem recipiens eandem . . alta et intelligibili voce perlegi et in vulgari nostro idiomate exposui et publicaui cuiusquidem precepti in fine dicte carte [contenti] tenor sequitur et est talis Insuper Jacobo Duncane de Merdrem balliuis nostris coniunctim et diuisim presentium tenore irreuocabiliter constitutis precipimus et firmiter mandamus quatenus vos seu vestrum aliquis ad prefatas terras et molendinum accedat et ibidem per terre et lapidis fundi lie clap et happer vt moris donationem statum sasinam et possessionem hereditariam realem actualem et corporalem totarum et integrarum illarum quarteriarum seu quarte partis ville et terrarum de Coclerathie [etc. as above] prefato Georgio Gordoune de Bleirdenie suis heredibus et assignatis vel ejus procuratori presentium latori juxta formam prescripte carte in omnibus et per omnia indilate tradatis vel tradat ad quod faciendum nostram plenariam et irreuocabilem tenore presentium potestatem In cuius rei testimonium huic presenti carte preceptum sasine in se continenti manu nostra vt sequitur subscripte sigillum nostrum proprium est appensum apud Essilmont vigesimo die mensis Novembris anno domini millesimo quingentesimo octuagesimo septimo coram his testibus domino Patricio Gordoune de Auchindoun milite Jacobo Abircromby et magistro Francisco Cheyne de Crage et sic subscribitur George Erll of Huntlie Post cuiusquidem precepti lecturam et publicationem vt supra dictus Georgius Gordoune dictum Jacobum Duncane balliuum antedictum humiliter et cum instantia requisivit etc. . . . . et in signum huiusmodi possessionis dictus balliuus sibi elegit unam bouem arabilem nigri coloris cornuatam et appretiari fecit ad nouem liberas pecuniarum huius regni super quibus etc. . . . . Acta erant hec etc . Presentibus ibidem Joanne Strachin in Balquharne Joanne Lyonne in Gerrie Wilhelmo Wat in Coclerathie Joanne Reidfurd illicdem Joanne Micheall illicdem et Joanne Gordoune seruitore dicti Jacobi Duncan de Merdrem testibus ad premissa rogatis pariterque vocatis.

> Et ego vero Georgius Cheyne clericus diocesis Aberdonensis regali auctoritate notarius publicus etc.

ABSTRACT OF III.

Instrument of sasine attesting that on December 2, 1587, "George Gordoune of Coclerachie" produced a charter (with precept of sasine) by George, Earl of Huntly, in favour of said George Gordoune—which precept describes the lands as "the fourth part of the town and lands of Coclerachie, the fourth part of Newbiging and croft of Futtie, and the fourth part of the mill of Coclerachie now called myll of Ryalbane, with the mill lands, and the fourth part of the multures of the forsaid lands, of the wood and groves, and the fourth part of Cruikit Haiches lying on the north side of the water of Bogy occupied by John Strachin," and enjoins sasine to be given to "George Gordoune of Bleirdenie," and was signed and sealed at Essilmonth on November 20, 1587, before Sir Patrick Gordoune of Auchindoun, James Abircromby and Mr Francis Cheyne of Crage—and that sasine was given by James Duncan of Merdrem, in presence of John Strachin in Balquharne, John Lyonne in Gerrie, William Wat in Coclerachie, John Reidfurd there, John Micheall there, and John Gordoune, servant to the said James Duncan of Merdrum; the notary being George Cheyne.

IV.

Omnibus hanc cartam visuris vel audituris Georgius Marchio de Huntlie Dominus de Enzie et de Gordoun et Badzenot hereditarius proprietarius terrarum aliorumque infrascriptorum Salutem in Domino sempiternam. Quia virtute cuiusdem contractus initi et confecti inter nos cum consensu et assensu nobilis et potentis principis Ludovici Lennocie ducis Comitis de Dernelie Domini de Tarbolton Methuen et Aubignay et Georgii domini Gordoun et Francisci Gordoun filiorum nostrorum pro eorum interesse super terras aliaque subscripta ab vna et Georgium Gordoun de Coclarachie et Elizabetham alias Bessie Duncan ejus sponsam partibus ab altera pro summa sex millium marcarum vsualis monete regni Scotie nobis per dictum Georgium Gordoun gratanter et integre persoluta predictum Georgium et dictam ejus sponsam heredes suos et assignatos in terris aliisque subscriptis modo subsequente infeodare tenemur prout in dicto contractu de data presentium latius continetur Noveritis igitur nos cum consensu et assensu personarum suprascriptarum dedisse concessisse vendidisse alienasse et hac presenti carta nostra confirmasse . . memoratis Georgio Gordoun et Elizabethe alias Bessie Duncan ejus sponse eorumque alteri diutius viventi in conjuncta infeodatione et heredibus masculis dicti Georgii Gordoun et assignatis quibuscunque hereditarie totas et integras terras nostras tres quarterias seu quartas partes davate terrarum de Coclarachie viz. ville de Coclarachie et crofte vocate crofte de Futtye terrarum de Newbiging et Lytle Mylne et tres quarterias nostras molendini de Coclarachie molendini de Ryalebane nuncupati terrarum molendinariarum multurarum et sequelorum eiusdem cum omnibus et singulis earundem domibus . . . jacentes infra vicecomitatum de Aberdene vnacum decimis garbalibus dictarum trium quarteriarum. . . . Tenendas et habendas totas et integras prefatas tres quarterias . . . de me heredibus meis

masculis et assignatis . . . Reddendo inde . . . vsualis monete regni Scotie . . .
Et nos vero prefatus Georgius Marchio de Huntlie . . . prefatas tres quarterias . . .
contra omnes mortales varrantizabimus . . . Insuper dilectis meis Johanni Leyth in
Bucharne et vestrum cuilibet . . . In cujus rei testimonium huic carte nostre ex
chirographo magistri Roberti Bissat scribe manu nostra subscripte sigillum nostrum
est appensum apud Huntlye vigesimo primo die mensis Maij anno domini millesimo
sexcentesimo decimo septimo coram his testibus Hugone Gordoun de Cultis Patricio
Mortimer filio quondam Johannis Mortimer de Cragivar Johanne Andersone in
Dunbennan et dicto Magistro Roberto Bissat.

To the charter this note is appended :—

Sasina data 23 Maij 1617 per Johannem Leyth in Bucharne balivum Hugoni
Gordoun attornato dictarum terrarum inter septimam et octauam matutinam pre-
sentibus ibidem Alexandro Pyrie Gulielmo Gallan Alexandro Gib in Coclarachie et
Alexandro Laird servitore dicti Georgii testibus ad premissa vocatis et rogatis

M. R. BISSET, notarius publicus.

ABSTRACT OF IV

Charter by George, Marquis of Huntly, in favour of George Gordoun of
Coclarachie and Elisabeth, alias Bessie, Duncan, his spouse, of the three fourth
parts of the davach lands of Coclarachie, in implement of a contract of sale of same
date whereby the said Marquis sold the said lands for 6,000 merks to said George
Gordon and his spouse, reserving power of redemption   The charter is signed and
sealed at Huntlye May 21, 1617, in presence of Hugh Gordon of Cultis, Patrick
Mortimer son of the late John Mortimer of Cragivar, John Andersone in Dunbennan,
and Mr. Robert Bissat writer of the charter.

V.

Omnibus hanc cartam visuris vel audituris Georgius Gordoune de Coclarachie
hereditarius proprietarius terrarum aliorumque subscriptorum salutem in Domino
sempiternam.   Quia virtute cujusdem obligationis per me factae datae et concessae
dilectae meae Bessetae alias Elizabethe Duncan meae sponsae pro causis in eadem
contentis ipsam in vitali redditu pro toto tempore vitae suae in terris aliisque subscriptis modo subsequente infeodare teneor prout in dicta obligatione de data apud
Colpnay septimo die mensis Julii anno domini millesimo sexcentesimo decimo
septimo latius continetur Noveritis igitur me dedisse concessisse et hac presenti
carta mea confirmasse . . . memoratae Elizabethe alias Bessie Duncan meae sponsae
in vitali redditu pro toto tempore vitae suae totam et integram meam quarteriam seu
quartam partem davatae terrarum de Coclarachie viz. . . . jacentem in baronia de
Drumblait infra vicecomitatum de Aberdeen Tenendam et habendam . . . Insuper
dilectis meis   . . In cujus rei testimonium huic presenti cartae preceptum sasinae
in se continenti ex chirographo Magistri Roberti Bisset scribae manu mea subscriptae

sigillum meum est appensum apud Coclarachie octauo die mensis Augusti anno domini millesimo sexcentesimo decimo septimo coram his testibus Alexandro Gordoun in Mairdrum meo filio Johanne Gordoun in . . . ismilne et dicto Magistro Roberto Bisset

Alex' Gordoun vitns	George gordoune
Jhon Gordoun vitnes	of Coclarachye
	M. R Bisset witnes

ABSTRACT OF V.

Charter by which George Gordon of Coclarachie, being bound, by an obligation dated at Colpnay, July 7, 1617, to infeft his beloved spouse, Bessie Duncan, in certain lands in liferent, grants to the said Bessie Duncan his fourth part of the lands of Coclarachie in liferent. The charter is signed at Coclarachie August 8, 1617, in presence of Alexander Gordoun in Mairdrum, his son, John Gordoun in . . . and M' Robert Bisset, writer of the charter.

VI

Omnibus hanc cartam visuris vel audituris Georgius Gordoun de Coclarachie proprietarius terrarum molendinorum aliorumque subscriptorum eternam in Domino Salutem. Quia virtute contractus matrimonialis initi et confecti inter me pro me ipso et onus in me pro Georgio Gordoun nepote meo suscipientem et dictum Georgium Gordoun juniorem pro se ipso suoque interesse cum consensu Alexandri Gordoun de Merdrum et Magistri Gulielmi Gordoun medicine doctoris curatorum prefati Georgii Gordoun junioris pro eorum interesse dictumque Alexandrum Gordoun de Merdrum pro se ipso jure et titulo suo ab vna et Alexandrum Setoun de Petmedden pro se et onus in eum pro Griselda Setoun filia eius legittima [suscipientem] dictamque Griseldam pro se et suo interesse partibus ab altera de data presentium teneor et astringor prefatum Georgium Gordoun juniorem in villis terris molendinis aliisque subscriptis modo et forma infra designatis infeodare Noveritis igitur me dictum Georgium Gordoun de Coclarachie pro perimpletione illius partis dicti contractus matrimonialis penes hoc infeofamentum conficiendum et intuitu dicti matrimonii secundum formam eiusdem contractus dedisse concessisse alienasse et hac presenti carta mea confirmasse . . dicto Georgio Gordoun nepoti meo et heredibus masculis inter eum et prefatam Griseldam Setoun procreandis quibus deficientibus dicto Georgio Gordoun juniori et heredibus suis masculis et assignatis quibuscumque omnes et singulas villas et terras meas de Overblairtoun alias vocato Colpnay ad boream cum pendiculo eiusdem vocato Vastburne cum molendino jam pridem super terris de Overblairtoun edificato cum terris molen-dinariis multuris sequelis croftis et pertinentiis earundem villam et terras de Pettens cum omnibus earundem domibus . . . jacentes infra baroniam de Baheluie et vicecomitatum de Aberdeen Reservando Jeanne Gordoun domine de Crag vitalem

suum redditum terrarum de Pettens cum pertinentiis et dimedii pendiculi terrarum
de Wastburne juxta titulo quem de iisdem habet (sine periculo vitalis redditus dicte
Griselde· Setoun terrarum de Overblairtoun eiusdem et alterius medii
pendiculi de Wastburne et croftarum eedem dispositarum virtute dicti contractus)
necnon totam et integram quartam partem lie Davauche landis de Coclarachie viz.
. . . jacentem infra baroniam de Drumblaitt et vicecomitatum antedictum necnon
alias tres quartas partes meas dictarum terrarum vocatarum Davauch landis
de Coclarachie viz. . . . jacentes infra dictum vicecomitatum de Aberdeen . . .
Reservando tamen mihi et Bessete Duncan mee sponse vitales nostros redditus totius
dicte ville et terrarum vocatarum the Davache landis de Coclarachie . . . Et ego
vero dictus Georgius Gordoun de Coclarachie heredes mei . . . omnes et singulas
predictas terras . (exceptis vitalibus redditibus dicte Jeanne Gordoun et Griselde
Setoun et annuo redditu dicto Alexandro Gordoun trecentarum marcarum spectanti-
bus et exceptis vitali meo redditu et predicte mee conjugis terrarum suprascriptarum
cum pertinentiis vt premissum est) contra omnes mortales warrantizabimus . . .
Insuper dilectis meis . . . In cujus rei testimonium huic presenti carte mee preceptum
sasine in se continenti manu Magistri Gulielmi Barclay advocati scripte manu mea
subscripte sigillum meum proprium armorum est appensum apud Coclarachie decimo
septimo die mensis Maii anno domini millesimo sexcentesimo vigesimo nono coram
his testibus Magistro Roberto Bisset de Lessindrum Alexandro Gordoun de Mardrom
Johanne Jessiman meo servitore et Magistro Roberto Petrie scriba.　　　　·

    Alexᵈ Gordoun Vitnes　　　　　　　　　　George gordoune

      M. R. Bisset witness　　　　M. Robert Petrie witness
      Jhon Jessiman vitnes

ABSTRACT OF VI.

    Charter by which George Gordoun of Coclarachie (in implement of a marriage
contract of same date between himself and his grandson George Gordoun, with consent of Alexander Gordoun of Merdrum and Mᵣ William Gordoun, doctor of medicine,
as curators of said George Gordoun, junior, on the one part, and Alexander Setoun
of Petmedden and his daughter, Grissell Setoun, on the other part) grants to George
Gordoun, his grandson, "the town and lands of Overblairtoun otherwise called
Colpnay on the north with the pendicle of the same called Vastburne, with the mill
. . . and the town and lands of Pettens . . . lying within the barony of Baheluie and
county of Aberdeen (Reserving to Jean Gordoun, lady of Crag, her liferent of the
lands of Pettens . . .), as also the fourth part of the davauche lands of Coclarachie
. . . as also the other three fourth parts of said davauch lands of Coclarachie . .
(Reserving to himself and his spouse, Bessie Duncan, their liferents of said davauch
lands of Coclarachie)" The charter was written by Mᵣ William Barclay, advocate,
and signed at Coclarachie May 17, 1629, in presence of Mᵣ Robert Bisset of Lessindrum, Alexander Gordoun of Mardrom, John Jessiman, servant to George Gordoun,
senior, and Mᵣ Robert Petrie, writer

VII.

Omnibus hanc cartam visuris vel audituris Georgius Gordone de Coclarachie hereditarius proprietarius terrarum aliorumque subscriptorum eternam in domino salutem. Noveritis me pro observatione certe partis literarum dispositionis per me Grissille Settone mee conjugi in vitali redditu durantibus omnibus sue vite diebus de data presentium factarum datarum et concessarum proque causis onerosis inibi expressis assedasse . . . prefate Grissille Settone mee conjugi in vitali redditu durantibus omnibus sue vite diebus totam et integram quartam partem ville et terrarum de Coclarachie quartam partem ville et terrarum de Newbigging quartam partem crofte de Futtie cum duabus davatis terrarum de Garrie ac quartam partem molendini de Coclarachie nunc vocatum molendinum de Ryalban cum terris molendinariis . . . jacentes infra dominium de Drumblait et vicecomitatum de Aberdein ad me hereditarie spectantes necnon totas et integras meas alias tres quarterias seu quartas partes dictarum terrarum de Coclarachie crofte de Futtie Newbigging et molendini de Coclarachie . . jacentes vt supra . . Insuper dilectis meis . . . In cujus rei testimonium huic presenti carte mee manu Andree Massie notarii publici scripte manuque mea subscripte sigillum meum proprium armorum est appensum apud Aberdein decimo quinto die mensis Decembris anno domini millesimo sexcentesimo quadragesimo tertio coram his testibus magistro Alexandro Davidsone advocato Richardo Rutherfuird burgensi burgi de Aberdein et Andrea Massie predicto.

ABSTRACT OF VII.

Charter by which George Gordon of Coclarachie (in implement of letters of disposition of same date) grants to Grissell Seton, his spouse, his fourth part of Coclarachie and also the other three fourth parts, in liferent The charter was signed at Aberdeen, December 15, 1643, in presence of Mr. Alexander Davidson, advocate, Richard Rutherfuird, burgess of Aberdeen, and Andrew Massie, notary, writer of the charter.

VIII.

Omnibus hanc cartam visuris vel audituris Georgius Gordoune de Cocklarachie hereditarius proprietarius terrarum molendini aliorumque subscriptorum salutem in domino sempiternam. Noveritis me pro perimpletione mee partis cuiusdam contracti matrimonialis inter me ab vna et Elizabetam Fraser relictam quondam Willielmi Meldrum de Haltoune ab altera partibus de data presentium initi et confecti virtute cuiusquidam contracti dictam Elizabetam Fraser in vitali redditu et pro omnibus sue vite diebus in terris molendino aliisque subscriptis modo subsequente infeodare teneor igitur dedisse . . . prefate Elizabete Fraser . . . totas et integras tres quarterias davate terrarum de Cocklarachie viz. . ac etiam totam et integram illam alteram quartenam seu quartam partem dicte ville et terrarum de Cocklarachie . . . tanquam principales necnon totas et integras villas et terras de Altoune et Newtoune de Monedies terras et villam de Whytmuire terras et villam de Muireailhous villas et terras de Myresyde et villas et terras de Carnehills . . . omnes jacentes infra parochiam de Aberchirder et vicecomitatum de Banff et hoc in speciale varrantum et securitatem dicte Elizabete Fraser . . . In cujus rei testimonium presentibus (per Patricium Fraserum scribam Edinburgi scriptis) manu mea subscriptis sigillum meum est appensum apud Fraserburghe die mensis tredecimo Decembris anno domini millesimo sexcentesimo quadragesimo quinto coram his testibus Alexandro Frasero de Philorth Joanne Fraser de Pittulie Joanne Baird clerico vicecomitatus de Banff et dicto Patricio Frasero testibus ad premissa vocatis rogatis et requisitis.

ABSTRACT OF VIII.

Charter by which George Gordoune of Cocklarachie (being bound by a matrimonial contract of same date between himself and Elizabeth Fraser, relict of the late William Meldrum of Haltoun, to infeft the said Elizabeth in the liferent of certain lands) grants to said Elizabeth Fraser in liferent the three fourth parts of the davach lands of Cocklarachie . . . and also the other fourth part . . . as the principal lands, and also, as warrandice lands, "the towns and lands of Altoune and Newtoune of Monedies, the town and lands of Whytmuire, the town and lands of Muireailhous, the towns and lands of Myresyde, and the towns and lands of Carnehills . . . all lying within the parish of Aberchirder and county of Banff". The charter was signed at Fraserburgh, December 13, 1645, in presence of Alexander Fraser of Philorth, John Fraser of Pittulie, John Baird, sheriff clerk of Banff, and Patrick Fraser, writer, Edinburgh, writer of the charter.

IX..

In Dei nomine amen. Per hoc presens publicum instrumentum cunctis pateat evidenter et sit notum quod anno incarnationis dominice millesimo sexcentesimo sexagesimo quarto mensis vero Maii die vigesimo quarto regnique S D. N. Caroli secundi Dei gratia Magne Britanie Francie et Hibernie regis illustrissimi fideique defensoris anno decimo sexto In mei notarii publici ac testium subscriptorum presentia in fundis terrarum molendini terrarum molendinariarum aliorumque subtusscriptorum personaliter comparuit Petrus Chalmer servitor Elisabethe Fraser domine de Cocklarachie procurator pro et nomine Issabelle Meldrum filie legittime quondam Willielmi Meldrum aliquando de Haltoun habens et tenens suis in manibus quendam contractum matrimonialem initum et confectum inter Johannem Forbes de Asloune pro seipso et onus in se suscipientem pro Willielmo Forbes ejus filio legittimo natu maximo et dictum Willielmum Forbes pro seipso cum speciali consensu memorati Johannis Forbes sui patris et utrumque cum uno consensu et assensu

ab vna et dictam Issabellam Meldrum ab altera partibus de data apud Cocklarachie
sexto die Maii proximo elapso Quis contractus continet preceptum sasine subinsertum
in fine ejusdem. . . . Quemquidem contractum . . . prefatus Petrus Chalmer. . . .
Waltero Forbes de Blacktoun balivo in hac parte per dictum preceptum specialiter
constituto presentavit . . . cujus precepti sasine saltem partis hujus in favorem
dicte Issabelle tenor sequitur et est talis And for infefting of the said Isabell
Meldrum in her conjunct fee and warrandice lands particularlie aboverehearsed, the
said John Forbes, elder of Asloun hes made . . . Walter Forbes of Blacktoun . . .
his baillies in that pairt requyring and desyring them . . . to passe . . . and give
and deliver . . . possession of the saids ten chalders victuall besyds the customes
(reserving two chalders of the saids ten in maner abovementioned) yeirlie to be
uplifted foorth of the saids toûnes and lands of Dorrisaill, the Muir Badinapeat, the
croft called the Brigend of Alfoord and of that pleughe of the Maynes called the
Overtoun, and in speciall warrandice of the samen, of so much rent foorth of the
saids lands and Maynes of Asloun and miln of the samen with the miln . . . as will
be answerable and equivalent to any prejudice or distres the said William Forbes
or Issabell Meldrum his said future spous shall sustayne during her lyfetyme through
want of any pairt or portioun of her lyferent lands abovewritten, to the said Issabell
Meldrum. . . . In witnes whereoff both the saids parties have subscribed thir
presents with their hands (writtin be Alexander Cuie, servitor to Robert Sharp,
shereff clerk of Banff) day yeir and place forsaids befor thir witnesses Adam Forbes
late tutor of Brux and John Forbes and James Miln servitors to the said Elisabeth
Fraser. . . . Post cujusquidem contractus . . . perlecturam etc. . . . Coram his
testibus Roberto Forbes filio legittimo dicti Johannis Forbes de Asloun Petro
Taylior in Asloun Willielmo Greinlaw servitore dicti Willielmi Forbes et Waltero
Innes servitore dicti Walteri Forbes de Blacktoun et diversis aliis ad premissa rogatis
et requisitis.

Ego vero Walterus Simson clericus Aberdonensis diocesis . . .
notarius publicus etc.

ABSTRACT OF IX.

Instrument of sasine attesting that on May 24, 1664, Peter Chalmer, servant
of Elisabeth Fraser, lady of Cocklarachie, as procurator for Issabella Meldrum, lawful
daughter of the late William Meldrum of Haltoun, produced a matrimonial contract
(dated at Cocklarachie, May 6, 1664) between John Forbes of Asloune and William
Forbes, his eldest lawful son, on the one part, and the said Issabella Meldrum, on
the other part, by which she is to be liferented in ten chalders victuall of Dorrisaill,
Muir Badinapeat, the croft called the Brigend of Alfoord, and of that pleughe of the
Mayns called the Overtoun, and in special warrandice, in so much rent of the Mains
of Asloun and mill thereof as will be equivalent to any prejudice sustained by want
of any part of her liferent lands; and that Walter Forbes of Blacktoun, as bailie,
gave sasine in common form, in presence of Robert Forbes, lawful son of said John

Forbes of Asloun, Peter Taylor in Asloun, William Greinlaw servant of said William Forbes, Walter Innes servant of said Walter Forbes of Blacktoun, and other witnesses; the notary being Walter Simson.

X.

In Dei nomine amen   Per hoc presens publicum instrumentum cunctis pateat evidenter et sit notum quod anno incarnationis dominice millesimo sexcentesimo septuagesimo nono mensis vero Decembris die decimo sexto et anno regni S. D N Caroli secundi Dei gratia Magne Britannie Francie et Hibernie regis fideique defensoris trigesimo primo   In mei notarii publici subscribentis et testium subscriptorum presentiis personaliter comparuit egregius vir Georgius Keith de Northfeild tanquam actornatus et in nomine Anne Baird filie legitime honorabilis viri domini Jacobi Baird de Auchmedden militis et sponse apparentis honorabilis etiam viri Johannis Gordon de Cocklarachie . . . et accessit unacum discreto viro Johanne Symson in Cocklarachie balivo in hac parte dictorum Johannis Gordon et Elizabethe Fraser domine de Cocklarachie ejus matris per preceptum sasine subscriptum ad effectum subtusmentionatum specialiter constituto ad solum et fundum terrarum aliorumque subscriptorum habens et suis in manibus tenens quendam contractum matrimonialem initum et confectum inter dictum Johannem Gordon cum speciali avisamento et consensu dicte Elizabethe Fraser sue matris pro omni jure vitalis redditus. . . et dictam Elizabetham pro seipsa et eos unanimi consensu et assensu ab una et dictum dominum Jacobum Baird et Jacobum Baird de Auchmedden juniorem ejus filium legitimum natu maximum pro seipsis et onus in se suscipientes pro dicta Anna Baird et eandem Annam pro seipsa cum dicti sui patris et fratris consensu partibus ab altera datum apud Auchmedden et Cocklarachie tertio et decimo quinto diebus mensis Decembris instantis virtute cujus contractus dicti Johannes Gordon et Elizabetha Fraser contemplatione matrimonii tunc contracti brevique (Deo juvante) solemnizandi inter dictum Johannem Gordon et Annam Baird dictam Annam in conjuncta infeodatione et vitali redditu durantibus omnibus sue vite diebus in totis et integris terris aliisque subscriptis viz. . . infeodare tenentur . quemquidem contractum matrimonialem preceptum sasine in se continentem dictus Georgius Keith . . . dicto Johanni Symson . . . exhibuit et presentavit . . . cujus precepti sasine tenor sequitur et est talis Attoure to the effect the said Anna Baird may be infeft and saised in the lands and uthers abovewriten . . . the said John Gordon and Elizabeth Fraser . . . hes made and constitute   . John Symson in Cocklarachie . . . their balzies in that part commanding and requiring them . . to passe and give and deliver state and saising .   off all and haill the said two pleughes off land off the mayns off Cocklarachie, the pleughe off land off Meikletowne, the towne and lands off Fittie, the towne and lands off Coulles and haughe bewest the water off Bogie, the pleughe off land off Litlemilne with the newmilne off Cocklarachie milnelands multurs and sequelles theroff, the two crofts besyde the stainewarde and Broomhill croft . . . to the said Anna Baird in lyffrent .   reserving alwayes to the said Elizabeth Fraser her lyffrent off the said pleughe off land off Litlemilne, milne and milnelands off Cocklarachie, two crofts besyde the staniewarde and Broomhill croft . . In witnesse wheroff thir presents (written be John Urquhart servitor to the said Sir James Baird) are subscryved be bothe the saids parties with ther hands place day moneth and year off God respective abovewriten before thir witnesses Alexander master off Salton Alexander Bisset off Lessindrum James Gordon off Ardmellie William Symson notar publick in Turreff and the said John Urquhart George Keith off Northfield James Baird sone lawful to the said James Baird and John Symson servitor to the said John Gordon. . . Presentibus ibidem Roberto Duncan in Boigheid Johanne Young Thoma Skinner Georgio Mill Alexandro Browster et Johanne Ogston in Cocklarachie testibus ad premissa rogatis et requisitis.

Et ego vero Gulielmus Symson clericus Aberdonensis diocesis notarius publicus etc.

ABSTRACT OF X.

Instrument of sasine attesting that on December 16, 1679, George Keith of Northfield, as procurator for Anna Baird, daughter of Sir James Baird of Auch-medden, produced a matrimonial contract (dated at Auchmedden and Coclarachie December 3 and 15, 1679, and witnessed as above) between John Gordon of Coc-larachie and his mother, Elizabeth Fraser, on the one part, and Sir James Baird of Auchmedden, and James Baird, junior of Auchmedden, his eldest lawful son, and Anna Baird, on the other part, whereby the said John Gordon bound himself to infeft the said Anna Baird, his apparent spouse, in liferent in certain lands of Coclarachie, and that John Symson in Cocklarachie, as bailie, gave sasine in common form in presence of Robert Duncan in Boigheid, John Young, Thomas Skinner, George Mill, Alexander Browster and John Ogston in Cocklarachie, the notary being William Symson

XI

Marriage Contract between Alexander Leslie of Little Wartle and Janet Gordon, September 26, 1696.

At Coclarachie, September 26, 1696 years, it is aggreed finally ended and matri-monially contracted betwixt the parties following they are to say Alexander Lessly of Litle Wartle as haveing the undoubted heretable right of the lands and others underwrytten with the pertinents for himself on the one pairt and Mris. Jannet Gordone sister german to John Gordone of Coclarachie her brother for herself with his consent and he as takeing the sole burden on him for her and also with the speciall advyce and consent of Alexander Gordone of Auchintoule and James Gordone of Ardmeallie her other two brothers on the other pairt in manner . . . following . . . In contemplatione of whilk marriage . . the said John Gordone be thir presents binds . . . him . . . to . . . pay . · to the said Alexander Lessley . . .

(163)

the soume of three thousand merks . . . whilk soume . . . are accepted . . . in full contentatione and satisfactione to them of all bonds of provisione bairns pairt of gear deads third or other provisione naturall that they or ayther of them can ask or crave anie manner of way from the said John Gordone be or throw his deceis or be deceis of umquhill George Gordone of Coclarachie his father or umquhill Elizabeth Fraser his mother or be deceis of Charles Gordone his brother or ani wayes whatsomever . . . In witness wherof both the saids parties have subscribed thir presents with their hands (written be James Gordon second sone to William Gordone of Westseat) day moneth place and year of God abovewritten befor thir witnesses, Mr James Lessly eldest lawfull sone to Mr Alexander Lessly minister at Croill and the said William and James Gordone wrytter heirof.

XII.

Marriage contract between James Lunan and Anna Gordon, May 29 and 30, 1712.

At Logie and Culclarachie the twenty nynt and threttie day of May respective sevintein hundreth and tuelve yeires it is apoynted matrimonially contracted . . . betuixt the pairties following they are to say Master James Lunend eldest lawfull son to Master Alexander Lunend preacher of the Gospell att Daviot heretable proprietour of the lands teinds and others vnderwritten with advyce and consent of his said father and of Janet Elphingstoun his mother for all ryght of lyfrent . . . and the said Master Alexander Lunend as taikand burden on him for his said son and spous abovenamed and they all with one consent on the ane pairt and Mris. Anna Gordon second lawfull dochter to John Gordon of Culclarachie for herself with consent of her said father and he taikand burden in and upon him for his said dochter and they both with one consent on the other pairt in maner . . . following . . . in contemplation of quhilk marriage . . . the said Master Alexander Lunend . . . binds . . . him to . . . saise the said Master James Lunend his eldest lawfull son and the said Mris. Ann Gordon his futur spous . . . in the westsyd of the lands of Kirktown of Daviot . . . and also . . in the eastsyd of the said Kirktown of Daviot . . . lying within the parochen of Daviot and sherefdom of Aberdeen as also the libertie of ane weikly mercatt to be holden att the said Kirktown of Daviot and of ane yeirly fair or mercatt ther to be holden at St. Colme's day . . . Attoure . . . the said Master Alexander Lunen hes made . . . Alexander Gordon of Caldwells . . . his baillies in that pairt . . . In witness wheroff both the saids parties have subscribed thir presents with ther hands (written be William Gordon of Westseat) day moneth places and yeir of God abovewritten befor thir witnesses . . . Sir James Elphingstoun of Logie Patrick Lunen lawfull son to the said Mr Alexander Lunen . . . Sir Samuel Forbes of Foveran Robert Crookshank gardner at Culclarachie and the said William Gordon wryter forsaid.

GIGHT.

BY

JOHN MALCOLM BULLOCH, M.A.

NEW SPALDING CLUB.

Y

PREFATORY NOTE.

THE great source of information about the Gight Gordons is the *Privy Council Register*, and the importance of the family is so great, and their lawlessness is so vividly described there, that I have not hesitated to quote at length. The *Balbithan MS.* contains a good account of the family (pp 15-8). Dr. Temple in his *Thanage of Fermartyn* (pp. 72-8) gives a deduction based on the *Balbithan MS.* I have consulted a great many other authorities, who will be found cited in the course of the history, which is an enlargement of two different sets of articles contributed by me to the *Aberdeen Free Press*, November 11, 18 and 25, December 21, 1898, and March 25, 1899, to *Scottish Notes and Queries*, February, 1899-February, 1900. I have been unable to discover the whereabouts of the contents of the Gight charter chest I am indebted for help to Rev. Dr. Temple, Mr. Murray Rose, Rev. Dr. Milne, Fyvie; Mr. A. M Munro, Aberdeen; and others, notably Rev. Stephen Ree, Boharm; and Captain Wimberley, Inverness, who have read the proof sheets—a very laborious task. I have dealt in a more or less narrative fashion with the two most famous members of the family, Colonel John Gordon, who was implicated in the assassination of Wallenstein, 1634, and Colonel Nathaniel Gordon, the Royalist, who was executed at St. Andrews, 1646.

J. M. B.

118 PALL MALL, S.W.,
September 29, 1902.

THE LAIRDS OF GIGHT.

GEORGE GORDON, 2nd Earl of Huntly = PRINCESS ANNABELLA STUART.

SIR WILLIAM GORDON, I. of Gight.

GEORGE, II.	JAMES, of Cairnbannoch.	JOHN, IV. of Gight.
GEORGE, III. (now represented by several peers).	JOHN.	WILLIAM, V.
	COLONEL JOHN, Assassinated Wallenstein.	GEORGE, VI.

GEORGE, VII.

GEORGE, VIII.

GEORGE IX.

ALEXANDER DAVIDSON = MARIE GORDON, X.
of Newton. of Gight.

ALEXANDER GORDON, XI.

GEORGE GORDON, XII.

CATHERINE GORDON (Mrs. Byron),
XIII., last of Gight, died 1811.

GIGHT.

THE lands of Gight lie in the parish of Fyvie. The name "Gight" is
possibly derived from the Gaelic word *Gaothach*, pronounced "Ghuach,"
meaning a windy place. Locally it is pronounced "Gecht". The lands
have been held by two different branches of the Gordons since 1467
In that year they came into the possession of Sir William Gordon,
third son of George, second Earl of Huntly, and were held by his
descendants until 1787, when they were sold to the third Earl of
Aberdeen, representing the Gordons of Haddo, who are descended from
"Jock" Gordon of Scurdargue, the natural cousin of Elizabeth Gordon
who was the founder of the House of Huntly The Gight Gordons
have gained more notoriety than almost any other cadet in view of the
fact that Lord Byron represented their line, and by reason of their
extraordinary spirit of revolt which was exemplified in the poet's strange
career, and is summed up in a number of well-known "frets" —

> (1) Twa men sat down by Ythan Brae
> The ane did to the ither say—
> "And what sic men may the Gordons o'
> Gight hae been ? "

> (2) When the heron leaves the tree
> The laird o' Gight shall landless be.

> (3) At Gight three men a violent death sall dee,
> And efter that the land shall lie in lea.

The career of the first branch, which ended with the "unlucky" number,
the thirteenth laird, was certainly crowded with murder and sudden
death ; and from first to last was dominated by a spirit of revolt against
the established order of things unequalled in the history of any other
branch of the House of Gordon. Consequently, the career of the Gight
family has been a happy hunting-ground for the modern theorists on

"degeneracy," and a great deal has been written about the family, though, curiously enough, this is almost the first chapter-and-date investigation. It must however be admitted that in the case of the Gight Gordons, history completely verifies the traditionary character of the family. One may sum up the disasters which attacked the family in tabular form, so that the reader may see at a glance what to expect.

The 1st Laird of Gight *fell* at Flodden
 One son *killed* at Pinkie (?)
 One son-in-law was *murdered.*
 One son-in-law *fell* at Pinkie
 Three grandsons (including the 3rd Laird) were *murdered.*
 One grandson was *executed.*
 One grandson was *drowned*
 One grandson *fell* in Holland
 One grandson *fell* in Flanders
 One grand-daughter's husband was *murdered* (by her own brother)
  Two great-grandsons were *murdered*
  One great-grandson *assassinated* Wallenstein
  One great-grandson *fell* in Holland.
  One great-grandson died in *prison.*
  One great grand-daughter's husband was *poisoned.*
  One great-grand-daughter was *arrested* for an assault (on a man).
  One great-grand-daughter was *excommunicated.*
   One great great-grandson *decamped* to Germany
   One great great-grandson was *murdered.*
   One great great-grandson was *executed*
   One great great-grandson was *killed* in Paris (?)
    One great great great-grandson (8th Laird) *besieged* his own mother's house
     The 11th Laird (great-grandson of the 8th) was *drowned* (? *suicide*).
     His son,
      The 12th Laird, was *drowned* (? *suicide*) It was his daughter,
      The 13th and last Laird, who married Captain Byron.

The house of Gight, which is now a complete ruin, stands most picturesquely on the brink of a rocky eminence, looking down upon the beautiful valley of the river Ythan. I cannot say exactly when the house became a ruin. In May, 1644, the Covenanters had done much to destroy it, as related by Spalding (*The Trubles*, Spalding Club Edition, ii., 369):—

Thay [the Covenanters] tuke out the staitlie insicht and plenishing, sic as bedding, naiprie, veschell caldrouns, chandleris, fyre veschell, quhairof thair wes plenty ; kistis, cofferis, cabinetis, trvnkis, and all vther plenishing and armour (quhairof thair wes [of course] plentie . . .), quhilk thay could get careit on horss or foot, bot wes takin away south : togidder with the haill oxin, nolt, ky, horss, meiris, and scheip, quhilkis war vpone the said Maynes of Haddoche and Geicht, and not ane four footed best left that thay could get. When thir commodeteis wes plunderit and spolzeit, then thay began to wirk vpone the tymber warkis quhilkis war fixt, and thair thay cruellie brak doun the wanescot burdes, bedis, capalmries, tymber wallis, sylring, toome girnellis and the lyk, and maid fyre of all. Thay took out the iron yettis, iron stauncheouns of windois, brak doun the glassin windois and left nather yett, dur, nor wyndo onbrokin doun , and, in effect, left thame desolat befoir thay removit.

This was not the final finishing of the house; but I suspect that the actual decay of the place began during the absences of Mrs. Byron's grandmother in Banff and of her father in England. That the place was going to rack and ruin during his ownership is shown by the observation of the writer of the article on Fyvie in the new *Statistical Account* (1845) He says :—

The burial place of the family of Gordon of Gight is in the parish churchyard. Formerly it was within the old church, and, upon the new church being built, my predecessor acquainted the Honourable Mrs. Byron of the altered situation in which it stood as being now exposed ; and put in her view the propriety of raising some protection round it, but without success.

In Byron's time the castle was in ruins, for he described it in *Childe Harold's Pilgrimage* (canto iii., stanza 47) as—

Worn, but unstooping to the baser crowd,
All tenantless save to the crannying wind,
Or holding dark communion with the cloud.
There was a day when they were young and proud ,
Banners on high and battles passed below;
But they who fought are in a bloody shroud,
And those which waved are shredless dust ere now,
And the bleak battlements shall bear no future blow

Sir William Allan, M P., in the *Rose of Methlic*, describes the ruins thus :—

Like some old eagle's barren nest,
High perched upon a rocky crest,
The ruined castle, grim and grey,
Still beautiful in cold decay,
Looks down upon the glen beneath,
In silent majesty of death.

They were described in Sir Andrew Leith Hay's *Castellated Architecture of Aberdeenshire*, they were pictured by Mrs J B. Pratt in her husband's ·book on *Buchan* (1858) There is an excellent ground-plan of Gight Castle in Macgibbon and Ross's *Castellated and Domestic Architecture of Scotland*, 1888 (i., 322). The writers say :—

> The plan of the ground floor is well preserved, and is somewhat remarkable. It is on the L plan, but the door enters in the centre of one limb, and has a long passage running right through the building to the staircase, which is in the centre of the back wall. The same arrangement may be observed at Craig Castle. From a bend in the passage a shot-hole commands the entrance door. In the vault of the lobby adjoining the door there is a small compartment of ribbed and groined vaulting, which is a feature peculiar to several castles in Aberdeenshire. The kitchen has the usual large fire-place, and a service window to the stair. The other compartments, which are vaulted, were bakehouse and cellars, one having the private stair down from the hall The hall, which occupies the principal portion of the building on the first floor, was a spacious apartment, 37 ft. by 21 ft It is entered in a peculiar manner, by a stair through one of the window recesses, the stair to the cellar, which was also continued up to the upper floors, also entering from a similar door in the opposite side of the window recess. A small vaulted room is obtained between the hall and the private room, and the walls of the latter are riddled with wall chambers in the manner common in the fifteenth century. From the thickness of the walls, and the number of wall chambers and other features, this castle evidently belongs to the fifteenth century, although probably it was remodelled at a later date. The remains of the tympanum of a dormer window still existing seem to point to this

One of the most recent descriptions of the ruin appears in a notable parish history, *Methlick, Haddo House, Gight, and the Valley of the Ythan*, 1899, which was written co-operatively by members of the Methlick Free Church Guild. Mr. Alexander Keith, the editor of this volume, in describing the ruins (pp. 67-75), which are illustrated by wash drawings by Mr. David West, says :—

> The part of the castle in best preservation is the doorway, formed of large dressed stones Immediately above is a recess, where formerly had been the family coat of arms. Entering into the small dark porch, the visitor has his attention arrested by the finely groined arch, with the keystone in the centre. This stone [is] ornamented with symbols of Christ's passion and death. On the lower face, the pierced heart, surrounded by the crown of thorns, can be readily made out, while less clearly, on the sides, may be discovered the pierced hands and feet, the ladder, the hammer, the nails, the spear, and the reed Facing the doorway is a large room, with an opening in the wall directly opposite the entrance door of the castle. On the left is the kitchen with its huge chimney   . Proceeding up, either over the ruins of what had once been a large circular staircase, or by the remains of a smaller

and shorter stair, the great hall of the castle is reached, which had on its west side, where attack was least likely to be made, a large window. Amid the wrack and ruin . . . it is impossible to form an adequate idea of the appearance of the structure in its resplendent days. On the level of the hall [which is 37 ft. by 21 ft.] will be observed a triangular structure, consisting of three dressed stones, and surmounted by an ornamental carving. On the middle stone is a cross, and on the lowest are carved the letters M. A R, with a heart pierced by a sword at the extreme base. This is commonly supposed to have been the upper portion of a dormer window, the remains of a private chapel or oratory dedicated to the Virgin. [This seems to have been the chapel which the General Assembly had ordered to be demolished in 1608.]

The Arms of Gordon of Gight, as recorded 1775, are:—Quarterly: 1 and 4, Azure, a mullet argent between three boars' heads couped or; 2 and 3, Azure, on a fess engrailed between three pheons argent a buck's head erased of the field. Crest: a buck's head and neck affrontée issuing out of the crest wreath, charged on the breast with a star argent Motto: " Bydand ".

Sir William Gordon, I. of Gight.

(Killed at Flodden, 1513.)

Sir William Gordon, first of the House of Gight, was the third son of George, second Earl of Huntly (died 1500), by his second wife, Princess Annabella Stuart, daughter of James I. of Scotland She had been married to Lewis, Count of Geneva, son of Lewis, Duke of Savoy, but the marriage was dissolved owing to the intrigues of the French King. She married Huntly in 1459, and was divorced from him under Papal law in 1471.

The estate of Schives had belonged to the old family of Maitland. Sir Patrick Maitland died, leaving two sisters, Elizabeth and Janet. The second Earl of Huntly financed them, and they resigned Schives in his favour, as will be seen by the following documents now in the charter chest of Ellon Castle (transcribed by Mr. Murray Rose) :—

1467. *May* 25.—Elizabeth and Janet Maitland, sisters, heirs of Sir Patrick Maitland of Netherdale, become bound and " oblist till ane noble and michte lord, our deirist lord George Lord Gordon, master of Huntlie [afterwards 2nd Earl of Huntly], for his gret lordschips favour in maintenance, supply and help done till us in supplying, helping and following and recovery of our said fadyr heritage . . and alsua for ye helping and furthering of us till oure marriages and for gret somys of gold, silvuyr and other moveabils, gudes giffine till us   for the gret costs, expensis, travils, and labouris which the said lord has made.   ." When they are infeft in their father's property they will make resignation thereof in the favour of Huntly.—Dated at Methlick

1467 *June* 12.—Resignation of Janet Maitland, in pursuance of the above bond, of the lands in the hands of the king as superior —Dated at Methlick.

1467 *June* 12—The Royal Charter following on last, to George, Lord Gordon of Gight, Naterdale, Pettinbrinzeane and Drumnaketh —Dated at Perth.

The *Balbithan MS.* account of the whole affair runs :—

Sir Patrick Maitland Barron of Gight and Sheeves leaving only three [only two are mentioned in the charters] Daughters, Earle George got the gift of the Ward of their marriage, and his said third son William Gordon not being willing to marry any of the three daughters, Earl George provided them of other Husbands, with whom he transacted for the Lands of Gight and Sheeves, which he gave to his son the said William

The elder daughter Elizabeth is stated (Temple's *Thanage of Fermartyn*, p. 308) to have married "Jock" Gordon of Scurdargue, but the dates seem to suggest that "Jock's" consort was at least the aunt of Elizabeth mentioned in the charter of 1467. In the *Sir Name of Baird* (1870, p. 13) we are told that Huntly gave the other daughter, Janet Maitland, in marriage to her cousin-german, Thomas Baird, and with her the lands of Drumnaketh, Pettinbrinzeane and others in the Boyne, and several lands, fishings and houses about Banff, "particularly the lodging formerly belonging to Lord Airly and now to Lord Fife". This Maitland-Baird marriage, according to the same authority, took place in 1490, "and is instructed by the following writs " :—

1505. *April* 11—Discharge Thomas Baird and Janet Maitland, his spouse, to William Gordon of Gight, upon the payment of 3,000 merks in lieu of claims.

1506—Charter by George, Earl of Huntly, upon the lands of Drumnaketh, etc , to Thomas Baird and Janet Maitland, his spouse

The Maitlands retained some hold on the lands of Schives,[1] for they received a charter of infeftment from the king on July 6, 1672

---

[1] There is much difficulty in distinguishing Gight from Schives, the land and barony of which is described in 1582 as the "dominical lands of the manor of Gight" with various other lands. The difficulty is increased by this reference Captain Wimberley suggests that the barony may have been divided into at least two parts, distinct from the superiority He asks "If Lord Aboyne acquired the whole barony, how and when did the Maitlands get it to sell?"

(*Acts of Parliament*)   On August 3, 1674, Sir Richard Maitland of Pitrichie, one of the Senators of the College of Justice, and his son, Sir Richard (as noted in the *Records of Aboyne*, p 337), entered into a contract with Charles, Earl of Aboyne, whereby they sold to him the lands and barony of Gight, or Schivas, and, in terms of that contract, they resigned the lands.   Thereupon Charles II. granted a charter under the Great Seal of the lands and barony of Gight in favour of the Earl of Aboyne, dated Edinburgh, August 4, 1675.   On May 31, 1678, Sir Richard (the second) was served heir to his father, the Senator, in (among other places) the shady third part of Newton of Schivas, with the pertinents called Skillmanee, which lands were held "immediately in chief of Sir George Gordon of Gight and Robert Irvine of Fedderet, or either of them . . . in feu farm and heritage for yearly payment of 40 shillings Scots at two terms in the year".   He also held the double part of the towns and lands of Auchincrive from the same owners (*Antiq. Aberdeen and Banff*, iii., 76).   On January 28, 1681, Charles Maitland was served heir to his brother, Sir Richard, in the lands and barony of Gight, with the tower, fort, manor place and tithes, which were all held in chief of the king in free barony and heritage perpetually (*Ibid.*, iii., 559).

On October 8, 1479, Huntly gave the estate of Gight to his second son, Adam, who married Elizabeth, Countess of Sutherland, and who founded the Gordon line of the Sutherland family.   Huntly dated a charter "apud le Geych" on May 4, 1481 (*Ibid.*, ii., 271).   Adam exchanged Gight for Aboyne with his younger brother, William ("*familiaris armiger*"), on November 1, 1490 .—

Rex confirmavit cartam Georgei comitis de Huntlee et dom de Badienach— [qua—pro filiali affectione etc —concessit filio suo carnali Willelmo Gordoun—terras et baroniam de Scheves cum juribus et pertinentiis vic. Abirdene—quas Adam Gordoun filius carnalis ejusdem comitis, in excambium quarundam terrarum baronie de Oboyne, vic. predict, in manus dicti comitis personaliter resignavit   Tenend dicto Wil et heredibus ejus masculis de corpore legitime procreatis, quibus deficientibus heredibus dicti comitis quibuscunque reversuras   Faciend regi servitium forinsecum quantum de terris et baronia de Scheves pertinet, et dicto comiti tres sectas ad tria placita capitalia de Huntlee apud principale messuagium ejusdem, necnon debita et consueta servitia]   Test Alex dom de Gordoun, David Ogilvy de Tolmad, Pat. Grantuly, rectore de Glas, .John Andree, vicario de Botary, And Frasare et And. Nesbit —Apud Huntlee, 2 Oct , 1490 (*Great Seal*)

Another stage in the history of the estate was when Lord Huntly resigned Schivas, for on May 16, 1498, the king confirmed William's charter, settling the estate on him; failing him, on his brother, James, and failing him, on the earl and his heirs.

On January 4, 1510-1 (*Great Seal*), the king again confirmed the charter by William Gordon and Jonete Ogilvy, his wife (mentioned here for the first time).

On December 6, 1512, the king confirmed the charter by which William sold to Alexander Gray, burgess of Aberdeen, the lands of Newton of Schivas (*Ibid.*). This deal may explain the fact that Sir William was elected a burgess of Aberdeen in 1511-2, along with Robert Anthone, tailor (*Miscellany of the New Spalding Club*, p 45). It shows that William was borrowing money and that the worthy burgess of Aberdeen had money to lend.

On November 24, 1506, there is a deed of sasine in favour of John Gordon, son and heir of John Gordon, of Lungar, on charter of William Gordon of Schivas, of the lands of Petnagoak, in the barony of Schivas (Index to the Parkhill Charters, quoted in Temple's *Thanage of Fermartyn*, p. 309)

On May 2, 1508, William Gordon of Schivas was one of the witnesses to the protest of John, Earl of Crawford, respecting the lands of Park and Kellie.

Sir William Gordon, with his brothers, the Earl of Huntly and Lord Adam, fought at Flodden (September, 1513). Adam fled from the field; Sir William was found among the dead (*Earls of Sutherland*, p. 86).

He married Janet Ogilvie (who was alive in 1511), daughter of the laird of Boyne, "with whom he begat three sons and a daughter" (*Balbithan MS.*, p. 15). I suggest another son and another daughter:—

1. GEORGE, II. of Gight.

2. JAMES of Cairnbannoch   The *Balbithan MS.* makes James the third laird, but I cannot get corroborative evidence from official documents   As showing the difficulty of describing definitely the succession of the third and fourth lairds of Gight, the following statement (which contradicts itself) from the *Familie of Innes* (p 248) concerning Colonel John Gordon, who helped to assassinate Wallenstein, may be quoted —

"This Coll. John Gordon was near Cousin german once removed with John Innes of Leuchars, whos mother was Marjorie Gordon, dochter to William

Gordon [V.] of Gight, who was cousine german with the said Colonell Gordon. This Collonell Gordon's father was ane John Gordon sone to John Gordon of Kadenbanno, brother to ane Gilbert [really John] Gordon off Ardmachyer, who was father to William Gordon who fell in to be laird of Gight after the slaughter of Sir George. . . . This Collonell Gordon's father and William Gordon of Gight umquhill John Innes's grandfather war brother barnis. Collonell Gordon's guidsyr [was] Gordon of Kadenbanno and William Gordon of [Gight's father] was John Gordon of Ardmachy   Kaddenbanno and Ardmacher were twae brothers cadent neare cousins ather brothers or brothers sons off the laird of Gight."

James at first had the lands of Cairnbannoch, which means the "peaked cairn" (Macdonald's *Place Names of West Aberdeenshire*, p. 84). Cairnbannoch, which is mentioned in a charter of Fergus, Earl of Buchan, in 1214, had originally belonged to the Abbey of Deer (*Aberdeen and Banff*, p. 470). Almost the only fact about Cairnbannoch that I have discovered is the statement in the *Privy Council Register* that William Gordon, V of Gight, demolished the House of Cairnbannoch. James of Cairnbannoch married, according to the *Balbithan MS*, —— Cheyne, of the Straloch family. The *Balbithan MS.* says he begat two sons, "Alexander," who became laird of Gight, and William; but the third laird was undoubtedly George. I therefore give James's descendants as follows —

(1) WILLIAM, who, according to the *Balbithan MS.*, was drowned in the Bogie and left no issue.

(2) JOHN, of Milton of Noth, described in the *Balbithan MS.* as a natural son. He seems to have gone abroad, for he is stated in the *Familie of Innes* to have been killed at the "battle of Flanders". He is probably the "Captain Gordon" who, according to Ferguson's *History of the Scots Brigade in Holland*, was killed before Antwerp, August 13, 1584   Mr. Ferguson identifies him as the Gordon who served in the company of Colonel William Stuart in the brigade, 1579-81. He married Margaret Caldwell (*Familie of Innes*)   On his death she married John Nairn, and had Juda Nairn (whose husband, —— Gregor, merchant at St. Andrews, fell at the battle of Kilsyth "contra Montrose"). Margaret Caldwell married, thirdly, Lieutenant Weache, and had a daughter, Anna Weache, whose husband (Alexander Petrie, son of —— Petrie, minister of the Scots Church at Rotterdam) was Colonel Gordon's executor. Margaret Caldwell had by her first husband (John Gordon) a son—

COLONEL JOHN, who immortalised himself, in 1634, by helping to assassinate Wallenstein, the generalissimo of the Holy Roman Empire   He began life in the French army. Schiller, in his *Death of Wallenstein*, says that Gordon and Wallenstein "were pages at the Court of Burgau" at the same period. But this is merely poetical license. Certain it is that Gordon, though a Protestant, entered the army of the Emperor   Fischer (*The Scots in Germany*, p. 113) says that Schiller fused Walter Leslie and Gordon into one.   Schiller's Gordon is "merely a creature of the imagination History knows nothing of the days of his boyhood being spent together with Wallenstein at Burgau, neither is the Gordon of history the weak-minded old man such as Colonel Butler, the Irishman, describes him   It must be granted, however, that we know little enough of his life"   The Rev Walter Harte's *Life of Gustavus Adolphus*, London, 1759 (pp. 51-7), quotes Pufendorf to the effect that Wallenstein had "raised him from a private soldier".   Burton passed him over in *The Scot Abroad. The Dictionary of National Biography* does not refer to him ; and the local genealogists are quite at sea   You must go to the extensive literature (in German) on Wallenstein to catch the slightest glimpses of him.   The Protestantism of Gordon was so strongly marked that one of Wallenstein's correspondents (quoted by Förster in his *Life of Wallenstein*) declares that "der Calvinische Geist hat den Obrest Gordon zu einem Schelm gemacht", while Andrew Leslie, writing to Father John Seton in 1638 (as quoted in the *State Papers*), complains that "Colonel Gordon is not yet a Catholic" ; as if strenuous efforts had been made to convert him. This is all the more strange in that the Gight family was defiantly Catholic, and at this very moment was fighting the Covenant with inveterate determination   But Gordon was first and foremost a soldier, not a religionist.   Had he been that, he would have entered the army of the Protestant champion, Gustavus Adolphus —"that thundering scurge, that terror of Germanie," as Patrick Gordon calls him in *Britane's Distemper*   When or how Gordon entered the Austrian service I cannot say, but it was probably *via* France, and through the influence of Richelieu   Wallenstein's successes roused the jealousy of the hereditary princes of the empire, and he was dismissed in 1630 ; but, on the death of Tilly at Lech in 1632, he was recalled   On June 26 of that year Wallenstein appeared before Nuremberg, and on July 28 he was attacked vigorously by Gustavus   Gilbert Gordon of Sallagh, in his continuation of *The Earls of Sutherland* (p. 474), says that Gordon, who "is descended of the hous of Gight," had followed the Emperor (Ferdinand's) "parties since the last warrs in Germany   He was taken prisoner be the King of Sweden [Gustavus Adolphus] hard by the citie of Norenborgh, when he hade his leaguer about that town in defence thereoff   The King of Sweden issued out of his leaguer about Norenborgh with a party of a thousand foot and fyve hundredth hors, and rencountering with

Collonel Spaw, Leivetenant-Collonel John Gordon, Captain Walter Leslie [son of John Leslie of Balquhain], and others leading a stronger and greater partie of the emperialists, the king invaded them and beat them, after a long and sharp fight : killed the most part of them ; tooke Spaw, Gordon and Leslie prisoners, and sent them into Norembourgh. [Nuremburg, Nov., 1631] The king kept Leivetenant-Collonel Gordon prisoner with him six weekes, and then for his valour released him without ransome " They were complimented on their gallantry in the fight. But they were not allowed to leave the camp of the victors for five weeks, for Sir John Hepburn, Munro, and the other Scots soldiers in the strange army of Gustavus entertained them, and did not permit them to leave until the armies were once more ready to fight. The next great feature of the campaign was not Swede against Austrian, but Wallenstein against his own Emperor Wallenstein's victories had turned his head, and he plunged into a series of intrigues by which he hoped to gain high power, if not to found a dynasty. His treasonable enterprise had reached such a point that on January 24, 1634, the Emperor signed a secret patent removing him from his command Wallenstein was not to be baulked, so he resolved to deliver the town of Eger, which is about twenty-five miles from Karlsbad—to-day it has a population of some 19,000 souls—into the hands of the Protestant enemy On February 23 Wallenstein arrived in the little town with his friends and an army of a thousand men Leslie discovered the plot, and reported it at once to Gordon, who was the commandant of the town No time was to be lost to save the Emperor Before a courier could reach Ferdinand the Swedes might be hammering at the gates Only one alternative to surrender remained Wallenstein must be removed at once by the assassin's hand Gordon was loth to countenance the stroke He had fought with him on many a field, and had found him a great tactician and an inspiring leader In *The Death of Wallenstein* Schiller emphasises (without historic support) this disinclination when he makes Gordon say .—

> Seize him and hold him prisoner , do not kill him
> Murder's a black deed, and Nature curses it.

Gordon listened doubtfully to the advice of his staff. Leslie was all for immediate action , indeed, he is the heavy villain of the *Tragedy of Albertus Wallenstein*, by Henry Glapthorne, which was "acted with good allowance at the Globe on the Bank-side by His Majesty's servants " in London in 1639 In the first act Leslie tells Gordon :—

> This Wallenstein, like a good easie mule,
> Have I led on by th' nose to this rebellion;
> Forc'd with such venom as will spread
> Like swift infection through his soul.

There is no evidence that the tragedian's view is historical, but the play must have its villain. Colonel Butler, a fiery Irishman who commanded Count Tertzky's regiment, supported Leslie; the generalissimo must be despatched at once. "Think of his greatness," says Gordon in Schiller's play (in a passage which is a paraphrase of the speech in Glapthorne); "he's himself so mighty: he seems above his part." Gordon still hesitates, and Butler scouts him (in Schiller) as "poor, weak Gordon," who

> Prizes above all his fealty.
> His conscious soul accuses him of nothing
> In opposition to his own soft heart.

In the end Leslie and Butler triumphed, and a scheme was laid to nip the traitor's design in the bud. Wallenstein was staying at a house (which is still standing) on the tiny market-place. (A plan of the building and a copy of Gordon's signature will be found in Richard Wapler's *Wallenstein's letzte Tage*, Leipsic, 1884.) The chief officers of his staff, Count Tertzky, Count Kinsky, Colonel Illo and Colonel Neumann were invited by Gordon on Saturday evening, February 25, to a banquet in the Citadel. All went merry as a marriage bell for a time. Everybody was in the highest spirits, when, at a given signal, the room was filled with dragoons, who had been placed in the adjoining apartments. "Vivat Ferdinandus!" they shouted, as with drawn swords they rushed on the guests. Before such forces the Counts and the Colonels had no chance. Illo and Kinsky were despatched on the spot. Neumann tried to scramble to the kitchen to summon his servant, but was slain in the attempt. Tertzky managed to get his orderly, but the two were overpowered and fell. Thus, in a twinkling, five men fell to save Ferdinand and the Empire; though, if he had been guided by his religious creed, Gordon should have opened the gates to the Protestant troops. But the arch-traitor of all remained. Wallenstein's lodging had already been surrounded by loyal troops, and thither Gordon and his fellow-officers marched. To the last (Schiller's) Gordon protested, and was left to watch the door, while the Irishmen, Colonel Butler and Captain Devereux, accompanied by six Dutch soldiers, mounted the staircase to Wallenstein's room, which looked out on the street. He had just taken a bath, and was standing in his shirt at the windows listening to the tumult. Two of the

generalissimo's bodyguard and a servant had to be slain before
an entry was effected. Devereux ran Wallenstein through the
heart with his halbert, and the traitor sank without a sigh. The
Empire had been saved   At first it was rumoured that Gordon
himself had done the deed, but this is not so, though the drama-
tists must needs change history. The ingenious Glapthorne makes
Gordon say· "Come softly, and if my stroke miss, second me"
Gordon is then made to stab Wallenstein   Schiller even makes
Wallenstein harangue Gordon —

> How the old time returns upon me.   I
> Behold myself once more at Burgau, where
> We two were pages at the Court together
> We oftentimes disputed.   My intention
> Was ever good , but thou wert wont to play
> The moralist and preacher ; and wouldst rail at me
> That I strove after things too high for me.

Wallenstein then goes over his career, as a drowning man might
do , while Gordon bids him remember the "good old proverb " —

> Let the night come before we praise the day
> I would be slow from long-continued fortune
> To gather hope ; for hope is the companion
> Given to the unfortunate by pitying Heaven
> Fear hovers round the heads of prosperous men,
> For still unsteady are the scales of Fate

To which Wallenstein replies —

> I hear the very Gordon that of old
> Was wont to preach to me, now once more preaching

Gordon sent Leslie at once to the Emperor with the news. Leslie
was created Count of Neustadt, and made a great marriage by
wedding Princess Anna de Dietrichstein, the daughter of the
Prime Minister. Gordon was created a Marquis, and was made
Bearer of the Gold Key, as High Chamberlain to the Emperor.
Never before nor since have any natives of Aberdeenshire struck
a blow of such international import, for Wallenstein was the
Napoleon of his age , and his assassination in the town of Eger
on February 25, 1634, made all Europe, then writhing in the
Thirty Years' War, open its eyes in wonder.   Gordon visited
his kinsman, John Innes, at Leuchars in 1644, but "the intesten
trouble of Scotland diverted him " from buying an estate in Scotland. He died at Dantzig, and was buried at Delft, Sir John
Hurry, the famous Covenanting General, being at the funeral
(*Familie of Innes*, p. 248) He was never married, his property
being inherited by his half-sister, Anna Weache, who married

Alexander Petrie (son of Petrie, the minister at Rotterdam), whom
Gordon left as his executor. There was some squabble about the
property, in which Leuchars was involved. Gordon is said to have
killed a young man who was "halff brother to his sister, called
Weache". According to Steven's *Scots Church at Rotterdam* (1836),
a Col John Gordon died at Delft and left a legacy to the Church
in 1649 The same authority says that two silver communion
cups were presented to the Scots Church at Rotterdam by Alexander Petrie, one being inscribed "In memoria nobiliss. Dni
John Gordonii, Equst aur dn. de Smidars," etc. The cups are
now (1902) much battered, and the inscription indecipherable.
They have been lent to the Scots Church at Brussels The official
burial record of the Nieuwe Kerk at Delft, under date June 1, 1649,
gives "Johan Gordon, baron tot Sneidons [*sic*] Schrivius [Schivas?]
. . . collonel". In a MS. at Delft, written and illustrated by
Willem van der Lely, burgomaster at Delft, 1768, entitled *Col-
lectio Monumentorum sepulcralium*, etc., a reproduction of Gordon's
escutcheon is given, inscribed "Hic jacet sepultus Ds. Johanes
Gordonius, Scotus Eques auratus, dominus in Smipars [*sic*] et
Scrivan, Caesariae majestatis Chiliarcha orthodoxus, gubernator
Aegrae, imperatori Ferdinando 2do a cubiculis, obiit Dantisci
$\ddagger\ddagger$ decemb Ao 1648" (Information from the burgomaster of Delft,
who says that there is a little about Gordon in P. Fimareten's
Versameling van gedenkshikken in Nederland, Delft, 1777, and in
R. Boitet's *Beschrejving der Stadt Delft*, Delft, 1779) Colonel
Gordon's will continued to be a subject of dispute for nearly forty
years after his death Fountainhall records that on November 16,
1687, "Sir William Binning, late Provost of Edinburgh, pursued
Hope of Carse on the testament of Colonel Gordon. This cause
was *res hactenus judicata* in Holland and the Lady Carss assoylzied
there. Answered, the process there was upon is previledge, as
being *testamentum militare* but here it is not insisted on *super eo
medio* bot as holograph. and it is certain that *res judicata* takes no
place except the two lybells be both *super eodem medio*. . . . Lady
Kerss had shunned these papers upoun oath and to evade it had
reteired out of the kingdome to Holland and had assigned and
conveyed her joynture and all her effects, particularly this right,
to some confident for her son's behoff. Her son stated himself a
party, and the Court of Session directed (Nov. 23) two commissions,
one to Holland for her to depone anent the haveing, and to try, if
this defence was proponed there, to take of the *res judicata*, and
the other was direct to Lubick, where the testament was made,
if holograph testaments, by their law be probative The cost of

this process was of great importance, being upwards of 40,000 rix dollars; and Sir William [Binning] in journeys to Holland and in processes had wasted more than £1,000 stg. on it" (Fountainhall, *Historical Notices*, ii., 827-8).

3. JOHN, IV. of Gight.

4. THOMAS. Mr. Murray Rose, who has mislaid his precise reference, tells me that on April 6, 1537, Thomas Gordon, "brother to George of Schives," witnessed a charter at Huntly. Thomas does not appear in *Balbithan MS*, and I have found no other reference to him

5. BARBARA; daughter of the first laird. The term "procreatis" in the extract from the *Great Seal*, November 1, 1490, already quoted, proves that George, II. of Gight, who was born about 1502 was younger than his sisters. Married first William Hay of Lormy (Fraser's *Chiefs of Grant*, i., 520). In 1553 there was precept of sasine by George Earl of Erroll in favour of Barbara Hay as heir to William Hay of Lormy her father ("consanguineus noster") in the half of the town of Nether Leask (*Antiq. Abd. and Banff*, iii, 156). Barbara Gordon, who was probably the mother of this Barbara Hay, married secondly, in 1541, John Grant, the first laird of Ballindalloch (who was a widower at the time), and who was killed on September 11, 1559, by John Roy Grant of Carron As a sample of the idea that ill luck followed the Gight family, I may quote Sir Robert Gordon, who notes (in the *Earls of Sutherland*, p. 416) that, on the same day seventy-one years later (1630), when the "inverterat feid and malice" between the families were still rampant, John Grant of Ballindalloch, the great-grandson of Barbara Gordon's husband, killed James Grant of Carron Sir Robert Gordon looked upon this as "the providence and secret judgement of the Almightie God". He remarks —

John Roy Grant of Carron [the murderer of 1559] wes left-handed : so is this John Grant of Ballendallogh [in 1630] left-handed also : and moreover it is to be observed that Ballendallogh, at the killing of Carron [in 1630], had vpon him the same coat-of-armour, or maillie-coat, which John Roy of Carron had vpon him at the slaughter of the great-grandfather of this Ballendallogh [in 1559]. which maillie-coat Ballendallogh had, a little befor this tyme [1630], taken from James Grant in a skirmish that passed betuixt them. Thus wee doe sie that the judgements of God are inscrutable, and that, in his owne tyme, he punisheth blood by blood.

The "judgement of God," however, did not prevent Ballindalloch's being so harried by the Carrons that he had to "flie from the north of Scotland and live for the most pairt in Edinburgh". In 1553 the queen granted a charter to John Grant (murdered in 1559) George Gordon "miles," apparently the second laird of Gight, his brother-in-law, and Mr. William Grant appear in it as the "curatores" of Patrick Grant, who bought the land of Tullochcarron at this date. It was he who carried on the

Ballindalloch line   Barbara Gordon and John Grant, I of Ballindalloch, had (according to Fraser's *Chiefs of Grant*) with other issue —

PATRICK GRANT, II. of Ballindalloch, born before his parents' marriage, but legitimated October 22, 1542   He had five sons and three daughters, and was succeeded by his eldest son—

.   PATRICK GRANT, III. of Ballindalloch, who had a son—

JOHN GRANT, IV. of Ballindalloch, who had—

JOHN GRANT, V of Ballindalloch (died before 1690); had—

JOHN ROY GRANT, VI of Ballindalloch; married Anne Leslie of Balquhain.   Under him the estates became very much encumbered, and were taken possession of by his creditors, who sold them in 1727 to Colonel William Grant (of the regiment which is now the Black Watch), younger son of James Grant of Rothiemurcus, who thus became the founder of the present family of Grant of Ballindalloch.   John Roy Grant had a son—

CAPTAIN JOHN GRANT, who entered the Dutch service in 1708.   He died before 1763.   He had—

PATRICK LESLIE GRANT, who, though no longer holding the Ballindalloch property, became a laird by succeeding his cousin, Count Ernest Leslie, as Protestant heir (he 'verted from Roman Catholicism) to the lands of Balquhain, of which he was the twentieth laird. He died unmarried, and was succeeded by his sister,

ELIZA GRANT'S, husband, PATRICK LESLIE DUGUID of Auchenhove They had no issue   Duguid married a second time, and had a son, John, the 22nd laird of Balquhain, the ancestor of the present laird (Leslie's *Family of Leslie*)

6. CATHERINE GORDON   I think the "Catherine Gordon of Gight," who married James Innes of Rathmakenzie, as noted in the *Familie of Innes* (p. 201, and also in the *Great Seal*), was a daughter of the first laird, and

may have been named after his half-sister, Lady Catherine Gordon, who married Perkin Warbeck   James Innes was the son of Robert Innes of Cromy (that is Crombie, in the parish of Marnoch), who was the second son of Alexander Innes of that ilk (died 1491), armour-bearer to James III, by Janet Gordon, daughter of the first Earl of Huntly. James Innes of Rathmakenzie, who was his wife's cousin-german, fell at Pinkie, 1547, and his son—

> ALEXANDER INNES of Crombie, was brutally murdered in Aberdeen, 1580.   Innes of Invermarkie had quarrelled with Crombie, and tracked him to Aberdeen   Simulating a fit, and crying " Murder ! Murder ! A Gordon ! A Gordon !" outside Crombie's lodging at night, Invermarkie induced his enemy to come out, and then shot him dead, while his followers decorated the dead man's body with their dirks   Crombie's son, a young boy, escaped by the back door, afterwards finding shelter with his father's second cousin, Alexander Innes of Cotts, known as " Crag-in-Peril " on account of the part he played at the murder of Invermarkie.   " Crag-in-Peril," as we shall see, married his cousin german, a daughter of the fifth laird of Gight. (See the *Familie of Innes*, pp. 198, 201.)

SIR GEORGE GORDON, II. OF GIGHT.

(*Son of I.*)

The second laird of Gight was a minor when his father, Sir William, fell at Flodden.   This is shown by the entry in the Exchequer Rolls serving him heir in accordance with the Act of Parliament passed after the battle :—

1516. *Sept* —Vicecomes respondebit pro 110 li de firmis terrarum et baronie de Scheves cum suis annexis, unitis tenen etc, cum pertinen jacentium infra balliam suam existentium in manibus regis per spatium 3 annorum ult elaps. sasina non recuperata et pro 40 li de relevio earundem, regi debitis per sasinam datam Georgeo Gordoun de eisdem apud Edinburgh 17 Sept, a r. 4 per dispensationem et statutum quondam s d. n regis predict. ut patet in retornatu (*Exchequer Rolls*, xiv., p 587).

The following items refer to the second laird :—

1522. *July* 15 —He was one of those who witnessed, in Lord Huntly's lodging in Edinburgh, Sir William Scott of Balweary's resignation of the lands of Parkhill in favour of his lordship (*Records of Aboyne*, p. 55)   The same authority tells us (p. 54), that he and his wife, Elizabeth, were parties (no date is stated) to a contract with Alexander Con of Auchry and William, his son, wherein it was stipulated that " so soon as Sir George or his heirs gets lands paying 80 merks penny mail in Buchan or

Garioch, and infefts said Alexander or William Con, or their heirs therein, by Charter and Sasine, they shall grant to said Sir George wadset right thereof, not to be redeemed for 10 years, for the sum of £800, and a fifteen years' tack after redemption ".

1528. *Oct.* 7.—The king confirms the charter by George Gordon, who had sold to Robert Maitland and Marjorie Garden, his wife, the lands of Auchincreif in Schivas The witnesses (at Aberdeen, Oct. 2, 1528) were Alexander Hay, Prebend of Turriff, Gilbert Hay of Schivas, Alexander Gordon, Mr. Gilbert Chalmers and Mr William Hay (*Great Seal*).

1530. *March.*—He witnessed the marriage contract between the fourth Earl of Huntly and Lady Elizabeth Keith (*Spalding Club Misc.*, iv., 139).

1530. *June* 25 —"Geo Gordoune of Geicht" was cautioner in £1000 that Alexander Fraser of Philorth would thole a great assise for the unjust acquittal of John Dempster of Auchterless (Pitcairn's *Criminal Trials*, 1, 148*).

1531. *Dec* 16.—Charter again confirmed, Gordon having sold "ingenioso juveni" Alexander Knowis, son and heir of the late James Knowis, burgess of Aberdeen, the lands of Newton of Schivas. Gilbert Menzies of Findon was young Knowis's tutor (*Great Seal*).

1532. *Feb.*—George Gordon, "of the Gycht," witnessed Hector Mackintosh's bond (*Spalding Club Misc.*, iv., 152).

1534 *May* 7.—Gordon's charter confirmed, he having sold to Laurence Ogilvy ("consanguineo suo "), Newton of Schivas and Boquhanyoquhy in Schivas— " Reservatis dicto Geo. arrendatione et fructibus dict. terrarum donec dict. Laurentius in terris de Newtoun molestaretur et regressu ad eas casu quo non molestaretur " (*Great Seal*)

George Gordon of Gight was witness of the warrandice of the lands of Migvie in favour of Walter Innes of Touchs This deed, which is among the Innes Charters at Floors, is undated, but as the Earl has the consent of his curator, Alexander, Bishop of Moray, it must have been within 1526-30 (Information from Mr. Murray Rose. See also *Exchequer Rolls*, xvi., 22)

1536. *June* 10.—George Gordon of "Gecht" witnessed, at Huntly, Garioch of Kynstairis bond (*Spalding Club Misc*, iv, 199).

1536. *Aug.* 23 —George Gordon of Gight witnessed, at Edinburgh, a charter to James Gordon of Coldstone (*Great Seal*).

1537. *Aug.* 31.—The Gordons are described for the first time as " de Geith " in the *Privy Council Register*. Till then they are described as " de Scheves ".

1538. *July* 31.—George Gordon of "Gycht" witnessed Lord Hume's bond at Edinburgh (*Spalding Club Misc.*, iv., 203).

1539 *Feb* 11 —The king confirmed the charter of George Gordon of Schives and Elizabeth Gordon, his wife, to the lands of Boquhanyochquhy, in the barony of Schives, which the said George resigned (*Great Seal*).

1539 *Dec.* 4.—John Abbot of Deer, having " sett in assedacioune to ane rycht honorabile man and our speciall louit frend, George Gordone of Scheues . . all and haill our lands of Carnebannocht, Auchtmontzell and Ardmauchtar . . . for all the termis . . . of nynetene yeris," charges his baillies to deliver sasine of the lands (*Antiq. Aberdeen and Banff*, iv., 552).

1540 *Feb.* 11.—The king confirmed the charter by Gordon to his wife in the lands of Boquhanochquy, which Gordon had resigned *personaliter* (*Great Seal*)

1540. *April* 18.—George Gordon, "baron of Gight," as "oure" lord of [illegible] Gray of Schivas figures in a march dispute about the lands of Sanquhat, the Master of Erskine's property, Auchnagatt and Guiltors (Aberdeen Papers, *Hist. MSS. Com*, 5th Report, Appendix, p. 609)

1543 *July* 18—Gordon's charter was confirmed on his selling to David Gordon in Savoch the lands of Newton of Schivas (*Ibid.*). On July 24 George Gordon of "Schewh" signed a bond made by Cardinal Beaton and others for mutual defence (*Gairdner's Letters . . . of Henry VIII.*, i., 508).

1546. *Sept* 3.—He witnessed, at Stirling, a charter of Alexander, Lord Elphinstone, dealing with the lands of Corgarff, Skellater and others (Aberdeen Papers, *Hist. MSS. Com*).

1546. *Aug.* 13.—The protection of Gight was proclaimed at the Cross of Aberdeen by Thomas Hunter as follows: "Maria dei Gracia Regina Scottorum, Omnibus probis hominibus suis ad quos litere pervenerint salutem Sciatis nos dilectum nostrum Georgium Gordon de Schevas terras suas homines suos universas earundem silvas posessiones ac omnia bona sua mobilia et immobilia sub firma pace et protectione nostra juste suscepisse Quare firmiter imhibemus ne quis malum molestiam injuriam seu gravemen aliquod inferre presumat injuste super nostram plenariam forisfacturam. . . Apud Edinburgh decimo tertio die mensis Augusti anno regni nostri quarto" (Information from Mr. Murray Rose)

1546. *Oct.* 5.—He was served heir to his father, William Gordon of Schivas, in the lands of Littil Geych within the barony of Schivas (*Inquisit. Speciales*). George had not got sasine on Little Gight as a minor in 1516, probably because it had been let on tack.

1546. *Nov.* 15.—The sheriff will answer for £3 6s. 8d. of fermes of the lands of Litill Geych, lying in the barony of Scheves and within his own bailiary, being in the hands of the King of the term of St Martin's last past, sasine not having been executed: and for £6 13s. 4d. for relief of the same due to the Queen for sasine granted to George Gordon: date as above (*Exchequer Rolls*).

1547. *March* 27.—George Gordon witnessed, at Edinburgh, a charter dealing with the Earl of Atholl (*Great Seal*).

1547. *May* 8.—The king confirmed the charter by Gordon and his wife, Elizabeth Gordon, in the lands of Little Gight, Boquhannochquhy (with mill), which George resigned. On the same occasion he witnessed, at Edinburgh, one of Lord Huntly's charters On *May* 10, George Gordon of Schivas witnessed a deed at Edinburgh (*Ibid.*).

1547. *May* 20—He appeared, with some other lairds, on behalf of William Lord Ruthven, who brought before the Privy Council the dispute he had with Patrick fourth Lord Gray (*Privy Council Register*).

1547. *September* 10.—Sir Robert Gordon (*Earls of Sutherland*, p. 128) says that "Gordon of Gight" was killed at Pinkie. It certainly was not the second laird

1548 —He witnessed the contract of marriage between John, Lord Forbes, and Margaret, daughter of the fourth Earl of Huntly Forbes afterwards repudiated the lady, and this added fuel to the feud between the Gordons and the Forbeses, in which the third laird of Gight lost his life (*Records of Aboyne*, p. 469).

1562. *Oct* —George Gordon of Gight, along with the lairds of Haddo, Abergeldie and Lesmoir (all Gordons), were ordered to keep within the burgh of Edinburgh, and "remain within the same and four miles thereabout till freed by the Queen's Majesty" (*Privy Council Register*)

1563 *Sept* 8.—Queen Mary presented to the Commendator and Convent of Aberbrothock George Gordon of Schivas ("eques auratus") and his wife Elizabeth to be their hereditary tenants in the lands of Monkshill, the Kirklands, Mill, and brewhouse of Fyvie, and the lands of Ardlogy, previously held by George, formerly Lord Gordon (*Antiq. Abd. and Banff*, iii, 550).

1564 *Oct* 12.—George Gordon, "knycht," and George Gordon, "younger" of Gight, and eighteen others were arraigned before the Privy Council for the "crewale invassion of William Con of Auchry and hurting and wounding of him in divers parts of his body to the great effusion of his blude; and striking and draging with a brydill three of Con's cottars and otheris" "My Lord of Cassillis, My Lord Barthwik, The Lord of Colsgaile, Hew Kennedy of Barquhynaycuire, procurators for the pursuers" The prolocutors for the panel were Mr Tho. McCalzane, Mr David Borthwik, George Baird of Auchmaddy, Mr. Tho Gordoune. "Becaus sufficient noumer of Barronys and Pearis compeirit nocht to pass upon Assyise of the saidis Lairdis of Geycht elder and younger, the Justice ordanit Souarties to be ressauit of thame, for thair comperance the thred day of the next Justice-aire (Aberdeen) or soner vponne xv dayes warnyng to vnderly the law for the saidis crymes." *Verdict*—"Acquittis James Cheyne and the other pannels." "The Lord of Pittindreych, George Johnestonne of Alychtmond, Mr Duncan Forbes of Monymusk, and John Forbes of Fynzeak were the only Barons on the Assise Among the Absentees was William Gordoune of Auchindoune" (Pitcairn's *Criminal Trials*, i., 453)

1565. *Nov.* 29 —George Gordon "miles" was served heir in the lands of Schives to his father William, who had been killed in 1513 (*Retours*). He probably considered the sasine in his minority as insufficient If his mother survived till 1565 and had infeftment in conjoint fee in certain lands he could not serve himself as heir to his father in these lands until after his mother's death, as they were for all practical purposes her property till then in consequence of settlement of marriage.

1568 —George Gordon of "Shives, knycht," signed a bond for the Queen's service (*Spalding Club Misc*, iv, 157) On June 27, 1568, he witnessed, at Huntly, the Laird of Macintosh's bond of manrent to the Earl of Huntly (*Ibid.*, iv., 225).

1570. *March* —Vicecomes respondebit pro £148 de firmis terrarum de Newtoun, Schives, etc. . . existentium in manibus regis et suorum predecessorum per spatium quinquaginta quinque annorum et unius termini ultimo preteritorum partim ratione warde et partim sasina non recuperata videlicet, decem annorum priorum ratione warde et relinquiorum annorum ac termini sasina non recuperata, et pro 53s 4d de relevio earundem: regi debitis per sasinam datam Georgio Gordoun de Scheves (*Exchequer Rolls*, xx., 406). This entry gives a clue to Gight's age.

1570. *July 29.*—George Gordon of Gight was one of the arbiters for the Earl of Sutherland in a dispute (Fraser's *Sutherland*, Book ii., p. 140).

1573. *Oct. 21.*—Vicecomes respondebit pro £12 de firmis totarum integrarum terrarum de Littill Folay . . . existentium in manibus domini regis per spatium unius anni et unius termini ultime elapsorum sasina non recuperata: et pro £8 de relevio earundem regi debitis per sasinam datam Georgio Gordoun (*Exchequer Rolls*, xx., 449).

The second laird married Elizabeth Gordon, daughter of Robert Gordon of Fetterletter, son of James Gordon, I. of Haddo. Cullen in his diary (*Spalding Club Misc.*, ii., 58) records that Elspet Gordon, Lady Schives, "depairtit at Aberdeen" on June 10, 1587. The *Balbithan MS.* (p. 54) says that the second laird had no issue, but the 1564 extract from Pitcairn already quoted seems to show that he had a son.

GEORGE GORDON, III. OF GIGHT.

(*Son of II.: killed* 1579.)

After full consideration of all the documentary facts, I am compelled to forego the *Balbithan MS.* theory of the early Gight succession in favour of another as follows:—

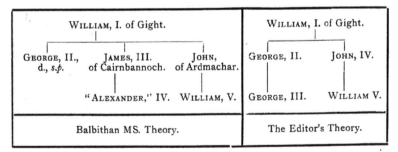

| | Balbithan MS. Theory. | | The Editor's Theory. |

I abandon the *Balbithan MS.* with reluctance, because as a rule it is very correct: but it is unquestionably wrong in calling the fourth laird, who, it says, married Agnes Beaton, "Alexander"; while there is undoubted evidence that John of Ardmachar was served heir to Schivas. I can find no documentary evidence whatever to show that James of

Cairnbannoch ever succeeded to Gight ; while the 1564 reference in Pitcairn, already quoted, to the two George Gordons, elder and younger
of Gight, strongly suggests that the two were father and son.   When
George, III. of Gight, died his daughter was served heir to him (1580),
while in 1581 his uncle John of Ardmachar was served second heir to
him.   In any case, George III. was undoubtedly a grandson of the
first laird, and represented the third generation of the Gordons of Gight.
Very little is known about him.   As I have shown, he was delated in
1564 with George Gordon of Schivas, " knycht " (II of Gight), for
the " crewale " invasion of Con of Auchry.   The following items also
refer to him ·—

1568.—George Gordon, "appearand" of Gight signs a bond for the Queen's
service (*Spalding Club Misc.*, iv., 157).

1575-6   *March* 10.—On Sept 13, 1580, John Leslie, of Balquhain, sheriff
Wardatar of Aberdeen, acknowledges the receipt of £168 16s. 1½d. from the fermes
of the lands and barony of Scheves (except certain lands in which Elizabeth Gordon,
this laird's daughter, was conjointly infeft) of £37 10s. 3d , and of £20 9s. from the
relief of the excepted lands, all due to the Crown by sasine granted March 10, 1575-6,
to George Gordon of the same (*Exchequer Rolls*)

1576.   *May* 24.—George Gordon of "Geych" witnessed at Edinburgh a caution
of Adam Gordon of Auchindoun on behalf of Allan Balfour (*Privy Council Register*)

1576.   *June* 26.—George Gordon was one of the witnesses (at Huntly) of a
deed, by which George, fifth Earl of Huntly, directed precept to Alexander Gordon
of Toldow, his baillie, for infefting John Gordon, "now of Kennertie," as heir of late
Thomas, his father, in the lands of Braeruddoch, holding in chief of the granter in
blench ferm (*Records of Aboyne*, p. 128)

1576.   *Oct* 26.—George Gordon of Geycht finds surety to re-enter Linlithgow
(*Privy Council Register*)

1577.   *Nov.* 22.—The king confirmed Gight's charter   " qua—pro observatione
promissi facti quondam Mariote Ogilvy, domine de Melgem, pro variis gratitudinibus
sibi ante complementum matrimonii sui prestitis "—he sold to Agnes Betoun, his
wife (and daughter of Lady Melgum), " during her lifetime," various lands, including
Gight ("cum turre et fortalicio "). The deed was witnessed at Gight on Oct 20,
1577, by Gilbert Auchterlony (possibly a relative of the wife of his cousin, William
Gordon, fifth laird, who married Isobell Ochterlony), John Gordon, servant of the
laird ; John Gordon of Audiaill, and Mr. Patrick Bisset, burgess of Edinburgh
(*Great Seal*).

1579.   *Jan.* 30 —The king confirms the charter—"factam per Guilielmum
Craig, dominum liberi tenementi de Craigisfintray ac terrarum subscript et M. Tho.
C, advocatum ac feoditarium earundem "—by which to implement a contract of
date December 18 and 22, 1578, a fourth part of the lands of Tullimald, in Turriff,

had been sold to George Gordon and Agnes Betoun his wife (*Great Seal*). On *Dec.* 10, 1579, the king granted to Patrick Cheyne of Esslemont ("pro bono servitio") these same lands which Gordon and his wife resigned. A daughter of the first laird married a Cheyne of Pennan (*Ibid.*)

1579. *Feb.* 20 —Although there had been an act of caution on Nov. 6, 1576, by John Blacader of Tulliallane for the appearance of George Gordon of Gight when required, and also for the good behaviour of him and his under pain of £5,000, it is complained that Gordon "hes not keipit gude reule in the cuntrie sen the dait foirsaid of the said act, in sa far as he continewallie sen syne hes resset within his place of Geycht William Gordon, sone to John Gordon of Ardmauchar, oure Soverane Lordis rebell, and at the horne for act and part of the cruell slauchter of umquhill Thomas Fraser of Straichin, and upoun diverse utheris landis within his boundis and jurisdictioun, lyke as the said Williame presentlie dwellis and remanis upoun the said George proper landis and heretage of Litile Ardoch, quhairin he hes remanit this lang tyme bigane, suppleit, intercommonit with, fortiffiit and manteinit be him". It is represented therefore that the said Blacader, cautioner for Gordon of Gicht, "hes incurrit the foirsaid pane of five thowsand pundis". Letters of summons having been issued, and "the said Johnne Blacader of Tullyallane compeirand be Robert Erskin his sone in law and procuratour, quha enterrit and presentit personalie the said George Gordoun of Geycht, and tuke instrumentis that the said Johnne had satisfied and fulfillit the command of the saidis letters in that part," and there being no appearance for the prosecution in the person of the Lord Treasurer, the King's advocates or any other official, the said George Gordon of Geycht "askit instrumentis that his said souirtie and he had obeyit and fulfillit the command of the charge of the saidis letters, and that nane compeirit to persue him according thairto, and that he sould not be haldin to answer in tyme cuming, quhill he be first lauchfullie and ordourlie chairgit and his expenssis payit" The Lords admit this protest of Gordon, "finding and declairing notwithstanding that the said Johnne Blacader, his cautioun, standis obleist as afoir according to the said act" (*Privy Council Register*)

1579. *Feb.* 26 —Caution was given by George Gordoun of Geycht for himself that he will appear personally before the Council at any time on a month's warning, and also that he, his kin, tenants and servants "sall keip gude reule in the cuntrie in the menetyme under the pane of £5000". In respect of this caution the Laird of Geycht for himself, the previous caution for him made by Johnne Blacader of Tulliallane is ordered "to be deleit, sa thot na executioun pas upon the same in tyme cuming" (*Ibid.*).

1579. *March* 2 —Representation by George Gordon of Geycht that he finds himself in difficulties in the matter of the caution he has given for his good behaviour in lieu of the former caution given for him by Blacader of Tulliallane. The conditions of this band "he myndis and sall, God willing, observe and keip, and continew trew and obeedient subject to his Majestie"; but private parties have interpreted the band as entitling them to pursue him, for their own ends, in civil causes betwixt them and his tenants. Therefore "gif his Hienes and Lordshippis sall not yit gif thair interpretatioun how far, and to quhome, and for quhat caus the said band maid be him sall extend, he sall be continewallie trublit and callit upoun wrangus and sinister narrationis of sic as seikis na thing les then the observatioun and keiping of gude reule and quietnes of his Majesteis obeydient subjectis, to the greit hurt of the said George, his freindis and servandis". His petition accordingly is that the King and Council "wald gif thair declaratioun quhidder the samyn sould extend for the said George obeydience and keiping of gude reule to his Hienes in tyme cuming allanerlie, or gif ony his Majesteis subjectis sould tak occasioun thairby, upoun sinister narratioun to be maid be thame, to call and persue him at sic tymes as pleisses thame thairupoun" The decision is in his favour, for it "ordanis and commandis the Secretar and his deputis to direct na letters for calling of the said George Gordon of Geycht for contraveming of the act abovewrittin, without it be upoun speciale occasioun committit be him aganis the Kingis Majesteis self or his auctoritie, and that upoun directioun of his Hienes with avise of his counsale and na utherwyise" (*Privy Council Register*).

1579. *June* 4.—George Gordon of Scheves was one of a commission of justiciary (*Exchequer Rolls*).

1579. *Dec.* 7 —Caution in 2,000 merks by George Gordon of Gicht and Alexander Lindesey of Vane, James Leirmonth of Dersy, James Leirmonth apparent of Balcomy, Michael Balfour of Monquhany, and David Farrett of that ilk, for the good conduct of David, Earl of Crafurd, who is licensed to go abroad for three years (*Privy Council Register*).

The third laird took a leading part in the bitter Gordon-Forbes feud, conducted under the direction of Adam Gordon of Auchindown (the notorious Edom o' Gordon), son of the fourth Earl of Huntly. In the famous ballad of the burning of the Forbes stronghold at Towie (1571), the imprisoned lady is made to express a preference for Gight. Although she declines to come down to Edom, she declares:—

> But gi'e me Cluny, Craig, or *Gight*,
> Or gi'e me young Lesmoir,
> And I'll gi'e owre my bonny hoose
> To ony o' the four.

In the beginning of 1574, according to Sir Robert Gordon of Gordonstown's history, Gight went across to France with Edom o' Gordon and six other gentlemen, and was entertained by Charles IX. They were followed by Arthur Forbes, son of Lord Forbes, who attempted to assassinate Auchindown. The French king sent out his guards, who, with the aid of the Gordons, killed Forbes. Auchindown recovered (dying in 1580). Gight had to pay the penalty of the act, for late in

1579, or early in 1580 (Sir Robert Gordon gives 1579), he fought a duel with John Lord Forbes—the *Privy Council Register* calls his antagonist Alexander Forbes, younger of Towie—on the shore of Dundee. The *Privy Council Register*, under date January 30, 1580, refers to the affair thus:—

> For sa meikle as upoun the occasioun of sum contentious wordis quhilk is laitlie happanit to fall out in presence of the Kingis Majestie betuix umquhill George Gordoun of Geicht on the ane part and Alexander Forbes younger of Tollie on the uther part, quhairupoun schortlie eftir followed baith thair slauchteris, the kin and freindis alsua of baith the saidis parties ar movit in quarrell and contraversie, ayther of thame aganis utheris · quhilk, gif the samyn be not removed and taiken away in tyme be sum mid and indifferent way to thair ease and weill, gretar inconveniensis is abill to follow, to the trubling of the gude and quiet estait of the haill cuntrie

Sir Robert Gordon (*Earls of Sutherland*, pp. 174-5), who gives the name of Gordon's antagonist as John Lord Forbes, describes the affair in the following terms —

> The cause which the Lord Forbes pretended for this slaughter was that the Laird of Gight had given him some injurious words before the [Privy] Councell, which wes then by the lords reconciled in some measure. Yit the Lord Forbes returning into the north [apparently after the Council meeting in Edinburgh] did watch the Laird of Gight when he landed at the ferrie of Dundie, wher the Forbesses shott him vnawars with musketts, besyd the wundmilne upon the shoar. He fought with them a long tyme after he wes shott and wounded, and pursued them eagerlie vntill he wes oversuayed with their multitude. So he died feighting with great courage among them, haveing killed some of them at that instant. The Laird of Auchindoun [Adam Gordon] went about to pursue the Lord Forbesse by the lawes of the kingdome for this slaughter, bot such wes the great malice of the ring-leaders then at court against the Gordons (the King being minor) that he culd have no justice at that tyme, and so Auchindoun delayed the mater, thinking to repair that wrong by some other occasion; bot he wes prevented by death [in 1580. The Privy Council tried to stop the feud in 1580, but it was still going on as late as 1587, when the Council again intervened.]

George Gordon married Agnes Beaton (she was alive in 1597), natural daughter of Cardinal David Beaton (murdered 1546) and Mariota Ogilvy, described in the *Great Seal* as Lady of Melgem, and in G. E. C.'s *Complete Peerage* as sister of Lord Ogilvy. She had a whole sister, Margaret Beaton, who married the tenth Earl of Crawford. An important reference to Agnes Beaton occurs in the *Great Seal* :—

> 1577. *Nov.* 22.—The king confirmed the charter of George Gordon of Schives which " pro observatione promissi facti quondam Mariote Ogilvy domine de Melgem

pro varus gratitudinibus sibi ante complementum matrimonii sui prestitis—venditit Agneti Betoun conjugi sue, filie dicte Mar, pro tempore ejus vite"—the lands of Gight and others, to be held by the king.   John Gordon of "Audiaill" is one of the witnesses

Agnes Beaton, after George Gordon's death, married (before January, 1583) Sir Patrick Gordon of Auchindown, Sheriff-Depute of Aberdeen-shire (killed at the battle of Glenlivat, Oct. 1594), the brother of Edom o' Gordon (her first husband's old friend) and of the fifth Earl of Huntly.   Thus the Gights and the Huntlys were once more brought together.   On July 26, 1597, Dame Agnes Beaton, Lady Auchindoun, complained to the Privy Council that in—

1595. *Dec.*—Johnne Mulwart and Callum McCandrachie stole from her, at night, furth of her lands of Inach, 66 wedders. They had been convicted by an assize in a Court held at the place of Cambrathok, on November 20 last, by William Gordoun of Dasky, bailie to the Laird of Grant   They had, however, found caution for payment to her of the prices of the said wedders within 15 days thereafter, viz.: Mulwart had found for his cautioner Duncane Grant, brother of the Laird of Grant, and McCandrachie had found for his cautioner Johnne Miller   The 15 days are long bygone, but the complainer after divers applications has received no satisfaction from principals or cautioners   The complainer appearing by Mr Williame Harte, her procurator, the said principals and cautioners for not appearing are to be denounced rebels (*Privy Council Register*).

By her husband, the laird of Gight, she had only one child, a daughter, Elizabeth, and from her many noblemen of to-day are descended.   These descents are so curious that I venture to work out a few of them   The daughter was—

ELIZABETH.   She was served heir to her father, June 23, 1580 (*Inquisit. Generales*).   She was under the guardianship of her step-father, Sir Patrick Gordoun of Auchindoun (*Great Seal*), and married Sir George Home of Spot, High Treasurer of Scotland, afterwards Earl of Dunbar.   In 1582 her step-father contracted with John Gordon (IV of Gight) on her behalf to sell Schives to the latter's grandson, George (VI. of Gight)   This may corroborate the *Balbithan MS.* as showing that while the main estate went in the male line—to her granduncle, John—yet she had certain rights in the property as the descendant of a younger son.   On Nov. 15, 1595, William Gordon of Gight and Lady Elizabeth Gordon, with the consent of Sir George Home of Spot, resigned the lands of Cairnfechil, Auchinlech, the mill of Fechil and the lands of the Fechil in favour of Robert Maitland, Glenchincreiff, which had been granted "quondam Joanni Gordon de Geycht" (*Great Seal*)   On May 22, 1596, Elizabeth Gordon and her

husband, Home, were granted the lands of Derington (*Great Seal*). Home
was created Baron Hume of Berwick in 1604, and advanced to the Earldom
of Dunbar in 1605. He attended King James VI into England, and was
made K.G. in 1608. He died suddenly at Whitehall on January 29,
1611-2. Some say he was poisoned, which ought just to have been a
Gordon's luck, for her father and her step-father had been killed and her
maternal grandfather murdered. Lord Dunbar left no male issue, and his
earldom became dormant (G. E. C.'s *Complete Peerage*, iii, 201). His barony
seems to have vested in his two daughters and co-heirs, Anne and Elizabeth. These were as under :—

The Earls of Home

(1) LADY ANNE HOME married Sir James Home of Coldingknows, and had
   JAMES HOME, who succeeded to the Earldom of Home as third Earl in
      1633. He married Lady Jane Douglas, daughter of Lord Morton,
      grand-daughter of the fifth Earl Marischal, and was succeeded by
      his three sons in turn
   ALEXANDER, 4th Earl of Home (died *s p* about 1674).
   JAMES, 5th Earl of Home (died July 22, 1706)
   CHARLES, 6th Earl of Home (died August 20, 1706) He had
      ALEXANDER, 7th Earl of Home (died 1720). He had
         WILLIAM, 8th Earl of Home (died 1761), and
         ALEXANDER, 9th Earl of Home (died 1786) He had
            ALEXANDER, 10th Earl of Home (died 1841) He had
               COSPATRICK, 11th Earl of Home (died 1881). He had
                  CHARLES, 12th and present Earl of Home Born 1834.

The Earls of Suffolk.

(2) LADY ELIZABETH HOME, a second grand-daughter of the fourth Laird of
   Gight, married, in 1612, Theophilus Howard, 2nd Earl of Suffolk
   (died 1640) She died August 19, 1633, at the Tower in Greenwich
   Park, of which her husband was keeper She had four sons (three
   of whom succeeded to the Earldom in turn) and five daughters.
   Her immediate male issue became extinct in 1745, on the death of
   the 10th Earl of Suffolk (the 11th Earl succeeded, as descending
   from her husband's brother, the second son of the first Earl) Before
   going into the Suffolks in the main line, I may refer to Lady
   Elizabeth's daughters, still represented.
   (v) ELIZABETH married as his second wife in 1642 Algernon Percy, 4th
      Earl of Northumberland, and became the grandmother of Lady
      Elizabeth Percy, who was married three times before she was
      sixteen, and who was dealt with at some length by the present

writer in the *English Illustrated Magazine* of March, 1898 The
Earldom of Northumberland became extinct (1670) in Lady
Elizabeth's father, the fifth Earl. Her son, Algernon Seymour,
by her third husband (the Duke of Somerset), was created Earl
of Northumberland in 1749. The latter's daughter married Sir
Hugh Smithson, who succeeded to the Earldom, in 1750, and
was created Duke of Northumberland in 1766 This Smithsonised
Percy was the ancestor of the present Duke

(vi) MARGARET married, in 1640, Roger (Boyle), 1st Earl of Orrery, who
is represented in the main line to-day by the Earl of Cork. In
this connection I may recall the fact that the fourth son of the
8th Earl married (in 1845) Eleanor Vere, daughter of Alexander
Gordon of Ellon. She is well known as a writer on gardening
under the initials " E V B.".

(vii) FRANCES married Sir Edward Villiers, and became the mother of
the 1st Earl of Jersey, and the ancestor of the present Earl

In order to place clearly the descent of Lady Elizabeth Home's sons (who
succeeded each other), I rearrange them thus :—

(ii) GEORGE (Howard), 4th Earl of Suffolk (1625-1691), succeeded his
brother, the third Earl (see below), and was succeeded by his brother

(iii) HENRY, 5th Earl of Suffolk (1627-1709), who had
HENRY, 6th Earl of Suffolk (1670-1718), who had
CHARLES, 7th Earl of Suffolk (1693-1722). He was succeeded
by his uncle,
EDWARD, 8th Earl of Suffolk (1671-1731), who was succeeded
by his brother,
CHARLES, 9th Earl of Suffolk (1675-1733). He had
HENRY, 10th Earl of Suffolk (1706-1745), who exhausted Lady
Elizabeth Home's male issue. I now return to the eldest son

THE BARONS HOWARD DE WALDEN.

(i) JAMES (Howard), 3rd Earl of Suffolk (1620-1689), died without male
issue, his Earldom going to his brother (as above), and his barony
of Howard de Walden falling into abeyance between his daughters
(G. E. C 's *Complete Peerage*, iv., 265).
LADY ESSEX HOWARD married, in 1667, Edward (Griffin), 1st Baron
Griffin, but her male issue became extinct in 1799, when her
right to the Barony of Howard de Walden went to the issue
of her sister,
LADY ELIZABETH HOWARD (1656-1681), married Sir Thomas
Felton, Bart , and had
ELIZABETH FELTON, married, in 1695, John (Hervey), 1st Earl
of Bristol, and had

Lord Hervey, died (in 1743) before his father, and had

George William, 2nd Earl of Bristol (1721-1775).

Augustus John, 3rd Earl of Bristol (1724-1779).

Frederick Augustus, 4th Earl of Bristol and Bishop of Derry, 1730-1803, whose daughter, Elizabeth, married, as his second wife, the 5th Duke of Devonshire (see Vere Foster's *Two Duchesses*). He had

Lord Hervey (1757-1796), who left a daughter,

Elizabeth Hervey, married Charles Rose Ellis (1771-1845), who was created Baron Seaford in 1826, and by him had

Charles Augustus (Ellis), 2nd Baron Seaford, who got the Barony of Howard de Walden on petition (1807). He had

Frederick (Ellis), the 7th Baron Howard de Walden, the father of the present peer,

Thomas, 8th Baron Howard de Walden, born 1880.

Frederick William (Hervey), the second son of the Bishop, succeeded as 5th Earl in 1803, and was created Marquis of Bristol in 1826. He died in 1859, having had

Frederick, 2nd Marquis of Bristol (1800-1864). He had

Frederick, 3rd and present Marquis of Bristol (born 1834).

John Gordon, IV. of Gight.

(Son of I.: died before 1592.)

The Gight family had been so unlucky in the matter of male issue that the estates reverted, in the person of the fourth laird, to a son of the first, for the third laird, who left an only daughter, was succeeded by his uncle, John Gordon, who had held the lands of Adiell in Strichen, and also those of Ardmachar.

1577. *Oct.* 20.—John Gordon of Audiaill witnessed charter by which George Gordon of Gight made provision for his wife, Agnes Beaton (*Great Seal*, Nov. 22, 1577).

1581. *July* 31.—John Gordon of Adiwill was served heir of entail to his nephew, George Gordon of Gight (*Retours*).

1581. *Nov.* 21.—John Gordon of Adiell (or Adiwell) was served heir special to his nephew George in the lands of Schives with superiority (*Inquisit. Generales*).

1581. *Dec.* 21.—Vicecomes de Aberdeen necnon marusfeodi ejusdem, vice-comes dicti vicecomitatus de Abirdene in hac parte ex deliberatione dominorum consilii specialiter constitutus, respondebunt pro £96 de firmis totarum et integrarum terrarum et baronie de Scheves, cum superioritate, tenentibus, tenandriis et libere-tenentium servitiis, jacentium infra balliam suam, existentium in manibus Supremi domini nostri regis per spatium duorum annorum aut eo circa ultime elapsorum sasina non recuperata : et pro £48 de relevio earundem, reservato tamen vitali redditu totarum et integrarum terrarum et aliarum particulariter subscriptarum, que sunt partes et pendicule prefate baronie Schives. . . Elizabethe Gordoun domine vitalis redditus earundem, pro toto tempore vite sue, necnon reservato vitali redditu totarum et integrarum terrarum et aliarum subscriptarum, que etiam sunt partes et pendicule prefate baronie de Schives, videlicet . . . cum partibus, pendiculis, annexis, et con-nexis, domine Agnete Betoun, domine vitalis redditus earundem, pro toto tempore vite sue ; regi debitis per sasinam datam Joanni Gordoun de Adyell [Edinburgh, 2 Dec.] (*Exchequer Rolls of Scotland*, xxi., 461-2).

1585. *April* 5.—The king confirms the charter by John Gordon of Gight (which, with the consent of William, his son and apparent heir) for fulfilment of a contract entered into between Sir Patrick Gordon of Auchindoun, tutor dative to Elizabeth, daughter and heir legally served to the late George Gordon of Scheves and in name of Agnes Betoun his spouse on the one part, and the said John in name of Marjorie Gordon his spouse and the said William for himself and in name of Eliza-beth Auchterlonie his spouse on the other part, of the date at Aberdeen, 3rd January, 1582-3, granting to his grandson, George Gordon, eldest son of the said William, the lands and barony of Scheves, etc Reserving to the said John elder, Marjorie, William elder, and Elizabeth Auchterlonie, their life rents as outside the terms of the contract between the said John and William, of date 1582, with precept of sasine directed to Alexander Gordon in Stanehouse. Reserving also to Elizabeth, Lady of Gight, her life rent of the lands and pertinents, etc The witnesses are William Gordon of Auchindoir, three advocates (William Davidson, John Cheyne and Patrick Cheyne), and Captain John Gordon [the last probably being Ardmachar's son, who was executed for the Donibristle affair of 1592] (*Great Seal*)

He seems to have taken part in the great Keith feud of 1587 which the Gordons waged, for, according to the diary of George Clark, school-master of Deer, quoted in Gordon's *Scots Affairs* (vol. i., p. xxxiii.), the lairds of Lesmoir and Gight, and Captain (John ?) Gordon, the latter's son, slew, Nov. 28, 1587, John Keith of Cryallie. This would seem to be a different slaughter from that of John Keith of Clachriach which occurred a few days later, Dec. 2, 1587. The Keith feud, as I shall show later, was going on merrily as late as 1597, when the Town Council of Aberdeen intervened. In the *Border Papers* (i., 309) there is a mysterious reference to a slaughter by the " Larde of Gicht," for Hunsdon, writing to Walsingham, Feb. 2, 158⅞, says :—

The King . . . sent specially to Huntley to know whether hee woulde obeye and performe that comanndement which the King had sent unto him, or noe . which was, that hee shoulde put from him those Jessewites which resorted unto him and that he shoulde come to Eddinborrowe and bring the Larde of Giche with him who killed the Earle of Marches kinsman to aunswer the lawe ; who aunserd that if hee might bring his frinds and forces with him hee would bring the Lairde of Giche to underlaye the law—otherwise not.

It is difficult to say when the fourth laird died. It is stated in Pitcairn's *Criminal Trials* (iii , 64) that the "laird of Gight was killed at the Battle of Balrinnes, Oct. 3, 1594". If " John " was at the battle of 1594, he must have been more than eighty years of age. Sir Robert Gordon, in the *Earls of Sutherland* (p. 227), mentions the laird of Gight among those who were " hurt " in the battle "John" is described as " quondam " in the *Great Seal* under date November, 1595, and yet his son, William, the next laird, is described as "de Geyht" in the *Great Seal* under the date February 4, 1591-2. The *Balbithan MS.* says John married the first laird of Lesmoir's daughter. Captain Wimberley, in the *Gordons of Lesmoir* (p. 17), calls her Marjory. Patrick Grant of Rothiemurcus was surety, March 3, 1592-3, for Marjory Gordon, "*relict*" of John Gordon of Gight, in 500 merks, not to assist the Catholic Earls (*Privy Council Register*). Thus it is extremely difficult to say when the fourth laird died.

The fourth laird had four sons and (possibly) seven daughters :—

1. WILLIAM, V. of Gight
2. JOHN was admitted a Burgess of Guild of Aberdeen, September 17, 1582. He is remembered by reason of his share in the murder of the Bonny Earl of Moray, at Donibristle, in Fifeshire, February 7, 1591-2 The Earl of Huntly and his brother-in-law were commissioned to arrest the Earl of Bothwell, who escaped to Bute One of his partisans, the Earl of Moray, took refuge at Donibristle There he was besieged by Huntly and a party of forty Gordons, including William and John Gordon Huntly sent the latter to summon Moray from the castle ; Gordon was fired on and mortally wounded Huntly then fired the castle, and Moray fled with Patrick Dunbar, Sheriff of Moray. The pair were pursued and murdered among the rocks by William Gordon of Gight and the laird of Cluny. Calderwood (*History of the Church of Scotland*, v., 145) declares that John (" Captain ") Gordon was " left for dead at Dinnybrissell ". " His hatt, his purse, his

gold, his weapons were taken by one of his own companie . his shanks
were pulled off   He was taken into the Earle of Moray's mother [the
Baroness Doune, née Lady Margaret Campbell, daughter of the 4th Earl
of Argyll], and was cherished with meate and drinke and clothing. A rare
exemple ! She brought him over with her sonne's corps to seek justice "
Gordon protested that he was brought "ignorantlie" into the business:
" but confessed the Lord had brought him to his shamefull end for his
menie other great offences ". Wounded as he was, he was executed at
Edinburgh (12th February) five days after the murder; and "hes man was
hangitt" (Pitcairn's *Criminal Trials*, 1, 358). Lord Moray's mother,
according to Calderwood, "caused draw her sonne's picture as he was
demaimed, and presented it to the King in a fyne lane cloath with
lamentations and earnest suite for justice". She supported her case by
exhibiting the three bullets that were found "in the bowelling of the bodie".
One of these she presented to the king, another to some one else (not
named). She kept the third to preserve her sense of revenge. On June,
1593, according to the Balquhain Charter, No 659, quoted in the *History
of the Family of Leslie* (iii, 64), "Marjory Gordon, relict of Captain
John Gordon, brother of William Gordon of Gight, granted a letter of
reversion of the lands of Kirkhill, containing the sum of 3000 merks, in
favour of John Leslie of Balquhain". The *Balbithan MS* says that the
Captain married the "laird of Shevthins daughter Affleck, with whom he
begat two daughters, and was killed at Dinnibersell without more succession". Captain Gordon's widow, Marjorie Auchinleck, afterwards
married Robert Burnet, parson of Oyne, who figures in Barclay's protocol,
1601, as having a large claim on the Gight estates on behalf of his wife
(Davidson's *Earldom of the Garioch*, p. 242).

3 ALEXANDER was a soldier. The *Balbithan MS.* says that he was "killed at the
wars in Holland," but Sir Robert Gordon's statement (*The Earls of Sutherland*, p 180) is probably the more correct. " The yeir of God, 1585, Captane
Alexander Gordoun (brother to William Gordoun of Gight) wes governor
of the fort of Tour-Louis, besyd Antwerp, when it was rendered to the
Duke of Parma which fort wes manfullie defended by Captane Alexander
Gordoun a long tyme against the Spaniards, with the losse of much of his
owne blood, and the lyves of many of his souldiers. Then wes he maid
governor of Bergen-op-zom by Prince Maurice his excellence, and therefter
maid Colonell of a Scottish regiment [This regiment was probably part
of the Scots Brigade in Holland, for, according to Ferguson's history of
the same, an Alexander Gordon served in Col William Stewart's Regiment,
1579-81] In end, coming home to visite his friends in Scotland, he wes
slain in Monteith by some evill willers who had secretlie layd ane ambush
for him " The issue of this Alexander is not quite clear. According to
the *Balbithan MS* he married "a gentlewoman in Holland, and begat
with her

(1) CAPTAIN ALX^R GORDON in Holland. This Alexander married Holland, and begat

> A son, who was a captain anno 1633." According to Mr. James Ferguson's *History of the Scots Brigade* there was an Alexander Gordon in Captain James Scott's company in 1639.

Sir Robert Gordon (*Earls of Sutherland*, p. 180) gives a different account of Alexander Gordon's issue. He says that he " mareid Jacobee Pedralis of Aungadere, ane Italian gentlewoman, by whom he had tuo sons " :—

(2) GEORGE.

(3) CAPTAIN JOHN, who was slain in Holland. There is a good deal in Mr. Ferguson's *Scots Brigade* about a Captain John Gordon who was reported in 1609 to have been absent from his regiment for six months. His company fell into a very bad state and was discharged. In 1618 his case was still before the States of Utrecht, to whom he made references to the services done by his father in Brabant. The Captain John Gordon mentioned in the *Earls of Sutherland* had according to that authority (p. 180) a son, ALEXANDER.

4. GEORGE. The *Balbithan MS.* says he was killed " by the Master of Monteith". But the *MS.* has mixed him up with his brother, Alexander, for George Gordon, according to Sir Robert Gordon (*Earls of Sutherland*, p. 217), was " slain at Harlam in Holland". He does not appear in the *Scots Brigade in Holland*. The *Balbithan MS.* says he married " Lady of Skillmaroch " (possibly Skillmanee which formed part of Schivas, or Skillymarno in Deer) and had a daughter.

5. MARGARET, married as his second wife, Alexander Chalmers of Strichen. Her brother, William (V. of Gight), murdered her husband's step-father, Thomas Fraser of Strichen, on Christmas Eve, 1576, at Old Deer. Her son, John Chalmers, took part in the fight at Donibristle, 1592. Margaret Gordon, according to the *Balbithan MS.*, married secondly " the laird of Philorth's brother ".

6. CATHERINE married John Keith of Clachriach (*Great Seal*), who was murdered, December 2, 1589, at the Justice Port, Aberdeen, by her brother, William. This led to a feud between the Gordons and the Keiths. She was probably the mother of William Keith (brother of George Keith of Clachriach), who (with her nephew, John Gordon of Ardlogie) waged a deadly war on Leask of that ilk, 1616.

7. ELSPET, married Arthur Garden of Banchory, who was the son of George Garden and Isobel Keith, daughter of John(?) Keith, laird of Troup (brother of the 5th Earl Marischal). According to the " Birth Brieves," published in the *Spalding Club Miscellany*, they had

> ALEXANDER GARDEN of Banchory, who married Janet Strachan, and had

GEORGE GARDEN, captain in the German army He probably was the Rittmaster who initiated General Patrick Gordon of Auchleuchries into the ways of foreign service. The mother of the Rev. Dr. William Garden Blaikie was descended from this family. A Major Garden, "laird of Troup," son to the laird of Nether Banchory, died May, 1662 (*Scottish Notes and Queries*, 1st series, vii., 54)

8. ISOBELL, married (1) —— Hay, and (2) Patrick Grant of Rothiemurcus (*Balbithan MS.*) According to Fraser's *Chiefs of Grant* (1 , 509), P. Grant of Rothiemurchus married *Jean* Gordon, daughter of "the Laird of *Echt*"; where Echt is evidently a slip for Gight. On May 17, 1616, Captain John Gordon was served heir of Jean Gordon, Lady of Rothiemurcus, his father's sister (*Retours*). This confirms Sir Robert Gordon's account of Alexander's (3) issue as given above

9. A daughter married Patrick (?) Sinclair of Auchynachie (*Balbithan MS.*) John Sinclair, brother to the laird of Auchynachie, took part in the attack made by the Gights on the Hays of Brunthill in 1616 (to be referred to), and Patrick Sinclair of Auchynachie took part in the sixth laird of Gight's attack on his mother-in-law, Lady Saltoun, in 1618.

10. A daughter married —— Gordon, brother of the laird of Haddo (*Ibid*).

11. Daughter married, according to the *Familie of Innes* (p. 201), John Innes of Blackhills, and was the mother of "Crag-in-peril" ("sister-son to the laird of Gight"), who married his cousin Marjorie Gordon, daughter of the fifth laird of Gight

WILLIAM GORDON, V. OF GIGHT.

(Son of IV.: died 1604.)

William Gordon, the fifth laird of Gight, son of John, the fourth laird, by Margaret Gordon of the Lesmoir family, seemed to have been impelled by the double dose of Gordon blood in his veins to outdo his predecessors in a spirit of rebellion The check which the advent of the Kirk implied lashed him into a fury of revolt, and this was accentuated in the conduct of his seven stalwart sons, and several of his grandsons, including the eighth laird of Gight, and his cousin, Nathaniel Gordon of Ardlogie, whom the Kirk at last beheaded (1646).

Before he succeeded to Gight in 1592, William had made himself a terror. Let me summarise his career :—

No date.—According to Colonel Leslie in the *History of the Leslies* (iii , 296), he killed William Leslie (son of William Leslie, first of Warthill), who had married a daughter of Gordon of Auchindoir. Gordon was really quarrelling with Troup of Begshall, and Leslie seems to have interfered. At any rate, he was killed more by accident than design.

1576 *Dec.* 23.—*The murder of Thomas Fraser.*—On this date William Gordon killed Thomas Fraser of Strichen (step-father-in-law of Gordon's sister, Margaret, who had married Alexander Chalmers) Fraser and Gordon appear to have met at the village of Old Deer Some quarrel occurred between them on the way home. Gordon followed Fraser, and coming up with him on the bridge which spans the Ugie, struck him a blow with his sword, killing him on the spot. Gordon was afterwards obliged to pay 5,000 merks as compensation for the murder. Lord Saltoun, who tells the story in this way (*Frasers of Philorth*, ii , 148-9), scouts the origin of the quarrel as given in Anderson's *History of the Family of Fraser.* Anderson gives an account of how the estate of Strichen first came into the possession of one of the name; but this is "altogether incorrect". He says that Isobel Forbes, " daughter of Forbes of Corfurdie, had taken as her first husband William Chalmers of Strichen This person's elder brother, George Chalmers, had been long abroad and there was little chance of his returning. William died in possession of the estate. His widow sometime after married Thomas Fraser, son of Philorth, who assumed the title of Strichen. But the old proprietors, unwilling to part with their inheritance, threatened to dispossess him, and their disputes led to several fruitless conferences The Chalmers in their necessity had recourse to Gordon of Gight He and Fraser met at Old Deer in the hopes of effecting a compromise, but the overtures of either party meeting with contempt, Gordon in a rage followed after Fraser, and coming behind him at the Bridge of Deer, laid him dead with one blow of his two-handed sword." Anderson quotes *MSS. of the Strichen Family* and the *Wardlaw MSS* , "but the evidence of charters shows how little dependence can be placed upon those MSS From the charters the whole story seems to have been an invention of the authors of the MSS , and it is highly improbable that the quarrel which took place between Thomas Fraser and Gordon of Gight could have any connection with the purchase of Strichen."

1582. *May* 9 —William Gordon, "apperand of Gycht," was made a free Burgess of Aberdeen.

1584. *April* 5 —The following charter (of which a partial translation has already been given under John IV.) is very important for its genealogical information Rex confirmavit cartam Joannis Gordoun de Geycht—[qua, cum consensu Willelmi G. filii sui et apparentis heredis—ob perimpletionem contractus initi inter Pat. Gordoun de Auchindoun militem, tutorem dativum Eliz. G filie et heredis legitim, deservite quondam Georgii G. de Scheves, et nomine Agnetis Betoun ejus sponse, ab una, et dictum Jo. ac nominibus Marjorie Gordoun sponse sue et dicti Wil, et dictum Wil. pro ipso et nomine Eliz. Auchterlownie ejus sponse, ab altera partibus, de data apud Abirdene, 3 Jan 1582—vendidit nepoti suo Georgio Gordoun filio seniori dicti Wil —terras et baroniam de Scheves, viz terras dominicales maneriei de Geicht cum turre et fortalicio, hortis et pomariis, terras de Littill Geicht cum molendinis granorum et fullonum, terras de Fadounhill, Brukilleisseit, Blakhillok, Mylnebreche, Swanfurde, Bawquhannachie cum molendino, Middlemure, Cow(k)-stoune, Mekill Ardoch cum molendino, Carnorie, Newsait, Littill Ardoch, Lentathe, Baythnagoakis major et minor, Auchincreiff, Monletie, Newtoun de Scheves et Skelmanay, cum tenentibus etc. advocatione ecclesiarum et capellaniarum, salmonum piscatione super aqua de Ithane, vic. Abirdene :—Tenend. dicto Geo. et heredibus masc. ejus de corpore legit. procreandis ; quibus deficientibus, Joanni G. filio secundario dicti Wil , et heredibus etc. (*ut supra*): quibus def, Willelmo G. filio tertio genito dicti Wil , et heredibus etc. (*ut supra*): quibus def heredibus masc. quibuscunque dicti Wil senioris, de rege :—Reservando dictis Jo. seniori Marjorie, Wil. seniori et Eliz. A. vitalem redditum, juxta tenorem contractus inter dictos Jo. et Wil , initi de data . . 1582 .—cum precepto sasine directo Alexandro Gordoun in Stanehous :—Reservando insuper Eliz. Gordoun domine de Geycht vitalem redditum terrarum et pertinen. ratione tertie aut conjuncte infeodationis—Test. Wil. Gordoun de Auchindoir, Magistris Wil Davidsoun, Jo. Cheyne, Pat Cheyne, advocatis, capitano Jo Gordoun ·—Apud —— 1582] (*Great Seal*).

1587 *Jan* 12.—William Gordon of "Geicht" and George Gordon of Crichie (his son-in-law ?) were caution for David Craik (*Privy Council Register*)

1587-97 —*Vendetta with the Keiths.*—Caution in £1,000 was given on May 20, 1587, by John, son and apparent heir of John Gordon of Cairnburrow, that William Gordon should cause rebuild and repair the place of Cairnbannoch, lately demolished by certain persons at his command, in as good state as "before the douncasting of the same," at the sight of John Gordon of Pitlurg, George Gordon of Kindrocht, Michael Fraser of Stonywood, Johnne Fraser of Crichie, and Gilbert Hay of Park, or any three of them conjunctly, between this date and 20th June next. Sir George Ogilvy of Dunlugas gave caution, £2,000, that William Gordon of "Geyth" should not harm John Keith, fiar of Troup, brother of George, Earl Marischal, and his tenants of the lands of Cairnbannoch. On Dec. 2, 1587, William Gordon murdered his sister's husband, John Keith of Clachriach. On Nov. 28, 1587, the lairds of Lesmoir and Gight and Captain (John ?) Gordon (the brother of William), who was beheaded for his share in the Donnibristle affair (1592), killed John Keith of Cryallie (Diary of George Clark, quoted in the preface to Gordon's *Scots Affairs*, vol. i., p xxxiii). For the murder of Clachriach young Gight had to fly, and he was harboured at Linlithgow by Huntly, who declined to surrender him to the king. Notwithstanding the Acts of Parliament (and especially the Act 1584, c. 17, iii., 301) forbidding litigants to come to courts except in " sic noumer and cumpany as the saidis actis provydis, under the pane of incurring the cryme of convocatioun of his Hienes lieges," yet the king is informed that George, Earl Marischal, and the friends of the late Johnne Keyth of Glak on the one side, and William Gordoun of Geych and his accomplices on the other side (which latter are charged to answer in the Tolbooth of Edinburgh upon 5th January next for the slaughter of the said late Johnne), intend to come, with a convocatioun of their adherents respectively, to the said diet Now there being among them " sindrie deidlie feidis," both parties are charged under the penalty above written to repair to the said Tolbooth, with no more attendance than is authorised by the said Acts of Parliament (*Privy Council Register*). The Keith feud was going on merrily as late as 1597, when (on April 29) the magistrates of Aberdeen thought it necessary to dispatch the Bishop of the Diocese and his man, as an ambassador to Gight and Inverugie, "so as to secure peice betuix the lairds of Gycht and [Keith of] Benholme". But his lordship's mission was a failure, for on December 30 George, Earl Marischal, and his wife, Margaret Ogilvy, John Keith, Captain of Dunnottar, and James Hog in Ballyedrie, complained to the Privy Council that Alexander Keyth in —— and his accomplices had been convicted of having stolen from the said lady a gray horse and from Hog two mares. But because the culprit was a Keith, the assize had continued the pronouncing of doom upon him till they had "devysit ane forme of death to him," and in the meantime had delivered him to the said captain, to be kept in the said castle. He had escaped thence, and the complainers have ever since used all diligence not only for his re-apprehension, but also for recovery of the said goods At last they had found the animals "gangand and pasturand" upon the lands of Gight, in the possession of Gordon of Gight and certain of his tenants Thereupon they had attached the goods and desired the laird of Gight to make restitution of them, offering to "verifie the horse and meiris challengeit". The laird of Gight however not only refused to deliver up the said goods, but "maist malicioushe and cruellie," accompanied by George Gordon (and three others), and divers other of his men, all armed with hagbuts, pistolets, jacks, steelbonnets, swords, gauntlets and other weapons, pursued the said Hog, and those with him at the said challenge, and wounded them in divers parts of their bodies. Farther, ever since the said Alexander's escape he had been resetted and maintained by Gight. The pursuers appearing by Mr. George Fraser, their procurator, the laird of Gight for neither appearing, nor having entered Keyth as charged, is to be denounced rebel (*Ibid.*).

1589. *April* 10—Gight was commanded as a rebel to surrender his castle within six hours after being demanded (*Ibid*).

1590. *Dec.* 16.—He had to find caution in £10,000 for the preservation of good order on his estate (*Ibid.*) By the Act of Parliament passed in July, 1587 (*Acts*, iii, 461-467), all landlords and bailies on the borders and in the Highlands on whose lands broken men dwell are required to find sufficient sureties within fifteen days after being charged under pain of rebellion, that they, and all for whom they are "bound to" answer by the general bond, shall keep good rule in the country, and also that they shall make themselves and their men answerable to justice. Accordingly certain persons are ordered to find caution to the effect foresaid.

1591 *June* 30.—The lairds of Gight, Auchindoun, Cluny, Lord Huntly and others had got commissions to arrest the laird of Grant, who on this date got the commission suspended (*Ibid.*).

1591-2. *Feb.* 7 —*The murder of the "Bonny" Earl of Moray.*—Gight took part in the affair at Donibristle, for which his brother Captain John was executed. Sir Robert Gordon (*Earls of Sutherland*, p 216) says that it was the Laird of Gight who actually killed the Earl "among the rocks of the sea". On March 22, 1592, the Privy Council denounced the Earl of Huntly and others concerned in the affair. William Gordon of Gight, and others, having failed to appear "at ane certain day bigane as charged to answer touching the last tressounable raising of fyre and burning of the place and houssis of Dunnybirsell and slauchter of umquhill James, Erll of Murray, and certane uthiris being thairin," are to be denounced rebels This order was merely for form's sake and by way of legal sequence to a charge previously given. In fact the Earl of Huntly and his associates were now free from all chance of pursuit. David Moysie in his *Memoirs* noticed that Huntly had warded himself by arrangement in Blackness Castle on March 10, but that his associates had neglected to ward themselves at the same time in Edinburgh Castle as had also been arranged The minutes of proceedings in the Earl's case are "suspiciously scanty" in the Register of Council. It was a disagreeable affair, and a good deal may have been left purposely unregistered On March 9, 1593, William Gordon's arrest "for treasonable fire raising and burning of the place of Dynnibirsill" was again ordered. On March 16, however, he was relaxed from the horn (*Privy Council Register*).

1593. *Feb.* 11.—The king gave ("*pro bono servitio*") and gave anew ("*de novo*") to William Gordoun "*de Geicht*" the lands "vocatas lie Mures de Fyvie," which included Maktarie, Blachrie, Badichellis, Murefundlands and Swanford, which William Meldrum of Moncoffer, brother of George of Fyvie, resigned "*pro hoc infeofamento conficiendo*" (*Great Seal*).

1593. *March* 1.—William Gordon was one of those who witnessed at Aberdeen a bond of caution in £20,000 that Lord Huntly should keep the peace (*Privy Council Register*).

1594. *Oct.* 3.—Calderwood says that the laird of Gight was killed at the battle of Glenlivet (*History of the Church of Scotland*, v., 351), but this is not so, for he got remission in 1603 (*Spalding Club Misc.*, iv, 159).

1595. *July* 26.—The king confirmed the charter of Sir Richard Cockburn of Clerkingtoun, junior. With the consent of Patrick Barclay of Towie and William Meldrum "de Haltoun," he had sold the lands to Gight and his wife, Isobel

1595. *Feb.*—John Carey writes to Burghley that the Duke of Lennox had frustrated most of Huntly's friends, including "Geithe" (*Border Papers*, ii, 15).

1595. *Nov* 15.—The king granted the lands of Carnefechill, Auchinlek and Pittrichie to Robert Maitland of Auchincrieff, who had sold them to William Gordon of Gight and Elizabeth Gordon (*Great Seal*)

1595 *April.*—He was excommunicated (Calderwood's *History*, v., 366).

1596 *March.*—The General Assembly ordered his arrest, and, a little later, that he should be "chargeit to come south" (*Acts of Assembly* · Bannatyne Club, Part III., pp. 873, 877).

1596 *March* 24.—At the General Assembly of the Kirk in Edinburgh (the sixtieth of the series of General Assemblies since the Reformation, and an unusually memorable Assembly) a memorial representing grievances was sent to His Majesty, who was urged, amongst other things, "to cause the lairds of Cluny, Geicht, and a number of others, to enter themselves in ward" (*Privy Council Register* and *Booke of the Kirk of Scotland*, v., 409, 417).

1597. *Jan.* 27.—William Gordon was made a burgess of Aberdeen (*New Spalding Club Miscellany*).

1597. *June* 24.—William Gordon was one of the sureties to George, Earl Huntly, who gave caution in £20,000 that he would not communicate with Jesuits. The bond was subscribed at Aberdeen on this date (*Privy Council Register*).

1598. *July* 25.—William Gordon of Gight, as cautioner for John Innes, *alias* McCarie, elder, burgess of Elgin (who was accused as art and part in the slaughter of the wife of the provost of Elgin), is fined 400 merks, being double of the penalty prescribed by the Act of Parliament, because he was at the horn. Who this John Innes was I do not know: his too-name was McCarie: his Gight connection may point to his belonging to the Inneses of Blackhills (Pitcairn's *Criminal Trials*, ii., 42).

The vendetta with the Mowats.—Having tired of his feud with the Keiths and the Kirk, Gight turned his attention to the Mowats and the Hays. On Sept. 10, 1601, Magnus Mowat of Balquholie (a deduction of whose family appeared in *Scottish Notes and Queries*, Dec. 1898, Jan. 1899), complained to the Privy Council that, although he is heritably infeft in the lands of Balmelie and others after specified, and he and his predecessors have peaceably possessed the same past memory of man, yet Williame Gordon of Geicht, John and Alexander, his sons, and George Gordoun in Bridgend, envying the pursuer's possession, and not content to live in peace "as it becomis Christianis," continually trouble and molest him For example: (1) In May, 1601, the said George, having the roum of Brigend adjacent to the complainer's lands of Balmelie, built a fold dyke within the bounds of the pursuer's said lands; and, while Johne Mowat, servitor to the complainer, endeavoured to stay the erection of the same, the said George and his brother, armed with lances, swords and pistolets, shot the said John with a pistol and afterwards wounded him with a sword, (2) Upon June 5 Gordon of Geycht and the said George, in Brigend, with others to the number of twenty men, all armed with hagbuts, pistolets, swords and lances, came to the lands of Balquholie, "raid athort and trampit doun the cornes sawin thairupoun," wounded Robert Catto, servitor to the complainer, "with ane reach of ane pistolett on the face," hurt Andro Jaffray, likewise his servitor, with a sword in the shoulders, and afterwards presented a pistolet at Thomas Cheyne, also complainer's servant; (3) Upon June 6 the said John Gordon, accompanied by the said George and others, to the number of 300 persons, on horse and foot, all armed with jacks, hagbuts, spears, steelbonnets, swords and gauntlets, came again to the said lands of Balquholie, and tramped down and destroyed the corns; (4) Upon June—John and William, sons of the said John Gordon of Gight, accompanied by a number of "evill disposed persons," came to complainer's lands of Lescraigie, Galstoun and Bromhill, broke up the doors and windows of his tenants' houses, sought them for their slaughter, and, having apprehended William Smythe, one of the said tenants, struck him in his own house, and carried him as prisoner to the place of Gight Charge had been given to the said William Gordon of Gight, William and Adam Gordon, his third and fourth sons, Robert Dalgleische in Staniehous of Gight, Walter Maitland, servitor to the said William Gordon, and others, John Gordon, second son of the laird of Gight, George Gordon at the Brigend, Patrik Gordon and others, servitors to the laird of Gight, and others, to appear on Sept. 10 and answer; and now the pursuer appearing the order is to denounce all the defenders for non-appearance (*Privy Council Register*)

How the Laird of Gight defied the law.—On Sept 27, 1601, Alexander Chalmer, messenger (according to his complaint to the Privy Council on October 24), executed letters raised against William Gordon of Gight by Magnus Mowat, apparent of Balquholie, charging him to answer for certain crimes and to find law surety to Mowat. While returning from the place of execution Chalmer was pursued by a number of Gordon's men, and violently brought back to the laird of Gight, who at first sight of the officer would have shot him with a pistolet if he had not been stayed by some persons present "He then hurlit him within his hall, tuik the copyis" of the said letters, believing them to be the principal letters, and "kaist thame in a dische of bree," and forced the said officer "to sup and swallow thame, held ane drawne dagger foiranent his hairt, avowing with mony horrible and blasphemous aithis to have thrust the dager throw his hairt gif he had not suppit the saidis copyis; and efter that the said officer, for feir and saulftie of his lyfe, had swallowit the saidis copeis, the said laird getting some previe informatioun that the principall letters wer yet extant and that the copeis wer only destroyit, he come to the said officer in a new rage and furie, raif the principall letters onte of his sleif, raif thame in peices, and kaist thame in the fyre" Gordon not appearing, the order is to denounce him rebel This bit of bravado seems to have become quite historic, for twenty-eight years later (that is in 1629) Luke Simpson complained to the Privy Council of an attack that had been made on him by James Wishart of Potterrow, who told him when he came to serve a summons, "Luke, the Laird of Gight caused ane messenger eat his awin letters". When Luke reminded Wishart that Gight "wes caused pay als weill thairfore," Wishart struck him in the face. On Oct 17, 1601, the Marquis of Huntly was rebuked for carelessness in the execution of the laws within the bounds of his northern lieutenancy, and especially for his laxness in dealing with Gordon of Gight "And how that now of lait thair wes a maist vyld contempt and indignitie done to his Majestie be William Gordoun of Geycht, quha, to the contempt and dishonnour of his Majestie, forceit and compellit ane officer of armes to supe his Majesteis letters, quhilkis the said officer had put to executioun againis him." Accordingly, his Majestie, in presence of the Council, commands the Marquis to apprehend the said Gordoun of Geycht and to bring him "quick or deid" to his Highness, or if the said Gordoun escape apprehension, then to do his utmost in holding him furth of the bounds of his office and to assist the King's servants in intromitting with the goods and house of the culprit

The Mowat vendetta prolonged until the year 1610 —On Feb. 16, 1604, George, Earl Marischal, was caution for Magnus Mowat, fiar of Balquholly, not to harm

William Gordon of Gight. On Feb 24, 1604, the warrant of the Privy Council was subscribed by Lord Fyvie, commanding James Prymrois, clerk, to receive the Marquis of Huntly as caution for William Gordon of Gight for the indemnity of the laird of Balquholly, and to receive William Chalmer of Drumlettie as surety for Gight for his compearance before the Council On March 1, 1604, Chalmer gave caution in 2,000 merks for William Gordon; and on March 14, 1604, George, Marquis of Huntly, gave caution for William Gordoun of Gight and his servant, 5,000 merks not to harm Magnus Mowat, fiar of Balquholie Mr Alexander Cumyng, advocate, registers and writes the bond, which is subscribed at Leith, February 23, before Alexander, laird of Spynie, John Gordon of Cairnburrow, John Gordon, his son, John Gordon of Pitlurg. On June 14, 1606, Robert Drummond of the Dole of Carnock was caution for Andrew Meldrum of Drumbrek in £100 to answer before the Council on July 17 to the complaint of Magnus Mowat, fiar of Balquholie, for coming with the laird of Gight to his place On May 23, 1608, Sir Thomas Ker of Hilton was caution for Gight's second son, John, to appear before the Privy Council in answer to complaints by Magnus Mowat and not to harm Mowat. On July 28, 1610, James Gordon of Lesmoir was caution in 100 merks for Patrick Gordon, in Tulloch, sometime domestic servitor to the late William Gordon of Gight, to answer before the Council on Nov. 22 to the complaint of Magnus Mowat. On the latter date Patrick Gordon complained to the Council against Mowat for suspension of horning " as he has never been lawfully charged is most innocent, and had nevertheless found caution in 100 merks to answer this day and to pay 10 merks for his escheat to the Treasurer, the horning should be suspended simpliciter". Pursuer appearing, but not the defender, the Lords suspend the horning (Privy Council Register).

A midnight attack on Turriff —1601. *July* 18 —A complaint was made to the Privy Council on Sept. 10, 1601, by Alexander Coupland and William Duffus, inhabitants of Turriff, Ralph Anslie, servitor to Francis, Earl of Erroll, and Alexander, Master of Elphingstoun, as follows Upon July 18 last Johne Gordoun, second son of the laird of Geicht, accompanied by Patrik Gordoun, servitor, and George Troupe, burgess in Aberdene, came to the town of Turriff and pursued Coupland and Anslie for their lives, wounding Anslie beyond hope of recovery William Gordoun of Geicht, being informed of what had happened, and having "enterit in communing" with George Hay, parson and minister of Turriff, the said minister had given him his word that the whole of the inhabitants of the said town should be answerable for any injury done to himself, his son, or any of his company; whereupon the laird of Gight had departed, and all the inhabitants, thinking themselves thereby secure for the time, had retired to rest Yet, in spite of this agreement, William Gordon of Gight, George Gordon, his son and apparent heir, William and Adam, also his sons, and others, and Patrik Gordon (servitor), George Gordon at the Brigend (and three servitors), and many others, came to the town of Turriff that same night at twelve o'clock, all armed with long guns, spears, and pistolets, and "oppresst the haill toun". More especially, they went to the dwelling-house of

William Duffus, and "thair tuik him furth of his bed, and brocht him to the gait, he being sark allane; quhair the laird of Geicht seeing him, drew his sword, and had slaine him, unles ane of his cumpany keppit the straik upoun ane lang gun. Thairefter the said William Duffus fled for feir of his lyfe, quhilk the Laird of Geicht persaveing, cryit, 'Lett him not away, bot schuite him', quhairupoun dyvers schottis wer schot at him with pistolettis, muscattis and hacquebuttis. In end, he was schot with ane muscat with nyne bulletis in dyvers pairtis of his body, quhairby the said Williame remanis in sic danger of his lyfe as na man knawis quhat houre he sall die." Charge had been given to the defenders above written to appear on Sept. 10 and answer, and now the said William Duffus, appearing for himself and the other pursuers, the Lords ordain the defenders to be denounced rebels for non-appearance (*Privy Council Register*).

1601. *Oct.* 30 —A commission was granted to the Earl of Erroll of justiciary against Gordon of Gight and the rebels who adhered to him: William Gordon of Gight, John, Adam and William, his sons, George Gordoun, sometime at the Brigend of Turreff, now in Little Geycht, Patrik Gordoun, servitor, and others, on account of recent counts brought against them. The execution of this commission against the said laird of Geicht is superseded, however, till Nov. 15 next (*Ibid.*). Gight, however, had escaped across the Border, for on Nov. 21, 1601, Sir John Carey, the Governor, writes to Cecil: "Ther is a leard of Scotland named the Leard of Gethe, wiche for some particulars amongest themselves hathe byn thought fitt bey the Kinge to be banyshed for a tyme his owen counterey: whoe hathe mad choyse to com hether tyll his remission be granted and tyll the Earle of Arrell can be gred withe him. This Lerd of Gethe is the onley prinsepall man of the Earle of Huntleyes howes, and on that hathe ever parted him in all his actyones, and is on that maye doe most and knowes most of the earles mynd of aney man livinge." On Dec. 17, 1601, Carey again writes: "For the Earl of Huntly's offer by Gethe, I shall as you direct let it fall. Yet I would have been glad that it might have been accepted at the least with thanks if but to have kept them from doing ill, for no man living in Scotland has more power to harm his Majesty, and is therefore worth keeping in good terms" (*Border Papers*, ii, 775-6).

1602. *Jan.* 17.—As notwithstanding the promise made by George, Marquis of Huntly, and his obligation by an Act of Council (see Oct. 17, 1601) to keep William Gordon of Geycht furth of his lieutenancy while at the horn for the "vyld contempt and indignitie" done to the King's officer, the said Gordoun has returned within the realme and has passed home, or at least haunts the said bounds, there is order to charge the Marquis to enter Gordoun before the Council upon —— to answer (*Privy Council Register*).

1603 *Feb.* 22.—William Gordon of Gight was one of the sureties in 4,000 merks that the Marquis of Huntly should appear before the Privy Council on April 10 (*Ibid*).

1603 *Oct.* 17 —William Gordon of Gight gave caution for Robert Birney in Brakley Tarves 1,000 merks not to harm James Gordon of Haddo, or Johnne

Gordoun of Tirelt. Mr Lawrence registers the bond, subscribed at the Kirk of Tarves, 6th October, before William Prot, George Pringle, William Kar, William Steward, Johnne Meldrum, William Gordoun, and William Leslie, notary public (*Privy Council Register*) •

1605. *April*—William Gordon was put to the horn for not paying to William Buchan and James Anderson, burgesses of Aberdeen, the sum of 200 merks with £54 as principal and 40s. for expenses On Aug. 15, 1605, it was reported to the Privy Council that Gordon "remains at the horn unrelaxed". The Lords ordered the captain of the guard to apprehend him and "remove his family furth of his house and inventory his goods for his Majesty's use" (*Ibid*).

1605. *His death*—William Gordon died in this year, and in death gave nearly as much trouble as when in life, for he was buried with Roman Catholic honours. On January 3, 1607, the king sent a letter from Whitehall to the Privy Council of Scotland "concerning the mode of dealing with noble men suspected in their religion". In the course of the epistle his Majesty said. "And heirwith we are specialie to recommend unto you that exact tryall be taikin of these two verie heynous offenceis committed at the two severall buryallis and funerallis of the Lord Ogilvy and Laird of Geicht, quhairin ther wes sum superstitious ceremoneis and rittes used as gif the profession of papistrie had bene specialie licenced and tolerated, and upon the knauledge of the authouris of those insolenceis, owre plesour and will is that ye do presentlie commit thame, and efter the examination of all the particular circumstances in that mater that ye acquent us thairwith to the effect that we may returne bak unto yow owre will and pleasour thairin". At Edinburgh, April 2, 1607, Sir Thomas Hamiltoun, King's Advocate, complained to the Privy Council as follows: "Notwithstanding the Acts of Parliament against 'superstitious and popische rates,' yet at the burial of William Gordoun of Geycht, George Crawford, now servitor to —— Hay of Urie, of the special causing of George Gordoun, now of Geycht, bore a crucifix on a spear immediately before the corps the whole way in the place of burial, the said George being present on the occasion and assisting at this superstitious and popische custom" (*Privy Council Register*).

William Gordon married Isobel Ochterlony, daughter of (William ?) Ochterlony of Kelly (*Balbithan MS.*). In the charter chest of Lord Morton (*Hist. MSS Com*, 2nd Report, Appendix, p. 184) there is a letter from " Dame Elizabeth Gordon Lady of Gycht," under date 1597. Alice Lady Morton declined to let me examine it. Isobel Ochterlony died in May, 1604, and like her spouse was buried according to the rites of the Roman Catholic Church. On April 2, 1607, Sir Thomas Hamilton, the King's Advocate, complained to the Privy Council that at the funeral David Wilson, tenant of part of the lands of Gight—

By command of George Gordon, now of Geycht, the Lady's son, careyed ane crucifix upoun ane speir immediatelie before the corps of the said umquhill Issobell the haill way to the place of her buriall. Charge had been given to George Gordon, David Wilsoun and George Crawfurd to answer, and now pursuer appearing, but none of the defenders, the Lords, after hearing the depositions of certain witnesses, find the libel proved against Gordoun in both points, and also the charge against Crawfurd, and therefore ordain both to enter in ward in the Castle of Edinburgh within eighteen days after being commanded under pain of rebellion (*Privy Council Register*). On May 13, 1604, John Melville, painter in Aberdeen, was summoned by the Presbytery for painting the crucifix

William Gordon and his spouse, Isobel Ochterlony, had seven sons and seven daughters. All the boys followed in the footsteps of their sire—one of the daughters, even, was charged with a brutal assault on a man ; and the grandchildren of the laird (the sons of his sons and of his daughters alike) became notorious The issue of the fifth laird was as follows :—

1. GEORGE, VI. of Gight.
2 JOHN, of Ardlogie. He was the father of the famous Royalist, Nathaniel, and himself was a redoubtable warrior. In 1601 he took part in the Turriff Raid, to which I have referred. But his chief contribution to the history of his house was his connection with a dare-devil gang of marauders, called the "Societie and Companie of Boyis," or "Knights of the Mortar" (who are fully described in the *Privy Council Register*) They went about the country as champions of Rome, but their real object was plunder On January 20, 1607, the Privy Council wrote a letter to the Marquis of Huntly calling on him to suppress the "Societie" as follows: "After owre verye hairtlie commendationis to your goode Lordships. We ar informed of a very great insolence begun, and like to grow to a greater hicht, within the boundis of your Lordshipis office be Johne Gordoun, callit of Gycht, —— Forbes of Corsindae, Patrik McInneis, and some otheris, who, having associat unto thameselffis ane nomber of deboscheit and laules lymmaris calling thameselffis 'The Societie and Companie of Boyis,' they haif most unlauchfullie and seditiouslie bound thameselffis in ane fellowschip with aithis, vowis, and protestationis of mutuall defence and persute, and that every one of thair quarrellis salbe common to all, and that the purpois and interprise of ony one of thame salbe prosequuted, bakkit, and followit onte be the haill societie aganis all and quhatsomevir without respect of personis Lyke as thir same lymmaris keepis thameselffis togidder, committing open and avowed reiffis, heirshippis and utheris enormities in all pairtis quhair they may be maisteris and commandaris. Quhilk proude and detestable attempt, as it is odious to be hard of in a peaceable estate, subject to a Prince whom God hes armed with pouer and force able to suppress the same, so the same caryis with it no little sclander and prejudice to your Lordshippis honour

and credit.—That within your boundis quhair your Lordship may command suche ane handfull of lymmaris dar presome to attempt such interpriseis. And we are certane that the knaulege hairof being broght to his Majestie will mak his heynes wonderfully till admeir your Lordshippis lang patience and connivence in not apprehending, punisheing and suppresseing of thir lymmaris and what constructionis may be made heirupon to his Majestie agains your Lordship we remit to your Lordshippis consideratioun. Alwayes we are heirby to requeist and desyre your Lordship that, with all convenient speede, you tak orderis for apprehending of the saidis personis and some otheris the chieftanes of that laules societie and present thame heir befoir the Counsell, and that your Lordship prosequute with fyre and swerd the haill raist of thair followaris and nevir leaf of the persute of thame while thay may be apprehendit, punist and altogidder supprest, as you respect his Majesteis service, the peace of the countrey, and your awne credite, honnour, and reputatioun, and as your Lordship wold estew that hard censure and constructioun whiche his Majestie may mak of your behaviour in this point. Sua we committ you to God." On July 13, 1607, Ardlogie (supported by Alexander Copland of Udoch, Patrick Con of Auchry and his son, and Robert Udny of Tilliecorthy) raided the lands of Magnus Mowat of Balquholly, their neighbour. On July 29 Mowat returned the compliment by taking away the peats of Auchry and of Mrs. Patrick Copland of Udoch, widow (possibly the mother of the aforesaid Alexander, who in 1603 had been charged with assaulting Magnus Mowat, apparent of Balquholly, at the fortalice of Freswick, Caithness). In 1616 he waged war on William Leask of Kelly, whose daughter seems to have married his brother Adam. He was also implicated in the brutal murder of Francis Hay. In 1618 he helped, according to the *Privy Council Register* of June 11, 1618, his brother Alexander and his "suster's son, William Gordon of Saphak, to raid the lands of Sir William Keith of Balmuir, a civile, obedient, and ansuerable subject who never offendit thame". An account of this affair will be found in the account of Ardlogie's brother, Alexander. On March, 6, 1618, Ardlogie went on horseback with a sword in his hand to the "ball greene of Kellie" when Sir William Keith was at the place of Kellie, "rode up and down the greene, making provocatioun to him to have come furth, and with schouting and crying he utterit the wordis following, ' Up thy hairt, Ardlogie!'" I think this John was the John Gordon of Ardlogie who offered to raise levies for the King of Denmark's army (1626-7), for which Scotland raised 14,000 men. On March 8, 1627, Captain James Sinclair of Murkill got a commission to raise 3,000 men. Ardlogie undertook a "charge" in Murkill's regiment, and received his Majesties "moneyes," and gave his bond for "lifting and transporting of thame toward Germanie". He failed to do so, for on July 25, 1618, the Privy Council reported that he

"hes most undewtifullie and unworthilie failyied in performing his conditioun, sua that after ane yeares patience and attending his discharge of
. dewtie he is at last for that caus denunced his Majesteis rebell and put to
the horne, quhairat he hes remained this lang tyme, as he does yitt,
unrelaxt, to the high and proud contempt of his Majesteis auctoritie and
·disappointing and hindering of his Majesteis service ". The Council there-
· fore requested Lord Huntly to arrest him, " for we know very weill if your
lordship kythe in this earand (as we perswade our selffis you will) thair is
no possibilitie that the said Johne can escape your lordships hands " (*Privy
Council Register*). In 1634 John of Ardlogie helped the Huntly Gordons
to avenge themselves on Frendraught for the burning of Viscount Aboyne,
robbing Alexander Innes, minister of Rothiemay, of his ryding horss
(*Troubles*, i , 48). He was denounced as a rebel, and ordered (in 1635) to be
arrested. He seems to have escaped to Germany, for it is apparently he
who is referred to in a letter from Andrew Leslie to Father John Seton
(dated March 26, 1639), and quoted in the Domestic Series of *State
· Papers* (*Charles I* , 1638-9, p. 569) : " I have tasted of your Germany   . .
· Colonel Gordon [of Wallenstein fame ?] is not yet a Catholic   He has
·had a cousin [Ardlogie would have been his cousin-german] by him, who
is lately dead, called John Gordon of Ardlogy, his brother's son [this is
· nonsense in any case], who married the Provost of Melrose's daughter."
·The *Balbithan MS.* says that Ardlogie married the daughter of Captain
·Thomas Keir and had four sons and two daughters

> (1) ADAM took part in the attack made by the sixth laird of Gight, his
> uncle, on Sir Harry Wood of Bonnyton (when he is described as
> " appearand " of Gight) in 1624 (to which I shall refer) In 1625
> he was admitted to the Scots Men at Arms in France by Huntly,
> who was captain in the corps, and who made his first muster at
> Leith, July, 1625. Adam Gordon, who had Patrick Gordon of
> ·Boghead (his uncle ?) as one of his cautioners, promised that he
> should " dewlie observe and keip the haill mustoris dewlie preparit
> with ane man and tua horse, armit in all peices with ane case of
> pistollis at sic place and tyme as the said capitaine [Huntly] should
> appoint " (*Spalding Club Miscellany*, iv). I think he must be the
> Gordon referred to by Robert Innes, the nephew of John Gordon
> of ·Ardlogie, who wrote to his brother, the laird ·of Leuchars,
> ·from London, July 15, 1636, as follows (*Familie of Innes*, p. 225):
> "Young Arlogie I think be this tyme be deid. The·nycht befor I
> ·cam· to Parris [he] was run throw the bodie by·on[e] Achterfoall.·
> ·Arlogie being ·wery drunk persuit the wther in stritts. My Lord
> . ' [Gordon] ·was wery cairfull off him . . . He told ·me he thocht he
> could not live tuo dayes."

> (2) JOHN is described by Spalding (i , 355) as " second son," and (ii.,

324) in 1644 as "goodman of Ardlogie". He joined in the attack (1634) on the laird of Frendraught, who had burned up Lord Aboyne in 1630, and was denounced as a rebel He went to Berwick in June, and returned in November, 1640 (Spalding's Troubles, L, 293. In the latter month, while drinking at Fyvie, he shot Sergeant Forsyth, of Lieutenant Fotheringham's musketeers, dead. The Gordons got clear away, and Fotheringham was afterwards (Jan 16, 1641) drummed out of the army in public, the degradation taking place at the Cross of Aberdeen, when the hangman broke the sword of the lieutenant, who was then "convoyit out of the toune, throw Futters port, to seik his fortoun" (ibid, 11, 4). He was alive in January, 1647 (Acts of Parliament), when he "received assurances without acting" On June 27, 1655, a John Gordon got a pass to go to Poland or Sweden (Calendar of State Papers). I think that this John Gordon of Ardlogie must have been the one who married Isobel Innes, one of the three daughters of Jerome Innes, minister of Fyvie, and son of the first laird of Edingight. The genealogy at this point is very puzzling, for this Isobel may have been John's mother, not his wife, though the dates seem to indicate the latter supposition At any rate John Gordon of Ardlogie and Isobel Innes had a daughter, Elizabeth Gordon, who married her distant kinsman, John Innes of Edingight (probably about 1659), and (possibly) had three sons and a daughter. One of these sons, John, sixth of Edingight, was the father of Alexander Innes of Rosieburn, and the grandfather of Katherine Innes, Mrs. Byron's mother (See Colonel Innes' Chronicles of the Family of Innes of Edingight)

(3) NATHANIEL, the daring Royalist, was probably the third son of old Ardlogie. He was the only member of the Gight family that ever met his death on the scaffold (Jan 20, 1646). Few of the Cavaliers present such a dashing figure as Nathaniel Gordon. Indeed, he is so picturesque that I fancy Scott, who considered him one of "the bravest and best soldiers in Europe," had he ever written a romance of Aberdeenshire, might possibly have taken Gordon for his hero: the unusual length of a note in Border Minstrelsy points that way. In addition to his escapades as a soldier, the gay Gordon did not leave it to the imagination of the romancer to supply a "love interest," for, as became a man of the same ancestry as Byron, and with the amatory Montrose as his leader, he could spell Woman as well as War. I fancy Nathaniel must have been a trained soldier from the fact that he was entrusted with important commands by Huntly and Montrose, and is constantly spoken of as "Major Gordon" Bishop Wishart speaks of him as having

served gallantly "both abroad and at home". The fact that his mother was a daughter of the Provost of Melrose, and that his father died in Germany, indicates that the Ardlogie family were not stay-at-homes; and it is just possible that his kinsman, Wallenstein's assassin, may have given him a taste of fighting in the Empire. He crosses our path first in the very year (1634) when Europe rang with Wallenstein's death, and during the next decade he figures constantly in the annals of the Loyalists who defied the Covenant. In November, 1634 (Spalding's *Troubles*, i., 48), he joined the band of Gordons who set about avenging the death of the first Viscount Aboyne, who had been burned at Frendraught Castle four years before—for family feuds were carried on with the vigour of invincible vendettas. They "spolzeit" cattle from Crichton They stole the minister of Rothiemay's "ryding horss". They took "sum moneyis fra Mr. Robert Jamesoun, minister at Mairtyne Kirk, violentlie and maisterfullie". They hanged one of Crichton's friends, suspected of being a spy, "most cruellie vpone the gallous neir to Strathbogie". They drove off 260 oxen and 360 sheep from Frendraught They burned up the corn-yard of the Mains of Frendraught, "quhairin thair wes standing four scoir stakis". They effected an entrance at the house of Rothiemay, and "took it up royallie," killing a large number of sheep for their banquets. Some of these they "saltit, sum they rvistit, and sum they eitit freshe," while they compelled Frendraught's tenants to replenish their larder with "meill, malt, cokis, customs, and pultrie". The laird of Frendraught went to Edinburgh and laid his case before the Privy Council. One day a herald in "cot armes, with sound of trvmpit," rode forth to summon the "misdoeris" to answer to the Crown He met the band on the road between Banff and Elgin, only to be told that they intended to be avenged on Frendraught Of course the "misdoeris" did not appear before the Privy Council; and the bulk of them, including Nathaniel Gordon, were declared rebels. Ever a favourite with women, the dashing young cavalier was harboured by the lady of Rothiemay (*née* Katherine Forbes), whose son had also been burned. She got nearly a year's imprisonment in Edinburgh for her trouble (being liberated in the autumn of 1637), but Nathaniel escaped and lived to fight another day. Whether he left the country with his father, who, as noted, died in Germany in 1638, I cannot say In any case, he does not reappear in the great struggle till June, 1639, when he captured Ogilvy of Powry in a hand-to-hand struggle near Elsick (Gordon's *Scots Affairs*, ii, 275) In June, 1640, he left for Berwick with George, Lord Gordon (the elder brother of Viscount

Aboyne, who had been burned at Frendraught) (Spalding's *Troubles*, 1, 293), and he is absent from the pages of Spalding until the spring of 1644, the most violent year of his restless career.   In Feb., 1644, as Nathaniel and his friends were plundering the lands of Taarty, belonging to the learned Dr. Dun, of Aberdeen, they encountered a band of Covenanters, who were bound on a similar errand to the estates of some persistent Loyalists.   The Covenanters were routed and disarmed, and cam schamefully back againe to Aberdene (Spalding's *Troubles*, ii., 322).   Encouraged by this success, the little band of Loyalists kidnapped the Provost and Magistrates of Aberdeen on March 19, 1644.   At seven o'clock in the morning nine cavaliers—Irvine of Drum and his brother, Seton of Shethin, Meldrum of Iden, Innes of Tipperty, Sir John Gordon of Haddo, Sir George Gordon of Gight, John Gordon of Ardlogie and his brother, Major Nathaniel Gordon—at the head of sixty or a hundred horsemen—the number differs according as your authority is Loyalist or Covenanter—rode into the town, kidnapped Patrick Leslie (the Provost), ex-Bailies Robert Farquhar and Alexander Jaffray, and Dean of Guild John Jaffray, and within four-and-twenty hours had clapped them in Huntly's stronghold at Strathbogie The poor burghers were kept there till April 2, when they were transferred to Auchindoun, another Gordon keep; nor were they set at liberty until May 7, when the Marquis of Argyll appeared on the scene and rescued them ' ῀ ʿii., 324).   On April 5, 1644, Nathaniel made a daring deal on his own account which got him into trouble with his chief, Lord Huntly   A Danish herring smack, which had been taken by an English pirate and depleted of its crew, drifted into Aberdeen Bay   Nathaniel Gordon, assisted by twenty musketeers, seized the prize, and clapped the Englishmen who had been put on board in the Tolbooth.   The pirate duly made its appearance to claim the prize.   Nathaniel promptly arrested the pilot and the skipper, who turned out to belong not to the pirate, but to an English man-of-war.   In retaliation the pirate began to harry the local shipping, and even made a descent on the land at Belhelvie.   The fishing population, which suffered most, complained to Lord Huntly, who reproved Nathaniel "veray bitterly" for taking the prize without his permission Gordon, hitherto an obedient soldier, resented the reproof   He was indeed so "angrie that he hastellie took his leive and left the Marques' service".   Just before taking that step, however, he had been one of the force (300 strong) which (on April 24) had raided the town of Montrose, where he is said to have killed a bailie, Alexander Peirson   The laird of Drum tried to set fire to the

town twice, but Gordon "pat out the samen"—which surely more
than counterbalanced his slaughter of the worthy bailie.　On
April 29 he sent in his resignation to Huntly, offered his services
to the marquis' son, Lord Gordon, and when they were refused,
"leivit be him self." (Spalding's *Troubles*, ii, 339-52).　But he could
not live long "be himself".　If he had been wise he would have
got out of the country, for the forces of the Kirk were quickly
closing round the Cavaliers.　On May 8 the Covenanters made a
dead set on the Gight country as the hotbed of the Loyalist cause
in the north.　Kelly, where Sir John Gordon of Haddo lived,
surrendered; the House of Gight was captured, the young laird
managing, however, to escape; Gight and Haddo were marched
off to Edinburgh as prisoners; while a reward of 18,000 marks was
offered for the "inbringing" of Lord Huntly "quik or deid," and
"sic vther soumes" for young Gight and Nathaniel Gordon.　So
Nathaniel put all his private grievances aside, for he "luikit for no
better himself, if he hapnit to cum in [to the Covenanters'] handis".
He therefore resolved to fight it out to the death, and "defend him
self als long as he could".　His policy, however, was not the
negative one of mere defence　He opened a positive campaign of
attack by setting upon the merchants of Aberdeen and Dundee
who assembled at St. James' Market in Elgin on July 24.　The
merchants came back to Aberdeen 14,000 marks the poorer, and
Lord Gordon was despatched to arrest Nathaniel and his friends.
His lordship returned without his "pray, and the honest men
gat no amendis" (*ibid.*, ii.; 392)　Then came a brief respite,
for Nathaniel, eager to escape the ban of excommunication,
agreed to a truce with the Covenanters, and even allowed the
redoubtable Andrew Cant to reprove him, Nov., 1644　Spalding
describes all this as "politique".　On Feb. 6, 1645, however, he
signed the Royalist Bond of Union (*History of the Clan Gregor*, ii,
92)　By the following March Cant's power had crumbled to pieces
The ministers "fled for feir", there was no sermon in "either of the
Aberdenis"; and on Sunday, March 9, Nathaniel marched into the
town with a hundred Irish dragoons, got the keys of the Tolbooth, set
free the prisoners, and seized all the available arms　On March 15
Sir John Hurry, the Covenanting general, came into the town, to find
Nathaniel and his friends "drinking cairleslie" in their lodgings.
Hurry's men killed Captain Donald Farquharson, who had married
Margaret Gordon, of the Abergeldie family, and two or three other
Cavaliers　Nathaniel once more escaped with his life, losing Lord
Huntly's best horse, which had been lent to him, for he had re-
gained the favour of his chief (Spalding's *Troubles*, ii, 453-5).　But

he could not really escape, for fighting was in his very blood, and soon he got a chance of showing his mettle, for the deciding battles of the great struggle followed fast on one another In each of these he occupied an important post, commanding the right wing of Montrose's army either alone or in conjunction with some one else. His bravery is described in glowing terms in *Britane's Distemper*. He was present at the battle of Auldearn (May 9), and afterwards helped young Graham to rescue his sister, Lady Margaret Stirling of Keir, from Linlithgow, where she had been imprisoned after being captured (on the very day of the battle) by the Kirk. At the battle of Alford (July 2) he hacked his way through a lane of the enemy, bidding his musketeers throw aside their weapons and hamstring the horses with their dirks. Once again he escaped, but he left Lord Gordon a corpse on the field which Montrose won so dearly. He also fought at the battle of Kilsyth, August 15 The periods between these battles were filled in with escapades which sorely troubled the Covenanters. For instance, some time in the September after Kilsyth, the ragged rebels whom Nathaniel and Lord Ogilvie commanded quartered themselves on the Rev Bernard Sanderson, the minister of Nithsdale. They "brake vp his cofferis, chistis, and almries; carried away his whole bedding and the haill abuilzements" of '' minister and his wife They "brunt and spoyled his buekis, chistis, chyres, stoolis, and vther tymber work"—for a camp fire had to be kept going; and they ate up "his haill cornes vpon his gleib"—for even dashing cavaliers could not live on loyalism alone The unfortunate parson fled to Carlisle for "safety of his lyff", while his servants and "motherless childring" took to the "hillis and mountaines, destitute bothe of food and harbourie". This escapade cost the Crown 1,200 merks, for that was the compensation voted to Sanderson by the Scots Parliament. Then Nathaniel's luck turned, for he was captured after the battle of Philiphaugh (September 13), and marched off to Edinburgh in triumph by the Covenanters (*Earls of Sutherland*, p. 529) He was charged with the deadly crime of having taken upon him to "rise in arms, and to remain with, fortify, assist, and supply James Graham, the avowed enemy of this kingdom, leader of that rebellious army, which lately this year by-gone has infested this kingdom and troubled the peace thereof". The gay Nathaniel parleyed with the Presbyterians. There is even a subtle irony in the fact that his answers to the Court—still preserved in the Duke of Montrose's charter chest (*Hist. MSS. Commission*, 2nd Report, Appendix, pp 174-5)—have Scripture texts scribbled on the back But the Court closed its ears to all entreaties, for it knew that his release would mean renewed trouble. So it declared him guilty, and condemned him to die as a traitor. The execution took place at the Cross of St Andrews on January 20, 1646, the maiden or guillotine being brought from Dundee for the purpose. Gordon was the first of the prisoners, who included Sir Robert Spottiswood, to mount the scaffold Wishart's account of him (as translated by Mr. Morland Simpson in the *Deeds of Montrose*, p. 169) is memorable :—

When he saw death so near he bitterly lamented the sins of his youth. Just before his death a paper was thrust into his hands to sign, in attestation of his penitence. To this he readily put his name. At the same time he called God and His angels and all who were present to witness that, if there were anything in that document derogatory to the King and his authority, he utterly disowned it. He was then absolved from the sentence of excommunication laid upon him for an adultery he had committed long before. Amidst the profound pity of the spectators he laid his head upon the block.

Even in death, however, Nathaniel was not at rest, for Parliament and Presbyteries continued to wrangle over him for five years at least. His estate was a matter of dispute (*Acts of Parliament*, vi., part 2, p 227). He seems to have had no ready money towards the end of his career, for Robert Keith, the minister of Deer, advanced 200 merks, and Elspet Donaldson, widow of an Aberdeen burgess, lent 100 merks to support Nathaniel in prison and to afford him decent burial. Gordon, however, declared to the end that 500 merks were due to him by Janet Gordon, the widow of William Gordon of Tulloch, and he directed in his last will and testament that his creditors should be paid out of this, the residue going to his wife, Grisel Seton—probably of the Shethin or Udny families. But Mrs Gordon of Tulloch resolutely declined to pay the 500 merks, and the poor parson of Deer had to appeal to Parliament as late as 1649 to help him to get back his money. Nathaniel's wife Grisel must have had to practice the patience of her great namesake, for he was fancy-free, and did not let the marriage vow interfere with his inclinations Cant had once criticised his polygamous instincts, whereon Nathaniel wrote the parson a letter which "fleyet him to the hairt, and causit him to remove out of the toun" of Aberdeen. Nathaniel afterwards confessed his sin, "but God knowis," says Spalding (ii., 431), "if this humiliatioun wes fra his hairt". Long after his death his emotional misdemeanours were torturing the conscience of the Presbytery of Strathbogie, which persecuted Jean Gordon, "Lady Alter"—she is sometimes called "Lady Glengerak"—from 1645 to 1651 on the ground that she had borne one child to Nathaniel and another to his comrade-in-arms, Captain Mortimer. The Duke of Fife's first known ancestor, Adam Duff in (not of) Clunybegg, gave evidence in this case. He told the Presbytery (January 19, 1650) that the lady "vas in a barne of his fourteen days or thereaboutt, and for anything that he or the vomen thereaboutt could perseaue, shoe vas vith child" (*Presbytery Book of Strathbogie*). A contemporary ballad (preserved by Peter Buchan) pictures Nathaniel as serenading a widow:—

Widow are ye sleeping yet ?	If I promised to marry you,
Or widow are ye waking ?	My dow, but an' my dawty;
Ye'll open the gin, let me come in,	And if I promised to marry you
And me your only darling. .	I'm sure I'm nae sae fauty.

Despite all this pillorying, however, Nathaniel Gordon remains a picturesque, almost likeable, figure in history. He is referred to in the ballad of the "Gallant Grahams":—

Nathaniel Gordon, stout and bold,
Did for King Charles wear the blue.

Patrick Gordon in *Britane's Distemper* (p. 168) declares that he was "weel belowed euen by his enemies". He was "too walourous a cauelyre". Wishart says he was "famous for his courage and military skill," and that he was "a brave, faithful gentleman" who had "great influence in his own country". Nathaniel had a son—

ADAM, who was served heir to his "gudsir," Jan 2, 1656 (*Inquisit. Gen*). He was possibly the Adam Gordon of Ardlogie who was at Konigsberg in 1659, for General Patrick Gordon of Auchleuchries, the friend of Peter the Great, sent letters home to Scotland by him (Patrick Gordon's *Diary*)

(4) GEORGE helped his father in 1634 to steal the horse of Alexander Innes, the minister of Rothiemay, who was deposed in 1647, when he was succeeded by James Gordon, the well-known parson of Rothiemay (Spalding's *Troubles*, 1, 48). He may have been the George Gordon, one of his tenants at Lethenty, who in 1622 went forth to do battle on his own account with two brothers named Ferguson, at Newburgh. Undeterred by the fact that the day was the Sabbath, he struck one of them with "his faldit neiff upoun the faice and head, and thereby damneist and feld him deid to the ground," and then "verrie barbarously cuttit off his right lug". Not satisfied with this barbarism, he pursued the other brother with a drawn sword, and "cutt ane grite peece of his harne pane" (*Privy Council Register*). George of Lethentie was accused by William Durhame, fiar of the Grange, Henry Ramsay of Ardownie,

and Mr William Murray in Ardownie, of helping Sir George
Gordon of Gight to "minass" them, 1631 (*Privy Council Register*).

(5) Daughter married John Gordon, son to Knockespock (*Balbithan MS*).

3. WILLIAM took part in a raid on Turriff (July, 1601), and was put to the horn.
He disappears from all records after this date. The *Balbithan MS.* says
he was "killed in Turreff".

4. PATRICK held the farm of Boghead on the Gight estate, in 1695 its poll tax
was set down at £9 14s. In 1601 he murdered Robert Catto, servant of
Mowat of Balquholly (*Privy Council Register*). On July 2, 1606, Sir John
Lindsay of Wodray and Sir William Ochterlony of Kellie were caution to
the Council for Patrick Gordon, brother to the laird of Gight, not to
harm Archibald Douglas and Magnus Mowat, fiar of Balquholly. He
was implicated with his brother Adam in an assault on Fraser of Stoneywood and Fraser of Durris in Aberdeen, 1609 On July 23, 1612, Sir
Thomas Hamilton of Byres, the King's Advocate, and Alexander Bannerman of Waterton, and others, complained to the Council that Patrick
and Adam Gordon, brothers of George Gordon of Gight, pursued Bannerman and his friends for their lives in Aberdeen and wounded two of
Bannerman's servants. Moreover, they "daily since this assault and
insolence hes borne and worne hagbutis and pistolletis, and ridden and
gon thairwith publictlie and avowedlie in all pairtis" of the country to
attack pursuers. The Lords find defenders guilty of the assault and wounding, and ordain them therefore to enter in ward in the Tolbooth of Edinburgh, there to remain at their own expense till further order be taken
with them in the matter, but assoilzie them from the charge of having
worn hagbuts and pistolets, pursuers having failed in proving that
particularly. In 1615 he was implicated in the attack on the Hays In
1616 William Leask, of that ilk, complained that Patrick and his brothers,
John and Alexander, had annoyed him for eighteen months On Nov. 4,
1617, he was asked by the Privy Council to leave the country On Sept.
10, 1623, a complaint was tendered to the Privy Council by the King's
Advocate and George Thomson, Writer to the Signet, to this effect:
Patrick Auchterlony of Bonhard owed various sums of money to the said
George Thomson, who had with great patience waited for payment, but
at last was constrained to raise letters of horning and then a caption
against his debtor On —— May, 1623, while Auchterlony was in Dundee, Thomson charged the provost and bailies of that burgh to apprehend him. Auchterlony, being warned, absented himself, and the complainer caused his horse, which was valued at £12, to be poinded in
part payment. For this cause alone Auchterlony resolved to have the
complainer's life, and in company with Patrick Gordoun, brother of
George Gordon of Gight, and others, lay in wait for complainer, who
was to ride from Dundee to Forfar, there to appraise the horse anew at
the market-cross. When he was seen on his way thither, Patrick

Gordoun, at Auchterlony's instance, leaped on horseback, and "haveing tua chargit pistollettis at his belt," rode after Thomson Gordon, on overtaking Thomson, demanded "how he durst be so bald as to poynd" his kinsman Auchterlony's horse (Patrick's mother, it may be remembered, was an Ochterlony). Thomson "simplie ansuerit that he understoode that his Majesteis auctoritie was a sufficient warrand", whereupon Patrick "most proudlie said that, yf he haid all the warrands that the King hes, he sould mak him repent the doing thairof, and without ony forder (speeches?) pullit furth ane of the saidis pistollis frome his belt, and thairwith gaif the said George a cruell straik and wound on the rycht side of the head, and then gaif him ane uther cruell and deadlie straik and wound a little above his left eye, and thairby almost dammeist him dead". The complainer fled for safety to a house near, when Gordon "bendit" one of his pistols and rode furiously after the complainer "to the said house gavell," but some well-disposed neighbours "stayit him and convoyit him away". Pursuer appearing personally, while the two defenders do not appear, the Lords order them to be denounced rebels. Patrick was engaged in a vendetta in 1625 to avenge the case of his illegitimate son William. He had been anxious that this son should marry Margaret, the only daughter of John Cushnie, Culsalmond. The girl, however, set her heart on one Richard Gordon. He was the son of Iohn Gordon of Drymies (a cadet of Craig). Richard was servitor of Leslie of Wardes (a brother, Oliver, was servitor to the laird in 1627); he was put to the horn in 1623 for the "felloun and cruell slaughter of John Johnston in Inverurie," and in 1622 had been denounced as having worn hagbuts for three years, and "shoit thairwith at deir, rae, and wyld foull" Patrick Gordon heard of the intended wedding in September, 1625, and he immediately sent his son William "with a nomber of¡laules personis" to Cushnie's house, "of purpois to haif ravished" the girl. They offered "grite violence both to hir fathir and mother," hurt "diverse of hir familie," and "perforce caryed away the said Margaret Cushnie, band hir upon a horse behind ane of thame, and at last the said William verie barbaroushe did force hir" By the aid of the justices of the peace she was rescued, and shortly afterwards married her Richard. The Gights resolved to be avenged. They lay in wait for Richard, "soght him divers tymes, and [at] last, rancountering him betuix Tillyfour and Newton of Colsalmond, he wes violentlie assaultit and persewit of his lyffe by the said Patrik, accompanyed with Johnne Gordoun of Ardlogie, his brother [the father of the notorious Nathaniel, executed in 1646], Johnne Gordon of Knockespock [who had married the latter's sister], and a nombir of thair complices, who, nochtwithstanding of the said Richart his humble salutatioun unto thame, and of his submissive intreatie for Godis peace and his majesties, did hurt and wounde bothe him and his hors". At last Richard was "constrayned in his just and necessar defence to stand to the saulftie of his lyffe, and haveing a pistoll about him, wheras no prayer nor intercession availlit him, he shoit " Patrick "with the pistolett". Patrick succumbed to his wounds, "acknawledgeing at the verie houre of his death his fault and just deserving, and did freelie acquite and pardoun the said Richart". Richard appealed to the king for pardon. His Majesty referred his petition to the Privy Council (Feb 12, 1626), and summoned both parties (July 4, 1626). None of the Gight Gordons appeared however, and the Council found Richard entitled to at least a year's protection, "the reason why they did not go further having apparently been that though the slaughter committed had been in self-defence, yet Richard Gordon, in having a pistol about him at all, had incurred the penalties imposed by the Acts against useing or wearing fire-arms". When Cushnie wanted to return home from Edinburgh, he was afraid lest his action against the Gights would "mak thame the more violent and insolentlie disposed aganis him, sua that he cannot live in the cuntrey for feare of thair trouble and persute". So the Council (July 6, 1626) wrote to the Marquis of Huntly. "We haif thoght goode to recommend the honnest man [Cushnie] to your Lordshipis protectioun and saulf-gaird, earnestlie requeisting and desiring your Lordship to tak the patrocinie and defence of him, and so to provide for his indempnitie aganis the rage and malice of the said William Gordoun and his partakeris as they may be restreaned and awed by your Lordshipis countenance and auctoritie from harmeing of him, and that he may repose in peace and follow out his adois without feare or danger of thair persute". On August 1, 1626, caution was given by Mr Patrick Dunbar, fiar of Westerton, in 2,000 merks, that Adam Gordon, son of John Gordon of Ardlogie, would not molest Richard Gordon, "son to John Gordon of Drummoureis" (in 1627 he is described as of Drymies), Oliver, John and Patrick, his brothers, George Gordon of ——, John Cushnie in Newton of Culsalmond, nor their families. On August 23, 1626, the Council again wrote to the king relating what they had done in the matter. On March 13, 1627, Mr. John Paip, younger, advocate, as procurator for the cautioner, registered a bond of caution by James Gordon, fiar of Tillielt, in 3,000 merks, "that George Gordon, apparent [and afterwards VII.] of Geyght, will not molest Richard Gordon, John Cushnie in Cowcraigs, Isobell Hervie, his spouse Margaret Cushnie [Mrs. Richard Gordon, his daughter], Olipher Gordoun, servitor to the Laird of Wardes, John Gordon, servitor to Lord Gordoun, and Patrick Gordon in ——, brothers to the said Richard, nor their families, tenants, etc., in terms of lawburrows raised by them, with clause of relief". The bond written by John Lessell, notary, at the new Kirk of Deer, is dated at the Mill of Kellie, March 8, 1627. The feud, however, as related in the *Privy Council Register*, did not stop there. On May 16, 1628, Oliver Gordon, brother of Richard Gordon aforesaid, complained

to the Council about the Gight Gordons. He told how he had been "upoun
the Linkes of Aberdeen [on a date not stated, in this year] ryding upoun
my awin hors, haveing a course to have runne with John Johnestoun,
servitor to the Laird of Cluny". John Gordon, Ardlogie (brother of
Patrick), who had hate and malice against him, getting notice of this,
came on horseback to the links, "with a bendit hacquebutt in his hand and
a paire of pistoletts at his belt, and John Dalgleische, his servant, running
at his hors foote with a paire of pistolets at his belt and a gwune in his hand".
When Ardlogie saw Oliver he made his way to him behind his back and
would have shot him unawares, if Johnstone had not called on him to
save himself. Ardlogie fired, but his hagbut misgave, whereupon Oliver,
who had neither sword nor armour upon him, having left the links and
"sett spurres" to his horse, was followed by Ardlogie, who had his hagbut in hand "readie bendit" to shoot. Oliver craves the Privy Council
for a summons against Ardlogie.   Patrick Gordon married Margaret
Erskine of Ardestie, Forfarshire (*Balbithan MS.*). On July 18, 1642, the
king confirmed the charter (dated May 29, 1613) by the late Sir Henry
Lindsay (13th Earl of Crawford) to Alexander Durham of Downiemylne,
Forfar, with a precept of sasine to Patrick Gordon.   Janet Durham
married Robert Erskine of Ardestie, whose son resigned these lands to
the sixth laird of Gight in 1623 (the year that Sir Henry Lindsay died).
It will be remembered that Patrick Gordon committed a brutal assault
on George Thomson, writer to the signet, on the highway near Dundee
in 1623, when the lawyer had apparently been settling this business with
him.   This was the third alliance of the Gight Gordons with Forfarshire women, for Patrick's father, William, V of Gight, married an
Ochterlony, while his brother, George, VI. of Gight, married Isobell
Wood of the House of Bonnyton. The *Balbithan MS.* says that Patrick
Gordon "has issue". A son (whose Christian name is not given) was
denounced in August, 1634, for joining in the attacks on the laird of
Frendraught. Two of his sons were—

> JOHN   He was served heir to his father, Patrick, on June 4, 1630
> (*Inquisit. Gen*), and may have been the one who figured in the
> Frendraught vendetta.
> WILLIAM, illegitimate, was concerned in the attack on Richard Gordon,
> as already described.

5. ADAM. He was a fighter, like all his brothers. He was implicated with his
brother Patrick in an assault made on Fraser of Stoneywood and Fraser of
Durris in Aberdeen, 1609. On July 6, 1609, he, his brother Patrick, and
several other Gordons, "to the number of six score persons, all armed
with certain weapons, including hagbuts and pistolets, came at night to
the house of Robert Davidsoun in Abirdene, where the complainers were
for the time, pressed violently to enter therein for their slaughter, and

would have succeeded if they had not been stayed by some good people ".
The next day the defenders followed complainers with drawn swords and
with "bend hagbuts and pistolletis" while they were repairing from Newtown of Abirdene to the Auldtoun, and would have slain them if they had
not been stopped by the magistrates at the port of the said burgh   When
called on to appear before the Privy Council a few of the gang did so, and
were found guilty.   In June, 1612, Adam and his friend Francis Hay of
Logierieve, who was to kill him three years later, and his brother Patrick
Gordon, attacked Alexander Bannerman of Waterton and two of his servants "to the effusion of thair blood in grite quantities" (*Privy Council
Register*).   Adam fought a friendly sword duel with his comrade Francis
Hay (son of George Hay of Ardlethan, cousin-german to the Earl of Erroll).
Hay was defeated, and in pique shot Gordon dead (Dec. 15, 1615)   Three
days later Hay was captured in the house of William Hay of Logierieve
by George (the laird of Gight) and John and Alexander, the brothers of
Adam.   He was carried by them to their "awne ludgeing," the Bonnie
Wife's Inn, in the Gallowgate of Aberdeen, and tried before a packed
jury by a clansman, John Gordon of Clubsgoul, Sheriff of Aberdeen.
The whole case is detailed at length, on account of its extraordinary
lawlessness and ferocity, in the description of the next laird, the sixth,
who took his brother Adam's death very much to heart   Adam Gordon
had got into a trouble with a woman, for on October 6, 1608, he promised
the Presbytery of Ellon (Mair's *Records*, p 76) to marry Isobell, daughter
of William Leask of that ilk   Whether the marriage ever took place I
cannot say (the *Balbithan MS.* does not supply the name), but he declared
that he was willing "to satisfie for entycing" her out of her father's
house, to pay five merks, and make repentance in the Kirk of Ellon
Adam at any rate took umbrage at the House of Leask, for on July 24,
1615, he was put to the horn at the instance of the King's Advocate and
Alexander Leask in Balschamphie, Thomas Fidler there, and William
Smyth in the Mains of Leask.   On August 2, 1615, his arrest was ordered
for not appearing before the Council in answer to a charge of wearing
hagbuts and pistollets, and committing acts of oppression on the said
pursuers   On July 25, 1616, William Leask, apparent of that ilk, complained to the Privy Council that "in the previous December George
Gordon of Gight and William Hay, his son-in-law, attacked him on the
highway, the former with a drawn sword and the latter with two swords
pulled out of one scabbard.   George broke his weapon upon Leask's
head and his son-in-law struck him in divers places through the clothes
Pursuer appearing personally, and the defender George Gordon not
appearing, the Lords ordered him to be denounced rebel.   Later on, Leask
complained to the Council that he had been annoyed for eighteen months
by John, Patrick, Alexander and Robert Gordon of Gight, and William
Keith, who was probably their nephew.

6. ALEXANDER, "in Burngraynes" (so described in the *Privy Council Register*), took part in the murder of Francis Hay. He was denounced as a rebel in 1616 for attacking Leask of that ilk. He was also prosecuted as a Papist. The most notable events in his career were his attacks on Sir William Keith of Balmure. On August 11, 1617, the Lords of Secret Council reported that "of lait thair has ane unhappie accident fallin oute betuix" James Forbes of Blakstoun on one part, and the late William Keith, brother to the Goodman of Clachriach, and Alexander Gordon, brother to the laird of Gight, on the other, wherein Keith was killed and Forbes taken a prisoner by Keith's friends The next we hear of Alexander Gordon is as an enemy of Sir William Keith of Balmure, for on June 4, 1618, it was reported by Keith to the Privy Council that "mony insolencyis" had been committed on him by John Gordon of Ardlogie, his brother Alexander in Burnegraynes, and William Gordon of Saphak, "thair suster sone". On March 10, 1618, according to Keith's story, the three went armed to the land of Kellie, belonging in liferent to Keith's wife, Dame Margaret Bannerman, rode about in a bragging and insolent manner near to the place where pursuer happened to be staying, and endeavoured to provoke him to come forth. They then went to some of his cottars who were near at hand, and told them "that they were come thair to fetche a bair". Disappointed in their desire by the interference of pursuer they rode away to the Kirk of Methlik, where some masons were at work setting up a loft for pursuer. The masons had been warned of their wicked purpose, and so escaped the assault which defenders had intended to make upon them " With drawin swerdis in thair handis thay enterit in the kirk and raid athorte the said Sir Williame's and his said spous landis, searcheing and seeking thair tennantis, demanding of all personis thay mett gif thay wer" Keith's men, and "compellit thame with mony threatningis and minassingis to sweir upoun thair swordguardis that thay wer not thair men". When James Ewing, in Little Methlick, one of Keith's men, who dwelt near the Kirk, heard of the affray and came to see what was wrong, the three Gordons "schamefullie and unhonnesthe, without respect or regairde had to his grite age, perseuit him of his lyff, and he haveing humelie beggit mercie of thame, saying he wes a friend and had nothing to do with thame, thay commanded him to cast his sword frome him, quhilk he haveing done for saulftie of his lyff, thay then of new perseuit him of his lyff, and had not faillit to haif slane him, wer not be the providence of God, his awne bettir defence, and help of some personis present, he wes fred from thame" Pursuers appearing personally, and defenders not appearing, the Lords order the three defenders to be denounced rebels. According to the Privy Council report of June 11, 1618, the three Gordons were not content with this swaggering and "lawles forme to injure and trouble gentlemen thair nichtbouris (who yf the reverent respect and regaird of

(227)

his Majesteis authoritie and obedience restreanit thame not, wald mak the saidis personis to content thameselffis with ressoun and to forbeare thair foleyis). Thay misheanthe, shamefullie, and unhonnestlie come be way of hamesuckin to the dwelling house and corneyaird of Mr. Johnne Mersair, a harmless, innocent minister, and finding him single and allone at his meditatioun with a booke in his hand, thay invadit and perseuit him of his lyffe, housit him in his house, and fleeing to his horse gaif him a nomber of straikis with swerdis, and hurte and woundit him; assezeit him in his house; brasheit his durris with grite jestis; held in bendit pistollis at his windois of purpois to haif shoite him yf thay had gottin a sight of him, and thay had not failed to haif rissen fyre and brinte the house and the said Mr. Johnne within the same, wer not, be the providence of God, some gentilmen and nightbouris, hairing of thair cruell and barbarous purpois, come and releist the said Maister Johnne. For the quhilkis barbarous and detestable insolencyis the saidis Johnne, Alexander and Williame Gordonis being callit and convenit afoir his Majesteis justice and chargit to find cautioun to haif underlyne the lawis, thay absentit thameselffis frome thair tryall, refused to find cautioun, and wer thairfoir, upoun the 18 day of Aprile (1618), denunceit rebellis and putt to the horne, quhairat they remane as yitt unrelaxt, hanting all publict placeis and societie of men as yf thay wer laughfull and obedient subjectis, heighlie to the offence of owre Soverane Lord and misregaird of law and justice. And quhairas the uncontrolled ressett and supplie quhilk the rebellis findis in the cuntrey, not onlie fosteris thame in thair impietie and rebellioun, bot encourageis otheris insolent and lawles personis to adhere unto thame, and the Lordis of Secreit Counseill haveing resolved examplarlie to punishe all suche personis as sall gif ony ressett, supplee or comforte to thir rebellis so lang as thay continew in thair rebellioun, and to the effect all pretext of excuse salbe tane frome thame, yf thay or ony of thame sal happin to offend in this case . . . command, charge and inhibit all and sindrie his Majesteis liegeis and subjectis be oppin proclamatioun at all placeis neidfull that nane of thame presoome nor tak upoun hand to ressett, supplee, nor intercommoun with the saidis rebellis, furneis thame meate, drink, house nor harborie, nor haif intelligence with thame, privatlie nor publictlie, be letteris, messageis, nor no other maner of way during the tyme of thair rebellioun, certifeeing thame that sall failyee or do in the contrair that they sall be callit, persewit and punist thairfoir with all vigour." On July 27, 1619, the Marquis of Huntly, who had been charged at the instance of Sir William Keith and Mr. John Merser to produce Burngraynes and his brother Ardlogie before the Council, protested, and as the pursuers did not appear the protest was admitted. On Jan. 27, 1620, the horning against Ardlogie, who had found caution in 1,000 merks to appear before the Council, which he did, was relaxed. On June 4, 1618, John Hedderwick in Boddam complained to the Privy Council that on the night of April 4, 1618, Alexander Gordon, brother to the laird of Gight, Johne Sinclair, brother of ——— Sinclair of Achannachie, and George Bruce, servitor to the said Alexander, all armed with swords, hagbuts and pistollets, assaulted him at the place of Fortrie, "shote tua billotis throw his richt thie, and with ane lance ran him throw the same thie". They then struck him to the ground and wounded him very seriously in the head. Alexander Gordon did not appear before the Council and was put to the horn According to the *Balbithan MS*, Alexander Gordon married a Hay

7. ROBERT. He took part in the Hay and Leask affairs, and on Nov. 4, 1617, he and his brother Patrick appeared before the Privy Council and "actit thameselffis to depairt and pass furth of this cuntrey for obedyence of his Majesteis decreit". He was one of a band of raiders who, in 1634, entered the lands of "Lady Frendraught," "spyling and laying of the same waist, and hanging one of her tenants at Strathbogie". The Aberdeen Town Council was ordered (December, 1634) to arrest him, but declined the task. In July, 1636, the Privy Council issued a proclamation for his arrest in connection with this affair According to the *Balbithan MS.*, he married a daughter of Ogilvie of Kempcairn

8. JANET. The *Balbithan MS.* says that one of the fifth laird's daughters married a Leith of Harthill. Dr. Davidson in his *Earldom of the Garioch* notes that John Leith, second of Harthill, married as his second wife a Janet Gordon, whom I take to be Gight's daughter. Dr. Davidson further adds that Leith had by his first wife (Beatrice Fraser) a son John, third of Harthill, the notorious rebel who broke out of the Tolbooth of Aberdeen, July, 1640; and that it was his son Patrick who was executed as a rebel in Edinburgh, Oct 26, 1647 (at the age of twenty-five) Now Spalding (*Troubles*, 11, 392) speaks of this Patrick as the "cousing" of Nathaniel Gordon Hence I am inclined to believe that ——— Gordon of Gight married John the third, not the second, laird of Harthill, as Dr. Davidson says In any case, the Spalding reference makes it clear that Patrick Leith was descended from a Gight Gordon (whereas Dr. Davidson's statements make no relationship at all). She was either the mother or the grandmother of "young Harthill," who was hand-in-glove with Nathaniel Gordon, notably in the raid on the Aberdeen merchants at St James' Fair, Elgin, July 24, 1644, and at the capture of Forbes of Craigievar's troopers at Inverurie on Sunday, Feb 23, 1645

9 CHRISTIAN made a good match by marrying, as his first wife, Sir Adam Gordon of Park. George Jamesone painted the portraits of Sir Adam and his spouse, which are now in the possession of Mr. Gordon Duff of Park and Drummuir; but whether the lady was Christian Gordon or Helen Tyrie, Sir Adam's second wife, I cannot tell (John Bulloch's *George Jamesone*, p 138) As the Park genealogy will be treated in another volume, I shall content myself here with tracing it out only in regard to the Duff

connection, because it is the first landed family with whom we can connect the Duke of Fife. The eldest son of Sir Adam was—

SIR JOHN GORDON of Park, who married Margaret, daughter of Sir James Sibbald of Rankeillor, in 1631, and had—

> (i) SIR JOHN GORDON, created a baronet in 1680   The baronetcy became extinct in 1804
>
> (ii) SIR GEORGE GORDON of Edinglassie, Sheriff of Banff   He had, with other issue, a daughter—
>
>> JEAN GORDON, married William Duff of Dipple (grandson of the much-disputed Adam Duff in Clunybegg), and became the mother of the first Earl Fife, and ancestor of the Duke of Fife (Temple's *Thanage of Fermartyn*, p 121)

10. ANNA married, according to the *Balbithan MS*, (1) Alexander Gordon of Tulloch, son of Alexander, III. of Cracullie, and (2) Thomas Gordon of Pittendreich, the fourth son of Sir Thomas Gordon of Cluny (by Elizabeth Douglas, daughter of the Earl of Angus), and brother of Sir Alexander Gordon of Cluny and of Patrick Gordon of Ruthven, who wrote *Britane's Distemper*. Pittendreich was implicated in an attack in Aberdeen, March 26, 1644 (Spalding's *Troubles*, p. 330). Sir Thomas Gordon of Cluny was caution to the Privy Council for the sixth laird of Gight in connection with the murder of Francis Hay in 1617. On Feb 28, 1629, Anna Gordon, spouse to Thomas Gordon of Tulloch, was infeft in the lands of Pittendreich. On June 4, 1674, Thomas Gordon of Pittendreich was given as the liferenter of Tulloch, the laird of which was then a minor (*Records, of the Meeting of the Exercise of Alford*, p. 225)   By her first husband (Alexander Gordon of Tulloch) she had—

> WILLIAM GORDON of Tulloch, who went to France with a corps of men in March 5, 1642, and was made a captain (Spalding's *Troubles*, ii., 125). He married the laird of Cluny's daughter (*Balbithan MS.*), Janet Gordon, who (as a widow) was due Nathaniel Gordon 500 merks in 1646. He had two sons—
>
>> ALEXANDER GORDON of Glengarroch
>>
>> THOMAS GORDON of Garioch.

11. JEAN married George Gordon of Crichie. The *Balbithan MS.* (p. 107) gives the name of "Cushney". But Crichie is unquestionably correct. Crichie, who was a cadet of Lesmoir, had first married Katherine McIntosh, by whom he had Adam of Bogholl (*Balbithan MS.*, p. 45). He then married Jean Gordon, by whom he had—

> WILLIAM GORDON of Saphak, described in the Privy Council Register as the sixth laird of Gight's "suster sone"   William assisted his uncle, Alexander Gordon in Burnegraynes, to raid the lands of Sir William Keith of Balmure in March, 1618 (Nathaniel Gordon's father also being implicated). He was put to the horn   On June 9, 1619, George Gordon of Gight was caution for him and Harry

Gordon in Haddo not to molest William Keith and John Merser.
On July 8, 1619, William complained to the Privy Council as
follows: "He is informed that he is denounced as a rebel at the
instance of Sir William Keith, Merser, and the King's Advocate for
not appearing to answer to a charge of wearing hagbutis" coming
to the lands of Kellie and near to Sir William Keith's house, " and
in defiance of him ryding and courseing thair horse foiranent his,
searcheing of the said Sir William his maisonis at the kirk of
Mathelick, who wer building to him ane dask thairintill, of purpois
to haue slane thame, compelling his awne men to sweir vpon naiked
swerdis that thay wer not his servandis, invaiding and perseuing
the said Mr. John Merser of his lyff within his awine barneyard,
houseing him within his house and besedgeing him thairin a lang
space". Pursuer appearing personally and defenders not appearing,
and pursuer pleading that he was not lawfully charged, had given
caution of £500 for obedience, and had offered £20 for his escheat,
the Lords suspend the process until the principal letters of horning
are produced   The *Great Seal* calls his wife Elizabeth Forbes and
mentions him as late as 1620.   The *Balbithan MS.* calls him simply
"William Collonell Gordon"   He had, as noted, a brother by his
father's first wife, Katherine McIntosh (*ibid.*, p 45)

ADAM of Bogholl (*Great Seal*).   He was one of several Gordons, including William of " Saquhan," who granted a bond in 1606 to
Patrick Gordon of Ruthven, author of *Britane's Distemper*, Aug. 28,
1616.   "The just..e be the mouth of Thomas Young, Dempster of
Court, ordanit Adam Gordoun of Boigholl [as cautioner and surety
for the entry of John Gordon of Clubsgoul, the judge who "tried"
Francis Hay] to be vnlawet in the pane of ffyve hundreth merkis
for the nocht entrie : and that the said John Gordoun sall be
denuncet our Soverane Lordis rebell and put to his hienes horne,
and all his moveabill guides to be escheited " (Pitcairn's *Criminal
Trials*, III, 401).   On July 16, 1620, Adam Gordon of Bogholl,
was cautioner for Harry Gordon of Haddo, who was accused of
the slaughter of John Johnston, servant and near kinsman to the
laird of Caskieben, and was "unlawit for nocht entrie of the said
Harie in the pane of 200 merkis " (*ibid.*, III , 48).

12. LUCY (?) married James (?) Mowat of Balquholly (*Balbithan MS*).   Mr. Hay
in his *Sinclairs of Rosslyn* says that " Lucy Gordon, daughter of the laird
of Gight," married " James Mowat of Balquholly," and had a daughter—

MARGARET MOWAT, who had two illegitimate children (Patrick and
John) to the Hon. William Sinclair, second son of the fourth Earl
of Caithness   These boys were legitimated in 1607   The second
of them—

REV JOHN SINCLAIR, was the ancestor of Sir John Sinclair, the

compiler of the *Statistical Account of Scotland,* and of the present
baronet of Ulbster, and the Archdeacon of London.

13 ELSPET (or ELIZABETH) was a sister worthy of her brothers' exploits She
married, in 1600, James Cheyne of Pennan, a James Cheyne (possibly of
Esslemont) being charged by the Ellon Presbytery (Feb 11, 1600) with
having performed the ceremony, he "having no function in the ministrie"
(Mair's *Presbytery of Ellon,* p 32). Cheyne belonged to a very lawless family.
On March 23, 1619, John Gordon of Buckie made a series of complaints
to the Privy Council about Elspet and her husband. "Of late," he says,
"in his absence they had molested his tenants on the lands of Esslemont,
compelling them with oppin force and violence to yeild unto quhat sumevir
is demandit of them." In June, 1617, Elspet and her spouse went to the
dwelling-house of Alexander Anysoun in Cairnhill, tenant of pursuer,
assaulted him in a very cruel manner, and swore that he would have his
life unless he removed from that town and the lands of Esslemont, or
paid "in name of blak maill" a number of cayne fowls and a yearly
pension From Nov., 1617, to Feb., 1618, Elspet and her husband had
gone to the pursuer's barnyard of Esslemont and taken away corn for
the use of their horses and cattle. On a night of May, 1618, they went
to the dwelling-house of John Petrie in Esslemont and Issobell Tillery,
his spouse, broke up the doors, made themselves masters of the house,
opened lockfast "loomes," etc , and took away "the haill meite, drink,
meill, beiff and muttoun being within the same". When the tenants
requested them to depart, Cheyne set upon Petrie with a sword and
dagger, and would have slain him had he not escaped from the house.
Thereupon Cheyne "cryit for fyre," and endeavoured to burn the house
He was prevented by some neighbours who had gathered together. In
July, 1618, Cheyne went to the pursuer's lands of Carstane and assaulted
Johnne Ligertwood, another tenant, whom he felled to the ground. He
then demanded some meal and malt from Johnne Ligertwood, but was
refused. Thereupon Cheyne went to Ligertwood's house and took a
number of hens, capons, and other fowls He swore that if he were
again denied, he should neither eat nor drink till he had taken Ligertwood's life. When the latter raised letters of lawburrows against Cheyne,
that worthy vowed that he would take his life "in caise he gaif his aith
that dreides him bodelie harme". It is further stated that Petrie having
asked the said Elspet Gordon to "forbeir suche unseamelie forme of
doing," she thereupon "consaueing ane heich offence aganis him in the
hicht of his distemperit passioun and unreulie humour, pat violent hand
on him, and schamefullie and unhonnestlie strak and dang him with hir
handis and feit in sindrie pairtis of his body and left him for deid". Her
husband has so often threatened to burn pursuer's houses, cornyards, etc ,
that his tenants and servants intend to "leave of the labouring of his
lands and to cast the same in his hands". Pursuer appearing and the

said James Cheyne appearing for himself and his said wife, the Lords
assoilzied the defenders because pursuer had failed to prove the charges

14 MARJORIE married, before 1587, her cousin-german, Alexander Innes of
Cotts, who was known as "Crag-in-Peril". His mother was a daughter
of the fourth laird of Gight. (I may note in parenthesis that her husband's
grand-niece, Jane Innes, who died in 1727, married Thomas Pitt, the
ancestor of Lord Chatham and William Pitt. A table giving the full
connection between the Inneses and Pitts was published in *Scottish Notes
and Queries*, June, 1898. A very elaborate table of the Pitts appears
in Lady Russell's *Swallowfield and its Owners* p 195.) Marjorie had a
strain of the family blood, for there was "sum intrigue" between her
and Innes, the marriage coming off "abruptly," though she was really
"contracted with the Laird of Tolly Barclay" (*Familie of Innes*, p. 201)
They had seven sons and two daughters :—

(1) JOHN INNES of Leuchars was his mother's son. In 1612 he and
several other boys, including two Gordons (of course), were arraigned before the Aberdeen Town Council for a series of riots in
the Grammar, Song and Writing Schools of the city. On December 1 they took possession of the Song School, "lang before
the superstitious tyme of Yeuill, against the laudibill acttis and
statutes maid thairanent obefoir, nochwithstanding that souertie
wes found be thame that thay sould not tack the schulles at that
time nor na uther tyme of the year; and that thay sould observe
gude ordour and discipline within the saidis schullis". They were
also charged with carrying guns and with "schouting thairwith
alswell on the nicht as on the day". Their "greit deids of oppres-
sionne and ryottis" included their forcible entry of the citizens'
houses, and "bracking up thair durris and windowis and maisterfullie tacking of thair fouillis, pultrie, breid, and vivaris". They
also looted the country carts which brought "fewall and vivaris
cumeing to this burghe and mercat thairof" (Spalding Club,
Extracts from the Council Register of Aberdeen). The ringleaders
were imprisoned in the Tolbooth. This John Innes began life in
the French army with his distant kinsman, Colonel Gordon (of
Wallenstein notoriety) His eldest son married Marjorie Geddes,
daughter of James Geddes of Auchenreath, and had eighteen
children, including—

JOHN INNES of Leuchars, who married, at the age of forty-nine,
Elizabeth Gordon, daughter of Sir George Gordon of Edinglassie, the latter being his father's first cousin His wife's
sister married William Duff of Dipple John Innes had no
issue.

(2) ALEXANDER INNES entered the English service, and was attached
successively to Buckingham, Stafford, and the King. He was

once employed on a State mission to Holland (*Familie of Innes,* p. 208).

(3) JAMES INNES was also in the English (Royalist) service, and was made a prisoner by the Parliamentary army at Windsor, 1643

(4) PATRICK INNES of Mefts was employed by the Earls of Argyll and Huntly.

(5) GEORGE INNES had a pair of colours in Lord Spynie's regiment, raised for service with Gustavus Adolphus, 1621   He was laird of Caldcots ; married Isobel, daughter of Adam Gordon of Park ; and was ancestor of Cosmo Innes the antiquary.   The *Balbithan MS.* (p. 36) erroneously calls him *John* Innes

(6) ROBERT INNES was also worthy of his mother's son.   On Aug. 7, 1621 (*Privy Council Register*), his uncle, the laird of Gight, had to appear on his behalf as cautioner in 500 merks that the boy should not disturb Marion Strachan, relict of John Innes of Leuchars (probably his aunt), and John Dunbar, notary public, burgess of Elgin, and their families   The bond is dated at Coittis, July 20, 1621, and is witnessed by, among others, James Rutherfuird, Provost of Elgin.   He entered the French army, and afterwards served with the English Royalists (*Familie of Innes,* p 208)

GEORGE GORDON, VI. OF GIGHT.

(*Son of V. : died in prison,* 1640.)

This laird, the eldest of the fifth laird's seven sons, carried on the family traditions with unswerving fidelity, and his life was one long struggle against law and order   He had arrived at that point of culture when a man is able to formulate the philosophy of his conduct. According to the *Privy Council Register,* he once said to his wife—

I can tak no rest   I knaw I will die upon a scaffald.   Thair is ane evil turne in my hand, quhilk I avow to God presentlie to reform (*Privy Council Register,* July 2, 1618).

Secondly, we are informed by the same authority that Gight thought that it was

A cryme unpardonable in the person of ony of his rank or within to resset or schaw favour to ony person aganis whome he beiris querrell.

The Council ultimately labelled him as

A most rebellious and disobedient person, who, by a concourse of a nombir of odious crymes, [had] made himself in a kynd eminent abone offendaris of the heichest degree

As a final evidence of his evil reputation, let me quote Lord Dun-fermline, who, writing to Lord Binning on Feb. 18, 1616 (Fraser's *Earls of Haddington*, ii , 134), says :—

The insolence and misrewll committed by Geight can nather be vncouthe to yiow nor me that knaws the humouris of thase folkes, althocht wee might hawe hoped that the good ordour of all the rest of the countrie might hawe tempered thame suim better.

Gight simply revelled in his effrontery, and, after the manner of a Jack Shephard, he once bragged that (*Privy Council Register*)

He knew the Wynd of the Tolbuith, and how to gyde his turne [and that he had had to do] with the gritest of Scotland, and had outit his turnis aganis thame.

Let me demonstrate these *obiter dicta* by the leading incidents in his career, extending over a period of six and forty years (1594-1640) :—

1593. *April* 12.—George Gordon, fiar of Gight, and others, having failed to appear to underlie such order "as sould haue beine prescrivit to thame tuicheing the observatioun of peax and quietnes in the cuntrie," are denounced as rebels (*Privy Council Register*).

1594. *Dec.* 26 —Robert Betoun of Balfour became surety in 5,000 merks for George Gordon, apparent of Gight, to keep ward in the place of Bonytoun or any other place besouth the Tay. On Feb. 13, 1595, this bond was deleted (*Ibid.*). Note that the third laird of Gight, who died in 1578, had married a daughter of Cardinal David Beaton, while the sixth laird himself was captured in 1640 by a Captain Beaton

1602. *Nov.* 23.—The contract between George Gordon, fiar of Gight, and Mr. Robert Maitland on the third part of the lands of Auchincruive is recorded (*Sasine Register*)

1605. *Oct.* 19 —John Gordon of Buckie had to offer caution of £2,000 that Gight should not harm Archibald Douglas of Bennettle (*Privy Council Register*).

1606 *Feb.* 8.—George Gordon of Gight, " *haeres masculus et talliae* Willielmi Gordoun de Geicht, patris," was served heir in the lands of Badichill, Over and Nether Murefundlands, Over and Nether Suanfurde, Blacrie, and Mactarrie (*Inquisitiones Speciales*).

1607 —A "witch " named Malie Wyse was said to live on the lands of Gight (Mair's *Ellon*)

1607. *July* 3 —A priest named William Murdo, examined by the Privy Council, declared that he "understandis Mr. David Law as he belevis [is] bruther to the Bischop of Orknay, who is ane preist and not as yit ressavit in the ordour of Jesuitis, bot is desyreous to be thairin, and that Mr. David Law come to this cuntrey some yeiris syne frome Pareis, as the deponer rememberis, and the deponer knew him not afoir he come to this cuntrey bot as a young scoller in Pareis And the deponer knowis that he remanit a quhyle with young Geycht, and with his sister in Buchane, with whom he maid his residence   Examinat upoun that part of the writting beiring 'Estate preterita visitavi loca in quibus peregrinatus fuerat Machareus noster pie memorie,' etc., quhat placeis thir wes wher M'Quhirrie had hantit of auld, deponis that it wes with the Laird of Geycht in Buchane and no uther part, and deponis that he remanit in the wynter with William Leslie of Conrak and the rest of the partis contenit in his former depositioun " (*Privy Council Register*)

1609   *March* 16 —Alexander, Lord Elphinstone, successfully petitioned the Privy Council for letters against George Gordon of Gight, James Gordon, apparent of Newton, John Gordon of Ardlogie, and others, for resetting and supplying John Meldrum of Ordley, who, on May 13, 1607, was put to the horn at the complainer's instance for not obtempering the decreet obtained by Andro Meldrum, now of Drumbek, before the Lords of Council and Session on March 14, 1607.

1610. *February* —The Bishop of Moray assured the king that Gight had shown himself a "great furderar and favourer of peace "

1612. *September* 29, 30.—The Synods of the diocese of St Andrews north of the Forth ordered Gight's excommunication to be intimated from its kirks (*Minutes of the Synod of Fife*), which was pillorying him again in 1614

1615. *June* 15 —The king confirmed the charter by Henry Wood of Bonytoun, who sold to Gight, his son-in-law, the lands of Cuikburnes, "cum pendiculo," Tullybrex (*Great Seal*).

1615. *December.*—Gight was summoned by the Privy Council for breaking a sword across the head of the laird of Leask, whose daughter had been abducted in 1608 by his brother Adam

GIGHT'S REPUDIATION OF THE "TREW" RELIGION.—Between 1597 and 1616 Gight carried on a constant battle against the "trew religion ".   In this he was supported by his wife, Isobel Wood, of the Bonnyton family.   The Woods were Papists, and the Presbytery Records of Ellon (which Mr. Mair has summarised) teem with reference to their heresy.   Gight was in constant conflict with the Reformed Church, and was accused of harbouring "masse priests," who went about the country disguised as "medicinars".   On June 12, 1594, he was one of the north countrymen charged to appear before the King and Council to answer for good rule and loyalty, to answer concerning "persute and invasioun of his Majesteis declairit tratouris, rebellious and unnaturall subjectis, tressounable practizaris and conspiratouris aganis the trew religioun presentlie professit within this realme, his Majesteis persone and estate, and libertie of this cuntrey".   On July 11, 1594, Gordon was denounced as rebel in connection with this edict.   In November, 1594, "young Geicht and Clunie" were received by the Duke of Lennox, who had been left in Aberdeen by the king as his lieutenant in the north   The Duke " tooke up vigourouslie the penalteis of the commoun people that obeyed not the proclamatiouns, but compounded easilie with the assisters of the rebels.   He had power to receave to peace whom he pleased   He had avaritious and craftie counsellers left with him " (*Privy Council Register*)   In 1597 the Presbytery of Ellon learned that Gight (who then lived at Little Ardo) and Isobel Wood had " laitlye caused ane popish priest to baptise ane bairne to them ". Gight retorted that the minister of Tarves had declined to baptise " ye first of ye four bairnes ".

Gight and his wife excommunicated, 1601.—In January, 1601, Mrs. Gordon was excommunicated, " as nothing is seen in her bot contumacie," and in the following September Gight was excommunicated He had a fear of this sentence—extraordinary in a man of his turbulent type—and gave "the brethren" a trying time. On April, 1601, he was summoned to Aberdeen by the Presbyteries of Aberdeen and Ellon under pain of excommunication, but he did not appear. A letter was received from the Marquis of Huntly pointing out that George had ridden south with him " chairgit in his majesties adois ". Gordon himself sent a letter, adding in addition to Huntly's excuse, that his brother-in-law, young Wood of Bonnyton, was in danger of his life at Edinburgh, " and to be executed as he fearit this xxiii of Aprile " The brethren put off the examination of Gordon until May 8, when he duly appeared Sentence of excommunication was deferred until July 1, under certain conditions, among them that he should have the Confession of Faith read to him and attend the Kirk of Methlick. On July 24 he was summoned by the Presbyteries for failing to fulfil the conditions. His father, William, appeared in his absence and produced " tua testimionallis, testifeand his diseass, quhilkis the presbyteries fand irrelevant, becauss thair was na offer maid thairwith that he wald satisfie " But upon his father's " ernist " request, the pronunciation of sentence was again postponed. He was summoned again on Aug. 7, but did not appear. Instead, he sent a servant with a letter, written from Kelly, on Aug. 6̨. He declared that he had a "deadlie diseass," which made him unable to leave the country, although the brethren might think this "ane fenyeit excuise. Befoir God I persuaid my selff that I haue fewe daies to leve in respect of yeiris." He offered to ward himself in his house to receive " nane quha is excommunicat (my bed fellow being exceptit)," and that he would confer with them when his " deidlie secknes dois permitt ". He had simply a terror of excommunication, and went on to say: " I heir offeir, giff thair is nathing can satisfie yow [if] I remane Catholick, bot my bluid and wardlie wraik, to enter my selff   . in ony place ye pleiss till opponit, and giff it sall pleiss Majestie and your wisdomes of the Kirk of Scotland sa to tack my bluid for my professioun, quhilk is Catholick Romane, I will maist willinglie offere it for the same". The brethren were dissatisfied and summoned him (for the fourth time) on Aug 14. Instead of appearing he sent his father, William The brethren excommunicated him on Sept. 20 (*Aberdeen Kirk Session Records*, pp. 178-183, Mair's *Presbytery of Ellon*, pp. 7-11).

Gight summoned as a Papist by the Privy Council—On Oct 24, 1601, he appeared before the Privy Council on the charge (which he denied) of having often, notwithstanding divers proclamations to the contrary, resetted Mr. Johne Hamiltoun, who has made "schamefull defectioun and apostacie fra the treuth," and been " a trafficquar and practizar aganis the lauchfull authoritie and government of Princeis," and the Council ordered him, on a caution of 5,000 merks, to enter in ward in the burgh of Montrose, and remain there till freed by his Majesty, "to the effect in the meanetyme he may have conference with the ministeris, and be resolvit be thame in sic heidis and pointis of his religioun quhairin he standis in doubt". Sir David Wode becomes his surety On March 2, 1601, Sir Johnne Lindsay of Wodheid was caution in 5,000 merks that Gight should repair to his own house of Ardoch and remain there, going monthly, if his health permit, to the burgh of Abirdene, where he is to reside eight days every month, occupied in conference with the Bishop of Abirdene and Presbytery thereof for his resolution in such points of religion as he stands in doubt of. He is to continue in the said ward and eight miles thereabout till freed by his Majesty If he be so visited with "disease and seiknes" that he cannot repair to the said burgh, he shall monthly advertise the said Bishop and Presbytery thereof, with a request to send some one to reason with him on the said matter. On April 13, 1602, Huntly was charged by the Privy Council to enter certain Papists still at large in the north (Gight included) before the King and Council. In 1604 he was accused of having carried a crucifix on a spear at his mother's funeral. On Feb. 18, 1608, the captain of the guard was ordered to apprehend him and inventory his goods as he had been excommunicated, and had remained a long time unrelaxed from the horn. On April 28, 1608, John Dempstair and certain other officers of the guard reported to the Council that they had apprehended him in the north in the company of Francis, Earl of Erroll, "who, however, had prevented them from fully executing their warrant, alleging that he was a councillor himself, and would enter Gordon before the Privy Council when charged". Erroll was ordered to "compeir befoir the Counsell and to exhibit the Laird of Geycht" In 1608 the General Assembly ordered the "downcasting" of Gight's private chapel (Mair's *Ellon*). In 1609 the Privy Council summoned him for sheltering a Jesuit, Walter Murdo, "a traffiquair and practizar aganis the lauchfull authoritie and government of Princeis ". He was ordered, under a caution of 5,000 merks, to confine himself to the burgh of Montrose, where he was to confer with the ministers.

Gight banished.—On Feb. 1, 1614, he was ordered to go abroad and remain there "dureing all the dayis of his lyftyme," without skaith to his person or property, provided he attempt nothing against the king or the present religion (*Privy Council Register*). On July 2, 1616, a commission under the signet was granted to the captain and lieutenant of the guard to apprehend Gight, as "ane profest and avowed Papist," who, "in the pryde of his heart, contemning and disdaining all kynd of procedeur, alsweill ecclesiastique as criminall," has made himself eminent above other offenders, especially by the wearing of hagbuts, the assault on the brethren of Brunthill and the murder of Francis Hay, and his refusal to appear for trial. Since he was put to the horn for these crimes he had been summoned before the High Commission of the Kirk for practising against the religion, but he had refused to appear.

THE VENDETTA WITH THE HOUSE OF HAY, 1615-23.—The feud between the Gordons of Gight and the House of Hay is unparalleled even in the history of the Gordons for its ferocity. It arose from several causes, and as usual had a basis in friendship and relationship In the first place, Gight felt that he had to avenge the death (in a duel, Dec 15, 1615) of his brother Adam, at the hands of Francis Hay of Logierieve, who had been his bosom companion, and second, there seems to have been some disagreement between his son-in-law, William Hay, son of the eighth Earl of Erroll, and the Hays of Brunthill. The vendetta assumed almost national importance, so that the Earl of Dunfermline thought it worth while to write to the king, Dec 23, 1617 (*Letters to King James VI*, Maitland Club, 1835)· "Your Sacred Majesty agreed [the Marquis of Huntly and Lord Erroll] and thair freindis in a particuler perrollus deadlie feade [which] was fallin out amongs thameselffis, and lykelie to haue maide great truble betuix thame for the slauchter and bloode betuix Laird of Gight Gordon and ane brother of the Erll of Erroll's and some otheris his freindis".

The capture of Francis Hay, who killed Adam Gordon in a duel, 1615.—Adam Gordon fell on Dec. 15, 1615. Three days later, according to the statement of the King's Advocate before the Privy Council (April 16, 1616), "George Gordoun of Geycht, William Hay, his son in law, Johnne, Alexander, Robert and Patrik Gordonis, his brether, James Baird, William Gordoun in the Maynis of Geycht, Johnne Sinclair, bruther to the Laird of Achannachie, Andro Nicolson, servitor to William Hay, Patrik Clynthe in Ardiffery, Thomas Bisset, servitour to the Laird of Geycht, and Johne Gordoun, Scheref-depeite of Abirdene, with utheris thair complices, and with convocatioun of hes Majesteis leigeis to the noumir of —— personis, all of thame being privat men, cled with no lauchfull warrand, pouer, auctoritie nor commissioun, and being bodin in feir of weir, with invasive forbidden and unlauchfull wapponis, and convocat and assemblit togidder, the said Laird of Geycht come in a hostile and weirlyke maner to William Hay his dwelling house of Logyruiff, quhair umquhill Francis Hay, his Majesteis frie leige, wes for the tyme. [They] invironed and belayit the house on all sydis, upoun set purpoise, provisioun and resolutioun to have assedgit the same, and in end to have ressin fyre, gif any oppositioun had bene maid to thame in the deleverie of the said Frances. And haveing assaylled the said William Hay within his awne house a certane space with mony threatning and minassing speitcheis, in end thay forcit him for eschewing of thair barbarous crueltie . . . to grant thame acces in his house. And thay, usurping upoun thayme his Heynes royall pouer and auctoritie, took the said Frances prisouner and transportit him, guairdit with a nomber of men in armes, to the burgh of Abirdene Comeing thair about ten of the cloke at nicht, thay committit and detenit him presoner in thair awne ludgeing in the Gallowgait of Abirdene callit the Bony Wyffis Inne the space of fourty-aucht houris,—to witt, quhill the twentye day of the said moneth at ellevin of the clock in the foirnoone, suffering no persone of his kin and freindschip to haif access unto him nor to confer nor intercommoun with him in this meanetyme."

Gight arranges a sham trial of Hay—"Gycht in this tyme directit his messageis and letteris to the haill baronis and gentilmen of the cuntrey thairaboute who profest him freindschip and goodwill, intreating thame to come and assist him in the acting of that detestable, violent, and barbarous tragidie which he had in handis. Quhairupoun thair come flocking unto him frome all the cornaris of that province nomberis of baronis and gentilmen in airmes Being all assemblit togidder to the nomber of twa hundreth people in airmes, and the Laird of Geycht—thinking himselff of sufficient pouer, force and strength to do his turne and to resist quhatsumevir thing sould be intendit be ordour of law or utherwyse for defence of the said Frances his lyff, he being backit, assistit and accumpaneit with the haill nomber of personis foirsaidis in airmes—brocht the said Frances frome thair ludgeing the said twenty day at elevin of the clock in the foirnoone." Hay was carried "alangis the hie calsay to the Tolbuith of Abirdene, quhair Johne Gordoun of Clubbisgoul, scheref-depeite of Abirdene, ane of thair awne complices and direct pairtie with thame in all that mater, wes attending, he being the cheife persone whose advise, counsaill, and directioun and opinioun thay followit in the prosequtioun of this haill busynes. And he being guiltie in his awne conscience before God of partialitie and preocupyit opinioun, and knawing weill aneugh that the tyme of his priviledge, gif he ony had, wes expyrit, he, notwithstanding to the offence of God, contempt of his Majestie, and scandaill of the justice of the cuntrey, most presumptuouslie, arrogantlie, and with ane evill conscience, usurpit upoun him the place of judge and presentit himself and sat down in judgement "

Hay was refused the benefit of legal advice.—"Mr. William Barclay, advocate, wes prepairit to haif compeirit for defence of the said Frances lyff, and had mony gude reasonis and exceptionis aganis the pretendit judge, as partiall and incompetent, being pairtie aganis his jurisdictioun as expyrit (the defendair not being tane reid hand), aganis the tyme (as not being cited upoun fyftene dayis wairning) and aganis the actioun as excludit, becaus the pairtie [Adam Gordon] slayne be Frances died at the horne for divers criminall causis, quhairof the horningis wer reddie to produce. But the said scheref-depute, Laird of Geycht, and thair freindis being foirsene thairof, and understanding weill aneugh that ony ane of thir exceptionis according to the course of law and justice wald haif frustrat and maid void that dyet, and thay, being bent and resolvit to haif the said Frances lyff, thay directit George Leslie of Kincraigie to the said Mr William Barclay with a commissioun dischargeing him upoun the perrell of his lyff to come and speik for the said Frances [They told Barclay] gif he compeirit that, howevir thay wald reverence his Majesteis seate during his being thair, thay sould put twenty quhinyearis in him efter he wes anes doun the stair. And some uther advocatis in the toun were boistit, threatnit, and minassit gif in any wayis thay spak in that mater. And some of the said Frances freindis, who wer prepairit to come to Abirdene to dischairge that dewtie unto him, quhilk became thame, thay wer adverteist and forwairnit to come upoun thair gaird, or utherwyse upoun thair hasard and perrell. And sua the poore gentilman, being bereft of the benefite of lauchfull defence quhilk God and nature has indifferentlie allowed unto all men, and debarrit fra speiche, company and conferrence of his freindis and advocatis, who durst not assist him for feir of that unlauchfull assemblie of forces, he wes enterit upoun pannell and put to the knawledge of ane assise selectit and chosen be the pairties thameselffis, and who wer so far addictit unto thame as no doubt wes had of the said Frances convictioun. Lykeas he wes convict be thame of the said slauchter, and sentence of death pronuncit aganis him to losse his head."

(240)

Hay condemned to death by a packed court and brutally murdered by the Gordons —
" After the pronunceing of quhilk sentence the pretendit usurping judge deliverit the
said Frances to the pairtie, to be demanit as thay thocht good, who took him bak to
thair awne privat prisone agane, and keipit him till the nixt day. And chuseing the
tyme of sermone for his executioun about seven in the cloik in the morning, to the
effect the eyis of these who delytit to heir the preiching of Godis word sould not be
polluted, nor thair hairtis grevit with that act worthie of no uther spectatouris bot
the cruell actouris, thay being all convenit in airmes as afoirsaid, took the said
Frances doun the closse of thair ludgeing oute at a backyette, and caryit him to a
holl betuix tua mottis, not a rig lenth or tua fra the said dure, quhair they crowned
thair tragidie with so butcherly mangling the poore gentilman with sex severall
straikes upoun his shoulderis, hind head and neck, as the lyke hes nevir, or seldome,
bene sene or hard."

The Gordons then make an attack on the victim's kinsmen, the Hays of Brunthill,
1616 —The Gights, however, were not satisfied with the brutal murder of Francis
Hay. They made a daredevil attack on the Hays of Brunthill (who had sheltered
Francis) in " a most raigefull crueltie," for the laird of Gight thought it a " cryme
unpardonable in the persone of ony of his rank or within to resset or schaw favour
to ony persone aganis whom he beiris querrell" So on February 1, 1616, the laird
of Gight, his brothers Alexander, Patrick and Robert, his son-in-law, William Hay,
his servants, James Baird and William Gordon, in the Mains of Gight, Andrew
Milne, falconer, John Sinclair, brother to the laird of Auchanachie, Andrew Nicolson,
servant to William Hay, and Andrew Cantlie, " all bodin in feir of war, and haveing
hagbutis and pistolletis upoun thair personis," did battle with the Hays According to the complaint of the King's Advocate to the Privy Council (April 16, 1616),
Gight was informed by a spy sent out by him that William, George and Patrick
Hay, the sons of Alexander Hay of Brunthill, were " at ane brydaill at the mylne of
Ardiffrie, within twa flicht shott of thair fatheris dwelling hous and upoun Frances
Erll of Erroll his proper land and heritage of the barony of Slaines ". The Gordons
" raid about the house in a bragging forme, purpoislie to have trayned " the Hays
out. The Hays, knowing that their lives were in imminent danger, sent out their
brother George without " swerd or weapone " to parley with the intruders In " most
gentill termes " he desired them to " go away in peace and not to crave moir blood,
seeing ther wes aneugh already gottin. Bot so far wer they [the Gordons] frome
giving care to the intreaty of the said George, that most feirslie, schamefullie and
cruellie they set upoun the said George and his saidis tua brethir, and invaidit and
perseuit thame of thair lyveis, hurte the said Williame deadlie in the oppin of the
head with a swerd eftir he wes schote throw the thie with a hagbute, gaif the said
George tua deidlie strykis, ane on the head and ane upoun the left hand, sua that he
is mutilat of tua fingeris, and strak the said Mr. Patrik through the body, and left
thame all lyaid upoun the ground for dead, suirlie beleving thay had bene dead,
utherwyse thay had not left thame quhill thay had bene dead, and thay left ane
hagbute and pistollet behind thame." According to the King's Advocate (on March

12) it was the laird of Gight who "schote a lang hagbute at William Hay, quhair-with he schote him throw the thie," and then attacked Patrick and George It was also stated that the laird's son-in-law, William Hay, presented a pistol at Patrick Hay, "quhilk misgaif, and that thaireftir he stoggit him with a rapper"

The Laird of Gight gives the Privy Council a different version —The laird of Gight, who did not appear as ordered before the Privy Council, had quite a different story to tell He declared that, as there was "some question, controversie and difference standing betuix" his son-in-law, William Hay, and the latter's mother, Dame Agnes Sinclair, Countess of Erroll, he (the laird of Gight) travelled for the "freindlie setling of the materis forsaidis standing questionable ". He arranged a tryst between Hay and his mother at the Kirk of Cruden In the evening, he, his son-in-law, his servant Baird, and two other "husband men," left the house of Hay, which was near the church. They were "single and thame allanes with ganging staulffis in thair handis walking on fute for seiking ane flicht to the said Laird of Geycht his halk upoun the watter of Cruden. They come alongis the said watter neir unto the mylne of ——, perteining to the said William Hay, in a verie peciable and quiet manner, lippyning for nothing les then ony oppin violence or injurie to have bene done to thame be ony persone or personis. Notwithstanding, it is of treuth that Maister Patrik, Williame and George Hayis, sones to Alexander Hay of Brunthillis, being in ane oisler house neir unto the said mylne, quhair they had spent the most pairt of that day in the intertenyment of thameselffis with excesse, and persaveing the said Laird of Geycht walking on his fute with ane staulf in his hand as said is, upoun a deidlie malice and privat grudge consavit and borne be thame in thair hairtis aganis him resolvit at that tyme to have his lyfe. And for this effect the said Mr. Patrik Hay, him allane comeing first furth of the said house, verie tantanlie, scorn-fullie, and disdanefullie schoutit and cryit the falconeris cry, and said 'Wow, wow, schit schew!' and the said Laird of Geycht, not knawing at first who it wes, nor quhat the mater meanit, patientlie comportit with the speitcheis foirsaidis, bot heireftir persaveing that it was Mr. Patrik Hay, for eschewing of forder trouble thay went directlie fordwart alongis the said watter, comporting with the injurie foirsaid. And the said William Hay, bruther to the said Mr. Patrik, comeing then furth of the said house, thay both, airmed with swerdis, came trotand eftir the said complenaris; and the said William Hay, brother to the said Erll of Erroll, haveing went to thame to ask of thame quhat thay meanit, and to haif dissuadit thame fra committing ony oppin violence aganis his said father-in-law, thay directlie past by him, pullit out thair swerdis, and most feirslie set upoun the said Laird of Geycht, and schamefullie, cruellie, and unmercifullie invaidit and perseuit him of his lyff. And he having fled from thame a grite space, thay, accompanyit with the said George Hay, thair said third bruther, followit him over the bra of the mylne dame of the said mylne (fra quhilk place he could not flie ane fute farder), and thair the saidis thrie brether most cruellie and unmercifullie invaidit and perseuit him of his lyff, lichtit all thrie upoun him at once with thair drawne swerdis, cuttit doun thairwith his pickadill upoun both his sheulderis, strak him on his bak in the said mylne dame, and had not faillit to have slayne and drownit him thairintill (his said son-in-law and his said servand being singlit frome him and haldis fast be the persones present for the time) wer not, be the providence of God, the said Laird of Geycht his said servand, who bore his halk, pat ane hagbute in his hand, which he then accidentlie caryed for slaying ane craw to the halk, (and) the said Laird of Geicht defendit himselff thairwith   And the saidis personis also cruellie and unmercifullie invadit and perseuit the said William Hay and —— Baird of thair lyveis, and thay narrowlie eschapit with their lyves."

How the Privy Council tried in 1616 to bring the Gordons to justice.—The Privy Council found it a difficult task to bring the Gordons to book   On Feb 8, 1616, the Council ordered all the parties to appear, the laird of Gight and his son-in-law, Hay, under pain of 5,000 merks each   On March 12 Hay appeared, and he and the laird of Gight, together with the latter's brother, John, who did not appear, were ordered to enter their persons in the Tolbooth of Edinburgh within fifteen days   The laird's brother, Alexander, was denounced as a rebel, and all his movables were to be escheated for his non-appearing   On behalf of the Brunthill victims, Mr. David Rattray, minister at Cruden, appeared and declared that they were unable to travel—their father in respect of his "aige and seikness," and the three sons in respect of the "hurtis and woundis quhilkis they ressavit".   On April 16 the King's Advocate detailed the whole story at great length   It was stated that the laird of Gight, "feiring the event of his tryall, and takand upoun him the ignominie and guilt of that cryme, he abstentit himselff and compeirit not" before the Council   James Gordon of Knockespock appeared to excuse the absence of the defenders, all of whom were absent except William Hay, Gight's son-in-law   So the Lords ordered that the laird of Gight, his brothers John and Alexander, together with John Gordon of Clubisgoul (the sham judge of Francis Hay) and Gight's servant, James Baird, should enter their persons in the Tolbooth   William Hay was delivered to the lieutenant of the guard to be similarly confined   The charge against Gight's brothers, Robert and Patrick, and against John Sinclair, Adam Nicolson, William Gordon, Patrick Bisset and Patrick Cantlie was found not proven so far as the actual capture of Francis Hay was concerned, though they were all put to the horn in respect of the attack on the Brunthill Hays in February.

The Hays accused of making an attack on the Laird of Gight.—The quarrel took a new turn in June, 1616, when the Hays attacked the Gordons, for, according to the complaint (Feb 25, 1617) by the King's Advocate and the laird of Gight, the Hays, accompanied by George Hay of Achairne and Johnne Fraser of Crechie, "with utheris, thair compliceis, all bodin in feir of weir and with hagbutis and pistolletis prohibite to be worne be the lawis of this realme, come upoun the —— day of the said moneth of Junij, ryding upoun horsbak, to the said George [Gordon] his landis of Birnes, and searcht and socht the said George throughout all the pairtis of his saidis landis, raid about the housis of the same, and had not faillit to have slane him upoun set purpois, provisioun and foirthocht felloun wer not be the providence of God he come not thair that day"   The Gordons appeared personally, as also did George and William Hay, the latter presenting a testimonial under the hand of

Mr. David Rattray, minister at Cruden, stating that Mr Patrick Hay was sick and confined to bed The other defenders, George Hay of Auchquhairney and George Fraser of Crechie, not appearing, and the said William and George Hay having admitted that they had worn hagbuts and pistollets since the beginning of trouble with pursuer, but without ever having done harm to any person, the Lords assoilzie George and William from the charge of assault because they have denied the charge on oath. They excuse the absence of Mr. Patrick, and order the other defenders who have not answered the summons to be denounced rebels.

General indictment of Gight and his "odious crymes," July, 1616 —On July 6, 1616, the Privy Council resolved to punish Gight, not only on account of the Hay affair, but also as a Papist. He was described as "ane profest and avowed trafficquing Papist and adversair to God and his treuth, having shaikin af his dewtie and alledgeance to his Majestie, his obedience to the laws and discipline to the Kirk, and in the pryde of his hairt contempning and disdaining all kynd of procedour that can be used aganis him. [He] hes of laitt gevin prooffe of a most rebellious and disobedient persone, and by a concurse of a number of odious crymes hes maid himself in a kynd eminent above offendaris in the heichest degree." The laird had been "chairgit to haif compeirit befoir the Lordis of his Majesties Previe Counsall to haif underlyne such ordour as sould haif bene tane with him for ob- serveing of his Majesteis peace and keiping of goode reule and quietnes in the cuntrey, as alsua to haif answerit to ane complaint maid upoun him for his Majesteis Advocatt for his Hienes witnesse for bearing and wearing of hacquebuttis and pistolletis and persute of the brether of Brunthill hard by thair fatheris dwelling house". But the laird, "takand the cryme upoun him, and disdaneing either to gif obedience to his Majestie or to purge and cleir himself of the said cryme, absentit himself and compeirit not befoir the saidis Lordis to haif answerit upoun his usurpeing of his Majesties princlie power and auctoritie in the unlauchfull taking of umquhill Frances Hay, and for the barbarous and butcherlie murdering of him he lykewyse tooke the cryme upoun him and absentit himself, for the quhilk decreit and sentence is gevin and pronunceit, and letteris of horning direct aganis him for entrie of his personie in wairde within the Tolbuith of Edinburgh. And alsua upoun the said xxviiij day of Marche, Alexander Gordon, brether to the said George Gordon of Geycht, wes denunceit rebell and putt to the horne be vertew of letteris raisit at the instance of his Majesties Advocat for his not compeirance personallie at ane certane day before the saidis Lordis to have answerit to ane complaint maid upoun him tuitcheing the bearing and wearing of hacquebuttis and pistolettis as the saidis letteris execute, indorsate, and registrat beiris And siclyke upoun the fourt and sex dayis of Julij instant Alexander, Patrik, and Robert Gordonis, brether to the said George Gordon of Geycht, James Baird and William Gordon, in the Maynis of Geycht, Andro Mylne, falconer, Andro Nicolsoun, servitor to William Hay, son in law to the said George Gordon of Geycht, and Patrik Cantlie in Ardiffrie, wer denuncit rebellis and putt to the horne be vertew of letteris raisit at the instance of his Majesties Advocat foirsaid for not compeirance personallie

before the saidis Lordis of Secreit Counsall at ane certane day bigane to haif
ansuerit to ane complaint maid upoun him be his Majesties said Advocat for the
persute and invasioun of the forsaidis brether of Brunthill with unlauchfull and
forbidden waponis in maner and at the tyme specifeit and content in the saidis
letteris as the samyn beiris. . . . Quhairfore the Lordis of Secreit Counsall hes
gevin and grantit and be the tennour hairof gevis and grantis full power and commissioun, expres bidding and chairge to the Capitane or Leutennant of the Gaird and
to suche of the Companie of the Gaird as salbe direct be thame to convocate his
Majesties liegeis in armes, and to pas, search, seik, and tak the personis rebellis
foirsaidis quhairevir thay may be apprehendit, and to bring, present and exhibite
thame befoir the saidis Lordis to be tane ordour with as apperteynis, as alsua to pas,
persew, and tak thair houses" (in customary form).

The King intervenes in the Gordon-Hay vendetta.—At last the king himself intervened. Writing to the Privy Council from Bletso (July 24, 1616), with "most
princelie, wyse and judicious direction," his Majesty said· "We once hard of ane
aggreiance betwene the Hayes and Gordons, but are not the les now certified of
the contrarie, and that the saidis Hayes are now resolved to urge the benefit
and executioun of our lawes allsweill against the unlauchfull imprisonaris and
putteris to death of thair late kinsman, Francis Hay, as against the invaderis
and hurteris of the brethren Brunthill. In whiche regaird and upoun the not
aggreiance of the afoirnamed parteis wee have thocht good to recommend unto
yow two thingis which yee are accordinglie to performe. The first is that yee proceed
with all care and diligence to a full and exact tryall of the committeris and acces-
saries guiltie of the foirsaidis crymes, especiallie of the unlauchfull committment
and executioun of the said Frances Hay, and that this done, yee caus do justice
against the offendaris according to the merite and qualitie of the cryme quhairof
thay salbe fund culpable. The next thing whiche we are to recommend to yow is
(after due triall and punishement of the delinquentis) to urge the foirsaidis pairties to
reconcile and aggrie. For, as a reconciliatioun can not upoun equall termes intervene betweene guiltie and innocent, so is it necessarie that justice preceid for
making the guiltie pairtie innocent by punisheing offendaris, that thairefter a
freindschip and aggreiance may be performed betuix the pairties so made innocent
on both sides And what in this case we have prescribed, the lyke yee ar to
observe and use as a rule and square to direct yow in all incidentis of this or the
lyke nature, knawing that as wee rigne not precario bot a frie and absolute king, so
we will nather suffer the reconciliatioun of pairties amongst thameselffis to intersept
the dew course of justice in the punishment of crymes whairin we have interesse,
nor that the lauchfull instance of pairties interessed against suche malefactoris to
be punished by the hand of our justice salbe ane occasioun of discorde amongst the
freindis of suche pairties therefter. And so, not doubting bot yee will proceid to the
performance of the premisis with that care and diligence that the consequence of the
mater, and wee for our satisfactioun do require, wee bid yow fairwell "

Special precautions taken for the trial of the Gordons in Edinburgh, Aug., 1616.—
The extraordinary intimidation at the "trial" of Francis Hay in Aberdeen gave

the Crown authorities such a fright that when they resolved to try the Gordons in Edinburgh they took extraordinary precautions. On August 27, 1616, they issued a proclamation for keeping of the peace in Edinburgh on the approaching day of law for the trial of parties concerned in the taking and execution of Francis Hay. "Forsamekle as althocht by divers actis and proclam(ationis) maid and publeist heirtofoir the convocatioun of his M(ajesties) liegeis for backing of pairties to dayis of law be pro(hibite) and dischairgit under divers pases mentionet and (contenit in) the actis maid theranent, notwithstanding (the Lordis) of Secreit Counsall ar informed thair is grite nomberis of people come to this burgh for assisting and backing the pairties haveing entres in persute and defence at the dyet appointit befoir his Majesties Justice in the Tolbuith of Edinburgh upoun the xxviij day of August instant for the taking and executioun of umquhill Frances, it is to be suspected that some inconvenientis sall fall oute betuix thame within this burgh to the breck of his Majesties peace without remeid be providit : Thairfore the saidis Lordis ordanit ane maiser to pas to the mercat croce of Edinburgh and utheris placeis neidfull and thair be oppin proclamatioun to command and chairge all and sindrie his Majesties liegeis and subjectis who ar alreddy come or that salhappin to come to this burgh to attend and await upoun the said day of law, or for ony uther caus or occasioun quhatsumevir, that thay and everie ane of thame observe his Majesties peace, keepe goode reule and quietnes ane with another, and that thay nor nane of thame presoome nor tak upoun hand to invade or persew ane another, nor to mak provocatioun of offence or displeasour ane to another by worde, deade, countenance, toukeing, nor by na uther maner of way, under quhatsumevir collour or pretext under the pane of deade.—certifeeing thame that failyeeis or that sall happin to do in the contrair that thay salbe takin, apprehendit, and the pane of deade salbe execute upoun thame withoute favour or mercye · and to command and chairge and inhibite all and sindrie his Majesties liegeis and subjectis that nane of thame presoome nor tak upoun hand to accompany ony of the saidis pairties to the bar the day foirsaid without ane warrant in wryte from the saidis Lordis to be grantit upoun the petitioun and desyre of the pairtyis persewar and defendair under the pane of warding of thair personis and forder punishement at the discretioun of his Majesties Counsall."

The outlawing of Francis Hay's unjust judge, John Gordon of Clubisgoul.—According to the MSS. collections of Sir James Balfour, preserved in the Library of the Faculty of Advocates, and printed in Pitcairn's *Criminal Trials* (iii, 39), John Gordon of Clubisgoul, who had been summoned with Gight and his accomplices for Hay's slaughter, appeared before the justice and his deputes in the Tolbooth of Edinburgh, August 28, 1616, accompanied by "sum gentilmen of the name of Gordon". He came with outward "show and apperance," and petitioned the Council to let some gentlemen of his name assist him at the bar   This was granted "to sex persones selected and maid choise of be himselff.   The Erll of Erroll came lykewayes heir for persute of that mater, he having procurit ane Licence from the Counsell convenit at Abirdene for his cuming heir." He also "cravit licence that he might go to the Bar to assist the persute of that mater, bot in regaird he wes excommunicat it was not thought expedient that he sould go in persone to the bar, becaus it wes suspectit that the excommunication would be objectit aganist him to debar him from proces. And als becaus His Maᵗⁱᵉˢ Advocat was pairtlie persewar in the Letteris who wold prosecute that mater, als weill as if the Erll war present. The Court being fensit, the justice, Justice Clerk, with the haill memberis of the Court, and the parteis persewaris being all present, and the Sheref-depute being constantlie looked for to compeir, he notwithstanding absentit himselff, and is thairfoir declairet fugitive and his cautioneris vnlauit." This was but a formal beginning of the proceedings against the main culprit, Gordon of Gight himself.

Gight complains to the Council about their injustice to him in the Hay affair, 1617.—On January 16, 1617, the laird of Gight complained to the Council that he had been put to the horn wrongfully for not entering into ward to answer three charges: (a) the pursuit of William, George and Mr. Patrick Hay; (b) the slaughter of Francis Hay; and (c) his not appearing to answer the complaint anent the trouble between him and the brethren of Brunthill As he was never lawfully charged to enter his person or to appear, and as he had found caution in 6,000 merks to appear this day, and will make payment of 200 merks to the treasurer for his escheat, he pleads that the hornings should be suspended Pursuer and the King's Advocate appearing personally, the Lords, in respect of the laird's appearance, suspend the letters of horning. They order him to find caution in the sum of 5,000 merks to keep the peace, and to appear before them to answer for the said crimes, and to find caution in the Books of Adjournal for his appearance before the justice to the same effect under the said pain of 5,000 merks. Caution is to be found within forty-eight hours. On Jan. 14, 1617, William Hay was ordered to be set at liberty, the laird of Gight being made his cautioner. February 26 was appointed as the day of Gight's appearance, and as the Council learned that there would be "grite contestatioun and reasoning betuix the pairties, and that divers questionis, objectionis, ansueris and replyis" would require good advice and deliberation, "the saidis Lordis hes appointit and nominat and be the tennour heirof nominatis and appointis the personis following—thay ar to say, Sir Richard Cokburne of Clerkintoun, knicht, Lord Previe Seale; Sir Williame Levingstoun of Kilsyith; Sir Andro Hammiltoun of Ridhous; Sir Alexander Drummond of Medop; and Sir James Skeene of Currihill—to be assessouris to our Soverane Lordis Justice, and to assist him with thair advise and opinioun in suche thingis as salbe propouned in that judgement".

The Marquis of Huntly and the Earl of Erroll ordered to intervene.—On February 20, in view of the "hairtburning, private grudge, and miscontent" which the whole vendetta had occasioned, the Council ordered that the officers of arms should "pas to the Mercat Croce of Edinburgh" and charge the Marquis of Huntly, "as chief to the said Laird of Geycht," and Francis, Earl of Erroll, as to the brether of Brunthill, "as alsua the pairtyis thameselffis, and the haill noblemen, baronis, and gentlemen of thair name, and all thair servandis, followaris, and propper dependaris, who ar alreddy come to this burgh or sall come to the same to attend and awaitt upoun the said day, and for assisting and baking of one of the pairties, that they immediatelie addresse thameselffis to thair ludgeingis within this burgh [of Edinburgh] and conteene thameselffis thairin, and onnawayes come furthe thairof withoute licence of the

saidis Lordis had and obtenit to that effect, and that the pairtyis thameselffis onnawayes presoome to come to the Justice Court quhill the magistratis of the said burgh
of Edinburgh come and mak thair convoy and addresse to the same under the pane of
rebellioun, etc, with certificatioun. And siclyke to command, chairge, and inhibite
all and sindrie personis that nane of thame be fund walking upoun the streetis of
this burgh efter the ringing of the ten hour bell at night under the pane to be takine,
apprehendit, wairdit, and punist as accordis."

　　The trial of Gight was a fiasco.—The trial proved a sheer fiasco. On Feb. 26,
1617, the Court met as appointed, the prosecutors being Lord-Advocate Oliphant
and Marjorie Keith, the mother of the deceased Francis Hay, while as prolocutors
for the defence were Gordon of Cluny, the Laird of Strathdon, Thomas Nicolson
elder, and Alexander Peebles and Robert Fairlie, advocates. By consent of both
parties the trial was adjourned till the 28th, Gordon of Cluny becoming cautioner in
5,000 merks for the appearance then of Gordon of Gicht. "Upon the 26 Februar,"
writes Calderwood, "the Crosse of Edinburgh was taken doun. The old long stone,
about fortie foots or thereby in length, was translated by the devise of certaine
mariners in Leith from the place where it stoode past memorie of man to a place
beneath in the Highe Street without anie harme to the stone, and the bodie of the
old Crosse was demolished and another buildit, whereupon the long stone or obelisk
was erected and sett up on the 28th Marche." When Feb 28 came round the Lords
of Secret Council thought it expedient for "mony goode respectis and considera-
tionis tending to the observation of his Majesteis peace within the burgh that
the justice courte now presentlie sitting for tryeing of the Laird of Geycht anent
the unlauchfull taking and detening of umquhill Francis Hay and for persuite
of the brether of Brunthill sall sitt no (langer this nyght nor fyve of the cloke
at nyght and so lang heirefter as this mater salbe of continewance), that the
Courte (sitt no langer bot till fyve of the cloke nyghtlie), and ordanes the (clerk of)
Counsall to (go and make intimation heirof to the justice) and to desire him to
conforme himself in this mater accordinglie". The second day of the trial (Feb.
28) is described at length in Pitcairn's *Criminal Trials* (III., 419-422). Sir William
Hart and Alexander Colville were the judges. The prosecutors, as on the first day,
were Lord-Advocate Oliphant and Marjorie Keith, mother of the deceased Francis
Hay, but with George Hay, brother of the deceased William Hay, fiar of Brunthill,
and George Hay, his brother, now conjoined with them; as prolocutors for the
pursuit were named the Earl of Erroll, Lord Oliphant, Lord Yester, and Alexander
Keith of Ludquharne; and the prolocutors for the defence now named were the
Marquis of Huntly, the Earl of Eglinton, Viscount Lauderdale, Lord Ochiltree, Mr
Thomas Nicolson, and Mr. Alexander Peebles. After a good deal of ingenious
argumentation between the laird of Gight's counsel and the Lord Advocate, the
trial was adjourned to the following day (1st March), Gordon of Cluny continuing his
caution for the laird of Gight. The Court duly met for its third sitting on March 1
as appointed. From Pitcairn (III., 422-424) it appears that, in consequence of the
illness of Sir William Hart, the single judge on the bench that day was Mr. Alexander Colville, and that it was pleaded on behalf of Gordon of Gight that Colville

could not be lawfully a judge in the case, because he was fourth of kin to the Countess of Erroll, whose husband was a party to the pursuit, and that the sitting was consumed in argument pro and con on this question between the counsel for Gight and the Lord Advocate. There was again adjournment to the present 4th March, on which day, as appears from Pitcairn (iii., 424-427), Mr. James Bannatyne of Newtyle presented his commission and took his place on the bench along with Mr. Alexander Colville, and much of the proceedings consisted in argument pro and con on a declinature submitted in retaliation by the Lord Advocate of the competency of Drummond of Medhope and Hamilton of Redhouse to be assessors on the trial, in respect that they were both related to the Marquis of Huntly, and therefore likely to be prejudiced in favour of Gight. The question was left un-decided and the Court again adjourned. Since the 4th March, the third day of the sittings, there had been adjourned sittings on the 7th, the 8th, and the 11th and 12th (see Pitcairn, iii, 427), where it appears that the pursuers had abandoned their declinature of the assessorships of Drummond of Medhope and Hamilton of Redhouse, and that on the 11th and 12th there were very prolix disputations on the merits of the case

The trial stopped —On March 13, which was the eighth day of the trial, there was a stop in the proceedings, which is recorded thus : " The Justice and Assessouris for obedience of ane warrand of the Lordis of Secreit Counsall producet be my Lord Justice Clerk, continewis this Justice Court and all forder disputatioun in this cause to the auchtene day of Junii nixtocum". The warrant is signed by the Chancellor, Marr and Binning. The trial was postponed on June 18 to June 27, when, according to Pitcairn, "the Justice be directioun of the Kingis Majestie de-clairit be my Lord Advocat continews all forder disputatioun in this process and tryell of the particular crymes respective content in that summondis to the third day of the next justice-air of the sherefdome quhair the parteis, alsweill persewaris as defendaris, duelles (Aberdene), or soner upon xv dayes wairning : and ordanis the Laird of Geicht to find caution for his compeirance to the effect and in maner above written, under the pane of 5,000 merks, conforme to his Majesteis directioun re-portit to his Majesteis Advocat as said is ". Gight found William Gordon of Rothiemay his surety.

Erroll objects to Huntly.—On July 27, 1617, the Lords of Secret Council decided on the proposition laid before them by the king "tuitching" the exemption craved by Francis, Earl of Erroll, from the office and judgment and jurisdiction of sherriffship of George, Marquis of Huntly, which the Earl desired " be insert in his Majesteis decreit, and sentence arbitrall to be gevin and pronuncet be his Majestie upoun that submissioun, maid unto his Majestie be the said Marques takand the binding on him for George Gordoun of Geycht and Johnne Gordoun, lait scheref-depute of Abirdene, on the ane pairt, and the said Erll of Errole, takand the burdyne on him for the fader and bairnes of Brunthill and for the moder and freindis of umquhill Frances Hay, on the other pairt ". The Lords, understanding that the submission pro-ceeded not upon any deeds done by the Earl and the Marquis, " or upoun ony con-troversie or debait standing amangis thameselffis, bot onlie upoun the occasiounis fallin oute betuix thair freindis, and that thay ar no forder bundin bot to caus thair freindis underly and obey his Majesteis decreit and sentence to be pronunceit betuix thame; and considering thairwithall that a schereff-principall can not be ansuerable *in criminalibus* for his depute, seeing the cryme is personall and the punishement dew thairfoir aucht onlie to be execute upoun the persone guiltye: Thairfoir the saidis Lordis findis that his Majestie in his decreit and sentence can not of law decerne the said exemptioun seeing thair is no suche mater submittit, and his Majestie can not pas the boundis of the submissioun; and yf the said Erll hes ressoun for him to seik the said exemptioun he wil be hard thairupoun befoir the Lordis of Counsell and Sessioun".

The King settles the vendetta.—"It was the King himself," says the editor of the *Privy Council Register* (vol xi.), "that had thought the trial worthy of his own interposition during his visit to Edinburgh. He wanted the trial arranged so that it should run aground by being transferred to Aberdeen. Then he took the whole affair into his own hands, and resolved to settle it by a royal decreet arbitral which the parties should be invited to accept." So on August 20 the Privy Council sent letters to Lord Huntly and Lord Erroll summoning them to Edinburgh on Sept 8 in "peciable maner, accompanyed onlie with thair houshalde servandis, and to keepe thair ludgeings quhen thay come heir" Huntly was ordered to bring Gight and his brother, John Gordon of Ardlogie Erroll was to bring the three brothers Hay of Brunthill On Sept 10, 1617, there appeared before the Privy Council the Marquis of Huntly, George, Lord Gordon, the laird of Gight, and his son-in-law, Hay, Sir Alexander Gordon of Cluny, Gordon of Abergeldie, and John Gordon of Buckie, on the one part; and the Earl of Erroll, his son, Lord Hay, his brother, —— Hay, Nathaniel Keith, and the brothers Hay of Brunthill, on the other It was "signifiet" to the two parties that the king had pronounced his sentence arbitral in the dispute, and that it "wes his Majesteis will and pleasour that afoir his decreit wer showne unto thame that thay sould be reconsiliat and aggreit, and promeis to stand to his Majesteis decreit and sentence foirsaid. And thay being demandit yf thay wer content to conforme thameselffis to his Majesteis will and plesour on this point, thay declairit that in all reverence and humilitie thay wold acquiesce to his Majesteis will and plesour. Therefore in testificatioun of thair willing obedience to his Majestie, thay choppit handis, one with another, and promeist to burie all formair greiffis, displeasouris, and unkyndnes standing amangis thame, and to stand and underly and fulfil the decreit and sentence gevin and pronunceit be his Majestie betuix thame."

A recrudescence of the feud, 1617.—Even then, however, the dispute was not settled, for on January 31, 1618, the King's Advocate and William Hay, Gight's son-in-law, petitioned the Council as follows: Despite the publication of the decreet in the matter of the feud between them and the "brether of Brunthill," and the "chopping" of hands in presence of the Council, the said Williame Hay, when walking on the links, less than a mile from his house, on ——, was attacked by William Hay, younger of Brunthill, and Mr. Patrik Hay, on horseback, and armed with hagbuts and pistollets. Petitioner having his "led horse" with him made his escape. The brothers thereupon retired to an "oistlar" house at the Kirk of '——, on the highway home, and there hid themselves. They assembled together twelve horsemen and twenty footmen all armed, but petitioner, suspecting the ambush, rode home another way. On —— November last "the said Johnne Hay" assaulted David Nicolsoun, petitioner's servant, in Patrik Blak's booth in Abirdeene   All these persons are guilty of carrying forbidden weapons, and should be ordered to appear before the Council. The petition is signed "Sir W Oliphant"; on the back, "Fiat ut petitur, P. Pollok".

The final settlement.—On June 29, 1623, Mr Robert Learmonth, advocate, as procurator for the dischargers, registers a discharge by Francis, Earl of Erroll, and William Hay, fiar of Brunthill, and George and Mr. Patrik Hay, his brothers, to James Prymrois, clerk of the Privy Council, for £2,000 consigned in his hands by George Gordon of Gight, for obedience of part of a decree arbitral pronounced by the king as judge and arbiter chosen by George, Marquis of Huntly, and the said Earl of Erroll, dated at Carlisle, August 6, 1617, and registered in the books of Council and Session on September 10 thereafter   The discharge is dated at Slains, May 26, 1623. Witnesses John Hay, burgess of Aberdeen, Alexander Davidson, John Hay and David Syme, servitors to the Earl of Erroll, and Walter Hay, inserter of the date and names of witnesses. On the same date there is an acquittance by Erroll and the Hays   The discharge is signed "Errol"; "Wm. Hay, w^t my hand"; "George Hay, w^t my hand", "M P Hay, with my hand"; "Alex^r Davidsone, witness", "W. Hay, witnes"; "J. Hay, witnes", "apud Edinburgh, nono Junij, 1623". Mr Robert Learmont, advocate, as procurator for Erroll and William, George and Patrik Hay, "consentis to the registratione of this above writtin discharge in the buikis of Secreit Counsall " (*Privy Council Register*).

1618. *April* 10—This day Mr. James Lawtie, advocate, as procurator for William, Lord Blantyre, and George Gordon of ——, gave in a document for registration bearing that they had become cautioners for George Gordon of Gight, that he shall not molest James Cuming in ——, Johnne Andersone, George Grede (?) ——, Williame —— of Methlick, James Hay in —— Methlick, George his brother, John Raith there, and —— their families and tenants   The act of caution, which was written by Thomas Crombie, writer, was signed at Leyth on April 10, 1618, by the said parties before Mr. Andro Skene of Chapeltoun, Mr. James Buchane, son of the laird of ——, William Hammyltoun, "my servitor," and Alexander Blair (*Ibid.*)

GIGHT'S ATTEMPT TO BLACKMAIL HIS DYING MOTHER-IN-LAW, THE DOWAGER LADY SALTOUN, 1618.—Gight's next venture was an attempt to blackmail his mother-in-law, Lady Saltoun   In 1617 he married at Rothiemay, as his second wife, Lady Jean Lindsay (who had married, in 1607, Sir John Lindsay of Kinfauns and Carraldstone, son of the twelfth Earl of Crawford). She was the daughter of George Abernethy, seventh Baron Saltoun (died 16), by his wife (married 1588), Lady Margaret Stewart, daughter of the fourth arl of Atholl, Chancellor of Scotland, who had married Lady Elizabeth Gordon, daughter of the fourth Earl of Huntly. The parson of Rothiemay was suspended for celebrating the marriage, Gight being a Roman Catholic (*Frasers of Philorth*, ii , 63). Gight got two step-daughters.

His wife's sister, Lady Margaret Abernethy, married Sir Alexander Fraser of Philorth, and became the mother of the tenth Baron Saltoun, the first Fraser to bear that title It may be remembered that Gight's father, William, killed Thomas Fraser of Strichen in 1576. He had been married less than a year when he tried to blackmail his mother-in-law, old Lady Saltoun, who was lying at the point of death at Corncairn (which was afterwards bought for Gight's brother-in-law, and called Park), to make a will in his favour. The whole case was recited before the Privy Council on July 2, 1618, when Patrick Livingstone of Inchorsie, his brother, Mr. William, and the King's Advocate made this complaint.

Gight intimidates the dowager's adviser, Patrick Livingstone.—On April 20, 1618, Gight, accompanied by George, his eldest son, James Baird, and John Alschinner, his servants, and others, all armed with pistollets and other weapons, went to Corncairn, "quhair umquhill Dame Margaret Stewart, Lady Saltoun, lay seik for the tyme, and quhair he looked to have found the said Patrik And missing him thair, being informed that he wes riddin to the place of Tullidone, to the baptisme of his susteris bairne, he addrest him selff with als speid and come to the said place Quhairof notice being gevin to the said Patrik, he and all these that wer with him come furth and mett the said George, ressavid him with all schawis of hairtie love and kyndnes, and he acquat thame with suche outward formes of goodwill and hairtynes as thay could haif wished, and past with thame to denner, intertennying pleasant and familiar discourseis at the denner, with mony promisis and attestationis of his best affectionis to the said Patrik and his wyff. And efter denner thay accumpaneid him to his horsse, looke-ing for nothing les then that he had ony bad or sinister purpois in his hairt aganis the said Patrik. Bot afore he took horsse he called the said Patrik asyde unto him, and, in presence of the minister of Rothemay, he begun to questioun him anent the testament and latter will maid be the said laite lady, and quarellit the said Patrik for suffering hir to mak ony testament, as gif it had layne in his pouer to have stayed hir, alledgeing that all that scho had wes his birth right, and that no utheris had interesse thairto And the said Patrik . verie mòdesthe and soberlie ansuerit him that it wes the laydis will to mak a testament for the weele of hir oyis, and that he had no reasoun, nather lay it in his pouer, to stay and hinder hir, and that he wald quite his pairt of the said testament for ane plak, so as he micht have his releif of twa thousand merkis quhairin he stood ingadgeit as cautionair to him self for the said lady." Gight, "not being content with this the said Patrikis ansuer, burst furth in moist bitter and passionat speetcheis aganis him, protesting and avowing with mony horrible aithes that he sould stryk ane daigger to the said Patrikis hairt, and that he sould cleive him to the harne pane unles he causit the said testament ather to be nullit or reformit to his contentment. And the said George, his sone, presentit ane bend pistollet to the said Patrik, of purpois and intentioun to have schote and slane him thairwith. And he and his said sone and thair complices had not faillit at that tyme to have tane some unhonnest advantage of him, wer not thay stayit be the gentilmen present and in company with the said Patrik for the tyme. And so, finding him selff disapoint of his blodie and wicked purpois at that tyme, he past away with mony threatningis to have the said Patrikis lyff gif the testament wer not reformit agane the nixt meeting."

A second attempt to threaten Patrick Livingstone.—"And schoirtlie thairefter the said lady haveing send for the said Mr. Williame to confer with him upoun some particulairis concerning hir estaite, and he accordinglie haveing address him selff unto hir, the said George, being informed thairof, and that the said Mr. Williame wes riddin to Rothemay to his said bruther, quhair he hes dwelt thir sax yeiris bigane," resolved to "tak some advantage of thame at that tyme, [and] accumpaneid with George Craufurd, William Pratt in Monkishill, Johnne Abirnethie, his servitor, and Williame Essillis in Fettircarne, with utheris his compliceis, bodin in feir of weir, with pistolletis prohibite to be worne, as said is, came upoun the sext day of Maij last to the said place of Rothemay. And the said Mr. Williame, persaveing him comeing, he address himself to meete him, expecting all freindlie and kynd useing of him, in respect of the mony good officeis done be the said Mr. Williame to him and the mony promeisis of freindship maid be him to the said Mr Williame. And at the said Mr. Williame's first meeting with him, he, persaveing the said Patrik walking some space asyde with the minister of Rothemay, he brak at him in a grite raige and furie, and with verie grite difficultie wes he stayed be some personis present for the tyme. And the said Mr. Williame, being informed that Sir James Skene of Currie-hill, ane of the nomber of the Lordis of Prevey Counsaill, wes than newlie lichtit at the Kirk of Rothemay, he past unto him, acquentit the said Sir James with the lawles and insolent cariage of the said Laird of Geicht, and humelie desyrit him, as ane of his Majesteis Prevey Counsaill, to bind the said Laird to the peace Quhilk the said Sir James did."

Gight tries to confront old Lady Saltoun herself.—When Skene returned south "the said Laird of Geycht, being forgetfull of the promeis maid for keiping of the peace, he upoun the thretene day of Maij last directit and send his awne wyff, his eldest sone, Johnne Abirnethie, and Andro Wood to the place of Corncarne in commissioun to the saidis Patrik and Mr. Williame, that thay sould caus the said testament be reformed to his contentment, or ellis it sould be the darrest testament that evir wes maid in the North And the said Lady Saltoun being delt with to reforme the said testament, scho planelie declairit that scho wold not alter ane word thairof Quhilk answer being returnit to the said George, he wes so incensit and commovit thair-with that upoun the morne thaireftir, being the fourtene day of Maij, he, accum-paneid with George Gordoun, his eldest sone, James Baird in the Mayne of Geicht, William Prat in Munskishill, William Stewart in McTarie, George Gordoun in Lethentie, Walter Ogilvy in Dudweik, Patrik Sinclair of Achannachie, Johnne Abirnethie, Johnne Alexander, and Alexander B'oun, servitoris to the said Laird of Geicht, with convocatioun of his Majesteis eigeis to the noumer of ten personis, all bodin in feir of weir, with jackis, secrites, teil-bonnetis, tua-handit swerdis, and utheris wapponis invasive, and with pistolletis, prohibite to be worne as said is, come to the place of Cornecarne, quhair he thocht to have surprysit the saidis Patrik and Mr. Williame at denner tyme ar evir thay had bene war of him. And quhen he come to the place, finding the yettis oppin, he appointit tua of his servandis to guard the yet, and he send ane uther up to the hall to try and persave quhair thay wer sitting, resolveing gif thay had bene togidder to have slane thame at that same instant Bot, seeing be the providence of God the said Patrik wes a little before riddin to Rothemay,·he directit his servand, James Baird, to the said Mr. Williame, desyreing him to come and speik with him."

Gight makes William Livingstone his prisoner —Mr William, " being sitting at his denner, he rais presentlie frome the table and went unto him single and allane, without company or wapponis, dreiding no harme of him, seeing as the said Mr. Williame apprehendit all his miscontentment wes aganis his said bruther. And quhen the said Mr. Williame come unto him, his servandis past betuix the said Mr Williame and the yet, and thairby cutt him schorte of all meanis of retreate to the house. And he himselfe enterit in most dispytfull and railling speetcheis aganis him, commanding the said Mr. Williame presentlie to gif him satisfactioun in that mater of the testament, or ellis he sould have the said Mr. Williame's hairt bloode, and that he sould wasche his handis in his blood. And the said Mr. William, haveing oppossit aganis his furie his awne innocence and impossibilitie to gif him contentment in that mater quhairwith he burdynit him, and then the respect quhilk he aucht to carey to his Majestie and his lawis, and the havie wraith and judgement of God that wold still persew him gif he medlit with the said Mr Williame his innocent blood, yit nothing could content him, bot with horrible aithes he avowed that nane sould releve him out of his handis, and that he sould ding a sword throughe thame that durst presome to releve him, uttering in this meanetyme mony disdanefull speetcheis aganis his Majestie and his lawis, saying that he knew the Wynd of the Tolbuith and how to gyde his turne, and that he hes had to do with the gritest of Scotland, and had outit his turnis aganis thame, and in this forme he detenit and held the said Mr. Williame the space of tua houres as a prisonner under his power, dureing the quhilk haill space the said Mr. William evir expectit that he sould have put violent handis on his persone, and that he sould have tane his lyff. And at last he propossit this overture unto the said Maister Williame—that he wold spare his lyff gif he wold bring his bruther out of Rothemay unto him Quhilk propositioun being with reasoun rejectit be the said Mr. Williame, as a mater unworthie to be hard of, and most unnaturall to have bene performit on his pairt, he than urgeid the said Mr. Williame to go with him to Rothemay, and that he sould tak on with him, and that he sould decyde his querrell with the said Mr. Williame and his bruther. Quhilk being of the nature of ane challange, he wes forcet to undirtak the same, purpoislie to be red and quite of the said George truble. And so, thay being sinderit, he past in to the place, and with grite intreaty wes moved to tak some refreschement, and then to ly doun and tak rest; bot he wes so far distemparit and careyed with a cruell purpois of revenge as he could tak no rest, bot rease immediatlie, saying to his wyff, ' Jeane, I can tak no rest. I knaw I will die upoun a scaffold. Thair is ane will turne in my hand, quhilk I avow to God presentlie to performe ' And with that he maid searche for the said Mr Williame, sua that he wes constrayned to reteir himselff to ane 'quiet chalmer and to hyde him selff." The next move in the game shows the vengeful pertinacity of Gight.

A raid on Rothiemay in search of Patrick Livingstone —" Persaveing that he could not get the said Mr. Williame, he with all haist, accumpaneid with George Gordoun, raid to Rothemay thinking to have surprysit the said Patrik unawaris. Lyke as he being walking in quiet maner afoir the yet, he wes almoist surprysit of him, and with grite difficultie relevit himself within the house The yettis quhairof being closed and locked, he chapped verie rudlie at the yet, crying and schouting unto the said Patrik to come furth that he micht have his hairt blood; bot finding him self frustrat of his wicked purpois, he come back immediatlie to the place of Cornecarne, resolved to have had the said Mr. Williame's lyff, avowing with mony horrible aithes that he sould nevir see Geycht till he had the said Mr. Williame and his brotheris lyff, and that it sould coast him his lairdschip of Geycht or he sould have thair lyveis, saying thay had bound him to the peace, and that he caired not for the peace, he had doubled out his turne aganis the best in Scotland, and that he sould go mad, lyke Richie, the foole, gif he wer not revengeit upoun thame. And he remanit in the place all that day and tua dayis thaireftir threatning the deeing lady to reforme hir testament. And finding hir constant in hir resolutioun to stand be that quhilk scho had done, he send commissionaris to the saidis Patrik and Mr. Williame to Rothemay, quhairunto the said Mr. Williame had reteirit him selff in the nicht for eschewing of his raige and furie, commanding thame outher to caus him ressave satisfactioun in that mater of the testament, or than assuire thame that no house in the North sould keepe thame, and behavit him selff so ruidlie and insolentlie within the place of Cornecarne in the sicht and presence of the diseasit aiget lady that without all doubt he haistned hir death, quhilk fell out that tyme."

The decision of the Privy Council in the case.—Gordoun appeared for himself, his son, James Baird, Williame Pratt, Williame Stewart, George Gordoun, Johne Alexander, Alexander Broun, and Williame Eshillis; George Crawfurde and Walter Ogilvy did not appear. The Lords find that the laird "hes verie injurioushe boistit, minassit and threatnit" defenders, and that his son, "who is bot ane young boy under his pouer and commandement," has been suffered to carry pistollets in his company, and therefore order him to be committed to the Castle of Edinburgh, therein to remain at his own expense till he present his said son before the Lords, and till he be liberated by them. He is also to pay a fine of 500 merks to the treasurer, and not to depart till he have paid the same. "And whereas thair hes bene divers complaintis formarlie maid to the saidis Lordis aganis him, sua that it is verie evident and liklie that he will not be reclamed frome his oppressioun nor halden under obedience of the law, unles some strait course and ordour (be) tane with him and his said sone," order is therefore given that the said laird and his said son find caution in 10,000 merks each to keep the peace, and to appear before the Lords when called upon to do so, in £500 each not to wear hagbuts and pistollets, and shall also find lawburrows in 5,000 merks each. The Lords order George Craufurde and Walter Ogilvy to be denounced' rebels. On July 9 Gight "exhibited" his son George to the Council, who committed him to the Castle of Edinburgh, where he was to remain at his own expense during their pleasure. On July 16 Gight and his son were fined 500 merks for wearing pistolets They had to find caution in 10,000

(255)

merks to appear before the Council when called, lawborrowis to the two Livingstones in 5,000 merks, and £500 caution not to wear hagbuts. Adam Gordon of
Park, Gight's brother-in-law, and George Chalmer of Cowburtie, became caution for
old Gight, who in turn was caution for his son until the time of the latter's marriage,
when he was to be presented to the Lords by his father to find new caution for himself. On Feb. 14, 1622, Gight informed the Council that he was finally reconciled
to the Livingstones, and that "all quarrellis, contraverseis, eilistis and dabaittis
standing betuix thame are removed and tane away, and thay stand under most
hairty termeis of frendschip," so that now Patrick and William desire no such
caution "Lykeas thay ar attending at the doore, and being callit will compeir,"
and will renounce and pass from the caution so far as they are concerned.

Gight's protest against the Council's finding.—As touching the remaining points of
keeping the peace, Gight and his son declare that they are hardly used, being law-
abiding subjects, and ever ready to appear for trial on all complaints that can be made
against them. "Thair is no uther baronis nor gentlemen in the country putt under
this forme of cautioun, and to injoyne conditionis to thame, and to hold bondis over
thair headis with the lyke quhairof no uther guid subjectis ar burdeyneit within this
kingdome, it caryes a foull and havie imputatioun aganis thame, as gif thay wer brokin
men, aganis whome the course of law could have no executioun, and in this caise
thay ar in a maner seperat frome the whole rest of the subjectis of the kingdome,
and sett by be thameselffis with a mark of reprotche over thair headis, whilk is a verie
grite greif unto thame; and thay ar expoisit to the malice of all the malitious
toungis in the countrey, who takis hold of this cautionarie that thay underly to
misprese thame at thair pleasour." As for George Gordoun, younger, "he wes
bot a young boy the tyme of that complaynt, and wes onlie in company with
his father at that tyme, and rakleslie laid a pistolett upoun him, being ignorant
of the law, and nevir afoir nor sinsyne wes thair any complaynt maid upoun
him. And sieing the saidis George Gordoun, elder, and George Gordoun, younger,
ar ansuerabill and lawbyding subjectis, and as the saidis Lordis knawis ar bleist
with good estaittis and fortnis quhilkis thay will be loathe foolishelie to haisard
or perrell to thair awne wrak, besydeis the haisard of the law, humblie thairfoir
beseikand the saidis Lordis to exoner thame of this cautionarie and of all thay (that)
may follow thairupoun, sua that thay leive in the rank and conditioun of the re-
manent baronis and gentilmen of the countrey, and that the saidis Lordis wold this
day accept of the compeirance of the said George Gordoun, younger, and declair the
said George Gordoun, elder, his act satisfeit in that poynt and he simpliciter fred
thairof." Mr. William Livingstoun being called in, appears for himself and his
brother, and the petitioners being also present, declares that he and his brother
are reconciled with them, and do renounce the caution for indemnity. The Lords
therefore exonerate the petitioners and their cautioners from the burden of the indemnity; they also relieve the elder Gordoun from his cautioning of his son, and
ordain the son to find caution for himself in £500 that he shall not wear hagbuts.
They find, however, that it is not expedient that the elder Gordon should be altogether freed from caution for keeping the peace and appearing before them, but

they modify the amount from 10,000 merks to 2,000 merks, and order him to find new caution in that sum, and also in £500 not to wear hagbuts Adam Gordon of Park and George Chalmer are freed from their responsibility (*Privy Council Register*).

1618 *July* 30.—The king granted to the laird and his second wife (Jean Abernethie), and erected into a free barony, the lands of Many (consisting of Lyntoun, Cothill, Cowhill, and Altersait) in Belhelvie, which William Forbes of Craigievar and Patrick Forbes of Corse, his brother, resigned (*Great Seal*).

1619. *June* 10.—The king confirmed the charter by James, Earl of Buchan, by which they sold to Gight the lands ("irredimabiliter") of Fetterletter and Lethentie This Earl of Buchan was the first of the Erskines who held the title He was the son of Lord Mar, and married Mary Douglas, *de jure* Countess of Buchan. On March 22, 1617, they held a charter of the Earl James to themselves and the longest liver, with remainder to male issue (*ibid*).

1619. *Jan.* 14.—The king ratified the charter by George Gordon, the next laird, of these lands, granted to Andrew Meldrum, second son of the late Andrew Meldrum of Fyvie.

1619. *June* 10 —Gight and the King's Advocate complained to the Council that Andrew Meldrum of Drumbek had worn hagbuts and pistollets since January, 1618, and "gangis thairwith in all pairtis of the cuntrey quhair he hes occasioun to repair, and useis the same for his particulair revenge upoun all suche personis aganis whome he beiris querrell". Pursuers appearing personally, and defender appearing by Mr. Rodger Mowat, advocate, because of his "infirmitie and inhabilitie to compeir notoure and knawne," the Lords find the charge of having carried pistollets proven, and order defender to keep ward in Edinburgh during their pleasure, and to find caution in 200 merks to keep the peace (*Privy Council Register*)

1621. *Nov.*—In the Minute Book of Processes we find mention of "letteris against Gordon of Geight and utheris papists to appear" (*ibid*)

1623. *Jan.* 30. — Gight sold to Patrick Gordon of Nethermuir and the latter's heir, George, the lands of Cuikburnes (in Logie-Buchan), Many, Leyton, Cothill, Cowhill, and Altersait (in Belhelvie) (*Great Seal*). According to the *Collection for a History of the Shires of Aberdeen and Banff* (p. 285), Menie was bought in 1623 from Gordon of Gight by William Seton of Udny, and after that mortgaged (1659) by Sir Robert Graham of Morphie to Robert Kerr, burgess in Aberdeen.

GIGHT'S ATTACK ON HIS BROTHER-IN-LAW, SIR HARRY WOOD OF BONNYTON, 1623 — Gight became hard up—a condition demonstrated by the sales of his lands. Having failed to squeeze his second wife's mother, old Lady Saltoun, he turned on his first wife's brother, Sir Harry Wood of Bonnyton According to Wood's complaint to the Privy Council (April 28, 1624), Gight suddenly appeared on Sunday, July 20, 1623, in the parish kirk of St. Vigeans, where Wood was sitting "in his awne dask, in a verie modest and quyet maner". He was accompanied by William Gordon of Chapeltoun, John Abernethy and George Ireland (*alias* Abercrombie), his servitors, John Gordon of Ardlogie, Adam Gordon his son, John Gordon, son to the goodman of Knockespock, Andrew Cook in Meny, Andrew Udny, servitor to the laird of Foveran, Thomas Shewan, messenger in Brechin, and others, "all bodin in fear of wear, with swords, long dagours, buffell coites, secreitts, plait sleives, steil hattis, with plait stringis, gantellitts," and other weapons   They rushed into the kirk with drawn swords, when the parson "after the ending of the sermone wes at his prayer, and rusheing throw the kirk, and overtradeing weomen and bairnis who wer sitting upoun thair kneyis at the prayer, they come directlie to the complenaris dask, quhair he wes lykewyse upoun his kneyis at his prayer, and shamefullie and unhonnestlie invadite and perseuit him as he supposeit of his lyff, shouting and cryeing 'Traitour be tane,' holding thair drawne swordis and dagouris in thair handis in threatning maner gif he maid ony resistance, sua that he wes constrained to yeild to the necessitie and to rander himself in thair will".

Sir Harry taken prisoner.—Then, "he haveing in modest and sober maner demandit of thame the cause and reasoun of thair so lawles and insolent proceidour aganis him, the said Laird of Geyght, out of the pryde and malice of his hairt, replyit and ansueirit that he wald knaw no law, and that the complener sould goe with thame nil he wald be quhair they pleasit.   And sua they caried him as prisonnar with thame to his awne house of Lethem, quhilk they supprysed and tooke, locked the yetts thairof, held his wyff and children out of the same, and with drawne durkis and daigers thrattenit his servandis within his house, and keipit him captive and prisonner within the said hous, suffering non to come neir him, or acces unto him, and in end presentit unto him ane bond conteining diverse gritt soumes of money and uther hard conditionis, quhilkis thay wald nowise reveill unto him, and propoussed unto him thane to subscrye the bond   And he, preferring the saiftie of his credite to onything that might follow and happin upon that bond, he subscryvit the same, not knowing the tennour nor contents thairof   And dureing the time that thay remained within his house thay sett thair haill horse upon a shote of his best infeild aittis, and held thame thairon till they eate, trade, and distroyit the same; and suche of his servandis as preast to turne the horse thay minassit of thair lyffis."

The punishment of Gight—Parties having been called, the pursuer was personally present, as also the laird of Gight for himself and in the name of John Gordon of Ardlogie, Adam Gordon, his son, John Gordon, son to the guidman of Knockespock, Andrew Cook, and Andrew Udny, for whom he declared he would answer in this case, but the said John Abernethie, George Ireland, and Thomas Shewan did not compear.   The laird of Gight, having referred the proof of the matter simply to the pursuer's oath, and pursuer having deponed to the above effect, adding that had the laird of Gight "presentit unto him a wreit concerning the liveing of Bonnytoun he would have subscryveit it at that tyme," the Lords "finds and declairs that the said John Gordoun of Ardlogie, Adame Gordoun, his sone, and John Gordoun, sone to the guidman of Knokespak, come with the said laird of Geight to the kirk at the time foirsaid, and in a verie tumultuous and unseemlie maner, haveing tua drawne swordis in thair handis, patt violent handeis in the said Laird of Bonnytoun without chargeing and arreisting of him be ane officiar, and quhen the said Laird of Bonnytoun asked of Geyght quhair his officiar wes and be quhat warrand he tooke him, the Laird of Geight answeirit that 'I will tak yow and be answeirable to the Counsall,' and finds and declairs that the said Laird of Bonnytoun subscryveit the bond foirsaid, he being Geight's prisonnar for the tyme", which being "ane verie gritt insolence against the said Laird of Bonnytoun, of a wicked and pernicious praeparative and example, and to the braik of his Majesteis peace," the Lords ordain the laird of Gight to be committed to ward in the Tolbooth of Edinburgh, and to remain there upon his own charges till released, also to pay to the treasurer a fine of 500 merks, to the poor of St. Vigeans parish 200 merks, "for the offence committed be him within the kirk foirsaid," and to the witnesses for their expenses £5 for every horseman and forty shillings for every footman. They also ordain him to present before them the said John Gordon of Ardlogie, Adam Gordon his son, and John Gordon, son to Knockespock, that they may be committed to ward and otherwise punished. Finally, they ordain the lairds of Gight and Bonnyton to find caution acted in the books of Council in 5,000 merks each to keep the peace towards each other. On April 29, 1624, John Leith, fiar of Harthill, Harry Ramsay of Ardownie, and Patrick Gordon, indweller in Edinburgh, were cast in 5,000 merks for Gight not to molest Wood or his family; also in £5,000 that on his being released from the Tolbooth he will keep ward in Edinburgh till he pay the fines for his insolence to the laird of Bonnyton, and until released by the Council; with clause of relief, signed "Jon Leythe, Henri Ramsay, Patrik Gordoun, George Gordoun of Gichtt". On the same date Alexander Ramsay, fiar of Arbikie, gave caution in 5,000 merks for Wood not to harm Gight. On May 3, 1624, Henry Ramsay of Ardownie was caution in 2,000 merks that Gight would present his nephew, Adam Gordon, younger of Ardlogie, and also young Knockespock to the Council on June 1. On the same date there is caution by Gight in £1,000 for Henry Ramsay, elder of Adney, and in 1,000 merks for Henry Ramsay, fiar thereof, his son, not to molest Mr. Williame Durehame, apparent of Lumquhy, nor his family. On the same day Mr. John Paip, younger, advocate and procurator for the dischargers, registers an acquittance by Sir Henry Wardlaw of Pittreive, knight, to John Aitkyne, in name of George Gordon of Gight, for 500 merks, being the fine imposed upon Gordon for his assault upon Wood of Bonnyton. Dated at Edinburgh, May 3, 1624 (*Privy Council Register*).

GIGHT AND HIS FRENCH GOVERNESS —The poverty of Gight, which was only increased by these expensive attacks on his relatives, is strikingly illustrated by the remarkable letter about his daughter's French governess which the Privy Council wrote to Lord Huntly, his chief, as follows, under date September, 1623 "After oure verie hairtlie commendationis to your goode lordship, it has bene complenit unto us be Mr. Johne Paip, writter, that he haveing causit denunce the Laird of Geyght, eldair, and putt him to the horne for non payment to him of the soume of iijᵐ iijᶜ merkis money as principall and iijᶜ merkis of expenssis, that the said Laird notwithstanding, in contempt of the law and justice, lyis still at the horne without ony purpois or intentioun to mak payment of the said soume. We understand, althoght Mr. Johnne his name be used in this mater, that the soume nevirtheles is the proper debt of a strangeair, a Franshewoman, who thir divers yeiris bigane hes had and still hes the charge of educatioun of one of the said Laird his doghtoris, and intertenyis and furnissis hir verie honnestlie in hir apparell and dyet, and bringis hir up in all verteous exerciseis beseameing a young gentlewoman of hir birthe, and this soume is a grite pairt of the chargeis deu to the poore strangear for that caus; quhairin the said Laird oversees himselff verie far in neglecting suche a point of dewtie to a strangear who hes had and still hes such a care of his doghter, and he gevis hir mare nor just caus to blame the justice of this kingdome, whilk in a mater of this kynd hes provin and provis so frindles unto hir.　　The consideratioun whereof hes moved us to recommend the same to your Lordship requeisting and desiring your goode Lordship to deale with the said Laird to haif some regaird of his credite and dewtie in this point, and to mak tymous and thankfull payment to the said Mr. Johnne of this soume.　　Quhairin yf he shall mak ony refuise or delay, that then your Lordship, according to the dewtie of your office, apprehend him and committ him to warde till he purge this hoirning.　We doubt not bot your lordship in your awne honourable regaird to justice and to the furtherance of a poore strangear to justice will so behave yourselff heirin as by your meanis the poore strangear may haif ressoun.　Wherein as yow sall do that whiche to your honnour and dewtie in this caise apperteynis, so yow will do us a singulair pleasour　And so committing yow to Godis protectioun, we rest your Lordships verie loving freindis, Mar, Roxburgh, Melros, Lauderdaill, Arskine, Ar. Naper, S W. Oliphant, Kilsaithe."

1623. *Nov*—The Minute Book of Processes notifies "Alexander Annand a cautioner for the appearance of Gordon of Geight" (*Privy Council Register*).

1623. *Dec.* 24.—The king granted to Gight the lands of Ardestie, Murdrum, and part of Downykeane in Forfar, which Robert Erskine of Ardestie (son of the late Robert) resigned, and the lands of Carlonge and Newbigging in Forfar, which (the 14th ?) Lord Crawford resigned.　It will be remembered that the third laird of Gight's sister-in-law (Margaret Beaton) married the tenth Earl of Crawford (*Great Seal*).

1628. *April* 18.—Sasine to George Gordon, younger of Gight, of the town and lands of Chapelton of Schivas (*Aberdeen Burgh Sasines*)

1629. *April* 1—Gight sold the lands of Many to William Seton of Udny and Marjory Innes, his wife, for 40,000 merks (*Great Seal*).

1631. *June* 19.—Gight was ordered (on July 5) by the Privy Council in his absence to enter into ward at the Edinburgh Tolbooth for attacking "Mr" William Murray in Ardownie after the sermon in the parish kirk of Monfuthe　Murray was dining with Jerome Lindsey when Gight enticed him "farre out of the toune," and then "er ever he wes awar . . . strake out a nomber of straikes .　. and had not failed to have slaine him, wer not his [Murray's] awne better defence".　On *July* 5 William Durham, fiar of Grange, Henry Ramsay of Ardownie and "Mr." William Murray in Ardownie complained that Gight whose "turbulent dispositioune is not unknowne . . . daylie troubles and molests us and others gentlemen dwelling about him, threatning us with all sort of violence, by hacquebuts, pistolets and uthers forbidden weapouns"　Gight was ordered to find £1,000 caution to desist (*Privy Council Register*)

1631 *July* 27.—Gight and his brother John of Ardlogie with a gang of armed men were charged before the Privy Council with having on this date gone to the Kirkton of Rayne to kill John Leith of Harthill, which they would have done "if some noble weomen and ladeis had not interceedit " (*ibid.*).

1633 —George Gordon of Gight owed Patrick Wood in Little Ardo 4,600 merks on the lands of Chapelton of Schivas (*Spalding Club Misc*, iii, 132)

1634. *Nov.* 13.—Gight was ordered by the Privy Council to arrest those who had attacked the laird of Frendraught (Spalding's *Troubles*, i., 421).

1635. *July* 3.—He was caution that his son-in-law, Coxton, John Innes of Leuchars and others should not harm Innes of Balvenie (*Familie of Innes*, p. 230).

1639. *Feb.* 14.—He took part in the first Raid of Turriff (Spalding, i., 137).

1639. *April* 16.—Gight, who throughout the Covenanting struggle "kythit" with the anti-Covenanters, was one of a deputation to Lord Aboyne, then at Percok, to request him not to go south, as the country was "heidles" (*Ibid*, i, 172).

1639. *May* 8.—Gight was one of another deputation who, supported by eighty horse and sixty foot, "cam to the kirkyeard of Ellon, and send to the laird [Kennedy] of Kermvk, being in his owne hous of Arduthie, desyring him to refuse the countrie covenant, and to subscrive the Kingis covenant." Kennedy refused (*Ibid.*, i., 181).

1639. *May* 10.—Gight, the young laird of Cromartie, with some other lairds, intended to "cum to the place of Tolly Barclay, and thair to tak out sic armes, mvscatis, gvnis, and carrabinis as the lairdis of Delgatie and Tollie-Barclay had plunderit from the said young laird of Cromartie out of the place of Balquholly [which belonged to the Mowats, who were relatives of Gight]; bot it hapnit the Lord Fraser and maister of Forbes to sie thair cuming. Thay manit the houss of Towy, cloissit the yettis, and schot diuerss schotis fra the houss heid, whair ane seruand of the laird off Geichtis wes schot, callit Dauid Prat. . . . Heir it is to be markit that this wes the first blood that wes drawin heir sen the beginning of this covenant" Gight's party ultimately retreated, "thinking it no vassalage to stay whill thay war slayne: syne, but more ado, rode their way" (*Ibid.*, i., 182).

1639. *May* 13.—Gight took part in the Trot of Turriff, when the Royalists surprised the Covenanting Committee (*Ibid.*, i., 185).

1639. *June.*—Montrose and his artillery attacked the castle of Gight, which was well defended by the laird and Colonel Johnston. The siegers, however, withdrew to Aberdeen (on June 3) when they heard that a Royalist army was approaching. Spalding says the soldiers left the siege, " but more skaith " (*Ibid.*, i., 201; *Britane's Distemper*, p. 23).

1639. *July* 10.—On this day it was reported to the Presbytery of Ellon that Gight had "come to ye Kirk of Ellon upon ye Saboth day, and having maid some ryding throuche ye toun of Ellon which wes scandelous ". Gight (at a subsequent meeting) declared that "he cam not to the Kirk of Ellon to mak ony convocatione, nor to offend or to irritat any gentleman there, but onlie to visit ye laird of Ochterellone and Mr. David Leache [the minister], to tak with him the young laird of Foveran [his grandson], wha was in Ochterellone [the lad's mother, Gight's daughter, having died in the early part of the year]". He said he was sorry if he had offended any of the brethren (Mair's *Records of the Presbytery of Ellon*, p. 141).

1640 *April.*—Gight began to fortify his house with "men, mvskat, meit, and drink, and vther devysis of defenss," in view of Monro's advance (Spalding, i., 265)

1640. *June.*—Gight, described as a "seiklie, tender man, being by chance at this samen tyme in Montross,'is takin by ane Capiten Betoun, and had to [the Tolbooth of] Edinbrugh with the rest; his houss of Ardessie [in Forfarshire] pitifullie plunderit, becauss he wes ane papist and out stander aganes the good causs' (Spalding, 1, 285). , Upon caution he had "libertie of frie waird within the toune".

1640. *Nov.* 17.—He "wes confynit in the toun, whair old Geicht departit this lyf" in November (*Ibid*, 1, 285), "either through age or greefe or bothe together. He was a Papist in his profession. That was eneuch indytment against him" (Gordon's *Scots Affairs*, III, 200).

1640. *Dec.* 30 —"Collonell Maister of Forbes send out to the intaking of the place of Geicht ane capiten with 32 soldiouris. The hous is randerit be the lady, becaus none laird wes there. Aluaies scho cam in and delt so with the collonell that they were all removit and cam bak agane to Abirdene" (Spalding, 1., 375)

Gight was twice married: (1) before 1597 to Isobell, the daughter of Sir Patrick Wood of Bonnyton—the name of his lands in Udny and in Forfarshire (see a deduction of the Woods in *Scottish Notes and Queries*, Nov., 1898); and (2), before May 18, 1617, to Jean, daughter of George Abernethy, seventh Baron Saltoun, and widow of Sir John Lindsay of Kinfauns. She was involved, it may be remembered, with her husband, Gordon, in his attack on her mother, in 1618. Dr. Temple (*Thanage of Fermartyn*, p. 264) says that James Gordon, son of James, IV. of Newton, married "the lady of Gight, but had no issue". The dates suggest that the lady was probably the widow of the sixth laird of Gight, but I cannot verify Dr. Temple's assertion. The second laird of Newton (the brother of Sheelagreen) was hand-in-glove with the Gights in their war against the Covenant, and was executed for his share in the rising (1644). Mr. Mair, in his *Presbytery Records of Ellon* (p. 8), notes that Gight's first wife (Isobell Wood) bore him at least five children before 1597. The *Balbithan MS.* says that the first wife bore Gight two sons and three daughters, and that his second wife bore him a son and a daughter.

1. GEORGE, VII of Gight

2 JOHN assisted his nephew, the eighth laird, to raid the town of Montrose. He was imprisoned in Edinburgh, 1644, with his brother, the seventh laird, who was granted, through his agent, Thomas Gordon, 300 merks to "menteyn" himself and his brother in prison (June 19, 1644, *Acts of Parliament*)

3 ALEXANDER is referred to in a charter of 1642 as the son of Sir George Gordon and Lady Jean Abernethy Like his father and his uncle Patrick, he married a Forfarshire woman, Lilias, second daughter of Sir William Menteith of Kers. In 1642 the king confirmed the charter

of 24th February, 1636, by the seventh laird, in implement of a marriage contract of the same date to Lilias, second daughter of Sir William Menteith of Kers, promised spouse of Alexander Gordon, in life-rent, to continue during her widowhood, and in fee to Alexander and his heirs by Lilias, whom failing to said Sir George and his heirs by said Jean, whom failing to heirs and assignees whatsoever of said Sir George. In 1636 he got the estate of Ardestie, in Forfarshire, from Robert Erskine (*Great Seal*). His father was known as "Old Ardestie" (Gordon's *Scots Affairs*), he having probably got that estate through his first wife, Isobell Wood, who was a Forfarshire woman. He, too, had dealings in 1630 with Alexander Durhame of Downiemylne In 1642 the king confirmed a charter (dated 18th February, 1631) by Alexander Lindsay of Potterlie to Alexander Gordon for a payment of 16,000 merks by his nephew (the seventh laird).

BARBARA married Sir John Turing, both of them "recusants," 1623 (Mair's *Presbytery of Ellon*, p 67) A royal charter of July 29, 1623 (the year when they were recusants), shows the marriage contract between Barbara Gordon and Sir John Turing of Foveran was dated at Gight, August 3, 1620. On January 5, 1629, she renounced her right in the Mains of Gight in favour of her father. Her husband was present at the battle of Worcester, 1651, and had been created a baronet, 1639. He lost his lands at Foveran, which his house had held for three centuries. He had by Barbara Gordon a son, George, who was alive in 1644 (*Troubles*, ii , 330), but predeceased him By his second marriage (in 1652) he had a son, who died unmarried in 1682, when the representation of the family devolved on the (first) baronet's nephew, the ancestor of the present baronet, who lives at Chichester. Barbara Gordon died early in the beginning of 1639, and Lord Huntly, whose "ant" she was (according to Spalding's *Troubles*, i., 137), attended her funeral. The Turings are dealt with in the *Thanage of Fermartyn* (pp. 565-572).

5. MARY married Alexander Innes of Coxton, who was concerned in the anti-Covenanting struggle, but was pardoned, 1647 (*Acts of Parliament*). On January 5, 1629, she renounced Little Gight and Faldonhill She died August 20, 1647 (*Familie of Innes*) She is buried at Lhanbryde (Jervise's *Epitaphs*)

6. LILIAN married the Hon. William Hay of Fetterletter, son of the eighth Earl of Erroll, by Lady Agnes Sinclair, daughter of Lord Caithness (*Privy Council Register*). He quarrelled with his mother in 1616 (*Ibid*), and helped his father-in-law to attack the Hays of Burnthill (1616), to which I have already referred. On January 5, 1629, Lilian renounced her rights in Meikle Ardo and Carnerie, with the consent of her husband, in favour of her father.

7 —— GORDON. The *Balbithan MS.* says Gight had a daughter by his second wife. _ I cannot verify this.

George Gordon, VII. of Gight.

(Son of VI.)

I do not know when the seventh laird was born, but he was described by the Privy Council in 1618 as "ane young boy". His career was almost as stormy as his father's   Its leading events are as follows :—

1618.—Gight, though "a young boy," helped his father, in April and May of this year, as I have shown, to worry old Lady Saltoun, his step-grandmother, into altering her will. On July 2 the Privy Council ordered the lad to be imprisoned in Edinburgh. On July 9 his father "exhibited" him, and committed him to the castle, "therein to remain at his own expenses during their Lordships' pleasure".

1623   Aug. 20.—Complaint by the King's Advocate against John Forbes of Pitsligo, George Gordoun, fiar of Geicht, Robert Innes of Balvennie, Alexander Bannerman of Elsick, Alexander Annand of Auchterellon, George Gordoun of Newtoun, Johne Leith, apparent of Harthill, and Johne Burnet of Campbell, who since 1617 had worn hagbuts and pistolets and shot at wild fowl and deer in contravention of the laws   The pursuer appeared personally, with all the defenders (except George Gordoun, fiar of Gight, who is therefore ordained to be denounced rebel) (Privy Council Register).

1623. Nov. 21.—Alexander Annand of Arduthie was caution in 1,000 merks for George Gordon, fiar of Gight, to appear before the Council on Sept. 10 and answer a charge of wearing hagbuts and pistolets (Ibid)

1624   July.—He took part with his father in the raid on Sir Harry Wood of Bonnyton, his uncle, in the Kirk of St Vigeans.

1633.—George Gordon, younger of Gight, owed 100 merks to the miller of Towie (Spalding Club Misc., iii , 132)

1636. Dec. 20.—The Privy Council granted him letters of protection against his creditors for a year, repeating the favour in 1638

1640. June 11.—"The young laird of Geicht is forsit be Marschall and Monro to cum in ; and vpone Frydday the 11th of Junij he cam to Aberdein befoir the counsall of warr. He getis 48 houris protectioun. Ane challenge of combat past betuixt him and [Alexander Fraser] the laird of Phillorth. Marschall getis word, sendis ane pairty of soldouris for him (to eschew this fight), and took him out of his naikit bed, lying in Mr. Thomas Lilleis house in Old Abirdein. Geicht (wnder protectioun) mervallis at this bussines, not knowing Marischallis purpoiss. Aluaies he gettis libertie from the capiten that took him to ryde beside him (who wes also horst) over to the toun, and speik with Marschall. The capiten, seing his horss bot ane litle naig, wes content   and so thay ryde on with his soldiouris whill thay cum to the Justice Port, whair Geicht schiftis the capiten and all his keiparis, and be plane speid of foot he wynis cloiss away, to all thair disgraces, and to Germanie goes he"

(Spalding's *Troubles*, i., 287). He may have lived in Germany with his kinsman, Colonel John Gordon, who assassinated Wallenstein, and who had seen John Gordon of Ardlogie die in 1638 He spent part of the time in England as the next item shows

1642. *April* 20.—On this date King Charles wrote this letter, which has been discovered in the Record Office by Mr. Murray Rose: "Charles, by the Grace of God King of Great Britain, France and Ireland, Defender of the Faith, To all and sundry to whom these presents shall come, Greeting: Seeing that a noble and most brave knight, George Gordon of Gight, faithful to us and beloved, one of the lords of our bedchamber, descended of the most noble house of Huntley in Scotland, has so proved his fidelity to us in the late troubled times, that not only did he for two years perform the duties of commander of a troop of horse and company of foot in our service with the highest credit, but also out of his great zeal on our behalf defrayed at his own expense the charge of both companies; and that after the pacification of Berwick fresh troubles having broken out in England, he proceeded thither, and there being made a Colonel by us, he for the space of a whole year conducted himself with the highest bravery and merit And now that peace has been restored, he asks our permission to depart; and we being desirous not only to accord to him our benign permission, but also to grace him with this passport as a testimony of his fidelity and bravery. Therefore we earnestly desire all Kings, Princes, and States others, our Friends and Neighbours through whose countries he may pass, or in which he may give evidence of his bravery, as well as their vice-gerents and other magistrates and goodmen: and we strictly enjoin our subjects that they afford to the said George Gordon full freedom and power of going, abiding and returning with his household and goods, permitting none to molest or injure him, but rather afford him all offices of humanity, benevolence and friendship which every one expects to be rendered to himself: and they may rest assured that whatever aid they shall confer on this excellent man will be very grateful to us, and will be willingly rewarded by us as occasion offers, and we have caused this passport to be given under our regal hand and seal, in our Court at York, the twentieth of April, 1642, and of our reign the eighteenth year."

1643 *Feb.* 20.—The king granted to Robert Cruickshank, junior, and Alexander Burnet, senior, merchant burgesses of Aberdeen, their heirs and assignees whatsoever, the lands and barony of Geight, which belonged to George Gordon of Geight, son and heir of the late Sir George, and were valued 8th November, 1642, at 16,800 libs. (*Great Seal*)

1643 *June* —"Schir George Gordon, elder of Geicht, cam hame out of Germanie," where he had been for three years (Spalding's *Troubles*, ii, 254).

1643. *July* 31.—The king grants to James, Earl of Airlie [the laird's brother-in-law], his heirs and assignees whatsoever the Kirklands of Gight, etc., etc, and the other lands and tacks of teinds on July 18, 1643, at 11,504 merks Gight was in hiding in Germany from 1640 to 1643 During this period his creditors seem to have fallen on his assets, and that may have caused him to come "out of Germany" in 1643, as Spalding tells us

1644. *March* 19 —He was one of the band of Royalists who rode into Aberdeen and captured Provost Leslie, Robert Farquhar and Alexander Jaffray, "lait bailhes," and John Jaffray, Dean of Guild, and took them to Strathbogie, and then to Auchindown (*Troubles*, ii., 324-5).

1644 *March* 26—He and his son accompanied the Marquis of Huntly to Aberdeen (*Ibid.*, ii, 330).

1644. *April.*—He was one of the band that went to Banff, "took in the toune but contradictioun, mellit with the keyis of the tolbuith, took frie quarteris, and plunderit all the armes thay could get, buffill cotis, pikis, pistollis, suordis, carrabinis, yea and money also Thay took from Alexander Winchester, ane of the bailleis thairof, 700 merkis, quilk he [had] as ane of the four collectouris of the taxationis, and loane siluer of Banff, and fra —— Schand in Doun thay plunderit some moneis. Thay causit the balleis (for Doctor Douglass thair prouest had fled) and tounesmen subscrive and sueir the band denying the last Covenant. . . . Thay also took from George Geddess, ane vther of the saidis four collectouris, 500 merkis of taxatioun and loane siluer *Geicht keepit all the moneyis*, about 2,500 merkis.   Thairefter thay rode to Muresk, perseuit the place, and being randerit, thay took the Laird with thame ; syne returnit to Innervrie, quhair thay met with the Marquis " (*Ibid.*, ii, 342)

1644. *May* 1.—He rode through Old Aberdeen with a company of about 60 horse, bearing "new quhyte lances in thair handis," to Strathbogie " (*Ibid* , ii , 352).

1644. *May* 9.—The house of Gight was "randerit" by the laird to the Covenanters. Gight was captured (though his son escaped). "Thair is ane capitan with about 24 soldiouris put within the place of Geicht, quhilk wes weill provydit with meit and drink and other necessares ; and quhairin thair wes store of ammvnitioun, pulder and ball, with victuall in girnellis aboundantlie" (*Ibid.*, ii., 359).

1644. *May* 13.—Gight and the other prisoners, his brother John, and Sir John Gordon of Haddo, were brought to Aberdeen "throw the lynkis". The Aberdeen Town Council spent £26 13s. 4d. in entertaining Patrick Chalmers, the lieutenant of the horse troop, "that cam as convoy with Haddo and Gight," and his men (*Spalding Club Mis* , v., 161)   Haddo and Gight were taken to Edinburgh. In June the Parliament (see *Acts of Parliament*) granted Gight liberty to write to his wife and get the services of an "ypothecarie" because of the "weakness of his bodie".   He also asked to be relieved of the "burdene of his interteanment of his brother" [John], who was in prison with him.   Parliament granted him 300 merks, through his agent, Thomas Gordon.   In July he was granted permission to see his wife and his daughter, Barbara In the same month witnesses against him were granted £20 each.   In June, Mr George Sharpe, the minister of Fyvie, had complained to Parliament that Gight owed him "87 bolles victuell and £251 13s. 4d. of his stipend," which the laird was ordered to pay up.   Haddo was tried in July, and condemned and executed (July 19, 1644) Gight's trial was postponed till January, 1645. Meantime he escaped

1647. *Jan.* 5 —He was pardoned by Parliament.

1648. *Feb* —The Commission of that General Assembly declared of Gight and Gordon of Ardlogie that the Presbyteries where they lived were overawed.

1648. *May.*—He was summoned by Parliament to appear for the "cryme of malignancie for his complyand with the rebels, assisting of them in the rebellion, or being accessorie or active himself in said rebellion ". A messenger-at-arms was ordered to "warne and charge the said —— Gordon" personally "giff he can be apprehendit " The proclamation for his arrest was to be exhibited at the market crosses of " the head burghe of the shyre quhair he dwellis " (*Acts of Parliament*)

Gight married Lady Elizabeth Ogilvy, daughter of the sixth Lord Ogilvy of Airlie (died 1616) and sister of the first Earl of Airlie (died 1648), whose wife (a daughter of the Earl of Haddington) is the heroine of the well-known ballad, " The Bonnie Hoose o' Airlie ". In 1624 Gight was described as an " apostate," and his wife as a " recussant " (Mair's *Presbytery of Ellon*, p. 67).

1. GEORGE, VIII. of Gight.

2. A son (*Balbithan MS*).

3 BARBARA was allowed to visit her father in Edinburgh Jail, July, 1644 (*Acts of Parliament*).

GEORGE GORDON, VIII. of GIGHT.

(*Son of VII.*)

This laird followed precisely in the way of his ancestors ; and even surpassed them by an attempt to oust his own father from the estates His career runs thus :—

1635.—He was a student at King's College, Aberdeen (*University Register*)

1642 *July.*—He married Keith, the laird of Ludquharne's daughter, while his father was still in Germany. Keith was a Covenanter, which may account for Spalding's statement (*Troubles*, ii , 175) that young Gight " fell [at this time] in sum variance with his awin mother," at the instigation of Ludquharne, " as wes thocht ". He wished to enter into possession, as his father, who was in Germany when the seventh laird died, was never infeft " thairintill ". " The lady ansuerit scho would not deliuer these wreittis (hir husband being absent) without his consent. Quhairvpone, be Ludquharnes assistans, thay resolue to tak in the place of Geicht, whiche scho schortlie manis, and stoutlie defendis. Thay tak in barnes and laiche bigging to sie if thay could get the yetis opnit, and schot in at the hall wyndois, quhair ane William Gordone wes schot through the schulder blead." The affair reminds one of the plight of the lady's sister-in-law, who had been besieged in the " Bonnie Hoose o' Airlie " two years before. In the present attack on " Lady Gight," her brother, the Earl of Airlie, " heiring of his sisteris distress," remonstrated with Lord Huntly on the subject. The Marquis " satlit" the business at Leggitisden " betuixt Geicht

(who cam thither) with the ladie his mother". Spalding relates a curious incident.
When Gight was returning from Leggitisden, "weill content of the agriement,
Johne Lesk, ane of his owne folke, schooting ane volay with ane hagbut of found for
joy (lying at the seige of Geicht), hes hand wes schot fra him, and schortlie thairefter
[he] deit. This hagbut of found in the trubles wes plunderit be Ludquharne, the
said Johne Lesk being in his company, out of the place of Foverane; so he gat his
reward, and this seige dissoluit."

1644   *Feb. 23.*—A band of Covenanters, who had set out to raid the lands
of several lairds who would not sign, met a troop of loyalists, including young Gight,
who were plundering the lands of Dr. Dun at Taartie. The Covenanters were
"schamefullie dvng bak, thair armes tane fra thame, and routit pitifullie. . .
Quhairat our Committee of Aberdene . . . wes heichlie offendit" (Spalding's
Troubles, ii., 322).

1644. *March 26.*—Young Gight and a number of Royalists met Lord Huntly
in Aberdeen. Young Gight, Drum and Haddo, and some horsemen were left in
charge of the town, which Huntly left (*Ibid.*, ii , 330).

1644. April 22.—Young Gight and a band of Royalists left Aberdeen and
crossed the Bridge of Dee. At two o'clock in the morning of April 24 they entered
the town of Montrose, "dang the toune's people [who were on the watch] fra the
calsey to thair houssis, and out of the foirstaires thay schot desperatlie, bot thay
war forssit to yeild by many feirfull schotes schot aganes thame; quhair vnhappelie
Alexander Peirsone, ane of thair bailleis, wes slayne". The raiders then tried to
charter an Aberdeen ship, then lying in the harbour, to carry off the town's "cartowis". But the provost had taken refuge in the vessel, which "schot fyve or six
peices of ordinans disperatlie amongis " the Royalists, "with about fourtie mvscattis,
quhair by the gryte providens. of God thair wes bot onlie tuo men killit and sum
hurt". The Royalists then "brak the quheillis of the cartowis, for moir thay could
not do, nor brak them thay micht not, and threw thame over the schoir to mak
thame vnserviceable ". They afterwards plundered the shops of the town, and
"cruellie spolzie ritche merchandice, clothis, silkis, veluotis, and other costlie wair,
siluer, gold and siluer wark, armes, and all vther thing, quhairat the hieland men
wes not slow. Thay brak up a pype of Spanish wyne, and drank hartfullie. Thay
took Patrick Lichtoun, lait Provost," and another man prisoner. "Thay left Mon-
troiss in wofull cace, about tuo efternoone "—not a bad twelve hours' work. "Syn
that samen nicht [they] went to Cortoquhy to meet with the Erll of Airlie [young
Gight's uncle], who heiring of the Marques of Argyllis cuming wold not give thame
entrie " As a consequence, thirty-two of the party who lingered plundering the
town of Montrose were captured by the Covenanters, and taken to Edinburgh
(*Ibid* , ii , 347-8). A few days' before old Gight had plundered the town of Banff.
A reward of 18,000 merks,was offered for the capture of young Gight (among others),
"quik or deid ".

1644. *May 9* —When old Gight surrendered his house to the Covenanting
party at this date, "his sone, the young laird, escaipis with tuo or thrie, and being
weill horsit, lap the park dykes and saiflie wan away in presens of the soldiouris

lying about the place, who follouit, but cam no speid to thair gryt greif" (*Troubles*, 11 , 359).

1645. *Feb.* 20 —Young Gight and his friends apprehended at Percock " Alexander Forbes *alias* Plagne, a bussie bodie in the good causs," who was carrying Covenanting despatches to the Committee at Elgin (*Ibid ,* ii., 448)

1645. *Feb.* 24 —Young Gight and his friends took two of Forbes of Craigievar's troop "lying cairleslie in thair naikit bedis within thair quarteris of Innervrie Thay took thair horss, thair moneyis, thair apparell, and armes, and gave the men libertie to go; whairat Cragiwar wes heichlie offendit " (*Ibid.,* 11 , 449)

1645. *July.*—He was wounded at the battle of Alford (*Earls of Sutherland*, p. 526).

Gight—whose career after this point is obscure—was certainly lucky to have escaped with his head, for his friends fell thick in the struggle, as follows :—

1644 *July* 19.—Sir John Gordon of Haddo, his neighbour, was executed at Edinburgh.

1645 *July* 2.—Lord Gordon, his chief's son, fell at the battle of Alford.

1646 *Jan* 20.—Nathaniel Gordon, his kinsman, was executed at St Andrews.

1647. *Oct.* 26.—John Leith, younger of Harthill, his cousin, was executed at Edinburgh

1649. *March* 22 —The second Marquis of Huntly, chief of his clan, was executed at Edinburgh

Considerable ambiguity exists about the name of his wife. Spalding says (*Troubles*, ii., 174) he married (in July, 1642) a daughter of Sir William (?) Keith of Ludquharne (whose ancestor, Sir John Keith, had been killed at Flodden). He seems to have married as his second wife Lucretia, daughter of Robert Irvine of Fedderat by his wife Elizabeth Campbell, daughter of Sir Duncan Campbell of Glenurchy, who was married in 1621 (*MS. Pedigree*, by Col. Forbes-Leslie at Drum Castle). According to Row, whose Journal was printed in *Scottish Notes and Queries*, Jan., 1894, Dame Anna Forbes, " Lady Gight," daughter to the Lord Forbes, died Sept. 14, 1667, aged 67. According to Macfarlane's *Genealogical Collections* (ii., 244), " Arthur Forbes of Eight married Anna Forbes, daughter to my Lord Forbes . . and the said Arthur to his second Lady married Barbara Forbes, daughter to the Laird of Asloun . . .". Hence in Row *Gight* is probably a slip for *Eight*. The mention of this lady, however, seems to give some semblance of truth to the ballad entitled " Gight's Lady," which Peter Buchan printed. In this ballad the lady says:—

> First I was lady o' Black Riggs,
> 　And then into Kincraigie,
> Now I am the Lady o' Gight,
> 　And my love he's ca'd Geordie.

> I was the mistress o' Pitfour,
> 　And madam o' Kincraigie,
> And now my name is Lady Anne,
> 　And I am Gight's own lady

The ballad describes how Gight went after "Bignet's lady". He then got into prison, and owned first to having stolen "ane o' the King's best brave steeds," and "sold him in Bevany"; secondly, to having killed five orphans for their money. A ransom of 10,000 crowns is then put on "Geordie's" head. His wife then

> Spread her mantle on the ground,
> 　Dear but she spread it bonny;
> Some gaed her crowns, some ducadoons,
> 　And some gaed dollars mony

Gight, of course, is saved, and his spouse prepares to ride off with him, when he announces his unswerving devotion to her rival. "A finger o' Bignet's lady's hand is worth a' your fair body". And he is made to stab her to the heart.

> Now a' that lived intil Black Riggs,
> 　And likewise in Kincraigie,
> For seven lang years were clad in black,
> 　To mourn for Gight's own lady.

Historically, I cannot verify the ballad at all. Peter Buchan makes a third laird of Gight (killed in 1578) the hero of this affair, but I fear that Buchan is simply guessing at the truth. The eighth laird of Gight, at any rate, had two children (although the *Balbithan MS.* says he "begat a daughter and dyed").

1. GEORGE, IX. of Gight

2. MARIE. On July 16, 1684, there is a discharge and renunciation by her to her brother of 12,000 merks, "contained in heritable bond by him, with consent of Dame Elizabeth Urquhart, his spouse, to his said sister, of date April 20, 1683. whereby for security of said sum he bound himself to infeft his said sister in an annual rent of £480, furth of the town and lands of Newseat, Ardoe, etc., in the Parish of Tarves". At Aberdeen, May 22, 1684 (*Aberdeen Sasines*, xii., 57) She seems to have been the "Mrs. Mary Gordon of Gight" who was married on June 2, 1691, to Lieut.-Colonel John Gordon The marriage ceremony was performed by

the minister of Fyvie before the Laird of Meldrum and the Laird of Knockleith. The Lieutenant-Colonel is spoken of in the *Poll Book* as "the laird of Gight" in 1695 On Sept. 30, 1697, "Lieut. Col John Gordon of Gight" was a witness to the baptism of Margaret, daughter of Mr. George Dalgarno, minister at Fyvie (*Fyvie Register of Baptisms*) Lieut.-Col. Gordon and his wife Marie had a daughter—

ELIZABETH, baptised by the minister of Fyvie, in presence of John Gordon of Rothnie, William Pantoun in the Miltoun of Fyvie and others, June 12, 1694 (*Ibid.*) What became of this Elizabeth I cannot say. She is mentioned in the *Poll Book*.

SIR GEORGE GORDON, IX. OF GIGHT.

(*Son of VIII.*)

Very little is known about this laird. Dr. Temple, in the *Thanage of Fermartyn*, dismisses him with four-and-twenty words Almost the only fact I can discover about him is that he was a Commissioner of Supply in 1678 and 1685 (*Acts of Parliament*). In 1682 Lord Aberdeen sent a present of plums to Gight's gardener (Aberdeen Papers, *Historical MSS. Commission*, 5th Report, p. 609). In a sasine of 1685 Gight is described as "Knight, Baronet". The following item from the *Register of Aberdeen Sasines* (xii., 137) throws some light on him, suggesting that the family had fallen into debt :—

1685. *Jan.* 15.—Discharge and renunciation by George Keith of Knock, Sheriff-Depute of Kincardine, to Sir George Gordon [ninth] of Gight, and George Gray of Schivas, his cautioner, of £3,000, which he agreed to pay in consideration of the sums contained in a heritable bond by the deceased Sir George Gordon [eighth] of Gight to Nathaniel Keith in Aden, of date December 30, 1642, and registered February 1, 1649, in and to which bond the said Nathaniel constitute the deceased Major George Keith of Whytriggs, father of the foresaid George, cessioner and assignee by his assignation of date September 11, 1656. Whereupon the said Major, having raised letters of horning against the said deceased Sir George Gordon, and by virtue thereof caused charge him to pay to the said Major the sums of money foresaid, which being suspended by the said deceased Sir George Gordon, the said umquhile Major obtained dereet of suspension before the Lords of Council and Session on November 16, 1667, against the said Sir George Gordon, whereby they found the saids letter and charges orderly proceeded, and decern the same to have effect, and be put to further execution, etc. At Aberdeen, December 4, 1684.

The ninth laird married his kinswoman, Elizabeth Urquhart, only daughter of Patrick Urquhart of Meldrum (1611-1664) by Lady Margaret Ogilvie, who was the daughter of the first Earl of Airlie, and the cousin of her husband, for it will be remembered that the seventh laird of Gight had married the sister of the first Earl of Airlie. Gight died before 1695, for his wife was described (*Poll Book*) in 1695 as the "duager of Gight," and was living at the Mains of Gight. Among her servants occurs the name of Donald M'Queen. He may have been the hero of the ballad called "Donald M'Queen's Flicht wi' Lizie Menzie," quoted by Peter Buchan. Donald is said to have tempted her with a cheese as a love philtre! It is certain, however, that Lizie Menzie was not "Lady of Fyvie" in the sense of being the wife of the last Earl of Dunfermline, as Buchan makes out. According to the *Poll Book*, Mrs Magdalen Crichton, relict of Laurence Oliphant, son of Lord Oliphant, was living at Woodhead of Gight in 1695. Lady Gordon, who was alive in 1704 (*Privy Council Register*), afterwards married Major-General Thomas Buchan of the Auchmacoy family, who died in 1721 (without leaving issue), at Ardlogie, the jointure house of the Gights (Joseph Robertson's Preface to the *Diary of General Patrick Gordon*). Buchan met General Patrick Gordon in Edinburgh on June 20, 1686. He had served in France and Holland, and was made a Major-General by James II. in 1689. The tombstone that marks the resting-place of the Gights stands in the churchyard of Fyvie. One side of it bears a coat of arms, of date 1685, with the letters "S[ir] G[eorge] G[ordon]" and "D[ame] E[lizabeth] U[rquhart]" in the body of it, surmounted by the Gordon motto, "Bydand," and at the base runs the Urquhart motto, "By sea and land". The ninth laird had an only daughter—

MARIE GORDON, X of Gight

MARIE GORDON (MRS. DAVIDSON), X. OF GIGHT.

(*Daughter of IX.: died* 1740.)

She was the only child of the ninth laird I think that this is made quite clear by the following extract from the *Register of Sasines*, Aberdeen (XII., 514) :—

1687. *June 22.*—Sasine on Charter under the Great Seal to Marie Gordon, only lawful daughter procreated between Sir George Gordon of Gight and Elizabeth Urquhart, his spouse, and the heirs male of her body: which failing to the eldest heir female without division of her body, and the heirs male or female of her body: and the said heirs as well male as female, and the heirs of taillie and provision nominated by the said Sir George, and succeeding to his lands and estate shall assume the sirname of Gordon and insignia of the family of Gight, etc, of the lands and barony of Gicht, *alias* Schives . . . At Whythall, April 4, 1685. Sasine on June 13, 1687. George Gordon in Gight is a witness.

There is a curious difficulty in connection with the tenth laird, involved in the presence of two John Gordons on the estate—a Captain John in 1685, and a Lieutenant-Colonel John in 1695 Captain John figures in two references :—

1685 *February 23.*—Sasine on disposition by Dr. Patrick Urquhart [uncle of the tenth laird of Gight], Professor of Medicine in King's College, Aberdeen, and Elizabeth Muir, his spouse, with consent of Sir George Gordon of Gicht, Knight, Baronet, to Captain John Gordon, sometime tutor of Glenbucket, for an annual rent of £60 Scots, corresponding to the principal sum of £1000: furth of the town and lands of Little Gicht, mill and mill lands of Ardo, lying in the parishes of Fyvie and Tarves. At Aberdeen, May 20, 1684: Sasine on January 30, 1685 (*Aberdeen Sasines,* vol xii, folio 171).

1708. *February 12*—Sasine on letters of obligation by William Keith of Ludquharne [the eighth laird of Gight had married a Keith of Ludquharne], with consent of Lady Jean Smith, his spouse, and George Keith, their second lawful son, to Agnes Gordon [of the Badenscoth family], relict of Captain John Gordon, tutor of Glenbucket, and George Gordon, his eldest son, of an annual rent of £40 Scots furth of two crofts of the town and lands of Stirlinghill, sometime possessed by Alexander Bruce and George Darg, lying in the parish of Peterhead. At Boddam, December 13, 1707 · Sasine on December 31, 1707 (*Ibid,* xix, 412).

The "tutor of Glenbucket" was the grandson of Sir Adam Gordon of Glenbucket, by his second wife, Helen Tyrie. Sir Adam's first spouse was Christian, a daughter of the fifth laird of Gight. The other John, the Lieutenant-Colonel, figures in the *List of Pollable Persons in Aberdeenshire,* 1695 (ii., 289), where the "laird of Gight" is stated to be "Livetennent-Collonell John Gordon" (to the amount of £996 13s. 4d Scots) His wife is stated to be "Dame Mary Gordon," and his daughter "Mrs. Betty Gordon". Now, who was this Lieutenant-Colonel John Gordon? Was he the first husband of Marie, the tenth laird, or was his wife Marie the daughter of the eighth and the aunt of the tenth laird; and did he assume the guardianship of her

(273)

lands during her minority? The laird of Gight's valuation in the
parish of Ellon in 1695 was £149 16s. The valuation of the lands of
Gight was £996 13s. 4d. Scots, as follows :—

	£	s	d
Lieut.-Col. John Gordon should pay of the proportion of the valued rent £1 11s, effeirand to the duty of the saids lands in his own labouring, but its absorbet in the highest, in which he is raited, being £24 Scots· *inde* with the generall poll is	£24	6	0
Dame Mary Gordon, his lady, and Mrs. Bettie Gordon, his daughter	0	12	0
Their servants and cottars	14	10	4
	£39	8	4
Maynes of Gight (occupied by Dame Elizabeth Urquhart, "Duager of Gight," and cottars)	25	4	8
Little Gight	8	3	8
Swanfoord	3	8	8
Milne of Gight	3	16	4
Blackhillock	4	15	6
Lethentie	6	15	6
Fadonhill	5	2	4
Cottoune	4	12	0
Millbrecks . . . .· .	10	11	6
Brucleseat	2	6	0
Fetterletter	9	15	4
Stonhouse	2	1	8
Munkshill	10	15	0
Woodhead of Gight, occupied by Mrs. Magdalen Crighton, relict of Mr. Laurence Olyphant, son to Lord Olyphant [Patrick, sixth Lord Oliphant, married as his second wife Mary, daughter of James Crichton of Frendraught], Mrs. Bettie Gordon, James Gordon, gentleman, Anna Gordon, spouse to Alexander Whyte, an officer in the army in Flanders, but indigent; and others .	21	17	6

"Lady" Marie Gordon, who was the first woman laird of Gight,
married at Fyvie, Nov. 2, 1701, Alexander Davidson, younger of Newton
of Culsalmond. The witnesses were "the laird of Cubardie, the lairds of
Knockleath, Banchrie, and many others". On the margin the "Lairds
of Newton and Lady Gight" are given (*Fyvie Register of Marriages* in
the Register House). The marriage contract, dated Edinburgh, October

20, 1701, is referred to in the *Register of Aberdeen Sasines* (xix., 559) thus :—

> 1712 *June* 26.—Sasine on (1) contract of marriage between Alexander David-
> son, younger of Newton of Culsalmond, with consent of Alexander Davidson, his
> father, on the one part, and Lady Mary Gordon, heiress of Gight, with consent of
> Lady Elizabeth Urquhart, her mother, for infefting her in liferent after the decease
> of the said Alexander Davidson, now her future spouse, in 22 chalders victual
> furth of the one or other half of the lands, mills, etc, of Newtoun of Culsalmond,
> Williamstoun and Melinsyde, by letters of resignation by the said Mr. Alex-
> ander Davidson, his father: contained in the said contract, which is dated at
> Edinburgh, Oct. 20, 1701. Also, on (2) charter of resignation by the Queen to the
> said Alexander Davidson and the said Mary Gordon of the said lands. At Edin-
> burgh, June 22, 1711, and registered June 5, 1711. Sasine in ——, 1712.

There should have been a certain irony in this alliance, because, while the Gight family had been notorious law-breakers, the Davidsons had for generations been administering the law as "advocates" in Aberdeen Yet the Gight lawlessness was uninfected by the marriage, for Alexander Davidson exhibited (so late as 1704) an extraordinary contempt for the law, so that his progeny may be supposed to have had a good share of Gight morality in their blood. It was part of his marriage contract that Davidson should pay the debts of his mother-in-law, who had married General Buchan. Davidson apparently re-gretted this arrangement, for, in 1704—at which date the contract had not been registered—he borrowed a copy of the contract from his mother-in-law, through James Hamilton of Cobairdy. Then followed a curious lawsuit, which is condensed from the *Privy Council Register* in Chambers's *Domestic Annals* (iii., 304), under date September, 1704 :—

> When the [Gight] family creditors applied for payment of their debts, Davidson
> did not scruple to send them, or allow them to go, to the old Lady Gight and her
> husband (General Buchan) for payment. Beginning to feel distressed by the
> creditors, old Lady Gight sought back the copy of the contract for her protection;
> but, as no entreaty could induce Davidson to return it to Cobairdy, she was forced
> to prosecute the latter for its restitution Cobairdy, being at length, at the instance
> of old Lady Gight and her husband, taken upon a legal caption, was, with the
> messenger, John Duff, at the Milton of Fyvie, on his way to prison, 16th September,
> 1704, when Davidson came to him with many civil speeches, expressive of his regret
> of what had taken place. He entreated Duff to leave Cobairdy there on his parole
> of honour, and go to intercede with General Buchan and his wife for a short respite
> to his prisoner, on the faith that the contract should be registered within a fortnight,
> which he pledged himself should be done Duff executed this commission success-

fully, but when he came back Davidson revoked his promise. It chanced that another gentleman had, meanwhile, arrived at the Milton, one Patrick Gordon, who had in his possession a caption against Davidson for a common debt of £100 due to himself Seeing what stuff Davidson was made of, he resolved no longer to delay putting his design in execution; so he took Duff aside and put the caption into his hand, desiring him to take Davidson into custody, which was immediately done In the midst of these complicated proceedings, a message came from Mrs Davidson, entreating them to come to the family mansion, a few miles off, where she thought all difficulties might be accommodated. The whole party accordingly went there, and were entertained very hospitably till about two in the morning (Sunday), when the strangers rose to depart, and Davidson came out to see them to horse, as a host was bound to do in that age, but with apparently no design of going along with them. Duff was not so far blinded by Gight's hospitality as to forget that he would be under a very heavy responsibility if he should allow Davidson to slip through his fingers Accordingly he reminded the laird that he was a prisoner, and must come along with them; whereupon Davidson drew his sword, and called his servants to the rescue, but was speedily overpowered by the messenger and his assistant, and by the other gentlemen present   He and Cobairdy were, in short, carried back as prisoners that night to the Milton of Fyvie. This place, being on the estate of Gight, Duff bethought him next day that, as the tenants were going to church, they might gather about their captive laird, and make an unpleasant disturbance; so he took forward his prisoners to the next inn, where they rested till the Sabbath was over   Even then, at Davidson's entreaty, he did not immediately conduct them to prison, but waited over Monday and Tuesday, while friends were endeavouring to bring about an accommodation This was happily so far effected, the Earl of Aberdeen and his son, Lord Haddo, paying off Patrick Gordon's claim on Davidson, and certain relatives becoming bound for the registration of the marriage contract. From whatever motive—whether, as alleged, to cover a vitiation in the contract, or merely out of revenge—Davidson soon after raised a process before the Privy Council against Cobairdy, Gordon and Duff for assault and private imprisonment, concluding for £3,000 of damages; but, after a long series of proceedings, in the course of which many witnesses were examined on both sides, the case was ignominiously dismissed, and Davidson decerned to pay 1,000 merks as expenses.

Fountainhall refers to this affair in his *Decisions of the Lords of Council* ·—

1708 *July* 15 —Mr. Alexander Davidson of Newton, having married Anne [Marie] Gordon, the heretrix of the lands of Gight, it was represented to him that the debt affecting the estate was only £40,000, whereon, by his contract of marriage, his father obliged himself to advance that sum to disburden the lands, and accordingly paid it in; but after the marriage debts emerged double of that sum, and far above 100,000 merks; and being pursued by [Patrick?] Gordon of Cults for a debt owing to him by Gight, and he insisting, *primo loco*, to have him made liable for the annual rents of that sum, he alleged that being unluckily engaged for that family, he finds the debts so insuperable, and so far exceeding the value of the estate, that he is willing to renounce and abandon the whole to the creditors, upon liberating him of the debts that had so unexpectedly and surprisingly emerged on that estate, even though he should lose the £40,000 advanced by his father. . . The Lords thought Mr. Davidson's case very hard, to make him liable in the annual rents of the debts far exceeding the rents of his wife's land; yet, *ita lex scripta est*, the same was now turned into a fixed known custom and law Only, he was thus far relieved, but the Lords did not think him liable in the principal sums, but left them to affect the lands by adjudication and other diligence for securing that.

In 1702 Alexander Dunbar, the laird of Monkshill, received from Mary Gordon and her husband a precept of *clare constat*, whereby the town and lands of Monkshill were declared redeemable by them as superiors, for the sum of 3,000 merks (*Thanage of Fermartyn*, p. 80)

Davidson died about 1716. His widow seems to have died in 1739 or in 1740, for on 29th January, 1740, their son, Alexander, was served heir to his mother. Alexander Davidson and Mary Gordon had—

1. GEORGE DAVIDSON, born and baptised May 20, 1704. Mr. Alexander David-son, elder of Newtone, sponsor· witnesses, James Ogilvie at miln of Airdo, Adam Panton in Litlegight, Patrick Chalmers in the Newtown and Alexander Wilson in Buchquhandachie (*Fyvie Register of Baptisms*)

2. ALEXANDER DAVIDSON, born and baptised Jan. 30, 1707 Major Generall Buchan and Alex Davidson, Laird of Newton, present The Earl of Huntly, the Laird of Cockstown, the Laird of Pitmeden, god-fathers (*Ibid.*).

3. ALEXANDER DAVIDSON, born and baptised May 16, 1711, by Mr George Dalgarno, minister of Fyvie, at the Milne of Williamston in the parish of Culsalmond, Alexander Davidson, Laird of Newton, elder, Thomas Buchan, Major Generall, were present and several others (*Ibid*).

4 ALEXANDER GORDON, XI of Gight

5 ELIZABETH DAVIDSON, married James Gordon of Techmuiry, and died at Faichfield on October 1, 1788, in the eighty-fifth year of her age (*Scots Magazine* (1, 518), which calls her "sister of Alexander Gordon of Gight") I may note that Dr. Temple (*Thanage of Fermartyn*, p. 76) says she "married, in 1767, Alexander Innes of Breda and Cowie ". This is a mistake The Elizabeth Davidson whom Innes married was the daughter of William Davidson, Provost of Aberdeen from 1760 to 1762. The Provost died in 1765 (A M. Munro's *Memorials*, p. 240).

6 ISOBEL DAVIDSON, baptised Dec. 11, 1705, married (as his first wife) William Fordyce of Monkshill, Aquhorties, who bought the lands of Monkshill from her brother, Alexander, in 1744 (*Thanage of Fermartyn*, p. 80) She was dead before 1738, when Fordyce married Margaret, daughter of

Walter Cochrane of Dumbreck, Provost of Aberdeen (*Scottish Notes and Queries*, May, 1900). Isobel Gordon had one son—

WILLIAM FORDYCE of Monkshill, Captain in the Marines, who was the grandfather of Sir Fitzroy Kelly, Attorney-General, 1858-9. Captain Fordyce sold Monkshill to George Gordon, XII. of Gight, in 1768

7. JEAN DAVIDSON, born and baptised June 1, 1709, Jean, Countess of Dunfermline being the godmother (*Fyvie Register of Baptisms*), who married Andrew Robertson of Foveran (Temple's *Thanage of Fermartyn*, pp. 76, 575). They had a son—

JOHN ROBERTSON of Foveran, who married Mary, daughter of David Stewart of Dalguise, Provost of Edinburgh, and died 1826 He was succeeded by his son—

ANDREW ROBERTSON of Foveran. He sold the estate of Foveran to David Gill of Aberdeen, to Alexander Mitchell of Ythan Lodge, and to Miss Christina Mackenzie (*Ibid.,* p 575).

ALEXANDER GORDON, XI. OF GIGHT.

(*Son of X.: born 1716; drowned 1760.*)

Alexander, the eleventh laird, was baptised May 25, 1716, the Earl of Huntly, the Laird of Cockstoune and the Laird of Pitmeddan being godfathers, and Alexander Gordon in Bochelle and William Panton at the Miltoune of Fyvie witnesses (*Fyvie Register of Baptisms*). In accordance with the sasine on charter granted to his mother (June 22, 1687), he assumed the "sirname of Gordon and insignia of the family of Gight". Dr Temple calls him "Alexander Davidson Gordon," but I can find no authority for this middle name. On his tombstone he is called "Alexander Gordon," while the *Service of Heirs* describes him (in 1735 and 1740) as "Alexander Gordon or Davidson".

He was served heir to his father in Newton, Wrangham, Glenistoun, Skares and Melvinside on January 10, 1735; to his grandfather, Alexander Davidson of Newton, on January 10, 1735; to his granduncle, James Davidson of Tillymorgan, who died September, 1720, in Tillymorgan, Sauchieloan, Graystone and Catdenaill in Culsalmond, January 10, 1735; to his mother, January 29, 1740

The eleventh laird, soon after his accession, redeemed from Elizabeth Smith (who was a sister of "Tiftie's Annie") and her son, William

Dunbar, the wadset of Monkshill, by paying up the 3,000 merks due thereon. In 1744 he sold the lands to William Fordyce of Aquhorties, his brother-in-law (*Thanage of Fermartyn*, p. 80). In 1768 the latter's son, Captain William Fordyce of the Marines, resold Monkshill to the next laird of Gight, George Gordon, and the burden of 4,000 merks was discharged by the payment of this sum to Isobell Fordyce, his mother.

He married Margaret Duff, born Dec. 20, 1720 ; died at Banff, Nov. 13, 1801 (*vide* Gight tombstone) She was the daughter of Patrick Duff of Craigston (uncle of the first Earl Fife, and founder of the Duffs of Hatton). This alliance was interesting from several points of view besides Byron's famous love affair with his cousin, Mary Duff. The Duffs represented everything that the Gordons of Gight did not. They were never reckless—especially where money was concerned ; for their rise is one of the most wonderful stories of success, and was mainly due to brains as applied to commerce. Sometimes (as I argued at considerable length in *Scottish Notes and Queries*, May, 1898) their brains led them into literature (Sir M. E. Grant-Duff and his brother, Mr. Douglas Ainslie, are cases in point to-day), and it might be advanced that Byron was a good deal indebted to this strain in his blood for his literary instincts. In any case, it may be taken for granted that the Gight family increased their balance at the bankers during the reign of Margaret Duff, despite the fact that she had a large family, and apart from the annexation of the Davidson estates.

The eleventh laird of Gight lived at a period when the landed gentry had ceased to go out to slaughter their neighbours, and, in turn, get killed for their trouble. But, like so many of his ancestors, he met a violent death (at the age of forty-four), for he was drowned in the river Ythan, on January 24, 1760. The *Aberdeen Journal*, in recording the event, says : " He was an honest, inoffensive gentleman, an affectionate husband, indulgent parent, sincere friend, master, and good Christian. He had frequently found benefit to his health by using the cold bath, and he had the misfortune to perish in the water of Ythan, while he was bathing, being suddenly swelled with melted snow " ! In his plenitude of grief, as you will note, the reporter's sense of syntax failed him (for surely no man ever succumbed to an overdose of melted snow); and I am further inclined to believe that the journalistic reticence of 1760 may have led him to gloss the fact of suicide. Scotsmen in

1760 had not become slaves to the tub so much as to induce them to bathe in ice-covered rivers in the depths of winter. Furthermore, the victim's son, the next laird of Gight, is said to have drowned himself in the Bath Canal, though no obituary notice I have seen mentions the fact.

Mrs. Gordon, with all the common-sense tenacity of her race, survived her spouse for forty-one years, having a jointure of £55 11s. on the Gight estate to the very end. She took herself to Banff, where she lived with her sister, in a three-storeyed house in Low Street. She practically brought up her granddaughter, Mrs. Byron, whose reckless marriage must have shocked her, though it did not prevent her from entertaining her great-grandson (Lord Byron) at Banff when he was about seven or eight years old. In Dr. Cramond's *Annals of Banff* (i, 228-237) will be found various legends about Byron's boyhood in Banff, and a letter which shows what an illiterate speller old " Lady Gight ". was The eleventh laird of Gight and his spouse had no fewer than twelve children — nine sons and three daughters. Beyond the appearance of their names on the Gight tombstone at Fyvie and the *Register of Baptisms*, I have been able to discover nothing about them, so that I imagine most of them died young Only the eldest of them took the name of Gordon. The rest were Davidsons, as follows:—

1. GEORGE GORDON, XII. of Gight, born Nov. 14, 1741.
2. ALEXANDER DAVIDSON, baptised Nov. 26, 1744 (*Fyvie Register of Baptisms*). He was at Marischal College, 1758-62 He got his father's estate of Newton in 1760. He was a captain in General R. Dalrymple-Horn-Elphinstone's regiment, the 53rd Foot, and married the General's daughter, Jean, by whom he had three daughters, including Mary and Margaret, who died unmarried, having sold the estate of Newton to the grandfather of the present proprietor, Mr. A M Gordon of Newton (*Private information*).
3. PATRICK DAVIDSON, baptised Dec 19, 1745, before the laird of Techmuirie and Mr. Milne (*Fyvie Register of Baptisms*).
4. JOHN DAVIDSON, baptised Nov 30, 1749 (*Ibid.*).
5 WILLIAM DAVIDSON, baptised July 24, 1750 (*Ibid.*).
6. JAMES DAVIDSON, baptised Nov. 24, 1752, before William Stuart of Achorachan and George Gray, servitor to the laird of Gight (*Ibid.*)
7. ARCHIBALD DAVIDSON, baptised Oct 15, 1754 (*Ibid.*) Dr. Temple (*Thanage of Fermartyn*, p. 77) says he was a lieutenant in the same regiment as his brother, namely, the 53rd Foot, and that he infefted, by clare constat, in

1787, his niece, Catherine Gordon (Mrs Byron), in the lands of Melvinside, Gleniston, and others in Culsalmond. He appears to have been unmarried

8 ROBERT DAVIDSON (Temple's *Thanage of Fermartyn*, p. 77).

9. ADAM DAVIDSON (*Ibid*)

10. MARY DAVIDSON ⎱ twins. baptised Jan 9, 1736
11. MARGARET DAVIDSON ⎰

12. ELIZABETH DAVIDSON, baptised Nov. 14, 1742 (*Fyvie Register of Baptisms*), died at Banff, June 20, 1804, having survived all her family She erected the tombstone to her father and mother and brothers and sisters in Fyvie churchyard.

13. MARY DAVIDSON, baptised Dec. 29, 1743 (*Ibid.*).

14. MARGARET DAVIDSON, baptised Oct 19, 1747 (*Ibid.*), she died 1764

GEORGE GORDON, XII OF GIGHT.

(Son of XI. born 1741 ; drowned 1779)

With this laird the male line of the Gight family became extinct for the second time—it had really ended in the ninth laird, his great-grand-father. The twelfth laird was baptised in the manor place of Ardlogie, Nov. 14, 1741, by the Rev. Thomas Scott, minister of Fyvie, in the presence of "the Lady Gight and William Knight, servitor to the laird of Gight" (*Fyvie Register of Baptisms*). He was served heir to his father in April 18, 1760. On these letters, and a certified rent-roll of £1470 13s. 4d , he was enrolled a freeholder in Aberdeenshire. On Sept. 14, 1771, sasine was granted in favour of George Gordon of Gight on the lands of Minmore and others, in the parish of Inveravon, Banffshire, proceeding on a charter and disposition of the Duke of Gordon (*Banff Sasines*).

He revived the old alliance between the Gordons and the Inneses, by marrying Catherine Innes, the daughter of Alexander Innes of Rosieburn (1701-1761), who was Sheriff-Clerk of Banffshire, and Provost of Banff for five terms of office. This Alexander Innes had married Catherine Abercromby (1708-1784), second daughter of Alexander Abercromby of Glassaugh, M.P. for Banffshire (from 1706 to 1727 ; he died 1729). The graves of the Inneses and the Russells are in Banff church (*Annals of Banff*, ii., 358-9) The connection between the Gordon and Innes families, which began in the sixteenth century, will be more clearly understood from the accompanying table :—

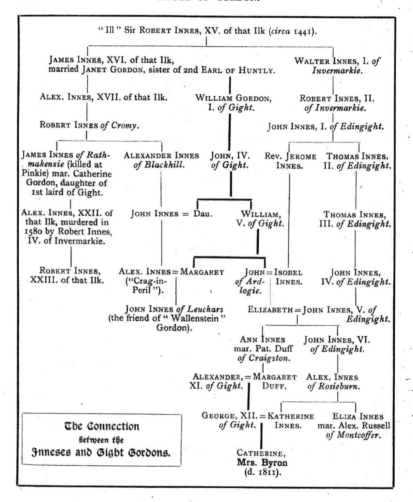

The Connection
Between the
Inneses and Gight Gordons.

It will be noticed that the twelfth laird of Gight and his wife were second cousins (see Colonel Innes' *Chronicle of the Family of Innes of Edingight*, 1898). The marriage contract between them is dated June 2, 1763, and is (or was) in the possession of Mrs. Katherine Russell

Jack, the wife of John Jack, Inspector-General of Hospitals. I am
indebted for the digest of it to the late Dr. Garden Blaikie, who perused
it after writing his articles on the Gight family in the *Scotsman* (Sept.
24, 1896), where he repeated the old blunder that the twelfth laird
had married Catherine Duff.

The contract secured for Mrs. Gordon a jointure of £1,000, the trustees being
General James Abercromby of Glasshaugh, M.P. (died 1781), her uncle ; Captain Aber-
cromby, his eldest son, Thomas Innes of Rosieburn, her brother (1749-1784), and
John Innes of Edingight (the Duffs, Gordons, Abercrombys and Inneses being closely
intermarried). The property consisted of the Barony of Gight, which comprised
Mains of Gight, Potts and Carfulzie, town and lands of Millbrecks, Blackhillock,
Swanford, Fawdonhill, Little Gight, Middlemuir, Balquhynachie, Miln of Ardo,
Corn and Walk Milns of Gight, Miln lands and Stonehouse of Gight, Coal town
thereof, Fetterletter (comprehending Ardlogie and Woodhead), the town and lands
of Windyhills (comprehending Blackhills); the town and lands of Lethenty and
Bruckleseat, the town and lands of Newseat, the town and lands of Little Folla, with
the miln of Balquhydaches, etc, in the parishes of Fyvie and Tarves. The contract
also provided very explicitly that should the succession fall to a daughter, she must
marry either a Gordon or one who would assume that name

The children of the marriage are said to have been brought up by
the laird's mother, who lived at Banff His youngest daughter died
there in 1777, and this seems to have weighed on the mind of the laird,
who is described by Dr Kiernan, an American writer on degeneracy, as
"a victim of periodical melancholia". The laird made a will, dated
Dec. 19, 1777 :—

Whereas I have no heirs male procreate of the marriage betwixt me and
Katherine Innes, my present spouse, I am resolved to settle my lands and barony of
Gight and whole estate upon my daughters and their heirs, and in order and in
manner after-mentioned: By these presents I do give, grant and dispone, with the
reservations, etc , to and in favour of myself, whom failing by decease, to Katherine
Gordon, my eldest daughter procreate betwixt me and the said Katherine Innes, my
present spouse, and the heirs male to be lawfully procreate of her body, and the
heirs whatsomever to be lawfully procreate of their body, the eldest heir female in
case the succession shall devolve upon females, always succeeding without division,
and excluding heirs portioners: which failing, to the heirs female to be lawfully
procreate of the body of the said Katherine Gordon, and the heirs whatsomever
to be lawfully procreate of their bodies: which failing, to Margaret Gordon, my
youngest daughter, procreate betwixt me and the said Katherine Innes [and the heirs
of her body] . . which failing, to my own nearest heirs and assignees heritably
and irredeemably the lands of Gight, comprehending the particular towns, teinds and
others after-mentioned, namely the Mains of Gight, comprehending Potts, with the

tower, fortalice and manour place thereof, houses, bigging, yards, orchards and pertinents thereof; the town and lands of Millbrecks, Blackhillock, Swanford, Fawdonhill, Little Gight, Meiklearde and pendicle called Middlearde, Middlemuir, Balquhynachie, Milne of Ards, Corn and Waulk milns of Gight, Miln Lands, multures, sucken and sequels of the said Miln, Stenhouse of Gight, Coaltown thereof, Fetterletter, comprehending Ardlogie and Woodhead, the town and lands of Windiehills, comprehending Blackhills, the town and lands of Lethintie and Bruckleseat, the town and lands of Newseat, the town and lands of Coaltown, with pendicle called Little Folla with the miln of Balquhynachie, miln, lands, multures, sucken, sequels and pertinents thereof, together with the haill houses, biggings, yards, orchards, tofts, crofts, outsetts, insetts, mosses, muirs, marshes, woods, fishings, pasturages, meadows, commonty, common pasturage, annexis, connexis, dependencies, pendicles, and haill prevaleges and pertinents thereof, with the teind sheaves of the said haill lands all lying within the parishes of Fyvie and Tarves and the Sheriffdom of Aberdeen, all which lands, teinds and others aforesaid with certain other lands were erected into a haill and free barony called the barony of Gight, and the Manner Place of Gight is declared to be the principal messuage conform to Charter, etc., as also all and haill the Burgh of Barony of Woodhead of Fetterletter lying within the said lands and barony of Gight, with burdens, etc

In the beginning of 1779 Gordon made another disposition :—

Whereas I purchased some time ago from Captain William Fordyce, of the Maines, the property of the lands of Monkshill, teinds and fishings, and I having afterwards purchased the superiority of the fishings after mentioned, the same were conveyed and disponed in favour of Thomas Innes of Rosyburn, in liferent during all the days of his lifetime, and to me George Gordon of Gight, my heirs and assignees whatsoever in fee and, as I have no heirs male procreate of my own body, I am resolved to settle the said lands of Monkshill and teinds thereof with property, the superiority, and the superiority of the fishings after mentioned in favour of myself, and after my decease, upon Katherine Gordon, my eldest daughter: . all and haill the town and lands of Monkshill, with the teinds and feu-duties thereof, houses, biggings, yards, tofts, crofts, pendicles and pertinents of the same whatsoever lying within the Barony of Gight, parish of Fyvie, and Sheriffdom of Aberdeen, as also all and haill that half nets fishing of salmon fish in the river of Don near the city of Old Aberdeen, with all the privileges, etc., which sometime belonged to the deceased James Colinson, burgess of Aberdeen, to me George Gordon, whom failing by decease, the said Catherine Gordon, my eldest daughter, and the other heirs substitutes in manner aforesaid

Gordon seems to have gone to Bath in search of health, and committed suicide in the canal there, on Saturday, January 9, 1779. The only reference to the fact of suicide is in a letter which his daughter wrote to her solicitor at the time of her son's proving his title before taking his seat in the House of Lords I have not seen the letter. Mr.

Prothero (*Byron's Letters and Journal,* i., 3) just states that Gordon committed suicide. I have searched all the available newspaper files in vain for any information on the point. The *Bath Chronicle* of Jan. 14, 1779, recorded that

> On Saturday evening last [January 9] died here George Gordon, Esq. of Gight, in the county of Aberdeenshire, descended from an ancient family, and possessed of considerable estate. He was a gentleman of great probity, much esteemed by his acquaintance for the generosity and goodness of heart, and will be sincerely regretted by many to whom he was a warm friend and liberal benefactor.

The *Aberdeen Journal* (of 25th Jan.) stated

> On Saturday, the 9th curt., died at Bath, George Gordon, Esq. of Gight. It is hoped his friends will accept this as a sufficient notification of his death

He was buried "under Mr. Pierce's stone by the font," in Bath Abbey, Jan. 15, 1779 (*Register of Bath Abbey*, Harleian Society, ii., 465). Colonel Alexander Campbell was buried "in George Gordon's ground by the font," April 24, 1779. Had he committed suicide, would he have been buried in the abbey? A tablet to Gordon, in the extreme south-east corner of the abbey, bears the inscription :—

GEORGE GORDON, Esq.
of Gight
in the Shire of ABERDEEN
Died 9th of Jany. 1779.

His widow survived him a few years. Her will was proved by her daughter, Catherine, before the Commissary of Aberdeen on January 16 ("last"), and confirmed on Feb 22, 1783, Thomas Innes of Rosieburn and John Innes of Edingight being cautioners. The "relict of the deceased George Gordon" is returned as having died "upon the —— day of —— last".

> The executrix [Catherine] gives up and acknowledges to be resting to the defunct as executrix nominated by the now deceased Miss Margaret Gordon, her daughter, conform to her last will and testament, dated Dec. 1, 1779 . . . the principal sum of £1,500 sterling contained in the said deceased George Gordon of Gight his bond of provision to the said Miss Margaret Gordon, dated Aug. 24, 1776 . . . : also another £1,500 contained in an additional bond of provision by the said George to the said Margaret, dated Dec. 19, 1777

The twelfth laird and his wife had three daughters—

1. CATHERINE, XIII and last of Gight
2. MARGARET, born 1766 ; died at the Bristol Hot Baths, March 7, 1780 (*Scots*

Magazine) In her will, of which her sister Catherine was executrix, and which was confirmed Feb. 22, 1783—Thomas Innes of Rosieburn and John Innes of Edingight being the cautioners — she is described as "youngest lawful daughter" of the deceased George Gordon of Gight.

3. ABERCROMBY. The *Aberdeen Journal* of Feb. 3, 1777, records that "On Tuesday last, died at Banff, Miss Abercromby Gordon, youngest daughter of George Gordon, Esq. of Gight. Her relations and friends will please accept of this notification of her death." In the churchyard of Banff there is an inscription: "An affectionate and sorrowing parent places this memorial of his attachment upon the grave of a promising and beloved daughter, Abercromby Gordon, who in the bloom of life was cut off by a fever in Banff in January, 1777"

CATHERINE GORDON (MRS BYRON), XIII. AND LAST OF GIGHT.

(*Daughter of XII.: died* 1811.)

Catherine Gordon was the last of her line, and ended the first of the two branches of the Gordons who have held the lands of Gight. She became mistress of the estates on attaining her majority, for she was served heir to her father in September, 1785, by which date she had taken the very step to lose everything—by marrying John Byron. Her whole life up to this point had been that of loss after loss. Her mother had died while she was a mere child. One sister died in 1777; her father died in 1779; her only other sister died in 1780. Her mother's trustees, General Abercromby and Thomas Innes, died respectively in 1781 and 1784 Her maternal grandmother, Mrs. Innes, died in 1784, so that, by 1785, the Gight family had reduced itself to the young heiress, her paternal grandmother (*née* Duff), and her aunt, Margaret Davidson. The heiress started her career (according to Moore) with £3,000 in cash, two shares of the Aberdeen Banking Company, the estates of Gight and Monkshill, and the superiority of two salmon fishings on the Dee. She was "a stout, dumpy, coarse-looking woman, awkward in her movements, and provincial in her accent and manners" (Prothero's *Byron*), but "proud as Lucifer" (as her son said) "and very headstrong". She considered herself quite a great personage, and her idea of her own superiority was doubtless increased by her having lived in "England," and figured among the beaux of Bath like a Society

GIGHT   123

lady. Bath proved her ruin, for it was there she met and married
Captain Byron The marriage register (as quoted in Peach's *Historic
Houses of Bath*, 1886) runs as follows (although Cordy Jeaffreson, in the
Real Lord Byron, 1883, declares that the marriage, which he describes
as a sham elopement, took place in Scotland):—

> John Byron, Esquire, of the parish of St. Peter and St. Paul, in the city of
> Bath, a widower, and Catherine Gordon, of the parish of St. Michael, in the same
> city, spinster, were married in this church [St. Michael's, Bath] this thirteenth day
> of May, in the year one thousand seven hundred and eighty-five [May 13, 1785],
> me, John Chapman, Rector. ·
> This marriage was solemnized between us
>
> [Signed] John Byron.
Catherine Gordon
>
> In the presence of Sarah Hay [and Dr.] Alexander Hay.

It is a curious fact that the bride was the third Catherine Gordon who
had married an alien adventurer. Lady Catherine Gordon, the daughter
of the second Earl of Huntly, married, in 1495, the French impostor,
Perkin Warbeck ; while Lady Catherine Gordon, the daughter of the
second Marquis of Huntly, married, about 1659, the Polish traitor,
Count Andreas Morsztyn.

The Byron mating was almost incredible from every point of
view, and, of course, it turned out impossible. Byron was notorious ;
Catherine Gordon was a nonentity. Byron was handsome; she was
very plain. Byron was bankrupt; she had a good balance at her
bankers—doubtless exaggerated by herself (unconsciously) and by the
people of Bath (through ignorance) This, and this alone, may be
taken as the reason of the marriage. Byron had borne down on Bath
with the view of getting an heiress, for the £4,000 a year which he had
enjoyed for five years lapsed in 1784 on the death of his first wife, the
former Marchioness of Carmarthen. He found himself up to the ears
in debt within a few months.   ·

Let me recall Byron's story briefly, familiar though it is Captain
John Byron was the eldest son of Admiral the Hon John Byron (who was
in turn the second son of the fourth Lord Byron), by Sophia Trevanion
of Carhays, Cornwall (whose pedigree will be found in Burke's *History
of the Commoners*, 1833, i., 253-5). The Byrons had become a bye-word.
The fifth Lord (who was in Aberdeen as a captain in the Duke of

Kingston's Horse, March 20, 1745-6) made himself notorious by reason of his killing his kinsman, William Chaworth, in a duel, fought in a tavern in Pall Mall, in 1765. The Admiral (1723-1786) started life by being wrecked on the coast of Chili, in 1741 (he wrote a book about it); and, as a Don Juan of fifty summers, he again found himself on a dangerous coast, for he set up an establishment in London for his wife's ex-maid (*Town and Country Magazine*, Dec., 1773). His handsome son, Captain John Byron, regarded him as an excellent model, for he ran away, in December, 1778, with the beautiful, but bored, Marchioness of Carmarthen, Baroness Conyers in her own right, and daughter-in-law of the 5th Duke of Leeds. The town rang with the scandal (see *ibid.*, Jan., 1779, and *Bon-Accord*, August 19, 1898). Byron had the temerity to marry the lady, June, 1779. She bore him one child, the famous Augusta. She kept him in pocket-money, and departed this life, in France, Jan. 27, 1784, the victim of "consumption and his ill-usage".

At this crisis Catherine Gordon crossed his path. Whether he piqued her or petted her I do not know; but the blasé bankrupt man-about-town (*aetat* 30), with the memory of his beautiful Marchioness constantly before him (in the face of her daughter), went one day to St. Michael's, Bath, with the dumpy little "heiress" (who had a Scots accent), and the tragedy of her line reached a climax   A legend is related in the *Memoirs of Robert Chambers* (p. 287) about Catherine Gordon's marriage with Byron. In 1784 (the year in which Byron's first wife died) Miss Gordon, who was present at a performance in Edinburgh of Mrs. Siddons, as Isabella, in *The Fatal Marriage*, was " carried out of her box in hysterics, screaming loudly the words caught from the great actress, 'Oh, my Biron! my Biron!' A strange tale was therewith connected. A gentleman, whom she had not at this time seen or heard of, the Honourable John Biron, next year met, paid his addresses, and married her. It was to her a fatal marriage in several respects, although it gave to the world the poet, Lord Byron." The marriage was not welcomed by Miss Gordon's relatives, especially her economical grandmother. It was tabooed even by her neighbours. Peter Buchan published in his collection of ballads (1828, p. 258) the following verses, which he says were " written by a Scottish bard who had been dissatisfied with the marriage of Miss Gordon":—

O, whare are ye gaein', bonny Miss Gordon ?
  O, whare are ye gaein', sae bonnie and braw ?
Ye've married, ye've married wi' Johnny Byron,
  To squander the lands o' Gight awa.

This youth is a rake, frae England he's come ;
  The Scots dinna ken his extraction ava ;
He keeps up his misses, his landlord he duns ;
  That's fast drawin' the lands o' Gight awa.

The shootin' o' guns, and rattlin' o' drums ,
  The bugle in woods, the pipes in the ha',
The beagles a' howlin', the hounds a' growlin'—
  These soundings will soon gar Gight gang awa'

A curious echo of the note of dismay which Captain Byron struck among the Aberdeenshire gentry has come down to us in the shape of a diary kept by Alexander Russell, Mrs. Byron's cousin, the son of the co-commissioner on her estates. In this document, now owned by his grandson, the present laird of Aden, Russell describes a visit he paid the Byrons in September, 1785, when he was seventeen. Russell was "much struck by the extravagance of the establishment, and much impressed by the descriptions of fashionable society given by Captain Byron". No doubt the gallant captain entertained the lad of seventeen to an account of his own amours—including his flight with Lady Carmarthen ; while the exploits of old Q., who was then *the* man-about-town, would be related. Boys, however, will be boys, for the laird of Aden tells us that his grandfather joined in "dancing the lands of Gight awa'" to the sound of the pipes in the "ha'," which scandalised the ballad writer, and gives a graphic account of these merry meetings :—

He was also greatly edified, and not a little shocked, by seeing a copy of a recently published work, called *La Nouvelle Heloise*, which he discovered on Captain Byron's table, and which in no way harmonised with Tillotson's sermons, which, to judge by previous entries in his diary, had been the young man's favourite reading. He also relates how greatly alarmed he was one Saturday night lest wild Captain Jack should dance on into the Sabbath. He therefore retired to bed at 11.30, but, to his great relief, the reels left off before the clock struck midnight. It would appear that Mrs. Byron and her young son paid frequent visits to her aunt and uncle at Aden.

The Aberdeenshire "gentry" could not tolerate Byron (the clash-ing of his reckless temperament with their cautious outlook on life must

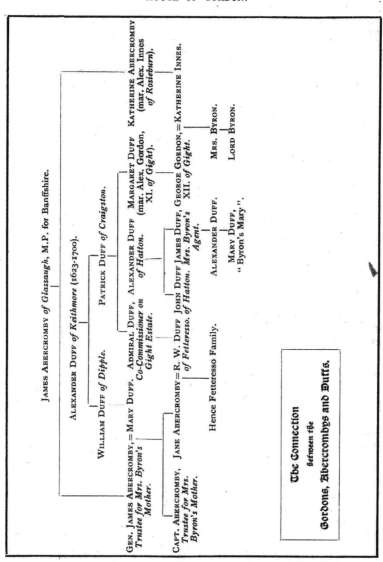

JAMES ABERCROMBY of *Glassaugh*, M.P. for Banffshire.

ALEXANDER DUFF of *Keithmore* (1623-1700).

PATRICK DUFF of *Craigston*.

WILLIAM DUFF of *Dipple*.

ADMIRAL DUFF, Co-Commissioner on *Gight Estate*.

ALEXANDER DUFF of *Hatton*.

MARGARET DUFF (mar. Alex. Gordon, XI. of *Gight*).

KATHERINE ABERCROMBY (mar. Alex. Innes of *Rosieburn*).

JOHN DUFF of *Hatton*.

JAMES DUFF, Mrs. Byron's Agent.

GEORGE GORDON, XII. of *Gight*. = KATHERINE INNES.

MRS. BYRON.

LORD BYRON.

GEN. JAMES ABERCROMBY, = MARY DUFF, *Trustee for Mrs. Byron's Mother*.

R. W. DUFF of *Fetteresso*.

ALEXANDER DUFF.

MARY DUFF, " Byron's Mary ".

CAPT. ABERCROMBY, *Trustee for Mrs. Byron's Mother*.

JANE ABERCROMBY = of *Fetteresso*.

Hence Fetteresso Family.

The Connection *between the* Gordons, Abercrombys and Duffs.

(290)

have been very comic), although he seems to have gone half way to meet them, by living at Gight and adopting his wife's name, by calling himself " John Byron Gordon ". Their repudiation of him was shown when he tried to vote in the Parliamentary election of February, 1786, when George Skene of Skene, backed by the Whig Duffs, offered himself as member for Aberdeenshire against James Ferguson of Pitfour, the nominee of the Tory Gordons Byron's vote was disallowed, although he put himself forward as " John Byron Gordon of Gight ". A squib of the period (reprinted in Davidson's *Earldom of the Garioch*) dismisses him thus :—

> And there was an Englishman, married in haste
> To an heiress that suited him just to his taste,
> Yet his right of attendance at court was not clear,
> So they sent him to dance it at home for a year

It is interesting to note that Lord George Gordon also tried to vote ·—

> There, too, was the Lord of the Protestant mob,
> Who came post a long way to assist at the job;
> And yet, when he came, no assistance could grant,
> For no oath he would take but the old Covenant

Very soon after this Mrs. Byron suffered further degradation. Unlike her mother, her grandmother, and her great-grandmother, she had no marriage settlement—which shows how little she had profited by the Duff strain in her ; and her husband's creditors fell upon her income. The stocking was very soon emptied. The Aberdeen Bank shares went for £600. The timber on the estate was cut down and sold, to the amount of £1,500. Monkshill was sold in 1787 to James Hay of Brigend, Lord Aberdeen's factor, bringing in (with the superiority of the Dee fishings) £480. Meantime £8,000 had been borrowed on the Gight estate, and it too had to go—Byron and his wife having left it for good in the summer of 1786, when they went to Hampshire in the first instance, and then to Cowes (not to France, as Moore makes out).

Some very interesting correspondence, dealing with the sale of Gight, was published (for the first time) by the Rev. Dr Milne of Fyvie in the supplement to his parish magazine (February, March and April, 1886). In order to understand the nexus of the families involved in these disputes the table on the preceding page should be studied.

On July 15, 1785, Alexander Duthie wrote from Aberdeen to the laird of Aden as follows:—

Mr. Innes, Breda, has been in the country for some time, and I have not yet seen him since I got your last letter, but I know he has refused payment of a number of drafts upon him from Mr. Byron Gordon, which were returned protested. I suppose he had heard from the lady. For some days past a rumour has gone thorrow in the town that Capt. Byron and his lady were parted, which I am afraid is too true, for late last night Mr. Byron arrived here in a chaise and four without any other person. What has become of the lady I know not. He has not an acquaintance here, nor is he recommended to anybody. Mr. Innes is not in town. So what the Captain intends nobody knows. It is said he is going to Gight.

On November 25, 1785, Duthie, who seemed to have been confidential agent of the Russell family, wrote to Russell:—

Mr. Innes [who came to Aberdeen on Nov. 24] says that Captain Byron had wrote to his father to see if he would advance money for paying off the debts of Gight upon an heritable security, to be granted by Captain Byron and his lady, but as yet they had got no return. Mr. Innes is going next week to Gight to see if there is any return from the Admiral. If not, he proposes to take an heritable security in his own name for the debts of Gight, and to convoy it to some person who will lend the money.

Captain Byron (writing from his mother's birthplace, Carhays, in Cornwall, on August 22, 1786) addressed the following remarkable letter to the co-commissioners of the Gight estate, namely Admiral Robert Duff (I. of Fetteresso, who died 1787), Mrs. Byron's grand-uncle, and Alexander Russell of Montcoffer, who had married her aunt (Eliza Innes):—

Gentlemen,—I received yours this instant, with your copy, and am perfectly satisfied with the determination, except in one respect, namely, the coach-horses going to Mr. Stewart, Mill of Arden, as Mrs Byron Gordon is at S[outh] Warnborough, a house I have taken in Hampshire, and I being obliged to be here on business, I can only give you my sentiments with regard to the bond Mr. Watson has signed, therefore the other two must be given up. With respect to the sale, I have wrote to Lord Aberdeen and Fyvie. When I get their answers I will send them to you with our resolutions. I think it is the best way to dispose of the Estate as soon as possible, as I see no end to the expense we may incur.

I hope Mr. Duff, as soon as the money is got, will remit a certain sum to us, as we have been obliged to borrow of Mr. Hay, our factor, when we thought we should have been relieved by Mr Duff on the 20th June, and I beg Mr. Duff will make out to the Commissioners the sums we are indebted to him, and that the produce of the bond may be sent immediately to me, and also the amount of the meal rent due, etc., may be sent us —I am, etc., etc.,   JOHN BYRON GORDON.

James Duff (fourth son of Alexander Duff, I of Hatton), Sheriff-Clerk of Banffshire, who was Mrs. Byron's agent, communicated (on September 18, 1786) with Russell as follows :—

Dear Sir,—Some posts ago I had a letter from Mr. Byron Gordon in answer to the one wrote when you was here, copy of which is subjoined ; to it I shall refer when I again hear from him as to the price I shall advise you In the meantime I have wrote Mr. Hay, the factor, to get back the horses from Mr Stewart. I have delayed the roup proposed, as Mr. Byron says nothing of it; by this there can be no inconveniency. At last the proposed loan from Cairnbanno I think will take place, and as there is now no time to be lost it will be necessary for you to fix some day to be here next week—when Mr. Abercrombie is ready to attend in order to finish the transaction, the papers being now all in my custody, and Mr Byron's affairs require despatch, so in course will expect to hear from you.—I am, Dear Sir, etc., etc ,   JAMES DUFF.

As there is no regular post to you, [I] have sent this by express, so as to have time to advise the gentlemen the day you are to be here.

On August 16 Mr. Russell got a letter from a Mrs. Clerk .—

I am sorry to hear from every quarter that the estate of Gight is to be sold for certain. I wish you and Mrs. Byron's friends could only get but £100 a year secured to her, but I will not meddle in it, for I have done all I can for her, poor unhappy creature!

Mrs. Byron, for her part, did not approach the Commissioners in the first instance. Doubtless she thought that she had put herself out of court by marrying the *roué ;* and yet she felt herself so much in his power, through her affections (the point is exceedingly interesting in a woman of her hard instincts), that she demanded protection against herself, as well as against her husband. She approached the Commissioners through her kinswoman, Miss Urquhart of Craigston, to whom she wrote from South Warnborough, on November 13, 1786, in this strain :—

It is by Admiral Duff and Mr Russell of Montcoffer's advice that we sell the estate [of Gight] You know they are the Commissioners, and if they act as my friends they should see that there is a proper settlement made upon me, the best that I could wish or expect would be ten thousand pounds; and I would have that settled in such a manner that it would be out of Mr. Byron's power to spend, and out of my own power to give up to him, though I should wish to have the power of spending it myself, or to leave it to any lady I pleased, though I am not sure if that could be done; though if it could I should wish it. I suppose if that could not be done, it might be settled in such a manner that he could not spend it, and that I could not give it up to him, but that I might leave it to him if I was to die I should not wish to appear in it myself or that Mr. Byron should know that I wrote or spoke to any one on this subject, because if he did he would never forgive me, but I should wish it to be done without my appearing in it   Admiral Duff is certainly the best person, but I should wish that he would not mention me in it, but as if it came from himself, and as being my uncle, that he thought it his duty to demand and see properly settled upon me   For God's sake mention it to nobody but who is necessary, and I beg that your answer to this letter you will send under cover to my maid, Mrs. Bawn, at South Warnborough, near Hartford Bridge, Hampshire. I trust to youre friendship.

This letter was duly communicated by Miss Urquhart to Admiral Duff. In order to reach his colleague (Russell) it was communicated by Miss Urquhart to Miss Helen Innes, who sent it to her brother-in-law, Russell   Miss Innes wrote (from Banff, November 30, 1786) :—

If anything could be done to secure her, you will be best judge what steps are proper, now that she sees the necessity of it herself. [Up to this point Mrs. Byron would seem to have repudiated the interference of her relatives] It will be an act of charity in her friends to do what they can for her   Miss Urquhart is desirous that it should not be mentioned to any person here, as you will see that it would not be proper that Mr. Byron should hear of it, and she has mentioned it to nobody but me.

There was great difficulty in selling the estate ; Alexander Gordon of Letterfourie, who had married Alexander Russell's daughter Helen (by his first wife), was anxious to buy it.   The estate was at last put up for sale on December 12, 1786, but was withdrawn.   Mr. J. Buchan, W.S., offered £16,000.   Gight was at last bought in 1787 for £17,850, by the third Earl of Aberdeen, for his son, Lord Haddo, the descendant of that Sir John Gordon of Kellie (or Haddo) who had lost his head for the very same cause which the Gight Gordons had followed with impunity. The prevalent idea that the family of Gight was pursued by an unlucky fate—crystallised, as I have shown, in several " frets "—was expressed at this period by a legend related by Moore, who repeats the gossip of a correspondent, to the effect that, shortly before the sale of Gight, a number of herons, which had nested for years in a wood on the banks of a large loch at Gight, called the Hagberry Pot, flew over to Haddo When Lord Haddo was informed of this, he said : " Let the birds come, and do them no harm, for the land will soon follow ".   The omniscient " Thomas the Rhymer " had prophesied that

> When the heron leaves the tree
> The laird o' Gight shall landless be.

The evil fate did not end with the old Gight family, for Lord Haddo met his death on the "Green of Gight," by being thrown from his horse (October 2, 1791), leaving several children, including the future Premier (labelled by Byron "the travelled Thane, Athenian Aberdeen"), and the Hon. Sir Alexander Gordon, Wellington's A.D.C., who was killed at Waterloo. Haddo's death was believed to fulfil "Thomas the Rhymer's" prophecy:—

> At Gight three men a violent death shall dee,
> And efter that the lands shall lie in lea,

which was completed by a servant from the home farm being killed in a similar way. Mr. James Davidson (of the Scottish Employers' Liability and General Insurance Company) tells me that the prophecy was fulfilled in 1855 or 1856, when James Davidson, Bridge of Methlick (my informant's father), was commissioned to destroy the outhouses at Gight and turn the land into lea. A youth named Main, son of Francis Main, a "dyker," set about the work of demolition light-heartedly, with the remark: "Thomas the Rhymer made a mistak' for aince, for the place will be ca'ed doon withoot a third man bein' kilt". He had no sooner said this than a wall fell and killed him. Mr. Davidson vividly remembers the washing of the blood-stained blankets in which young Main had been carried away.

Mrs. Byron was not much better off even after the estate was sold. On Dec. 10, 1786, Mrs. Duff, the mother of Mary, whom Byron fell in love with and who married Robert Cockburn, wrote to Russell from Bath "with reference to our poor niece," Mrs. Byron. She says that a joint letter had been written to Byron representing to him "the justice and necessity of securing £3,000 or £4,000 out of the estate of Gight for their joint lives, the principal to go to the survivor, the annuity not to be touched by the debts of either. To ask for more would have given Byron an excuse to grant nothing." Mrs. Byron saw nothing like the £10,000 which she wished to be settled on her. The whole proceeds of the sale, £17,850, were mopped up by her husband's creditors, except £1,122, which was required to pay her grandmother (née Duff) an annuity of £55 11s 1d., and £3,000 for herself, which was lent by the trustees to Mr. Carsewell of Rathillet, Fifeshire. It says much for Mrs. Byron's thrift that this capital sum, £4,122, was untouched during her remaining life of twenty-four years, for her son inherited it intact on her death, and by his will (dated 12th August, 1811) directed that it should be used to pay off certain legacies and debts.

After the sale of Gight, Captain Byron and his wife seem to have gone to Chantilly, to escape the duns who had not yet been satisfied. Mrs. Byron was reported, in September, 1787 (*Annals of Banff*, i., 236), to be "big with bairn". She returned to England about the close of 1787, and, on January 22, 1788, she gave birth to the poet, at 22 Holles Street, off Oxford Street, London. The house, which used to be marked by a metal medallion, was pulled down years ago, and the site is now occupied by the huge drapery establishment of John Lewis & Co., whose business notepaper bears a bust of Byron, and who have erected in a niche in the wall a statue to mark the site of the historic spot.

The birth seems to have reconciled Mrs. Byron to her family, for Mr. Duff of Fetteresso and the Duke of Gordon (Jane Maxwell's husband)—whose line she despised, ignorantly supposing her own to be descended from the real Gordons—were the godfathers. As a specimen of the confusion in Byron biography, I may note that R. C. Dallas declares that the poet was born at Dover; while Sir Cosmo Gordon goes the length of saying that the event occurred at Gight. Shortly before the boy's birth Mrs. Byron sent her step-daughter, the six-year-old Augusta, to the child's grandmother, the Dowager Lady Holdernesse.

Mrs. Byron, probably to gratify her relatives, and also for the sake of economy, took up her residence, in 1790, at Aberdeen, which she made her headquarters for the next eight years. But for her son's succeeding to the baronage of Byron (in 1798) she might have lived and died in Aberdeen, and Byron's genius might have been choked in consequence. She lived at different periods in Virginia Street (apparently with a Mrs. Cruickshank, "on the shore," to whom she wished a letter addressed to her in January, 1791); in two different houses in Queen Street, and at 64 Broad Street, which was demolished in 1901. The last is her best known residence. This house kept up the traditions of literature by sheltering Dr. John Mackintosh, the author of the *History of Civilisation in Scotland*. She sometimes spent her summer holiday in a little cottage off the South Stocket Road, called Honeybrae, which has been demolished to make way for the voracious villa (*Aberdeen Free Press* of July 26 and September 4, 1898, and *Evening Express*, January

19, 1899). Mr. George Walker (author of *Aberdeen Awa'*) learned this fact from a Mrs. Black (who was Mrs. Byron's servant) or her son. Mrs. Black, who was a member of the George Street U.P. Church, died in the forties. The west room of the first floor of the villa used to be pointed out as the room occupied by Byron. It has been said that Villa Franca, in the South Stocket Road district, was the house in which Byron stayed. As the house had at that time been recently built by old Peacock, the dancing master, for his own residence, it is unlikely that he would have let it for summer lodgings. Mrs. Byron's grandmother seems to have forgiven her, for Byron and his mother visited (on one occasion at least) the veteran dowager (*née* Duff) at Banff. Some illustrated articles by Rev. W. Rogerson on Byron's connection with Aberdeen were given in *Bon-Accord*, May 8-July 10, 1902.

Her husband continued to worry her till his death (by suicide?) at Valenciennes, on August 2, 1791, aged thirty-six. Moore declares that he paid her two visits at Aberdeen, apparently with the object of getting money out of her. The fear of herself, which she had expressed to Miss Urquhart five years before, proved too true, for, though she had been ruined by the Captain, she gave him more than she could spare, and got £300 into debt. The interest on this debt reduced her income to £135 a year, and it was not until the jointure of £1,122 fell to her (by her grandmother, the dowager's, death, in 1801) that she was able to clear her feet. It was probably one of her husband's visits that made her write, from Aberdeen, the following piteous letter to her uncle, Alexander Russell of Montcoffer, on January 24, 1791. As quoted by Dr. Milne, the letter runs thus :—

Dear Sir,—I wrote to your son some time ago about some business, which I suppose he has told you of. I wrote Mr. Duff at the same time, and I meant to have wrote to yourself, but, as Mr. Russel was at Fetteresso, I wrote to him. They both called on me, and your son said he did not think you would have any objection to do what I requested of you. I said I would write to you, but he said that was not necessary, as he would tell you of it, and as I have heard nothing to the contrary you will have no objection to sign the enclosed paper; it will be doing me a very particular favour, and I will feel very grateful for it. I am in great want of the money. The paper is this: Lord Aberdeen to advance me a hundred pounds at present out of the twelve hundred pounds settled on me at Lady Gight's death, but in case both me and Mr. Byron should die before my grandmother, he will not lend the money without the trustees guarantee any conveyance of mine, or Mr. Byron by a formal deed, which is the same thing as becoming bound for the money. I really do not perfectly understand the settlement, but I believe if Mr. Byron or myself was to die before Lady Gight, my son when he came of age, if he was to insist on it, could make them pay him the money, but I am not certain. But as the sum is only £100, Mr. Duff, Fetteresso, has signed the paper, and Mr. Watson and Mr. Clark at Edinburgh have agreed to sign it when it is signed by you and Mr. Duff. Indeed, Mr. Watson seemed to wish your son also to sign it, but in that he may do as he pleases The paper is made out by Dr. Thom, who was in possession of all my papers, and made it out accordingly. Therefore I hope you will have no objection to sign it when the rest have agreed, as it is only for £100, and there is four of you, and it is only running the risk of £25 in case Mr. Byron and me was to die before Lady Gight. If I was not in great want of the money I would not ask it, and it would be doing me a great favour. I beg you would return it as soon as possible. I hope all your family are well I beg to be kindly remembered to my aunt. I hope she is pretty well in her health, and believe me, dear sir, your affectionate niece,

C. BYRON GORDON.

Mrs. Byron spent the summer holidays in 1795, 1796, 1797 and possibly 1798 with her son in the house of James Robertson at Ballaterich (Michie's *Records of Invercauld*, pp 166, 391). She left Aberdeen in 1798, on her boy's succeeding to the title, and never came north again, so far as I know. Her life in England, spent mainly at Newstead during the next thirteen years, is too well known to be recapitulated here. But, as typical of her temperament, I may quote a letter (see Prothero's *Byron*) she wrote to one of her neighbours at Newstead, in September, 1809, as it recalls the violent boundary disputes which her ancestors had carried on with one another at the point of the sword. I retain her italics.

Sir,—I must *insist* on your confining yourself to your own premises, or at least not coming on Lord Byron's Manor to hunt and commit *trespasses*, which you have been so *long* in the habit of doing that you now, I suppose, fancy you have a right to do so; but I am fully *determined* to convince you to the contrary. Pray, Sir, do you suppose that I will remain here and *tamely submit* to every *insult* from you? If you think so you will find yourself extremely mistaken.

I cannot send out my Keeper but he must be abused by you on Lord Byron's own Manor. You presume on his absence to *insult* a *Woman* and assault an Old Man; that is, you insult his Mother, and injure the Property, attack the Persons and threaten the Lives of his Servants. In short, your language is unbecoming, and your behaviour totally unworthy, a Gentleman. To a man of courage these are *harsh truths*, but they are *truths nevertheless*.

I will now take the trouble to inform you that Lord Byron's Tenants shall be no longer annoyed by you with *impunity*, but that a prosecution will be immediately instituted against you for *divers trespasses* and *one assault.* You are surely not so ignorant as not to know that breaking down fences and riding through fields of standing corn with your Hounds are *unjustifiable, arbitrary,* and *oppressive* acts, and will not be submitted to in a *free country,* even if you was the *first Man* in it. I will not suffer my Keeper to be abused or interrupted in the execution of his duty, and he has my *positive* orders to use every possible means to destroy the Foxes   Lord Grey de Ruthyn's poaching and these abundant, noxious Animals have nearly deprived this *once* excellent Manor of game, and the Woods on this estate shall not continue to be a *Depôt* for your vermine, and *I'm determined to extirpate* the breed here, and to suffer so great a nuisance no longer.   If the breed of Fox-hunters could be as easily got rid of, the benefit to society in general would be great.   No earths shall be stopt on Newstead, as I shall encourage neither Foxes nor their Hunters on these premises.

I understand the earths have been stopt, and whoever shall be found at that work shall have sufficient cause to regret it, and care shall be taken to watch for them —I remain, Sir, etc., etc ,

C. G BYRON

Mrs. Byron died at Newstead on August 1, 1811.   Moore says she succumbed to "a fit of rage, brought on by reading over an upholsterer's bill "—so that she died as she had lived.   A few days before her death (July 23, 1811) Byron had written to her : "You will consider Newstead as your house, not mine: I'm only a visitor ".   She was taken ill so suddenly that Byron, who was living in London, did not reach Newstead in time to see her die   He was very much affected by her death.   "Thank God," he wrote one of his friends, "her last moments were most tranquil.   I am told she was in little pain, and not aware of her situation   I now feel the truth of Mr. Gray's observation : 'That we can only have one mother'.   Peace be with her."   Moore relates that

On the night after his arrival at Newstead, Mrs. Byron's maid, on passing the room where the body lay, heard a heavy sigh from within.   On entering the room she found Byron sitting in the dark by the bed.   When she spoke to him he burst into tears, and exclaimed: "Oh, Mrs By! I had but one friend in the world, and she is gone!"   On the day of the funeral he refused to follow the corpse to the grave, but watched the procession move away from the door of Newstead. then turning to Rushton, bade him bring the gloves, and began his usual sparring exercise, Only his silence, abstraction, and unusual violence betrayed to his antagonist the state of his feelings.

Mrs. Byron was buried in the vault in the chancel of Hucknall Torkard Church, Notts, where Byron and his daughter lie.   The chancel door opens directly on the slab which covers the Byron vault, and over its lintel is a mural tablet to the memory of the Countess of Lovelace, " Ada, sole daughter of my house and heart," whose coffin is beneath.   A plain marble slab let into the wall, nearer to the communion slab, marks the site of Byron's grave.   There is also a slab of rosso-antico marble let into the pavement immediately above the spot where the body of Lord Byron lies.   In the vestry there hangs a small escutcheon little more than a foot square, painted on silk, and bearing on the reverse the following inscription :—

The Honourable Cath. Gordon Byron of Gight,
Mother of Geo. Lord Byron,
And lineal descendant of the Earl of Huntley,
And Lady Jane Stuart,
Daughter of King James the First of Scotland,
Died in the 46th year of her age,
August 1st, 1811

Mr Charles B. Doran, writing to the *Pall Mall Gazette* many years ago, remarked :—

This magniloquence and pride of birth, lofty enough to befit a mausoleum, contrasts painfully with the poverty of the material on which it is presented to the eye. The silk is dingy, tattered and faded, falling away from the sides of the wooden frame to which it is stitched, and the inscription, which is on ordinary cardboard, in rude letters, as if drawn by a careless schoolboy, with only a miserable attempt at colouring, is fast becoming illegible   The contrast between the pride of long descent in the inscription, and the poverty perceptible in the decayed scrap of silk and ragged bit of pasteboard, is painful in the extreme.

The Rev J. E. Phillips, the vicar of the church, tells me that the escutcheon " is in a good state of preservation, and is in a handsome frame ".   I venture, however, to think that its former decay was more symbolic of Mrs. Byron's sad life.

Byron drafted a will on August 12, 1811, in consequence of his mother's death, by which he decreed that the £4,200 which came to him (through his mother) from the sale of Gight, four and twenty years previously, should be used to pay legacies and debts.

What was Byron's attitude to his mother ?   The question is very difficult to answer, for his own letters are as contradictory as the stories of his biographers   For instance, Rogers, in his *Table Talk*, gives two versions in these stories :—

(1) A lady, resident in Aberdeen, told me that she used to sit in a pew in St. Paul's Chapel in that town, next to Mrs Byron's, and that one morning she observed the poet (then seven or eight years old) amusing himself by disturbing his mother s devotions: he every now and again gently pricked with a pin the large round arms of Mrs. Byron, which were covered with white kid gloves.

(2) Professor Stuart, of the Marischal College, Aberdeen, mentioned to me the following proof of Byron's fondness for his mother. *Georgy*, and some other little boys, were one day allowed, much to their delight, to assist at a gathering of apples in the Professor's garden, and were rewarded for their labours with some of the fruit *Georgy*, having received his portion of apples, immediately disappeared, and on his return, after barely an hour's absence, to the query where he had been, he replied that he had been " carrying some apples to his poor dear mother ".

One of Byron's schoolfellows contributed an impression of the pair to the ramshackle *Appreciation of Byron* written by Sir Cosmo Gordon in 1824, as follows :—

[Mrs. Byron] was a lady of very staid and sober habits Her face was comely, and her air that of a lady, but her stature was diminutive, and she was too much *en bon point* for being accounted handsome. Notwithstanding, her son was all to her: she was all to her son: and the attentions which the mother showed to her son were more than repaid by the fondness which the son evinced for the mother.

Byron himself has described her thus :—

My mother was as haughty as Lucifer, with her descent from the Stuarts and her line from the old Gordons—not the Seyton Gordons, as she disdainfully termed the ducal branch [of course she was quite wrong]. She told me the story, always reminding me how superior *her* Gordons were to the southern Byrons, notwithstanding our Norman and always masculine descent.

He treated her with dignity, for he always addressed her on letters as the " Hon. Mrs. Byron," although, of course, she had no claim to the epithet (see the long series from 1808 to 1811, quoted in R. C. Dallas's *Life of Byron*, i , 77-121, and ii., 1-31). Beaconsfield sketched Mrs Byron under the name of Mrs. Cadurcis in *Venetia*, published in 1837. He gives a lurid picture of the lady :—

Mrs Cadurcis, since she was a widow, has lived in strict seclusion with her little boy. But I am afraid she has not been in the habit of dining as well as we have to-day. A very limited income. . . . [She was] a short and very stout woman with a rubicund countenance, and dressed in a style which remarkably blended the shabby with the tawdry. . . Mrs. Cadurcis was a great workwoman . . . not able to walk for any length of time . . Puffing, panting and perspiring, now directing her waiting woman, and now ineffectually attempting to box her son's ears, Mrs. Cadurcis indeed offered a most ridiculous spectacle " Take that, you brat," shrieked

the mother [when Lord Cadurcis mimicked her], and she struck her own hand
against the doorway   . Mrs. Cadurcis threw the cage at her son's head.   . Mrs.
Cadurcis went into an hysterical rage. then suddenly jumping up, she rushed at her
son . . . Mrs Cadurcis remained alone in a savage sulk. . . . [There was] a renewed
burst of hysterics from Mrs. Cadurcis, so wild and terrible, that they must have been
contagious to any female of less disciplined emotions than her guest. [She succumbed to] the most violent epileptic fits (chaps. i -xvii.)

The latest investigator of Byron's " degeneracy " is an American
professor, Dr James G. Kiernan, who contributed a series of articles on
Byron to the *Alienist and Neurologist* (reprinted in the defunct London
Humanitarian, 1899).   He sees degeneracy in Mrs. Byron's " predilec-
tion for quacks " (who tortured her boy's lame foot), and in her
" premature obesity "   Dr. Kiernan, coming to the subject with the
microscopic eye of the specialist, which sees " stigmata " everywhere,
mentions her father's suicide, and adds, on what authority I know
not, that " other members of the family were suicides ".   He sums up
Mrs Byron thus :—

Mrs Gordon was a woman of very unbalanced temperament   At the theatre
in Edinburgh she went into convulsions, shrieking about her love to "Mad Jack"
[Byron] on seeing Mrs Siddons as Juliet.   She half-worshipped, half-hated, her
blackguard husband, and fell into grand hysteria at his death.   Her mental defects
were the theme of comment by the poet's schoolfellows   "Your mother's a fool,"
said a schoolboy to Byron.   "I know it," was his curt reply, followed by an ominous
silence.   A more exasperating mother for a sensitive, passionate child cannot be
imagined than this vehement, undisciplined woman, who had fits of ill-temper hourly,
and who rarely passed a week without a wild outbreak of hysteric rage   Lavish of
kisses to the child when good-humoured, she was lavish of blows when he incurred
her capricious displeasure   In a later stage of his infancy, instead of fearing, he
hated her.   Once, after pouring coarse abuse and profanity upon him, she called him
a "lame brat".   At this the glare came from the child's eyes that so often flashed
from them in after-time.   Whilst his lips quivered and his face whitened from the
force of feeling never to be forgotten, he was silent, and then said, with icy coldness,
"I was born so, mother," and he turned away from the woman who dared not follow
him   The scene was in the poet's mind when he told the Marquis of Sligo that it
was impossible for him to love Mrs. Byron as a son ought to love a widowed mother
The scene was still in his mind when, three years before his death, he wrote the first
words of *The Deformed Transformed*—

Bertha · Out, Hunchback!
Arnold   I was born so, mother.

[Mrs Byron's] features had that exaggeration of the Scotch type which constitutes
arrest of facial development   She was by no means devoid of the shrewdness and

ordinary intelligence of inferior femininity. She was capable of generous impulses to the persons whom, in her frequent fits of uncontrollable fury, she would assail with unwomanly violence. Mrs. Byron's early education was remarkably neglected at a time when Scottish young ladies of her station were exceedingly well educated, and the contrast between them and the women of the lower class [whom Dr. Kiernan says Mrs. Byron "reached"] was enormous She found that her husband, to whom she had sacrificed her fortune, was the meanest kind of a profligate, who did not hesitate to leave her practically penniless, burdened with her own infant and the daughter [Augusta] of [his] first wife [Lady Carmarthen], whom she seems to have treated with all the kindness possible to an ill-regulated nature

Dr. Kiernan, of course, may be exaggerating Mrs Byron's incapacities; but, to my mind, there can be no doubt that she came of an utterly impossible race, and came at the fag end of it, when mere ebulliency of spirit had passed into a form of actual insanity on the one hand (as illustrated by her father), and of enfeebled physique on the other (as shown by the rapid decay of the family) The biographers of Byron (few of them Scots by the way) have, in the absence of the necessary genealogical knowledge, sketched Mrs. Byron's family by starting and guessing from her backwards I have reversed the process, and the two results are identical. A crude engraving of Captain Byron's bust is given in the *Town and County Magazine* of 1779, and Mr. R. E. Prothero tells me that a Mr. Hemmell, who resides in London, owns another portrait Mrs Byron's portrait, painted by Thomas Stewartson in 1806, is in the possession of Mr. John Murray, of Albemarle Street, and is reproduced by photogravure in Mr Prothero's edition of Byron's *Letters and Journals* (i., 194).

GEORGE GORDON, LORD BYRON.

Aberdeen has never produced a really great poet (a writer in the *Scots Observer* once hinted it never would); but it has made the most of its share of half of one, by creating a great saga round Lord Byron. Born January 22, 1788, in Holles Street, London, Byron spent only eight years (1790-8) of his life in Aberdeen and the north, but into that brief and boyish period many legends and some passions (the possession of which at such an age only proves Byron the more degenerate) have been laboriously packed. This is not the place to biograph Byron; but I must indicate the sources of information on his life in Aberdeen.

The influence of Aberdeen on Byron (besides that of his mother, which I have already dealt with) lasted until 1801, when (as a boy of thirteen) he left the school at Dulwich taught by Dr. William Glennie (born 1761), who was an Aberdonian, the son of Rev. John Glennie, D.D , minister of Maryculter, and brother of Dr George Glennie, Professor of Moral Philosophy, Marischal College. Byron had two Aberdonians, the sisters Agnes and Mary Gray, for his nurses   Moore has drawn them in bright colours   When Agnes Gray married Alexander Melvin of Aberdeen, Mrs. Byron was present at the christening of her first-born, who was called George Byron Melvin   Byron gave him a gold watch, which passed to the child's brother (Alexander Melvin), and from him to his aunt, Mary Gray, who gave it to Dr Ewing of Aberdeen   It is now in the possession of the widow of Major Ewing, the doctor's son, who lives at Taunton, and reproductions of the back and front of it were given in the *English Illustrated Magazine* (1897), along with reproduction of the younger Kay's portrait of Byron (at the age of seven), equipped as an archer.   Byron is said to have stayed for a time with Agnes Gray (Mrs. Melvin) at 177 Barron Street, Woodside, which was known as " Byron's Hall " (see Morgan's *Annals of Woodside,* pp. 105-6).   Mary Gray was in attendance on Byron at Nottingham in 1799.   (An article on his stay at Nottingham, by Mr J. A. Hammerton, appeared in *The Sketch* of September 22, 1897.)   Moore has presented the Grays as being very kind to Byron, but Hanson (quoted in Prothero's *Byron,* i., 10) gives a very different story.   Writing to Mrs. Byron on September, 1799, Hanson says :—

Her [Mary Gray's] conduct to your son was shocking   It was the general topic of conversation at Nottingham   Byron told me that she was perpetually beating him, and that his bones sometimes ached from it , that she brought all sorts of company of the very lowest description into his apartments , that she was out late at night; and he was frequently left to put himself to bed, that she would take the chaise boys into the chaise with her, and stopped at every little alehouse to drink with them.   But, madam, this is not all; she has even traduced yourself.

The Aberdeen period of Byron's life has been fully dealt with by Moore (who is generally the only authority quoted by north country writers).   Byron's boyhood in Aberdeen was described at length in *Harper's Magazine* (August, 1891), by Dr. Garden Blaikie (who told me that his article was very much cut down), and by Mr. Prothero in the *Nineteenth Century,* 1898.   Dr. Blaikie says :—

[At the age of five Byron was sent to the school of " Bodsy " Bower, in Longacre, the schoolroom being] a room like a wareroom, perhaps 25 or 30 feet long, low in the ceiling, with three or four small windows, ill-glazed and ill-cleaned, the walls and roof begrimed with dust, the rough, unwashed floor worn here and there into holes, suggesting excellent quarters for the rats below

Altogether, the school was so uncongenial that his mother took Byron away, and engaged private tutors, two of whom became ministers of the Church of Scotland. Mr Ross was a man of mature years, and Byron says : " Under him I made astonishing progress, and I recollect to this day his mild manners and good-natured painstaking " Of his other tutor, afterwards Rev. Dr. Joseph Paterson, Montrose, who died in 1865, at the age of ninety-two, Byron says :—

Afterward I had a very serious, saturnine, but kind young man, named Paterson, for a tutor He was the son of my shoemaker, but a good scholar, as is common with the Scotch He was a rigid Presbyterian also

Dr. Blaikie forgot to mention that David Grant, the compiler of *The Beauties of Modern British Poetry*, was one of Byron's tutors. He afterwards had a side school at Buffle, and used to boast to my maternal grandfather, Andrew Malcolm, M A., schoolmaster of Cushnie, that he had taught Byron.

· Byron ended his school experience at Aberdeen as a pupil at the Grammar School, then in the Schoolhill The best description of his schooldays is that which was written by Mr. Morland Simpson for *The Sketch* (June 22, 1898), where facsimiles of two pages of the register, with his name inscribed, " Geo Bayron Gordon "—superinscribed, " Dom de Byron " —were reproduced. The school registers show his name entered quarterly, from January 29, 1796, to the quarter which began (or ended) on June 18, 1798 (his granduncle, whom he succeeded in the peerage, died May 19, 1798) On January 29, 1796, he was in the second class. But Dr. Blaikie declared (*Harper's Magazine*) that Byron entered the school in November, 1794, along with Dr. Blaikie's father. I think that is probable, for he would have entered the first class (the registers before 1796 have not been preserved, if they ever existed) The last survivor of this class was Charles Winchester, advocate. I may note that Winchester was distinctly literary. In 1802 he was writing most of the articles in the *Intruder*, a penny-halfpenny octavo, issued by J. Burnett, Aberdeen, which at least reached a twenty-sixth number.   Winchester also translated the memoirs of that bombastic Jacobite, the Chevalier Johnstone.   Another contemporary of Byron at the Grammar School, though not in the same class, was William Knight, afterwards Professor of Natural Philosophy in Marischal College (1822-44).   He used to relate that Byron, who was his junior by two years, once tore his jacket, and was recompensed by a sound thrashing (*Alma Mater*, vi., 96).

Dr. Glennie's school at Dulwich, which Byron attended (1799-1801), is fully described in Harnett Blanch's *History of Camberwell* (pp 388-92). Byron thought it a " damned place ".   On going to Harrow he made a companion of Charles David Gordon (died 1826), son of David Gordon, XIV. of Abergeldie.   Two letters he wrote to Gordon (August 4 and 14, 1805) are quoted by Prothero (*Letters of Lord Byron*, 1., 69 and 77). In one of them he says .—

> I recollect passing near Abergeldie on an excursion through the Highlands; it was at that time a most lovely place.   I suppose you will soon have a view of the eternal snows that summit the top of Lachin-y-Gair, which towers so magnificently above the rest of our *Northern Alps*.   I still remember with pleasure the admiration which filled my mind when I first beheld it, and, further on, the dark, frowning mountains which rise near Invercauld, together with the romantic rocks that overshadow Mar Lodge.

Rev J G. Michie (*Records of Invercauld*, p. 389) is responsible for the statement, which is new, that Byron visited Invercauld in the autumn of 1803.   A ghillie told Mr. Michie that

> His lordship rested often and looked at the scenery.   He was very quiet, and did not often speak to me   When we began to climb the crags of Loch-an-uan, I thought he would not be able to scramble up, for he was rather lame, and I offered to assist him, but he would not have any help from me   When we got to the top he sat a long time on the edge of the rocks looking about him, but seldom asked me any question.

Byron was then a boy of fifteen and a half, and was much more likely to have been struck with the glories of " dark Lochnagar " than he could possibly have been on his earlier visits as a boy of nine or ten

Apropos of Byron's famous verses, I may note that a poem, in pretty much the same measure, appeared in the *Aberdeen Magazine* of October, 1798.   The first verse runs thus :—

Ye hills and high mountains surrounding Mount Battock,
Ye groves and bright fountains, ye surely can tell
How sportive and merry, my ewes, I've been with you,
How now I must bid thee, sweet mountains, Farewell.
I drove from the cot to the hill where I tended
My ewes, and my lambs from the wolf I defended
The charms of sweet Nature my pleasure so blended
I sang like a lark in the Glen of Lochlee

The verses were said to be the work of a "young shepherdess, whose images were drawn from the bleatings of her flock, the story of the skylark, and the wild flowers blooming in her native vale". Byron was living at Ballaterich in the summers of 1795-1797 and possibly 1798, and is said to have been courting Mary Robertson, his host's daughter. Is it possible that he wrote the verses, figuring as a "young shepherdess"? He was just nine at the time.

It is interesting to remember that Robert Louis Stevenson found a great inspiration within sight of "dark Lochnagar," for, as he wrote (*McClure's Magazine*, September, 1894), it was while recruiting in "Miss Macgregor's Cottage," Braemar, that he "ticketed" his performance *Treasure Island.*

There was a schoolboy [staying at the same time in Miss Macgregor's cottage] He had no thought of literature : it was the art of Raphael that received his fleeting suffrages, and with the aid of pen and ink and a shilling box of water colours, he had soon turned one of the rooms into a picture gallery My more immediate duty towards the gallery was to be showman but I would sometimes unbend a little, join the artist (so to speak) at the easel, and pass the afternoon with him in a generous emulation, making coloured drawings On one of these occasions I made the map of an island : it was elaborately and (I thought) beautifully coloured · the shape of it took my fancy beyond expression it contained harbours that pleased me like sonnets and, with the consciousness of the predestined, I ticketed my performance "Treasure Island"

I have already referred to the elaborate compilation of notices of Byron's residence in Banff in Dr. Cramond's *Annals.* A photograph of the pear tree in the garden of the old manse, which Byron is said to have robbed, has been taken by Rae of Banff, and was reproduced in *The Sketch* (April 13, 1898)

Byron has been credited with at least two amazing love affairs while he was in Aberdeen. Patrick Morgan (in the *Annals of Woodside*, p. 105) mentions an incredible affair he had with a Woodside girl,

"Lexy" Campbell. As Byron was only nine years old at the time it is inconceivable that "poor 'Lexy'" should have "lost caste by this affair," as Morgan declared, and if her subsequent career was "unfortunate," Byron was surely not responsible. Byron himself and Moore told the extraordinary story of his "passion" for his kinswoman, Mary Duff, of the Hatton family. Like many points in Byron's career, the identity of Mary is in dispute. The late Mr R W. Duff of Fetteresso declared she was a Duff. Rev. J G. Michie (*Records of Invercauld*, p. 391) says she was Mary Robertson, the daughter of James Robertson of Ballaterich, with whom Byron lodged in the summers of 1795, 1796, 1797 and possibly of 1798 The girl was Byron's senior by six years. A good summary of the controversy was contributed by Mr. Robert Anderson to *Scottish Notes and Queries* (December, 1892), and is re-stated in Mr. A. I. McConnochie's book, *The Royal Dee* (pp. 103-4). Mr. Michie (*Records of Invercauld*, pp. 389-95) goes over the ground elaborately. The "box" bed in which Byron slept at Ballaterich now serves as a cheese press at Dee Castle, a short distance to the east of the Robertsons' cottage. Mary Robertson married an excise officer, and died in Aberdeen in 1867; while Mary Duff married the excise officer's *raison d'être*, a wine merchant, Robert Cockburn, by whom she had four sons. Her portrait, taken after death (a somewhat gruesome sight), was reproduced in *Scottish Notes and Queries* (December, 1892). Dr. Blaikie suggested that Byron may have been in love with two Marys at once The idea is at least permissible in the great Byron saga.

Aberdeen is at this moment attempting to equip its strangely unstatued streets with a statue of Byron; but the movement has been attended by some extraordinary difficulties. Aberdeen has always assumed a curiously half proud, half shame-faced, allegiance to Byron. For instance, it was Dr. Alexander Kilgour (died 1874) who compiled a very frank (and anonymous) biography of Byron, under the title ·—

Lord Byron, from authentic sources, with remarks illustrative of his connection with the principal literary characters of the present day. "Dead scandals form good subjects for dissection."—*Don Juan.* London: Knight & Lacy, Paternoster Row; Aberdeen: W Gordon, A. Stevenson, D. Wyllie, and L. Smith, 1825 [Printed by William Aitken: pp. xvi , 207.]

The preface to the volume contains a few rather unreliable statements as to Byron's family history, and a few anecdotes about his residence in Aberdeen But nothing is extenuated.

Byron has six descendants still living (September, 1902). By his marriage (in 1815) with Anne Isabella (1792-1860), daughter of Admiral Sir Ralph Milbanke, sixth baronet (in 1856 she became entitled to the Barony of Wentworth by the death of her cousin the third Baron Scarsdale), he had an only child—

HON. ADA AUGUSTA NOEL, born December 10, 1815, in Piccadilly Terrace, London. She married, on July 8, 1835 (as his first wife), William King, eighth Lord King, Baron of Ockham. He was created Viscount Ockham and Earl of Lovelace in 1840, and took the additional name of Noel in 1860. He died, Dec. 29, 1893. She died, November 27, 1852, and was buried beside her father at Hucknall, Notts. She had:—

(1) HON. BYRON NOEL KING, Viscount Ockham. He was born, May 12, 1836, and succeeded to the peerage as Baron Wentworth, on the death of his grandmother (Lady Byron), in 1860. He died unmarried, September 1, 1862.

(2) RALPH GORDON KING-MILBANKE, the second and present Earl of Lovelace, born July 2, 1839. He succeeded his brother in 1862, and his father in 1893. Lord Lovelace assisted in editing the new edition of Byron issued by Mr. Murray. He married (1) in 1869 Fannie (died 1878), daughter of Rev. George Heriot; and (2) on December 30, 1880, Mary Caroline, daughter of the Right Hon James Stuart-Wortley (son of the first Baron Wharncliffe), by whom he has no issue. His half-brother (Lionel) is heir to the title. By his first wife Lord Lovelace has a daughter—

LADY ADA MARY KING-MILBANKE, born Feb. 26, 1871. She is, of course, the most direct descendant of Byron, belonging to the second generation now alive. She belongs to the fifteenth generation of the Gights.

(3) LADY ANNE ISABELLA NOEL KING-MILBANKE, born 1837, married, June 8, 1869, Wilfrid Scawen Blunt, poet, politician, and Arab horse-breeder. They have only one child—

JUDITH ANNE DOROTHEA BLUNT. She married, on February 2, 1899, at the Roman Catholic Church of Zeytun, Cairo, the Hon. Neville Stephen Bulwer-Lytton, second son of the second Earl Lytton, and grandson of the novelist Bulwer-Lytton. This is a most interesting literary alliance; the bride being the great-granddaughter of a poet (Byron) and the daughter of another (Blunt); the bridegroom being the grandson of a novelist (Bulwer-Lytton) and the son of a poet ("Owen Meredith"). The bride was given away (in her father's absence) by Lord Cromer (whose son, the Hon. Roland Baring, acted as best man). The honeymoon was spent at Heliopolis,

and the young couple were escorted part of the way by a bodyguard of mounted Bedouins They have—

 (1) NOEL ANTHONY SCAWEN BULWER-LYTTON, born April 7,
   1900
 (2) ANNE BULWER-LYTTON, born August 24, 1901. These
   children represent the sixteenth generation of the
   Gordons of Gight.

HOUSE OF GORDON.

APPENDICES TO VOLUME I.

LISTS OF GORDONS IN SCOTLAND.

NEW SPALDING CLUB.

PREFATORY NOTE.

THE appendices to this volume form part of the editorial scheme to supply a quarry as well as a structure—illustrated by the deductions of Abergeldie, Coclarachie and Gight, which show to what use the quarry may be put. They are intentionally confined to Scotland to begin with; and present in a handy form trustworthy information regarding the Gordons who owned land, studied at the Scots Universities, entered Parliament, or joined certain branches of the clerical and legal professions.

I.—THE RETOURS AND SERVICES OF HEIRS.

This appendix has been prepared—a very laborious task —by Mrs. Skelton, to whom the best thanks of the Club are due. The *Retours* and the *Services of Heirs*, though known to professional genealogists, are not always accessible. The entries have been extracted from the following works, which, while well known, are not easy to manipulate :—

Inquisitionvm ad Capellam Domini Regis Retornatarvm qvæ in pvblicis archivis Scotiæ adhvc servantvr abbreviatio [Edited by Thomas Thomson, Keeper of State Documents] Printed by command of his Majesty George III. in pursuance of an address of the House of Commons of Great Britain. Folio. Vols. I. and II., 1811, Vol. III., 1816.

Decennial Indexes to the Services of Heirs in Scotland. Commencing January 1, 1700. [Only the first two volumes, edited by John M. Lindsay, and comprising ten decades, down to 1800, have been indexed here.] Edinburgh: Printed for Her Majesty's Stationery Office Folio Vol. I (1700-49), 1863, Vol II (1750-99), 1870

The *Retours* were printed under the direction of Thomson, by command of the Crown, which, in answer to a petition from the House of Commons, dated July, 1800, appointed (in 1806) Commissioners to provide "for the better arrangement and preservation and more convenient use" of the Public Records Thomson (born 1768, died 1852), who was appointed Keeper of the Records in 1806, edited a long series of volumes, the most important of which were the *Acts of the Scots Parliament.* To the *Retours* he contributed a most instructive and highly condensed preface, which has to be studied closely. The *Retours* in Thomson's volumes, which come down to 1699, are in Latin and are arranged chronologically in each of the sections formed by the nature of the service as described below. The *Services*, which are in English, are a continuation of the *Retours*, but are arranged alphabetically in sections, each of which covers ten years. In this appendix will be found every person of the name of Gordon who was served heir of land in Scotland for two and a half centuries (1546-1800).

By the law of Scotland, on the death of a person possessed of freehold property, such property did not immediately become vested in the heir of the deceased person, but remained in abeyance until the person claiming to be the heir of the deceased person had established the fact of his kinship. Such being the case, it followed of course that some procedure was necessary to enable the person claiming to be heir or, for brevity, "the claimant," to have it judicially declared that the claimant was the heir to and entitled to succeed to and enjoy the lands of the deceased person, who is hereafter called "the ancestor". This judicial declaration was obtained in the following manner: On the death of the ancestor an order was issued by the Court of Chancery to the local judge (usually the sheriff) to make an inquiry into these points :—

(1) What were the lands the ancestor owned when he died.
(2) Whether the claimant was in fact the heir of the ancestor.
(3) Whether the claimant was of age.
(4) What was the value of the lands.
(5) Of whom, as feudal lord, the lands were held.
(6) By what feudal services the lands were held; in other words, what was the nature of and the incidents of the tenure.
(7) In whose possession the lands in question then were
(8) How the lands came to be in the possession of the person holding them and how long they had been so held

The document or order addressed to the sheriff commanding him to make the inquiry was called the " Brieve of Succession ". The local judge or sheriff had jurisdiction for a certain defined district only. Therefore, if the ancestor owned lands in various parts of Scotland it was necessary for a " Brieve of Succession" to be issued to the sheriff of every district involved. But, in order to avoid the same proceedings being gone through in different districts, an innovation was made, by which an officer of the Court of Session was appointed to make the inquiry concerning all the lands of the ancestor, wherever those lands might be situated.

The proceedings upon the Brieve of Succession were held before a judge and jury, and were described as a Service. When those proceedings were held before the local judge or sheriff they were called "Special Service," or "Service of an Heir in Special," for they related to lands in one district only ; whilst the proceedings before the officer of the Court of Session were called "General Service," or " Service of an Heir in General," as they related to all the lands of the ancestor, wherever those lands were situated

The verdict of the jury was transmitted to, and the " Brieve of Succession" was returned to, the Court of Chancery, where it was recorded, and an extract of the record was given to the claimant, and the extract so given was called the " Retour of the Service".

We have no certain knowledge of the ancient practice as to the registration of the " Retours of Service," but Thomson surmised that the verdict of the jury was retoured to Chancery " as a necessary step towards the feudal investiture of the heir," that is to say, the act by virtue of which the claimant was placed in possession of the lands of his ancestor. Thomson also notes :—

> That the original inquisitions were again delivered to the private party (the claimant), and not merely an extract, as at present, may be fairly conjectured from the many originals which yet remain in private custody.

In addition to the two classes of Inquisitions retoured to Chancery there were retours to a " Brieve of Tutory " and to a " Brieve of Idiotry or of Furiosity ". The former was for the purpose of ascertaining the person who ought to be appointed tutor to a claimant who was a minor. The latter was for the purpose of ascertaining the mental incapacity of the heir to the ancestor. If it were found that the heir was mentally incapable of managing his own affairs, then it was further found who was his nearest relative of proper age and capacity upon whom that management devolved.

There were two other sorts of retours, one as to the estimated value of the whole of the lands of a county or district ; the other for the purpose of ascertaining the real estate of which persons whose lands were forfeited for treason were in possession for five years preceding the dates of forfeiture.

Thomson sums up the importance of the Retours very neatly :—

> With certain limitations it [the Retour] may be considered as exhibiting an authentic history of the transmission by inheritance of the far greater part of the landed property of Scotland as well as that of the descent of the greater number of its considerable families during the course of the two last centuries. That part of the Record which precedes the date of the Scottish Statute of 1681 " concerning the

Election of Commissioners for Shires," derives a peculiar importance from its affording the appropriate evidence of a certain class of Freehold Qualifications.

Where are the ancient records of Chancery ? Some remarks by Lord Stair on a judgment of the Court of Session of 1624 throw light on the point. Stair says that "Services before the year 1550 were sufficient to satisfy . . . because at that time the books of Chancery were destroyed by war".

It ought perhaps to be explained that the contractions " A. E. " and " N. E. " in the *Retours* stand for " Auld Extent " and " New Extent ". These terms are explained by Skene in his *De Verborum Significatione*, 1597.

> EXTENT of landes signifies the rents, profites and issues of the samin, quhairof there is twa kindes, the AULD EXTENT and the NEW EXTENT. For it appearis that the rentall and valour of lands hes bin taxed and liquidat to ane certain sum of silver, conforme to the profites and dewties quhilk the lands payed at that time [the time of the Alexanders] quhilk is called the Auld and first Extent Bot because the revenues and dewties of land be progresse of time did increase and grow mair and mair, ane vther taxation and extent was made in the time of peace, as the former extent, conforme to the profites augmented as saide is quhilk is called, the New, or second, Extent.

The preface to the *Service of Heirs*, written by Mr. John M. Lindsay, describes the different kinds of heirs under Scots law as follows —

> *Heir.*—The term " Heir," without qualification, means nearest heir at law.
>
> *Heir of Line.*—This term means the same thing.
>
> *Heir of Conquest.*—The word " Conquest " means real property acquired by purchase or otherwise than by inheritance When a man dies intestate and childless in Scotland his inherited property goes to his immediate younger brother or heir of line, but his " Conquest " goes to his immediate elder brother (or to that brother's issue) as heir of conquest
>
> *Heir Portioner* means one of several females, or their issue, succeeding jointly.

Heir of Provision means an heir having right by settlement or will in the Scots form

Co-heir of.Provision means one of several heirs having right by settlement or will in the Scots form.

Heir Male of the Body and of Provision.—An heir is served in these terms when the lands stand destined to male descendants, excluding all female descendants and the issue of all females.

Heir Male and of Provision.—An heir is served in these terms when the lands stand destined to heirs male general—that is, not to male descendants only but also to other heirs male, collaterals or ascendants.

Heir of Entail, Taillie or Tailzie means an heir succeeding under the destination of an entail.

Heir "cum beneficio inventarii" means an heir who, doubting his predecessor's solvency, gives in an inventory of all his predecessor's real property, and thus obtains legal exemption from liability beyond the value of that property.

The index has been arranged on the following principle : 1. *Christian name,* the surname, which is, of course, always "Gordon," being omitted ; 2. the *place name* first mentioned ; 3. the *date* of the Retour or the Service. Where two dates are given the second refers to the registration.

II.—The Poll Book of Aberdeenshire.

This invaluable work was printed in two volumes (aggregating xxiv. and 1309 pp.) in a handsome quarto in 1844 under the title :—

List of Pollable Persons within the Shire of Aberdeen. 1696. Aberdeen. Printed by William Bennett, MDCCCXLIV.

The volumes were printed under the direction of Dr. John Stuart from the folio manuscript of 1541 pages, in the possession of General Gordon of Cairness, bearing the title :—

The Book or List off Poleable persons within the Shire off Aberdein and Burghs within the same : containing the names off the haill persones poleable and polemoney payable be them, conform to their respective capacities, according to the Act off Parliament anent Pole-Money daited the 25th day of June 1695 Faithfullie extracted ffurth of the Principall Lists of poleable persons off each paroch within the shyre, as they were reported by the Commissioners and Clerks for the severall paroches appointed for that effect. By William Hay collector appointed off the Polemoney payable ffurth off the said shire. And revised and examined by an quorum of the Commissioners of Supplie off the samen shyre and attested by them the first day of April 1696.

The MS. was submitted to the (old) Spalding Club, who relegated the printing of it to a committee of county gentlemen. The present appendix of Gordon entries has also been compiled by Mrs. Skelton. The late Mr. A. Dingwall Fordyce, of Fergus, Ontario, a great enthusiast on Aberdeenshire genealogy, made an index (of persons only), a model of neatness and accuracy. It is a MS. quarto of 271 pages, and is now in the possession of the New Spalding Club, to whom Mr. Dingwall Fordyce presented it in May, 1891. It is entitled :—

Extracts alphabetically arranged (Special and General) from the Poll Tax Book of Aberdeenshire (1696). (Special, pp 1-148 General, pp 151-262.) With list of orthographical variations. Synopsis of special extracts (S).

The Poll Tax was first imposed in May, 1693, to pay arrears due to the country and the army. Exceedingly unpopular, it was farmed out by the Government to Lord Ross and others for the sum of £44,000 stg. of tack duty. But in July, 1695, an Act was passed for turning the tack of the poll into a collection, on the ground that

The levying of money by pole was new, and as the countrey and others concerned had not observed the rules and ordinences contained in the Act of Parliament thereanent, the tacksmen were unable to pay the stipulated tack-duty unless they were allowed to exact the penal-

ties imposed by the Act, which would have tended to the disturbance
and oppression of the whole kingdom : therefore his Majesty liberated
the said tacksmen from the said tacks and tack duty, providing that
they should make just count and reckoning of all their intromissions
with the said Pole-money as if they had been only collectors

The Poll Tax was again put in force in 1695 (payable first
at Martinmas, the term being afterwards extended to October
15) to increase the army and navy.   The tax amounted to six
shillings per head, leviable on all except "poore persons" and
children under the age of sixteen, and "in families of all these
persons whose pole doth not exceed £1 10s Scots".   In addition to the six shillings, a cottar having a trade had to pay six
shillings more.   The following grading also was imposed ·—

Seamen	12 shillings Scots		
Tenants (on their valued rent)	$\frac{1}{100}$ part		
Merchants (with from 500 to 4,999 merks) . .	£2	10	0
,, (,, ,, 5,000 to 9,999 ,,) . .	4	0	0
,, (,, 10,000 merks and over) . .	10	0	0
Gentlemen (" so holden and repute ") . .	3	0	0
Heritors (with below £50 valued rent). .	0	20	0
,, (,, from £50 to £199) . . .	4	0	0
,, (,, ,, £200 to £499) . . .	9	0	0
,, (,, ,, £500 to £999) . . .	12	0	0
+ 2s. 6d. for each child *in familia*			
,, (with £1,000) . . .	24	0	0
+ £3 for each child *in familia*			
Lords	40	0	0
Viscounts	50	0	0
Earls	60	0	0
Marquises	80	0	0
Dukes	100	0	0
Widows (whose husbands would have been worth £1 10s. poll or over) . .	$\frac{1}{3}$ husband's poll		
Heiresses were subject to the same poll as their predecessors would have been			
Notaries, procurators and messengers-at-arms .	4	0	0

Writers, not to the Signet, Agents, Clerks of Inferior
    Civil Courts, Macers and Under-Clerks of
    Session .   .   .   .   £6 o o
Advocates, Writers to the Signet, sheriffs, doctors   12 o o
Commissioned officers in the Scots army . . two days' pay

The total tax collected in Aberdeenshire amounted to
£28,148 7s. 1d. Scots, or £2,345 13s. 7d. stg.

III.—Students at the Scottish Universities.

These lists have been compiled, partly from printed, partly
from manuscript sources, by Mr. P. J. Anderson. To each
name is prefixed the first year of the class to which the student
belonged.

The names of students at University and King's College,
Aberdeen, and at Marischal College and University, Aberdeen,
are taken from Mr. Anderson's *Roll of Alumni at University
and King's College*, 1596-1860 (Aberdeen University Studies :
No. 1. 1900), and his *Fasti Academiæ Mariscallanæ*, 1593-
1860. *Vol. II. : Officers, Graduates and Alumni* (New Spalding
Club, 1898).

The names of Glasgow graduates are taken for the period
prior to 1727 from the late Mr. Cosmo Innes' *Munimenta Universi-
tatis Glasguensis*, Vol III. (Maitland Club, 1854); for the period
subsequent to 1727, from Mr. W. Innes Addison's *Roll of the
Graduates of the University of Glasgow*, 1727-1897 (Glasgow,
1898). Mr. Addison has kindly supplemented the information
to be found in his admirable volume by furnishing the names of
all non-graduate alumni of the name of Gordon during the same
period, 1727-1897.

The names of Edinburgh graduates are taken from the late
Mr. David Laing's *Catalogue of the Graduates in the Faculties of
Arts, Divinity and Law of the University of Edinburgh since its*

Foundation (Bannatyne Club, 1858); and *List of the Graduates in Medicine of the University of Edinburgh from* 1705 *to* 1866 (Edinburgh, 1867). The Matriculation Albums of the University for the period 1634 to 1860 have also been searched for Gordon alumni by the Rev. Walter Macleod, Edinburgh, and the results incorporated with the extracts from the lists of graduates. The entries in the Edinburgh Albums are unfortunately very meagre and yield but slight means of identification.

None of the St. Andrews records have as yet been printed. Mr. J. Maitland Anderson, librarian to the University, has obligingly searched the Matriculation and Graduation Registers (1429 to 1879) for Gordon entries.

An attempt has been made to identify in the various University lists the Gordons who appear in Dr. Hew Scott's monumental work, *Fasti Ecclesiæ Scoticanæ the Succession of Ministers in the Parish Churches of Scotland from the Reformation A.D* 1560 *to the Present Time.* 3 vols. Edinburgh, 1866-71. The Gordons of the *Fasti* that have not been traced in the Universities are added in a separate list.

IV.—SCOTS MEMBERS OF PARLIAMENT.

The Gordons in this list are taken from Mr. Joseph Foster's *Members of Parliament, Scotland, including the Minor Barons, the Commissioners for the Shires and the Commissioners for the Burghs,* 1357-1882, *on the basis of the Parliamentary Return,* 1880, *with Genealogical and Biographical Notices.* London, 1882.

V.—MEMBERS OF THE FACULTY OF ADVOCATES, OR WRITERS TO H.M. SIGNET.

For the lists of Gordons who have been members of the Faculty of Advocates the best thanks of the Club are due to

Mr. J. T. Clark, Keeper of the Advocates' Library, who furnished the names for the present publication.

The names of Gordons who were Writers to the Signet are taken from Dr. T. G. Law's *History of the Society of Writers to Her Majesty's Signet, with a list of Members of the Society from* 1594 *to* 1890. Edinburgh, 1890.

J. M. B.

4th March, 1903.

ABBREVIATIONS.

A. E. .	.	Auld Extent
c. b. inv. .	. .	cum beneficio inventarii
conq.	.	conquest
d. .	. . .	daughter.
E. .	. . .	Extent.
f .	. . .	filius *or* filia.
gen. .	. .	general.
h. .	. . .	heir *or* hæres
hh. .	. .	hæredes.
I. de Tut. .		Inquisitio de Tutela.
I de Poss. Quinq	.	Inquisitio de Possessione Quinquennali

I. G		.	Inquisitio Generalis
I S .	. .	.	Inquisitio Specialis.
masc.		.	masculus.
N E.	. .	.	New Extent
port	. .	.	portioner, portionarius, *etc.*
prov .	. .	.	provision
s .	. .	.	son.
S H	.	.	Service of Heirs.
sp. .	.		sponsa.
spec .	.		special.
Supp.	. .	.	Supplement.
wid. .	. .	.	widow

APPENDIX I.

GORDONS MENTIONED IN SERVICES OF HEIRS IN SCOTLAND, FROM 1545 TO 1799.

—— de Baldornie, est fatuus et naturaliter idiota   I. de Tut., 26 Feb 1647

—— of Culvennan. *See* **Joan**, Barholme   S. H., 24 Jan. 1718

A., advocate. *See* **Robert**, Aberdeen   S. H., 24 Jan. 1712

Adam, Lieut. in Gen. Maitland's Regiment. *See* **Ann; Joan;**
    Theodosia   S. H., 27 June 1717

,,   de Aberlour. *See* **James**, Aberlour   I. G., 19 June 1697

,,   of Ardlogie, s. to Colonell Nathaniel, h of John of Ard-
    logie, his gudsir   I. G, 2 Jan. 1656

,,   of Ardoch, to his father Alexander of Ardoch—h gen.
                                           S. H., 9 May; 1 June 1753

,,   of Ardoch, to his father, Alexander of Ardoch, who
    died—March, 1753—h male spec. in the manse
    and croft of the Treasurer of Ross, and in
    Thomsonshill and part of Gallowbank, Ross-
    shire   S. H, 2 Sept.; 4 Oct 1757

,,   captain, of Auchanachy. *See* **Elizabeth**, Jamaica
                                           S. H., 23 Aug. 1782

,,   younger of Cairnfield, to his brother John, advocate,
    who died 11 April, 1793—h. spec. in the Barony
    of Linturk, including Drumdargue, Claymiln, etc.,
    Aberdeenshire   S H., 16 Aug.; 28 Aug. 1793

,,   s. of James of Cochlarachie. *See* **Charlotte**, Coch-
    larachie, **Harriet**, Cochlarachie   S. H., 9 Aug. 1779

,,   Sir, of Dalphollie. *See* **William** of Dalphollie
    I. G, 10 Dec., 1700; S. H.,   Dec. 1700,   S. H, 26 Feb. 1702

,,   goldsmith in Edinburgh. *See* **Helen**, Edinburgh   S. H., 6 May 1767

Adam, goldsmith in Edinburgh. *See* **William,** Edinb. S. H , 20 Nov. 1735

,, f. Alexandri aliquando in Chapeltoune de Eslemont, h
Adami, mercatoris in Leith, patrui   I. G., 27 Oct. 1698

,, in Leith *See* **Adam,** *supra.*

Agnes, wife of Geo. Gordon, minister at Alves, to her brother
David Brodie of Pitgaviny—co-h of prov. gen.
S H., 28 Oct 1746; 29 Jan. 1747

,, *See* **Margaret,** Auchlean   I. S (Wigton), 26 Oct. 1652.

,, h. Jacobi de Barnebarroch, avi,—in 3 mercatis et 10
solidatis terrarum de Gaitgill-Makilvernok,—25
solidatis terrarum de Gaitgill-M'Nische;—25
solidatis terrarum de Gaitgill olim occupatis per
quondam Fynlaum Watsoun, extendentibus in
integro ad 5 libratas terrarum antiqui extentus
infra parochiam de Barge.—A.E. 5l.; N.E. 15l.—
6 mercatis terrarum de Barnebarrache et Barnehowrie, cum principali mansione de Barnebarrach
et molendinis de Barnebarrach et Barnehowrie
antiqui extentus, infra parochiam de Colven.—
A.E 4l.; N.E. 12l.   I. S (Kirkcudb), 29 July 1602

,, h. port. praedicti Joannis [de Blaikat] in terris praedictis
See **Catharine,** Blaikat   I. S. (Kirkcudb.), 29 Oct. 1548

,, h. port. praedictae Margaretae [Blaket], sororis—in undecima parte dictarum terrarum. *See* **Catharine,**
Blaket   I. S. (Kirkcudb.), 14 April 1552

,, to her father Alexander of Crogo, writer in Edinburgh—
h. port and of line gen.   S H , 23 June; 30 June 1789

,, wife of Wm. Glendonwyne of Glendonwyne, to her sister
Mary, d. of Alex. of Crogo, who died 1790—h.
of line spec. in ½ of Crogo, including Knockclairn,
etc., and in ½ of Auchinreoch, etc., Kirkcudbrightshire   S. H., 4 Dec ; 30 Dec. 1790

,, above designed, to her father Alexander of Crogo, who
died in May or June, 1774—h of line spec. in
Barmark and in Upper and Nether Caldows,
Kirkcudbrightshire   S. H., 4 Dec.; 30 Dec. 1790

,, wife of Thos. Gordon, baker, Dumfries, to her father
William Kirkpatrick, merchant there—co-h. of
prov. gen.   S. H., 29 Mar.; 8 April 1794

Agnes, Crawford, wid. of Robert Gordon, sailor, Leith, to her
    brother James, brazier, Canongate—h. port. gen.
                                 S. H , 16 Sept. ; 18 Sept. 1766
    ,,   to her father Robert, sailor in Leith—co-h of prov
       gen.   S. H., 21 June ; 23 June 1791
    ,,   Janeta Frazer, f. Joannis Frazer aliquando fabri ferrarii
       burgensis de Inverness, procreata inter eum et
       Agnetam Gordoun, h port. Jacobi, fabri murarii
       in Inverness, avi,—Janeta, Margareta, et Maria
       Gordouns, hh. port. dicti Jacobi, patris,—in annuo
       redditu 16ol., correspondente 4,000m. de villa
       et terris de Salterhill, pro principali, et de villa
       et terris de Ettils, in parochia de Kinnedder, in
       speciale warrantum dictarum terrarum —E. 1d.
                                     I. S. (Elgin), 31 Nov. 1690
    ,,   Elizabeth Kirko, h. Agnetae Gordoun, matris, et
       Bessetae Gordoun, materterae,—in 20 solidatis
       terrarum antiqui extentus de Over Whytesyde,
       infra baroniam de Haliwood.—E. 2½m
                               I. S (Dumfries), 23 May 1662
    ,,   Maxwell, sp. Roberti Gordoune junioris de Shirmers,
       h. lineae gen. Gulielmi Maxwell, junioris de
       Monreith, fratris   I. G., 2 June 1681
    ,,   Maxuel, sp. Roberti Gordoun junioris de Shirmers, h.
       lineae gen. Gulielmi Maxwell senioris de Monreith,
       avi   I. G., 2 June 1681
Al., of Kinaldie. *See* **Janet,** Kinaldie.   S H , 9 Sept. 1740; 17 June 1741
Alexander, h. conq Patricii, fratris germani immediate junioris
                                 I. G., 8 Oct. 1633
    ,,   captain in the Earl of Orkney's regiment of foot
                                S H , 20 Aug. 1733
    ,,   burgensis de Abirdeen. *See* **John,** Knokleyth
                       I. S. Supp. (Aberd.), 12 Jan. 1579
    ,,   magister, f. legitimus quondam Joannis burgensis
       de Abirdein, inter illum et quondam Elspetham
       Crombie, h port. Domini Thomae Crombie de
       Kemnay militis, avunculi,—in terris praedictis.—
       E. 40s.   I. S (Aberd.), 20 July 1649
    ,,   burgensis de Aberdein   *See* **Juliana**   I G., 12 Jan. 1677

Alexander, burgensis de Aberdeen. *See* **George,** Aberdeen I. G., 19 July 1690

,,   in civitate veteris Aberdoniae, f. magistri Thomae
          in Kethocksmilne, h. Georgii de Nether Bodome,
          fratris germani,—in villa et terris de Neather
          Boddome cum parte vocata the Bass;—villa et
          terris de Over Boddom, infra parochiam de Insh.
          cum decimis.—A.E. 2l.; N.E. 8l.   I. S. (Aberd.), 22 June 1698

,,   merchant in Aberdeen, to his brother George of
          Sands, advocate—h. gen.   S. H , 18 April, 21 Apr. 1732

,,   barber in Aberdeen   *See* **Charles,** Warsaw S. H , 30 Aug 1733

,,   bookseller, Aberdeen.   John Largie, sergeant in
          Mackay's regt. of foot, to his aunt, Isabella
          Largie, wid. of Alex. Gordon, bookseller, Aber-
          deen—h. gen.   S. H. Supp , 20 Jan 1744

,,   residing in Aberdeen, to his father Alexander, ship-
          master there—h. gen.   S. H., 8 Nov.; 15 Nov. 1783

,,   shipmaster in Aberdeen.   *See* **Alexander,** *supra.*

,,   of Aberdour.   *See* **George** of Aberdour
                          S. H., 1 June 1791; S H , 4 Jan 1792

,,   of Aberdour.   *See* **William** of Aberdour   S. H., 20 Mar. 1793

,,   de Abirzeldi.   *See* **William,** magister, Abirzeldi
              I S. (Aberd.), 30 May 1601; I. S. (Aberd.), 17 June 1607,
                              I. S. Supp. (Aberd.), 31 July 1613

,,   de Achomachie.   *See* **Catherine,** Achomachie
                                  I. S. (Fife), 19 May 1698

,,   Penrose (Cumming) of Altyre, etc., to Sir William
          Gordon of Gordonstoun, bart.—h. of tail and
          prov. gen.   S. H., 25 May; 10 June 1795

,,   merchant, Amsterdam, to his father Robert of Cairn-
          field, Banff—h. male of prov. gen. S. H., 10 May; 27 June 1718

,,   of Ardoch.   *See* **Adam** of Ardoch
                          S. H., 1 June 1753, S. H., 4 Oct. 1757

,,   de Arradoull, h. Jacobi de Arradoull, fratris germani,
          —in villis et terris de Arradoull extendentibus ad
          8 bovatas terrarum, infra dominium de Einzie et
          parochiam de Raphane.—E. 2ol., etc., feudifermae
                                  I. S. (Banff), 23 Jul. 1663

,,   de Arradoull.   *See* **George,** de Arradoull
                                  I. S. (Banff), 18 Oct. 1692

                          (328)

Alexander, of Auchindolly, M.D. in Dumfries. *See* **Robert,**
   Bristol   S. H.,   6 Nov. 1778
,,   de Auchinreath. *See* **John** de Combrie   I. G., 15 Apr. 1665
,,   major-generall, of Auchintoull, Banff, to his father
   Alexander of Auchintoull—h. gen.   S. H., 27 June , 27 July 1713
,,   of Auchintoull. *See* **Alexander,** *supra.*
,,   major-general, of Auchintoul. *See* **Alexander** of
   Dorlathers   S. H., 30 July 1753
,,   of Auchintoul. *See* **Catharine** of Auchintoul S. H., 14 Sept. 1768
,,   of Auchleuchries. *See* **James** of Auchleuchries
        S. H., 23 Apr. 1751 ; S. H.,   2 Aug. 1768
,,   of Auchmunziel.   Alexander Forbes, son of Robt
   Forbes of Auchmunziel, to his gt. grandfather,
   Alexander Gordon of Auchmunziel—h. of prov.
   gen   S. H. Supp., 13 May 1745
,,   of Auchredy, to his father James of Auchredy—
   h. gen.   S. H., 18 Aug ; 2 Sept. 1709
,,   of Auchredy. *See* **James,** Auchredy   S. H., 25 Jan. 1740
,,   in the Customs at Ayr. *See* **Charles,** New York
          S H., 26 Mar. 1782
,,   de Balcray. *See* **Hugh** de Grange   I S. (Wigton), 23 Feb. 1608
,,   de Balery. *See* **Robert** de Bandane   I. G.,   2 Jan. 1607
,,   de Barnbarroch. *See* **James,** Barnbarroch
       I. S (Kirkcudb.), 21 Apr. 1556
,,   Barskeoche. *See* **Roger,** in Schirmers
       I. de Tut. Supp , 23 July 1577
,,   in Barskeoche. *See* **Roger,** in Schirmers
       I. de Tut. Supp., 23 July 1577
,,   de Barskeoche. *See* **George,** Barskeoche
   I. S. (Kirkcudb.), 27 Oct. 1607 ; I S (Wigton), 31 Oct. 1607 ;
       I. S (Kirkcudb), 10 Oct. 1609
,,   de Beldorney. *See* **George,** Beldorney
       I. S. (Banff), 20 Feb. 1627
,,   of Birkenburn. *See* **William** of Birkenburn S. H , 24 Apr. 1724
,,   h. Patricii de Brasmoir, patris   I. G , 18 Apr. 1626
,,   de Birsmoir, h. Patricii de Birsmoir, patris,—in
   terris et villa de Carnday, continentibus Auldtoun
   de Carnday, Over et Nether Cairndayis, Lin, cum
   molendino de Lin vel Carnday, et decimis garbali-

bus, in baronia de Cluny, infra parochiam de
  Kinairnie.—A.E. 40s., N.E. 8l.   I S. (Aberd.), 27 Sept 1637

Alexander, de Brasmoir, h. Patricii de Brasmoir, patris I. G., 5 Dec. 1665

,, de·Birsmoir, h. Joannis de . . avi   I. G., 7 Apr. 1666

,, of Blelack. *See* **John** of Blelack   S H., 16 Mar. 1723

,, merchant in Bordeaux, to his brother Charles,
    merchant in Edinburgh—h. of conq. gen.
                  S. H., 27 Jan. ; 31 Jan. 1728

,, in Borderside of Kelly   *See* **George,** in India
                        S. H , 2 Dec. 1793

,, merchant in Boulogne, to his father William,
    merchant there, once banker in Paris—h. gen.
            S. H., 11 Sept ; 19 Sept. 1729

,, merchant in Boulogne *See* **Robert,** Boulogne
                      S. H., 31 Dec. 1755

,, merchant in Boulogne. *See* **Robert** of Hallhead
          S. H., 8 Dec. 1759, S. H., 12 Dec. 1760

,, *See* **Joan,** Brokloch   I. S. (Kirkcudb.), 13   1615

,, of Cairnburrow. *See* **John** of Airthlock   S. H., 24 Dec. 1703

,, of Cairnborrow. *See* **John** in Finties   S. H., 11 July 1710

,, de Camdell, h. Jacobi de Tillisoules, patris   I. G., 18 Aug. 1696

,, son of W[illiam] of Campbelltoun, to his aunt
    Henrietta dau. of S. Broun of Mollance—h. port.
    gen. c. b. inv.   S H., 13 Feb. 1762

,, of Campbellton, to his father William of Campbell-
    ton, who died 18 Aug. 1785—h. spec. in Balma-
    cample or Campbellton, and Nether Campbellton,
    in the parish of Twynholm, Kirkcudbrightshire
              S. H., 5 May ; 16 Sept. 1789

,, to his father Alexander of Carltoun—h. gen. c. b.
    inv   S. H , 26 Aug. ; 5 Sept. 1743

,, of Carletoun. *See* **Alexander,** *supra.*

,, of Carleton, to his grandfather Nathaniel of Carle-
    ton—h. of taillie and prov. gen.   S. H , 3 Feb.; 16 Feb. 1773

,, of Carleton, to his grandfather Nathaniel of Carleton
    —h. gen.   S H., 23 Feb. ; 29 Mar. 1774

,, of Carlton *See* **John** of Carlton   S H., 30 Aug. 1790

,, younger of Carlton. *See* **John** of Carlton S. H., 30 Aug. 1790

,, de Castraman, h. Issobellae Muirhead, matris,—in 5

mercatis terrarum antiqui extentus de Castraman
et Darregoune, infra parochiam de Girtoun.—A.E.
3l 6s. 8d.; N.E. 1ol. I. S (Kirkcudb), 20 Mar. 1610

Alexander, de Castramen. *See* **Elspet,** Castramen
 I. S. (Kirkcudb.), 30 Jan 1644

,, in Chapeltoune de Eslemond. *See* **Adam,** Chapeltoune I. G., 27 Oct 1698

,, de Clone. *See* **William,** Clone
 I. S. Supp. (Wigton), Jan. 1596

,, de Clonyeard, h. masc. Joannis de Clonyeard,
 patris,—in 5 mercatis terrarum de Clonyeard, infra
 parochiam de Kirkmaden in Rynis.—A.E. 5m.,
 N.E. 1ol. I S (Wigton), 22 Feb. 1687

,, of Cloves *See* **Charles,** Cloves S. H., 28 July 1718

,, h masc. domini Thomae de Cluny militis,
 patris,—in villa et terris de Carvechin, Thornywray, Corsistane, Periesmylne, Sleauche cum
 park, Adamstoun, Silverhillok, Weistroune,
 Mutehillok, Boigheid, Newtoun ;—tertia parte
 villae et terrarum de Garie ;—bina parte terrarum
 de Chappeltoun ;—tertia parte de Wedderburne,—
 bina parte de Brumhill ;—tertia parte de Thomastoun ;—bina parte de Comalegie ; in baronia de
 Kynmondie per annexationem.—A E. 19m., N.E
 5ol. 13s. 4d. I. S. (Aberd.), 11 July 1607

,, h. talliae Georgii f Georgii de Cochlarrachie, fratris
 immediate senioris I. G., 24 July 1661

,, of Coldwells. *See* **Elizabeth,** Coldwells; **Isobel,**
 Coldwells S. H , 7 Feb. 1766

,, of Coldwells. *See* **Elizabeth,** Coldwells S. H., 1 Sept.1780

,, of Coldwells *See* **Fabian,** col. Polish service
 S. H., 23 Sept. 1783

,, in Collarhead, once in Achynachie. *See* **Alexander,**
 of Edintore S. H., 29 June, 9 July 1742

,, h. prov. Alexandri in Corriedoune, patris I. G , 8 Oct. 1633

,, in Corriedoune. *See* **Alexander,** *supra.*

,, of Crogo, writer in Edinburgh. *See* **Agnes,** Crogo ,
 Mary, Crogo S. H., 30 June 1789

,, of Crogo. *See* **Agnes,** Crogo S H , 30 Dec. 1790

Alexander, de Culvenen.　*See* **William** de Culvenen　I. G.,　6 Feb. 1679
　　,,　　of Culvennan　*See* **William** of Culvennan　S. H.,　4 Mar. 1703
　　,,　　of Cumry.　*See* **Catharine,** Cumry
　　　　　:　　　　　　　　　　　　　　　S H , 24 Feb. ; 27 Feb. 1779
　　,,　　portioner of Dallachy.　*See* **John,** Dallachy S. H.,　21 Aug. 1727
　　,,　　of Dorlathers, to his uncle Major-General Alexander
　　　　　of Auchintoul—h. gen.　　　　　S. H., 24 July ; 30 July 1753
　　,,　　in Drumfald.　*See* **Patrick,** Drumfald　I. G.,　19 July 1684
　　,,　　Spalding-Gordon, advocate, to his uncle Samuel
　　　　　Spalding of Dullarg—h. gen.　　S. H., 3 Feb ;　3 Feb. 1790
　　,,　　h. Alexandri in Dunce, patris　　　I. G.,　9 Mar. 1609
　　,,　　in Dunce.　*See* **Alexander,** *supra.*
　　,,　　de Erlestoun, h. Joannis de Erlestoun, patris,—in
　　　　　1 mercata terrae de Erlistoun ;—1 mercata terrae
　　　　　de Mylntoun ,—1 mercata terrae de Ardoch ;—
　　　　　dimidia mercata terræ de Over Barley ,—dimidia
　　　　　mercata terrae de Blaquharne ,—1 mercata terrae
　　　　　de Knokgry, et 2½ mercatis terrarum de Marbrok,
　　　　　cum molendino de Erlestoun, in dominio de
　　　　　Erlestoun et parochia de Dalry.—A.E. 7m. 6s. 8d.;
　　　　　N.E. 22m. 6s. 8d.—dimidietate terrarum de Quhyt-
　　　　　park.—E. 8l. 3s. 4d.—terris de Airdis, Over,
　　　　　Middill et Nather, in dominio Gallovidiae subtus
　　　　　Crie.—E. 20l. 3s. 4d etc.—40 solidatis terrarum
　　　　　antiqui extentus de Monydow ,—40 solidatis ter-
　　　　　rarum ejusdem extentus de Barmoffatte in baronia
　　　　　de Kirkpatrik-Durhame —E 11l. I.S. (Kirkcudb.), 23 Oct. 1628
　　,,　　de Earlestoun, h. Elizabethae unius haeredum por-
　　　　　tionariarum Joannis de Blaiket aviae,—in duo-
　　　　　decima parte 14 mercatarum terrarum de Blaiket et
　　　　　Lag, cum duodecima parte molendini de Blaiket
　　　　　antiqui extentus, in parochiis de Ure et Girtoun
　　　　　respective.—A.E. 15s. 6d. et tertia parte 2d. ;
　　　　　N.E. 46s. 8d.　　　　　　I. S (Kirkcudb.), 29 July 1634
　　,,　　of Earlstoun.　*See* **William,** Mr of Earlstoun
　　　　　　　　　　　　　　　　　I S. (Kirkcudb.), 23 Jan. 1655
　　,,　　nuper de Earlstone.　*See* **William,** Magister de
　　　　　Earlestone　　　　　　I de Poss. Quinq.,　3 Sept. 1686
　　,,　　de Earlstone, h. Alexandri de Earlstone, avi　I. G.,　4 Apr. 1700

Alexander, de Earlstone *See* **Alexander,** *supra.*

,,   of Earlstone, Kirkcudb., to his grandfather Alexander
of Earlstone—h. gen.   S H , 4 April 1700 , 29 Jan   1711

,,   of Earlstone   *See* **Alexander,** *supra.*

,,   of Earlstoun.   *See* **Thomas,** Earlstoun   S. H.,   5 Feb   1724

,,   s. of G., writer in Edin , to his g^{d}father George,
messenger there—h. gen.   S. H., 29 April ;   3 May 1704

,,   writer in Edinburgh.   *See* **Elizabeth,** Auchinhalrigg
S. H , 20 Feb. 1724

,,   of Edintore, to his uncle Alexander in Collarhead,
once in Achynachie, who died   —h. male spec.
in 1,371 merks over the lands of Cotts in the
parish of Longbryde, Elgin   S. H., 29 June ;   9 July 1742

,,   of Edintoir.   *See* **Isobel,** Midmar   S. H , 22 Apr   1763

,,   in Old Manse of Fintray.   *See* **Elizabeth,** Fintray,
Jean, Fintray   S. H , 22 Mar. 1775

,,   to his father Robert, postmaster in Fochabers—h
gen.   S. H., 31 July 1733 ; 21 Jan. 1734

,,   of Forskan.   *See* **John** of Drumquhynle   S. H ,   4 Mar. 1713

,,   in Garlerge.   *See* **John,** Garlerge
I. G., 28 July 1657 , I S. (Kirkcudb), 28 July 1657

,,   de Glengerrack.   *See* **Charles** de Glengarrack
I. S. (Banff), 29 Nov. 1692

,,   (or Davidson) of Gight, son of Lady Mary of Gight,
to his father Alexander Davidson of Newtoun,
who died   Feb. 1712—h. male spec in the
Newtoun of Wranghame, Glenestoun, Skares,
Melvinside, etc., Aberdeenshire   S. H., 10 Jan. , 20 Feb. 1735

,,   (or Davidson) of Gight, to his grandfather Alexander Davidson of Newtoun—h gen.
S. H., 10 Jan. , 20 Feb. 1735

,,   of Gight, to his granduncle James Davidson of
Tillimorgan who died   Sept. 1720—h. of line
and prov. spec. in Tillimorgan, Sauchenloan,
Graystone and Catden, all in the parish of Culsalmond, Aberdeenshire   S. H., 10 Jan. ; 20 Feb. 1735

,,   (or Davidson) of Gight, to his grandfather Alexander Davidson, of Newtoun—h. of line and of
prov. gen.   S. H., 28 July 1739 ; 18 Feb. 1740

Alexander (or Davidsone), of Gight, to his father Alexander
    Davidson of Gight—h. of prov. gen.
                        S. H., 28 July 1739; 18 Feb. 1740

  „   (or Davidson) of Gight, to his mother Mary of
        Gight—h. male and of prov. gen. S. H., 29 Jan., 18 Feb. 1740

  „   (or Davidsone) of Gight, to his granduncle George
        Davidson of Cairnbrogie—h of prov gen.
                        S. H., 8 April, 9 May 1740

  „   (or Davidson) to his father Alexander (or Davidson)
        of Gight, who died   Jan. 1760—h of taillie and
        prov. spec. in Newtoun of Wrangham, Glen-
        niestown, Skairs, Mellenside, etc., Aberdeenshire
                    S. H. Supp., 18 Apr.; 29 Apr. 1760

  „   (or Davidson) of Gight   *See* **Alexander,** *supra*

  „   (or Davidson) of Gight. *See* **George,** Gight
            S. H , 29 Apr. 1760; S. H., 1 May 1777

  „   of Glendaveny. *See* **Jean,** Glendaveny   S. H , 10 Aug. 1774

  „   to his father William of Greenlaw—h. gen. c. b
        inv.   S H., 7 Nov.; 23 Nov. 1758

  „   merchant in Greenock. *See* **Archibald,** Greenock
                      S. H., 18 Aug. 1739

  „   captain, portioner of Hassingtoun. *See* **George** of
        Gordonbank   S. H., 11 Sept. 1772

  „   advocate. *See* **James,** of Hilton, doctor   S. H., 22 June 1736

  „   Spalding-Gordon of Holm. *See* **Alexander** Spald-
        ing-Gordon, of Shirmers   S. H., 22 May 1778

  „   Spalding-Gordon of Holm. Samuel Spalding,
        physician, Devizes, to his brother Alexander
        Spalding-Gordon of Holm, who died 5 Nov. 1794
        —h spec c. b. inv., in Killochy, Knocksley,
        Hardlands, and Cubbox   S. H Supp , 28 Oct ; 1 Nov. 1799

  „   Duke of Gordon, to his father Cosmo George, Duke
        of Gordon, who died 5 Aug. 1752—h. male and
        of line spec. in the Marquisate, Earldom and
        Lordship of Huntly, etc., Aberdeenshire; Braes
        of Enzie, Banffshire; Lochaber, etc., Inverness-
        shire   S. H., 9 Feb.; 25 Mar. 1754

  „   Duke of Gordon to his father Cosmo George, Duke
        of Gordon—h. gen.   S. H., 9 Feb.; 25 Mar. 1754

Alexander, formerly Wemyss, surgeon in Huntly. *See* **Francis,**
    Craighall   S. H , 15 Mar 1791
    ,,   in Kelly. *See* **George,** in India   S. H., 2 Dec. 1793
    ,,   magister, h. Elspetae Crombie sponsae quondam
    Joannis, matris,—in equali dimidietate terrarum
    et baroniae de Kemnay, comprehendente terras
    dominicales de Kemnay vulgo Auldmaynes,
    Litlemaynes, et Mylntoun de Kemnay nuncupatas,
    cum parte dictarum terrarum nuncupata Insche
    de Mylntoun de Kemnay, et petia terrae nuncupata
    Haugh de Slugartie, jacente ex boreali parte aquae
    de Don ;—terras de Elisounwall ,—molendinum
    de Kemnay ;—terras de Over et Nether Auchqu-
    hoythies, Racharrald, Boigfur, Glenheid, Parkhill,
    ·Les-changie, croftas ejusdem, Wreattoun, Pektillim,
    croftam de Paradyce, croftas terrarum dominicalium
    de Cobleseat, salmonum piscariam super dictam
    aquam de Don, cum cymba portatoria lie ferrie-
    boat ; omnes unitas in baroniam de Kemnay —
    A E. 55s ; N.E 11l. xix.   I. S. (Aberd.), 2 Mar. 1648
    ,,   Vicecomes de Kenmuir. *See* **John,** magister, Ken-
    muir   I. S. (Kirkcudb.), 20 Sept 1698
    ,,   of Kilgour. *See* **John** of Kilgour   S H., 18 Dec. 1723
    ,,   of Kings-grange, collector of customs, Montserrat,
    America, to his brother Brigadier-General Patrick,
    of Kingsgrange, who died   Aug. 1776—h spec.,
    c. b. inv. in Grange, Kilquhenidie, etc.
                               S. H., 14 Oct. , 22 Oct. 1777
    ,,   of Kinmundy. *See* **James** of Techmuirie
    S H., 2 Feb. 1727 , S H , 18 April 1735 , S H., 17 July 1741
    ,,   in Kinnedour. *See* **Lewis,** Kinnedour   S. H., 6 Aug. 1718
    ,,   of Kirkland. *See* **Elizabeth,** Kirkland , **Margaret,**
    Kirkland   S. H., 3 Dec 1731
    ,,   of Kirkland. *See* **Alexander** of Littleknox   S H., 6 May 1788
    ,,   in Kirkmabrick   *See* **John** de Cairnfeild   I. G , 11 Jan. 1687
    ,,   de Knockbrex. *See* **Samuel,** Dumfries
                               I. de Tut , 4 April 1683
    ,,   de Knockgray   *See* **William** de Dundeugh
                         I. de Poss. Quinq., 31 Aug. 1682

Alexander, h. masc. Georgii de Lesmoir, patris,—in terris de
     Grodie, in baronia de Kynnadie —A.E. 10s., N.E.
        361.   I. S. (Aberd.), 3 Oct 1600
  „   h. Georgii de Lesmoir, patris,—in terris de Glascow
     forrest in baronia de Carnecrumlem, et per annexa-
     tionem in baronia de Glencuthill.—A.E 20s;
     N.E. 4l.   I. S (Aberd.), 20 Dec. 1600
  „   de Lesmoir. *See* **James** de Lesmoir
                       I. S. (Aberd.), 10 Apr. 1610
  „   Sir, of Lessmore, to his cousin Sir William of
     Lessmore, who died 15 Sept. 1750—h. male
     spec. in parts of Chappeltown, of Weatherburn,
     of Broomhill, of Carnlogie, Sleeack, etc.
                S. H., 23 Jan., 23 Apr. 1751
  „   Sir, of Lesmoir, bart., to his brother Captain John
     —h. of conq. gen.   S. H., 28 Mar ; 27 Apr. 1764
  „   Sir, of Lesmoir, bart., to his grandfather Sir James,
     of Lesmoir, bart.—h. male gen.
            S. H., 23 Oct. 1765; 24 July 1766
  „   of Letterfourie, to his father James of Letterfourie
     —h. gen.   S H , 12 July, 15 July 1791
  „   of Letterfourie, to his brother James of Letterfourie
     —h. gen.   S. H., 12 July; 15 July 1791
  „   of Letterfourie *See* **James** of Letterfourie S H , 13 Feb. 1798
  „   of Little Cocklaw, to his brother James of Little
     Cocklaw—h. gen.   S. H., 7 Feb. 1766 ; 7 Dec. 1771
  „   of Littleknox, to his grandfather Alexander of
     Kirkland—h. of line and conq gen.
               S. H , 26 Apr.; 6 May 1788
  „   of Littleknox, to his grandfather John Cannon of
     Littleknox—h. of line and conq. gen.
               S. H., 26 Apr.; 6 May 1788
  „   in Lochans. *See* **Robert,** Lochans
         I. G., 25 Apr. 1615; I S. (Kirkcudb.), 10 Oct. 1615
  „   in Lochanes. *See* **James,** Lochanes
                 I. S. (Kirkcudb.), 29 Oct. 1633
  „   of Logie. *See* **Robert** of Logie   S. H., 11 Oct. 1752
  „   de Mercartnay. *See* **James** de Mercartnay
                 I. S. (Kirkcudb.), 3 Nov 1607

Alexander, de Mundork   *See* **John,** Mundork   I. G , 30 Aug. 1626

„   de Over Barskeoche. *See* **John** de Over Barskeoche   I. S. (Kirkcudb.), 24 Feb. 1631

„   f. Gulielmi de Pinkaitland. *See* **Patrick,** Pinkaitland   I. G., 8 Feb 1690

„   de Pitlurg, h. Roberti de Pitlurg, avi,—in villis et
terris de Over Kinmundy et terris dominicalibus;
—villa et terris de Dourie;—villa et terris de Miln-
breck, cum molendino;—villa et terris de Milnhill,
villa et terris de Pettiemarkhouse,—villa et terris
de Smallburne;—villa et terris de Kinknockie, in
se comprehendente villam et terras de Auldtoun
ejusdem,—Nethertoun alias Welstrype, et alias
Pettindreichseat, Backhill alias Barackseat, in
baronia de Kinmundy et parochia de Deer, erectis
in baroniam de Kinmundy.—A.E. 5l.; N.E. 2ol.
I. S. (Aberd), 5 Oct. 1692

„   de Pitlurg, h. masc. Roberti de Pitlurg, patris,—
in terris de Pitlurges, et terris de Auquhorties
superiore et inferiore vulgo Over et Nether, cum
molendino de Auquhorties vocata Turnash, et
crofta terrae de Pittinfure vocata Letochie, extendente ad 1½ davatam terrae, infra baroniam de
Keith et parochiam de . . .—E. 22l. 6s. 8d. feudifirmae   I. S. (Banff), 11 Oct. 1698

„   to his father James, minister at Rosenath—h. gen.
S. H., 23 July 1707 ,   Mar. 1708

„   in Scheilgrein   *See* **James** in Drymmeis   I. G., 1 July 1614

„   of Shirmers, to his father William of Shirmers,
who died   Jan. 1716—h. spec. in the lands of
Cubbox and in 6,000 merks over Garlorgs, etc.
S. H., 23 June; 21 Sept. 1719

„   of Shirmers. *See* **Robert** of Shirmers
S. H., 24 Oct. 1755, S. H., 8 July 1756

„   Spalding-Gordon of Shirmers, to his father Alexander
Spalding of Holm—h. gen.   S. H., 20 May; 22 May 1778

„   de Siddera, h. Alexandri de Siddera, avi   I G., 27 July 1647

„   de Siddera. *See* **Alexander,** *supra.*

„   de Siddera, h. Joannis de Siddera, patris   I. G , 27 July 1647

(337)

Alexander, de Siddera, h. Joannis apparentis de Siddera, fratris

I. G., 27 July 1647

„ de Stradowne, mente captus fatuus et furiosus,—et
Georgius Marchio de Huntlie frater legitimus natu
maximus dicti Alexandri,—propinquior consanguineus patris dicti Alexandri   I de Tut., 3 Oct 1606.

„ Comes, h. Joannis Comitis Sutherlandiae, patris,—
in comitatu Sutherlandiae, et omnibus terris
ejusdem comitatus, cum castro de Dunrobyn,
piscationibus in aqua salsa et dulci, advocationibus
ecclesiarum et capellaniarum, infra vicecomitatum
de Inverness.—A.E. 500m ; N E. 1,000m.

I. S. (Sutherl.), 8 July 1573

„ de Swellend. See **Helen,** Swellend   I. S (Aberd.), 1 Jan. 1669

„ of Techmuirie. See **James** of Techmuirie   S. H , 1 Aug. 1729

„ de Torquhane. See **John,** Torquhane

I. S. Supp. (Kirkcudb), 30 Oct. 1582

„ magister, de Tulloche   See **William** de Tulloch

I. S. (Banff), 7 Dec 1637

„ of Tulloch, h. of William of Tulloch, his father,—in
the lands of Nether Tulloch, with the croft and
ferrie coble upon the water of Done, within the
parochin of Monymusk;—the lands of Over
Tulloch and Dipstoun, with the wood and salmond
fishing upon the water of Done, within the
parochin of Monymusk and regalitie of Sanct-
androis.—E. 24l.—The lands of Little Abercatie
lyand as forsaid ,—the half of the lands of Noth,
in the baronie of Strathbogie, in warrandice of the
lands of Abercatie —E. 12l. 8s   I. S. (Aberd.), Nov. 1656

„ of Wardhouse, s. of John of Beldorny, to his
granduncle Arthur of Wardhouse, who died
Oct 1760 — h. of taillie and prov. spec. in
Wardhouse and in Old Glanderston, etc

S. H. (Aberd.), 2 Sept. 1763

„ h. magistri Rogeri, patris,—in 5 mercatis terrarum
de Welcrage (vel Balcrage) antiqui extentus, in
parochia de Candidge —E 20m 6s. 8d

I. S. (Wigton), 31 Oct. 1598

Alexander, of Wardhouse, to his cousin Catherine of Wardhouse (wife of Capt. George Sempill), who died
5 Feb. 1762—h. of taillie and prov. spec. in
Cookshill, Garryhill, Fechlachie, Kinclune, etc
         S. H. (Aberd.), 12 Aug , 2 Sept.1763
 ,, of Wardhouse. *See* **Charles** of Wardhouse S H., 5 Sept 1770
 ,, of Whiteley. Margaret Grant at Dalmenach, to
her uncle Alexander Gordon of Whiteley, Sheriff-
Depute of Moray—h. port. gen S. H., 3 Dec , 29 Dec 1783
 ,, of Whiteley. *See* **Janet,** Hillockhead S. H., 29 Dec. 1783
 ,, of Woodhall, to his brother George (son of Alexander
of Woodhall), who died   —h spec. in the
tenandry of Woodhall, including Knockendunce,
Tripslaw and Waddelum, Haddington
         S. H , 18 Aug , 20 Oct. 1746
 ,, of Woodhall. *See* **Alexander,** *supra.*

Ann, to her father Adam, Lieut. in Gen. Maitland's regiment—
  h. port. gen   S. H., 16 Apr. , 27 June 1717
 ,, d. of F[rancis ?], shoemaker in Aberdeen. *See* **James,**
Aberdeen   S. H., 17 Jan. 1799
 ,, domina, h dominae Margaretae Irving, sponsae Caroli
Comitis de Aboyn, matris   I. G., 17 June 1665
 ,, d. of Js. of Banchory, to her aunt Ann, dau. of Rt.
Cumming of Birness—co-h. of prov. gen. S. H., 7 May 1740
 ,, to her brother Major Thomas of Clerkseat — co-h. of
prov gen   S. H., 12 Sept. ; 17 Sept 1740
 ,, wife of W. Forbes, gardener, Dunrobin, to her brother
Robert, s of George, tacksman of Culmaly—h.
port. gen   S. H., 24 May 1769
 ,, Brown, wife of John Gordon, writer in Edinburgh, to her
son Francis—h. of prov. gen S H., 28 Nov 1717 ; 27 June 1718
 ,, Brown *See* **John,** writer, Edinburgh S. H Supp. ; 31 Dec. 1719
 ,, Edinburgh. Isobel and Margaret Cheyne to their mother
Ann Gordon, wife of Charles Cheyne, merchant in
Edinburgh—h port ·gen S. H., 13 Nov. , 19 Nov. 1771
 ,, wife of Dr. And. Brown, Falkland, to her father Thomas, prof.
of philosophy, Aberdeen—h. gen. S H., 15 July ; 26 July 1799
 ,, to her brother John of Gordonbank—h. port. gen.
         S H , 6 Apr ; 21 Apr. 1796

Ann, h. Georgii feoditarii de Kincaldrum, f. fratris, — in
terris propriis baroniae de Kincaldrum comprehendentibus terras dominicales de Kincaldrum,
Buchtiehillok, et molendinum de Kincaldrum ,—
dimidietatem terrarum de Carrot ,—tenandriam
terrarum de Kincreich —A.E. 4l 10s , N E. 18l.
—terris templariis de Kincaldrum in parochia de
Methie.—E. 3s. feudifirmae　　　 I S. (Forfar), 16 Jan. 1662

　,,　Broune sp. Joannis Gordone junioris de Kingoodie, h.
Joannis Broune mercatoris in Edinburgo, avi
　　　　　　　　　　　　　　　　　I. G , 17 Aug. 1697

　,,　wife of John, farm servant in Main, to her father John,
farm servant, Elgin—h. gen.　S. H., 2 Dec 1772 ;　7 Jan 1773

　,,　d. of Francis of Miln of Kincardine, to her brother Hugh
of Miln of Kincardine—h gen.　　S H., 4 July , 4 Aug 1766

　,,　wife of Lieut. Thomas Stewart in Keithmore, to her father
Francis of Mill of Kincardine, who died　　 Oct.
1747—h. spec. in the lands, mill and mill lands
of Kincardine　　　　　　　　S. H , 3 Aug. , 26 Sept 1770

　,,　wife of George Gordon of Sheilagreen, to her father James
Donaldson of Cocklaw—h gen　S H., 16 Apr. ; 19 Apr. 1746

　,,　wife of George Gordon of Sheilagreen.　*See* **James,**
Sheilagreen　　　　　　　　S. H , 22 April ; 10 June 1747

Archibald, s. of Peter of Ardmeallie.　*See* **James,** Ardmeallie
　　　　　　　　　　　　　　　　　S H , 11 Apr. 1753

　,,　merchant in Greenock, to his father Alexander,
merchant there—h gen.　　S. H., 14 Aug ; 18 Aug. 1739

　,,　of Halleaths, to his father Gilbert of Halleaths—
h gen., c. b. inv　　　　S. H., 20 Mar., 30 Mar. 1790

　,,　of Minidow.　*See* **Gilbert,** Dumfries
　　　　　　　　S H., 12 June 1754 ; S H , 23 Aug 1759

Arthur, of Wardhouse.　*See* **Catharine** of Wardhouse
　　　　　　　　S H., 14 Feb 1761, S. H., 30 Sept. 1761

　,,　of Wardhouse.　*See* **Alexander** of Wardhouse
　　　　　　　　　　　　　　　S. H , 2 Sept. 1763

Barbara.　*See* **Christina,** Branelane　　I S (Aberd.), 6 Oct. 1669

　,,　wife of James Gordon of Hilton, M.D., to her sister
Ann, d. of Rt. Cumming of Birness—h port. of
line and prov. gen.　　　　　　S. H , 7 May 1740

Barbara, wife of Dr. James Gordon. *See* **John,** Pitlurg

S. H., 29 Jan 1783

,, *See* **Margaret,** Kirkwall   I. S (Orkney) 25 Nov.
1656; I G., 16 Dec. 1656; I S. (Orkney), 8 Feb 1662

Beatrix, h port. praedicti Joannis [de Blaikat], patris,—in
terris praedictis. *See* **Catharine,** Blaikat

I. S. (Kirkcudb.), 29 Oct. 1548

Benjamin, of Balbethan, to his father James of Balbethan—
h. gen.   S H., 7 Feb.; 24 April 1739

Bessie. *See* **Agnes,** Over Whytsyde   I. S. (Dumfries), 23 May 1662

Catharine Wardlaw, wife of James Gordon, merchant in Aberdeen, to her mother Henrietta Colin—h gen.

·   S H., 1 May; 4 May 1787

,, sp. Alexandri Gordone de Achomachie, h port
Joannis Martine de Lattons, patris, — magis-
ter Thomas Martine incola in St. Androws f
Elizabethae Martine f dicti Joannis Martine,—et
Margareta Leitch sp. Alexandri Ferrier ballivi de
St. Androws, et f Helenae Martine f dicti Joannis
Martine, hh port. dicti Joannis Martine, avi,—in
terris de Auchintrochane alias Midle, Wester, et
Norther Lathons vocatis, infra regalitatem Sancti
Andreae.—A.E 6s 8d , N.E. 26s. 8d.

I. S. (Fife), 19 May 1698

,, of Auchintoul, to her brother Alexander of Auchintoul, who died 30 Mar., 1768—h. of line and
prov. spec., in Auchintoul, etc., Banff; and in
Lathers, etc , Aberd. and Banff   S. H., 12 Aug.; 14 Sept 1768

,, of Auchentool. *See* **Frederica,** Auchentool   S H , 28 Aug. 1798

,, wid. of Alex. Forbes of Blackford, to her brother
James of Badenscoth—h. port. of line and prov.
gen.   S. H., 1 July; 10 July 1778

,, h. port. Joannis de Blaikat (qui obiit in conflictu de
Pinkiecleuch), patris,—in 14 mercatis terrarum de
Blaikat et Lag antiqui extentus, in parochiis de
Girtoun et Ur.—E. 3m. 6s 8d. I. S. (Kirkcudb.), 29 Oct. 1548

,, h. port Margaretae, sororis,—in undecima parte
10 solidatarum ex 9 mercatis terrarum de Blaket,
cum undecima parte molendini de Blaket, ex-

tendente ad 11 denariatas terrarum.—A.E. 11d.;
N.E 33d —6 denariatis terrarum de 5 solidatis 6
denariatis terrarum ex 5 mercatis terrarum de Lag
antiqui extentus in parochia de Ur et Girthoun.—
A.E. 6d.; N.E. 11d.   I. S. (Kirkcudb.), 14 Apr. 1552

Catharine, wife of George Rose, to her cousin David Bridges in
     Bullcamp, Suffolk—h. port. gen.   S H., 4 Feb.; 12 Feb. 1777

,,   Scott, wid. of Alex Gordon of Cumry, to her
     nephew, Patrick Scott-Hepburn of Kingstone—
     h. port. gen.   S. H , 24 Feb.; 27 Feb. 1779

,,   to her father Doctor James of Fechell, who died
     Aug., 1723—h. port. spec in the lands of Fechell
     in the parish of Ellon   S. H., 17 July; 29 Aug. 1741

,,   wife of John Byron, to her father George of Gight—
     h. of prov. and in gen.   S. H., 30 Sept., 21 Oct. 1785

,,   wife of Jas. Baird, merchant, Glasgow, to her grand-
     father John, physician there—co-h. of prov. gen.
           S. H., 30 May, 18 June 1792

,,   to her brother George of Glengerrick, who died in
     May or June, 1747—h. port. and of line spec.
     in the barony of Glengerrick, including Auchivis,
     Berryleys, Newmiln of Strathisla, etc, Banff
           S H., 16 Aug.; 25 Aug. 1748

,,   Kelly   *See* **George,** India   S. H., 2 Dec. 1793

,,   of Wardhouse, wife of the Hon. Captain G. Sempill,
     to her father Arthur of Wardhouse—h. of taillie
     and prov. gen.   S. H., 14 Feb. 1761

,,   of Wardhouse, wife of Captain G. (Gordon) Sempill,
     to her father Arthur of Wardhouse—h. gen.
           S. H., 28 Sept.; 30 Sept. 1761

,,   of Wardhouse.   *See* **Alexander** of Wardhouse
           S. H., 2 Sept. 1763

Charles, of Abergeldie, to his father Patrick of Abergeldie—h
     male of line and prov. gen.   S. H., 29 July, 25 Oct. 1737

,,   of Abergeldie, to his father Patrick of Abergeldie—
     h. male of taillie and prov. gen.   S H., 19 Aug.; 8 Sept. 1738

,,   of Abergeldy, to his grandfather Charles of Abergeldy
     —h. gen.   S. H., 8 July; 25 July 1768

,,   of Abergeldy.   *See* **Charles,** *supra.*

Charles, of Abergeldie. *See* **Peter** of Abergeldie.   S. H., 18 May 1798
  ,,   Comes de Aboyn. *See* **Ann,** domina, Aboyn   I G , 17 June 1665
  ,,   Capitanus. *See* **Rachael,** Aberzeldie   I. G., 1 Mar. 1798
  ,,   de Blelock. *See* **Isobel,** Blelock   I. G., 19 Feb 1698
  ,,   of Blelack. Charles Gordon Rose, g^{d}son of Hugh
        Rose of Tilliesnaught, to his g^{d}uncle Charles
        Gordon of Blelack—h. of line and prov. gen.
                    S. H. Supp., 9 July ; 17 July 1788
  ,,   Hamilton, advocate. *See* **Helen,** Boquhen ; Edin-
        burgh   S. H.,   Oct. 1771 ; S. H , 14 Aug. 1754
  ,,   de Bracco, h. Joannis de Bracco, patris,—in villa et
        terris de Bracco, cum terris dominicalilbus de
        Bracco ac pendiculis earundem vocatis Raebids et
        Whytwalls ;—terris et forresta de Drumkentoun ,
        —villa et terris de Glashea et pendiculis earundem
        vocatis Reidfoord, cum molendino de Glashea et
        privilegio baroniae, infra baroniam de Knoking-
        lews.—A E. 2m. ; N.E. 8m.   I. S. (Aberd.), 15 Sept. 1682
  ,,   merchant in Brechin, to his granduncle Charles of
        Glengarroch—h. male and of prov. gen.
                    S. H , 1 Mar ;   7 Mar. 1748
  ,,   of Buthlaw, to his uncle John of Buthlaw, advocate,
        who died   July 1775—h. of prov. spec. and
        the lands, mains and manor place of Newtyle,
        Drums, Mains of Buthlaw, Cadgerhill, etc.
                    S. H., 2 Apr. ; 26 Apr. 1776
  ,,   of Buthlaw. *See* **Thomas** of Buthlaw   S. H., 22 Feb. 1797
  ,,   to his father Alexander of Cloves—h gen.
                 S H., 20 May ; 28 July 1718
  ,,   in Dumfries, to his brother John, writer there—h.
        gen.   S. H , 6 Feb. ; 15 Feb. 1796
  ,,   merchant in Edinburgh. *See* **Alexander,** Bordeaux
                    S. H., 31 Jan. 1728
  ,,   to his father James at the Mill of Esslemont—h. gen.
                 S. H., 29 Mar.,   3 May 1744
C[harles], of Fetterangus. *See* **William,** Fetterangus   S. H., 13 Aug 1768
  ,,   magister, de Gardenstoune   *See* **Robert,** magister,
        Gardenstoune   I. G.,   5 Dec. 1674
  ,,   of Glenderrich. *See* **George** of Glenderrich   S. H , 8 Jan 1734

Charles de Glengarrack, h masc. Alexandrı de Glengarrack,
    patrıs,—ın terris de Over et Nether Auchınhuives
    et Bernelıes cum Alehouse et Alehousecrofts ;—
    terrıs et vılla de Glengerack, Alnecardoch, et
    Corbıescraıg, cum communı pastura in terrıs de
    Greenes de Kınbaldıe, Balnamaın, et Altmore, et
    potestate aedıficandı molendınum super easdem
    terras, ın baronıa de Strathila et regalıtate de
    Kınlose ;—2 bovatıs terrae de Newmilne de
    Strathıla ;—terrıs de Nether Kınmınıtıe vocatıs
    Overseat de Nether Kınmınıtıe ;—molendıno de
    Strathıla vocato Newmylne vel Overmylne de
    Strathıla, cum crofta terrae adjacente ın baronıa
    de Strathıla et regalitate de Kınlose ,—burgo
    baronıae de Newmıll, cum prıvılegıo forı hepdo-
    madarıı et 4 nundınarum annuatım ;—omnıbus
    unıtıs et erectıs ın baronıam de Glengerack.—
    A.E.   ; N.E. 77l. 14s. 6d.   I. S. (Banff), 29 Nov. 1692
,, of Glengerrick. *See* **George** of Glengerrick   S. H., 3 Oct 1746
,, of Glengarroch. *See* **Charles**, merchant ın Brechin
    S. H , 7 Mar. 1748
,, magıster. *See* **Robert**, magıster, Gordonstoune
    I. S. (Sutherl.), 22 Apr. 1675
,, Hamılton, of Newhall, advocate. *See* **William** of
    Newhall   S. H., 20 Apr. 1763
,, Hamılton, of Newhall, advocate. *See* **Henrietta** of
    Braelangwell   S. H., 29 Jan. 1787
,, s. of Peter, New York, to his brother Alexander ın
    the Customs at Ayr—h. of conq gen.
    S..H., 5 Mar.; 26 Mar. 1782
,, s. of G., merchant, Peterhead, to hıs grandaunt
    Catharıne M'Ronald or Forbes there—h. gen.
    S. H., 6 Mar ; 13 Aug. 1767
,, of Sheelagreen, captain, to hıs father Wılliam of
    Sheelagreen, who dıed   May, 1773—h. spec. ın
    Wranghams, Sheelagreen, wıth Manor Place,
    Boghıllock, etc., all in the parısh of Culsalmond,
    Aberd.   S. H., 4 Mar.; 11 Mar. 1776
,, of Wardhouse, to his brother Alexander of Wardhouse,

who died 24 Nov. 1769—h. of tail and prov.
spec. in Cookshill, Garryhill, Drummalachies,
Kinclune, Nether Kildrimmie, Wellhead, etc.,
Aberd. S. H., 13 Aug.; 5 Sept. 1770

Charles, of Wardhouse, to his father John of Beldorney, who
died 6 Oct. 1760—h. spec. in the lands of
Succoch, in the parish of Mortlach, Banff
S. H., 9 June; 11 Aug. 1777

„ merchant in Warsaw in Poland, to his father Alexander,
barber in Aberdeen—h gen. S. H , 21 July; 30 Aug. 1733

Charlotte, to her brother Adam, s of James of Cochlarachie
—h. port gen. S. H., 4 Aug.; 9 Aug. 1779

Christian, wife of And. Howison, Grammar School, Aberdeen,
to her brother Major Thomas Gordon of Clerk-
seat—h. prov. gen. S. H., 4 Nov. 1740

„ to her father James of Barns—h. port. gen
S. H., 6 Oct. 1739; 20 Nov. 1740

„ in Kininvie. Alexander Leslie, in Achnahandock,
to his mother Christian Gordon, wife of Robert
Leslie, in Kininvie—h. gen. S. H. Supp., 4 June, 12 June 1745

„ d. of T., in Lagan of Glenrinnes, to her grandfather Duncan Cumming of Letter Wandoch—h.
port. gen. S. H., 16 Jan. 1703

Christina, Marjoria, Barbara, Jeana et Issabella, hh. port.
Joannis de Branelane, patris,—in terris de New-
merdrum ;—terris de Brothow cum molendino de
Finglennie, alias vocato Crawsmill [? Cransmill],
—terris de Longley de Garbet, infra parochiam
de Esse et Ryne.—E.   . I. S. (Aberd.), 6 Oct. 1669

„ h. port. Jacobi Melvill de Hervistoun, avunculi,—
in dimidietate terrarum maneriei de Hervistoun
in barronia de Kinneff.—A E 20s.; N.E. 4l.—
dimidietate tenementi et dimidietate 4 croftarum
in territorio de Covy infra constabulariam ejusdem.—E. 2s. I. S. (Kincard.), 15 Mar. 1617

„ Hackett, sp. Roberti Gordoune de Chappeltoune, h.
port. Walteri Hackett de Meyen, patris I. G., 17 Oct. 1671

Clement, apud Water de Leyth. *See* **John**, in Water de
Leyth I. G , 22 June 1631

Cosmo, advocate, to his father John of Cluny—h. male and of
    line gen.   S. H., 21 Mar.;   Mar. 1770

Cosmo Alexander, to his mother Euphemia Mackintosh, wife
    of Patrick in Strone of Badenoch—h. gen.
                      S. H., 19 Apr.; 4 May 1737

Cosmo George, duke, to his grandfather George, duke, who died
    20 Nov. 1728—h. male spec. in the Marquisate
    of Huntly, Aberd.; Cabrach, Banff; Tulundie,
    Inverness; Ballormie, Elgin   S. H., 20 Oct.; 22 Oct. 1731

    ,,   duke, to his grandaunt Jean, Countess of Dum-
    fermling, who died   —h. spec. in
    the Lordship of Fyvie, including the lands, mains
    and mill of Fyvie, Minies, Urquhart, Fochabers,
    etc., Elgin   S. H., 1 Aug.; 13 Aug. 1733

    ,,   duke. *See* **Alexander,** duke   S. H., 25 Mar. 1754

David. *See* **Thomas**   I. G., 29 July 1697

    ,,   h. magistri Thomae scribae signeto regio, patris   I. G., 7 June 1690

    ,,   of Drumrash. *See* **Robert** of Drumrash   S. H., 24 Feb. 1773

    ,,   de Gordounstoune. *See* **Nathaniel,** Gordounstoune I. G., 22 Mar. 1681

Davida, to her brother John of Gordonbank—h. port. gen.
                       S. H., 6 Apr.; 21 Apr. 1796

Ebenezer, weaver in Perth. *See* **William,** Forfar   S. H., 7 June 1799

Elizabeth, wife of Alex., W.S., to her gt-gt-grandfather Robert
    of Achinhalrigg and Curfurroch—h. gen.   S. H., 20 Feb. 1724

    ,,   *See* **John** de Airdis   I. S. (Kirkcudb.), 4 Nov. 1610

    ,,   to her father James of Barns—h. port. gen.
                     S. H., 6 Oct. 1739; 20 Nov. 1740

    ,,   Nicolson, wife of Wm. Gordon, factor at Brox-
    month, to her brother William Nicolson, mer-
    chant, Edinburgh—h. gen.   S. H., 19 Nov.; 25 Nov. 1746

    ,,   to her father Alexander of Coldwells—h. port. of
    prov. and in gen.   S. H., 20 Dec. 1765; 7 Feb. 1766

    ,,   to her father Alexander of Coldwells—h. port. and
    of prov. gen.   S. H., 29 Aug.; 1 Sept. 1780

    ,,   (or Reid), of Cross of Monally. Margaret Phin,
    wife of Thos. Johnston, goldsmith in Montrose,
    to her gdmother Elizabeth Gordon, wife of Al.
    Phin of Achanassie—h. of prov. gen.
             S. H. Supp., 19 April; 26 April 1750

Elizabeth. *See* **Alexander** de Earlestoun   I. S. (Kirkcudb), 29 July 1634

,,   wife of Alexander, writer in Edinburgh, to her great-granduncle John of Achinhalrigg, who died —h. of conq. spec. in the toun and lands of Achinhalrigg, Banff   S. H , 1 Nov. 1723; 20 Feb. 1724

,,   to her mother Margaret Christie, wife of Alexander in Old Manse of Fintray—h. port. gen. S. H , 11 Mar.; 22 Mar. 1775

,,   late in Forrest of Skene, to her father John, shipmaster in Aberdeen—h. gen. S. H , 16 Dec. 1775 , 14 Feb. 1776

,,   h. Georgii de Geicht, patris   I. G. Supp., 23 June 1580

,,   wid. of Patrick Heron of Heron, to her great-grandfather John of Troquhain—h gen.
   S. H., 10 Oct 1765; 27 Mar. 1766

,,   wife of George Gordon, surgeon, Hanover Parish, Jamaica, to her brother David Denham, writer, Edin.—h. gen.   S. H., 18 Feb. 1753

,,   h Patricii de Hillheid, patris   I. G.,   *   *   *

,,   d. of George of Jamaica, to her uncle Captain Adam of Auchanachy—h. of line gen.
   S. H., 15 Aug.; 23 Aug. 1782

,,   d. of George of Jamaica, to her uncle John of Auchanachy—h. of line gen.   S. H., 15 Aug.; 23 Aug 1782

,,   Maxwell. *See* **James** of Killilour I. S. (Kirkcudb.), 13 Jan. 1657

,,   to her father Alexander of Kirkland—h port. gen.
   S. H., 14 Oct.; 3 Dec 1731

Elspet, h. Alexandri de Castramen, patris,—in 5 mercatis terrarum de Castramen et Deriegowyne antiqui extentus, in parochia de Girtoun.—A.E 3l. 6s. 8d.; N.E. 1ol.   I. S (Kirkcudb.), 30 Jan. 1644

,,   Crombie *See* **Alexander,** Kemnay. I. S. (Aberd), 2 Mar 1648

,,   *See* **Margaret,** Kirkwall   I. S. (Orkney), 25 Nov. 1656; I. G., 16 Dec. 1656; I. S (Orkney), 8 Feb 1662

Ernest, of Cowbairdy, to his father James of Cowbairdy, who died May, 1773—h. spec. in Cowbairdy, now called Northleslie, including Hillockhead, Colliescroft, Bogheads, etc., in the parish of Forgue, Aberd.   S. H., 18 Aug , 13 Sept. 1773

,,   of Cowbairdie, to his great-grandfather Sir John of Park—h. male gen.   S H , 12 Feb.; 27 Feb. 1782

Ernest, of Cowbairdie, to his uncle Captain John of Park—h. of
        taillie and prov. gen.   S. H., 12 Feb.; 27 Feb. 1782
    Sir, of Park, Bart , to his uncle Captain John of Park,
        who died   Sept. 1781—h. of tail. spec. in the
        lands, barony, manor place and burgh of barony
        of Park, etc., in the parish of Ordiequhill, Banff
                      S. H , 25 Sept. , 17 Dec. 1782

Eufamia, h port. praedicti Joannis [de Blaikat], patris,—in terris
        praedictis. *See* **Catharine,** Blaikat
                    I. S. (Kirkcudb.), 29 Oct. 1548
   ,,   h. port. praedictae Margaretae [Blaket], sororis, in
        undecima parte dictarum terrarum. *See* **Catha-**
        rine, Blaket   I. S. (Kirkcudb.), 14 Apr. 1552
   ,,   Mackintosh. *See* **Cosmo Alexander**   S. H., 4 May 1737
   ,,   Gray, sp Patricii Gordoune, unius Satellitum Regis
        Galliarum, h. port. Isabellae Gray f. legitimae
        quondam Andrae Gray olim de Duninald, f. patrui
                        I. G., 15 Mar. 1642
   ,,   Gray, sp. Patricii Gordoune unius Satellitum Regis
        Galliarum, h. port. Andreae Gray olim de Duny-
        nald, patrui   I. G., 15 Mar. 1642

Fabian, col. Polish service, to his g^dfather Alexander of Cold-
        wells—h. male and of line and of prov gen.
                S. H., 16 Sept ; 23 Sept. 1783

F[rancis?], shoemaker, in Aberdeen. *See* **James,** Aberdeen
                      S. H., 17 Jan. 1799

Francis, of Crage, h. of John of Crage, his grandfather
                     I. G., 12 Sept. 1655
   ,,   of Craig. *See* **John** of Craig   S. H., 16 April 1729
   ,,   (formerly Wemyss), s. of Wm. Wemyss of Craig-
        hall, to his brother Alexander, formerly Wemyss,
        surgeon, Huntly, who died 22 Nov. 1790—h. of
        prov. spec. in the lands of Branley, in the parish
        of Alford, Aberd.   S. H., 25 Feb.; 15 Mar. 1791
   ,,   s. of John, writer in Edinburgh. *See* **Ann,** Edinburgh
                     S. H., 27 June 1718
   ,,   de Kirkhill, h. Hugonis de Kirkhill, patris,—in villa
        et terris de Kirkhill et Mostoun, cum toloniis et
        custumis nundinarum vocatarum Trewall faire,

infra regalitatem de Lindoirs et parochiam de
Kinethmont —E. 6l. 6s. 8d feudifirmae

I. S. (Aberd.), 29 June 1694

Francis, to his father George of Miln of Kincardin—h gen

S. H., 31 Oct.; 11 Nov. 1730

,,   of Mill of Kincardine, to his grandfather John of Glencatt, who died   , 1706—h. spec. in the
lands of Glencatt in the parish of Birse, Aberd.

S. H., 3 Oct.; 31 Oct. 1744

,,   of Mill of Kincardine. *See* **Ann,** Mill of Kinc.

S. H , 4 Aug. 1766; S. H., 26 Sept. 1770

,,   (formerly Grant), commander R.N., to his uncle
James of Knockespock, who died   April, 1768—
h. port and of line spec. in Auchlyne, Newbigging, Knockespock, Terpersey, etc., and fishings in the Don, Aberd.   S H., 7 March; 13 April 1770

,,   Sir, of Lessmore, Bart., to his brother George—h.
gen.   S. H., 10 Dec., 25 Dec. 1790

Frederica (or de Rosenwald), to her cousin Catharine of Auchentool, who died   June, 1797—h. of prov. spec. in
Auchentoul, etc., Banff, and in the lands and mains
of Laithers, etc., Aberd. and Banff S. H., 12 July; 28 Aug. 1798

G., supervisor of customs. *See* **Henrietta,** Dumfries   S. H., 10 Dec. 1776

,, writer, in Edinburgh. *See* **Alexander,** Edinburgh   S H., 3 May 1704

,, merchant, Peterhead. *See* **Charles,** Peterhead   S. H., 13 Aug 1767

Gabriel, magister, h. masc et prov. Joannis de Spedoch, patris

I. G., 24 June 1687

George, colonel. *See* **Isobel Mary,** Stevenson   S. H., 15 Aug 1799

,,   writer to the signet. *See* **James**   S. H., 24 Oct. 1749

,,   Duke. *See* **Cosmo George,** Duke   S. H , 22 Oct. 1731

,,   Dominus. *See* **John**   I. G. Supp., 9 Jan. 1630

,,   Dominus Gordoun. Jacobus Seattoun de Touche, h.
Alexandri Seatoun fratris germani Georgii Domini,
abavi proavi,—propterea quod dictus Jacobus Seatoun nunc de Touche est f. et h saltem apparens
h. Jacobi Seatoun de Touche qui ultimo decessit,
qui Jacobus fuit f. et h. saltem apparens h. Joannis
Seatoun de Touche qui Joannes fuit f. et h. Jacobi
Seatoun de Tullibodie, qui Jacobus fuit f. et h.

Walteri Seatoun de Tullibodie, qui Walterus fuit
f. et h. saltem apparens h. Domini Niniani Seatoun de Tullibodie militis, qui Ninianus fuit f. et
h. Domini Alexandri Seatoun de Tullibodie militis,
qui Alexander fuit f. et h. dicti Alexandri Seatoun
fratris dicti Georgii Domini, ac abavi proavi dicti
Jacobi Seatoun nunc de Touche   I. G., 23 April 1630

George, burgensis de Aberdein, h. Gilberti burgensis de Aberdein, patris   I. G , 22 April 1634

,,   f. natu maximus, et h. gen. Alexandri junioris mercatoris burgensis de Aberdeen, patris   I. G., 19 July 1690

,,   f. natu maximus Alexandri, h. gen. dicti Alexandri junioris mercatoris burgensis de Aberdeen, patris I.G., 19 July 1690

,,   professor in the University of Aberdeen, to his father
George of Rainieshill, who died   —h. spec.
in Slugmagullie, Over and Nether Rainnieshills,
and in part of Mamewhay, Aberdeenshire

             S. H., 25 Aug.; 30 Sept. 1731

,,   professor. *See* **Margaret,** Aberdeen   S. H., 26 May 1740

,,   merchant, Aberdeen. *See* **John** of Portland parish,
Jamaica   S. H., 29 June 1772

,,   professor of Oriental Languages, Aberdeen. *See*
Thomas, Professor of Philosophy, Aberdeen

             S. H., 15 Feb. 1775

,,   merchant in Aberdeen. *See* **John,** merchant in Aberdeen   S. H., 5 April 1796

,,   of Aberdour, to his father Alexander of Aberdour, who
died   June, 1785—h. spec in the lands and
mains of Aberdour and Coburty, etc., in the parish
of Aberdour   S. H., 29 April; 1 June 1791

,,   of Aberdour, to his father Alexander of Aberdour—h.
gen.   S. H., 30 Nov. 1791; 4 Jan. 1792

,,   of Aberdour. *See* **William** of Aberdour   S H., 20 Mar. 1793

,,   minister at Alves. *See* **Agnes,** Alves   S H., 29 Jan. 1747

,,   merchant in Annan, to his granduncle Enoch Johnston
(son of Simon Johnston, minister at Annan), who
died   —h. spec. in Seafield, Battlehills,
Matthewsmains, Broadwellgreen, etc., Dumfriesshire   S. H., 3 Aug., 9 Nov. 1738

George, to his father Captain John of Ards—h. gen.

S H , 12 June 1706; 13 Dec 1707

,,   de Arradoull, h Alexandri de Arradoul, patris,—in
terris et villa de Haughes de Killesmont ·—E.
5m. 6s. 8d , etc , feudifirmae.—villa et terris de
Haughes de Killesmont vulgo vocatis Forgie :—
E. 4l. 20d., etc , feudifirmae.—villa et terris de
Mossley (vel Messlie).—A.E. 12s. 6d , N.E. 50s.
—omnibus infra baroniam de Grainge, parochiam
de Keith et regalitatem de Kinlos   I S (Banff), 18 Oct. 1692

,,   h. Patricii de Auchinangzie, patris,—in terris de Litil
Folay.—A E 40s. ; N.E. 8l.   I. S. (Aberd.), 6 Oct. 1573

,,   h. Georgii f. Joannis de Auchinreoch, patris,—in 20
solidatis 3 mercatarum terrarum de Lytletoun
antiqui extentus, in parochia de Borg.—A.E. 20s.;
N.E. 3l.   I. S. (Kirkcudb.), 16 April 1616

,,   *See* **George,** *supra.*

,,   of Badenscoth. *See* **William** of Badenscoth   S. H., 12 Jan. 1714

,,   h. Alexandri de Barskeoche, patrui,—in 5 mercatis
terrarum de Auchinreoch antiqui extentus, in
parochia de Or infra dominium Gallavidiae —
A E. 3l. 6s. 8d.; N.E. 10l.—3 mercatis terrarum
de Strongassill, viz , 1 mercata terrae de Strongassill et Crocefald ;—1 mercata terrae vocata
Midmark;—dimidio mercatae terrae vocatae Cassinbrok alias Croce-William, et dimidio mercatae
terrae de Haw antiqui extentus, in parochia de
Kellis —A.E. 40s. , N.E 6l —Terris de Stron-
faskin, Largemore, Knokschene, Middill et Nether
Barskeochis, cum piscationibus ejusdem in aqua
de Ken, in parochia de Kellis ·—E 25l —4 mercatis
terrarum de Glenairne antiqui extentus in parochia
de Or.—A.E. 53s. 4d. ; N.E. 8l.   I. S. (Kirkcudb), 27 Oct. 1607

,,   de Barskeoch, h Alexandri de Barskeoche, patrui,—in
13 mercatis terrarum de Auchnaucht, Carnegayne,
et Inschanke, in superioritate earundem, in parochia
de Kirkmadyne in Rynnis ;—5 mercatis terrarum
de Cloinzeard, cum molendino ,—5 mercatis terrarum de Portinkorkie ;—5 mercatis terrarum de

Curochtie,—2½ mercatis terrarum de Cairne, extendentibus in integro ad 20 libratas 6 solidatas
8 denariatas terrarum.—A.E. 20l. 6s. 8d.; N.E.
61l.—5 mercatis terrarum de Kirkbryde·—A.E.
5m., N.E. 10l.—dimidietate 5 mercatarum terrarum de Drumoir, in dicta parochia de Kirkmadyne:
—A.E 2½m , N E. 5l —3 mercatis terrarum de
Cairnmultiburgh, in parochia de Insche.—A.E.
3m.; N.E. 6l.—5 mercatis terrarum de Kildonnan,
in dicta parochia de Kirkmadyne.—A.E. 5m.;
N.E. 10l. 10s.—anno redditer 110m. de 5 mercatis
terrarum de Drumoir et molendino ejusdem, in
dicta parochia   I. S (Wigton), 31 Oct. 1607

George de Barskeoch, h. Alexandri de Barskeoche, patrui,—in
16 solidatis terrarum de Bargalie, et 8 solidatis
terrarum de Barquhoyis antiqui extentus, in
parochia de Monygoif.—A.E. 24s.; N E. 3l. 12s.
                        I S. (Kirkcudb.), 10 Oct. 1609

„   de Barskeoche. *See* **John** de Barskeoche
                I. S. (Kirkcudb.) ; I. S. (Wigton), 8. Aug. 1633

„   h. Alexandri de Beldorney, patris,—in villa et terris
de Beldorney cum terris dominicalibus,—villa et
terris de Lynbanis cum molendinis ejusdem ;—
villa et terris de Eister et Wester Genllis (vel
Goullis) cum piscatione salmonum super aqua de
Doverne, in baronia de Kethmore alias Auchindoune.—A.E. 26s. 8d.; N.E. 5l. 6s. 8d.—tertia
parte villae et terrarum de Balcheirie, in dominio
de Inneitherauch [*sic.*] et parochia de Morthlie.—
A.E. 10s.; N.E. 40s.   I. S. (Banff), 20 Feb. 1627

„   de Beldornye, h. Georgii de Beldornye, patris,—in villa
et terris de Beldornye ;—villis et terris de Lym-
banes cum molendinis earundem ;—villis et terris
de Easter et Wester Goulis, cum salmonum piscatione super aquam de Doverne, in baronia de
Keythmoir alias Auchindoune,—tertia parte villae
et terrarum de Belchirie, in dominio de Invercher-
auche et parochia de Mortliche.—A.E. 16m.; N.E.
42l. 13s. 4d.   I. S. (Banff), 19 July 1638

George de Beldornye. *See* **George,** *supra.*

„   *See* **John** of Birkenbush   S. H., 23 Nov. 1758

„   of Buckie, to his father George of Buckie—h. gen.   ·

                                                 S. H., 8 Sept.; 14 Oct. 1730

„   of Buckie. *See* **George,** *supra.*

„   of Buckie, to his great-great-grandfather John of Buckie

             —h. gen.   S. H., 7 July; 11 July 1733

„   of Buckie. *See* **John** of Buckie   S. H., 1 Nov. 1757

„   magister, h. Georgii apparitoris Cantariensis, patris

                                                 I. G., 4 Feb. 1671

„   apparitor Cantariensis. *See* **George,** *supra.*

„   of Chappeltoun, minister at Drumblade, to his grand-

            father Robert of Chappeltoun—h. of prov. gen.

                                            S. H., 19 Feb. 1752

„   de Cochlarrachie. *See* **Alexander,** Cochlarrachie I. G., 24 July 1661

„   h. talliae Georgii de Cochlarrachie. *See* **Alexander,**

            Cochlarrachie   I. G., 24 July 1661

„   de Colholstane, h. Jacobi de Lesmoir, patris,—in terris

            de Balmad, Gerachtie, Crageheid.—A.E. 4l.; N.E.

            16l.   I. S. (Aberd), 23 June 1559

„   h. Jacobi de Creiche, patris,—in quarta parte terrarum de

            Eister Creichie;—quarta parte terrarum de Middel

            Creichie;—quarta parte terrarum de Creichnaheid,

            in baronia de Creichie.—A.E. 20s., N.E. 4l.

                              I. S. (Aberd.), 6 Oct. 1553 [1573]

„   tacksman of Culmaly. *See* **Ann,** Dunrobin , **Grizell,**

            Cromarty; **Janet,** Torbreck   S. H., 24 May 1769

„   merchant in Dumfries. *See* **James,** town clerk of

            Dumfries   S. H., 29 Mar. 1733

„   in Dundurcus, h. masc. Jacobi in Collie, patris,—in

            quinta parte villae et terrarum de Dundurcus,

            cum bruerii domo et acra terrarum ad eandem

            pertinente, et Rig terrae tanquam parte ejusdem,

            et salmonum piscatione super aqua de Spey, infra

            parochiam de Dundurcus, et baroniam de Bar-

            muckatie.—A.E. 6s. 8d.; N.E. 26s. 8d.

                         I. S. (Elgin), 29 April 1692

„   portioner of Dundurcas. *See* **James,** in Dundurcas

                                 S. H., 24 Sept. 1714

George, nuncius, h. port. Magistri Georgii Bonyman, scribae in
      Edinburgh, avunculi   I. G., 17 Sept. 1628
  ,,   wrytter messenger in Edinburgh, heir of Marione Bony-
      mane, his mother sister   I. G., 30 Oct 1658
  ,,   h. Magistri Roberti, scribae in Edinburgo, patris   I, G., 18 Aug. 1696
  ,,   Edinburgh. *See* **John** de Aberlour   I. de Tut., 30 July 1696
  ,,   in Edinburgh. *See* **James,** Aberlour   I. G., 19 June 1697
  ,,   messenger in Edinburgh. *See* **Alexander,** Edinburgh
       S. H , 3 May 1704
  ,,   writer in Edinburgh, to his brother James of Gordon-
      bank—h. gen.   S. H., 26 Jan. ; 28 Jan. 1738
  ,,   callender-keeper in Edinburgh. Hugh Mackay, son of
      Rt. Mackay, tenant in Syre, to his g^{d}uncle George
      Gordon, callender-keeper in Edinburgh—h. port
      gen.   S H. Supp., 10 Nov. ; 12 Nov. 1785
  ,,   callender keeper in Edinburgh. Margaret Mackay, to
      her granduncle George Gordon, callender keeper in
      Edinburgh—h. port gen. S. H. Supp., 10 Nov., 12 Nov. 1785
  ,,   son of John, junior, of Edinglassie, to his aunt Elizabeth
      Gray, who died   Dec. 1741—h. of line spec.
      in the barony of Balegarno, including part of
      Abernythe, etc., Perth   S. H., 5 April ; 5 April 1746
  ,,   *See* **John,** Sir, of Embo   S. H., 12 July 1717
  ,,   de Geicht. *See* **Elizabeth,** Geicht   I. G. Supp., 23 June 1580
  ,,   de Geicht. *See* **John** de Adiwell   I. G. Supp., 31 July 1581 ;
       I S. Supp. (Aberd.), 21 Nov. 1581
  ,,   de Geicht, h. masc. et talliae Willielmi de Geicht,
      patris,—in terris et villa de Badichillo, Over et
      Nether Murefundlands, Over et Nether Suan-
      furde, Blacrie, Mactarrie, molendino de Mag-
      tarrie; in baronia de Fyvie.—A E. 6l.; N.E. 24l.
       I. S. (Aberd.), 1 Feb. 1600
  ,,   de Geicht, h. Willielmi de Geicht, patris   I. G., 8 Feb. 1606
  ,,   dominus, de Geight. *See* **John,** Geight   I. G., 9 June 1630
  ,,   to his father Alexander, or Davidson of Gight, who
      died   Jan. 1760—h. male of line, taillie and
      prov. spec. in Gight, Fetterletter, burgh of barony
      of Woodhead of Fetterletter, etc
       S. H., 18 April; 29 April 1760

George of Gight, to his father Alexander (or Davidson) of Gight,
who died Jan. 1760—h spec. in Tilliemorgan,
Sauchinloan, Grayston, and Newseat in the parish
of Culsalmond S. H., 23 April; 1 May 1777

„ of Gight. *See* **Catharine,** Gight S. H., 21 Oct. 1785

„ writer to the signet *See* **James,** merchant in Glasgow
S. H., 8 Mar 1764

„ of Glen. *See* **William** of Crackville S. H , 25 Aug. 1748

„ of Glenderrich [*sic.*], to his father Charles of Glenderrich
—h. male gen. S. H., 4 Oct. 1733, 8 Jan 1734

„ of Glengerrick, to his father Charles of Glengerrick, who
died June, 1712—h male spec. in Auchives,
Berryleys, Glengerrick, Newmiln of Strathilla,
burgh of barony of Newmiln, etc. S. H., 19 Aug.; 3 Oct. 1746

„ of Glengerrick *See* **Catharine,** Glengerrick, **Magdalen,** Glengerrick; **Margaret,** Glengerrick S. H., 25 Aug. 1748 .

„ of Gordonbank, to his father George of Gordonbank—
h gen. S. H , 3 Aug , 29 Aug 1758

„ of Gordonbank. *See* **George,** *supra.*

„ of Gordonbank, to his brother Captain Alexander, port
of Hassingtoun—h. of conq. gen. S H., 13 Aug.; 11 Sept. 1772

„ of Gordonbank, to his father George of Gordonbank,
who died 24 Oct. 1783—h. spec. cum ben invent.,
in Rouchester or Spensrigg, Easter Howlaws, with
Manor Place, etc S. H., 18 Dec.; 13 April 1783

„ of Gordonbank. *See* **George,** *supra.*

„ H., 63rd Foot. *See* **Patience,** Haddington S. H , 23 Oct 1790

„ de Haddo. *See* **John** de Haddo I S (Aberd.), 21 April 1627

„ dominus de Haddo, miles baronettus, h masc. talliae et
provisionis domini Joannis de Haddo, militis baro-
netti, fratris,—in terris dominicalibus de Haddo,
—terris de Bicenquyn, Greenmyres, Lrarnes [*sic*],
Meikle Methlick, Andat, Brakley-Andat, Hilbraie,
Northseat-Andat et Archedlie;—terris de duabus
Methlicks vocatis Haddo;—predictis terris de
Archedlie cum piscatione super aquam de Ythan,
—annuo redditu 5l. de dictis terris de Archedlie,
Andat et Brackley-Andat,—unitis in baroniam de
Haddo.—A.E. 8l., N.E. 32l I. S. (Aberd.), 10 Sept. 1669

George, dominus de Haddo, miles baronettus, h. masc. domini
       Joannis de Haddo, militis baronetti, fratris,—in
       . terris de Kirktoun de Tarves, cum lie Diracroft ·—
       E. 5l., etc.—terris de Brackley, cum novo molen-
       dino, infra baroniam de Tarves, et regalitatem de
       Aberbrothok :—E. 6l. 13s. 4d.—terris de Tullielt
       —E. 4l.—extendentibus cum grassumis, etc., ad
       21l. 4s.—villa et Maynes de Kellie, et terris de
       Milntoun de Kellie, in baronia de Kellie :—E. 20l.
       13s. 4d.—terris de Sauchaik, in dicta baronia de
       Kellie,—duabus tertiis partibus terrarum de Bar-
       racke, infra dictam baroniam de Kellie :—E. 20l.—
       terris de Kinawine et terris de Auchmaledy, infra
       dictam baroniam de Kellie :—E.   .—terris
       de Collyne, et 2 bovatis terrarum de Andat, in
       parochia de Methlick:—E. 5l. 6s 8d.—terris de
       Newpark de Kelly ;—terris de Overhill, cum lie
       seat earundem vocato Thornron, infra baroniam
       de Auchterelloun.—A.E. 10s. ; N.E. 40s.   :
                           I. S. (Aberd), 10 Sept. 1669

,,   feoditarius de Haddoch *See* **John,** Haddoch   I. G., 6 Oct. 1612

,,   de Halheid, h. Patricii de Halheid, fratris,—in villa
       et terris de Halheid, et terris de Corquhinderland,
       infra parochiam de Cuschnie.—A.E. 3l.; N.E. 12l.
                     I. S. (Aberd.), 27 Feb. 1622

,,   of Hallhead. *See* **Robert**   S. H., 27 July 1758

,,   h. Willielmi, patrui,—in 3½ mercatis terrarum nuncu-
       patis Hodie,—dimidietate unius mercatae terrae
       vocatae Carsinbrok alias Corswillame, in parochia
       de Keiris (Kellis ?).—A.E.   ; N.E.   :—
       terris de Strongassill.—A E 46s. 8d. ; N.E. 7l
                 I S. (Kirkcudb.), 7 June 1614

,,   Marchio de Hunthe. *See* **Alexander** de Stradoune
                     I. de Tut., 3 Oct 1606

,,   Comes de Hunthe, h. Georgii Comitis de Hunthe,
       patris,—in tenemento, messuagis, etc., infra bur-
       gum de Elgyne.—A.E. 3l.; N.E. 12l. I. S. (Elgin), 20 July 1573

,,   Comes de Hunthe, etc., h. Georgii, Comitis de
       Hunthe, patris,—in terris de Inverrownes, Inver-

lochie, et Fortarlettir.—A.E. 4l. 3s. 4d.; N.E. 16l
13s. 4d.—terris et dominio de Strayththoun, et
jure patronatus capellaniarum earundem.—A. E.
40l.; N.E. 200l.—terris et dominio de Cul-
saivertlie, Engzie, et superioritate Forrestae de
Boyne.—A.E. 100l. 2s., N.E. 500l. 6s. 8d.—
Superioritate terrarum de Culfin, Auchamoquhy et
Auchamasse.—A. E. 11l.; N.E. 44l.   I. S. (Banff), 31 Oct. 1575

George, Comes de Huntlie, h. Georgii Comitis de Huntlie,
patris,—in terris, dominio, et baronia de Huntlie,
olim vocata baronia de Strathbogy.—A.E. 375m.;
N.E. 375l.—terris de Tent, Cluny, Aboyne, Glentaner, Glenmuick;—advocatione ecclesiae.—Ten-
endriae, A.E., 625m.; N.E. 625l.—Proprietatis,
A E. 375m.; N.E. 375l.   I. S. (Aberd.), 29 Nov. 1575

„   Comes de Huntlie, h. Georgii, Comitis de Huntlie,
Domini Gordoun et Badzenocht, patris,—in terris
de Culsavertlie et Enzie et dominio ejusdem, cum
superioritate Forestae de Boyne;—superioritate
terrarum de Culphyn, Auchannochie, et Aucha-
naschie.—A.E. 100l. 2s.; N.E. 500l 6s. 8d —
terris et dominio de Strathowne, et advocatione et
donatione capellaniarum earundem.—A.E. 40l.,
N.E. 200l.   I. S. (Banff), 18 Sept. 1581

„   Comes de Huntlie, etc   *See* **George,** Comes, *supra.*

„   Marchio de Huntlie, Comes de Enzie, Dominus
Gordoun et Baidzenoch, h. masc et talliae
Domini Patricii de Auchindoun militis patrui,—in
terris et baronia de Gartullie, viz.,—terris domini-
calibus de Gartullie, vulgo vocatis The Hiltoun;
—terris de Wylie-wray, Westseat, Faichhill,
Kirkhill, Mylnehill, Overkirkhill, Corne-Cothrache,
Schancher, Bordelseat, Fidlerseat, Gimpistoun,
Cokistoun, Duncanstoun, Stoidfaulde, molendino
de Gartullie;—terris de Pyperis-croft, Douppis-
croft, et Fetteis-croft, infra baroniam de Gartullie
—A.E. 12l.; N.E. 48l   I. S. (Banff), 6 May 1600

„   Marchio de Huntlie, etc., h. Georgii, Cŏmitis de
Huntlie, Domini Gordoun et Badzenoch, avi,—

in quarta parte davatae terrarum de Cochlarachie,
vocata Leslie-quarter, viz. quarta parte terrarum de
Cochlarachie;—quarta parte terrarum de Newbiging, cum quarta parte molendini;—quarta
parte Croftae de Futtie;—2 bovatis terrarum de
Garrie.—A.E 30s; N.E 6l.   I. S. (Aberd.), 13 Jan 1618

George, Comes de Huntlie, etc. *See* **George,** Marchio, *supra*

  ,, Marchio de Huntlie, etc, h Georgii Comitis de
    Huntlie, etc., patris,—in officio hereditario ballia-
    tus baroniarum, Schirarum et annuorum reddituum
    terrarum ad Episcopatum Abirdonensem spectan-
    tium in patrimonio, infra diocesin Abirdonensem,
    in vicecomitatiens de Aberdeen et Banf respective
             I S. (Aberd.), 9 Feb. 1627

  ,, Marchio de Huntlie, etc., h Georgii Comitis de Huntlie,
    etc, patris,— in officio haereditario balliatus
    baroniae et annuarum reddituum et terrarum
    ad episcopatum Abirdonensem spectantium in
    patrimonio infra diocesin Abirdonensem in vice-
    comitatiens de Banf et Aberdeen respective
             I. S. (Banff), 9 Feb 1627

  ,, Comes de Huntlie. *See* **George,** Marchio, *supra.*

  ,, Marchio de Huntlie, Comes de Enzie, Dominus Gordoun
    et Badzenocht, h Georgii, Marchionis de Huntlie,
    etc, patris   I G., 2 Aug. 1638

  ,, Marchio de Huntlie, etc., h. masc. Georgii, Marchionis
    de Huntlie, etc., patris   I. G., 2 Aug. 1638

  ,, Marchio de Huntlie. *See* **George,** Marchio de Huntlie,
    etc., *supra.*

  ,, Marchio de Huntlie, etc, h. masc. Georgii, Mar-
    chionis de Huntlie, etc., patris,—in terris et
    Comitatu de Huntlie ab antiquo dominio et baronia
    de Strathbogie nuncupatis; terris et baronia de
    Touch, Oboyne, Clunie, Glentanner, Glenmuk,
    Midmar, et Cabrach cum advocatione ecclesiarum,
    comprehendentibus terras de Carnburro, Asswan-
    ley, Invermarkie, Lesmoir,—terras de Cairnes,
    Drumdelgie, Boigmayn, Nather Drumdelgie,
    Outseat, Baidsyde, Boghauch, Intoun, Inche-

stomack, Drumquhuie, Dykheid, Mariefauld,
Ernequholfp, Brakles, Schinscharine cum brueriis
ejusdem;—terras de Cairne, cum brueriis earundem, Drumheid, Davidstoun, Midtoun de
Davidstoun, Nethertoun de Davidstoun Croft,
Wynderaw, Ordonald, Botarie, Westthrid, Eist
thrid, molendinum de Botarie, Bogforge, Midseat, Leadmorlauch, Auchquhanachie, Ovir Auchindrung, Nether Auchindrung, Davach, bruerii
croftam de Ruthven, Brighous, molendinum de
Ruthven, Ogstoun, molendinum de Ogstoun,
Whythill, Cormaleit et Cumray, cum pertinentiis; dominium de Oboyn;—terras, dominium et
baroniam de Cluny;—terras de Midmar,—terras
de Cabrach;—terras et dominium de Glentanner;
—terras de Glenmuck et Inchemarnok, cum sylvis
de Brakley;—terris de Tullich et Ballater, cum
sylvis et forestis de Morveing et Kilblain;—terras
de Chandmoir cum lacu;—terras de Parkhill, cum
Boghous et earundem sylvis parkwood nuncupatis;
—terras de Skippertie, Litill Sauchan, molendinum
earundem;—terras de Tilliemair, cum Boiggis,
Craiggearne et West-landis vocatis The Leyes of
Tullochaddie, cum foresta de Corrynie;—terras de
Eistir et Westir Cullairlies;—terras de Beltie;—
terras de Craigmyl;—terras de Mekle-Sauchine;—
terras de Cairnday,—terras de Kincraigie, Culqu-
horsie, Ardgowis;—terras de Kintocher;—terras
de Davan, Lochboig;—terras de Logy, Broomhill
cum Boig earundem;—quartam partem terrarum
de Wastoun,—terras de Birs Logie et Dansboig;
—terras de Litill Culquhed, Deirstanes, cum pastura et advocatione ecclesiarum;—terras de Balin-
vir et Cocklaw;—villam et terras de Casteltoun
de Aboyne;—terras de Wreatoun,—terras de
Ballnagowne;—terras de Bowtie, cum crofta vocata
Gilbert Mylnis-croft;—terras de Ovir et Nether
Formastounes;—terras de Drumgask;—terras de
Muirtoun;—terras de Balvade cum molendino de

Desk ;—terras de Mikle et Litill Gellanes ,—terras
de Eistir et Westir Brerodakis et Munnudaven ;—
terras de Kinkouis et croftam earundem ,—terras
de Ovir et Nethir Ballnacraigis ;—terras de Ferrar
cum cymba et crofta ejusdem, et tribus quarteriis
terrarum de Blackmylne cum molendino ,—terras
de Camesunnay et Hauch ;—terras de Meikle et
Litill Chandmoiris ;—terras de Chandord ,—terras
molendinarias de Dunatie cum molendino ;—terras
de Water-Erne ;—terras de Tulloch ;—terras de
Ballamoir et Ballabeg ;—terras de Balmeanie ;—
terras de Auchnarrane ;—terras de Blairglas ,—
terras de Mostoun et Ailhous-croft earundem ;—
terras de Myltoune de Calquholdstane cum molendino et Smiddiecroft ,—terras de Belhaine ,—terras
de Meikle Culsche, et Eister Culsche ,—terras de
Tulloch, et Ardochie cum molendino ;—terras de
Mylntoun de Culsche ,—terras de Pett, croftam
de Glentannar ;—terras de Coldhame, et superioritatem terrarum de Tullochowdy ;—terras de
Fochabers, Eister et Westir Abergardnyis, cum
pendiculo earundem vocato Pronny, et salmonum
piscaria super aqua de Dee et Glengardyne eisdem
spectante ;—molendinum de Abirgairdyne ;—terras
de Larie, et croftas vocatas Corieauchden et
Brigend, cum pertinentiis vocatis Tarnagowne et
Candacraige, cum molendino de Larie ;—terras de
Kirktoune, infra parochiam de Glengardyne ;—
binas dimidietates tam occidentalem quam orien-
talem terrarum de Mekle Culquholdstanes cum
molendino ejusdem ,—terras de Litill Culquholdstanes et Auchnarran, infra parochiam de Cromar ;
—terras de Auchtererne, Tulloche, Tannamoyne,
Blackmylne, infra parochiam de Coldstane ;—
terras de Corsindae, Kebbetie, Ordifork, Auchin-
kebbetie, Ranalloch, Tullicarne, in dominis de
Clunie ,—villas et terras de Tullieriache, Tulli-
wanis, Litill Tollmaidis, Tornavechin, Drum-
lawsie, Blairglaslie ,—terras de Mekle Tolmaidis ,

—terras de Tulliefour et Tulliekeirie, infra baroniam de Clunie ;—terras Sunhynnie, infra baroniam de Midmar, cum libero et communi pasturagio dictarum terrarum, unitas in dominium seu baroniam de Huntlie alias Strathbogie :—A E. 375m., N.E. 375l. in proprietate.—A.E. 625m.; N.E. 625l. in superioritate.—Quarta parte davatae terrarum de Cochlarachie vocata Leslies Quarter, viz. quarta parte terrarum de Newbiging ,—quarta parte molendini ejusdem ,—quarta parte croftae de Futtie, cum 2 bovatis terrarum de Garrie :—A.E. 30s. ; N.E. 6l.—Villa et terris subspecificatis, viz. solari tertia parte villae et terrarum de Knokleyth, cum crofta brueria ejusdem, et crofta vocata Bilboecroft, cum molendino de Knokleyth ;—villa et terris de Halseywalls, tam solari tertia parte quam bina parte earundem ;—solari tertia parte villae et terrarum de Lenschave et Lenschavebrae ,—solari tertia parte villae et terrarum de Haltoun de Ochterles, cum solari tertia parte villae et terrarum de Thomastoun, infra baroniam de Ochterles-Dempster ,—umbrali bina parte villae et terrarum de Logy Auldtoun, cum pendiculis nuncupatis Bus de Logy Auldtoun et Ladyboig, infra parochiam de Ochterles ;—solari tertia parte villae et terrarum de Cuschnie, quae est pars terrarum et baroniae de Ochterles Dempster ; unitis in baroniam de Knokleith .—A.E. 10l ; N.E. 10l.—terris de Cowlie :—E. 10l —terris de Carnfechill :—E. 6l.—terris de Petreiche :—E. 3l.—molendino de Fechill :—E. 5l.—terris de Brecklaw :—E. 6l. 13s.—terris de Craigie :—E. 6l. 13s. 4d.—terris ecclesiasticis de Tarves :—E. 5l.—terris de Tullicarlin .—E 46s. 8d.—terris de Tullihilt .—E. 4l.—molendino de Tullihilt ·—E. 4l. 13s.—terris de Auchartie —E. 46s. 8d.—terris de Auchinleck —E. 4l.—terris de Boigfekill.—E. 16l.—terris de Auchinhuive :—E 4l. 13s. 8d.—terris de Munkishill —E. 4l.—

terris ecclesiasticis de Fyvie:—E. 8l.—molendino de Fyvie:—E. 40s.—brasinis de Fyvie —E.
40s.—terris de Ardlogy·—E. 8l.—officio balliatus
terrarum predictarum, in baronia de Tarves et
Fyvie infra regalitatem de Abirbrothock —E.
94l. 6s. 8d.—E. 133l. 6s. 8d. in integro —terris
de Schevedlie, Ballnagowne, Ardragathill, Pow-
tochie, Pittindreich, Brome, molendino de Keig,
brasina et crofta ejusdem; terris de Dullab, In-
zeane, Litill Abircattie, Mekle Abircattie, Gren-
toun, Finzeauch, molendino ejusdem, Cowlie,
Auchterbege, Todlachies, Tulliequharrie, Edin-
durne, Tillispolie alias Ovir et Nethir Tullochies,
—terris de Cottirstane, alias Coldstane, Newtoune
de Coldstane, Pitlyne, cum molendino ejusdem
quae sunt propriae partes dominii et baroniarum
de Keig et Monymusk, infra regalitatem Sancti
Andreae; cum officio balliatus predictarum villarum et terrarum:—E. 249l. 11s. 8d —tenemento,
vulgo The Persone of Belhelvies Manse nuncupato,
infra canoniam veteris Aberdonie.—E. 3s 4d,
etc., et 2od. in augmentationem.—terris de
Kynmoir.—E. 1ol 16s. 4d.—Brueria de Kynmoir.
—E. 49s. et 3s 4d. in augmentationem —Omnes
in baroniam de Keyth et regalitate de Spynie:—
E. 13l. 8s 8d in integro.—tenemento vocato
mansum Thesaurarii Aberdonensis jacente ut
supra·—E. 13s. 4d —3s. 4d. in augmentationem.
Mansione vocato Forbes Mains in dicti canonia
veteris Aberdonie.—E 6s 8d.—12d. in augmentationem.—Balliatus officio baroniarum, etc., ad
Episcopatum Aberdonensem spectantium, jacentium in vicecomitatibus de Aberdeen et Banf respective.—E. valet defensionem dicti Episcopi et
Capituli, etc —dimidietate terrarum de Cochlarachie;—dimidietate terrarum de Newbiging,
cum molendino et crofta de Futtie ac in sexta
parte terrarum de Garrie —E 2ol. 6s. 8d.—6s. 8d.
in augmentationem; terris de Cultis, viz., terris

de Eister Cultis, Mekle Cultis, Pett, Tullichar-
dochet Coldhame, cum molendino, in parochia de
Tarlan·—A.E. 61.; N.E. 24l.—decimis garbalibus
villarum et terrarum de Milntoun et molendini
de Dunnatyr, Ferrar, Brarodaches, Craigtoun,
Wraetouns, Casteltoun, Boutie [? Bontie], Miltoun, et molendini de Boutie, Balnagown, Dal-
quhing, Milton, et molendini, dimidietatis terrarum de Brodland, — decimis terrarum de
Foulbog, Haugh, Mekle Candmoir, Litill Candmoir, Kandred, et Camosmeyr, infra parochias de
Oboyne et Tulliche; unitis ad terras de Cultis:—
E. 2s.—privilegio focalium in maresus, vulgo to
cast peittis, turvis, et clodds, in maresiis vocatis
The Moss of the Auldtoun of Halheid, infra
parochiam de Cushnie —E. 6 bollae brasii seu
hordei   I. S. (Aberd.),   2 Aug. 1638

George, Marchio de Huntlie, etc, h. masc Georgii, Marchionis de Huntlie, etc., patris,—in terris de Cul-
savertie et Enzie ac dominio ejusdem, cum
superioritate Forrestae de Boyne, unitis in
dominium, et comprehendentibus superioritatem
terrarum de Culphin, Auchannochie, et Auchan-
nassie, cum maneriei loco de Bogiegicht, et advocatione ecclesiarum;—terras de Ordinhuiffs, Burne-
syde, et Bogmuchellis;—terras de Inchdask, Kil-
birnies, et Kilpottie·—A E. 125l. 1s 8d.; N.E.
500l. 6s 8d —terris et baronia de Auchindoun et
Keithmoor comprehendentibus terras, maneriem,
et terras dominicales de Auchindean;—croftas de
Auchbelrowie et Lagan ,—terras de Keithmoor,
Clunybeg;—dimidietatem de Clunymoir,—terras
de Milntoun cum molendino ,—terras de Tulloch-
allane, Over et Nether Thowmanonis, Smyths-
toun, Boigfuird, Badcheir,—binam partem terrarum de Inverchinache et Schanvell;—tertiam
partem terrarum de Balloherve, cum forrestis de
Glenfiddiche et Blakwatter, et advocationibus capel-
laniarum·—A E 10l., N E 40l —in terris et

baronia de Gartullie continente Maynes de Gartullie vulgo vocatas Hiltoune,—terras de Wylie-
.wrae, Westseatt, Sauchinhill, Kirkhill, Fechill,
Milnhill, Over Kirkhill, Cornetochrache, Sounker,
Bordelseat, Fidlerseat, Gumpstoun, Cokstoun, Duncanstoun, Stodfauld, molendinum de Gartullie,
croftas vocatas Pyperis-croft, Fetterscroft, Doupes-
croft, infra baroniam de Gartullie.—A E. 12l ; N.E.
48l.—terris de Pitglassie ,—terras de Auchinhun-
dauch (vel Auchnahandach) infra baroniam de
Murthlak, cum multuris de Keithbeig.—E 16l. 12s.
8d. feudifirmae :—terris de Keithbeig jacentibus ut
supra.—E. 4l. 6d. feudifirmae:—terris et baronia de
Strathaven, cum turre de Drimmin (vel Drimannie);
—terris de Fotterletter, Inveruries, et Inverlochtie,
cum advocatione capellaniae de Petcashe, infra
ecclesiam cathedralem de Murray, et jurisdictione
balliatus dictarum terarrum dominii et baroniae,
quae baronia comprehendit villas et terras de
Over et Nether Drimminis, Dalmoir, Downens
Over et Nether, Litill Inverchebat, Eister et
Wester Inveruries, Inverlochie, Dalivrogat, Fetterletter, Thomebreak et 2 Torrens, Auchlony, Dal-
mabie et molendinum, Balliebeag, Dallienarache,
Knawlerge, Auchnateill, Keppache, Eister et
Wester Campbell, Ruthven et molendinum,
Thomachlagan, Crewthlie, Glenconiglass, Auch-
ruchane, et molendinum, Minnimoir, Auchorochan,
Thombae Auchdregine, Auchmarrow, molendinum
vocatum Rufreische, Baddienochall, et Suiarthour;
—forrestas de Glenaven, Glenbuilg, et Glenlivet;
—salmonum piscationibus super aquis de Aven et
Livet dictis terris adjacentibus cum advocatione
ecclesiarum ,—terras de Blairfudie cum molendino,
Ledauche, Tombrecach , — villis et terris de
Nevay, Auchnastrae, Auchnaveiche, Auldweiche,
et Tomalman, infra dominium de Strathaven ·—
A.E. 40l. ; N.E. 16ol. — turre, fortalicio, et
Maynis de Balvenie, Davach, et Letiche (vel

Letauch), Milntoun de Balvenie, et Tulloche,
devach de Bucharme, devach de Belliehaukis, et
Argarthnie;—villis et terris de Nether Clunie et
Parkmoir, infra dominium de Balvenie, extendentibus per annum ad 40 celdras victualium in
speciale warrantum terrarum de Ogstoun in
Elgin et Forres:—A.E. 4l.; N.E. 16l.—villa et
terris de Keithbeg in parochia de Murthlake —
E.   —terris de Over et Nether Ardwellis,
cum forresta de Blackwatter in dominio de Balvenie.—A.E. 3l.; N.E. 12l.—balliatus officio
barroniarum, shyrarum, etc., ad episcopatum
Aberdonensem spectantium, jacentium in vicecomitatibus de Aberdeen et Banf respective ·—E.
valet defensionem dicti Episcopi et capituli, etc.

I. S (Banff),   2 Aug. 1638

George, Marchio de Huntlie, etc., h masc. Georgii, Marchionis de Huntlie, etc., patris,—in terris dominii
de Gordoun, Huntlie et Fogo;—terris de Rum-
iltoun, — terris de Reidpeth Nether Redcleuch,
Wolstruther, Quikiswood, Spottiswood, Fawsyd,
Hekispeth, Malerstanes et Fawnis, propriis partib-
bus dictarum terrarum de Huntlie, Gordoun et
Fogo, cum jure patronatus capellaniae de Huntlie
vocatae Chantorie, infra dominium de Gordoun —
A.E. 50l.; N.E. 200l.   I. S. (Berwick),   2 Aug. 1638

    „   Marchio de Huntlie, etc., h. masc Georgii, Mar-
chionis de Huntlie, etc., patris,—in terris de
Ogstoun et Plewlandis cum molendino ventoso,
et privilegio nundinarum et fororum de Ogstoun
ecclesiae, unitis in baroniam de Ogstoun, pro
principali.—A. E 8l.; N E. 32l.—villa et terris
de Ballormie:—E. 16l.—villa et terris de Dunkintie, cum libertate effodiendi focalia lie fewall,
faill et divot in communitate de Caldcot et Greinis,
in baronia de Kilmaldrake.—A E. 40s; N. E. 8l.
—terris et baronia de Fochabirs, viz., Eister et
Wester Fochabirs, et burgo de Fochabirs;—
terris de Ardedarauche; molendino de Fochabirs,

infra baroniam et regalitatem de Urquhart, cum
privilegio liberi burgi, et foro publico hepdoma-
.datim die Sabbathi, et 4 liberis nundinis :—E
13l. 16s. 8d. feudifirmae.—tenemento infra burgum de Elgin cum horto.—A.E. 3s.; N E 12s.
—villa et terris de Sanct Andrewis-Kirkhill,
infra regalitatem de Spynie et baroniam de
Kilmalemak, cùm pastura et privilegiis · — E.
4l. 10s. feudifirmae —villa et terris de Cald-
coittis infra parochiam de Elgyn — E 4l.
.feudifirmae ·—bina parte villae et terrarum de St.
Andraes-Kirktoun, infra baroniam de Kilmalek —
E. 3l. feudifirmae ·—sexta parte villae et terrarum
de St Androes-Kirktoun, cum feudifirma 6l. de
sexta parte villae et terrarum de Sanct Androes-
Kirktoun vocata Gilmersyd, cum superioritate
ejusdem, in baronia de Kilmalemake ·—A.E. 4l.;
N.E. 16l.:—cymba superioris passagii super aqua
de Spey, cum terris de Baithill et crofta ejusmodi,
infra parochiam de Essill.—A.E 5s ; N.E. 20s.
—parte terrarum de Reidhall vocata Craigheid et
Hardleyis, infra parochiam de Essill.—A.E. 5s.;
N.E. 20s.　　　　　　　I. S. (Elgin),　2 Aug. 1638

George, in India, to his father Alexander, in Borderside of Kelly
　　　　—h gen.　　　　　S. H , 23 Nov.;　2 Dec. 1793

　,,　in India, to his mother Katherine Knows, wife of Alex.,
　　　in Kelly—h. of prov. and in gen　S. H , 23 Nov.;　2 Dec. 1793

　,,　son of Sir W. of Invergordon, bart. *See* **William** of
　　　Newhall　　　　　　S. H., 18 April 1766

　,,　surgeon. *See* **Elizabeth,** Jamaica　　S H., 18 Feb 1753

　,,　of Jamaica　*See* **Elizabeth,** Jamaica　　S H., 23 Aug 1782

　,,　fier of Kincaldrum. Alexander Bowar, fier of Kincreith,
　　　h of prov of George Gordoun, fier of Kincal-
　　　drum, in the proper lands underwryttin of the
　　　barronie of Kincaldrum, to wit, the dominicall
　　　lands and mayns of Kincaldrum and Buchtie-
　　　hillock :—A.E. 45s.; N E 9l.—the Templelands
　　　of Kincaldrum —E 3s of feu duty I. S (Forfar), 21 Jan. 1659

　,,　de Kincaldrum. *See* **Anna,** Kincaldrum　I. S. (Forfar), 16 Jan 1662

George, of Miln of Kincardin. *See* **Francis**   S H , 11 Nov 1730

,,   de Kirkdaill, h. prov. Rogeri de Quhytpark, fratris germani,—in 5 mercatis terrarum ex 20 mercatis
terrarum de Newtoun de Cardins antiqui extentus, in baronia de Cardines et parochia de Anwoth
—A.E 5m.; N.E. 10l.   I. S. (Kirkcudb), 20 Mar. 1628

,,   in Knokleyth. *See* **John,** Knokleyth

       I. S. Supp. (Aberd.), 12 Jan. 1579

,,   h linae Rogeri de Knokreochis, fratris   I. G., 17 April 1610

,,   de Lesmoir. *See* **James,** Lesmoir   I. S. (Aberd), 29 Nov. 1564

,,   de Lesmoir. *See* **Alexander,** Lesmoir   I. S. (Aberd.), 3 Oct 1600,

       I. S. (Aberd.), 20 Dec 1600

,,   *See* **Francis,** Sir, of Lessmore, bart   S. H., 25 Dec. 1790

,,   Alexander, clerk to Messrs. ·Ross & Ogilvie in London,
to his uncle Robert, W.S.—h. gen.

       S. H , 6 May, 30 May 1793

,,   de Nether Boddom   *See* **Alexander,** Vet. Aberdonia

       I. S. (Aberd.), 22 June 1698

,,   de Newtoun, h. masc. Jacobi de Newtoun, patris,—in
terris et baronia de Newtoun de Wranghame,
continente terras de Newtoun de Wranghame,
cum molendinis granorum et fullonum ·—E 66l.
13s. 4d.—terras de Pulquhyt ,—terras de Kirktoun
de Colsalmond ;—terras de Carnhill :—E. 32l. 4s.
—terras de Lettinghame ;—terras de Williamstoun, cum molendino de Williamstoun et astrictis
multuris baroniae de Wranghame, cum privilegio
custumae et lie toll nundinarum et fori de Sanct
Serffisfair, annuatim super solum dictarum terrarum de Wranghame, infra baroniam de Newtoun
et parochiam de Colsalmond.—E. 55l. 6s. 8d.

       I. S. (Aberd.), 10 June 1644

,,   merchant in Old Aberdeen. *See* **Jean,** Old Aberdeen ;
Helen, Old Aberdeen   S. H., 9 May 1776

,,   of Rainieshill. *See* **George,** professor, Aberdeen   S H., 30 Sept. 1731

,,   of Rothney, to his father William of Rothney—h male
and of line gen.   S. H., 29 July, 17 Aug. 1772

,,   of Sands, advocate. *See* **Alexander,** merchant in
Aberdeen   S. H , 21 April 1732

George, h. Wilhelmi de Schives, patris,—in terris de Littilgeych,
    in baronia de Schives.—A.E. 20s , N E 6l. 13s. 4d.
                           I S (Aberd.), 5 Oct. 1546

  ,,   Miles, h. Wilhelmi de Shawis, patris,—in terris et
    baronia de Shawis (Schevis).—A E. 12l.; N.E.
    48l.   I. S. (Aberd), 29 Nov. 1565

  ,,   *See* **James** de Strangaslyle ·   I. S. (Kirkcudb.), 29 Jan. 1650
  ,,   of Sheilagreen. *See* **Ann,** Sheilagreen   S. H., 19 April 1746
  ,,   of Shellagreen *See* **James,** Shellagreen   S. H., 10 June 1747
  ,,   commissary-clerk of Sutherland. *See* **Hugh** of Carroll
                                      S. H., 9 Feb. 1741
  ,,   de Tarpersie. *See* **William** de Tarpersie I S. (Aberd.), 16 Dec. 1635
  ,,   of Tarpersie. *See* **William** of Tarpersie I. S. (Banff), 29 Aug 1655
  ,,   de Terpersie, h. Gulielmi de Terpersi, avi I. G Supp., 5 Feb. 1696
  ,,   de Terpersie, h. Georgii de Terpersie, proavi
                                I. G. Supp., 5 Feb. 1696
  ,,   de Terpersie. *See* **George,** *supra.*
  ,,   de Thornbank, h. Wilhelmi de Thornebank, patris,—in
    villis et terris de Newmylne vulgo nuncupatis the
    Lonne;—villis et terris de Nethir Kinminitys;—
    molendino de Strathylae nuncupato the Ovir-
    mylne, infra baroniam de Strathylae, regalitatem
    de Kinloss, et parochiam de Keith.—E. 27l. 11s
    feudifirmae   I. S. (Banff), 21 Oct. 1667
  ,,   de Tillaquhowdie. *See* **John,** Tillaquhowdie
                            I. S. (Aberd.), 29 Nov. 1610
  ,,   of Troquhain. *See* **Patrick** of Troquhain   S. H., Dec. 1761
  ,,   of Troquhain. *See* **Patrick** of King's Grange S. H , 16 Mar 1774
  ,,   *See* **Alexander** of Woodhall   S. H., 20 Oct 1746
Gilbert, burgensis de Aberdein. *See* **George,** Aberdein I G., 22 April 1634
  ,,   collector of excise in Dumfries, to his father Archibald
    of Minidow, collector of excise in Dumfries—h.
    gen.   S. H., 12 June 1754
  ,,   collector of excise in Dumfries, to his father Archibald
    of Minidow, who died 3 May, 1754—h. spec. in
    193l. 12s 8⅔d. stg over Corsock, including Muir-
    parks, etc., and Maintroull, Kirkcudbrightshire
                    S. H , 10 Aug.; 23 Aug. 1759
  ,,   of Halleaths. *See* **Archibald** of Halleaths   S H , 30 Mar. 1790

Grizell, to her mother Nicolas Stewart, wid. of John of Greenlaw—h. gen. S. H , 5 Aug. 1737 , 23 Feb 1743

„ wife of D Sanderson, joiner, Cromarty, to her brother
Robert, son of George, Culmaly—h port. gen.

S. H , 13 Mar. , 24 May 1769

Harriet, wife of And. Stewart, W.S., to her brother Adam, son
of James of Cocklarachie—h. port gen

S H., 4 Aug ; 9 Aug. 1779

Helen, to her father James of Barns—h. port gen

S H , 6 Oct 1739; 20 Nov 1740

„ h. port. praedicti Joannis [de Blaikat], patris,—in terris
praedictis. *See* **Catherine,** Blaikat

I S. (Kirkcudb.), 29 Oct 1548

„ h port. praedictae Margaretae [Blaket], sororis,—in undecima parte dictarum terrarum. *See* **Catharine,**
Blaket I. S (Kirkcudb.), 14 April 1552

„ Blaiket Joannes Broun de Mollans, h. Joannis Broun
de Mollans, patris,—in 10 solidatis 11 denariatis
terrarum 9 mercatarum terrarum de Blaiket antiqui extentus, cum undecima parte molendini
earundem, in parochia de Wre, olim pertinentibus
Helenae Gourdoun matri quondam Joannis Broun ·
—10 solidatis 11 denariatis 9 mercatarum terrarum
de Blaiket, et undecima parte molendini, olim pertinentibus Thomae Maxwell de Arremyng ,—cum
sua parte, et parte Joannis Pillo croftae vocatae
Bonsak pertinentis praedictis 9 mercatis terrarum
de Blaiket ;—10 solidatis 11 denariatis terrarum 9
mercatarum terrarum de Blaiket, cum undecima
parte molendini ejusdem, olim pertinentibus
Willielmo Douglas de Eschtries ,—10 solidatis
11 denariatis 9 mercatarum terrarum de Blaiket,
cum undecima parte molendini ejusdem, olim
pertinentibus Joanni Gordoun de Beoche ,—10
solidatis 11 denariatis terrarum 9 mercatarum de
Blaiket, cum undecima parte molendini earundem,
olim pertinentibus Petro M'Dowell de Machir-
more ;—quae quidem quinque partes extendunt
in integro ad 54 solidatas 7 denariatas terrarum

(369)

praedictarum 9 mercatarum terrarum de Blaiket,
et quinque undecimas partes molendini ejusdem.
—A.E. 54s ; N.E. 8l. 3s 9d.   I. S. (Kirkcudb.), 23 May 1616

Helen. *See* **William,** Cambridge   S. H., 14 Jan 1761
,,   Cunnynghame, wife of Charles H. Gordon, advocate, to
    Janet Hay, dau. of Jn. Hay, writer, Edinburgh—
    co-h. of prov. gen.   S. H., 5 Aug., 14 Aug 1754
,,   wife of Charles Hamilton Gordon, advocate, to her
    father William Cunningham of Boquhen—h. gen.
                      S. H., 16 July 1746 ;   Oct. 1771
,,   to her brother Captain William, son of Adam, goldsmith
    in Edinburgh—h. gen.   S. H., 28 April ;   6 May 1767
,,   dau. of T. in Lagan of Glenrinnes, to her grandfather
    Duncan Cumming of Letter Wandoch—h port.
    gen.   S. H., 16 Jan. 1703
,,   to her father George, merchant in Old Aberdeen—co-
    h. of prov. gen.   S H., 13 Mar.;   9 May 1776
,,   h. Alexandri de Swellend, patris,—in villa et terris de
    Swellend, infra parochiam de Monniecaback.—
    A.E 5s. ; N.E. 20s.   I S. (Aberd.), 1 Jan. 1669

Henrietta, wife of David Urquhart of Braelangwell, to her
    father Charles Hamilton Gordon of Newhall—
    h. gen.   S. H , 25 Jan. ; 29 Jan. 1787
,,   wife of G. Gordon, supervisor of customs, Dumfries,
    to her sister Louisa, dau. of J. Douglas of Dornoch
    —co-h. of prov. gen.   S. H , 16 Dec. 1776
,,   wife of G. Gordon, supervisor of customs, Dumfries,
    to her sister Stewarta, dau of J. Douglas of Dor-
    noch—co-h. of prov. gen   S H., 10 Dec. 1776
,,   wife of Ts. Lockhart, commissioner of Excise, to
    her brother Wm of Newhall, advocate, who died
    11 Jan. 1778—h spec. cum ben invent. in St.
    Martin's, Ross-shire, Balblair, Cromarty ; and
    Milton, Lanark   S. H., 26 Sept 1780; 9 Jan. 1781
,,   dau. of Peter, at Miln of Smithstown, to her uncle
    John of Balgown—co-h. of prov. gen.
                S H , 15 Dec. 1785; 25 Jan. 1786

Henry, of Auchlyne. *See* **James** of Auchlyne   S. H., 12 July 1714
,,   de Avachie, h. Joannis de Avachie, patris   I. G , 25 Jan. 1687

Henry, de Avachie, h. Joannis de Avachie, patris,—in terris de
Avachie et Kinminitie cum molendino de Avachie,
Milnehaughe et villa molendinaria, infra Marchi-
onatum de Huntlie (olim Strathbogie) et nunc
regalitatem ejusdem .—E. 20l. 6s. 8d.—villa et
terris de Harthill;—villa et terris de Nether-
carden cum molendino ,—advocatione parochiae
et ecclesiae parochialis de Oyne —A E. 3l., N.E.
12l —terris de Kirktoun de Oyne et Alehouse
Croft, infra parochiam de Oyne et regalitatem de
Garrioch .—E 24l feudifirmae —villa et terris de
Torreis cum silvis et boges ;—terris de Ardryn
(vel Ardoyne) cum molendinis ,—terris de Newlands infra parochiam de Oyne et regalitatem
de Garrioch · — E. 20l feudifirmae : — 2 aratris
de Ryhill et Buchanstoun cum molendino de
Buchanstoun, infra parochiam et regalitatem
praedictas, cum decimis garbalibus .—E.
—terris de Oldrayne comprehendentibus villam
et terras de Oldrayne et Newlands ejusdem cum
molendino, viz bina parte molendini de Rayne,
et bina parte croftarum dicti molendini cum
bruerio lie Alehouse, infra villam de Oldrayne et
servitiis ;—tertia parte dicti molendini ;—dimidia
parte villae et terrarum de Newrayne et Barrell-
dyke ,—terris de Lentask (Lentush), Leusk, Kirktoune de Rayne ;—villa et terris de Threefields
et Bonitoun ,—molendino de Bonitoun, omnibus
infra parochiam de Rayne ,—tertia parte villarum
et terrarum de Bruxtoun, infra parochiam de
Tillinessle ·—E.   feudifirmae :—decimis
garbalibus dictarum terrarum.—A E. 3s., N.E
13s. 4d.   I. S. (Aberd.), 25 Jan. 1687

,,   of Blairmad. *See* **John,** Blairmad   S. H , 26 Jan. 1728
,,   de Creich. *See* **John,** Creich   I. S. (Wigton), 7 April 1663
,,   de Glassauch, h. Henrici de Glassauch, patris,—in terris
de Glassauch et Craigmylnes earundem et multuris,
in dominio de Fordyce —E 9l., etc , et 5m in
augmentationem, feudifirmae .—terris de Pethade-

lies vulgo nuncupatis Over et Nether Pethadelies,
et tertia parte mori de Pethadelie, cum communi
·pastura super binam partem praefati mori de
Pethadelie, et super montem de Fordyce jacentibus ut supra, cum piscationibus alborum piscium.
—E. 10 bollae frumenti   I S. (Banff), 12 May 1643

Henry, de Glassauch, h. Henrici de Glassauch, patris,—in villis
et terris de Forskan, in baronia de Ruthven.—E.
5l. 5s. 10d. feudifirmae   I S (Banff), 24 Aug. 1649

,,   de Glassauch. *See* **Henry,** *supra.*

,,   to his father Colonel Henry of Knockespack, who died
23 Aug. 1787—h. male and of taillie spec. in Auchlyne, Newbigging, Knockespack, Gordonfield, etc.
      S H (Aberd.), 9 Dec. 1789, 20 Feb. 1790

,,   colonel, of Knockespack. *See* **Henry,** *supra.*

Hugh, of Carroll, to his granduncle George, commissary-clerk
of Sutherland—h gen.   S. H., 18 Mar. 1740; 9 Feb. 1741

,,   of Carrol. *See* **John** of Carrol   S. H., 19 Dec. 1766

,   goldsmith in Edinburgh. *See* **Rachel,** Edinburgh   S H., 23 Jan. 1777

,,   de Grange, h. conquestus Alexandri de Balcray, f. fratris
avi,—in terris ecclesiasticis vicariae et rectoriae
ecclesiae parochialis de Kirkynner, cum mansione
et decimis garbalibus inclusis, infra parochiam de
Kirkynner, extendentibus ad 2 mercatas terrarum
antiqui extentus.—A.E. 2m., N.E. 11l 17s. 4d
et 3s. 4d. in augmentationem,.feudifirmae
      I. S. (Wigton), 23 Feb. 1608

,,   of Grange. *See* **John** of Grange   S. H., 18 Aug. 1701

,,   to his great-grandfather Hugh of Grange, who died
     h. spec. in Grange, Trave, Barrachan, Kirk-
christ, Killeman and Baltrostan, all in the parish
of Penningham   S H , 24 Jan.; 25 Jan. 1733

,,   of Grange. *See* **Hugh,** *supra*

,,   in Killileoch. *See* **Robert,** Killileoch   I. G , 12 June 1697

,,   of Miln of Kincardine. *See* **Ann,** Miln of Kincardine
      S. H., 4 Aug. 1766

,,   de Kirkhill. *See* **Francis** de Kirkhill.   I. S. (Aberd.), 29 June 1694

,,   of Kirkhill. *See* **John,** Kirkhill   S. H., 21 Jan. 1708

,,   son of Hugh of Kirkhill   *See* **John,** Kirkhill   S. H., 21 Jan. 1708

Isobel. *See* **Alexander,** Aberdeen   S. H . Supp , 20 Jan. 1774

  ,,   Ardmeallie.   Maria Meldrum sp. Davidis Stewart
commissarii de Murray; Issobella Meldrum sp.
Jacobi Gordone de Ardmeallie · et Elspetha Mel-
drum sp. magistri Davidis Cuming ministri verbi
Dei apud Breymurray, hh. port magistri Joannis
Hay de Logie, avunculi   I G , 16 Jan. 1674

  ,,   Maria Melldrum sp. Davidis Stewart commissarii de
Murray, Issobella Meldrum sp. Jacobi Gordon de
Ardmeallie et Elspetha Meldrum sp magistri
Davidis Cuming ministri verbi Dei apud Breymurray, hh. port. magistri Joannis Hay de Logie,
avunculi ;—in molendino de Gatus;—aratro de
Nethertoun, de Crimongorthe;—aratro de Longley
et dimidio aratri de Ovirtoun de Crimondgorth ,
—aratro de Lochhills ;—alio aratro terrarum de
Ovirtoun de Crimondgorth ,—villa et terris de
Strathlodlie, cum decimis garbalibus, infra parochiam et baroniam de Crimond, unitis in tenandriam de Logie-Crimond.—A.E. 15l.; N E 6ol.
     I S. (Aberd.), 16 Jan. 1674

  ,,   wife of James of Ardmelie, to her sister Mary Meldrum
(wid. of D. Stewart, commissary of Murray), who
died   —h. port. spec. in 5,000 merks
over Lechars, Glassells, Polglarses, etc
     S. H., 2 July; 3 Aug 1708

  ,,   sp. Willielmi Cuming de Auchry, h. Joannis de Balmade
praepositi burgi de Bamf, patris,—in 2 bovatis
terrarum de Eister Croylett .—E. 1l. 15s. 9d —2
bovatis terrarum de Newfortrie in baronia de
Strathillay et regalitate de Kinlos —E 3l. 11s. 8d.
     I. S. (Banff), 4 Dec 1673

  ,,   sp Willielmi Cuming de Auchry, h. Joannis de Balmade
praepositi burgi de Bamff, patris   I G., 4 Dec 1673

  ,,   h. Joannis de Balmade nuper praepositi burgi de Bamff,
patris,—in dimidietate salmonum piscationis super
aquam de Divorne subtus scopulis de Alvach vulgo
The Cruives of Alvach nuncupatis, adjacentibus
terris de Moncoffer, Govin, et Corskie, cum Corfe-

house ejusdem, et dimidietate trium croftarum de
Braesyid.—A E. 4s.; N E. 16s.—Salmonum pis-
. caria super aquam de Divorne Thainsett nuncupata.
—A E 3s.; N.E. 12s. I. S. (Aberd.), 18 June 1674

Isobel, h. Joannis de Balmade nuper praepositi burgi de Bamff,
patris,—in annuo redditer 100m. de terris de Brunt-
zairdis in dominio de Glendouachie I. S (Banff), 18 June 1674

,, dau. of Jas. of Banchory, to her aunt Ann Cumming,
dau of Robt. Cumming of Birness—co-h of prov.
gen. S H., 7 May 1740

,, to her father James of Barns—h. port. gen.
S. H., 6 Oct. 1739; 20 Nov. 1740

,, h. Caroli de Blelock, patris I. G , 19 Feb 1698

,, *See* **Christina,** Branelane I. S. (Aberd.), 6 Oct. 1669

,, to her father Alexander of Coldwells—h. port. of prov.
and in gen. S. H., 20 Dec. 1765; 7 Feb. 1766

,, wid. of Alex. Murray, minister, Duffus, to her mother
Rebecca Dunbar or Gordon or Anderson—h. port.
gen. S. H., 25 April; 5 July 1782

,, Lady Hamiltoun, wife of Sir Wm., to her father Sir
John Hamiltoun of Halcraig, a Lord of Session—
h. port. gen. S. H., 14 May 1708

,, Lady Hamiltoun, wife of Sir Wm. of Dalpholly, to her
brother John Hamiltoun of Halcraig, advocate—
h. port. gen. S. H., 14 May 1708

,, of Kirkhill, wife of P. Stewart, Birkhall, to her brother
John, son of P[atrick] of Kirkhill—h. of prov. gen.
S H., 8 Feb.; 15 Feb. 1764

,, George Forbes (Lochermick), merchant, Aberdeen, to
his aunt Isobel Gordon, wife of Alex Crombie,
merchant there—h of prov. gen.
S. H. Supp., 8 Feb ; 19 Sept. 1752

,, wid of Alex. Garrioch, minister at Midmar, to her
brother Alexander of Edintoir—h. gen.
S. H., 16 Feb.; 22 April 1763

,, **Mary,** wife of Dr. James MacNeill of Stevenson, to her
father Colonel George—h. of prov. and in gen.
S. H., 22 July, 15 Aug. 1799

J., of Hillhead   *See* **Mary,** Hillhead   S H , 31 Dec. 1712

James, to his father George, writer to the signet—h. of line
gen.   S. H., 11 Oct., 24 Oct. 1749

  ,,   **George,** to his father Alexander, captain in the Earl of
Orkney's regiment of foot—h. gen   S. H., 11 Jan.; 20 Aug 1733

  ,,   jeweller in Aberdeen, to his sister Ann, dau. of F[rancis ?],
shoemaker there—h gen.   S H , 26 Dec 1798, 17 Jan. 1799

  ,,   merchant in Aberdour. *See* **Katharine,** Aberdour   S. H ,   4 May 1787

  ,,   f. legitimus quondam Adami de Aberlour, h. Georgii
f. legitimi quondam magistri Roberti scribae in
Edinburgh, f fratris   I. G., 19 June 1697

  ,,   de Ardmeallie. *See* **Isobel,** Ardmeallie
I. G , I. S. (Aberd.), 16 Jan. 1674; S. H., 2 July, 3 Aug. 1708

  ,,   to his brother Archibald (son of Peter of Ardmeallie),
who died   Sept., 1741—h. of prov. spec in the
lands and barony of Zeuchrie, including Myreside,
etc , with salmon fishings   S. H., 5 April; 11 April 1753

  ,,   of Ardoch, rector of Banchory. *See* **John** of Ardoch
S. H., 21 Jan 1748

  ,,   of Ardoe, Episc. min. in Montrose   *See* **John** of Ardoe
S. H., 21 Jan. 1748

  ,,   de Arradoull. *See* **Alexander** de Arradoull   I. S. (Banff), 23 July 1663

  ,,   of Auchendolly. *See* **Robert** of Auchendolly   S. H., 23 April 1717

  ,,   of Auchleuchries, to his father Alexander of Auchleuchries
—h. male and of line gen.   S. H., 9 Mar.; 23 April 1751

  ,,   to his brother James [*sic*.], son of Alexander of Auchleuchries—h. of prov. gen.   S. H., 1 July; 2 Aug 1768

  ,,   son of Alexander of Auchleuchries. *See* **James,** *supra.*

  ,,   of Auchlyne, to his father Henry of Auchlyne, who died
May, 1707—h. spec. in Auchlyne, Clatt, New-
bigging, Rindriggs, etc.   S. H., 18 Dec. 1713; 12 July 1714

  ,,   of Auchlyne, to his grandfather James of Auchlyne—
h. of prov. gen.   S. H , 10 Aug.; 12 Aug. 1734

  ,,   of Auchlyne. *See* **James,** *supra*   S. H , 12 Aug. 1734

  ,,   of Auchredy, N. Aberdeen. *See* **Alexander** of Auchredy
S. H , 2 Sept. 1709

  ,,   son of Al. of Auchredy, to his mother Marjory Davidson
of Cairnbrogie (and wid. of Alex. of Auchredy),
who died 7 Mar , 1739—h spec in Cairnbrogie
with its mill   S. H. (Aberd), 21 Sept. 1739; 25 Jan. 1740

James, de Auchtirairne.　*See* **John** de Glascou-forrest

　　　　　　　　　　　　　　　　I. S (Aberd), 20 Dec 1574

　,,　of Badenscoth, to his father William of Badenscoth,
　　　　who died　　Aug , 1733—h spec in Badenscoth,
　　　　two parts of Brookhills, Blackhills, and Reidhills,
　　　　and ⅛ of Logiealton, with Bogues of Darlay, etc

　　　　　　　　　　　　　　　　S. H.,　9 Aug. 1737

　,,　of Badenscoth.　*See* **Catharine,** Blackford , **Jean,**
　　　　Rothie　　　　　　　　　　S. H , 10 July 1778

　,,　of Balbethan.　*See* **Benjamin** of Balbethan　S. H , 24 April 1739

　,,　of Balmeg.　*See* **Samuel,** Anworth　　S H , 9 Dec. 1794

　,,　**Farquhar,** to his father John of Balmuir, clerk to the
　　　　signet—h of prov gen.　　S. H., 21 Jan ; 8 Feb 1790

　,,　of Banchory.　*See* **Ann; Isobel,** Banchory　S. H., 7 May 1740

　,,　of Banchory. *See* **Thomas,** Banchory　S H., 23 Nov. 1751

　,,　of Bar.　*See* **John** of Overbar　　S H , 12 Nov. 1708

　,,　h. Alexandri de Barnbarroch, patris,—in 6 mercatis
　　　　terrarum de Barnbarroch et Barnchwry antiqui
　　　　extentus, cum 2 molendinis dictarum terrarum,
　　　　in parochia de Colven ;—3 mercatis 10 solidatis
　　　　terrarum de Gaitgill-M'Ilvernok ; — 25 solidatis
　　　　terrarum de Gaitgill-M'Illinsche antiqui extentus,
　　　　in parochia de Larg.—A.E. 7l. 15s.; N.E. 23l. 5s.

　　　　　　　　　　　　　I. S. (Kirkcudb.), 21 April 1556

　,,　de Barnebarroch.　*See* **Agnes,** Barnebarroch

　　　　　　　　　　　　　I. S. (Kirkcudb.), 29 July 1602

　,,　h. Willielmi f Jacobi de Barnebarroche, patrui　I G , 24 May 1627

　,,　de Barnebarroche.　*See* **James,** *supra.*

　,,　of Barns.　*See* **Christian, Elizabeth, Helen, Isobel,**
　　　　Mary, Barns　　　　　　S. H., 20 Nov. 1740

　,,　minister of Bellie, to his grandfather James, portioner
　　　　of Dundurcas, who died　　, 1751—h. spec in
　　　　the fifth part of Dundurcas, with salmon fishings
　　　　on the Spey　　　S. H. (Elgin), 30 May ; 12 June 1780

　,,　of Birkenbush.　*See* **John** of Birkenbush

　　　　　　　　　　S. H , 23 Nov 1758 , S. H., 15 June 1770

　,,　of Boytath.　*See* **Josiah** of Boytath　　S. H , 31 Oct. 1720

　,,　son of James of Boytath.　*See* **Josiah** of Boytath

　　　　　　　　　　　　　　　　S. H., 31 Oct. 1720

James, de Buittle   *See* **Robert,** Vicecomes de Kenmure, etc.

                                          I. S. (Kirkcudb.), 1 May 1645

,,   of Buittill. *See* **Robert,** Viscount of Kenmure

                                I. S. Supp. (Kirkcudb.), 23 Feb 1658

,,   of Cairstown. *See* **Sybil,** Cairstown   S. H., 29 May 1799

,,   of Campbellton, Argyll, to his father James of Campbell-

       ton—h. gen.   S. H , 27 Feb. 1705 ; 25 Jan. 1706

,,   of Campbellton. *See* **James** of Campbellton, *supra.*

,,   of Campbelltoun. *See* **William** of Campbelltoun

                S H., 28 Mar. 1724; S H., 26 Oct 1726

,,   son of James, watchmaker in Canongate, to his cousin

       Roger of Dendeuch—h. gen. S H , 26 Nov. 1736; 14 Mar 1737

,,   watchmaker in Canongate. *See* **James,** *supra.*

,,   de Careltoune, h. Gulielmi de Quhytpark, patris I. G , 20 Dec 1670

,,   of Carleton. *See* **Nathaniel** of Gordonstoun   S. H.,   Dec. 1702

,,   of Carlton *See* **John,** Sir, of Earlston, bart   S H., 5 June 1799

,,   of Cocklarachie, to his father John of Cocklarachie, who

       died 8 July, 1714—h. male spec in one-fourth of

       the Davach lands of Cocklarachie, with mill, etc

                       S H., 14 July, 24 July 1721

,,   of Cocklarachie, to his father John of Cocklarachie—

       h. gen   S. H., 14 July, 24 July 1721

,,   of Cochlarachie. *See* **Charlotte,** Cocklarachie ; **Harriet,**

       Cocklarachie   S. H., 9 Aug. 1779

,,   in Collie. *See* **George,** in Dundurcus   I. S. (Elgin), 29 April 1692

, ,,   of Cowbairdy *See* **Ernest** of Cowbairdy   S H , 13 Sept. 1773

,,   de Crackullie. Jacobus Calder f. Alexandri Calder de

       Aslowne, h. Jacobi Gordoun de Crackullie, avi

       materni   I. G , 18 Jan 1627

,,   de Craigcullie. Jacobus Calder de Aslowne, h Jacobi

       Gordoun de Craigcullie, avi materni,—in terris de

       Glengarrok, cum Outsett earundem Alrecardoch

       nuncupato, in baronia de Strathyla.—E. 20m et

       6s. 8d. in augmentationem   I S (Banff), 2 May 1629

,,   de Crago *See* **Thomas** de Crago I S (Kirkcudb.), 1 June 1620

,,   Craigie *See* **Janet,** Craigie   S H , 16 Feb. 1799

,,   tenant in Craigie *See* **John,** Craigie   S H , 14 Nov. 1799

,,   junior, de Craighlaw. *See* **William,** magister, de

       Earlston   I de Poss Quinq , 3 Sept 1686

James, of Craiglaw   *See* **Margaret,** Glenlaggan , **Janet,** Kirkowan   S. H., 10 Jan. 1736

" of Craighlaw   William Wallace of Craighlaw, son of
William Wallace of Galrigge, to his uncle James
Gordon of Craighlaw, who died 24 Nov. 1734—
h. of line spec in the barony of Craighlaw, in-
cluding Barnernie, Barhaple, etc.
S. H. Supp (Wigton), 11 Dec , 15 Dec. 1738

" de Creiche   *See* **George,** Creiche I. S (Aberd), 6 Oct. 1553 [1573?]

" of Crogo. *See* **John** of Crogo   S H., 17 Sept.1702

" h. Gulielmi in Culleindoche, patris,—in 2½ mercatis
terrarum 40 solidatarum terrarum de Killerne et
Torris antiqui extentus, in parochia de Anueth·—
E. 5l. 4s.—firmis feudifirmariis dictarum terrarum :—E. 5l. 4s —dimidia mercata terrae de Tor
extentus praedicti .—A.E 6s. 8d.; N.E. 20s.—20
solidatis terrarum de Marquother extentus prae-
dicti·—A.E. 20s. , N.E. 3l.—2 mercatis terrarum
4 mercatarum terrarum de Brooche antiqui extentus,
in parochia de Kirkdaill.—A.E. 26s. 8d., N.E. 4l.
I. S. (Kirkcudb.), 5 Dec. 1609

" in Cullingdoch. *See* **John,** Cullingdoch
I. S. Supp. (Kirkcudb), 5 June 1623

" de Daach, h. Jacobi de Daach, patris   I G., 30 Sept.1698

" de Daach. *See* **James,** *supra.*

" in Drymmeis, h. Alexandri in Scheilgrein, patrui I. G., 1 July 1614

" town clerk of Dumfries, to his brother George, merchant
there—h of conq gen   S. H., 24 Mar.; 29 Mar. 1733

" in Dundurcas, to his father George, portioner of Dundurcas, who died   Oct , 1710—h. male spec.
in a fifth part of Dundurcas with the brewhouse
thereon   S. H. (Elgin), 18 June, 24 Sept.1714

" portioner of Dundurcas. *See* **James,** minister of Bellie
S. H., 30 May, 12 June 1780

" *See* **Jonet,** Edinburgh   I. G., 31 Mar. 1657

" to his father James of Ellon—h gen   S H., 25 July, 29 July 1732

" of Ellon. *See* **James,** *supra.*

" of Ellon to his brother William (son of James of Ellon),
who died 27 Feb., 1732—h. male and of prov.

(378)

spec. iń the barony of Ellon, including Ardgrain
and Broomfield, Carmuiks, Auchterellon, etc
                       /
                        S. H., 22 Nov 1732

James, of Ellon   *See* **James,** *supra*

,,   of Ellon, to his father James of Ellon—h gen.
                      S H , 27 Feb , 11 July 1750

,,   of Ellon   *See* **James,** *supra*.

,,   doctor, of Fechill   *See* **Catharine,** Fechell ; **Jean,**
     Fechell ; **Mary,** Fechell   S H., 29 Aug 1741

,,   merchant in Forres, to his father James, merchant there
     —h. gen.   S. H , 17 Mar , 25 Mar. 1756

,,   merchant in Forres   *See* **James,** *supra*.

,,   to his father James, merchant in Forres—h gen
                   S. H , 16 Feb. , 20 Feb 1770

,,   merchant in Forres   *See* **James,** *supra*.

,,   merchant in Garmouth. *See* **Thomas,** New York S. H., 23 May 1770

,,   merchant in Glasgow, to his father George, writer to
     the signet—h gen   S. H., 2 Mar , 8 Mar 1764

,,   of Gordonbank. *See* **George,** writer in Edinburgh S H , 28 Jan 1738

,,   de Haddo *See* **Jonet,** Haddo   I S. (Aberd), 11 Feb 1625

,,   de Haddo. *See* **John** de Haddo
           I. G., 11 May 1630; I. S. (Aberd.), 11 May 1630

,,   in Halfmark of Castlemadie, to his uncle James Goldie,
     cooper in Straiton—h. gen   . S. H , 12 Aug.; 19 Aug 1783

,,   of Hilton, doctor, to his father Doctor John of Hilton—
     h gen.   S. H , 27 Sept 1735 , 15 Mar 1736

,,   of Hilton, doctor, to his granduncle Alexander, advocate
     —h. of conq gen.   S. H., 22 May ; 22 June 1736

,,   of Hilton *See* **Barbara,** Hilton   S. H., 7 May 1740

,,   of Hilton, M.D., to his brother Ludovic of Auchmull,
     merchant, Aberdeen—h of conq. gen.
                 S. H , 27 Mar ; 6 June 1744

,,   *See* **Robert,** miles in Hollandia   I G , 7 June 1637

,,   in Inverness. *See* **Agnes,** Inverness   I S (Elgin), 31 Nov. 1690

,,   smith, Jamaica *See* **Jean,** Bellahouston   S. H , 28 June 1799

,,   of Kerston, to his brother William of Kerston, who died
     Jan , 1750—h spec. in Bow of Kerston, How,
     Navershall, Mill of Kerston, Mill of Voy, etc.
                 S. H , 18 April ; 9 July 1763

James, of Killilour. Jeane Maxwell, spous to Thomas Cruik,
merchand burges of Dumfreis: Elizabeth Max-
, well, spous to James Gordoun of Killilour: and
Nicolas Maxwell, spous to James Hammiltoun,
portioner of Alrenning (Areeming)—hh. port. of
Thomas Maxwell of Alrenning, their father,—
in the 40 shilling land of Alrenning, within the
parochin of Kirkpatrick, Durhame.—E. 5l and 2d.
in augmentatioun   I S (Kirkcudb.), 13 Jan 1657

,,   tenant, Kinleith. *See* **Jean,** Leith   S H., 18 Aug. 1772

,,   h. Joannis de Knarie, patris,—in 1 mercata terra de
Knarie antiqui extentus, in parochia de Kirkpatrick
de Mure.—E. 26s 8d   I S. (Kirkcudb.), 12 Mar. 1605

,,   of Knockespeck *See* **Francis,** Knockespock   S. H , 13 April 1770

,,   formerly Brebner, chief judge of Grenada, to his uncle
James of Knockespeck, who died   April, 1768—
h port and of line spec in Auchlyne, Newbigging,
Knockespeck, Terpersey, and fishings in the Don
          S. H., 7 Mar.; 13 April 1770

,,   .of Knockespeck. *See* **James,** *supra.*

,,   h. Joannis, in Larg, patris,—in $2\frac{1}{2}$ mercatis terrarum
de Crailoche antiqui extentus, in parochia de
Inche.—A E 33s 4d ; N.E. 6l.   I. S. (Wigton), 9 Jan. 1638

, ,,   de Lesmoir.   *See* **George** de Colholstane
          I. S (Aberd.), 23 June 1559

,,   h. Patricii f. legitimi et naturalis Georgii de Lesmoir,
fratris germani,—in dimidia terrarum de Auch-
terarie, Tulloch, Tanameynen, Blackmylne.—A E.
30s.; N.E. 6l.   I. S (Aberd.), 29 Nov. 1564

,,   de Lesmoir, h Alexandri de Lesmoir, patris,—in terris
de Balmad, Gorauchie, Craigheid, Morleis, et
molendino de Balmad —A E 4l ; N E. 16l.
          I. S (Aberd.), 10 April 1610

,,   h. Jacobi apparentis de Lesmoir, patris   I. G., 15 Dec. 1637

,,   apparens de Lesmoir   *See* **James,** *supra.*

,,   dominus, de Lesmoir miles baronettus, h domini Jacobi
de Lesmoir militis baronetti, proavi   I. G., 9 June 1641

,,   dominus, de Lesmoir miles baronettus   *See* **James,**
supra.

James, domınus, de Lesmoir mıles baronettus, h. masc domını
Jacobi de Lesmoir mılıtıs baronettı, proavı,—in
terris subsequentıbus ın tenandrıa, vız. villa et
terrıs de Carveichınes, Thornewrae, Corsılstaıne,
—vılla et terrıs de Sliauche cum lie Park, Adamstoun, Silverhıllok, Wistroun, Mutehıllok, Boıgheid,
Newtoun ;—villa et terrıs de Perrısmılne ,—tertıa
parte villae et terrarum de Garıe ,—terris postea
mentionatıs ın superıorıtate tantum, vız. bına
parte vıllae et terrarum de Chappeltoune ;—tertıa
parte vıllae et terrarum de Wadderburne ;—bına
parte villae et terrarum de Thomastoun ;—bına
parte vıllae et terrarum de Comalegıe, ınfra baronıam de Kınmundie per annexatıonem ·—A E
11l. ; N.E. 44l —Terris templarııs de Fulzıement,
in baronıa de Auchdındour, cum officıo heredıtarıı
ballıvatus, et prıvilegıo lıberae regalıtatıs :—A E
5s ; N.E 20s.—38 rudıs terrarum ınfra terrıtorium
burgı de Essıe, quarum 22 ȷacent ex borealı parte
dıctı burgi, et 16 ex australı parte ejusdem burgı,
unıtis in barohıam de Newtoun de Garıe —A.E.
20s.; N.E. 4l.—Terrıs de Essıe, Belhennıe cum
terrıs vocatis Croft de Auchinleck, et loco manerıalı
de Lesmoır, ınfra baronıam et domınıum de Hunt-
lıe :—E. 20l —Dımıdıetate vıllae et terrarum de
Auldmaırdrum ın baronıa de Strathbogıe, cum
ȷure patronatus ecclesıae de Essıe, in dıcta baronıa
de Strathbogıe.—A.E. 10s.; N.E. 40s.

I. S. (Aberd), 24 Aprıl 1642

,, domınus, de Lesmoır. *See* **James,** *supra.*

,, domınus, de Lesmoır, mıles baronettus. *See* **William,**
domınus, de Lesmoır baronettus

I G., 19 Jan 1648, I. S. (Aberd.), 19 Jan 1648

,, dominus, de Lesmoır *See* **William** de Lesmoır

I. S. (Aberd.), 9 Oct 1672

,, feodıtarıus de Lesmore. *See* **William,** dominus, de
Lesmore   I G , 9 Oct 1672

,, Sır, of Lesmoır, baronet. *See* **Alexander,** Sır, of Lesmoır, baronet   S. H , 24 July 1766

James, in Lettach, to his grandfather John of Auchinhannock,
who died   —h. spec. in Cairnborrow,
. Newtoune, Nuick, Blackhills, etc , in security
         S H., 25 July 1707 ; 11 July 1710

 ,, de Letterfurie, h. Patricii de Letterfurie, patris,—in
manerie de Ferne ab antiquo monasterium de
Ferne nuncupata;—terris dominicalibus et terris
de Ferne;—villis et terris de Eister Ferne et
Wester Ferne;—molendino de Ferne,—terris de
Innercarrone;—terris de Downe Westra,—terris
de Muldarge;—terris de Ukades;—terris de Mil-
toune;—terris de Balleinochie;—terris de Mid-
ganie, Downe, Vostray;—terris de Muldarge;—
terris de Ukades,—terris de Miltoune;—terris de
Ballemukie;—terris de Middelganie;—terris de
Pitkerie;—terris de Easterganie,—terris de Was-
terganie, Mikillrane;—terris de Balblair;—terris
de Dowcroft,—terris de Brighouse;—terris de
Mylcroft,—terris de Veitland, et piscatione de
Brouache;—terris de Catboll-Fischer;—terris de
Leachclemok (vel Lachclawy);—terris de Smuith
(Tulliche ?) ;—terris de Littilrane;—terris de
Amote,—terris de Rytdue (Ryland ?);—4 brasinis
lie Ailhouses de Fearne;—terris vocatis Smythis
lands, Hartecroft (Bartyscroft ?), crofta vocata
Robiesoun Croft, crofta vocata Baildnaseaucht
(Ballineserache ?) alias Cotteris Dellingis, et 8
acris terrarum per piscatores de Ferne occupatis,
cum molendino, infra vicecomitatum de Innernes;
—quae quidem antea monasterio de Fearne tanquam pars patrimonii ejusdem pertinuerunt.—E.
337l. 13s.   I. S. (Ross), 19 May 1606

 ,, de Letterfurie, h. Patricii de Letterfurie, patris,—in
manerie de Feirne ab antiquo monasterium de
Feirne nuncupata;—terris dominicalibus et terris
de Feirne;—villis et terris de Eister et Wester
Feirne,—molendino de Feirne;—terris de Inner-
carron;—terris de Downy-Wostray;—terris de
Mildarge;—terris de Wkadas;—terris de Miltoun,

—terris de Ballemoky ;—terris de Middilgany ;—
terris de Pitkerie ,—terris de Eistergany ;—terris
de Westergany ;—M'Killrany ,—terris de Balle-
blair ;—terris de Dowcroft ;—terris de Baikhous ;
—terris de Milcroft ;—terris de Weitland et piscatione de Bouachy ;—terris de Catboll-Fischer ;—
terris de Lawchclawey ;—terris de Tulliche ;—terris
de Lyttillrany ,—terris de Aniot (Amote ?) ,—terris
de Ryland ;—4 brasinis lie Ailhouses in Feirne ,—
terris vocatis Smeitlands (Smithlands ?), Bartyis-
croft, crofta vocata Robiesoun's croft, crofta vocata
Balleneserache alias Cotteris Deillings, et 8 acris
terrarum per piscatores de Feirne occupatis, cum
molendinis, infra vicecomitatum de Innernes ;—
quae quidem terrae aliaque uniuntur in baroniam
de Feirne, quae baronia perprius ad monasterium
de Feirne tanquam pars patrimonii pertinuit —E.
337l. 13s   I S. (Ross), 19 Maii 1606

James, of Letterfourie, to his father Alexander of Letterfourie,
who died 16 Jan , 1797—h of line and prov. spec.
in Durn, Cruickshankscroft, Badenstrath, etc., in
the parish of Fordyce   S H , 11 Nov 1797; 13 Feb. 1798

,,   of Letterfourie. *See* **Alexander** of Letterfourie S. H , 15 July 1791

,,   sone of Johne, burges of Linlithgow, h. of Andrew
Monteith, portioner of Redding, his mother's
brother,—in the 4 oxgate of land on the south
syde of the towne and lands of Redding, within
the barony of Polmonth and late regalitie thereof,
with privilege of commontie in the muir of Red-
dingrig and Whytsiderig.—E. 4l., etc., of feu
duty   I. S. (Stirl), 22 June 1655

,,   of Little Cocklaw. *See* **Alexander** of Little Cocklaw
                S. H., 7 Dec. 1771

,,   h. Alexandri in Lochanes, patris,—in 20 solidatis 5
libratarum terrarum de Knok-Overgaltnay antiqui
extentus, in dominio de Torphichen et parochia
de Galtnay.—A.E. 20s.; N.E 3l.
          I. S. (Kirkcudb.), 29 Oct 1633

,,   de Mercartnay, h. Alexandri de Mercartnay patris,—in

5 mercatis terrarum de Glengoppok antiqui extentus, in baronia de Crocemichaell.—E 4l

I. S. (Kirkcudb.), 3 Nov. 1607

James, de Marcartney, h. masc. Jacobi de Marcartney, avi,—in
2 mercatis 11 solidatis et 8 denariatis terrarum de
Over Marcairtney antiqui extentus, in parochia de
Kirkpatrick-Durrame,—E. 3l. 16s 8d.

I. S. (Kirkcudb.), 13 Oct 1631

„ de Marcartney. *See* **James,** *supra.*

„ de Marcartney, h. Jacobi de Marcartney, avi,—in 5 mercatis terrarum de Glengappok antiqui extentus, in
parochia de Crocemichael et baronia ejusdem.—E.
3l 6s. 8d., etc. I. S. (Kirkcudb), 21 Jan. 1634

„ de Marcartney. *See* **James,** *supra.*

„ de Midmar. *See* **William** de Aberzeldie I. S. (Aberd.), 14 Mar. 1621

„ at the Mill of Esslemont *See* **Charles,** Mill of Esslemont S H , 3 May 1744

„ minister, Montrose. Robert, Ann, Catharine and Margaret, son and daus of Dav. Dickson, merchant
in Montrose, to their grandfather James Gordon,
minister there—co-hh of prov gen S H., 18 Oct. 1754

„ minister in Montrose. Mary, dau. of Alex. Thomson,
M.D., Montrose, to her grandfather James Gordon,
minister there—co-h of prov. gen. S. H. Supp., 18 Oct. 1754

„ h. Patricii f. legitimi quondam Patricii de Nethermuire,
fratris I. G., 21 June 1643

„ de Newark. *See* **Robert,** Killileoch I G., 12 June 1697

„ de Newton. *See* **George** de Newtoun I. S (Aberd), 10 June 1644

„ Sir, of Park, bart., to his father Sir John of Park, bart ,
who died Feb., 1713—h male and of line spec.
in the barony of Park S. H., 28 April ; 4 May 1713

„ Sir, of Park. *See* **William,** Sir, of Park S. H., 26 April 1728

„ son of Sir James of Park, to Ernest Leslie of Balquhain
—h. of prov. gen. S. H., 5 Jan ; 25 Jan. 1740 ;
S. H., 19 July; 15 Sept 1740

„ Sir, of Park. *See* **James,** *supra.*

„ of Pitlurg. *See* **John** (Cumming) of Birness S. H., 21 Jan 1756

„ Dr., of Pitlurg *See* **John** (Cumming) of Pitlurg
S. H., 19 Mar. 1774; S. H., 29 Jan. 1783

(384)

James, minister of Roseneath. *See* **Alexander**   S H.,   Mar. 1708

  ,,   de Rothimay, h Joannis de Rothimay, fratris germani

                                 I. G., 15 April 1665

  ,,   to his mother Ann Donaldson, wife of Geo. of Shella-

        green—h. gen.   S H., 22 April; 10 June 1747

  ,,   de Strangaslyle (vel Strangassyle), h. Georgii, patris

        —in 3½ mercatis terrarum de Strangaslyle (vel
Strangassyle) antiqui extentus, vulgo vocatis 1
mercata terrae de Strangasslyle et Carfauld;—1 mercata terrae vocata the Midmark,—1 mercata terrae
vocata the How, et dimidia mercata terrae vocata
Corsemark alias Corsewilliam, infra parochiam de
Kellis.—A.E. 3½m ; N.E. 7l.   I. S (Kirkcudb), 29 Jan 1650

  ,,   de Techmurie, h. magistri Jacobi de Zeochrie ministri

        verbi Dei apud ecclesiam de Rothiemay, patris,—
in terris et baronia de Zeochrie comprehendente
villas et terras de Myresyde ;—binam et tertiam
partem vulgo nuncupatas North et Southmyre-
sydes ,—villam et terras de Whytmyre ;—villam
et terras de Muiralehouse, cum salmonum piscaria
in aqua de Dovern ,—terras de Kirktoun de Aberchirder, Kairnehill, et Zeochrie, cum maneriei loco
et decimis Garbalibus, et privilegio liberi nundini
apud ecclesiam de Aberchirder vocati Marnoch
fair, et glebarum et focalium vulgo Leitt peats
in mossis baroniae de Auchintoule ;—multuris
dictarum terrarum et baroniae,—omnes olim in
baronia de Auchintoule, nunc in baronia de
Zeochrie et parochia de Aberchirder, et unitas
in baroniam de Zeochrie.—A.E. 3l. 10s.;
N.E. 10l.   I. S (Banff.), 21 Feb 1694

  ,,   of Techmurie, to his uncle Alexander of Kinmundy—

        h gen.   S H., 31 Jan.; 2 Feb. 1727

  ,,   of Techmuirie to his brother Alexander of Techmuirie—

        h. gen.   S. H , 31 July; 1 Aug. 1729

  ,,   of Tichmury, to his uncle Alexander of Kinmundie,

        who died   Sept., 1722—h spec. in Kinmundie,
Tarduff, two parts of Thundertoun, Denns, and an
annual-rent of 24l , over Inverugy S. H., 9 April , 18 April 1735

James, of Techmuiry, to his uncle Alexander of Kinmundy,
 who died Sept., 1722—h. of prov. spec in a
 share of a bond for 11,000 merks over Straloch
 S. H., 19 May; 17 July 1741; S. H , 3 June; 17 July 1741
 ,, of Teichmuiry, to his uncle Ludovic of Kinmundy, who
 died Aug., 1734—h. spec. in 7,000 and 18,000
 merks over Strathloche, etc., Banff; and in an
 annual-rent of 90 merks from Blackhill, etc
 S. H , 11 June 1747
 ,, de Tillisoules. *See* **Alexander** de Camdell I. G., 18 Aug. 1696
 ,, *See* **William** de Tulloche I. G., 8 Dec. 1626
 ,, de Zeochrie. *See* **James** de Techmurie I. S. (Banff), 21 Feb. 1694
Jane. *See* **Jean.**
Janet. *See also* **Jeonet, Jonet.**
 ,, Porter, wife of John Gordon, in Auchinhay, to her uncle
 David Milligan of Dalscairth, who died 25 Jan.,
 1798—h p. spec. in the superiority of Little
 Furthhead, in the parish of Urr S. H , 26 July , 12 Aug. 1799
 ,, wife of Joseph Nettleship, soldier 4th dragoons, to her
 cousin David Bridges, Bullcamp, Suffolk—h. port
 gen. S H., 4 Feb. ; 12 Feb. 1777
 ,, designed below, to her father John, in Edinburgh, late
 factor to Earl of Hopetoun—h. gen.
 S. H., 21 Dec.; 28 Dec. 1753
 ,, wife of William, late of Bennett's College, Cambridge,
 to her father the said John, who died 1 Nov.,
 1753—h spec. bonds over Langtoun, Burnhouses,
 Boghill, Cumledge and Simprim S. H., 4 April; 2 May 1754
 ,, (dau. of J., factor to Lord Hopeton) *See* **William,**
 Cambridge S. H., 6 Mar. 1761
 ,, wife of John Duff, merchant, Elgin, to her mother Ann
 Smith, dau. of Henry Smith of Smithfield—h. of
 prov. gen. S. H., 8 Jan. 1751
 ,, above designed, to her grandfather Henry Smith of
 Smithfield, merchant in Dundee—h. of prov. gen.
 S, H., 8 Sept.; 10 Dec. 1753
 ,, wife of Al. Duff of Hillockhead, to her brother Alexander
 of Whiteley, advocate, etc.—h port. gen
 S. H., 3 Dec.; 29 Dec. 1783

(386)

Janet. *See* **Agnes,** Inverness   I. S. (Elgin), 31 Nov. 1690

  ,,   Forbes, wife of Al. Gordoun of Kinaldie, to her sister
       Barbara, dau. of John Forbes of Leslie—h. port.
       gen.   S. H., 9 Sept. 1740; 17 June 1741

  ,,   wife of Js. M'Clellan, minister, Kirkowan, to her cousin
       James of Craiglaw—h. port. gen cum ben. invent
            S. H., 10 Jan. 1736

  ,,   David M'Clellan, to his mother Janet Gordon, wife of
       James M'Clellan, minister at Kirkowan—h. gen.
            S. H. Supp., 14 April; 17 June 1756

  ,,   wife of Jas. Gibson, carrier in Leith, to her brother James,
       tenant, Kinleith—h port. gen.   S. H., 14 Aug., 18 Aug. 1772

  ,,   to her father Robert, sailor, in Leith—co-h of prov. gen
            S. H., 21 June; 23 June 1791

  ,,   wid. of Jas. Gordon, Craigie, to her uncle John, son of
       Jas. Gray of Leithhead—h. of port. of line and
       prov. gen.   S. H., 6 Feb.; 16 Feb 1799

  ,,   wid of A. Sutherland of Torbreck, to her brother Robert,
       son of Geo, tacksman of Culmaly—h port. gen.
            S. H, 24 May 1769

Jean [*or* **Jane**], wife of John Lister. Thomas Litster (or Lister)
       to his mother Jean Gordon, wife of John Lister or
       Litster, merchant in Aberdeen—h gen.
            S H. Supp., 24 Nov.; 2 Dec. 1756

  ,,   wid. of Thos. Gordon, merchant, Aberdeen, to her brother
       James Barclay of Cairness, who died 4 Jan., 1765
       —h port. spec. c. b. inv. in Arthursnook, or Inver-
       north, port. of Cairness, etc.   S. H., 19 Mar.; 3 April 1766

  ,,   wid. of Thos. Gordon in Aberdeen, to her sister Mary
       Barclay, wife of John of Buthlaw—h gen.
            S. H., 19 Jan; 2 Feb. 1780

  ,,   in Aberdeen, to her father Walter, shipmaster there—co-
       h of prov. gen.   S H, 7 April; 22 April 1786

  ,,   dau. of W., shipmaster in Aberdeen   *See* **Ralph,** Aberdeen
            S. H., 13 July 1793

  ,,   wid. of John M'Culloch. John M'Culloch of Barholm,
       to his grandmother Jean Gordon, wid of John
       M'Culloch of Barholm—h. gen.
            S H. Supp., 30 Jan., 22 Aug. 1753

Jean [*or* **Jane**], and Jeonet, hh. port. of William of Barndrine,
their father,—in the merk-land of Barndrine, and
merk-land of Culskoy of auld extent, in the parochine of Kirkcowane.—A.E. 26s. 8d., N.E. 4l.

I. S (Wigton), 25 July 1654

„ wife of Jn. Livingston, collier, Bellahouston, to her father
James, smith, Jamaica—h gen   S H , 30 Mar., 28 June 1799

„ wife of Jn. Livingston, collier, Bellahouston, to her uncle
Thomas, wright, in Jamaica—h. gen.

S. H , 20 May; 28 June 1799

„ Irvine, wife of Wm. Gordon, wright, Blackhall, to her
brother John Irvine, merchant—h. port. gen.

S. H., 6 Feb.; 3 Mar. 1739

„ *See* **Christina,** Branelane   I. S (Aberd), 6 Oct 1669

„ wife of John Litster of Clerkseat, to Major Thomas Gordon
of Clerkseat—co-h. of prov. gen

S. H., 12 Sept ; 17 Sept 1740

„ (service led before the sheriff of Elgin)   John Roy, in
Carse of Kinnoir, to his mother Jean Gordon—
h. gen.   S. H. Supp., 31 Dec 1788; 21 Feb 1789

„ Lady, Countess of Dunfermling.   John Urquhart of Meldrum, to his aunt Lady Jean Gordon, Countess
Dunfermling—Protestant h. gen. cum ben. invent.

S. H. Supp , 5 Dec 1711; 9 May 1712

„ Countess of Dumfermling.   *See* **Cosmo George,** duke

S. H., 13 Aug. 1733

„ to her father Doctor James of Fechell, who died   Aug.,
1723—h port. spec in the lands of Fechell in the
parish of Ellon   S. H., 17 July; 29 Aug. 1741

„ to her mother Margaret Christie, wife of Alex., in Old
Manse of Fintray—h. port gen.   S. H., 11 Mar.; 22 Mar. 1775

„ Arbuthnott, wife of Alex. Gordon of Glendaveny, to her
brother Alexander George, s. of Dr. Thos. Arbuthnott—co-h. of prov. gen   S. H., 10 Aug. 1774

„ Rose, wife of Jn Gordon, custom officer at Methil, to her
brother James Rose, s of Js Rose of Culmony—
h. gen.   S. H., 11 Feb.; 4 Nov. 1774

„ to her father John, merchant in and a bailie of New
Galloway—h. port. gen.   S. H., 13 July 1790; 21 Nov 1791

Jean [*or* **Jane**], to her father George, merchant in Old Aberdeen
        —co-h. of prov. gen   S H , 13 Mar ; 9 May 1776
  ,, wife of Js. Leslie of Rothie, to her brother James of Badens-
        coth—h port of line and prov. gen. S H , 1 July; 10 July 1778
  ,, dau of Peter at Miln of Smithstoun, to her uncle John
        of Balgown—co-h of prov. gen.
                   S. H., 15 Dec. 1785 , 25 Jan. 1786
Jeonet. *See* **Jean,** Barndrine   I S. (Wigton), 25 July 1654
Joan, to her father Adam, lieutenant in General Maitland's
        regiment—h. port gen.   S. H , 16 April, 27 June 1717
  ,, wife to John M‘Culloch of Barholme, to her father
        Gordon of Culvennan—h. gen.   S H., 7 Jan. ; 24 Jan. 1718
  ,, wife of John M‘Culloch of Barholme, to her brother
        William of Culvennan—h. gen
                S H , 18 Dec 1717, 24 Jan 1718
  ,, wife of John M‘Culloch of Barholme, to her brother
        William of Culvennan, who died 29 May, 1716—
        h. spec. in Tonnielogochs, Shennantoun, etc ,
        Wigton and Balmae, etc.
             S. H. (Kirkcudb), 18 Dec 1717 ; 24 Oct 1718
  ,, f. legitima Rogeri sp Jacobi M‘Millann, filii legitimi
        Donaldi M‘Millann de Brokloch, h Alexandri,
        patris,—in 20 solidatis terrarum vocatis the Bluris
        de Barskeiche (Barskeoch ?) antiqui extentus, in
        parochia de Kellis.—A.E. 20s.; N.E 3l.
             I. S. (Kirkcudb), 13   1615
  ,, domina de Rothiemurkus *See* **John,** Rothiemurkus I. G., 17 May 1616
John, h. Patricii fratris germani domini Georgii, patris
                   I G. Supp , 9 Jan 1630
  ,, burgensis de Aberdein. Elspeta Cromby sp Joannis
        burgensis de Aberdein, h port. domini Thomae
        Cromby de Kemnay militis, fratris,—in terris et
        baronia de Kemnay, comprehendente terras do-
        minicales de Kemnay, vulgo Auld Maynes, Litil
        Maynes, et Milntoun de Kemnay nuncupatas,
        cum parte dictarum terrarum nuncupata Inche
        de Mylntoun, cum pecie terrae vulgo nuncupata
        Hauche de Slugartie ex boreali parte aquae de
        Don ,—terras de Elesinwall ,—molendinum de

Kemnay;—terras de Over et Nather Auchin-
quothies, Ratharrald, Bogfur, Glenheid, Parkhill,
Leschangis, croftas ejusdem, Wreatoun, Pick-
tillum, croftam de Paradyce, croftas terrarum
dominicalium et Cobleseatt, salmonum piscariam
super aqua de Doun, cum lie creives, super dictam
aquam, cum cymba portatoria lie Ferriboat, de
omnes unitae sunt in baroniam de Kemnay·—
A.E. 5l. 10s.; N E. 22l.—villa et terris de Craig-
earne tam solari quam umbrali dimidietate earundem, cum salmonum piscaria super aqua de Don,
in baronia de Cluny, et parochiis de Cluny et
Kemnay respective.—E. 40s.   I. S. (Aberd), 12 June 1644

John, burgensis de Abirdein. *See* **Alexander,** magister, Abir-
       dein   I. S. (Aberd.), 20 July 1649
,,   shipmaster in Aberdeen. *See* **Elizabeth,** late in Forrest
       of Skene   S. H., 14 Feb. 1776
,,   merchant in Aberdeen, to his father George, merchant
       there—h. gen.   S. H., 6 Feb ;   5 April 1796
,,   de Aberlour,—propinquior agnatus, id est consanguineus
       ex parte patris Georgii et Margaretae liberorum
       magistri Roberti scribae in Edinburgo I. de Tut , 30 July 1696
,,   de Aberzeldie. *See* **Rachel,** Aberzeldie   I G.,   1 Mar. 1698
,,   of Achinhalrigg. *See* **Elizabeth,** Edinburgh   S. H., 20 Feb. 1724
,,   de Adiwell, h. masc. ratione talliae Georgii de Geicht, f.
       fratris   I. G. Supp., 31 July 1581
,,   de Adiell, h masc. Georgii de Geycht, f fratris,—in terris
       et baronia de Schives cum superioritate.—A.E.
       10l. 12s. 4d. , N E 48l   I. S. Supp. (Aberd.), 21 Nov. 1581
,,   de Airdis, h. Elizabethae, matris, in 10 solidatis terrarum
       9 mercatarum terrarum de Blaikit antiqui extentus,
       et duodecima parte molendini et piscariae ejusdem
       in parochia de Ure.—A.E. 10s ; N.E. 30s.
                          I. S. (Kirkcudb.),   4 Nov. 1610
,,   de Airdis, h Joannis de Airdis, patris,—in dimidia parte
       terrarum de Quhytpark·—E. 7l. 10s., etc.—terris
       de Airdis, Over, Middell, et Nether, infra dominium
       Galvidiae subtus Crie.—E. 20l., etc.
                        I. S (Kirkcudb.), 30 July 1611

John, de Airdis   *See* **John,** *supra.*

,,   de Airdis, h ex conquestu Rogeri de Quhytpairk, fratris
           I. G. Supp., 18 Feb. 1612

,,   of Airthloch, to his cousin Alexander of Cairnburrow — h.
   male gen.   S H., 15 Dec.; 24 Dec. 1703

,,   of Ardlogie   *See* **Adam** of Ardlogie   I G , 2 Jan 1656

,,   of Ardoch, to his gt-grandfather James of Ardoch, rector
   of Banchory-Devenick, who died Dec , 1714 —
   h. spec in the town and lands of Ardoch with its
   mill and salmon fishings S. H., 12 Nov. 1747; 21 Jan. 1748

,,   of Ardoe, to his grandfather James of Ardoe, Episcopal
   minister in Montrose—h. gen.
         S H , 12 Nov. 1747 ; 21 Jan. 1748

,,   captain, of Ards, Longford   *See* **George,** Ards S H , 13 Dec. 1707

,,   de Aroquhain.   *See* **Roger** de Aroquhaine
         I. S (Kirkcudb), 27 Jan. 1674

,,   of Auchanachy   *See* **Elizabeth** of Jamaica S H , 23 Aug 1782

,,   feoditarius de Auchindoir, h Patricii, fratris I G., 20 Aug. 1633

,,   of Auchinhannok, h. of Johne of Auchinhannock, his
   father,—in the lands of Meikle Dumeth, within
   the barony of Mortlich.—E. 9l 12s , etc , of feu
   farm   I. S. (Banff), 25 Jan 1655

,,   of Auchinhannok.   *See* **John,** *supra.*

,,   of Auchinhannock   *See* **James,** in Lettach S H , 11 July 1710

,,   in Auchinhay   *See* **Janet,** Auchinhay
      S. H. (Kirkcudb.), 26 July , 12 Aug. 1799

,,   de Auchinreoch.   *See* **George,** Auchinreoch
         I S (Kirkcudb.), 16 April 1616

,,   of Auchlean   *See* **Agnes,** Auchlean I S. (Wigton), 26 Oct. 1652

,,   of Auchleuchries   *See* **Patrick,** Auchleuchries S. H , 17 Mar 1722

,,   of Avachie, h. of John of Avachie, his father I G , 29 Jan. 1659

,,   of Avachie.   *See* **John,** *supra.*

,,   de Avachie.   *See* **Henry** de Avachie
      I. G , 25 Jan. 1687 ; I S. (Aberd), 25 Jan 1687

,,   of Avochie, to his father Peter of Avochie, who died
   Jan , 1773—h spec. in Fingask, with its mill, and
   part of Carboig Moss S H (Aberd), 1 Dec 1779; 24 Jan. 1780

,,   of Balgown.   *See* **Henrietta, Jean,** Miln of Smithstoun
         S H., 25 Jan. 1786

John, de Balmade.　*See* **Isobel,** Auchry

　　　　　I. S. (Banff), 4 Dec. 1673; I. G., 4 Dec. 1673

„　de Balmade.　*See* **Isobel,** Balmade　　I S. (Aberd.), 18 June 1674;

　　　　　I. S. (Banff), 18 June 1674

„　clerk to the signet, to James Farquhar of Balmoor—co-h.

　　of taillie and prov. gen.　　　　S. H., 11 Jan.; 17 Jan 1764

„　writer to the signet, to James Farquhar of Balmoor—h.

　　of taillie and prov. gen.　　　S H, 2 April; 27 April 1765

„　of Balmuir, clerk to the signet.　*See* **James Farquhar,**

　　Balmuir　　　　　　　　　　　　　　S H., 8 Feb. 1790

„　de Barskeoche, h. Georgii de Barskeoche, patris,—in

　　terris de Stranfaskin;—terris de Largemoir;—

　　•　terris de Knokscheine;—terris de Midle et Nethir

　　Barskeoches, cum piscatione in aqua de Ken —

　　E. 25l.—3 mercatis terrarum de Strangassill, viz.

　　1 mercata terrae de Strangissil et Crocefad;—1

　　mercata terrae nuncupata Midmark;—dimidietate

　　mercatae terrae vocatae Cassinbrok alias Croce-

　　William, et dimidietate mercatae terrae de Haw

　　antiqui extentus, in parochia de Kellis:—A E

　　40s.; N.E 6l —4 mercatis terrarum de Glenarme

　　antiqui extentus, in parochia de Or.—A.E. 53s. 4d;

　　N.E. 8l.　　　　　　　I. S. (Kirkcudb.), 8 Aug. 1633

„　de Barskeoche, h. Georgii de Barskeoche, patris,—in 13

　　mercatis terrarum de Auchnaucht, Carnegawin et

　　Inchankis in superioritate, in parochia de Kirk-

　　madin in Rynnes;—5 mercatis terrarum de Clon-

　　zard cum molendino,—5 mercatis terrarum de

　　Portincorkie;—5 mercatis terrarum de Currochtie;

　　—2½ mercatis terrarum de Cairne, in parochia de

　　Kirkmadin.—A E. 20l 6s 8d.; N E 6il.—5 mer-

　　catis terrarum de Kirkbryd ut supra jacentibus:—

　　A.E. 5m., N E 10l —dimidietate 5 mercatarum

　　terrarum de Drummoir ut supra jacente.—A.E.

　　2½m., N.E. 5l.—3 mercatis terrarum de Cairne-

　　multiburgh, in parochia de Inche ·—A.E. 3m.;

　　N.E. 6l.—5 mercatis terrarum de Kildounan in

　　dicta parochia.—A E. 5m.; N.E. 10l 10s —anno

　　redditu 140m. de terris de Drummoir, in parochia

　　de Kirkmadin　　　　　I. S. (Wigton), 8 Aug. 1633

John, of Beldorny. *See* **Alexander** of Wardhouse   S H , 2 Sept. 1763

  „   of Beldorny. *See* **Charles** of Wardhouse   S. H , 11 Aug. 1777

  „   in Belgia. *See* **Margaret,** Glenbervie   I. G , 13 June 1691

  „   de Beoche, h. Jonetae, matris,—in 10 solidatis 11 denariatis terrarum 9 mercatarum terrarum de Blacket,
cum undecima parte molendini earundem antiqui
extentus, in parochia de Or ;—5 solidatis 6 denariatis 5 mercatarum terrarum de Lag extentus
praedicti, in parochia de Girtoun.—A.E. 16s 5d. ;
       N.E. 49s 3d.   I S. (Kirkcudb.), 13 Oct. 1607

  „   de Beoche *See* **Helen,** Blaiket   I. S. (Kirkcudb), 23 Maii 1616

  „   of Birkenbush, to his brother George—h. of conq. gen.
       S H., 21 May 1754; 23 Nov. 1758

  „   of Birkenbush, to his father James of Birkenbush—h gen.
       S. H., 21 May 1754; 23 Nov. 1758

  „   son of James of Birkenbush, to his uncle John of Dallachy
       h. gen.   S H., 29 May; 15 June 1770

  „   (Cumming) of Birness, to James Cumming of Birness
       —h. of taillie and prov. gen.
       S. H , 16 Oct.; 7 Nov. 1751

  „   (Cumming) of Birness, to his father James of Pitlurg—h
       gen.   S. H., 14 Jan ; 21 Jan 1756

  „   de   . *See* **Alexander** de Birsmoir   I. G , 7 April 1666

  „   de Blaikat. *See* **Agnes, Beatrix, Catharine, Euphemia,
Helen, Margaret, Mariota, Marjory, Sibyl,**
Blaikat   I. S. (Kirkcudb), 29 Oct. 1548

  „   de Blaiket *See* **Alexander** de Earlestoun
       I. S. (Kirkcudb.), 29 July 1634

  „   to his father Henry of Blairmad—h. gen
       S H., 22 Dec 1727; 26 Jan. 1728

  „   of Blelack, to his father Alexander of Blelack—h. gen.
       S. H., 5 Mar ; 16 Mar. 1723

  „   h. magistri Roberti pastoris ecclesiae apud Boatary, patris
       I. G., 27 July 1682

  „   h. Patricii de Brakay, patris,—in terris de Mydiltoun de
Knokinblewis, Brakay, Glaschaw, cum molendino
et silva ,—terris de Drumcrutten, infra dominium
de Garzeauch —A.E 10s , N.E. 40s
       I S Supp (Aberd), 31 Oct. 1586

John, of Brackay, h. of Maister Patrick of Brackay, his father,
in the toun and lands of Brackay and pendicles
thereof, callit Radbaddis and Whytwall ,—the
lands and forest of Drumkowane ;—the toun and
lands of Glaschea and pendicle thereof, callit Rad-
foord, with the mylne of Glaschea, within the
barronie of Knokinglewis ;—the toun and lands
of Mideltoun of Knockinglewis, within the lordschipe of Gareoch, and parochine of Inverurie.—
A.E. 40s ; N.E 8l —The teynd sheaves and personage teinds of the said lands of Mideltoun of
Knockinglewis.—A.E. 1d.; N.E. 4d.

                          I S (Aberd), 4 Feb. 1657

„ de Bracko, h. Joannis de Bracko, patris,—in villa et terris
de Bracko, cum terris dominicalibus de Bracko, et
pendiculis earundem vocatis Reabidds et Whyt-
walls ;—terris et forresta de Drumkeaton ;—villa
et terris de Glaschea, et pendiculo earundem vocato Redford, cum molendino de Glaschea, infra
baroniam de Knockinglews (vel Knockinglens).—
A.E. 2m.; N.E 8m   I. S (Aberd), 20 Sept 1678

„ de Bracko. *See* **John,** *supra.*

„ de Bracco *See* **Charles** de Bracco.   I. S. (Aberd), 15 Sept. 1682

„ de Branelane. *See* **Christina,** Branelane I. S. (Aberd), 6 Oct. 1669

„ salmon fisher, Bridge of Don. *See* **Margaret,** Aberdeen

                          S. H., 6 Feb. 1796

„ de Buckie, h. Joannis de Hiltoun, patris   I G., 15 Feb. 1673

„ of Buckie *See* **George** of Buckie   S H., 11 July 1733

„ of Buckie, to his father George of Buckie, who died
Mar., 1756—h. male and of line spec. cum ben.
invent. in Nether Freuchny, Easter Buckie, Bridge-
field, Rives, Stonnyfold, etc.   S H., 18 Oct.; 1 Nov. 1757

„ of Buthlaw, advocate. *See* **Mary,** Buthlaw

                      S H , 19 Mar. ; 3 April 1766

„ of Buthlaw, advocate. *See* **Charles** of Buthlaw S H., 26 April 1776

„ of Buthlaw *See* **Jean,** Aberdeen   S. H , 2 Feb 1780

„ de Carnefeild, h. magistri Gulielmi de Carnefeild, patris,
—in terris et baronia de Rothiemay.—A.E. 2ol.,
N E. 8ol.   I S. (Banff), 7 Maii 1633

John, de Cairnfeild, f natu max. Agnetae Halthorne f Joannis
Halthorne de Cairnfeild, h port. Joannis Halthorne
de Cairnfeild, avi,—et Margarete Halthorne, sp
Davidis Cairns de Torr, h port. dicti Joannis
Halthorne de Cairnfeild, patris,—in 5 mercatis
terrarum antiqui extentus de Cairnfeild, infra
parochiam de Longcaster, nunc in Kirkinder per
annexationem.—E. . .   I. S. (Wigton), 11 Jan. 1687

  ,,   de Cairnfeild, h. gen Alexandri in Kirkmabrick, patris

         I G., 11 Jan. 1687

  ,,   advocate. *See* **Adam,** younger of Cairnfield   S. H , 28 Aug 1793

  ,,   of Carlton, to his brother Alexander, younger of Carlton,
who died 17 July, 1775—h. of taillie and prov.
spec in the three merk lands of Meikle Carlton,
parish of Borgue   S. H., 5 May 1789; 30 Aug 1790

  ,,   of Carlton, to his father Alexander of Carlton, who died
23 May, 1778—h. of taillie and prov. spec. in the
six merk lands of Little Carlton, and in the kirk
glebe of Borgue   S. H , 28 May; 30 Aug. 1790

  ,,   de Carneborrow. *See* **John** de Innermarkie I. S (Banff), 4 Oct. 1628

  ,,   of Carrol, to his father Hugh of Carrol—h. male and of
line gen.   S. H , 17 Dec., 19 Dec 1766

  ,,   of Carron   *See* **William**   S. H , 18 May 1797

  ,,   de Cloinyeard. *See* **Alexander** de Clonyeard

         I S. (Wigton), 22 Feb. 1687

  ,,   de Cluny. *See* **Thomas,** dominus, Cluny

         I. S (Aberd), 13 April 1602

  ,,   of Cluny. *See* **Cosmo,** Cluny   S. H , Mar. 1770

  ,,   of Cochlarachie. *See* **James** of Cochlarachie   S H , 24 July 1721

  ,,   doctor, of Colliestoun, to his father Doctor John of Colliestoun, who died July, 1718—h. spec. in Collies-
toun, etc , with the superiority of Guthries' croft,
etc   S. H , 18 May; 8 July 1719

  ,,   doctor, of Collieston. *See* **John,** *supra.*

  ,,   de Combrie, h. Janetae f Alexandri de Auchinreath,
sororis   I. G., 15 April 1665

  ,,   of Coynach. *See* **William,** Coynach   S. H , 5 June 1719

  ,,   of Coynach   *See* **Thomas,** Coynach   S H , 16 Jan. 1724

  ,,   of Crage   *See* **Francis** of Crage   I G , 12 Sept 1655

John, of Craig, to his father Francis of Craig, who died   Sept.,
      1727—h spec. in Auchindore, with its mill, Fulzia-
      ments, Creack, Mains of Craig, Longlands, etc.

                                               S. H , 8 April , 16 April 1729
,, of Craig, to his father John of Craig—h gen
                                       S. H , 22 Jan ; 31 Jan 1743
,, of Craig. *See* **John,** *supra.*
,, to his father James, tenant in Craigie—h. of line gen
                                  S. H , 30 Oct.; 14 Nov. 1799
,, de Craigieheid. *See* **Lewis,** Craigieheid
                            I. de Poss. Quinq , 31 Aug. 1682
,, of Craigmyle, to his father. Richard of Craigmyle, advo-
      cate in Aberdeen—h. gen   S. H., 14 Dec., 24 Dec. 1763
,, de Crechlaw. *See* **William,** Crechlaw
                      I S. Supp. (Wigton), 31 Oct 1580
,, h. Henrici de Creich, patris,—in annuo redditu 106m. de
      5 mercatis terrarum de Polmowart antiqui extentus,
      in parochia de Crugletoun   I. S. (Wigton), 7 April 1663
,, of Crogo, Kirkcudb , to his grandfather James of Crogo—
      h. gen.   S H , 8 Sept , 17 Sept 1702
,, burgh clerk of Cromarty. Lilias, dau of Neil M'Kenzie,
      mason, in Cromarty, to her grandfather John
      Gordon, burgh clerk of Cromarty, who died
      1686—h. of prov. spec in a tenement in Cromarty
                 S. H. Supp , 3 Nov 1713; 25 Jan 1714
,, of Cruchley, to his father William of Cruchley—h gen.
                                S H , 17 Jan.; 7 Mar. 1732
,, h. Jacobi in Cullingdoch, patris,—in 2½ mercatis terrae
      40 solidatarum terrarum de Killerne antiqui ex-
      tentus, in parochia de Anweth·—E. 5l. 4s feudifir-
      mae .—feudifirmarum divoriis dictarum terrarum .
      —A.E. 5l. 4s.; N.E. 15l. 12s.—dimidia mercata
      terrae de Tor antiqui extentus, in dicta parochia
      —A.E. 6s. 8d. ; N.E. 20s. I. S. Supp. (Kirkcudb.), 5 June 1623
,, to his father Alexander, portioner of Dallachy—h. gen.
                              S. H , 27 Jan., 21 Aug. 1727
,, of Dallachy. *See* **John,** Birkenbush   S H., 15 June 1770
,, de Drumquhendle, h Gulielmi de Farsken, patris
                              I. G., 27 Oct. 1693

John, of Drumquhynle, to his father Alexander of Farskan, who
died —h spec. in Drumquhynle, etc ,
Aberdeenshire ; and portions of the muir of Cald-
holm, etc   S. H., 19 Dec. 1712 ; 4 Mar. 1713

„ late of Drumquhynle *See* **William** of Crabstoun S H , 4 Sept 1735

„ dyer in Bridgend of Dumfries. *See* **Robert,** Dumfries
S. H., 11 Feb. 1725

„ to his father Thomas, surgeon in Dumfries—h. gen.
S H., 13 Oct. 1764 , 31 Jan 1765

„ writer in Dumfries. *See* **Charles,** Dumfries   S. H , 15 Feb. 1796

„ dominus, de Eaynbo, h. Joannis de Eaynbo, patris
I. G., 25 Maii 1648

„ de Eaynbo. *See* **John,** *supra.*

„ dominus, de Eaynbo, miles baronettus   *See* **Robert,**
dominus, de Eaynbo, miles baronettus   I G., 5 June 1649

„ in Edinburgh, late factor to Earl of Hopetoun. *See* **Janet**
S H , 28 Dec. 1753 ; S. H , 2 May 1754

„ in Edinburgh, late factor to Earl of Hopetoun *See*
William, Cambridge   S. H., 14 Jan 1761 , 6 Mar. 1761

„ merchant, Edinburgh   Christiana Sim, in the parish of
New Deer, Aberdeenshire, to her uncle John Gor-
don, merchant, Edinburgh—h of line gen
S H. Supp , 14 June ; 14 Aug. 1762

„ writer in Edinburgh. *See* **Ann,** Edinburgh
S. H , 28 Nov. 1717 ; 27 June 1718

„ writer, Edinburgh, Nicolas-Dick, wife of Jn. Ferguson,
Laribert, to her cousin Ann Broun, wid of John
Gordon, writer, Edinburgh—h of line gen
·   S. H. Supp , 31 Dec 1719

„ of Edinglassie *See* **William** (now Gray)   S. H , 3 June 1742

„ junior, of Edinglassie. *See* **George,** Edinglassie S. H., 5 April 1746

„ farm servant, Elgin   *See* **Ann,** Main   S H., 7 Jan. 1773

„ Sir, of Embo, to his brother George, son of Sir John of
Embo—h of prov. gen.   S H., 8 June, 12 July 1717

„ Sir, of Embo *See* **John,** Sir, *supra*

„ Sir, of Embo, bart , to his grandfather Sir Robert of Embo,
bart., who died   1693—h spec. in Embo,
Hiltoun or Bellaknuik, Achinthesaurer, etc.
S. H., 10 Jan. ; 13 Nov 1721

John, Sir, of Embo, to his father Sir John of Embo, bart., who
.   died 14 April, 1760—h. spec. in Embo, Hilton or
Bellaknuck, and Auchintheasurer
S H. (Sutherland), 19 Feb. ; 22 April 1761

„   Sir, of Embo, bart. *See* **John,** Sir, of Embo, *supra.*

„   de Erlestoun. *See* **Alexander** de Erlestoun
I. S. (Kirkcudb), 23 Oct 1628

„   of Errlstoune   *See* **Mr. William** of Errlstoune
I. S. (Kirkcudb.), 2 Oct 1655

„   John, Sir, of Earlston, bart., to his cousin James of
Carlton—h. male gen.   S. H., 1 June, 5 June 1799

„   s. of Rt of Farnachtie. *See* **Mary** (or Farquhar)   S. H , 23 Dec. 1737

„   in Finties, to his cousin Alexander of Cairnbarrow, who
died   —h. male and of conq spec in
Cairnbarrow, Balnacraig, Cairnmore, etc.
S. H., 25 July 1707 ; 11 July 1710

„   h. of John, s. to Alexander in Garlerge, his father   I G., 28 July 1657

„   s. to John, who was s. to Alexander, in Garlarg, h of
Robert of Knoxbreck, his granduncle,—in the 3
marke land of Knoxbreck ,—the 8 marke land of
Barloche (or Barlock), and the 22 shilling land
of the 4 mark land of Kinzeontoune, within the
parochin of Kirkanders and lordshipe of Galloway,
stewartry of Kirkcudbright and sherriffdom of
Wigtoun ·—E. 9l. 5s 8d —ane annuelrent of 8om
furth of the 9 markland of Inglistoune, and 16
pound land of Kirkanders, within the pareoche of
Kirkanders, now of Borg be annexatione
·   I S. (Kirkcudb), 28 July 1657

„   s. to Alexander in Garlerge   *See* **John,** *supra*

„   de Garveri. *See* **Robert,** Garverie   I S (Kirkcudb.), 6 Feb. 1672

„   h Patricii fratris germani domini Georgii de Geight
militis, patris   I. G., 9 June 1630

„   de Glascou-forrest, h. Jacobi de Auchtirairne, fratris
germani,—in dimidia terrarum de Auchtirairne,
Tulloch, Tannamoyne, et Blackmylne.—A.E. 40s.;
N.E. 6l.   I S (Aberd), 20 Dec. 1574

„   M.D., of Glasgow, to his brother William in Port-Glasgow,
formerly merchant, Glasgow—h. gen.
S H , 8 Dec., 24 Dec. 1762

John, physician, Glasgow   *See* **Katharine; Mary**   S H., 18 June 1792

  ,, of Glenbucket, to his father John of Knockspack, who
died   Oct., 1704—h spec in Over and Nether
Knockspack, etc., in the parish of Clatt

                                            S H., 26 Jan.; 5 Feb 1705

  ,, of Glencatt. *See* **Francis** of Mill of Kincardine S H., 31 Oct 1744

  ,, of Gordonbank. *See* **Ann,** Gordonbank, **Davida,** Gordonbank; **Mary,** Gordonbank   S. H , 21 April 1796

  ,, of Grange, to his brother Hugh of Grange—h. gen

                                        S H , 5 Aug , 18 Aug. 1701

  ,, Dr., of Greencastle, in the island of Jamaica. *See* **Robert**
Home   S. H , 26 Aug. 1776

  ,, of Greenlaw   *See* **Grizell,** Greenlaw   S. H , 23 Feb. 1743

  ,, of Grievshop, to his father William of Grievshop, who
died   Oct., 1778—h. spec in Grievshop and
Brundiascrook, etc , and in six acres of Forrescrook, etc.   S. H., 7 Dec ; 26 Dec. 1778

  ,, h. Georgii feodatarii de Haddoch, patris   I G , 6 Oct 1612

  ,, de Haddo, h masc. Georgii feodatarii de Haddo, patris,—
in terris de duabus Methlickis cum pertinentiis
vocatis Haddo ;—terris de Archedlie cum piscaria
super aqua de Ythane ,—superioritate annui redditus 5l. annuatim, solvendi domino Forbes de
praedictis terris de Archedlie , terris de Andat et
terris de Braiklay-Andat, unitis in baroniam de
Meikill Methlick.—A.E. 8l. ; N E. 32l

                                    I. S (Aberd.), 21 April 1627

  ,, de Haddo, h masc. Jacobi de Haddo, avi,—in terris de
New-park de Kellie ,—terris de Overhill cum saitt
vocato Thornerone, infra baroniam de Auchterellone.—A.E. 10s.; N.E. 40s   I. S (Aberd.), 11 May 1630

  ,, de Haddo, h. Jacobi de Haddo, avi   I G., 11 May 1630

  ,, dominus de Haddo miles baronettus, h masc. domini
Joannis de Haddo militis baronetti, patris,—in
terris de Kirktoun de Tarves cum Diracroft ,—
terris de Braklay et Tullilet, cum novo molendino
super eisdem terris constructo, infra baroniam de
Tarves et regalitatem Abirbrothok ·—E. 21l. 14s
—villa et Maynes de Kellie ;—terris de Mylntoun

de Kellie in baronia de Kellie —E. 20l 13s 4d.—
terris de Sauchak in dicta baronia de Kellie,—
duabus tertiis partibus terrarum de Barrake in
dicta baronia·—E. 20l. — terris de Knawin, et
terris de Achmaledye infra dictam baroniam·—
A.E.   ; N.E   .—terris de Collyne et
Andat, in parochia de Methlik:—E 5l. 6s. 8d.—
terris de Litle Methlick, infra parochiam de Meth-
like·—A.E   ; N.E.   .—terris de
Newpark de Kellie;—terris de Overhill et Seat
earundem vocato Thornerone, in baronia de
Auchterellon.—A.E. 10s ; N E. 40s.

I. S. (Aberd.), 14 May 1647

John, dominus de Haddo. *See* **John,** *supra.*

    ,,   dominus de Haddo miles baronettus   *See* **George,** do-
minus de Haddo

I. S. (Aberd.), 4 Sept. 1669; I. S (Aberd.), 10 Sept. 1669·

    ,,   de Halheid. *See* **Robert,** Hallheid   I. S. (Aberd.), 3 Oct. 1553

    ,,   h. masc Patricii de Halhead, patris,—in villis et terris
de Corqwhinderland et Halhead, infra baroniam
de Cushney.—E. 10l.   I. S. (Aberd.), 28 Sept 1683

    ,,   de Hiltoun. *See* **John** de Buckie   I. G., 15 Feb. 1673

    ,,   Doctor, of Hilton. *See* **James** of Hilton   S H , 15 Mar. 1736

    ,,   in Inchmore, to his uncle John of Laussie—Protestant
h. port. gen   S. H., 21 Feb.; 18 Mar. 1741

    ,,   de Innermarkie, h. prov Joannis de Carneborrow, patris,
—in villa et terris de Edinglassie cum molendino
fullonum,—villa et terris de Ovir Glenmarkie,
cum Bowplaces, et privilegio liberae baroniae,
infra dominium de Balveny:—A.E. 35s.; N.E. 7l
villa et terris Tumethis, cum brasina et pendiculo
Letachoirne nuncupata, infra diocesim Aberdonensem.—E. 22l.   I. S. (Banff), 4 Oct. 1628

    ,,   *See* **Alexander,** magister, Kemnay   I. S (Aberd.), 2 Mar. 1648

    ,,   the Hon., of Kenmore, to his brother the Hon. Robert of
Kenmore—h. gen.   S. H., 29 Jan.; 16 Feb. 1742

    ,,,   the Hon., of Kenmore. *See* **William** of Kenmore   S. H , 14 Feb. 1770

    ,,   John of Kenmore, to his brother William of Kenmore,
captain, 1st foot, who died   Feb , 1772—h. male

of line and prov. spec. in Barcaple, Culquha, Kenmore, salmon fishings in the Dee, etc.

S. H., 13 Nov.; 12 Dec. 1772

John, of Kenmore, to his father John of Kenmore, commonly called Viscount Kenmore, who died   1769— h. male spec. in the 5 merk lands of Over Culquha and Bridgend   S. H., 18 Feb ; 23 Feb. 1774

„ of Kenmore. *See* **John** of Kenmore, *supra.*

„ of Kenmore, to his brother Captain William of Kenmore, who died   1771—h. male and of prov. spec. in the ten pound lands of Tarscrechan and Dalbeatty, with woods and fishings   S. H , 8 Mar.; 22 Mar. 1774

„ of Kenmore, to his uncle Robert of Kenmore, commonly called Viscount Kenmore, who died in 1740 or 1741—h. male spec. in the lands of Buittle, with fishings in the Urr   S. H., 7 April ; 19 April 1777

„ Vicecomes de Kenmuire, dominus de Lochinvar, h. Joannis Vicecomitis de Kenmuire, domini de Lochinvar, patris,—in 19 mercatis terrarum de Kenmure, et Lagane, cum molendinis et piscationibus earundem ,—20 mercatis terrarum de Balmaclelland et Park, cum molendinis et piscationibus earundem, unitis in baroniam de Kenmuire, in parochiis de Balmaclelland et Kellis respective: —A.E. 39m.; N.E 117m.—10 libratis terrarum de Torskraichane et Dalbetie, cum molendinis et piscationibus, in parochia de Ur —A E. 10l , N.E. 30l.—34 mercatis terrarum de Glenskyreburne et over Polcrie cum molendinis et piscationibus ;—3 mercatis terrarum de Pollincrie in parochia de Anuath ,—4 mercatis terrarum de Ewinstoun, Blakcraig, et Knoknone ,—6 mercatis terrarum de Hardlandis et Moniebuy, in parochia de Balmaclelland .—A.E 47m ; N E. 141m.—5 mercatis terrarum de Bellingait ;—5 mercatis terrarum de Knoknarling (vel Knokmarling) et Darselloche ;— 5 mercatis terrarum de Garlarg et Blakmark, extendentibus ad 10 libratas terrarum antiqui extentus vocatis Catbellie, in parochia de Kellis,

cum molendinis et piscationibus,—5 mercatis
terrarum de Laggane ;—3 mercatis terrarum de
Litle Kirkbryd ;—20 solidatis terrarum de Clauchreid ;—2½ mercatis terrarum de Killigoune ;—1
mercata terrae de Milmark ;—1 mercata terrae
de Slaithes (vel Slaichtis) ;—1 mercata terrae de
Marchohar in parochia de Annuath ·—A.E. 20l. ;
N.E. 60l.—terris et baronia de Erlstoun extendente ad 40 mercatas terrarum antiqui extentus,
cum molendinis et piscationibus, advocatione
ecclesiae vocatae St. Johne's Kirk de Dalry, in
parochia de Dalry, omnibus unitis in baroniam
de Erlstoun:—A E. 32m 12s , N E. 98m. 9s. 4d.
terris et baronia de Gelstoun, viz. 3 mercatis terrarum de Glenzarrok ;—20 solidatis terrarum de
Litle Quhythill ;—20 solidatis terrarum de Potterland ;—3 mercatis terrarum de Kirkmurine et
Glen ;—4 mercatis terrarum de Mekill Quhythill
et Galdowbank ;—20 solidatis terrarum de Newlandis ;—7½ mercatis terrarum de Arilland ;—12
mercatis. terrarum de Inglestoun ;—molendino de
Gelstoun ;—8 mercatis terrarum de Bairdland
cum piscationibus, in parochia de Gelstaines
(Gelstoun ?) .—A.E. 42m. ; N.E. 126m.—terris et
baronia de Corsmichaell subtus mentionatis, viz.
2½ mercatis terrarum de Fuffok alias Suffok ;—5
mercatis terrarum de Irnealmerie ,—5 mercatis
terrarum de Auchindolie ;—5 mercatis terrarum
de Largmen (Largnain) ,—2½ mercatis terrarum
de Irnfillane ,—5 mercatis terrarum de Culgruff ;
—5 mercatis terrarum de Tradill alias Treddill ;
—5 mercatis terrarum de Mollance ;—5 mercatis
terrarum de Hillintoun ;—5 mercatis terrarum de
Harybraund ,—10 mercatis terrarum de Croftis ;—
5 mercatis terrarum de Glengappok ,—terris dominicalibus lie Maynis de Greinlaw, cum lie Kayne
Peitts et bundayworks baroniae de Crocemichaell ,
—5 mercatis terrarum de Irnemsbie ,—10 mercatis
terrarum de Chapalerne ;—2½ mercatis terrarum de

Clairbraund, cum advocatione ecclesiae parochialis
de Corsmichaell :—E. 213l. 6s 8d.—5 mercatis
terrarum de Litle Drybrughe;—5 mercatis terrarum de Drumjarg;—5 mercatis terrarum de
Irnefillane;—5 mercatis terrarum de Irnecraig,—
5 mercatis terrarum de Mekill Drybrughe;—5
mercatis terrarum de Chapmantoun,—5 mercatis
terrarum de Blakerne;—5 mercatis terrarum de
Arnminnie;—5 mercatis terrarum de Kilnottrie;
—molendino granario de Corsmichaell;—5 mercatis terrarum de Gerrentoun;—2½ mercatis terrarum de Blakpark, cum advocatione ecclesiae de
Corsmichaell —A E. 57m 6s 8d ; N.E. 172m
6s. 8d.—decimis garbalibus, etc., ecclesiae parochialis et parochiae de Kirkmabrek:—E. 20l.—unitis
in baroniam de Corsmichaell;—6 mercatis terrarum
de Culreache et Grobtail, in parochia de Girtoun :
—A.E. 4l.; N E. 12l.—10 mercatis terrarum de
Lochfergus;—5 libratas terrarum de Blakstokar-
toun,—3 mercatis terrarum de Litle Stokartoun;
—10 mercatis terrarum de Mekill Sypland;—15
mercatis· terrarum de Bombie, cum molendino
granario ejusdem;—10 mercatis terrarum de Bal-
greddane;—10 mercatis terrarum de Auchinflour;
—mansionis loco de Kirkcudbrycht;—Newmylne
de Kirkcudbrycht, in parochia de Kirkcudbrycht;
—8 mercatis terrarum de Chappeltoun, in parochia
de Kirkcanders;—12 mercatis terrarum de Laich-
borg;—3 mercatis terrarum de Blakcraig, infra
parochiam de Borg;—5 mercatis terrarum de
Cambletoun;— 50 solidatis terrarum de Ovir
Maynis;—1 mercata terrarum de Mark;—6 mercatis terrarum de Glengepe;—2½ mercatis terrarum de Fuffok;—5 libratis terrarum de Kempletone
et molendino granario;—5 libratis terrarum de
Over Campstane;—5 libratis terrarum de Nather
Campstane, in parochia de Tuynem.—A.E. 139m.
40d.; N E 417m. 10s.—10 libratis terrarum de
Balmangane cum piscariis, infra parochiam de

Sannik·—E. 40l. 13s. 4d. feudifirmae .—terris et
baronia de Larg, viz. 40 solidatis terrarum de
Culgow ;—40 solidatis terrarum de Litlepark ,—
20 solidatis terrarum de Glennamar ;—40 solidatis
terrarum de Drummauch Glengerrane ,—20 solidatis terrarum de Barrauchle ;—10 solidatis terrarum de Torqunik ;—10 solidatis terrarum de
Craignyne,—15 solidatis terrarum de Pulbrebboy,
Laggane, et Brokloche ,—1 mercata terrae de Kirre-
draucht ;—burgo baroniae de Mongof, cum liberis
foris et hebdomadalibus macellis, et fortalicio de
Larg, in parochia de Monygoif :—A.E. 11l. 40d. ;
N.E 33l. 10s.—3 mercatis terrarum de Drumrasche
antiqui extentus, cum advocatione ecclesiae de
Partone ;—5 libratis terrarum de Trallallane alias
Glenlawis, cum molendinis granarum et fullonum ;
—2 mercatis terrarum de Ervie ,—1 mercata terrae
de Barsell (vel Bardell) ,—40 solidatis terrarum
de Over Bordland et Barsell ,—terris de Glengun-
zeok, et terris vocatis lie tuentie schilling land,
omnibus infra parochiam de Partoun .—A.E. 14l.;
N.E 42l.—terris de Cuill, Corra (vel Turre), Cor-
battane (vel Torbattane), Dilderane, et Guffokland
in baronia de Buittill.—E. 54l. 12s —Fischear croft
de Kirkcanderis et insula de Kirkcanderis, parte
dimidietatis terrarum de Kirkcanderis, in parochia
de Kirkcanderis, et dominio galvidiae :—E. 4s. 8d.
—terris de Cleurie (vel Clanrie);—terris de Laggane ;—terris de Garverrie ,—terris de Tullinach
(vel Cullenach), in dominio de Galloway subtus
Crie, cum parte liberae forestae de Buchan :—E.
24l. 6s —terris de Muirfed, Cuill, Blairis, et Craig,
extendentibus ad 10½ mercatas et 40 denariatas
terrarum antiqui extentus ;—7 mercatis terrarum
de Barhassie ;—4 mercatis terrarum de Burnes ;—
36 solidatis 8 denariatis terrarum de Spittell ,—
30 solidatis terrarum de Cullinacne (vel Cullin-
dache) ·—E. 49l. 8s.—26 solidatis 8 denariatis
terrarum de Culcrainzie et Garhorne, vulgo nun-

cupatis Culchronchie et Garquhir ;—4 mercatis
terrarum de Lochinkit·—E 12m 10s.—2 mercatis
terrarum de Knarie et Bar antiqui extentus —E.
.—terris de Litle Hals·—E. 43s 4d. ,
—terris de Glenquikin et Dargavall extendentibus
ad 2½ mercatis terrarum antiqui extentus, infra
baroniam de Ferrie de Crie.—E. 3l. 12s. 8d.

I S. (Kirkcudb), 17 Mar 1635

John, Vicecomes de Kenmuire, etc   *See* **John,** *supra*
  ,,   Vicecomes de Kenmure, etc   *See* **Robert,** Vicecomes de
      Kenmure

I S. (Kirkcudb.), 1 May 1645 ; I. S (Wigton), 1 May 1645

  ,,   Comes de Kenmuir, etc   *See* **Robert,** Comes de Kenmuir

I S. (Kirkcudb), 14 Jan 1662

  ,,   magister, h masc et provisionis Alexandri Vicecomitis
de Kenmuir, patris,—in 19 mercatis terrarum
antiqui extentus de Kenmuir et Laggan ;—20
mercatis terrarum de Balmaclelland et Park,
unitis in baroniam de Kenmuir ,—5 mercatis terrarum de Ballengate ;—5 mercatis terrarum de
Knocknarling, Darselloch, Ramsell, superiore et
Midle Orchyeards ,—5 mercatis terrarum de Gar-
lurg, extendentibus ad 10 libratas terrarum antiqui
extentus vocatas Catbellie ,—terris et baronia de
Earlstoune, extendentibus ad 40 mercatas terrarum
antiqui extentus, cum advocatione Sancti Joannis
de Daleg (vel Dalry) ;—terris et baronia de Gelstoune, comprehendente 3 mercatas terrarum de
Glensawock ,—20 solidatas terrarum de Whythills;
20 solidatas terrarum de Potterland ,—3 mercatas
terrarum de Kirkmyre et Glen ,—4 mercatas terrarum de Meikle Whythills et Shadowbank ,—20
solidatis terrarum de Newlands ;—7½ mercatas
terrarum de Ayreland ;—12 mercatas terrarum de
Inglestoune, cum molendino de Gelstoune, M'
Braicks et Barniewater, et 8 mercatas terrarum
de Broadland ;—in terris et baronia de Crossmichaell, comprehendente 2½ mercatis terrarum
de Fuffock ;—5 mercatas terrarum de Irnmyre ;—

(405)

5 mercatas terrarum de Auchindalie;—5 mercatas terrarum de Fargarie;—2½ mercatas terrarum de Irnefillan;—5 mercatas terrarum de Trodlie alias Tradlie;—5 mercatas terrarum de Mollans;—5 mercatas terrarum de Hillingtoune;—5 mercatas terrarum de Heribrand;—10 mercatas terrarum de Crofts;—10 mercatas terrarum de Glenguppoch; —in terris et terris dominicalibus de Greenlaw, cum canis et lie bound days work baroniae de Crossmichaell,—5 mercatis terrarum de Irnehills; —10 mercatis terrarum de Chappeliron,—2½ mercatis terrarum de Clowbrand et Auchinhay, cum advocatione de Crocemichaell;—5 mercatis terrarum de Meikle Dryburgh,—5 mercatis terrarum de Chapmantoune;—5 mercatis terrarum de Blackyearne;—5 mercatis terrarum de Kilnotrie, cum molendino granario de Crocemichaell;—5 mercatis terrarum de Geiringtoune;—2½ mercatis terrarum de Blackpark,—5 mercatis terrarum de Irnecraig, et 5 mercatis terrarum de Blairney;— 10 libratis terrarum de Jerse, Katharinae, et Debaitie;—terris de Bargalie et Barhoyse;—34 mercatis terrarum de Glenskairburne et Over Paltries; —terris de Kaillcora, Corbatoun, Dildovan, et Suffolk (Fuffok).—A E. 298m., N E. 894m.— terris et baronia de Gordonstoune.—A.E. 40m., N.E. 120m —terris et baronia de Toungueland, alias vocata tenandria de Endrig, in baronia de Toungueland, cum officio ballivatus deputati terrarum, etc., pertinentiam ad monasterium de Toungland.—E. 219l. feudifirmae

I S. (Kirkcudb.), 20 Sept. 1698

John, of Kilgour, once of Garlie, to his father Alexander of Kilgour—h. gen.   S. H , 15 Nov.; 18 Dec. 1723

,,   junior, de Kingoodie. *See* **Ann,** Kingoodie   I. G., 17 Aug. 1697

,,   to his brother Hugh, s. of Hugh of Kirkhill—h. gen.

S. H., 10 Jan.; 21 Jan. 1708

,,   s. of P. of Kirkhill. *See* **Isobel** of Kirkhill   . S. H., 15 Feb. 1764

,,   de Kirkland. *See* **Jonet,** Kirkland   I. S. (Kirkcudb.), 18 Nov. 1617

John, de Knarie. *See* **James,** Knarie.—E. 26s. 8d

I. S. (Kirkcudb), 12 Mar 1605

„   Knockbrex. *See* **Samuel,** Dumfries   I. de Tut.,   4 April 1683

„   f quondam Georgii in Knokleyth, h. Alexandri burgensis
de Abirdeen, patrui,—in octo bovatarum terrarum
de Creichnalaid infra parochiam de Fyvie ·—A.E.
10s. ; N E. 40s —terris de Rodgerseitt jacentibus
ad umbram ·—A.E 20s. ; N.E. 4l.—dimidietate
terrarum de Creichnalaid vocata the Overseitt of
Creichnalaid, infra parochiam praedictam.—A E
20s., N E 4l   I. S Supp. (Aberd.), 12 Jan 1579

„   of Knockspack   *See* **John** of Glenbucket   S. H.,   5 Feb 1705

„   in Larg. *See* **James,** Larg   I. S. (Wigton),   9 Jan. 1638

„   h. prov. Rogeri de Largmore, patris,—in 5 mercatis ter-
rarum de Garverie antiqui extentus vocatis Over,
Midle, and Nethir Garveries, infra parochiam de
Kells.—E. 7l 3s. 8d   I. S. (Kirkcudb.),   8 June 1669

„   de Largmoir, h. Joannis de Largmoir, avi   I G., 16 Aug. 1695

„ ·   de Largmoir   *See* **John,** *supra*

„   of Laussie   *See* **John,** in Inchmore   S H , 18 Mar. 1741

„   de Law, h. Joannis de Law, patris   I G., 23 June 1696

„   de Law. *See* **John,** *supra*

„   sailor, Leith, to his father Robert, sailor there—h gen.

S. H , 7 Sept. ; 30 Nov. 1778

„   to his father Robert, sailor in Leith—co -h. of prov gen

S. H , 21 June ; 23 June 1791

„   captain. *See* **Alexander,** Sir, of Lesmoir, bart.   S. H , 27 April 1764

„   burges of Linlithgow. *See* **James,** Linlithgow

I. S. (Stirling), 22 June 1655

„   dominus de Lochinvar, miles   *See* **Robert,** dominus de
Glen, miles   I. S. (Dumfries) ; I. S. (Kirkcudb.) ;

I. S. (Roxbr) ; I. S. (Wigton), 5 Nov. 1604

„   de Lochinvar, h domini Roberti de Lochinvar militis,
patris,—in 2 mercatis terrarum antiqui extentus
de Conreath (vel Correath) alias Castelphairne,
in baronia de Glencairne:—A.E. 2m. ; N.E. 6m —
6 mercatis terrarum de Ovirkirktoun ;—6 mercatis
terrarum de Nathirtoun de Kirktoun ,—40 solidatis
terrarum de Quhytwilling in tenandria de Dryis-

daill, et infra senescallatum Vallis Annandiae .—
A.E. 10l.; N.E. 30l.—annuo redditu 20l. de terris
de Dalfibbill et Garrell   I S. (Dumfries), 20 Mar. 1628

John, de Lochinvar, h domini Roberti de Lochinvar militis,
patris,—in 19 mercatis terrarum de Kenmure et
Laggen, cum molendino et piscariis earundem ;—
20 mercatis terrarum de Balmaclellane et Park,
cum molendino et piscariis ;—unitis in baroniam
de Kenmure, in parochiis de Balmaclellane et
Kells respective :—A.E. 39m.; N.E. 117m.—10
libratis terrarum de Tarskerechain (vel Tarstrec-
hane) et Dalbetie cum piscariis, in parochia de
Ur:—A.E. 10l.; N.E. 30l.—5 mercatis terrarum
de Dunrod in parochia de Sannyk :—A.E. 5m.;
N.E. 10l.—34 mercatis terrarum de Glenskyer-
burne et Over Poltrie (vel Polcrie) ;—3 mercatis
terrarum de Pollintrie (vel Pollincrie), infra parochiam de Anueth ;—4 mercatis terrarum de
Ewinstoun, Blakcraig, Knoknone ;—6 mercatis
terrarum de Hardlands et Munibwy in parochia
de Balmaclellane :—A.E. 47m.; N.E. 141m.—5
mercatis terrarum de Bellingat ;—5 mercatis terrarum de Knockmarling et Darsallok ;—5 mercatis
terrarum de Garlarg et Blakmark, extendentibus
ad 10 libratas terrarum antiqui extentus vocatas
Catbellie, in parochia de Kells ;—5 mercatas terrarum de Laggan ;—3 mercatis terrarum de Litle
Knokbryde ;—20 solidatis terrarum de Clauchreid ;
—2½ mercatis terrarum de Killigowne ;—1 mercata
terrarum de Mylnemark ;—1 mercata terrarum de
Slaichtis ;—1 mercata terrarum de Meroquhir (vel
Mercoquhir) in parochia de Anueth :—A.E. 20l ;
N.E. 60l.—terris de Kirkcanderis cum molendino,
viz. Retray, Robeinstoun, Cumzentoune (vel Kin-
zentoun), Barloto (vel Barloco), Margrie, Knokbrex, et insula de Kirkcanderis, in dicta parochia
de Anueth —E. 21l.—terris et baronia de Erlstoun
extendente ad 40 libratas terrarum antiqui extentus, cum molendino, piscariis et jure patronatus

ecclesiae parochialis vocatae St. John's Kirk;—8
solidatis terrarum de Craiggulane in parochia de
Dalry, unitis in baroniam de Erlstoun .—A.E.
35l. 5s. 4d.; N.E. 105l. 16s.—terris et baronia
de Crocemichaell comprehendentibus 2½ mercatas
terrarum de Fuffok alias Suffok;—5 mercatas
terrarum de Irnealmerie;—5 mercatis terrarum
de Auchindolie.—5 mercatis terrarum de Largi-
men (Largnain?);—2½ mercatis terrarum de
Irnefullan;—5 mercatis terrarum de Culgrais;—
5 mercatis terrarum de Craddill alias Troddaill;—
5 mercatis terrarum de Millance;—5 mercatis terrarum de Hillingtoun;—5 mercatis terrarum de
Hairybrand;—10 mercatis terrarum de Croftis;
—5 mercatis terrarum de Glengopok;—terris et
terris dominicalibus lie Maynes de Greinlaw, cum
lie Kayne Pettis et Bwndaywarkis dictae baroniae
de Crocemichaell;—5 mercatis terrarum de Erins-
bie;—10 mercatis terrarum de Chapellane (vel
Chapelerne);—2½ mercatis terrarum de Clairbrand:—E. 213l. 6s. 8d.—5 mercatis terrarum de
Litill Dryburgh;—5 mercatis terrarum de Drumjarg;—5 mercatis terrarum de Irnefillane;—5 mercatis terrarum de Ernecraig;—5 mercatis terrarum
de Blairinnie;—5 mercatis terrarum de Meikill
Dryburgh;—5 mercatis terrarum de Chepman-
toun,—5 mercatis terrarum de Blackerne;—5
mercatis terrarum de Armynnie;—5 mercatis
terrarum de Kilnotrie,—molendino granario de
Crocemichaell;—5 mercatis terrarum de Garron-
toun;—2½ mercatis terrarum de Blakpark, cum
jure patronatus ecclesiae de Crocemichaell:—
A.E. 57m. 6s. 8d.; N.E. 172m. 6s. 8d.—decimis
garbalibus aliisque decimis ecclesiae parochialis
et parochiae de Kirkmabrek:—E. 20l.—omnibus
unitis in baroniam de Crocemichaell.—terris de
Amurfad (vel Aminfad), Cuill, Blaires et Craig,
extendentibus ad 10½ mercatas et 40 denariatas
terrarum antiqui extentus,—7 mercatis terrarum

de Balquassıe,—4 mercatıs terrarum de Burnes;
—36 solıdatıs 8 denarıatıs terrarum de Spıttell,
—30 solidatıs terrarum de Cullındache antıqui
extentus·—E. 49l. 8d.—26 solıdatıs 8 denarıatıs
terrarum de Culcrainzıe et Garhorne, vulgo nun-
cupatıs Kılchronchie et Garquhıll.—4 mercatıs
terrarum de Lochinkıt antiqui extentus —E ı2m.
ıos.—terris de Litlehals:—E 43s. 4d —terrıs de
Glenquıckın et Dargarvell extendentıbus ad 2½ mercatas terrarum antıqui extentus, infra baronıam
de Ferrıe de Crıe.—E. 3l ı2s. 8d.—terris et
baronia de Gelstoun comprehendente 3 mercatas
terrarum de Glenzarrok;—20 solıdatıs terrarum
de Litle Quhythıll;—20 solıdatis terrarum de
Potterland;—3 mercatas terrarum de Kırkmurrine
et Glen;—4 mercatas terrarum de Meıkle Quhythıll et Gıldowbank;—20 solıdatıs terrarum de
Newlandıs;—7½ mercatas terrarum de Arealand
(vel Arenland);—ı2 mercatas terrarum de Inglıs-
toun,—molendınum de Gelstoun,—8 mercatas terrarum de Bordland, infra parochıam de Gelstoun
—A.E 42m.; N.E. 84l.   I. S. (Kırkcudb.), 20 Mar. 1628 ı

John, de Lochınvar, h. domını Roberti de Lochınvar mılıtıs,
patris,—ın terrıs de Stıtchell ın baronia de Stıtchell.
—E. ıoom.   I. S. (Roxb), 20 Mar. 1628

„   de Lochinvar, h. domını Joannıs de Lochinvar mılıtıs,
avı,—in terrıs de Gordounstoun extendentıbus ad
dımidietatem de Glenken vocatam Kennyheıd,
Acked Nether (Aıkheıd, Monteir), Knokneman,
Stromekawane, et Hottorduscane, cum molen-
dıno granòrum de Bannahard;—lacu et capitalı
messuagio de Lochinvar, in baronıa de Grennan
per annexationem.—A E 24l ı3s 4d ; N.E 74l
I S (Kırkcudb.), 2 Feb 1630

„   domınus, de Lochınvar, mıles   See John, supra.

„   de Lochınvar, h domini Roberti de Lochınvar mılıtıs,
patris,—ın terris et baronıa de Larg, comprehendente 40 solıdatas terrarum de Culgow,—40
solıdatis terrarum de Lıtıl Park;—20 solıdatıs

terrarum de Glennairme,—30 solidatas terrarum
de Bartachlaw (Barbachlaw?);—30 solidatis terrarum de Drumnaucht et Glengarrane;—10 solidatas terrarum de Tarquinnok;—10 solidatas
terrarum de Craignyne,—15 solidatas terrarum
de Craignell;—15 solidatas terrarum de Powreck-
boye, Laggane et Brokloche, et mercata terrae de
Kereedrachat,—burgo baroniae de Moniegoff cum
foris et hepdomadalibus macellis;—fortalicio de
Larg in parochia de Moneygoffe.—A.E. 11l. 3s
8d.; N.E. 33l. 10s.   I. S. (Kirkcudb.),   2 Feb. 1630

John, dominus de Longormis et Decanus de Saulisberre, h.
masc magistri Laurentii domini de Glenluce,
fratris germani,—in tenandria de Glenluce, comprehendente maneriem seu locum de Glenluce;—
monasterium seu abbaciam de Glenluce,—burgum
baroniae seu regalitatis, et villam de Ballinglauch,
cum terris burgalibus olim ad abbaciam de Glenluce pertinentibus;—ecclesia de Glenluce rectoria
et vicaria ejusdem, et cappellanariis et altaragiis
capellae Mariae Virginis et Christi capellae, vulgo
Our Lady et Crystis chapell vocatis, et jure patronatus earundem;—decimis garbalibus ad dictas
ecclesiam, capellanarias et altaragias pertinentibus.—A.E. 5l; N.E. 20l.—terras croftas et piscarias subscriptas olim ab antiquo ad dictam
abbaciam et beneficium ejusdem pertinentes, viz.
croftas vocatas Kirkcrystis-chappell-croft ad Kil-
phillane jacentes ·—E. 13s. 4d.—croftam vocatam
Our Lady-chappell:—E. 38s.—croftam vocatam
lie Monkiscroft, jacentem infra parochiam de
Kirkcum:—E. 13s. 4d.—croftam vocatam Curie-
long (vel Turielong), Quhycruick ad jacentem ·—
E. 60 duodenae parvulorum piscium vocatorum
Whitings —2 piscarias super aquas de Pontantane
et Corswatteris, infra regalitatem de Glenluce —
E. 50s.—omnes erectas in tenandriam de Glenluce
                                   I. S. (Wigton),   6 June 1610

„   farm servant in Main.   *See* **Ann,** Main   S H,   7 Jan 1773

John, custom officer at Methil. *See* **Jean,** Methil

                                 S. H., 11 Feb.; 4 Nov. 1774

,,   to his father William of Minmore—h. male and of line
gen.   S. H., 24 Aug.; 27 Aug. 1767

,,   h. Willielmi in Monyboye, patris,—in 2 mercatis terrarum
de Cortas, et 2 mercatis terrarum de Glengep, in
baronia de Sanquhair.—A.E. 4m.; N.E. 12m.

                             I. S. (Dumfries), 25 May 1626

,,   h Alexandri de Mundork, patris   I. G., 30 Aug. 1626

,,   Sir (Sinclair), of Murkle, bart., to his father Sir Robert
Sinclair of Murkle, bart., who died 4 Aug., 1795—
h. male of line, taillie and prov. spec. in Isauld,
Broubster, Thurso, etc., Caithness, and in Stevenson, Haddington   S. H., 4 April; 18 April 1797

,,   h. Patricii junioris de Neathermuire, fratris germani I. G., 24 Mar. 1683

,,   of Nethermuir. *See* **William** of Nethermuir   S. H., 6 Mar. 1761

,,   of Nethermuir, to Patrick Garioch of Tulloch—h. of prov.
gen.   S. H., 13 June; 7 July 1789

,,   merchant in and a bailie of New Galloway. *See* **Jean,**
Sarah, New Galloway   S. H., 21 Nov. 1791

,,   de Ovir Barskeoche, h. Alexandri de Over Barskeoche,
patris,—in terris de Over Barskeoche et Drumbuy
antiqui extentus, in parochia de Kellis et dominio
Galvidiae.—E. 10l. 13s. 4d.—3 mercatis terrarum
de Auchlane extentus praedicti, in parochia de
Kirkcormok —A.E. 40s.; N.E. 6l.

                             I. S. (Kirkcudb.), 24 Feb. 1631

,,   of Overbar, to his father James of Bar—h. gen.

                               S. H., 5 Nov.; 12 Nov. 1708

,,   Sir, of Park, bart. *See* Sir **James** of Park, bart. S. H., 4 May 1713

,,   captain, of Park. *See* **Ernest** of Cowbairdie   S. H., 27 Feb. 1782

,,   Sir, of Park. *See* **Ernest** of Cowbairdie   S H., 27 Feb. 1782

,,   captain, of Park. *See* **Ernest,** Sir, of Park, bart. S. H., 17 Dec. 1782

,,   in Pitchash of Ballandalloch, to his brother William—h.
gen.   S. H., 21 Sept.; 22 Sept. 1738

,,   h masc. domini Joannis de Petlurg militis, patris,—in
terris et baronia de Kynmundie, viz. villa et terris
de Kynmundie;—terris de Mylnehill, Millbreck,
Durie, Pettimarkhous, Smallburne, Kinknokne,

Burngranis, alias Barraksait et Pettindreich seat;
—Carvethin, Thornywray, Corsilstane, Pireis-
mylne;—3 quartis partibus et tertia parte quar-
tae partis dimidiae terrarum de Drumblait, viz.
Sliauche, cum Park, Adamstoun, Silverhillok,
Weistroune, Mutehillok, Bogheid, Newtoun;—
tertia parte terrarum de Garie;—bina parte terrarum de Cheppiltoun;—tertia parte terrarum de
Wedderburne;—bina parte terrarum de Brumehill;
—tertia parte terrarum de Thomastoun;—bina
parte terrarum de Comalegie.—A.E. 20l.; N.E.
8ol.   I. S. (Aberd.), 31 Oct. 1600

John, dominus, de Petlurg, miles. *See* **John,** *supra.*
,,   h. domini Joannis de Petlurg, militis, patris   I. G., 31 Oct 1600
,,   dominus, de Petlurg, miles. *See* **John,** *supra.*
,,   de Petlurg, h. domini Joannis de Petlurg, militis, patris,
            —in annuo redditu 1ol. de terris de Mekil et Littil
            Bannagoakis, in baronia de Kelly.—A.E. 2s.;
            N.E. 8s.   I. S. (Aberd), 30 July 1603
,,   dominus, de Petlurg, miles. *See* **John,** *supra.*
,,   (Cuming) of Pitlurg, to his father John Gordon-Cumming
            of Pitlurg, who died   Feb., 1768—h. male of line,
            taillie and prov. spec. in parts of Mains of Birnes,
            with Manor Place, and in Menie with Mains and
            Manor Place   S. H., 1 Dec 1768; 31 Jan. 1769
,,   (Gordon-Cumming) of Pitlurg. *See* **John** of Pitlurg
                                               S H., 31 Jan. 1769
,,   (Cumming) of Pitlurg, to his grandfather Dr. James of
            Pitlurg, who died   Sept., 1754—h. male and of
            line spec. in Pitlurg with Manor Place, Urrquhor-
            ties with Tarnash Mill, etc.
                                   S. H., 15 Feb.; 19 Mar. 1774
,,   (Cumming) of Pitlurg, to his father John Gordon-Cum-
            ming of Pitlurg—h. gen.   S. H., 7 June; 12 June 1780
,,   Gordon-Cumming of Pitlurg. *See* **John** (Cumming) of
            Pitlurg, *supra.*
,,   (Cumming) of Pitlurg, to his grandmother Barbara Cum-
            ming, wid. of Dr. Jas. of Pitlurg—h. of line gen
                                   S H , 24 Jan.; 29 Jan. 1783

John, of Portland parish, county of Surrey, Jamaica, to his
     father George, merchant, Aberdeen—h. gen.
                              S. H., 18 June ; 29 June 1772
,,   h Roberti in Restalrig, patris   I G , 26 Aug 1697
,,   de Rothimey   *See* **James** de Rothimey   I G , 15 April 1665
,,   de Rothemay.   *See* **Patrick** Barclay, alias Gordon de
          Rothiemay   I. S (Aberd.),   5 Oct. 1698
,,   capitanus, h. Joannae dominae de Rothiemurkus, amitae
                              I. G , 17 May 1616
,,   de Siddera   *See* **Alexander** de Siddera   I G , 27 July 1647
,,   apparentis de Siddera   *See* **Alexander** de Siddera   I. G., 27 July 1647
,,   de Spedoch.   *See* **Gabriel,** Spedoch   I. G., 24 June 1687
,,   inspector of customs, Stromness   *See* **Sybil,** Cairstoun
                              S H., 29 May 1799
,,   h. Georgii de Tillaquhowdie, avi,—in terris de Litill-
          Follay, in parochia de Fyvie —A.E 40s , N E.
          81.   I S (Aberd.), 29 Nov 1610
,,   h. Alexandri de Torquhane, patris,—in 3 mercatis terrarum
          de Torquhane ;—1 mercata terrarum de Craig ;—1
          mercata terrarum de Barmorrow (vel Barkorrow),
          —3 'mercatis terrarum de Barinnie ;—4 mercatis
          terrarum de Mekill Mochrum antiqui extentus, in
          parochiis de Balmaclellane, Kellis, et Partoun.—
          A.E. 81 ; N E 36m.   I S Supp (Kirkcudb), 30 Oct. 1582
,,   h. Rogeri apparentis de Troquhain, patris,—in 40 solidatis
          terrarum de Auchinhay ;—1 mercata terrarum de
          Darnegarroch ;—1 mercata terrarum de Ovir et
          Nather Slougabeyis ;—molendino de Kirkpatrick
          cum a strictis multuris baroniae de Kirkpatrick,
          infra dictam baroniam de Kirkpatrick-Durhame ·—
          E. 17l. 4s —4 mercatis terrarum de Muill antiqui
          extentus, infra parochiam de Kirkpatrick de Mure et
          baroniam de Lochmaben per annexationem, parti-
          bus monastrii de Dundrennan .—E. 4m. 40d —
          40 solidatis terrarum de Kirktilbryd ,—20 solidatis
          terrarum de Marglev,—40 solidatis 40 denariatis
          terrarum de Bardarroch, infra parochiam de Kirk-
          patrick-Durhame.—E. 12l. 14s 4d
                         I. S (Kirkcudb), 29 July 1617

John, de Troquhane, h Joannis de Troquhane, avi,—in 3 mer-
c_atis terrarum de Troquhane ;—1 mercata terrae
de Craig ;—1 mercata terrae de Barmarrowe ;—3
mercatis terrarum de Blarennie antiqui extentus,
in parochia de Balmaclellane —A E 5l 6s. 8d ;
N.E 16l —terris de Bartaggart extentus praedicti,
in dominio Galvidiae subtus Crie et parochia praedicta ,—dimidia mercata terrae de Altaquhyt, parte
30 solidatarum terrarum de Arnelosche extentus
praedicti ,—5½ mercatis terrarum de Irnlantoun
extentus praedicti, in parochia de Tuyname.—
A.E. 6l. 13s 4d , N E 20l —5 libratis terrarum
de Barkaple extentus praedicti, in parochia de
Toungland —E 7l 10s , etc   I S (Kirkcudb), 9 Oct 1632
  ,,   de Troquhane. *See* **John** de Troquhane, *supra*
  ,,   of Troquhain *See* **Elizabeth,** Heron   S H , 27 Mar. 1766
  ,,   Lieut., E.I.C.S., to his father Lieut.-Col. the Hon John,
who died 31 Oct , 1778—h male spec in the
superiority of Tullich, etc , and forests of Morven
and Coblean, all belonging in property to Farquharson of Inverey   S H (Aberd), 2 April 1787
  ,,   the Hon., Lieut.-Col *See* **John,** Lieut , E.I.C.S., *supra*
  ,,   in Water de Leyth, h Clementis apud Water de Leyth,
patris   I G , 22 June 1631
  ,,   lieutenant, 30th foot, to his father Nathaniel of Whitehill
—h gen   S H , 12 Nov ; 26 Nov. 1794
Jonet. *See also* **Janet, Jeonet.**
  ,,   *See* **Juliana**   I. G., 12 Jan. 1677
  ,,   sp. magistri Thomae Davidson Clerici commissariatus
Abirdonensis, h. Jacobi de Haddo, patris,—in villa
et terris de Braklay, Tarves, Kirtoun de Tarves et
Diracroft ejusdem, infra baroniam de Tarves.—E.
14l.   I S (Aberd), 11 Feb. 1625
  ,,   *See* **John** de Beoche   I S (Kirkcudb), 13 Oct. 1607
  ,,   h port praedictae Margaretae [Blaket], sororis,—in
undecima parte praedictarum terrarum
     I. S (Kirkcudb), 14 April 1552
  ,,   de Colclarachie. Alexander Forbes, h. Jonetae Gordon,
port. de Colclarachie, matris,—in quarta parte

terrarum de Colclarachie;—dimidia sextae partis
terrarum et villae de Garry;—quarta parte terrarum et villa de Drumdornache, in regalitate de
Gareoche—A.E. 30s.; N.E. 10l.

I. S. (Aberd.), 23 June 1554

Jonet. *See* **John** de Combrie   I. G., 15 April 1665

,,   *See* **Thomas** de Crogo   I. S. (Kirkcudb.), 1 June 1620

,,   Blythman, relict of James Gordon, messinger, h. of
Helene Blythman, relict of Robert Paterson,
tailyeir burges of Edinburgh, her sister   I. G., 31 Mar. 1657

,,   h. Margaretae, f. legitimae quondam Laurentii domini
de Glenluce, sororis,—in annuo redditu 1000m. de
manerie seu loco de Glenluce et hortis ejusdem, et
decimis ad ecclesiam de Glenluce et ad capellanias
ejusdem pertinentibus   I. S. (Wigton), 18 May 1643

,,   Alexander Leythe, h. Elizabethae alias Bessie Leythe,
f. legitimae quondam Joannis Leythe de Harthill
inter ipsum et Jonetam Gordoun suam sp. novissi-
mam procreatae, sororis germanae   I. G , 15 July 1631

,,   h. Joannis de Kirkland, patris,—in 1 mercata terrae
antiqui extentus vocata Toddistoun;—tenemento
terrae in villa de Sanct Johannes clauchan, vulgo
nuncupata domus sub monte,—4 acris terrarum
et 1 dieta lie Daywark prati cum horto, etc., eidem
tenemento spectante, infra parochiam de Dalry·—
E. 8m. 6s. 8d —terris vocatis the Littill Kirkland
de Dalry, extendentibus ad 18 acras terrarum :—
E 5s. 4d.—omnibus in baronia de Carleton

I. S (Kirkcudb.), 18 Nov. 1617

Josiah, of Boytath, to his brother James, son of James of Boytath—h. gen. c. b. inv.   S H., 11 Oct.; 31 Oct. 1720

Juliana, sp. Gulielmi Rosset et Joneta, sp. Thomae Allane in
Ellone, hh. port. Alexandri, burgensis de Aberdein,
patris   I. G., 12 Jan. 1677

Katharine. *See* **Catharine.**

Kenneth, magister, f. et h. magistri Roberti de Cluny, procreatus inter illum et Margaretam M'Kenzie f.
domini Kennethi M'Kenzie de Coull ejus tertiam
sp., patris   I. G., 11 July 1699

Kenneth, h. prov. magistri Roberti de Clunie, procreatus inter
      illum et Margaretam M'Kenzie f. Kennethi
      M'Kenzie de Coull ejus sp , patris   I G , 26 Aug. 1699

,,   advocate, to his nephew Robert of Clunie, advocate,
      who died   April, 1729—h. of prov. spec. c. b.
      inv in the lands and mains of Clunie, and in
      Craig, Glentoun, Tilliecairn, Castletoun, etc.
                 S. H., 18 Nov. 1729; 28 Mar. 1730

,,   advocate, to his nephew Robert of Clunie, advocate—
      h. male and of line gen. c b. inv.
                 S. H. 18 Nov. 1729, 28 Mar. 1730

,,   of Cluny, advocate. *See* **Robert**   S. H., 17 Oct. 1741

Laurence, dominus, de Glenluce. *See* **John**, dominus de Lon-
      gormis   I. S. (Wigton), 6 June 1610

,,   dominus, de Glenluce. *See* **Jonet**, Glenbervie
                 I. S. (Wigton), 18 May 1643

Lewis, M.D , in Aberdeen. *See* **Robert**   S. H., 24 Jan 1712

,,   of Auchmull, merchant, Aberdeen. *See* **James** of Hilton,
      M.D.   S H., 6 June 1744

,,   frater Joannis de Craigieheid, inquisitor
                 I. de Poss. Quinq., 31 Aug 1682

,,   dominus, de Gordounstoune. *See* **Robert,** magister,
      Gordounstoune
          I. G., 5 Dec. 1674; I. S. (Sutherl.), 22 April 1675

,,   dominus, de Gordounstoune. *See* **Robert,** dominus de
      Gordounstoune
          I. G., 21 Sept. 1688, I. S (Elgin), 21 Sept 1688

,,   brother of Sir Robert of Gordonstoun *See* **Robert** S. H., 31 Dec 1722

,,   to his father Alexander in Kinnedour—h. gen.
                 S. H., 24 July; 6 Aug 1718

,,   of Kinmundy *See* **James** of Teichmury   S. H., 11 June 1747

Magdalene, to her husband John Stewart, minister at Drum-
      bleat—h. of prov gen   S. H., 6 April, 12 April 1763

,,   to her brother George of Glengerrick, who died in
      May or June, 1747—h. port. spec. in the barony of
      Glengerrick, including Auchives, Berryleys, New-
      miln of Strathisla, etc.   S. H., 16 Aug ; 25 Aug. 1748

Margaret. *See* **William,** magister   I. G., 11 Aug. 1668

,,   domina sp. Com. de Aboyn. *See* **Ann,** Aboyn I. G., 17 June 1665

Margaret, wid. of Professor Geo. Gordon, Aberdeen, to her
   brother George, s. of Geo Fraser, sub-principal
   there—h. port. gen.   S H , 26 May 1740

"   to John Davidson, her husband, s of Wm Davidson, merchant in Aberdeen—h of prov gen.
                 S. H., 12 Dec. 1746, 6 Jan. 1747

"   wife of Geo Birnie, innkeeper, Aberdeen, to her
   father John, salmon fisher, Bridge of Don—h.
   gen.   '   S. H., 16 Dec. 1795; 6 Feb. 1796

"   and Agnes, hh. port. of Johne of Auchlean, their
   father,—in the 10 merk-land of Auchlean comprehending the lands of Wood Hills (or Woodhills)
   and Husbandtoun, with the corne milne;—the 1
   merk-land called Markbreddan of old extent, within
   the parochin of Wigton —A E 11m ; N.E. 22l.
   —the 2 merk-land of Glenjorie, and 20 shilling-
   land of Glenchalmer of old extent, within the
   parochin of Glenluce.—E 18m. of feu farm
                  I S. (Wigton), 26 Oct. 1652

"   h port. praedicti Joannis [de Blaikat], patris,—in
   terris praedictis. *See* **Catharine**
                 I. S (Kirkcudb.), 29 Oct. 1548

"   *See* **Agnes, Catharine, Euphemia, Helen, Jonet,
   Mariota, Sibyl,** Blaket   I. S. (Kirkcudb.), 14 April 1552

"   Edwardes Makmarane, h. Margaretae Gordoun, matris,
   —in 11 solidatis 6 denariatis terrarum de 9 mercatis terrarum de Blakat, cum undecima parte
   molendini antiqui extentus, in parochia de Ur;—
   5 solidatis terrarum de Laig antiqui extentus, in
   parochia de Girtoun.—A E. 16s. 6d.; N.E. 49s 6d.
                 I. S. (Kirkcudb.), 24 July 1576

"   wife of Jn Black, senr. John Black, junr., merchant,
   Bordeaux, to his mother Margaret Gordon, wife
   of Jn. Black, senr., merchant there—h. gen.
             S H. Supp., 5 July; 22 July 1748

"   wife of Alex. Duff of Bracco. Margaret Duff, wife of
   Pat. Duff, advocate, Aberdeen, to her grandmother
   Margaret Gordon, wife of Alex Duff of Bracco—
   h. gen   S H. Supp., 1 June 1722

Margaret, Edinburgh. *See* **John** de Aberlour I. de Tut , 30 July 1696

 ,, Joanna Forbes, h. Margaretae Gordone, sp. Alexandri
   Forbes de Ester-Migtie, matris I. G , 10 June 1693

 ,, h. Margaretae Sinclair, matris,—in dimidietatie 4½
   mercatarum terrarum antiqui extentus baroniae
   de Erlistoun, extendente ad 2 mercatas et 40
   denariatas terrarum earundem subscriptarum, viz
   dimidietate mercatae terrae de Erlistoun ,—dimidietate mercatae terrae de Mylntoun ,—dimidietate
   mercatae terrae de Marnbrok ,—dimidietate mercatae terrae de Quhitlie ,—dimidietate dimidiae
   mercatae terrae de Dalclany ,—dimidietate dimidiae
   mercatae terrae de Glentie, in baronia de Erlistoun,
   et parochia de Dalry.—A.E. 30s. , N.E. 4l 10s.
       I. S Supp (Kirkcudb), 15 May 1593

 ,, *See* **Elizabeth, Jean,** Fintray S H , 22 Mar 1775

 ,, relicta magistri Joannis Irvine rectoris ecclesiae de ·
   Glenbervie, h. Roberti Gordoun f. Joannis in
   Belgia, fratris germani I. G., 13 June 1691

 ,, to her brother George of Glengerrick, who died in
   May or June, 1747—h. port. spec in the barony
   of Glengerrick, including Auchives, Berryleys,
   Newmiln of Strathisla, etc. S H., 16 Aug. , 25 Aug 1748

 ,, wife of William M'Millan of Glenlaggan, to her
   cousin James of Craiglaw—h port. gen. c. b inv.
       S H, 10 Jan. 1736

 ,, *See* **Jonet,** Glenluce I. S. (Wigton), 18 May 1643

 ,, Tait, wife of Wm. Gordon of Holm, to her brother
   Robert Tait, s. of Wm Tait of Lochenkitt—h
   gen. S. H , 20 Sept , 28 Nov. 1759

 ,, *See* **Agnes,** Inverness I S. (Elgin), 31 Nov. 1690

 ,, to her father Alexander of Kirkland—h. port. gen.
       S H , 14 Oct. , 3 Dec 1731

 ,, Barbara and Elspet, hh. port of William, merchand
   burges of Kirkwall, their father,—in the tenements
   of land underwritten, viz., that tenement of land
   with the yaird sometyme perteining to Robert
   Soulbie, lyand in the toune of Kirkwall, in that
   pairt thairoff callit the Laverock, within the schirrif-

dome of the earldome of Orkney and lordschipe of
Zetland ·—E. services as effeirs .—that ruinous
. hous and yaird quhilk was built and plantit upon
the peice of weste ground of nyntein foot of breid
in the Laverok of Kirkwall :—E. services as effeirs:
—that piece of quoy land callit Quoy-angrie extending in lenth to fyftie eight foots of measure,
within the pareoche of St. Olla.—E. 1 poynt
French wyne, and ane unce of sufficient toubalco,
of feu ferme :—ane annuelrent of 23l. 12d. furth
of the lands and heretages pertaining to Johne
Midhouse, and speciallie of the said John his
tenement of land lyand in the said toune of
Kirkwall in that pairt thairoff callit the burghe
beneath Sant Ollowes brige ·— E. 1d. blench
ferme ·—that tenement of land and yaird sometyme pertaining to John Gairner in Kirkwall, in
that pairt thairoff called the Laverock.—E. 4s. of
feu duty, etc.   I. S. (Orkney), 25 Nov 1656

Margaret, Barbara and Elspet, hh. port. of William, merchand
burges of Kirkwall, their father,—in a tenement
in Kirkwall :—E 40d.—a ruinous hous and yaird
in Kirkwall ·—E. 2 capones:—a piece of quoy-
land called Quoy-angrie within the parochin of
St. Olla ·—E. ane poynt of French wyne and ane
rowie of tubalco ·—ane annuelrent of 23 punds
12 penyes furth of lands in Kirkwall ,—a tenement
of land in Kirkwall —E. 4s and 12d. in augmen-
tation   I. S. (Orkney), 25 Nov. 1656

  ,,   Barbara and Elspet, hh. port. of Magnus Taillyer,
merchand burgis of Kirkwall, their uncle on the
mother syd   I. G., 16 Dec. 1656

  ,,   Barbareta et Elizabetha, hh. port. Magni Tailzeor
mercatoris in Kirkwall, avunculi,—in australi
parte tenementi terrae ex antiquo ad praeposi-
turam de Orkney pertinentis cum area et horto,
in urbe de Kirkwall .—E 33 asses 4d.—dimidio
tenementi terrae ac domus vocatae lie Innes, in
Kirkwall .—E. 1d. albae firmae —tenemento ac

domo cum duabus partibus hortorum apud littus
de Kirkwall :—E. saginatus capo ·—tenemento
terrae in lie Laverok-villae de Kirkwall :—E. 1
pondus candidae cerae, cum debito servitio:—
roume et terris de Waile, extendentibus ad 1
obulum terrae infra parochiam de Firth :—E. 19d.
scat silver, etc.—70 pedibus terrae in longitudine
et 43 pedibus in latitudine, in media urbe de
Kirkwall.—E. 10 asses, feudifirmae

I. S. (Orkney),   8 Feb. 1662

Margaret, d. of T. in Lagan of Glenrinnes, to her grandfather
Duncan Cumming of Letter Wandoch—h. port.
gen.   S. H , 16 Jan. 1703

Mariota, h. port. praedicti Joannis [de Blaikat], patris,—in
terris praedictis   I. S. (Kirkcudb.), 29 Oct. 1548

„   h. port. praedictae Margaretae [Blaket], sororis, in
undecima parte dictarum terrarum

I. S. (Kirkcudb), 14 April 1552

Marjory, h. port praedicti Joannis [de Blaikat], patris,—in
terris praedictis   I. S. (Kirkcudb.), 29 Oct. 1548

„   *See* **Christina,** Branelane   I. S (Aberd.), 6 Oct. 1669

„   Cairnbrogie. *See* **James,** Auchredy   S H., 25 Jan. 1740

Mary, wife of Jas. Farquhar in Aberlour, to her brother John,
s. of Rt. of Farnachtie—h. gen.

S. H., 20 June 1735 ; 23 Dec. 1737

„   to her father James of Barns—h. port. gen.

S. H., 6 Oct. 1739 ; 20 Nov. 1740

„   Butthlaw. *See* **Jean,** Aberdeen   S. H , 2 Feb. 1780

„   dame, wife of Sir Jas. Abercromby of Birkenbogg, to her
brother Robert, merchant, Aberdeen—h. gen.

S. H., 2 May ; 11 May 1732

„   Barclay, wife of John Gordon of Buthlaw, advocate, to
her brother James Barclay of Cairness, who died
4 Jan., 1765, h. port. spec. cum ben. invent , in
Arthursnook or Invernorth, part of Cairness, etc.

S. H., 19 Mar., 3 April 1766

„   to her father Alexander of Crogo, writer in Edinburgh—
h. port. and of line gen.   S. H., 23 June ; 30 June 1789

„   d. of Alex. of Crogo *See* **Agnes,** Glendonwyne   S. H., 30 Dec. 1790

Mary, to her father Doctor James of Fechell, who died Aug ,
1723—h. port. spec. in the lands of Fechell in the
parish of Ellon   S. H., 17 July ; 29 Aug 1741

„ lady, of Gight *See* **Alexander** (or Davidson) of Gight
S H., 20 Feb. 1735

„ of Gight. *See* **Alexander** (or Davidson) of Gight S H , 18 Feb. 1740

„ wife of Jn. Wilson, iron merchant, Glasgow, to her
g^dfather John, physician there—co-h. of prov. gen.
S H., 30 May ; 18 June 1792

„ to her brother John of Gordonbank—h. port. gen.
S. H., 6 April , 21 April 1796

„ wid. of J. Gordon of Hillhead, to her brother Robert, s.
of R. Ross of Auchlossen—h. port. gen.
S. H., 18 Dec.; 31 Dec. 1712

„ *See* **Agnes,** Inverness   I S (Elgin), 31 Nov 1690

„ wid. of James Irvine of Kincoussie Margaret Irvine,
to her mother Mary Gordon (wid. of James Irvine
of Kincoussie), who died April, 1742—h. spec.
in one-third of the lands of Fechell, in the parish
of Ellon   S. H. Supp , 2 June ; 9 June 1742

„ Walshe, sp to William Gordone of Munibuy, h. of
Johne Walshe, younger, of Collistoun, her brother
german, in the 4 pund land of Gribtoune within
the parochine of Halywood, and barronie of Grib-
bistoun :—A.E 4l ; N.E. 12l —the 20 shilling land
of Neithersyde (or Nether Whytsyde) ,—the 20
shilling land of Gibbistoun, within the pareoch of
Dunscoir and barronie forsaid.—A.E. 40s ; N.E.
6l   I. S (Dumf.), 20 Feb 1659

„ Walshe, sp. to William Gordoune of Munibuy, h. of
Johne Walshe, younger, of Collistoun, her brother
german,—in the 4 pund land of Boordland and
Cowansdykis, within the parochin of Alddistone :
—A.E 4l. , N.E 12l.—the 10 pund land of Loch-
drougand within the parochine of Kirkcormoch.
—A.E 10l ; N.E. 30l —xxv. 180
I. S. (Kirkcudb.), 20 Feb. 1659

„ h. Gulielmi de Robertoun, patris,—in 6 mercatis terrarum .
de Rotraix ;—3 mercatis terrarum de Robertoun ;

2 mercatis terrarum 4 mercatarum terrarum de
Kingzeantoun, molendino de Kirkcanders, in
parochia de Kirkcanders, et dominio de Galloway.
—E. 8l. 2s. I. S. (Kirkcudb), 8 Sept. 1668

Nathaniel, colonel. *See* **Adam** of Ardlogie I G , 2 Jan. 1656

,, of Carleton. *See* **Alexander** of Carleton S H , 3 Feb. 1773

,, of Carleton. *See* **Alexander** of Little Cocklaw
  S. H., 29 Mar 1774

,, h. Davidis de Gordounstoune, patris I G , 22 Mar 1681

,, of Gordounstoune, to James of Carletoun—h. of
  taillie and prov. gen. S. H , 12 Dec. 1702 , Dec. 1702

,, to his father Robert, s. of William of Holm—h. gen
  S H , 8 Aug., 22 Aug. 1724

,, of Whitehill *See* **John,** Whitehill S H , 26 Nov 1794

Nicolas. *See* Grizell, Greenlaw S. H., 23 Feb. 1743

Patience, wife of Geo. H. Gordon, capt 63rd foot, to her father
  Edward Stedman, minister, Haddington—h. port
  gen S H , 7 Oct , 23 Oct 1790

Patrick [*or* Peter] *See* **John** I. G Supp., 9 Jan. 1630

,, h. Roberti, fratris immediate senioris I G , 31 July 1622

,, *See* **Alexander** I. G , 8 Oct 1633

,, of Abergeldie. *See* **Charles** of Abergeldie
  S. H , 25 Oct 1737 ; S. H., 8 Sept 1738

,, of Abergeldie, to his father Charles of Abergeldie—h.
  male of taillie and prov gen. S H., 21 Feb ; 18 May 1798

,, of Aberlour, to his grandfather Patrick of Aberlour—h.
  gen. S H , 11 June, 5 July 1792

,, of Aberlour. *See* **Patrick,** *supra.*

,, of Ardmeallie *See* **James,** Ardmeallie S. H , 11 April 1753

,, de Auchinangzie. *See* **George,** Auchincingzie
  I. S. (Aberd), 6 Oct. 1573

,, *See* **John,** feoditarius de Auchindoir I. G., 20 Aug 1633

,, dominus de Auchindoun, miles *See* **George,** Marchio
  de Huntlie I. S (Banff), 6 May 1600

,, to his father John of Achleuchries—h gen.
  S. H., 10 Mar., 17 Mar. 1722

,, of Avochie. *See* **John** of Avochie S H , 24 Jan. 1780

,, de Brackay *See* **John,** Brakay I. S. Supp (Aberd), 31 Oct. 1586

,, Maister of Brackay. *See* **John** of Brackay I S (Aberd.), 4 Feb 1657

Patrick [*or* **Peter**] de Brasmoir. *See* **Alexander**, Brasmoir
                                                   I. G , 18 April 1626

    ,,   de Birsmoir. *See* **Alexander** de Birsmoir I. S (Aberd.), 27 Sept 1637

    ,,   de Brasmoir *See* **Alexander** de Brasmoir   I G , 5 Dec. 1665

    ,,   h. Patricii de Corachrie, patris   I. G , 31 July 1622

    ,,   de Corachrie. *See* **Patrick**, *supra.*

    ,,   *See* **Eufamia**, Duninald   I. G., 15 Mar. 1642

    ,,   f. natu maximus Alexandri in Drumfald, h Gulielmi in
          Millerriven, avi.   I. G , 10 July 1684

    ,,   watchmaker in Edinburgh, to his brother Thomas,
          watchmaker there—h. gen   S. H , 20 April ; 1 May 1746

    ,,   *See* **John**, Geight   I. G., 9 June 1630

    ,,   h Patricii de Gordounsmilne, avi   I. G , 6 Feb 1639

    ,, .   de Gordounsmilne. *See* **Patrick**, *supra.*

    ,,   h. Patricii de Gordonismyln, avi,—in villa et terris de
          Cottoun, cum novo molendino vulgo nuncupata
          Gordonsmylne, et crofta sub monte et crofta supra
          montem, vocatis lie Fold, lie Netherhauch et Inch,
          inter aquas de Don et lie Brayes ;—astrictis mul-
          turis villarum et terrarum de Cottoun, Capinstone
          alias Cabrostone, et croftarum seu riggarum Veteris
          Aberdoniae et territorii ejusdem, infra baroniam
          Veteris Aberdoniae lie Schire nuncupatam, et
          parochiam Divi Macharii.—E. 12l , etc., feudi-
          firmae   I S Supp (Aberd.), 24 July 1650

    ,,   de Gordonismyln. *See* **Patrick**, *supra*

    ,,   de Halheid, h. Patricii de Halheid, patris,—in villa et
          terris de Halheid ,—terris de Corquhinderland infra
          parochiam de Cushnie —A. E. 3l. ; N.E 12l
                          I S (Aberd.), 7 June 1617

    ,,   de Halheid. *See* **Patrick**, *supra.*

    ,,   de Halheid. *See* **George** de Halheid   I. S. (Aberd), 27 Feb 1622

    ,,   de Halhead. *See* **John**, Halhead   I. S. (Aberd.), 28 Sept. 1683

    ,,   de Hillheid. *See* **Elizabeth**, Hillheid   I. G.,   * * *

    ,,   of King's Grange, formerly of Troquhain, Colonel, to
          his father George of Troquhain, who died   July,
          1759—h. spec. in the 10 merk land of Grange and
          Wairdmeadow, in the parish of Urr
                   S. H., 21 Jan, ; 16 Mar. 1774

Patrick [*or* **Peter**], of Kings-grange, brigadier-gen.   *See* **Alex-**
          ander of Kings-grange   S H., 22 Oct. 1777
  ,,   of Kirkhill.   *See* **Isobel** (or Stewart) of Kirkhill S. H., 15 Feb. 1764
  ,,   *See* **James**, Lesmoir   I. S. (Aberd), 29 Nov. 1564
  ,,   de Letterfurie.   *See* **James** de Letterfurie   I. S. (Ross), 19 May 1606
  ,,   at Miln of Smithtoun.   *See* **Henrietta, Jean,** Miln
                                       S. H., 25 Jan. 1786
  ,,   *See* **James**, Nethermuire   I. G., 21 June 1643
  ,,   de Nethermuire.   *See* **James**, Nethermuire   I. G , 21 June 1643
  ,,   junior, de Neathermuire.   *See* **John**, Neathermuire I. G., 24 Mar. 1683
  ,,   New York.   *See* **Charles**   S. H., 26 Mar. 1782
  ,,   h. Alexandri, f. Gulielmi de Pinkaitland, fratris germani
                                    I. G., 8 Feb 1690
  ,,   Barclay alias Gordone de Rothemay, et Toure, h. Joannis
          Gordone de Rothemay, patris,—in annuo redditu
          104l. correspondente 2,600m. de villa et terris de
          Overtoune de Glenbucket et Fairntoull, infra
          parochiam de Glenbucket.—E. 1d. albae firmae
                        I S. (Aberd.), 5 Oct. 1698
  ,,   in Strone of Badenoch.   *See* **Cosmo Alexander,** Strone
                              S. H., 4 May 1737
  ,,   of Towie, to his grandfather Patrick Barclay of Towie,
          who died   —h. spec. in Blairmormonth,
          Crimondgorth, etc., on appraisement
                  S. H , 20 July 1712 ; 11 May 1713
  ,,   of Troquhain, captain, to his father George of Troquhain
          —h gen   S. H., 1 Oct. ;   Dec. 1761

Rachael, sp. Capitani Caroli, h Joannis de Aberzeldie, fratris
          germani   I. G., 1 Mar. 1698
  ,,   to her mother Rachel Robertson, wife of Hugh, gold-
          smith in Edinburgh—co-h. of prov. gen.
                  S. H , 15 Jan. ; 23 Jan. 1777

Ralph, shipmaster in Aberdeen, to his father Walter, shipmaster
          there—co-h. of prov. gen.   S. H., 7 April, 22 April 1786
  ,,   shipmaster in Aberdeen, to his sister Jean, d. of W ,
          shipmaster there—h. gen.   S. H , 6 July ; 13 July 1793

Rebecca, wife of Thos. in Speymouth, to her mother Rebecca
          Dunbar or Gordon or Anderson—h port gen.
                    S H., 25 April, 5 July 1782

Rebecca. *See* **Isobel**, Duffus   S H , 25 April; 5 July 1782
Richard, of Craigmyle, advocate *See* **John** of Craigmyle S. H., 24 Dec 1763
Robert. *See* **Patrick**   I. G., 31 July 1622
  „   son of A., advocate, to his uncle Lewis, M D , in Aber-
          deen—h. gen.   S. H., 8 Dec 1711 , 24 Jan. 1712
  „   merchant, Aberdeen. *See* **Mary,** dame, Birkenbog
                              S. H., 11 May 1732
  „   of Achinhalrigg and Curfurroch. *See* **Elizabeth,** Achin-
          halrigg   S. H , 20 Feb. 1724
  „   of Auchendolly, to his father James of Auchendolly, who
          died 28 Oct., 1708—h. spec. in Auchendolly and
          Trowdall in the parish of Corsmichael
                          S. H., 26 Feb ; 23 April 1717
  „   de Bandane, h. Alexandri de Balery, f. patrui   I G., 2 Jan. 1607
  „   h Roberti de Baranrine, patris,—in dimidio 6 mercata-
          rum terrarum de Barunreine, Barlimaine, Culstray,
          Kenmoir, Barquhaple, et Barbundie contigue ad-
          jacentium, in parochia de Kirkcowan ·—A.E. 40s.,
          N.E. 6l.—1 mercata terrae cum 40 denariatis ter-
          rarum vocatis Markbayne —A.E 16s 8d ; N.E
          50s —alia mercata terrae vocata Culvenane antiqui
          extentus.—A.E. 13s 4d., N.E 40s.
                          I. S. (Wigton), 20 Jan 1595
  „   de Baranrine *See* **Robert,** *supra.*
  „   magister, apud Boatary. *See* **John,** Boatary   I. G , 27 July 1682
  „   ⸌ to his father Alexander, merchant in Boulogne—h of
          prov. gen   S. H., 26 Dec.; 31 Dec. 1755
  „   s. of Alex., merchant, Boulogne-sur-mer. *See* **Robert**
          of Hallhead   S H., 12 Dec 1760
  „   merchant in Bristol, to his brother Alexander of Auchin-
          dolly, M D., in Dumfries, who died   Nov , 1777
          —h spec. in Auchindolly and Trowdale, in the
          parish of Crossmichael S H. (Kirkcudb.), 30 Oct.; 6 Nov. 1778
  „   of Cairnfield, Banff. *See* **Alexander,** Amsterdam
                              S. H., 27 June 1718
  „   de Chappeltoune *See* **Christina,** Chappeltoune I. G., 17 Oct. 1671
  „   of Chappeltoun. *See* **George** of Chappeltoun S. H , 19 Feb 1752
  „   magister, de Cluny. *See* **Kenneth,** Cluny
                    I G , 11 July 1699; I. G , 26 Aug 1699

Robert, of Cluny, advocate, to his father Robert of Cluny—h.
gen. S. H , 12 Dec.; 13 Dec. 1723

,, of Cluny. *See* **Robert** of Cluny, *supra.*

,, of Cluny, advocate, to his grandfather Robert of Cluny
—h. gen. S. H., 12 Dec.; 13 Dec. 1723

,, of Cluny. *See* **Robert** of Cluny, *supra.*

,, of Clunie, advocate. *See* **Kenneth,** Clunie S. H., 28 Mar. 1730

,, to his mother Elizabeth Malloch, wid. of Kenneth of
Cluny, advocate—h of prov. gen. S H., 11 Sept ; 17 Oct 1741

,, s of Geo , tacksman of Culmaly. *See* **Ann,** Dunrobin ,
Janet, Torbreck , **Grizell,** Cromarty S H , 24 May 1769

,, to John his father, dyer in Bridgend of Dumfries—h.
gen. S H., 12 Sept 1724 , 11 Feb 1725

,, of Drumrash, to his brother David of Drumrash, who
died Oct , 1771—h of prov. spec in Drumrash,
part of Threave, Grange, and Nether Kiltoun or
Hallmyre, etc. S. H. (Kirkcudb.), 29 Dec. 1772 ; 24 Feb. 1773

,, dominus, de Eaynbo, miles baronettus, h domini
Joannis de Eaynbo, militis baronetti, patris I. G , 5 June 1649

,, magister. *See* **George,** Edinburgh I. G., 18 Aug. 1696

,, magister, Edinburgh *See* **John** de Aberlour I. de Tut., 30 July 1696

,, magister, in Edinburgh. *See* **James,** Aberlour I. G., 19 June 1697

,, goldsmith in Edinburgh. Alexander Forbes, writer in
Edinburgh, to his uncle Robert Gordon, goldsmith
there—h. gen. S. H. Supp , 7 Oct ; 20 Oct. 1767

,, Sir, of Embo, bart. *See* **John,** Sir, of Embo, bart
S. H., 13 Nov. 1721

,, of Farnachtie *See* **Mary,** Aberlour S H., 23 Dec. 1737

,, postmaster in Fochabers *See* **Alexander,** Fochabers
S. H., 21 Jan. 1734

,, h. Joannis de Garveri, fratris,—in 5 mercatis terrarum
de Garverries antiqui extentus, vocatis Ovir, Midle
et Nather Garveries, infra parochiam de Kels.—E.
7l. 3s 8d. feudifirmae I. S. (Kirkcudb.), 6 Feb 1672

,, de Garwarrie. *See* **William** de Dundeugh
I. de Poss Quinq., 31 Aug. 1682

,, *See* **Margaret,** Glenbervie I. G., 13 June 1691

,, dominus, de Glen miles, h. domini Joannis de Lochinvar
militis, patris,—in 6 mercatis terrarum de Ovir

(427)

Kirktoun ;—6 mercatis terrarum de Nethertoun de
Kirktoun, cum 40 solidatis terrarum de Quhit-
wolling in tenemento de Dryisdaill, et Senes-
callater Annandiae·—A.E. 10l ; N.E 30l.—annuo
redditu 20l. de terris de Dalfabill et Garvald ac
molendinis, in comitatu de Bothuell ;—dimidia
parte terrarum de Drumragane extendente ad 2½
mercatas terrarum antiqui extentus :—A.E. 33s. 4d.;
N.E. 5l.—8 libratis terrarum nuncupatis Gillaga-
poch et Belliboycht antiqui extentus, in baroniae
de Glencarne et parochia ejusdem .—A.E 8l.,
N.E. 24l.—2 mercatis terrarum antiqui extentus
de Conraith alias Castelphairne in dicta baronia
de Glencarne :—A.E. 26s. 8d. , N.E. 4l.—2 mercatis terrarum de Corsbank in Robertmure, in
baronia de Sanquhar.—A E. 26s 8d ; N.E. 4l.—
2 mercatis terrarum de Corcas, et 2 mercatis
terrarum de Glengep, antiqui extentus, in dicta
baronia de Sanquhar.—A.E. 53s 8d.; N.E. 8l.

I. S. (Dumfr.),   5 Nov. 1604

Robert, dominus, de Glen miles, h. domini Johannis de Lochin-
var, militis, patris,—in 19 mercatis terris de
Kenmoir et Laggane ; — 20 mercatis terris de
Balmaclellane et Park, unitis in baroniam de
Kenmoir, in parochiis de Kellis et Balmaclellane :
—A.E 39m.; N.E. 117m.—10 libratis terrarum
de Torschrachane et Dalbaittie in parochia de Ur .
—A.E. 10l.; N.E 30l.—5 mercatis terrarum de
Dunrod in parochia de Sannik :—A.E. 5m.; N.E.
10l.—34 mercatis terrarum de Glen, Skyrburne, et
Over Polcrie, in parochia de Anweth ; 3 mercatis
terrarum de Pollincrie antiqui extentus in dicta
parochia de Anweth ,—4 mercatis terrarum de
Evinstoun, Blakcraig et Knoknone in parochia de
Balmaclellane ;—6 mercatis terrarum de Hardlands et Monyboy in parochia de Balmaclellane :
—A.E. 47m.; N.E. 141m.—5 mercatis terrarum
de Ballingait ,—5 mercatis terrarum de Knokmarling et Darsarloch ;—5 mercatis terrarum de

Garlarge et Blakmerk, extendentibus ad 10 libratas
terrarum antiqui extentus vocatas Catbullie, in
parochia de Kellis;—5 mercatis terrarum de
Laggane;—3 mercatis terrarum de Litill Kirkbryde;—20 solidatis terrarum de Clauchreid;—
2½ mercatis terrarum de Killigoune,—1 mercata
terrae de Mylmark;—1 mercata terrae de Slaychtis,
—1 mercata terrarum de Marcoither (vel M'Corhill),
in parochia de Anweth et baronia de Cardines:—
A.E. 20l.; N.E. 60l.—3 mercatis terrarum antiqui
extentus de Orquhir in parochia de Girthoun.—
A.E. 40s.; N.E. 6l.—2½ mercatis terrarum de
Lag, cum dimidio molendini granorum ejusdem
antiqui extentus, in parochia de Girthoun.—A.E.
33s. 4d.; N.E. 5l.—37 mercatis terrarum de
Gordounstoun extendentibus ad dimidietatem de
Glenken in baronia de Grennane, et 20 solidatis
terrarum de Cornavell in parochia de Kellis.—
A.E. 25l. 13s. 4d., N.E. 77l.—5 libratis terrarum
de Nether Barcappill ·—E. 7l. 10s., etc., firmae.—
5 mercatis terrarum de Kirkconnell et Blakmark
—E. 3l., etc., firmae.—10 mercatis terrarum de
Largmannoch :—E. 20m., etc., firmae.—2 mercatis
terrarum de Leoch —E. 49s. 4d, etc., firmae:—
5 libratis terrarum de Overculquha et Brigend :—
E. 18m., etc, firmae —5 libratis terrarum de
Netherculquha :—E. 10l, etc., firmae.—5 libratis
terrarum de Ballannane.—E. 10l., etc., firmae.—
5 libratis terrarum de Over Ballincrosche —E.
16m. etc., firmae.—5 libratis terrarum de Nether
Ballincrosche :—E. 10l., etc., firmae —5 libratis
terrarum de Argranane, Litillpark, et Graviscroft ·
—E. 5l. 3s., etc., firmae.—10 libratis terrarum vocatis Maynes de Toungland.—E. 20l.—granarum
molendino et astricta multura terrarum de Over-
barcappill, cum aquae ductu lie Milncroftis.—E.
6 bollae farinae avenaticae, etc.—astrictis multuris terrarum de Dunnop:—E. 4 bollae farinae
avenaticae, etc.—molendino fullonum —E. 10l.—
omnibus in parochia de Toungland.—quae quidem

firmae et pretia victualium, pultrearum et anserum
coacervatae, extendunt ad summam 161l 15s et
5l. in augmentationem, in integro 166l 15s.—
haereditario officio balliatus deputari terrarum,
dominiorum praediorum et aliarum quarumcunque
possessionum monasterii de Toungland ·—E valet
administrationem justitiae tenentibus et inhabita-
toribus —2 mercatis terrarum de Glenquickin et
Dargavell antiqui extentus, in parochia de Kirkmabrek ·—E. 3l. 10s 8d —5 libratis terrarum de
Eurig, cum molendino et astricta multura, in
parochia de Girthoun.—E. 20l 13s 4d firmae.—
3 mercatis terrarum villae vel lie Clauchand de
Girthoun cum decimis inclusis, in dicta parochia
de Girthoun.—E. 46s 8d firmae —terris ecclesiasticis et gleba ecclesiastica parochiae de Balmaclellane, cum mansione in parochia de Balmaclellane
—E. 6m. 6s. 8d.—4 mercatis terrarum de Lochinkit
antiqui extentus in parochia de Kirkpatrick of the
Mure ·—E. 5l. 6s 8d —10 mercatis terrarum de
Chapelerne antiqui extentus, in parochia de Crocemichael ·—E. 20m. etc.—annuo redditu 300m. de
4½ mercatis terrarum antiqui de Nether Hesilfeild,
in parochia de Rerik   I. S. (Kirkcudb), 5 Nov 1604

Robert, dominus, de Glen miles, h domini Johannis Gordoun
de Lochinvar militis, patris,—in terris de Stichell,
in baronia de Stichel.—E. 100m.   I. S (Roxb.), 5 Nov 1604

   „   dominus, de Glen miles, h. domini Joannis de Lochinvar, militis, patris,—in 8 mercatis terrarum de Over
Glasnycht vulgariter nuncupatis Garglasnycht;—
4 mercatis terrarum de Kilzeild,—2 mercatis terrarum de Killemore;—3 mercatis terrarum de
Kirkcryst;—2 mercatis terrarum de Barcrostane
cum molendino, etc, dictae baroniae de Glasnycht,
in parochia de Pennynghame, et officio balliatus
dictarum terrarum et baroniae de Glasnycht ·—E.
25l. 13s. 4d. feudifirmae —10 mercatis terrarum
de Ballinsalloch in Mers de Crie, in baronia de
Pennynghame —E. 14l. feudifirmae
                      I. S. (Wigton), 5 Nov. 1604·

Robert, magister, frater germanus domini Ludovici de Gordounstoune, h. magistri Caroli, fratris germani
junioris   I. G.,   5 Dec 1674

   ,,   magister, frater domini Ludovici, de Gordonstoune, h.
magistri Caroli, fratris germani immediate junioris,
—in terris de Pilrossie, Aucharrie, Newtoune,
Spanziddell et Flod cum decimis, infra parochiam
de Creich.—A.E. 22m., N.E. 24l.   I. S (Sutherl), 22 April 1675

   ,,   dominus, de Gordounstoune, h. domini Lodovici de
Gordounstoune, patris   I. G.,   21 Sept. 1688

   ,,   dominus, de Gordounstoun, h. masc. domini Lodovici
de Gordounstoun, patris,—in terris et baronia de
Dallas comprehendente particulariter multuras et
Miltoun de Dallas,—villam et terras de Halton,
Craigend, Blackhills, Torcastle, Toberbuie, Edin-
vil, Kinmor, Rimachie, Bellavraide, Leonach,
Succoch, Achnes, Bellachragan, et Alterhearnie,
infra parochiam de Dallas :—A.E. 1l. 17s. 6d. ;
N.E. 7l. 10s.—advocatione subdiaconatus Moravi-
ensis comprehendente decimas parochiarum de
Dallas et Auldearne, infra vicecomitatus de Murray
et Nairne respective ·—A.E. 1 rosa ; N.E. 1d —
unitis in baroniam de Dallas   I. S (Elgin), 21 Sept 1688

   ,,   (Sir) of Gordonstoun, to his father Sir Robert of Gordonstoun—h. gen.   S. H., 12 July, 24 Sept. 1705

   ,,   Sir, of Gordounstoun. *See* **Robert,** Sir, of Gordounstoun, *supra.*

   ,,   Sir, of Gordonstoune, to his father Sir Robert of Gordonstoune, who died   Sept., 1704—h. spec in
50,000 merks over Latheron, Knockinian, Week,
etc.   S H , 9 Feb. ;   6 Mar. 1714

   ,,   Sir, of Gordonstoune. *See* **Robert,** Sir, of Gordounstoune, *supra.*

   ,,   to his father Ludovic, brother of Sir Robert of Gordonstoun—h. male gen   S. H., 12 June ; 31 Dec. 1722

   ,,   Sir, of Gordonstoun. *See* **Robert,** *supra.*

   ,,   Sir, of Gordonston, bart., to his father Sir Robert of
Gordonston, bart.—h. of prov. gen.
               S. H., 30 April ;   6 May 1774

Robert, Sir, of Gordonston, bart. *See* **Robert,** Sir, of Gordons-
      - ton, bart., *supra.*

,,   Sir, of Gordonstoun, bart. *See* **William,** Sir, of Gor-
         donstoun, bart.   S. H., 26 Dec. 1776

,,   Sir, of Gordonstoun, bart. Henrietta Scott, Mar-
         chioness of Titchfield, to her granduncle Sir
         Robert Gordon, bart —h. of tail and prov. gen.
            S. H. Supp., 18 May; 22 June 1796

,,   Home, to his father Dr. John of Greencastle, in the
         island of Jamaica—h. gen.   S. H., 23 Aug ; 26 Aug. 1776

,,   incola in Haddingtoun, h Roberti incolae in Water of
         Leith, patris   I. G., 24 Jan. 1673

,,   h. Joannis de Halheid, avi,—in terris de Halheid et Col-
         quonderland, in baronia de Cushin (vel Cushnie).
         —A.E. 3l., N.E. 12l.   I. S. (Aberd.), 3 Oct. 1553

,,   to his father George of Hallhead—h. of prov. gen.
            S. H., 25 July; 27 July 1758

,,   of Hallhead, to his granduncle Alexander, merchant in
         Boulogne—h. gen.   S. H., 28 Nov.; 8 Dec. 1759

,,   of Hallhead, to his cousin Robert, s. of Alex., merchant,
         Boulogne-sur-Mer—h. gen.   S. H., 10 Dec.; 12 Dec. 1760

,,   miles in Hollandia, h. conq Jacobi, patrui   I. G., 7 June 1637

,,   s. of William of Holm. *See* **Nathaniel,** Holm S H., 22 Aug. 1724

,,   s. of Wm., junr , of Holme, to his grandfather William
         Tait of Lochenkitt—h. of prov. gen.
            S. H., 30 Aug.; 29 Oct. 1759

,,   f. legitimus quondam Hugonis mercatoris in Killileoch
         in regno Hiberniae, h Jacobi nuper de Newark,
         fratris, avi   I. G., 12 June 1697

,,   Vicecomes de Kenmure, dominus Lochinvar, etc., h.
         masc. et talliae Joannis Vicecomitis de Kenmure,
         domini Lochinvar, etc., nepotis patrui,—in 34
         mercatis terrarum de Glenschyrburne et Over
         Polcrie cum molendinis et piscariis, in parochia
         de Anuath —A.E. 34m., N.E. 82m.—terris et
         baronia de Erlistoun extendentibus ad 40 mer-
         catas terrarum antiqui extentus, cum molendinis
         et piscariis, et advocatione ecclesiae parochialis
         nuncupatae St. John's Kirk de Dalry, in parochia

de Dalry, omnibus unitis in baroniam de Erlistoun
—A.E. 32m.; N.E. 98m. 9s. 4d.—terris et baronia
de Gelstoun comprehendentibus 3 mercatas terrarum de Glenzarrok;—20 solidatas terrarum de
Littill Quhytill;—20 solidatas terrarum de Potterland ;—3 mercatas terrarum de Kirkmirrane et
Glen ;—4 mercatas terrarum de Meikle Quhythill
Gildowbank;—20 solidatas terrarum de Newlandis;
—7½ mercatas terrarum de Arieland ,—12 mercatas
terrarum de Inglistoun ;—molendinum de Gels-
stoun ;—8 mercatas terrarum de Boirdland cum
piscariis, in parochia de Gelstoun :—A.E. 42m.,
N.E. 126m.—terris et baronia de Corsmichaell
comprehendentibus 2½ mercatas terrarum de
Fuffok, alias Suffok;—5 mercatas terrarum de
Irnenalmrey ,—5 mercatas terrarum de Auchindolie ;—2 (vel 5) mercatas terrarum de Largmen
(Largnene);—2½ mercatas terrarum de Irnefillan ,
—5 mercatas terrarum de Culgruise (Culgruff) ,—
5 mercatas terrarum de Troddill alias Traddill ;—
5 mercatas terrarum de Mollance ;—5 mercatas
terrarum de Hillintoun ;—5 mercatas terrarum de
Hariebrand ;—10 mercatas terrarum de Croftis ,—
5 mercatas terrarum de Glengappok ;—terras dominicales lie Maynis de Greinlaw, cum lie Kayne
peitis et bundaywork baroniae de Corsmichaell ;—5
mercatas terrarum de Irnenisbie ;—10 mercatas
terrarum de Chappellerne ;—2½ mercatas terrarum
de Clourbrand (Clairbrand), cum advocatione et
jure patronatus ecclesiae parochialis de Corsmichaell :—E. 213l. 6s. 8d feudifirmae.—5 mercatas terrarum de Litteldrybrughe ;—5 mercatas
terrarum de Drumlarge (vel Drumjarg) ,—5 mercatas terrarum de Irnefilland ;—5 mercatas terrarum
de Erncraig ;—5 mercatas terrarum de Blairenne ,
—5 mercatas terrarum de Meikildrybrughe ;—5
mercatas terrarum de Chapmantoun ;—5 mercatas
terrarum de Blakerne ,—5 mercatas terrarum de
Armynie ;—5 mercatas terrarum de Kilnottrie ,—

molendınum granorum de Corsmıchaell;—5 mercatas terrarum de Gerrıntoun;—2½ mercatas terrarum de Blakpark, cum molendınıs et pıscarııs,
et jure patronatus ecclesıae de Corsmichael·—
A.E. 57m. 6s. 8d., N.E. 172m. 6s 8d.—decımıs
garbalıbus, etc., ecclesıae parochıalıs et parochıae
de Kırkmabrıck, omnıbus unitıs ın baronıam de
Corsmichaell·—E. 20l.—terris de Clennıe;—terrıs
de Laggane;—terrıs de Garvorie;—terrıs de Cul-
lındoch, cum parte forrestae de Buchane dıctıs
terrıs de Cullındach adjacente, ınfra domınıum de
Galloway subtus Crıe.—E. 24l. 6s. feudıfirmae.—
terrıs de Mureford, Cuıll, Blaıres, et Craıge, extendentıbus ad 10½ mercatas et 40 denariatas
terrarum antiqui extentus;—7 mercatis terrarum
de Barhassıe,—4 mercatıs terrarum de Burnes,—
36 solıdatıs et 8 denarıatıs de Spıttıll;—30 solidatıs terrarum de Cullındach antıquı extentus·—
E. 49l. 8s.—26 solıdatıs et 8 denarıatıs terrarum
de Culcranzie et Garhorne, nunc vulgo nuncupatis
Culcruquhy et Garquhir,—4 mercatıs terrarum de
Lochınkıt —E. 12m. 10s.—2 mercatıs terrarum
de Knarrıe et Bar:—E 4l.—terrıs de Lıtıllhals.
—E. 43s. 4d. et 10s. pro servıtııs, etc.—terrıs de
Glenquıkkın et Dargavell extendentıbus ad 2½
mercatas terrarum antıquı extentus, ınfra baronıam
de Ferrıe de Crıe:—E. 3l. 12s. 8d.—tenandrıa de
Endrig comprehendente 5 lıbratas terrarum de
Nether Barcapıll.—E. 7l. 10s., etc., feudıfirmae.
—5 mercatas terrarum de Kırkconnell et Blakmark:—E. 3l., etc., firmae.—10 mercatas terrarum de Barmanoch (vel Larmannoch):—E. 20m.,
etc., firmae.—2 mercatas terrarum de Beoch:—
E. 49s. 4d., etc., firmae.—5 lıbratas terrarum de
Overculquha et Brıgend.—E. 18m., etc., firmae.
—5 lıbratas terrarum de Natherculquha —E 10l.,
etc., firmae.—5 lıbratas terrarum de Ballanane:—
E. 10l., etc., firmae.—5 lıbratas terrarum de Over-
ballıncrosche:—E. 16m , etc , firmae.—5 lıbratas

terrarum de Netherballincrosche :—E. 10l., etc.,
firmae.—5 libratas terrarum de Argranane, Littill-
park, et Grayiscroft —E. 5l. 3s., etc., firmae.—
10 libratas terrarum vocatarum Maynis de Tungland.—E. 30l.—molendinum granorum de Tungland.—E. 6 bollae farinae avenaticae, etc—
molendinum fullonum de Tungland.—E. 10l.,
etc.—astrictas multuras, etc., de Tungland, cum
salmonum piscariis in aqua de Die, in baronia de
Tungland.—E. 4 bollae farinae avenaticae, etc.—
haereditario officio balivatus deputati terrarum
et possessionum ad monasterium de Tungland
pertinentium —E. 1d.—5 libratis terrarum de
Endrig cum molendino earundem, in baronia de
Kirkcryst, et cum molendinis et salmonum piscariis, omnibus unitis in tenandriam de Endrig
—E. 34l 13s. 4d.—5 libratis terrarum de Dunjope
antiqui extentus, in baronia de Tungland.—E.
12l. 6s. 8d , etc.—crofta terrae vocata Lanymossok
infra parochiam de Tungland.—E. 15s.

I. S. (Kirkcudb.),   1 May 1645

Robert, Vicecomes de Kenmure, etc , h. masc. et talliae Joannis
Vicecomitis de Kenmure, domini Lochinvar, etc.,
nepotis patrui,—in terris et baronia de Myrtoun
nunc vulgo nuncupatis terris et baronia de Cul-
creoche, comprehendentibus terras dominicales lie
maynis de Culcreoch ,—terras de Shalloche ,—
terras de Glenrassie,—terras de Barnkirk ,—terras
de Corsbie cum molendinis granorum et fullonum ;
—terras de Kerrewissell ;—terras de Skaite ;—
terras de Blackquarter ;—terras de Nather Glenchappell ,—terras de Over Glenchappell ,—terras
de Clonvill ,—terras de Keirchappell ,—terras de
Glenvarinoch ;—terras de Kirkcala ,—terras de
Over-Castelldonald et terras de Nether Castell-
donald, cum molendinis et piscariis, et cum
advocatione ecclesiarum, extendentibus ad 27
libratas terrarum antiqui extentus ,—in 5 mercatis terrarum de Barskeoch, infra baroniam de

Myrtoun-Herreis, omnibus unitis in baroniam de
Culcreoch —A.E. 27l.; N.E 81l.—10 mercatis
terrarum de Ballinschalloche, in lie moiss de Crie
et baronia de Penyghame.—E. 14l.　I. S. (Wigton),　1 May 1645

Robert, Vicecomes de Kenmure, dominus Lochinvar, h. masc.
et talliae Joannis Vicecomitis de Kenmure, domini
Lochinvar, f. patrui,—in 37 mercatis terrarum
antiqui extentus de Gordounestoun, cum molendino granorum earundem, in parochia de Dalry.—
A.E. 24l. 13s. 4d.; N.E. 74l.　I. S. (Kirkcudb),　1 May 1645

　,, 　Vicecomes de Kenmure, etc , h masc. et talliae Joannis
Vicecomitis de Kenmure, domini Lochinvar, f.
patrui,—in terris dominicalibus lie maynes de
Barnbarroch cum molendino, parte 5 libratarum
terrarum de Barnbarroch et Barglas :—A.E. 26s.
8d., N.E. 4l —4 mercatis terrarum de Balverinoch,
in parochia de Kirkinner —A E. 2l. 13s. 4d., N.E.
8l　　　　　　　　　　　I. S. (Wigton),　1 May 1645

　,, 　Vicecomes de Kenmure, dominus Lochinvar, h. masc.
Jacobi de Buittle, patris,—in 10 mercatis terrarum
antiqui extentus de Buittill, infra baroniam et
parochiam de Buittill —E. 16l. 6s. 8d. feudifirmae.
—astrictis multuris praedictarum terrarum :—E.
5m.—salmonum piscaria in aqua de Ur :—E. 10s.
—3 mercatis terrarum de Litill Kirkbryde :—1
mercata terrae de Slaithis antiqui extentus, infra
parochiam de Kirkmabrik —A.E. 4m.; N.E. 12m.
I. S. (Kirkcudb.),　1 May 1645

　,, 　Viscount of Kenmure, h. of James of Buittill, his father,
—in the 16 shilling land of Bargalie of auld extent;
—the 8 shilling land of Barhoys of auld extent, in
the parish of Minigaff.—A.E. 24s.; N.E. 3l. 12s.
I. S. Supp. (Kirkcudb), 23 Feb. 1658

　,, 　Comes de Kenmuir, h. Joannis Comitis de Kenmuir,
domini de Lochinvar, f patrui,—in 3 mercatis
terrarum antiqui extentus de Drumrasch, cum
advocatione ecclesiae parochialis de Bartoun ;—
4 libratis terrarum de Tratolan alias Glenlairis,
cum molendinis granarum et fullonum ;—2 mer-

catis terrarum de Ervie;—mercata terrae de Barsell;
—40 solidatis terrarum de Ovir Barland et Nether-
stell ;—terris de Glengunzeoch, et terris vocatis 20
shilling land, omnibus jacentibus infra parochiam
de Bartoun (Partoun ?).—A.E. 12l.; N E. 361

I. S. (Kirkcudb.), 14 Jan. 1662

Robert, the Hon., of Kenmore. *See* **John,** the Hon., of Kenmore

S. H., 16 Feb. 1742

,, of Kenmore, commonly called Viscount Kenmore. *See*
    John of Kenmore S. H., 19 April 1777

,, of Knoxbreck. *See* **John,** Garlarg   I S (Kirkcudb), 28 July 1657

,, sailor, Leith. *See* **Agnes,** Leith   S. H., 16 Sept. ; 18 Sept. 1766

,, sailor, Leith. *See* **John,** Leith   S. H., 30 Nov. 1778

,, sailor in Leith. *See* **Agnes,** Leith ; **Janet,** Leith ;
    John, Leith S. H., 23 June 1791

,, College of Lincluden. *See* **Robert,** the Rev., London
    S. H., 19 Mar.; 24 Mar. 1763

,, h. Alexandri in Lochans, patris,—in annuo redditu 70m.
    de 6 mercatis terrarum de Mekill Knokis antiqui
    extentus, in parochia de Buttill

I. S. (Kirkcudb.), 10 Oct. 1615

,, h. Alexandri in Lochans, patris   I. G., 25 April 1615

,, dominus, de Lochinvar, miles. *See* **John** de Lochinvar
    I. S. (Dumfr) ; I. S. (Kirkcudb.) ; I. S (Roxbr.), 20 Mar. 1628

,, dominus, de Lochinvar, miles. *See* **John** de Lochinvar
    I. S. (Kirkcudb.), 2 Feb. 1630

,, of Logie, to his father Alexander of Logie—h. gen.
    S H., 4 Oct. ; 11 Oct. 1752

,, the Rev., of Theobald's Court, London, to his father
    Robert, College of Lincluden—h. gen.
    S. H., 19 Mar. ; 24 Mar. 1763

,, W.S   *See* **George Alexander,** London   S. H., 30 May 1793

,, de Pitlurg. *See* **Alexander** de Pitlurg

I. S. (Aberd.), 5 Oct. 1692

,, de Pitlurg. *See* **Alexander** de Pitlurg   I. S (Banff), 11 Oct. 1698

,, in Restalrig. *See* **John,** Restalrig   I. G., 26 Aug. 1697

,, de Shirmers. *See* **Agnes,** Shirmers   I. G., 2 June 1681

,, of Shirmers, to his father Alexander of Shirmers—h.
    gen. S. H., 22 Oct. ; 24 Oct. 1755

Robert, of Shirmers, to his father Alexander of Shirmers, who
died June, 1735—h. spec. in the lands of Cubbox
in the parish of Balmaclellan

S H. (Kirkcudb.), 25 June, 8 July 1756

„ de Straloche, h. magistri Roberti de Straloche, patris,
—in villa et terris de Over Kinmundie cum terris
dominicalibus;—villa et terris de Dourie, Milne-
breck cum molendino Milhill, Pittiemarkhous,
Smallburne, Kinknackie comprehendentibus villam et terras de Auldtoun ejusdem, Nethertoun,
alias Welstrype, et alias Pittindreichs-seat, Backhill, alias Barrackseat, in baronia de Kinmundie
et parochia de Deer, unitis in baroniam de Kinmundie.—A.E. 5l.; N.E. 24l —terris et devata
de Bottarrie, comprehendentibus villam et terras
de Bottarie, Aucharne, Auchinloche, Boigferge,
Whytstaines, Claymyres, molendinum de Bottarie,
in dominio de Huntlie, et parochia de Bottarie —
E. 24l.—villa et terris de Fechill, Cobleseat, Coble-
croft, lie priviledge of ferrieing super aquam de
Ythan, Procurators-croft, per annexationem infra
dominium de Deer et parochiam de Elone.—E. 8
bollae victualium, etc. I. S. (Aberd.), 8 Oct. 1663

„ magister, de Straloche. *See* **Robert** de Straloche,
supra.

„ incola in water of Leith. *See* **Robert,** Haddingtoun

I. G., 24 Jan. 1673

Roger, de Aroquhaine, h. Rogeri de Aroquhaine, avi,—in 40 solidatis terrarum de Auchinhae;—mercata terrae de
Darnharroch (vel Darngarroch),—mercata terrae de
Ovir et Nether Slangabers,—molendino baroniae
de Kirkpatrick, omnibus infra baroniam de Kirkpatrick-Durhame.—E. 17l. 4s. feudifirmae.—40
solidatis terrarum de Kirkhillbryde, ac 20 solidatis
terrarum de Marglay,—40 solidatis et 40 denariatis
terrarum de Barndarroch, infra dictam parochiam
de Kirkpatrick-Durham.—E. 12l. 4s 4d. feudifirmae

I. S. (Kirkcudb.), 27 Jan. 1674

„ de Aroquhaine. *See* **Roger,** supra.

Roger, de Aroquhaine, h. Joannis de Aroquhain, proavi,—in
      terris de Bartaggart extendentibus ad 4 mercatas
      terrarum, infra parochiam de Balmaclellane :—
      E. 7l. 4d. feudifirmae.—5½ mercatis terrarum de
      Irlandtoune antiqui extentus, infra parochiam de
      Twynem.—A.E. 3l. 13s. 4d.; N.E.
                           I. S. (Kirkcudb.), 27 Jan. 1674

"   *See* **Joan**, Brokloch   I. S. (Kirkcudb.), 13 ... 1615

"   *See* **Thomas** de Crogo   I. S. (Kirkcudb.), 1 June 1620

"   of Dendeuch. *See* **James**, Canongate   S. H., 14 Mar. 1737

"   in Hill. *See* **William**, Hill   I. S. (Kirkcudb.), 6 Feb. 1672

"   de Holme, h. Wilhelmi de Holme, patris,—in 5 mercatis
      terrarum de Holme antiqui extentus, in parochia
      de Balmaclellane :—A.E. 5m.; N.E. 10l.—5 mer-
      catis terrarum de Fyntallachie antiqui extentus,
      in parochia de Kellis :—A.E. 5m.; N.E. 10l.—25
      solidatis ex 5 libratis terrarum de Ballannan an-
      tiqui extentus, in parochia de Tungland :—A.E.
      25s.; N.E. 3l. 15s.—annuo redditu 50m. de 16
      solidatis 8 denariatis terrarum de Barend antiqui
      extentus, infra parochiam de Balmaghie ·
                           I. S. (Kirkcudb.), 28 Oct. 1617

"   de Holme, h. Wilhelmi de Holme, avi,—in 1 mercata
      terrae de Monybwy antiqui extentus, in parochia
      de Balmaclellane.—A.E. 13s. 4d.; N.E. 40s.
                           I. S. (Kirkcudb.), 28 Oct. 1617

"   of Holm. *See* **William** of Holm   S H., 24 July 1735

"   in Ireland, to his granduncle Adam Black in Murehouse
      —h. gen. (Service led at Ayr)   S. H., 11 Mar.; 29 April 1729

"   in Ireland, to his cousin Margaret Black, d. of Adam
      Black in Murehouse—h. gen.   S. H., 11 Mar.; 29 April 1729

"   de Knokreochis. *See* **George**, Knokreochis   I. G., 17 April 1610

"   de Largmore. *See* **John**, Largmore   I. S. (Kirkcudb.), 8 June 1669

"   de Quhytpairk. *See* **John** de Airdis   I. G. Supp., 18 Feb. 1612

"   de Quhytpark. *See* **George** de Kirkdaill
                           I. S. (Kirkcudb.), 20 Mar. 1628

"   in Shirmers,—propinquior agnatus, id est consanguineus
      ex parte patris Alexandro, f. et h. apparenti quon-
      dam Alexandri in Barskeoche   I. de Tut. Supp., 23 July 1577

Roger, apparens de Troquhain. *See* **John,** Troquhain

                                        I. S. (Kirkcudb.), 29 July 1617

  ,,   magister. *See* **Alexander,** Welcrage   I. S (Wigton), 31 Oct. 1598

Samuel, s. of Wm., minister of Anwoth, to his grandfather

          James of Balmeg—h. of prov. gen. S. H., 15 Aug.; 9 Dec. 1794

  ,,   mercator burgi de Dumfreis,—propinquior agnatus,

          id est consanguineus ex parte patris Samueli et

          Joannae liberis Alexandri de Knockbrex I. de Tut., 4 April 1683

  ,,   in Jersey, purser, R.N., to his grandfather Robert

          M'Brair, messenger in Dumfries—h. of prov. gen.

                               S. H., 1 Dec.; 10 Dec. 1787

  ,,   Knokbrex. *See* **Samuel,** Dumfries   I. de Tut., 4 April 1683

Sarah, to her father John, merchant in and a bailie of New

          Galloway—h. port. gen.   S. H., 13 July 1790; 21 Nov. 1791

Sybil, h. port. praedicti Joannis [de Blaikat], patris,—in terris

          praedictis   I. S. (Kirkcudb.), 29 Oct. 1548

  ,,   h. port. praedictae Margaretae [Blaket], sororis,—in un-

          decima parte dictarum terrarum I. S. (Kirkcudb.), 14 April 1552

  ,,   d. of Jas. of Cairstoun, to her brother John, inspector of

          customs, Stromness—h. gen.   S. H., 13 May; 29 May 1799

T., in Lagan of Glenrinnes. *See* **Christian, Helen, Margaret,**

          Lagan   S. H., 16 Jan. 1703

Theodosia, to her father Adam, Lieutenant in General Maitland's

          regiment—h. port. gen.   S. H., 16 April; 27 June 1717

Thomas, magister. *See* **David**   I. G., 7 June 1690

  ,,   h. Davidis f. legitimi quondam magistri Thomae

          scribae signeto regio, fratris germani   I. G., 29 July 1697

  ,,   magister. *See* **Thomas,** *supra.*

  ,,   merchant, Aberdeen. *See* **Jean,** Aberdeen

          S. H., 19 Mar., 3 April 1766; S. H., 19 Jan.; 2 Feb. 1780

  ,,   Professor of Philosophy, Aberdeen, to his brother

          George, Professor of Oriental Languages there—

          h. gen.   S. H., 8 Feb.; 15 Feb. 1775

  ,,   Professor of Philosophy, Aberdeen, to his aunt Bethia

          Fraser—h. gen. (Service led at Aberdeen)

                               S. H., 8 Feb.; 15 Feb. 1775

  ,,   Professor of Philosophy, Aberdeen, to his aunt

          Catherine Fraser—h. gen. (Service led at Aber-

          deen)   S. H., 8 Feb.; 15 Feb. 1775

Thomas, Prof. of Philosophy, Aberdeen. *See* **Ann,** Falkland
S. H., 15 July 1799

,,   to his father James of Banchory—h. gen.
S. H., 9 Nov.; 23 Nov. 1751

,,   of Buthlaw, to his father Charles of Buthlaw, who
died   Jan., 1796—h. spec. in Newtyle, Mains of
Buthlaw, with mill, in the parishes of Foveran
and Longside   S. H., 17 Jan.; 22 Feb. 1797

,,   Major, of Clerkseat. *See* **Ann, Jean,** Clerkseat
S. H., 17 Sept. 1740

,,   Major, of Clerkseat. *See* **Christian,** Aberdeen
S. H., 4 Nov. 1740

,,   dominus, h. Joannis de Cluny, patris,—in villa et croftis
subscriptis vocatis terras Forrestae de Brass, viz.
Knokie-know, vulgo, the Lang Lidrik, the Spittal,
Glencatt, et Achabreck.—E. 10l. et 3s. 4d. in
augmentationem   I. S. (Aberd.), 13 April 1602

,,   dominus, de Cluny, miles. *See* **Alexander,** Cluny
I. S. (Aberd.), 11 July 1607

,,   to his father John of Coynach—h. gen.
S. H., 16 Jan.; 16 Jan. 1724

,,   Thomas of Coynach. *See* **Thomas,** in London
S. H., 16 Jan. 1799

,,   of Crathienaird, to his grandfather Thomas of Crathienaird—h. gen.   S. H., 7 July; 30 July 1767

,,   of Crathienaird. *See* **Thomas** of Crathienaird, *supra.*

,,   de Crogo, h. Jonetae unius duarum hh. port. Rogeri,
matris,—in dimidietate 5 mercatarum terrarum
antiqui extentus de Crogo, extendente ad 33 solidatas 4 denariatas terrarum infra parochiam de
Balmaclelland:—A.E. 33s. 4d.; N.E. 5l.—dimidietate 2½ mercatarum terrarum ejusdem extentus
de Holme de Dalquharne, extendente ad 16 solidatas 8 denariatas terrarum, infra parochiam de
Dalry.—A.E. 16s. 8d.; N.E. 50s.
I. S. (Kirkcudb.), 1 June 1620

,,   de Crogo, h. Jacobi de Crogo, patris,—in dimidietate
5 mercatarum terrarum antiqui extentus de Crago
extendente ad 33 solidatas 4 denariatas terrarum,

infra parochiam de Balmaclellane .—A.E. 16s. 8d.;

    N.E. 50s.   I. S. (Kirkcudb.), 1 June 1620

Thomas, baker, Dumfries. *See* **Agnes,** Dumfries

                                   S. H , 29 Mar.; 8 April 1794

   ,,   surgeon in Dumfries. *See* **John**   S. H., 31 Jan. 1765

   ,,   son of Alex. of Earlstoun, to his uncle Sir William of

        Aftoun, bart.—h. of taillie and prov. gen. S. H., 5 Feb. 1724

   ,,   watchmaker in Edinburgh. *See* **Patrick,** there S. H., 1 May 1749

   ,,   wright in Jamaica. *See* **Jean,** Bellahouston   S. H., 28 June 1799

   ,,   magister, in Kethocksmilne. *See* **Alexander,** vet.

        Aberdonia   I. S. (Aberd.), 22 June 1698

   ,,   in London, to his grandfather Thomas of Coynach,

        physician, Peterhead—h. gen. S. H., 8 Dec. 1798 , 16 Jan. 1799

   ,,   watchmaker in New York, to his father James, mer-

        chant in Garmouth—h. gen.   S. H., 18 May; 23 May 1770

   ,,   de Pettindreich, h. magistri Thomae de Pettindreich,

        patris   I. G., 2 Oct. 1663

   ,,   magister, de Pettindreich. *See* **Thomas** de Pettin-

        dreich, *supra.*

   ,,   in Speymouth. *See* **Rebecca,** Speymouth   S. H., 5 July 1782

W., shipmaster in Aberdeen. *See* **Ralph,** Aberdeen   S. H., 13 July 1793

 ,, Cambridge. *See* **William,** Cambridge   S. H., 14 Jan. 1761

Walter, magister, in Abirdene. *See* **William,** Abirdene

                                 I. S. (Aberd.), 29 Mar. 1615

   ,,   shipmaster in Aberdeen. *See* **Ralph,** in Aberdeen;

        Jean, Aberdeen   S. H., 22 April 1786

William, magister, scriba signeto regio, h. Margaretae sororis

                                 I. G., 11 Aug. 1668

   ,,   h. magistri Wilhelmi scribae signeto regio, patris

                                 I. G., 17 July 1688

   ,,   magister, scriba signeto regio. *See* **William,** *supra.*

   ,,   h. magistri Walteri in Abirdene, patris,—in manso

        olim spectante thesaurario de Abirdene, in canonia

        de Abirdene.—E. 13s. 4d.   I. S. (Aberd.), 29 Mar. 1615

   ,,   Earl of Aberdeen. *See* **William** of Fyvie S. H., 3 Dec. 1760

   ,,   Earl of Aberdeen. *See* **William,** the Hon., of Fyvie

                                 S. H., 23 May 1797

   ,,   of Aberdour, to his father Alexander of Aberdour—h.

        gen.   S. H., 28 Jan., 20 Mar. 1793

William, of Aberdour, to his brother George of Aberdour, who
    died   June, 1792—h. spec. in the barony of
    Aberdour, including Cowbog, Glassie, Windy-
    heads, etc.   S. H., 28 Jan. ; 20 Mar. 1793

,,   magister, h. Alexandri de Abirzeldie, fratris immediate
    senioris,—in terris baroniae de Abirzeldie, inclun-
    dentibus terras dictae baroniae de Abirzeldie,
    Eistoun de Glenculladyr, unitis in baronia de
    Abirzeldie.—A.E. 6l. ; N.E. 24l.   I. S (Aberd), 30 May 1601

,,   h. Alexandri de Abirzeldie, patris,—in terris de
    Grandoun, Inchmill [sic.], Perslie, et Craibstone.—
    A.E. 3l. 6s. 8d. ; N.E. 13l. 6s. 8d.
                     I. S. (Aberd.), 17 June 1607

,,   de Abirzeldie, h. Alexandri de Abirzeldie, patris,—in
    terris de Stering cum pendiculis, viz. Lymnoe,
    Auldschillauche, Tarrinschill, ceterisque pertinen-
    tiis earundem, extendentibus ad unam davatam
    terrae, infra dominium de Huntlie per annexa-
    tionem —A.E. 13s. 4d. ; N.E. 4m.—terris vocatis
    ly Lurgis tam in proprietate quam communitate,
    in baronia de Oneill, infra parochiam de Migmar.
    —E. 41s. feudifirmae   I. S. Supp. (Aberd.), 31 July 1613

,,   de Aberzeldie, h. Jacobi de Midmar, avi ex parte,
    patris,—in terris de Carnetrailzeane, cum mo-
    lendino, Ailhous, Mekilglasgow, Beildziestoun,
    Auchinvee, infra comitatum de Buchane.—A.E
    3l. ; N.E. 12l.   I. S. (Aberd), 14 Mar. 1621

,,   Sir, of Aftoun, bart. *See* **Thomas,** Earlstoun S H., 5 Feb. 1724

,,   minister of the parish of Alvie. James McGregor,
    at Glenmarkie, lieut., to his g^duncle William
    Gordon, parish minister of Alvie—h. of conq.
    and prov. gen.   S. H. Supp., 12 Aug. ; 26 Dec. 1788

,,   minister of Anworth. *See* **Samuel,** Anworth S. H., 9 Dec. 1794

,,   merchant in Ayr. William M'Croscrae, in Ayr, to
    his uncle William Gordoun, merchant there—h.
    gen.   S. H. Supp., 28 June , 15 Sept. 1736

,,   of Badensoch, to his father George of Badenscoth—
    h. gen   S. H., 17 Nov. 1713 ; 12 Jan 1714

,,   of Badenscoth. *See* **James** of Badenscoth S H., 9 Aug. 1737

William, (Gray), of Balligorno, to his grandaunt Elizabeth Gray

of Balligorno—h. of prov. gen.   S. H., 1 Sept.; 15 Sept. 1743

,,   of Barndrine. *See* **Jean**, Barndrine   I. S (Wigton), 25 July 1654

,,   *See* **James** de Barnebarroche   I. G., 24 May 1627

,,   of Birkenburn, to his father Alexander of Birkenburn,
who died 19 June, 1709—h. spec. in the town and
lands of Birkenburn in the parish of Keith

S. H., 28 Feb. 1721, 24 April 1724

,,   wright, Blackhall. *See* **Jean**, Blackhall

S. H., 6 Feb.; 3 Mar. 1739

,,   merchant in Boulogne, once banker in Paris. *See*
Alexander, Boulogne   S. H., 19 Sept. 1729

,,   factor at Broxmonth. *See* **Elizabeth**, Broxmonth

S. H., 19 Nov. 1746

,,   s. of W., Cambridge, to his g^dmother Helen Hepburn,
wife of J., factor to Lord Hopeton—h. gen.   S. H., 14 Jan. 1761

,,   s. of W., Cambridge, to his mother Janet (d. of J.,
factor to Lord Hopeton), who died   Sept., 1760
—h. spec. in bonds over Langtoun, Burnhouses,
Boghill, Cumledge, and Simprim   S. H., 29 Jan.; 6 Mar. 1761

,,   late of Bennett's College, Cambridge. *See* **Janet**,
Cambridge   S. H., 2 May 1754

,,   of Campbelltoun. *See* **Alexander**, Campbelltoun

S. H., 13 Feb. 1762

,,   of Campbelltoun, to his father James of Campbelltoun
—h. gen.   S. H., 9 Jan.; 28 Mar. 1724

,,   of Campbelton, to his father James of Campbelton,
who died   May, 1722—h. spec. in Spots, Orch-
yeardtoun, Glenshunnock, Bomby, and Conqui-
toun   S. H., 28 Sept. 1725; 26 Oct. 1726

,,   of Campbellton. *See* **Alexander** of Campbelton

S. H., 16 Sept. 1789

,,   magister, de Carnefield. *See* **John** de Carnefield

I. S. (Banff), 7 May 1633

,,   s. of Jn., Carron, to his uncle William M'Donald,
Jamaica, lieut. 79th regiment—h. of prov. gen.

S. H, 15 May; 18 May 1797

,,   h Alexandri de Clone, patris,—in 5 libratis terrarum
de Barsalloch antiqui extentus, in parochia de

(444)

Mochrum (excepto molendino) :—A.E. 5l.; N E.
15l.—2 mercatis terrarum de 3½ mercatis terrarum
de Clone in parochia praedicta:—A.E. 2m.; N.E.
6m.—1½ mercata vel 20 solidatis terrarum de dictis
3½ mercatis terrarum de Clone.—A.E. 20s.; N.E.
3l.—3 mercatis terrarum de Crossrie, in parochia
de Kirkcowen.—A.E 3m.; N.E. 9m.

I. S. Supp. (Wigton),   Jan. 1596

William, to his father John of Coynach—h. gen.

S. H., 4 Dec. 1718; 5 June 1719

„ of Crabstoun, to his father John, late of Drumquhynle
—h. male gen.   S. H., 20 Aug.; 4 Sept. 1735

„ s. of Wm. of Crackville, to his uncle George of Glengerrick, who died in May or June, 1747—h. port.
spec. in the barony of Glengerrick, including
Auchives, Berryleys, etc.   S. H., 16 Aug.; 25 Aug. 1748

„ of Crackville. *See* **William,** *supra.*

„ de Craig. *See* **William** de Dundeugh

I. de Poss. Quin , 31 Aug. 1682

„ h. Johannis de Crechlaw, patris,—in 2 mercatis terrarum de Mydmundork, de illis 6 mercatis terrarum
de Mundark antiqui extentus, in parochia de Kirke
.—A.E. 26s. 8d.; N.E. 4l.

I. S. Supp. (Wigton), 31 Oct. 1580

„ de Crauchlaw, h. Willelmi de Crauchlaw, avi,—in 5
mercatis terrarum de Largliddisdaill, alias Larg-
leviestoun nuncupatis, in parochia de Leswald;—
2½ mercatis terrarum de Kerdlachlene (vel Kere-
lauchleine), in parochia de Kirkmadyne in Rynnis.
—A.E. 5l.; N.E. 15l   I. S. Supp. (Wigton), 5 Oct. 1596

„ de Crauchlaw. *See* **William,** *supra.*

„ senior de Craighlaw. *See* **William,** magister de Earlstone   I. de Poss. Quinq., 3 Sept. 1686

„ de Craichlaw, h. Gulielmi de Craichlaw, avi,—in 20
solidatis terrarum de Bardochit cum molendino
antiqui extentus, infra baroniam de Earlestoun.—
E. 3l.   I. S. (Kirkcudb.), 7 July 1691

„ de Craichlaw. *See* **William** de Craichlaw, *supra.*

„ of Cruchley. *See* **John** of Cruchley   S. H., 7 Mar. 1732

(445)

William, in Culleindoche. *See* **James,** Culleindoche

I. S. (Kirkcudb.),   5 Dec. 1609

,,   de Culvenen, h. Alexandri de Culvenan, patris

I. G.,   6 Feb. 1679

,,   of Culvennan, to his father William of Culvennan—

h. gen.   S. H., 2 Mar.; 4 Mar. 1703

,,   of Culvennan, to his grandfather Alexander of Cul-

vennan—h. gen.   S. H., 2 Mar.; 4 Mar. 1703

,,   of Culvennan. *See* **William** of Culvennan, *supra.*

,,   of Culvennan. *See* **Joan,** Barholme

S. H., 24 Jan. 1718, S. H., 24 Oct. 1718

,,   de Dalphollie, h. domini Adami de Dalphollie, patris

I. G., 10 Dec. 1700

,,   of Dalphollie, to his father Sir Adam of Dalphollie—

h. gen.   S. H., 10 Dec.;   Dec. 1700

,,   of Dalpholly, to his father Sir Adam of Dalpholly,

who died   Sept., 1700—h. male spec. in St.
Martin's, etc., Ross and Cromarty, and Kilfeder,
etc.   S. H., 3 Feb.; 26 Feb. 1702

,,   Sir, of Dalpholly. *See* **Isobel,** Halcraig   S. H., 14 May 1708

,,   ' de Dundeugh, Gulielmus de Holme, Robertus de

Garwarrie, Alexander de Knockgray, Gulielmus
de Craig, fuerunt possessores quarundam terrarum mentionat. per spatium quinque annorum
immediate preceden. sententiam forisfacturae
contra illos pronunciatam per dominos justiciarii
sexto die mensis Julii anno dom. MDCLXXX.

I. de Poss. Quinq., 31 Aug. 1682

,,   h. Gulielmi de Dungeuch, patris   I. G.,   5 Jan. 1695

,,   de Dungeuch. *See* **William,** *supra.*

,,   Mr., of Earlstoun, h. of Alexander of Earlstoun, his

father,—in the lands of Earlstoun within the
parochin of Dalry, comprehending ane merkland
of Earlstoun ;—ane merkland of Mylntoun ;—ane
merkland of Ardoch ;—ane halfe merkland of Over
Barley ;—ane halfe merkland of Balwherne ;—ane
merkland of Knolgrey (Knockgrey);—2½ merkland
of Marbrock, with the mylne and milne lands of
Earlestoune .—A.E. 7½m., N.E. 22½m.—the halfe

(446)

of the lands of Quhytpark within the parochin of
Keltoun :—E. 7l. 10s. and 13s. 4d. in augmentationem —the lands of High, Over, Middell and
Nether Airds, within the lordship of Galloway
beneath Crie, and parochine of Kellis :—E. 20l.,
etc.—the 40 shilling land of Myndell (or Myndew):
—E. 5l 10s.—the 40 shilling land of Barnofarrie
(or Barmoffatie), within the barony and parochin
of Kirkpatrick-Durhame .—E. 5l. 10s.—the lands
of Over Marcairtney ·—E. 4l. 10s.—the lands of
Nether Marcairtney —E. 5l. 10s.—the lands of
Glengoppok.—E. 5m.   I. S. (Kirkcudb), 23 Jan. 1655

William, Mr., of Errlstoune, h. of John of Errlstoune, his
guideshir,—in ane croft of land callit Temple-
landcroft of Crocemichall, within the parochin of
Crocemichall ·—E ½m.—the ane merkland of Over
Glenhall (or Glenhowle), and half merkland of
Nether Barley of old extent, within the lordshipe
of Erlestoune and parochin of Dalry.—A.E. 1½m ;
N.E. 4½m   I. S. (Kirkcudb.), 2 Oct. 1655

„ magister, nuper de Earlstone et Alexander nuper de
Earlstone ejus f. et Gulielmus senior de Craighlaw pater Jacobi junioris ejus f fuerant hereditarii
possessores earundam terrarum specificat. per
spatium quinque annorum immediate preceden.
decimum nonum diem mensis Februarii anno dom.
MDCLXXX., in quo die sententia forisfacturae
contra illos per dominos justic. generalem, justic.
clericum, et justic. commissionarios pronunciata
fuit   I. de Poss Quinq., 3 Sept. 1686

„ (Duff), to his cousin Margaret Udny Duff (d. of Wm.
Duff of Braco), who died   —h. of taillie
spec. in Eden, with its salmon fishings, Aberd. ;
and in other fishings at Inverichtney, Banff
               S. H., 27 Mar. ; 4 April 1793

„ to his father Adam, goldsmith in Edinburgh—h. gen.
               S. H., ^5 Feb. ; 20 Nov. 1735

„ captain, son of Adam, goldsmith in Edinburgh. *See*
     Helen, Edinburgh   S. H , 6 May 1767

William (now Gray), g^dson of Jn. Gordon of Edinglassie, to
     . his g^dmother Mary Gray, sister of Elizth. Gray,
     Ballegerno—h. of prov. gen.   S. H , 3 June 1742
,,   s. of James of Ellon. *See* **James** of Ellon   S. H., 22 Nov. 1732
,,   de Farsken. *See* **John** de Drumquhendle   I. G., 27 Oct. 1693
,,   sometime merchant in Norway, to his father William
     of Farskine—h. gen.   S. H., 18 Jan.; 10 Feb. 1780
,,   of Farskine. *See* **William**, *supra*.
,,   s. of C. of Fetterangus, to his g^dfather Walter Stewart,
     minister, Ellon—co-h. of prov gen.
                       S. H , 22 July, 13 Aug. 1768
,,   bookseller in Forfar, to his father Ebenezer, weaver
     in Perth—h. gen.   S. H., 15 May; 7 June 1799
,,   of Fyvie, to his father William, Earl of Aberdeen—
     h. of prov. gen   S. H., 1 Aug.; 3 Dec. 1760
,,   the Hon., of Fyvie, General, to his father William,
     Earl of Aberdeen—h of prov. gen.
                 . S. H , 20 April; 23 May 1797
,,   de Geicht. *See* **George** de Geicht
              I. G., 8 Feb. 1606 ; I. S. (Aberd), 8 Feb. 1606
,,   Sir, of Gordonstoun, bart , to his brother Sir Robert
     of Gordonstoun, bart.—h. of prov. gen.
               S. H., 20 Dec. ; 26 Dec. 1776
,,   Sir, of Gordonstoun, bart. *See* **Alexander** Penrose
     (Cumming)   S H., 10 June 1795
,,   of Greenlaw. *See* **Alexander**, Greenlaw   S. H., 23 Nov. 1758
,,   of Grievshop *See* **John** of Grievshop   S. H., 26 Dec. 1778
,,   h. Rogeri in Hill, patris,—in 40 solidatis terrarum de
     Over Laggan antiqui extentus, infra parochiam de
     Parton.—A.E. 40s.; N.E. 61 I. S (Kirkcudb), 6 Feb. 1672
,,   *See* **George,** Hodie   I S (Kirkcudb), 7 June 1614
,,   de Holme. *See* **Roger** de Holme I S (Kirkcudb.), 28 Oct. 1617
,,   de Holme, h. lineae Gulielmi de Holme, avi   I. G., 29 Jan. 1642
,,   de Holme. *See* **William**, *supra*.
,,   de Holme. *See* **William** de Dundeugh
               I. de Poss. Quinq., 31 Aug. 1682
,,   of Holm. *See* **Nathaniel**, Holm   S. H., 22 Aug 1724
,,   of Holm, to his great-grandfather Roger of Holm—
     h. gen.   S. H., 15 July; 24 July 1735

William, of Holm. *See* **Margaret,** Holm   S. H., 20 Sept.; 28 Nov. 1759

  ,, Sir, of Invergordon, bart. *See* **William** of Newhall
                                S. H., 18 April 1766

  ,, junr., of Holme. *See* **Robert,** Holme   S. H., 29 Oct. 1759

  ,, of Kenmore, capt, to his father the Hon. John of
        Kenmore—h. of line and prov. gen. S. H., 6 Feb.; 14 Feb. 1770

  ,, of Kenmore. *See* **John** of Kenmore   S. H.; 12 Dec. 1772

  ,, Capt., of Kenmore *See* **John** of Kenmore   S H., 22 Mar. 1774

  ,, de Kennertie, h. Willielmi de Kennertie, patris I. G., 6 June 1628

  ,, de Kennertie. *See* **William** de Kennertie, *supra.*

  ,, de Kennertie, h. Willielmi, patris,—in terris et baronia
        de Kinnertie, viz. Meikle Kinnertie, Midel Kinner-
        tie, Muirtoun, Carnetoun, cum piscatione terrarum
        de Auldtoun de Kinnertie, et Schiphirdiis croft.—
        2 croftis de Burnsyde;—crofta de Watersyd.—A.E.
        3l., N.E. 12l.   I. S. (Aberd.), 6 June 1628

  ,, *See* **William** de Kennertie, *supra.*

  ,, of Kerston, to his granduncle William of Kerston,
        who died   Nov., 1688—h. spec. in Bow of
        Kerston, How, Navershaw, Mills of Kerston, and
        Voy, etc.   S H., 5 July; 18 Oct. 1744

  ,, of Kerston. *See* **William** of Kerston, *supra.*

  ,, of Kerston. *See* **James** of Kerston   S. H., 9 July 1763

  ,, *See* **Margaret,** Kirkwall   I. S. (Orkney), 25 Nov. 1656

  ,, dominus, de Lesmoir, baronettus, h. masc. domini
        Jacobi de Lesmoir militis baronetti, patris I. G., 19 Jan. 1648

  ,, dominus de Lesmoir, miles baronettus, h. masc. do-
        mini Jacobi de Lesmoir militis baronetti, nepotis
        fratris,—in villis et terris de Corveichines, Thorni-
        wrae et Corsalstane;—villis et terris de Sliache
        cum Park, Adamstoun, Silverhillock, Wistroun,
        Mutehillock, Boigheid, Newtoun;—terris de Perns-
        mylne (vel Peerismylne);—tertia parte villae
        et terrarum de Garie;—bina parte villae et
        terrarum de Chappeltoun;—tertia parte villae et
        terrarum de Wedderburne;—bina parte villae et
        terrarum de Broomhill;—tertia parte villae et
        terrarum de Thomastoun;—bina parte villae et
        terrarum de Comalegie, infra baroniam de Kin-

mundie :—A.E. 11l., N.E. 44l —terris templariis
de Essie, in baronia de Strathbogie ,—terris templariis de Fuilziement, infra baroniam de Auchindoir :—A.E. 5s. ; N.E. 5s.—officio haereditario
ballivatus, et privilegio liberae regalitatis, infra
bondas terrarum suprascriptarum ,—38 rudis seu
particatis terrarum infra territorium burgi de Rattray .—A.E 20s. ; N.E. 4l.—omnibus unitis in
baroniam de Newtoun-Garrie　　　I S (Aberd), 19 Jan. 1648

William, dominus, de Lesmore, h Jacobi feoditarii de Lesmore,
f. patrui　　　　　　　　　　　　　I. G., 9 Oct. 1672

,,　　de Lesmoir, h. domini Jacobi de Lesmoir, avi,—in
terris de Essie-Beltennie, cum terris vocatis croft
de Auchinleck, infra baroniam et dominium de
Huntlie :—E. 20l.—solari dimidietate villae et
terrarum de Auldmerdrum, in baronia de Strathbogie, cum jure patronatus ecclesiae de Essie.—
E. 1d.　　　　　　　　　　　　　I. S (Aberd.), 9 Oct. 1672

,,　　Sir, of Lessmore.　*See* **Alexander,** Sir, of Lessmore
　　　　　　　　　　　　　　　　　S. H., 23 April 1751

,,　　in Millerriven　*See* **Patrick,** Drumfald　I G., 19 July 1684
,,　　of Minmore.　*See* **John,** Minmore　S. H , 27 Aug. 1767
,,　　in Monyboye.　*See* **John,** Monyboye　I. S. (Dumf.), 25 May 1626
,,　　of Munibuy.　*See* **Mary,** Munibuy
　　　　　　　I S. (Dumf.) (Kirkcudb.), 20 Feb. 1659

,,　　of Nethermuir, to his father John of Nethermuir,
writer in Edinburgh—h. gen. S. H., 6 Dec. 1760 ; 6 Mar. 1761

,,　　of Newhall, to his father Charles Hamilton of Newhall, advocate, who died　　　Oct., 1761—h. of line
spec. c. b. inv., in W. St. Martin's, E Balblair,
etc., Ross ; W. Balblair, etc., Cromarty ; Milntoun,
etc., Lanark　　　　　　　S. H., 11 April , 20 April 1763

,,　　of Newhall, to his uncle George (s of Sir William of
Invergordon, bart.), who died　　　1752—h.
male and of conq. spec. in parts of the lands of
Brae called Meikle and Little Brae
　　　　　　　　S. H., 30 Jan. ; 18 April 1766

,,　　of Newhall, advocate　*See* **Henrietta,** Newhall
　　　　　　　　　　　　　　　S. H., 9 Jan. 1781

William, Sir, of Park, to his father Sir James of Park—h. gen.

                              S. H., 23 April; 26 April 1728

    ,,   de Pinkaitland. *See* **Patrick,** Pinkaitland   I. G., 8 Feb 1690

    ,,   *See* **John** in Pitchash of Ballandalloch   S H., 22 Sept. 1738

    ,,   in Port-Glasgow, formerly merchant, Glasgow. *See*

          John, M.D., of Glasgow   S H , 24 Dec. 1762

    ,,   de Quhytpark. *See* **James** de Careltoune   I. G., 20 Dec. 1670

    ,,   de Robertoun. *See* **Mary,** Robertoun

                          I. S (Kirkcudb.), 8 Sept. 1668

    ,,   of Rothney. *See* **George** of Rothney   S H., 17 Aug. 1772

    ,,   de Schives. *See* **George,** Schives   I. S. (Aberd.), 5 Oct. 1546

    ,,   de Shawis *See* **George,** Shawis   I. S. (Aberd.), 29 Nov. 1565

    ,,   of Shirmers, to his father William of Shirmers, who

          died   Sept., 1685—h. male spec. in Dalswinton,

          Cubbocks, Aronclosch, etc.

                  I. S. (Kirkcudb.), 20 Oct. 1713; 8 Feb 1714

    ,,   of Shirmers. *See* **William,** *supra.*

    ,,   of Shirmers *See* **Alexander** of Shirmers   S. H., 21 Sept. 1719

    ,,   of Sheelagreen *See* **Charles** of Sheelagreen, Cap-

          tain   S. H., 11 Mar. 1776

    ,,   of Sheelagreen   Alexander Hay (formerly Leith) of

          Rannas, Col (formerly Leith of ˉLeithhall) to

          William Gordon of Sheelagreen, who died 5 May,

          1773—h of prov. spec , in Seggieden and Edder-

          lick, in the parishes of Premnay and Kinnethmont

               S. H. Supp. (Aberd.) 14 April , 1 Aug. 1792

    ,,   de Tarpersie, h. Georgii de Tarpersie, patris,—in

          villa et terris de Erlisfeild et Seggiedene, infra

          parochiam de Kynnethmont :—A E. 3l. ; N.E

          12l —villa et terris de Badinscoth, cum pratis ex

          occidentali latere aquae de Ythane nuncupatis

          Crombie, cum molendino de Badinscoth, Redgill

          et Boiges de Badinscoth, cum bina parte terrarum

          de Brukillis, bina parte terrarum de Bakiehill ;—

          bina parte terrarum de Reidhill, infra parochiam

          de Auchterles —E. 1m   I. S. (Aberd.), 16 Dec. 1635

    ,,   of Tarpersie, h of George of Tarpersie, his father,—

          in the toune and lands of Culbuithlyes, with the

          halfe thereof, Donhead, and Quhittuties ;—the

shadow-halfe of the toune and lands of Maynes of
Buithraigie, within the chaymberie of Boyne and
parochin of Inverboyndie, for principal·—A.E.
4l ; N E. 16l.—the toune and lands of Auchyn-
dachie, Eistertoun, Westertoun, Hilhead, with
the mylne of Auchindachie, within the parochin
of Keithe, in warrandice of the foresaid lands.—
A.E 40s.; N.E 8l. I S. (Banff), 29 Aug 1655

William, de Terpersie. *See* **George** de Terpersie I. G Supp., 5 Feb 1696

„ de Thornebank. *See* **George** de Thornebank

I. S. (Banff), 21 Oct. 1667

„ de Tulloche, h. Jacobi, patrui I. G., 8 Dec. 1626

„ de Tulloch, h magistri Alexandri de Tulloche, avi,—
in terris de Auchinhovis, viz. Over et Nether
Auchinhovis, Berrieleyes, cum Ailhouse, et Ail-
housecroft, et communi pastura ;—terris vocatis
Grenis de Kinbade, Balnameine, et Ardmoire ;—
i aratro terrarum vulgo nuncupato the Vest Pleuch
terrarum de Midseat de Auchinhovis, extendente
ad 8 bovatas terrarum ;—terris de Corbiecraig et
Restrypis·—E. 25l., etc.—feudifirmae —terris de
Glengairock, cum Outseat, Alrecardoche nuncupato, in baronia de Strathila et regalitate de Kinloss.—E. 20m., etc., firmae I S. (Banff), 7 Dec. 1637

„ of Tulloch. *See* **Alexander** of Tulloch

I. S (Aberd.), Nov. 1656

APPENDIX II.

GORDONS MENTIONED IN THE LIST OF POLLABLE PERSONS WITHIN THE SHIRE OF ABERDEEN, 1696.

—— Sheriff Gordon. *See* **John**, Aberdeen.

Adam, Aberdeen (late of Inverebrie), and his lady, and Hellen, Jean and Anna, his children. II. 623, 624.

,, *See* **Alexander**, elder, merchant, Aberdeen.

,, of Auchanachie, Ruthen, and his wife, and George, his son; Elizabeth, his servant II. 434.

,, servant, Badivines, Alfoord. I. 404

,, of Balgonen, Keige. I. 461.

,, gentleman, tennent, Easter Camphell, Kincardin O'Niell (he classing himself as a gentleman), and his wife, and John, his son. I. 112.

,, younger, gentleman, tennent, Curfidlie, Kincardin O'Niell, and his wife, and John, Jean, Mary, Agnes, his children I. 112, 113.

,, servant, Drumdola, Forgue. II. 402.

,, gentleman, son, to umquhill Adam, sometime of Glenbucket, having renounced to be air to his deceist father [Adam] before the Sheriff of Aberdeen, and denies to be heritor. Jeane Douglass, lyverentrix of Glenbucket. [His brothers and sisters were] Robert, Alexander, Margaret, Helen, Jacabona (all these five children unprovyded). I 518.

,, deceist, sometime of Glenbucket, *ut supra*, one of the Commissioners appointed for the parish of Glenbucket. I. 517, 518

,, sub-tennent, Toune of Newbrough, Foverane, and his wife II. 169.

,, measson, Old Meldrum, Bethelnie, and his wife, and Margrat, his daughter. I 329.

,, gentleman tennent, Mill of Smistoun, Rhynie; Elspet, his servant. II. 450.

Agnes, 19 years of age, daughter of (   ) Gordon of Craig of Auchindoir, Auchindore. I. 505.

     ,,   *See* **John,** Craigstoune.

     ,,   *See* **Adam,** Curfidlie.

     ,,   servant, Garinsmilne, Culsalmond   I 267

     ,,   *See* **John,** tutor of Glenbucket, Peterhead.

     ,,   *See* **George,** Mosstoune.

     ,,   servant, Skeen. II 497.

     ,,   *See* **Alexander,** Whytewell.

Alaster, tennent, Altchaldach, Glenmuick, and his wife   I 173.

     ,,   servant. *See* **Patrick,** Geach

     ,,   tennent, Larie, Glengairdine, and his wife. I. 165

     ,,   tennent, Larie, Glengairdine, and his wife. I. 165

Alexander, barber, Aberdeen, and his wife. II. 604.

     ,,   Captain, Aberdeen. II. 623

[,,   ] Gordon, Provost, deceast ; Grissell Walker, his relict, Aberdeen ; James and Anna, her grandchildren. II. 613.

     ,,   deceast merchant, Margrat Cumming, Aberdeen, his relict, and Alexander, Francis and Elizabeth, her children. II. 612

     ,,   *See* **Alexander,** *supra.*

     ,,   elder, merchant, Aberdeen, and his wife, and Adam, George, Jean, Janet, his children   II 627.

     ,,   younger, merchant, Aberdeen   II 619.

     ,,   *See* **James,** junior, Aberdeen

     ,,   *See* **John,** late baillie, Aberdeen

[,,   of Abergeldie.]   *See* [**Euphemia** Graham], Ladie Dowager of Abergeldie.

     ,,   servant, Abergeldie, Crathie. I. 152.

     ,,   sub-tennent, Abergeldie, Crathie   I. 151.

     ,,   *See* **James,** Achmull

     ,,   *See* **William,** Adamstoun.

     ,,   tennent, Milne of Aden, Deer (one of the Commissioners appointed for the parish of Deer), and his wife and two children, George Rankine his son-in-law, and his two sisters. I. 610, 636.

     ,,   servant, Over Altrie, Deer. I. 617

     ,,   of Auchmunziell, Auchredie, Elizabeth Keith his wife, William his son, Jean his daughter. II. 27.

     ,,   *See* **George,** of Badenscoth

     ,,   of Barrack, Auchredie, Christane Grant, relict of deceased Patrick ;

Jean, Catherine, Janet, Mary and Elizabeth, his sisters; Janet, his servant. II. 24.

Alexander, gentleman, brother to and principal tenant of Charles of Blelack, Invernochtie, and his wife. I. 542.

„ gentleman tennent, Bogforth, Botarie, and his wife, and John, Euphemia, Jane and Margrat, his children. II. 438.

„ *See* **John,** Botarie.

„ gentleman tennent, Maynes of Brucklay, Auchredie, and his wife, and Anna, Barbray and Elizabeth, his children II. 13, 14.

„ tennent of John of Cairnborrow, Glass, and his wife. II. 460

„ gentleman tennent, Claymyres, Botarie, and his wife, and Alexander, his son and Arthour his servant II. 438.

„ *See* **Alexander,** *supra.*

„ *See* **John,** Cocklarachy.

„ son of ( ) Gordon of Craig of Auchindoir, Auchindore I. 505

„ of Coldwales, Ellon, his lady, and Alexander and John, his sons, and Jane and Margrat, his daughters. II. 258.

„ *See* **Alexander,** *supra.*

„ *See* **James,** Comry

„ *See* **John,** Cormellat.

„ tradesman, Coulie, Udnie, and his wife II 179.

„ tennent, Strait Craigs, Oyne, his mother and his daughter Margaret. I. 283, 284.

„ tennent, Craigtoune, Kincardin O'Niell, and his wife and daughter. I. 93.

„ sub-tennent, Cranstoune, Kildrumey, and Christian Tough, his wife. I 503.

„ *See* **John,** Cranstoune.

„ *See* **John,** Creagihead.

„ Mr., a portion of Cults, Glengairdine, sometyme belonging to Mr. Alexander, now to the Earle of Marr. I. 168.

„ grassman, Curmar, Kincardin O'Niell, and his wife I. 91

„ tennent in third pairt of Cushney, Auchterless, and his wife. II 391.

„ servant, Foverane. II. 149.

„ notar publict in Toun of Fraserburgh, and his wife, and sister-in-law, and three children. II. 100.

Alexander. *See* **Adam,** of Glenbucket.

,,   *See* **John,** tutor of Glenbucket, Peterhead.

,,   servant.   *See* **John,** of Hallhead

,,   servant of James Sievewright, tennent, Hillock, Kincardin O'Niell.
I. 91.

,,   merchant, Toun of Inverurie, Margratt Forbes, his spouse. I. 356

,,   servant, Maynes and Milne of Kindrocht, Streichen. I. 608.

,,   tennent, Kinharochie, Ellon, and Margrat Cowper, his spouse.
II. 247, 258

,,   gentleman, residing in Kinmundy, Longside   I. 593.

,,   *See* **John,** of Knockespock.

,,   *See* **James** [or] **John,** Knockespock.

,,   *See* Sir **James** of Lesmoir.

,,   herd, Letter, Skeen. II. 500.

,,   Leyes, Drumblate, and his wife. II. 276.

,,   *See* **John,** Littel Milne.

,,   Mr., minister of the Gospel at Logie, Logie Buchan   II 229.

,,   servant, Loynchirk, Tullich. I. 161.

,,   tennent, Milbreck, Deer, and his wife. I. 621.

,,   tennent, Muress, Tullich, and Beatrix, his daughter. I. 164.

,,   gentleman, Old Aberdeen, and his wife; two children, Hugo and
Margrat. II. 593.

,,   gentleman, and his wife and daughter, Old Aberdeen. II. 591.

,,   younger, Old Aberdeen. II. 557.

,,   sub-tennent, Parkhill, Kemney, and his wife. I. 369.

,,   of Pitlurg, Kinmundy, Deer, Katherine and Mary, Pitlurg's
sisters. I. 620.

,,   servant.   *See* **Duncan,** Moss Syde of Polwhit

,,   . *See* **George,** of Rothnie.

,,   gentleman, and tennent, Sandieston, Dumbennan, and Jean
Johnston, his spous, Alexander, his youngest son, Margrat and
Anna, his daughters, Anna, his servant. II. 421.

,,   *See* **Alexander,** *supra.*

,,   *See* **Hugh,** Scotshall.

,,   gentleman tennent, Milne of Skelmure and Corthicram, Deer,
his wife and daughter. I. 633.

,,   grassman, Stranduff, Kincardin O'Niell, and his wife. I. 94.

,,   yeoman, Threefield, Bonitoun, and Milne of Bonitoun, Rayne,
Anna and Helen, his daughters. I. 275.

Alexander, sub-tennent, Threefield, Bonitoun, and Milne of Bonitoun, Rayne, and his wife. I. 275.

,, servant, Tillegonie, Tarves. II. 205.

,, cairter upon the Maynes of Towie, Turreff. II. 356.

,, servant, Udney, Foverane. II. 162.

,, talzor, sub-tennent, Waterton, Ellon, and Barbra Ross, his wife. II. 242.

,, Whytewell, Logiedurno, Margaret Keith, his wife, Agnes, his daughter. I. 306.

,, herd, Whytewell, Tyrie. II. 62.

,, tennent, Midlepleugh, Nether Woodhill, Tarves, and his wife. II. 205, 206

Allen, servant, Mayns of Tillesnacht, Birss. I. 77.

Andrew. *See* **Robert,** stabler, Aberdeen.

,, servant *See* **Robert,** stabler, Aberdeen.

,, Auchmaludies, Bedlainis and Drums, Auchredie, and Katharine Mitchell, his wife II. 8.

,, grassman, Easter Earle Seat, Cruden, and Barbra Laurensone, his spouse. II. 133.

,, tennent, Ellenmorre, Kindrocht, and his wife, and his son. I. 130

,, Little Erdo, Methlick, and his wife. II. 218.

,, sub-tennent, Nether Riven, Loggiemarr, and his wife. I. 30.

,, tennent, Over Robiestoun, Dumbennan, and Bessie Taylor, his spouse, Elizabeth, his daughter II. 421.

Ann. *See* **John,** younger of, Fechill.

Anna. *See* **Adam** (late of Inverebrie), Aberdeen.

,, *See* [**Alexander**], Provost, Aberdeen.

,, *See* **John** (deceast), procurator, Aberdeen.

,, servant, Aberdeen. II. 623

,, servant, Achtidonald, Longside. I. 594

,, servant, Ardiffrie, Cruden, wife of Robert George. II. 103.

,, servant, Auchinhove, Lumphanan. I. 116.

,, *See* **James,** Achmull.

,, *See* **Hendry,** of Avachie.

,, *See* **Robert,** Bottarie.

,, *See* **John,** Bottarie

,, *See* **John,** Nether Achine.

,, *See* **Alexander,** Maynes of Brucklay.

,, *See* **William,** Buthlay

Anna. ane cottar-wife with John of Cairnborrow, Glass   II. 459.

,,   spouse to John Leith of Cardin, Oyne   I. 290.

,,   Chappletoun, Drumblate (given under)   II. 273.

,,   *See* **John,** of Cocklarachy.

,,   wife of Hierom Spence, son of Thomas Spence, Easter Collonoch, Dumbennan, and Janet Ferier, his spouse. II. 418

,,   wife of David Tyrie, gentleman tennent, Craighall, Kinethmond. I. 488

,,   *See* **John,** Creagihead.

,,   spouse to Alexander Ker, tennent, Drumnahoove, Kildrumey. I. 499

,,   *See* **George,** Mill of Fiddes.

,,   servant, Gairdnerhill, Kildrumey   I. 501.

,,   *See* **Robert,** Milne of Kinnoir.

,,   *See* Sir **James,** of Lesmoir.

,,   *See* **John,** of Nethermoor.

,,   *See* **Nathaniell,** Newnoth.

,,   spouse to William Thomson, skipper, Peterhead. I. 572.

,,   relict of Robert Forbes, gentleman, of Pittintagart, Migvie, and two children. I. 5.

,,   servant, New Rayne, Rayne. I 279.

,,   *See* **George,** of Rothnie.

,,   *See* **Alexander,** Sandieston

,,   servant. *See* **Alexander,** Sandieston.

,,   *See* **Alexander,** Threefield, Bonitoun

,,   Woodhead of Gight, Fyvie, spouse to Alexander Whyte, ane officer in the army in Flanders, but indigent. II. 295.

Arthur, Mr., gentleman, deceast. *See* **Robert,** Aberdeen.

,,   servant. *See* **Alexander,** Claymyres.

,,   *See* **John** of Law

Barbara, wife of James Cuie, cottar, Balmelie, Turreff. II. 362.

,,   *See* **Alexander,** Brucklay.

,,   daughter of (   ) Gordon of Craig of Auchindoir, Auchindore. I 505.

,,   *See* **John,** younger of Fechill.

,,   Toun of Gibstoune, Dumbennan, wife of Alexander Leith, gentleman, principal tacksman   II. 423

,,   wife to William Watsone, Kirktoune of Dyce, Cleatt. I. 467.

,,   tennent, Ramstoune, Monymusk, relict of ane gentleman I. 379.

,,   servant, Thomastoune, Auchterless. II. 383

Beatrix. *See* **Alexander,** Muress.

Bessie, servant, Anchendrume, Ruthen. II. 430.

   ,,   *See* **John,** Creagihead.

   ,,   Mrs. *See* Livetennent-Colonel **John,** of Gight.

   ,,   wife of Alexander Davidsone, weaver, Toun of Kirkhill, Kinethmond. I 491

   ,,   servant, Rotten Bog, Insch   I 258.

Bettie, Mrs , indweller, Woodhead of Gight, Fyvie   II. 295.

Catherine. *See* **John,** litster, Aberdeen

   ,,   relict of John Collisone of Skellmire, Aberdeen, and Barbra, her daughter   II. 615

   ,,   *See* **Alexander,** of Barrack.

   ,,   wife of William Craigmill, no trade, cottar, Maynes of Monymusk. I. 374.

[Charles, 2nd] Earl of Aboyne and his Lady. I 25, 43, 50, 54, 56, 157, 164, 178.

   ,,   of Auchanachie, Ruthen, Commissioner appointed for the parishes of Ruthen and Botarie ; his son and his wife. II. 429, 434.

   ,,   Laird of Blelack, Loggiemarr, one of the Commissioners for the parishes of Migvie and Tarland ; and his two daughters. I. 1, 33, 541, 542.

   ,,   gentleman, of Bogsyd, Kingedward   II. 323, 324

   ,,   *See* **John,** Borland

   ,,   *See* **William,** Buthlay.

   ,,   *See* **John,** of Hallhead.

   ,,   servant, Saphoke, Fyvie. II. 307.

Christian, servant, Aberdeen. II. 621.

   ,,   servant, Aberdeen. II 624.

   ,,   Afleck, Udnie, mother of James and Richard Findlay. II. 177.

   ,,   spouse of William Laing, tennent, Easter Auchlewchries, Cruden. II. 131

   ,,   *See* **John,** The Bogg.

   ,,   *See* **John,** of Cocklarachy.

   ,,   and Issobell, Comalagy, Drumblate. II. 274

   ,,   *See* **James,** Daach of Kinnoir.

   ,,   wife of John Lawsone, weaver, sub-tennent, Milne of Lenturk, Lochell. I. 435.

   ,,   mother to James Glennie, tennent, and Alexander Glennie, tradesman, Old Forrest, Rhynie. II. 451.

Christian, Old Meldrum, Bethelnie, and Margrat, her sister. I. 329.

   ,,   *See* **Hugh,** Scotshall.

Collin, harvest hook, Mid Toune, Glass. II. 458.

Daniell. *See* **Robert,** elder, merchant, Aberdeen.

David. *See* **William,** Buthlay.

Donald, cottar with Harie, Avachie, tennent, Maynes of Balquhollie, Turreff. II. 349.

   ,,   sub-tennent, Invercauld, Crathie, and his wife, and John, his brother. I. 147

   ,,   Invercauld, Kindrocht, and his wife. I. 132.

Duncan, servant, Aberdeen. II 630

   ,,   tennent, Blacharrage, Glenmuick, and his wife. I. 179.

   ,,   tennent, Cults, Glengairdine, and his wife   I. 168.

   ,,   servant, Knowheade of Cults, Tarland. I. 11.

   ,,   son of Margrat Wilson, tennent, Ferrer, Aboyne; William, his brother. I. 64.

   ,,   millart, Kirktoune, Drumblate, and his wife. II. 269.

   ,,   gentleman, Moss Syde of Polwhit, Culsalmond ; Margrat Mowat, his wife ; Alexander his servant. I. 261.

   ,,   servant, Sterrein, Glenmuick. I 172.

Elizabeth. *See* **Alexander,** deceast merchant, Aberdeen.

   ,,   *See* **Robert,** elder, merchant, Aberdeen.

   ,,   *See* **William,** alias Bogie, merchant, Aberdeen.

   ,,   servant, Loanhead, Aberdeen. II 627.

   ,,   *See* **James,** Achmull.

   ,,   *See* **William,** Adamstoun

   ,,   servant, Over Aden, Deer. I. 615.

   ,,   servant, Mill of Ashogle, Turreff. II. 345.

   ,,   servant. *See* **Adam,** of Auchanachie.

   ,,   *See* **Hendry,** Avachie

   ,,   *See* **Alexander,** of Barrack.

   ,,   *See* **Robert,** Bottarie. II. 438.

   ,,   *See* **Alexander,** Brucklay. II. 14.

   ,,   *See* **William,** Buthlay.

   ,,   a friend in the house of John of Cairnborrow, Glass. II. 458.

   ,,   Camalynes, Fyvie, daughter of Lucriss Steill, cottar woman. II 314.

   ,,   Chappeltoun, Drumblate II 273.

Elizabeth, wife to Alexander Hendersone, tennent, Toune of Cleatt, Cleatt
I. 465.

,, indweller, Cottoune, Fyvie. II. 293.

,, 10 years of age, daughter of ( ) Gordon of Craig of Auchindoir, Auchindore. I. 505.

,, *See* **Patrick,** elder of Cults.

,, servant to the Laird of Dyce. II. 507.

,, servant to the Laird of Echt. I. 213.

,, Urquhart, Dame Duager of Gight, Maynes of Gight, Fyvie.
II. 290.

,, *See* **John,** tutor of Glenbucket, Peterhead

,, *See* **John,** of Kirktoune of Glenbucket.

,, spouse to Alexander Reidfoord, Toun of Kirkhill, Kinethmond
I. 491.

,, *See* **John** of Knockespock.

,, servant, Links, Old Machar. II. 569.

,, *See* **George,** Millden.

,, *See* **John,** of Nethermoor.

,, *See* **John,** of Nethermoor.

,, widdow, tennent, Newtoun of Ardenrit, Cruden, John and
Charles Hay, her sons, Elizabeth her servitrix. II. 106, 123

,, servitrix. *See* **Elizabeth,** *supra.*

,, *See* **Andrew,** Over Robiestoun.

,, *See* **George** of Sweltoun.

,, *See* **John,** Torniechelt.

Elspeth, cottar woman, Newplace of Cairnbrogie, Tarves. II. 208.

,, Chappeltoun, Drumblate. II. 273.

,, and Janet, sisters, cottar women Corsgights, Auchredie. II. 4.

,, tennent, Litell Daach, Ruthen, Alexander Lith, her son. II. 433.

,, servant. *See* Sir **James,** of Lesmoir.

,, Mackterrie, Udnie, wife of Andrew Allan, and a son. II. 178.

,, servant, New Machar. II. 551.

,, grasswoman, Seggeden, Kinethmond, and her daughter. I. 486.

,, servant. *See* **Adam,** Mill of Smistoun.

,, servant, The Muir, Tullich. I. 156.

,, sub-tenant, Ellon. II. 241.

[Euphemia Graham], The Ladie Dowager ot Abergeldie, Glenmuick.
I. 171.

,, *See* **Alexander,** Bogforth.

Francis, Mr., chosen and appoynted with the Poll Commissioners for the
　　　　parish of Balhelwie. II. 521

　　　,,　　*See* **Alexander,** deceast merchant, Aberdeen

　　　,,　　*See* **William,** merchant, alias Bogie, Aberdeen.

　　　,,　　(16 years of age), son of the Laird of Craig of Auchindoir, Auchin-
　　　　　doir. I. 505.

　　　,,　　gentleman tennent, Easter Clova, Kildrumey, and Elspet Thom-
　　　　　sone, his wife I. 502, 503

　　　,,　　gentleman tennent, Smistoune, Rynie. II. 449.

George, first Duke of Gordon. I. 522, II. 325, 413, 424, 429, 435,
　　　　442, 448.

　　　,,　　first Earl of Aberdeen, Methlick (one of the commissioners appointed
　　　　　for the valuation of lands in 1673—Introduction), the Countess
　　　　　[Anna Lockhart, dau. of George Lockhart of Tolbreck] and
　　　　　sex ladys, my Lord Haddo, Mr. William, his Lordship's young-
　　　　　est son, Mrs. Mary Gordon, lawfull daughter to the deceast
　　　　　Sir George Gordon of Gight. I., x. 291, 306, 329, 361; II.
　　　　　5, 187, 209, 210, 253.

[　,,　] Lord Haddo　*See* **George,** Earl of Aberdeen, *supra*

　　　,,　　Anna Cumeing, Aberdeen, relict of [Alexander] Leask, minister at
　　　　　Maryculter, gentleman; William and Alexander, her children,
　　　　　Patrick and George Gordon, her grandchildren. II. 614.

　　　,,　　merchant, Aberdeen, and his wife, and Janet, Jean and Robert, his
　　　　　children. II. 618.

　　　,,　　younger, merchant, Aberdeen, and his wife, and George, his son.
　　　　　II. 628

　　　,,　　*See* **George,** *supra.*

　　　,,　　youngest, merchant, Aberdeen. II. 618

　　　,,　　Mr., servant, Aberdeen. II. 632.

　　　,,　　*See* **Alexander,** elder, merchant, Aberdeen.

　　　,,　　*See* **John,** late baillie, Aberdeen.

　　　,,　　taylor, Aberdeen, and his wife (Alexander and Christian Strachan,
　　　　　his wife's children), Robert, his son. II. 619.

　　　,,　　sub-tennent, Maynes of Aberdour, Aberdour, and his wife. II. 64.

　　　,,　　of Achline, Kirktoun of Dyce. II. 512

　　　,,　　servant, Ardiffrie, Cruden II. 104.

　　　,,　　*See* **Adam,** of Auchanachie.

　　　,,　　cottar, no trade, Auchinhive, Lumphanan, and his wife I. 118.

　　　,,　　servant, Auchinhove, Lumphanan. I. 116.

George, gentleman tennent, Westertoun of Auchleuchries, Cruden ; Jean Seaton, his spouse , Patrick, his son. II. 129, 131.

,, tennent, Backhillock, Glenbucket, and his wife. I. 521

,, of Badenscoth, Auchterless (Commissioner appointed for the parish of Auchterless) , Helen Keith, his lady, and Jean, his daughter , Alexander, George and William, his sons II. 375, 376, 379.

,, *See* **George,** *supra*

,, *See* **John,** of Cocklarachy

,, *See* **Hendrie,** Mill of Collithie

,, tennent, The Milne of Coull, Coull, one of the Commissioners for the parish of Coull, and his wife. I. 36, 37.

,, *See* **William,** Cragcullie.

,, gentleman tennent, Craigmelie, Dumbennan, and Jean Straquhan; his wife ; his sons, James, 24 years, and John, 10 years , his daughters, Margrat, 14 years, Janet, 8 years II. 415.

,, cottar, and his wife, Daach, Ruthen. II. 435.

,, *See* **John,** of Davedstone

,, cottar (no trade), Davieshill, Foverane, and his wife II. 165

,, (deceast), Jean Keith, relict of George, gentleman, Toun of Deer, Deer. I 619.

,, heretor of the Kirktoune of Dyce, Cleatt, his lady, two daughters and a son I 466

,, gentleman tennent, Little Erdo, Methlick, his wife and son. II. 209, 221

,, gentleman tennent, The Mill of Erdo, Methlick, and his wife II 225

,, gentleman tennent, Mill of Fiddes, Foverane , Margaret Pitendrich, his wife ; Anna, her daughter II 163, 164

,, servant, Findlatrie, Touch I 416

,, tennent, Formestoun, Aboyne, and his wife I 58

,, Sir, of Gight, deceast *See* **George,** Earl of Aberdeen.

,, sometyme in Garmoch ; Elizabeth Johnston his relict, gentlewoman, Rawes of Huntly, Dumbennan , James, their son , Girzell, their daughter. II 422

,, servant, Rawes of Huntly, Dumbennan. II. 419

,, servant, Kincardine, Kincardin O'Niell I. 105

,, heretor and possessor of the Mill of Kincardine, Kincardin O'Niell, and his wife I. 115

,, servant, Bridge Alehouss, Kintore. I 397.

George. *See* Sir **James,** of Lesmoir.

„   gentleman tennent, Millden and Fyfeshills, Balhelwie, and his wife, and George, John, Margrat, Jane and Elizabeth, his children. II. 522, 524

„   *See* **George,** *supra.*

„   tennent, Toune of Mosstoune, Kinethmond, and Agnes, his spouse I. 491.

„   grassman, Mountcoffer, Kingedward, and his wife. II. 322.

„   *See* **John,** of Nethermoor.

„   cottar, Overhill, Montwhiter. II 369.

„   yeoman, Kirktoune of Rayne, and his wife. I. 278.

„   servant, Reidbank, Ellon. II. 251.

„   *See* **Katheren,** Old Aberdeen

„   Laird of Rothnie, Wranghame, Culsalmond, Insch and Premney, one of the Commissioners appointed for the parish of Culsalmond ; Georg, his eldest son, Alexander, his second son, William, his third son, Anna, Jean, Janet and Margrat, his daughters. I. 239, 248, 260, 266.

„   *See* **George,** *supra.*

„   *See* **Hugh,** Scotshall.

„   servant, Mill of Shethin, Tarves II. 189.

„   Slioch, Boggyside, Drumblate, and his wife. II. 266

„   of Sweltoun, Dumbennan, gentleman tennent ; Jean Lesley, his spouse ; John his eldest son, ten years of age, George, his second son, five years of age ; Issobell, his daughter, twelve years of age, Elizabeth, his daughter, nyn years of age ; Mary, his youngest daughter, three years of age. II. 414.

„   *See* **George,** *supra.*

„   Laird of Tarpersie, Tillinessell, one of the Commissioners appointed for the parish of Tillinessell, and his lady, four daughters and two sons. I. 475, 482

„   messenger and gentleman, Tories, Oyne, Jean Jamessoun, his spouse. I. 288.

„   tennent, and maltman for his trade, Turriffe, Turreff, and his wife. II. 341, 346

„   servant, The Maynes, Tyrie, and his wife and his daughter. II. 62.

„   servant, Witingstain, Dumbennan, II 416

Gilbert, tennent, Bridgehouse, Deer, and his wife. I. 618.

Girzell. *See* **George,** Garmoch.

Harie, Avachie, tennent, Maynes of Balquhollie, Turreff II 348.

„   ane cottar, no trade, Bellastraid, Loggiemarr, and his wife. I. 29.

„   *See* **Hendrie,** Mill of Collithie.

„   *See* **Robert,** Milne of Raves of Huntly.

Helen. *See* **Adam** (late of Inverebrie), Aberdeen.

„   *See* Mr **Patrick,** King's College of Aberdeen.

„   servant woman, Wester Collonoch, Dumbennan, II. 418

„   *See* **John,** Craigstoune.

„   *See* **Adam,** deceist of Glenbucket.

„   *See* **John,** tutor of Glenbucket, Peterhead.

„   *See* **James,** Kirktoune of Rayne.

„   *See* **Alexander,** Threefield, Bonitoun.

Hendry, of Avachy, Kinnoir; Anna, his sister, 15 years; Elizabeth, his
        youngest sister, 12 years II. 426, 427

„   gentleman and tennent, Mill of Collithie, Gartly, and his wife, and
        Robert, Harie, George, Jean and Margrat, his children. II.
        446.

„   gentleman tennent, Droumheid, Ruthen, and his wife. II. 431.

Hugh (deceist), of Kirkhill, Kinethmond; his relict, Elizabeth Hay, married
        to Thomas Abercrombie, gentleman, Kirkhill, Kinethmond   I.
        491.

„   gentleman, Scotshall, Insch , Jean Duncan, his spouse ; George, Alex-
        ander, William and Patrick, his sons , Christian, Marjorie,
        Rebecca, Issobell, his daughters. I 249.

Hugo. *See* **Alexander,** Old Aberdeen.

„   tennent, Ellenmor, Kindrocht   I. 130

Issobell. *See* **James,** junior, Aberdeen.

„   *See* **Robert,** Aberdeen.

„   *See* **Robert,** elder, merchant, Aberdeen

„   servant, Aberdeen. II. 606.

„   servant, Aberdeen. II. 598.

„   wife of John Steuart, gentleman tennent, Maynes, Auchterless
        II. 384

„   *See* **Patrick,** Bracklamore.

„   *See* **John,** of Cocklarachy.

„   cottar, wife of William Hiltoun, cottar and a tradesman, Wester
        Collonoch, Dumbennan. II. 419

„   wife of William Dickie, weaver, Wester Corthieram, Lonmey. II
        41.

Issobell. *See* **John,** Coulie

„ Little Erdo, Methlick. II. 221.

„ servant, Keir, Balhelwie. II. 525

„ a little lass, servant, Nethertoune, Glenbucket. I. 519

„ servant, Glenmallen, Forgue. II 396

„ servant, Invereis, Kindrocht. I. 136

„ *See* **James** or **John,** Knockespock.

„ servant, Pitsligo. II. 87

„ servant, Prevon, Glass. II. 462

„ *See* **Hugh,** Scotshall

„ wife of William Thomsone, tennent, Seggeden, Kinethmond. I. 486.

„ *See* **George,** of Sweltoun

„ mother of John Littlejohn, sub-tennent of George of Sweltoun, Dumbennan II. 415.

„ cottar woman, Wester Craigie of Tarves, Tarves. II. 192.

„ servant, Thaynestoune, Kinkell I 349.

„ Tilitermont, Ruthen II. 432

„ servant. *See* **William,** Toloch

„ cottar, wife of John Smith, cottar, Westertoun, Dumbennan. II 418.

„ servant, Windiheads, Aberdour. II 67

Jacabona. *See* **Adam,** of Glenbucket

James. *See* **[Alexander],** Provost, Aberdeen

„ younger, merchant, Aberdeen II 631.

„ junior, Aberdeen, and his wife, and Alexander, Issobell and Janat, his children. II 628

„ weaver, Aberdeen, and his wife. II 610

„ tennent, Achmedy, Cabrach ; Isobell Reid, his wife, James, his son. I. 522.

„ *See* **James,** *supra*

„ *See* **John,** Achmedy.

„ gentleman, and principal tennent of the Tounes of Achmull and Lonend, Kinnoir, with his wife, James, Alexander, Jean, Elizabeth and Anna, his children, [   ] Barclay, his mother. II. 428.

„ *See* **James,** *supra*.

„ of Achredy, Ellon, his wife and eldest son II 255

„ *See* **William,** Adamstoun

James, no trade, cottar, Ardachie, Glengairdine. I. 170
,, of Ardmellie (portioner of Logie), Crimond II. 48.
,, servant, Arnedg, Ellon. II. 251.
,, grassman, Auchanachie, Ruthen, and his wife II 435.
,, servant, Auchendrume, Ruthen. II. 430.
,, tennent of the Laird of Craig of Auchindor and gentleman fermer, Milne of Auchindor, Auchindore, and his wife, and his sone, and two daughters. I. 506, 507.
,, gentleman tennent, Westertoun of Auchleuchries, Cruden, Elizabeth Leslie, his spouse. II 131.
,, elder of Auchlyne, Cleatt, his lady and daughter; Commissioner appointed for the parish of Cleatt I. 463, 469.
,, younger of Auchlyne, Cleatt, principal heretor of the lands of Cleatt, Newbiging and Auchminzie, his lady, two sons and two daughters. I. 463, 464.
,, tennent, Auldivallach, Cabrach, Janet Clerk, his spouse I 523
,, *See* **William,** Milne of Avachy.
,, gentleman, brother to the Laird of Badenscoth, Old Machar, Margaret Moir his wife ; a daughter called Mary. II. 564
,, sub-tennent, Balmurell, Crathie, and his wife. I 150
,, tennent, Bellandore, Glenmuick, and his wife. I 176.
,, weaver, Bogfoutouns, Forgue. II. 410
,, Bolnean, Tullich, and his wife. I. 158.
,, *See* **Robert,** Bottarie.
,, *See* **John,** Bottarie.
,, servant, Burnend, Ellon. II. 251.
,, and William, factors for the Lands of Buthlay, Longside. I 596.
,, Clocharbie, Kingedward, and his spouse. II. 320
,, sub-tennent, Wester Clova, Kildrumey. I. 500.
,, tincler, Cobairdie, Forgue, and his wife II. 401.
,, *See* **John,** of Cocklarachy.
,, tennent, Coldholme, Migvie, and his wife. I. 2, 3.
,, cottar, Mill of Collithie, Gartly, and his wife. II 447.
,, gentillman tennent, Comry, Ruthen, and his wife, and Alexander and Jane, his children. II. 433.
,, tennent, Corebeg, Glengairdine, and his wife I. 165.
,, yeaman tennent, no trade, Cowhill, Fyvie, and Issobell Blackhall, his wife II. 277, 287.
,, *See* **George,** Craigmelie

James, servant, Creaghall, Ellon. II., 258.

  „   servant, Cushney, Keirn. I. 446

  „   gentleman tennent, Daach of Kinnoir, Kinnoir, and his wife, and Thomas, James, Christian, their children. II. 425.

  „   *See* **James,** *supra*

  „   elder, of Daach, gentleman, Commissioner appointed for the parishes of Ruthen and Botarie II. 429, 435.

  „   cottar, no trade, Davieshill, Foverane, and his wife. II 165.

  „   Denend, Udnie, his wife and two daughters. II. 182.

  „   Douniehills, Peterhead, Jean Robertsone, his spouse, and Jean, their daughter. I. 566

  „   servant, Dumuoy, Drumblate. II 275.

  „   Mr., Drumblait. II. 274.

  „   *See* **[John],** Fechell.

  „   *See* **George,** Garmoch.

  „   cottar, Loanhede, Greenmyre, Foverane. II 167.

  „   Gullburne Croft, Finglanie, Rhynie, and his mother. II. 453.

  „   tennent of John, of Davedstone, Hillsyde, Botarie, and his wife. II. 441.

  „   cottar, and his wife, Kinkell. I 348.

  „   *See* **Thomas,** Kirktowne.

  „   hird, Knockandach, Lochell. I. 430.

  „   or **John,** tennent of John of Knockespock, Cleatt, Isobell his wife, Alexander his son, William his servant. I. 467.

  „   crofter, Knowhead, Alfoord, and Margaret Sharp, his wife. I. 409.

  „   Sir, of Lesmoir, Drumblate, one of the Commissioners appointed for the parish of Drumblate, his ladey; William, George, Alexander, John, Robert, his sons; Anna, Jean, Margaret, his daughters; Elspet his servant. I. 257, 517; II. 260, 453.

  „   servant, Lessundrums, Drumblate. II. 266

  „   sub-tennent, New Merdrum, Rhynie, and his wife II. 452.

  „   tennent, Mortlach, Ruthen, and his wife. II. 431.

  „   tennent, Overboddom, Insch, and Agnes Jamesone, his wife. I. 252.

  „   gentleman tennent, Parkhaugh, Glass, and his wife (his children, pollable in Murray, not with him) II. 456.

  „   Quilraxe, Tarves II. 204

  „   gentleman, Kirktoune of Rayne, and his spous; Margaret and Helen, their daughters. I. 277

James, wright, Reidheugh, Udnie, and [   ] Findlay, his wife   II. 175.

  ,,   Mr., merchant, Rothemay (deceast).   *See* **Katheren**, his relict; Old
          Aberdeen.

  ,,   tradesman, Brae of Scurdarge, Rhynie, and his wife.   II. 451.

  ,,   tennent, East Maynes, Seatoune, Aberdour, and his wife   II. 72, 76.

  ,,   of Seaton, Old Machar, Poll Commissioner for the parish of Old
          Machar; Marjorie Forbes, his lady, Margaret Scougall, his
          grandchild (no children *in familia*).   II. 552, 562, 563, 571.

  ,,   tennent, Easter Sluie, Kincardin O'Niell, and his wife.   I. 100, 101.

  ,,   Strathgirnick, Glengairdine, and his wife.   I. 167.

  ,,   servant, Strathgirnick, Glengairdine.   I. 166.

  ,,   sub-tennent of George of Sweltoun, Dumbennan, and Issobell Forbes,
          his wife.   II. 415

  ,,   Tarfatt, Streichen, and his wife.   I. 603.

  ,,   servant, Tearavell, Skeen.   II. 499

  ,,   Laird of Techmuine, Fraserburgh, one of the Commissioners appointed
          for the parish of Fraserburgh, has a valuation in Rathen Parish;
          his two sons and daughter.   I. 649; II. 90, 95.

  ,,   servant.   *See* **William**, Toloch

  ,,   Cottoune of Tonley, Touch, and Marjorie Makie, his wife   I 416.

  ,,   yeoman, Meiekle Warthill, Rayne, and his wife   I. 273.

  ,,   sub-tennent, Waterton, Ellon, and his wife.   II. 242.

  ,,   tennent, Whitehillock, Auchindore, and his wife.   I. 506, 508

  ,,   tennent, Whitewool, Kinethmond, and Jannet Leslie, his wife.   I
          488.

  ,,   servant, Milltoune of Whithouse, Tullich.   I. 157.

  ,,   gentleman, indweller, Woodhead of Gight, Fyvie, and Margaret Far-
          quharson, his spouse.   II 295

Jane.   *See* **Jean.**

Janet.   *See* **Alexander**, elder, merchant, Aberdeen.

  ,,   *See* **George**, merchant, Aberdeen.

  ,,   *See* **James**, junior, Aberdeen

  ,,   *See* **Robert**, merchant (himself not in the kingdom), Aberdeen

  ,,   servant, Old Aberdeen.   II. 585

  ,,   *See* **Alexander**, of Barrack.

  ,,   servant.   *See* **Alexander**, of Barrack.

  ,,   spouse to William Mackie, Brandsbutt, Inverurie.   I 357

  ,,   servant.   *See* **John**, of Cairnborrow.

  ,,   *See* **John**, of Cocklarachy.

Janet and Elspet, sisters, cotter women, Corsgights, Auchredie II 4
,, servant. *See* **John**, Creagihead.
,, *See* **George**, Craigmelie
,, spouse of George Cruickshank, elder, tennent, Edingerack, Premney. I 245
,, servant, The Maines, Ellon II 246
,, indweller, Maynes of Fyvie, Fyvie, and Agnes Wood, her daughter, past sixteen years. II 278
,, wife of James Mackie, cottar, no trade, with Dame Elizabeth Urquhart, Duager of Gight, Maynes of Gight, Fyvie II 291
,, *See* **Robert**, Milne of Raves of Huntly
,, servant, Invercauld, Crathie. I. 146.
,, servant, Easter Muress, Tullich. I 160.
,, servant, Peterhead. I. 556
,, spouse to Patrick Birny, Polleye, Oyne I 285
,, mother of Patrick Lessly of New Rayne, Rayne I 279.
,, *See* **George**, of Rothnie
,, servant, Scotstoun, Old Machar. II 572.
,, wife of John Wilke, tennent, Telongouss, Cleatt I 471.
,, servant, Tombae, Glenmuick. I. 174
,, *See* **Adam** (late of Inverebrie), Aberdeen
Jean [*or* **Jane**]. *See* **Alexander**, elder, merchant, Aberdeen
,, *See* **George**, merchant, Aberdeen
,, *See* **John**, elder, merchant, Aberdeen.
,, *See* **Robert**, merchant (himself not in the kingdom), Aberdeen.
,, servant, Aberdeen. II. 601
,, servant, Old Aberdeen. II. 587
,, *See* **James**, Achmull.
,, herd to James, gentleman, principal tennent of the Tounes of Achmull and Lenend, Kinnoir II 428
,, *See* **Alexander**, of Auchmunziell.
,, *See* **William**, Milne of Avachy.
,, *See* **George**, of Badenscoth
,, *See* **Alexander**, of Barrack.
,, wife of Robert Cumming of Birnes, Logie Buchan II 238.
,, *See* **Alexander**, Bogforth
,, *See* **John**, Miln of Bottarie
,, *See* **John**, of Cairnborrow.
,, *See* **Alexander**, of Coldwales

Jean. *See* **Hendrie**, Mill of Collithie.

„ *See* **James**, Comry.

„ daughter of ( ) Gordon of Craig of Auchindoir. I. 505.

„ *See* **John**, Craigstoune

„ servant, Creichie, Fyvie. II. 297.

„ *See* **Patrick**, elder, of Cults

„ *See* **Adam**, younger, Curfidlie.

„ wife to [Patrick] Coupland, minister of Cushney. I. 443

„ *See* **James**, Douniehills.

„ servant, Dumuoy, Drumblate. II. 275.

„ Fetterletter, Fyvie, nice of Jealls Taylor, spouse of Peter Will, yeaman tennent (no trade) II. 295.

„ *See* **Patrick**, Maynes of Gight.

„ *See* **John**, tutor of Glenbucket, Peterhead.

„ *See* **Patrick**, of Harlaw, Aberdeen.

„ wife of George Petrie, messenger, Rawes of Huntly, Dumbennan. II. 422.

„ servant, Kebettie, Midmar. I. 190.

„ *See* Sir **James**, of Lesmoir.

„ *See* **George**, Millden

„ wife of Peter Anderson, grassman, Newseat, Culsalmond. I 269.

„ *See* **Nathaniell**, Newnoth.

„ *See* **George**, of Rothnie.

„ servant, Scurdarge, Rhynie. II. 450

„ servant, Skeen. II. 497.

„ wife of William Lumsden, tennent, Stonebridges, Kildrumey I 503.

„ servant *See* **Thomas**, Tombreak.

John, late baillie, Aberdeen, and his wife and Alexander, George and John, his children. II. 622.

„ *See* **John**, *supra*.

„ litster, Aberdeen, and his wife, and Cathren, his daughter. II 626

„ elder, merchant, Aberdeen, his wife and daughter, Jean. II. 598

„ (deceast), procurator, Aberdeen, Mary Seaton, his relict; Anna, her daughter. II 615

„ saidler, Aberdeen, and his wife. II. 598.

„ servant, Aberdeen II. 621.

„ son to Sheriff Gordon, Aberdeen II 623

„ taylor, Aberdeen, and his wife; no child of age. II. 599.

John, Master, Commissar Clerk of Old Aberdeen; Elizabeth Irvine, his wife, and three children II. 552, 571, 592.

　,,　　Laird of Abergeldie, Crathie, Mrs. Bettie Ross [Rose] his lady. I. 150, 151, 166, 171.

　,,　　Abergeldie, Crathie, and his wife I. 152.

　,,　　gentleman tennent, Nether Achirie, and in Bridgend, Cruden, and Margaret Forbes, his spouse; Patrick and Anna, their children. II 105, 117.

　,,　　small tennent at Achmedy, Cabrach, and his wife; James, his brother; Janet Couper, his mother, widow. I. 522.

　,,　　tennent, Acholie, Glenmuick, and his wife. I. 178.

　,,　　*See* **William,** Adamstoun.

　,,　　of Knockespock, being ane heritor in Cleatt Parish, principal tennent for the time, of the toune and lands of Arclach, Dumbennan; Mary, his wife; John, his eldest son, 20 years; Alexander, his second son, 8 years, Elizabeth, his daughter, 12 years. Commissioner appointed for the parish of Dumbennan; Rachell, servant. I. 467; II. 413.

　,,　　*See* **John,** of Knockespock, *supra.*

　,,　　tennent, Ardally, Invernochtie, and his wife. I 539.

　,,　　tennent, Ardhunchar, Kildrumey. I. 497.

　,,　　tennent, Ardmenach, Glenmuick, and his wife. I. 176.

　,,　　gentleman fermer and tennent, Newtoune of Auchindor, Auchindore, and his wife, and his daughter, of one year of age. I. 506, 507

　,,　　servant, Mayns of Auchinive, Tarves. II. 191.

　,,　　Laird of Auchleuchries, Cruden, one of the Commissioners appointed for the parish of Cruden; Elizabeth Grant, his lady, and Patrick, his son. II. 102, 129.

　,,　　herd, Auchquharnie, Cruden. II. 132.

　,,　　servant, Maynes of Auchterfoull, Coull I 41.

　,,　　cottar, Balmurell, Crathie. I. 149.

　,,　　younger, sub-tennent, Balmurell, Crathie, and his wife. I. 149.

　,,　　indweller, Over Bellastrain, Glentaner, and his wife. I. 54.

　,,　　cottar, no trade, Bellatrach, Glenmuick, and his wife. I. 173.

　,,　　sub-tennent, Bellnagoun, Aboyne, and his wife. I. 57.

　,,　　*See* **Alexander,** Bogforth.

　,,　　Boghead, Drumblate. II. 272.

　,,　　tennent, The Bogg, Coldstone, and his wife, and Christian, his daughter. I. 18, 23.

John, gentleman tennent of the Earl of Aboyne, Borland, Glentaner, and his wife, and Charles, his son, Wiolet, his servant. I. 50, 51.

„ gentleman tennent, Miln of Bottarie, Botarie, and his wife ; John, James and Alexander, his sons , Jane and Anna, his daughters. II. 439

„ *See* **John,** *supra.*

„ gentleman, Mill of Bourtie, Bourtie. I. 330.

„ Broomhill, Echt, and his wife. I 209.

„ of Cairnborrow, Glass, Poll Commissioner appointed for the parish of Glass ; Elizabeth Innes, his ladie ; Bell Balfour and Jean, his grandchildren ; Elizabeth, a friend within the house ; Thomas, Janet, Margarett, servants. II. 455, 458.

„ cottar, Daach of Cairnwhelp, Botarie, and his wife. II. 436

„ servant, Daach of Cairnwhelp, Botarie II. 436

„ cottar, Daach of Cairnwhelp, Botarie, and his wife. II. 437.

„ *See* **Adam,** Easter Camphell.

„ Laird of Cocklarachy, Drumblate, and his lady, and Jannet, his sister ; George, Alexander and James, his sons, and Christian, Anna and Issobell, his daughters, the said children being under 16 years ; Margaret his servant. II. 271.

„ Cocklarachy, Drumblate, and his wife II. 272.

„ herd. *See* **William,** Codraine

„ *See* **Alexander,** of Coldwales.

„ sub-tennent, Colestone, Coldstone, and his wife. I 19.

„ tennent, Toune of Comistee, Forgue, and his wife. II. 412.

„ tennent, Corilar, Gartly, and his wife. II. 443

„ gentleman tennent, Cormellat, Ruthen, and his wife ; John and Alexander, his sons. II. 431.

„ *See* **John,** *supra.*

„ tennent, Coulie, Udnie, and his wife, and John and Issobell, their children II. 179

„ *See* **John,** *supra.*

„ The Laird of Fechell, Ellon ; Mrs. May and ( ) Gordones, his grandchildring ; James, his grandchyld. II. 257.

„ tradesman, Coull, and his wife. I. 37

„ weaver, Brae of Coynach, Deer, and his wife and daughter. I. 629.

„ *See* **George,** Craigmelie.

„ living for the time at Craigstoune, Kingedward, his valued rent being in the parish of Old Deer, and Jeane Lindsay, his wife ; Agnes, Jeane and Helen, his daughters. II. 327.

John, gentleman tennent, Cranstoune, Kildrumey ; Christian Leith, his
       spouse ; Alexander, his son. I. 502, 503.

  „   gentleman tennent, Creagihead, Ruthen, and his wife, and John, Alex-
       ander, Patrick, Anna and Bessie, his children ; Janet, his
       servant. II. 433.

  „   *See* **John,** *supra.*

  „   Mr., Mayns of Culter, Peter Culter, and his wife and daughter. II.
       475.

  „   *See* **Adam,** younger, Curfidlie.

  „   of Davedstone, Botarie ; John, George, Mary and Katren, his children.
       II. 440

  „   *See* **John,** of Davedstone, *supra.*

  „   Dukestone, Cushney. I. 442.

  „   servant, Eastbank, Crimond. II 45

  „   ] Laird of Edinglassie, has a valuation in the parish of Glass. II. 455.

  „   of Edintor, Lochell, not a resident here, but has a valuation. I. 434.

  „   tennent, The Maines, Ellon, and Elspeth Ligertwood, his spouse.
       II. 244, 246.

  „   of Erdo, Methlick. II. 224.

  „   younger of Fechill, Deer, one of the Commissioners appointed for the
       parish of Deer, heretor of the Lands of Reneston ; Jean Mait-
       land, his wife ; Katharine, Ann, Barbara, daughters to Fechill ;
       Katharin, his servant. I. 610, 620 ; II. 229.

  „   tennent, Ferrar, Aboyne. I. 62.

  „   tennent, Formestoun, Aboyne. I. 58.

  „   tennent, New Milne of Foverane, and his wife. II. 150, 151.

  „   servant, Gateside of Fuchell, Tarves. II. 200.

  „   Livetennent-Collonell, Laird of Gight, Fyvie, one of the Commissioners
       appointed for the parish of Fyvie, has a valuation in the parish
       of Logie Buchan ; Dame Mary, his lady, and Mrs. Bettie, his
       daughter ; Margaret his servant. II. 224, 276, 289, 290.

  „   tutor of Glenbucket, Peterhead ; Agnes, his lady ; Alexander, his son ;
       Elizabeth, Helen and Jean, his daughters. I. 569

  „   gentleman, of Kirktoune of Glenbucket, and his wife, and Elizabeth, his
       daughter. I. 521.

  „   tennent, Wester Glentoune, Keige ; Isobell Leitch, his spouse ; John,
       his son. I. 453, 455.

  „   *See* **John,** *supra.*

  „   herd, Haddo, Fyvie. II. 281.

John, of Hallhead, Cushney, one of the Commissioners appointed for the
        parish of Cushney, has valued lands in the parish of Tarland,
        and his ladie ; Patrick, Robert and William, his sons ; Patrick
        and Charles, his brothers ; Margrat, his mother ; Margrat and
        Marie, his sisters ; Alexander, his servant. I 13, 436, 440

[„   Dr.], Laird of Hilton, has valued rent in the parish of Old Machar
        II. 567.

„   *See* **Donald,** Invercauld, Crathie

„   sub-tennent, wyver, Invercauld, Crathie. I. 145.

„   *See* **Robert,** Kandakelle.

„   Meikle Kelle, Methlick, and his wife. II. 213.

„   servant, Kinkell. I. 348.

„   tennent, Town of Kirkhill, Kinethmond, and Jeane Andersone, his wife.
        I. 491.

„   Kirktoune, Echt, and his wife. I. 205.

„   tennent, Kirktoune, Glengairdine, and his wife   I. 166

„   of Knocks, commissioner appointed for the parish of Kinnoir. II. 424.

„   gentellman, and principall tennent of Littel Milne, Ruthen, and his
             wife ; Alexander, Thomas and William, his childring. II 429

„   herd, Miln of Knokleith, Auchterless. II 391.

„   Lark, Cabrach, no stock nor trade, and his wife. I 526

„   Laird of Law, Kinethmond, one of the Commissioners appointed for
             the parish of Kinethmond ; Anna Irvine, his ladie ; Arthur, his
             son. I. 484, 492

„   hird, Fermtoun of Lenturk, Lochell   I 435.

„   *See* Sir **James,** of Lesmoir

„   merchant, Mill of Kincardine, Kincardin O'Niell. I. 115.

„   elder, gentleman, of Mill of Kincardine, Aboyne, and his wife. I. 68.

„   *See* **George,** Millden.

„   tennent, New Morlichie, Kinbetach ; Margaret Reid, his spouse   I
        528

„   and his mother, Mueress, Tullich. I. 162.

„   tennent, Mueress, Tullich, and his wife. I. 162.

„   tennent, Mueress, Tullich, and his wife. I. 162.

„   of Myrestoune, his lands of Coynach, Deer. I 629.

„   of Nythermoor, Auchredie, one of the Commissioners appointed for the
             parish of Auchredie ; Elizabeth, his spouse ; George, Anna,
             Elizabeth, his children. II. 1, 10, 11.

„   gentellman and tennent, Overhall, Ruthen   II. 433.

John, tennent, Maynes of Philorth, Fraserburgh, and his daughter. II. 101.

,,   weaver, Pitsligo, and Magdalin Club, his wife. II. 80.

,,   Putmurchie, Lumphanan, and his wife. I. 128.

,,   cowherd, Kirktoune of Rayne, Rayne. I. 278

,,   servant, Strathaneltrie, Coull. I. 42.

,,   *See* **George,** of Sweltoun.

,,   servant, Mayns of Thorntoune, Bourtie I. 335.

,,   tennent, Tilitermont, Ruthen, and his wife. II. 432.

,,   tennent, Torniechelt, Cabrach ; Elizabeth, his spouse. I. 522.

,,   Laird of Rothimay, Lands of Towie, Fyvie. II. 314.

,,   tennent, Whyteside, Rathen, and his wife and mother-in-law. I. 639, 640.

,,   servant, Windiheads, Aberdour II. 68.

Katherine, spouse of William Grant of Creichie, Fyvie. II. 297.

,,   *See* **John,** of Davedstone.

,,   *See* **John,** younger, of Fechil.

,,   servant. *See* **John,** younger, of Fechil.

,,   relict of Mr. Alexander Forbes of Foveran. II. 149.

,,   Old Aberdeen, relict of Mr. James, merchant at Rothiemay ; Lues, her son, ane gentleman ; George, his brother. II. 586.

,,   sister. *See* **Alexander,** of Pitlurg, Kinmundy.

,,   wife of James Young, tennent, Seggeden, Kinethmond. I. 486

,,   of Mill of Skellmure and Quorthiecrame, Deer. I. 633.

Lewis, physician, Aberdeen. II 632.

,,   *See* **Katheren,** Old Aberdeen

,,   gentleman, deceist, of Belnastryne ; Margaret Irvine, his widow, Milne of Lenturk, Lochell. I. 435.

,,   servant, Miltoune of Cults, Tarland. I 10.

Magdalen, servant, Currfuttachie, Kincardin O'Niell. I. 110.

Margaret. *See* **Robert,** merchant (himself not in the kingdom), Aberdeen.

,,   *See* **William,** merchant (alias Bogie), Aberdeen

,,   servant, Aberdeen. II. 614.

,,   servant. *See* **Robert,** stabler, Aberdeen.

,,   servant, Aberdeen. II. 610.

,,   *See* **William,** Adamstoun.

,,   spouse to Alexander Ergo, grassman and smith, Auchleuchries, Cruden. II. 130

,,   Auchmaludies, Auchredie ; Elspet and Issobell Cummings, her daughters. II. 8.

Margaret, servant, Bithney, Forbes. I 449.

" spouse to James Davie, weaver, Blackhall, Inverurie. I. 363.

" *See* **Alexander,** Bogforth.

" mother of Alexander Mackenzie, weaver, Bogfoutouns, Forgue II. 411.

" wife of John Rainy, tennent, Upper Bracka, Pitsligo. II. 79

" servant, Burntstane, Toune of Burnfield, Kinnoir II. 428.

" servant. *See* **John,** of Cairnborrow.

" servant. *See* **John,** of Cocklarachy.

" *See* **Alexander,** of Coldwales.

" *See* **Hendrie,** Mill of Collithie.

" *See* **George,** Craigmelie.

" daughter-in-law of John Wilson, tennent at Darley, Auchterless. II. 381.

" wife of Alexander Walker, tennent, Alehouse of Drumbeck, Udnie and Susanna, servant. II. 173.

" spouse to William Hay, tennent, The Maines, Ellon, and her son. II. 244.

[" Learmont] Lady Duager of Lessmore, Daach of Essie, Rhynie; her husband was a knight baronet. II. 454

" wife of Thomas Chalmer, grassman, Mid Garnestoune, King-edward, II. 332.

" servant, Geach, Cabrach. I. 524.

" servant. *See* **Livetennent-Collonell John,** of Gight.

" *See* **Adam,** of Glenbucket

" *See* **John,** of Hallhead (mother).

" *See* **John,** of Hallhead (sister).

" servant, Rawes of Huntly, Dumbennan. II 419.

" spous to James Petrie, merchant, Rawes of Huntly, Dumbennan II. 420.

" wife of William Thomson, tennent, Knockespock, Cleatt. I. 468.

" *See* Sir **James,** of Lesmoir.

" maid-servant of the Laird of Lethendie, Logidurno. I. 298.

" *See* **George,** Millden.

" cottar woman, Mains of Nethermure, Auchredie. II. 11.

" *See* **Alexander,** indweller, Old Aberdeen.

" Old Aberdeen, relict of Mr. John Lundie, humanist in the King's College of Aberdeen II. 588.

Margaret. *See* **Adam**, Old Meldrum.
,,   ` *See* **Christian**, Old Meldrum
,,   tennent, Overboddom, Insch. I. 252.
,,   wife of Thomas Forbes, shoemaker, Newtoun of Premny, Premney I 241.
,,   grasswoman, Quithell, Deer. I. 636.
,,   servant, Nether Robiestoune, Dumbennan. II. 423.
,,   *See* **James**, Kirktoune of Rayne.
,,   *See* **George**, of Rothnie
,,   cottar, spouse to John Moir, cottar with Alexander, Sandieston, Dumbennan II. 421.
,,   *See* **Alexander**, Sandieston
,,   servant, Brae of Scurdarge, Rhynie. II. 451.
,,   servant, Seggeden, Kinethmond. I. 486.
,,   *See* **Alexander**, Strait Craigs.
,,   wife of [John Walker], the Parson of Tillinessell. I. 484.
,,   wife of John Menzie, Tolach, Cleatt. I. 474.
,,   widow, Wingstoun, Dumbennan II 417
Marjorie, Little Auchredie, Auchredie II 21.
,,   Auchmunziell, Auchredie; Christane Webster and Jannet Mathers her daughters II 27.
,,   spouse to John Pierie, merchant, Bethelnie, Old Meldrum. I. 328.
,,   spouse to James Thomson, notar publict, Cornhill, Knowhead, Kinbetach. I. 528.
,,   a friend in the house of John Farquharson of Fortrie, Blairmormonth, Lonmey. II. 33.
,,   servant, Glenhead, Kemney I 371.
,,   grasswoman, Glenstone, Culsalmond. I. 262.
,,   servant, Newbrough, Foverane. II. 169.
,,   and Helen, Old Aberdeen. II. 593
,,   spouse to James Strachan, Old Meldrum, Bethelnie. I. 328.
,,   *See* **Hugh**, Scotshall
Mark, no trade, sub-tennent, The Maynes, Aberdour, and his wife. II. 71.
Mary, daughter-in-law of John Cordiner, tennent, Mill of Allathan, Udnie. II 174.
,,   *See* **John**, of Knockespock, Ardach.
,,   *See* **James**, brother to the Laird of Badenscoth, Old Machar.
,,   *See* **Alexander**, of Barrack

Mary, servant, Bellamore, Glenmuick. I. 175

„   spouse to John Robertsone, Buchanstoun, Oyne I 285.

„   daughter of Gordon of Craig of Auchindoir, Auchindore. I. 505

„   servant, Crimond. II. 44.

„   servant of the Earle of Erroll, Cruden. II 103.

„   *See* **Adam,** younger, Curfidlie.

„   *See* **John,** of Davedstone.

„   wife of James Alexander, grassman, Daviot I. 315.

„   (Dame). *See* Livetennent-Collonell **John,** of Gight

„   laufull daughter to the deceast Sir George, of Gight. *See* **George,** Earle of Aberdeen.

„   *See* **John,** of Hallhead .

„   *See* **Robert,** Milne of Rawes of Huntly.

„   wife of Patrick Thomsone, merchant, Toun of Kirkhill, Kinethmond. I. 491.

„   wife of George Dyce, Knows of Durno, Logidurno. I. 293.

„   *See* **Alexander,** of Pitlurg, Kinmundy.

„   servant, Rora, Longside. I. 580.

„   *See* **George,** of Sweltoun.

Nathaniell, gentleman, Newnoth, Rhynie, and his wife, and Anna and Jean, his children , Agnes Hamilton, his mother-in-law; Thomas, her son. II. 452

„   of Old Noth, one of the Poll Commissioners for the parishes of Rhynie, Essie and Cabrach. I. 522 ; II. 448.

Patrick [*or* **Peter**], Mr , gentleman, humanist in the King's College of Aberdeen ; Mr Thomas, his son , Helen, his daughter II. 593.

„   Aberdeen, and his wife II. 611.

„   *See* **William,** merchant, alias Bogie, Aberdeen   II. 626.

„   Anna Cumeing, Aberdeen, relict of [Alexander] Leask, minister, Maryculter, gentleman ; William and Alexander, her children , Patrick and George Gordon, her grandchildren   II. 614

„   deceast. *See* **Alexander,** of Barrack.

„   tennent,· Bracklamore, Aberdour, and his wife, and Patrick and Isobell, his children. II. 63, 67.

„   *See* **Patrick,** *supra.*

„   *See* **John,** Nether Achirie.

„   gentleman tennent, Crofts of Nether Ardmachron and Dykesyde, Cruden ; Janet Stewart, his spouse. II. 105, 121.

„   *See* **John,** of Auchlewchries.

Patrick.   *See* **George,** Wastertoun of Auchlewchries

,,   tènnent, Broadsea, Fraserburgh. II 91.

,,   merchant, Kirktoune of Cabrach   I 525

,,   *See* **John,** Creagihead.

,,   gentleman, Culsh, Kildrumey   I. 497, 500

,,   elder, of Cults, Kinethmond, and his ladie ; Patrick and William, his sons ; Jean and Elizabeth, his daughters. I. 489.

,,   *See* **Patrick,** *supra.*

,,   servant, Meldrum, Bethelnie. I 319

,,   Little Erdo, Methlick, and his wife   II. 218

,,   younger, Little Erdo, Methlick, and his wife   II. 218.

,,   seaman, Fraserburgh, and his wife   II. 98

,,   weaver, Mayns of Frendraught, Forgue, and his wife and daughter. II. 405.

,,   tennent, Geach, Cabrach, and his wife ; Alaster, his servant. I. 523.

,,   cottar, no trade, with Dame Elizabeth Urquhart, Duager of Gight, Maynes of Gight, Fyvie, and Jean, his wife. II 291.

,,   son. *See* **John,** of Hallhead.

,,   brother *See* **John,** of Hallhead.

,,   of Harlaw, residenter in Aberdeen, has a valuation in the parish of Logidurno, and his wife, and William and Jean, his children. I. 291, 305 ; II. 625.

,,   of Haugh, Tullich. I. 159.

,,   sub-tennent, Kemney, and his wife   I. 367.

,,   *See* **Robert,** Milne of Kinnoir.

,,   tennent, Milltoune, Glenmuick, and his wife ; Patrick, his servant. I. 176.

,,   servant. *See* **Patrick,** *supra*

,,   of Nethermoor, Auchredie , Anna Strachen, his wife ; William, his son. II. 10.

,,   Newtoun of Premny, and Issobell Couper, his spous. I 241.

,,   Rathen, and his wife. I 645.

,,   *See* **Hugh,** Scotshall.

,,   servant, Mayns of Tillet, Tarves   II. 190.

,,   cottar (no trade), Mill of Udney, Udnie, and his wife. II. 184

Penelopy.   *See* **William,** Milne of Avachy

Rachel, servant   *See* **John,** of Knockespock, Arclach

Rebecca.   *See* **Hugh,** gentleman, Scotshall

Robert, merchant (himself not in the kingdom), Aberdeen, and his wife, and Janet, Margrat, Issobell and Jean, his children. II. 605.

,, elder, merchant, Aberdeen , no wife ; Daniell, Issobell and Elizabeth, his children. II 625.

,, junior, merchant, Aberdeen. II. 602.

,, servant of Patrick Culbert, barber, Aberdeen. II. 605

,, servant, Aberdeen. II. 632

,, servant. *See* **William,** younger, merchant, Aberdeen.

,, stabler, Aberdeen, and his wife, and Andrew, his son ; Andrew and Margrat, his servants II. 615.

,, son of Mr. Arthur, gentleman, deceast, Aberdeen II 623.

,, *See* **George,** merchant, Aberdeen.

,, *See* **George,** taylor, Aberdeen.

,, *See* **William,** merchant, alias Bogie, Aberdeen.

,, tennent, Abergarden, Glengairdine, and his wife. I. 165

,, *See* **William,** Adamstoune.

,, servant, Auchterlons, Ellon. II. 256

,, tennent of George, of Badenscoth, Darley, Auchterless, and his sister. II. 380, 381.

,, tennent, Birkenbrewll, Auchindore, no gentleman, no trade, one of the Commissioners appointed for the parish of Auchindore, and his wife. I 505, 516

,, gentleman tennent, Miln of Bottarie, Botarie, and his wife ; James, Anna and Elizabeth, his children II 438

,, *See* **Hendrie,** Mill of Collithie.

,, tennent, Dorlathers, Turreff ; Jean Massie, his wife, and his daughter II. 359

,, *See* **Adam,** of Glenbucket.

,, Sir, of Gordounstone, Ryehill, Oyne I. 284

,, *See* **John,** of Hallhead.

,, gentleman and tennent, The Milne of Raves of Huntly, Dumbennan ; Mary Buchan, his spouse ; Hary, his son ; Janet and Mary, his daughters. II 416.

,, merchant and indweller, Rawes of Huntly, Dumbennan (no wife nor bairns) II. 420.

,, tennent, Kandakelle, Glenmuick, and his wife, and Thomas and John, his sons. I 179

,, gentleman, and principall tackseman and tennent, Milne of Kinnoir, Daach of Kinnoir, and wife ; Peter and Anna, his children. II. 425

Robert. *See* Sir **James,** of Lesmoir.

   ,,   cottar, Mennes, Foverane, and his wife. II. 155

   ,,   servant, Newtoune, Culsalmond I. 260.

   ,,   Tillichetly, Alfoord, and Margaret Morgan, his wife I. 412.

Sophia, spouse of Thomas Smith, sub-tennent, Sandend, Cruden II. 134.

Susanna, servant *See* **Margrat,** Alehouse of Drumbeck, Udnie.

Thomas, Mr *See* Mr. **Patrick,** King's College of Aberdeen.

   ,,   merchant, Aberdeen, and his wife , no child of age. II. 599.

   ,,   Achighouse, Kindrocht, and his wife. I. 134

   ,,   cottar, Ardonald, Ruthen, and his wife. II 431.

   ,,   servant, Balvack, Monymusk. I. 376

   ,,   heretour of the Lands of Neather Boddom, Insch I. 250, 251.

   ,,   tennent, Milne of Bridgend, Aberdour II 70

   ,,   servant *See* **John,** of Cairnborrow.

   ,,   apprentice, Millne of Charletoun, Aboyne I. 60.

   ,,   servant, The Mill, Ellon II 259

   ,,   Doctor, of Craigellie, Rathen I. 650

   ,,   weaver, Curbanchrie, Cushney, and his wife I 442

   ,,   gentleman and tennent, Hallgreen, Ruthen, and his wife. II. 429.

   ,,   *See* **Robert,** Kandakelle.

   ,,   *See* **James,** Daach of Kinnoir.

   ,,   cottar, Kirktowne, Forbes, and his wife and James, his son I. 449.

   ,,   *See* **John,** Little Milne, Ruthen.

   ,,   Dr., doctor of medicine, Lonmay Parish , his lady; two sons and two daughters II. 38.

   ,,   *See* **Nathaniel,** Newnoth, Rhynie.

   ,,   crofter, Mean Pleugh, Alfoord, and his wife. I. 399, 400.

   ,,   tennent, Tombreak, Glenmuick, and his wife; Jean, his servant. I. 175.

William, Mr. *See* **George** Earle of Aberdeen

   ,,   merchant, alias Bogie, Aberdeen, and his wife, and Patrick, Robert, Francis, Elizabeth and Margaret, his children. II. 626.

   ,,   younger, merchant, Aberdeen, and wife; Robert, servant. II. 619

   ,,   weaver, Aberdeen, and his wife II. 603.

   ,,   tennent, Acholie, Glenmuick, and his wife. I. 178.

   ,,   gentleman tennent, Adamstoun, Drumblate, clerk and collector appointed for the parish of Drumblate, and his wife, and James, Alexander, Robert, John, his sons, and Margaret and Elizabeth, his daughters. II. 260, 261, 263.

William, grassman, servant of Charles, of Auchanachie, Ruthen, and his wife. II. 435.

,,   grassman, Old Auchindor, Auchindore, and wife; no child. I. 512

,,   *See* **Alexander,** of Auchmunziell.

,,   tennent of the Laird of Auchterelons, Ellon, and Cristan Anand, his wife. II. 256, 257.

,,   Mr., gentleman tennent, Milne of Avachy, Kinnoir, one of the Commissioners appointed for the parishes of Dumbennan and Kinnoir, and his spouse; James and William, his sons; Penelopy and Jean, his daughters. II, 413, 424, 427

,,   *See* **William,** *supra.*

,,   *See* **George,** of Badenscoth.

,,   gentleman tennent, Bankhead, Aberdour II. 71, 73

,,   tennent, Broomhead, Glass. II. 459.

,,   gentleman, Buthlay, Longside, and Elizabeth Martine, his spouse; Charles, Anna, Elizabeth and David, his children. I. 596.

,,   and James, factors for the Lands of Buthlay, Longside. I. 596

,,   tradesman, Calsiend, Udnie, and his wife. II. 174.

,,   servant, Carnie, Botarie. II. 437.

,,   *See* **Alexander,** Claymyres.

,,   gentleman tennent, Codraine, Gartly; John, his herd. II. 446.

,,   · weaver, Milton of Coynack, Deer, and his wife. I 630.

,,   son of (   ) Gordon of Craig of Auchindoir, Auchindore. I 505

,,   hird to (   ) Gordon of Craig of Auchindoir, Auchindore. I. 506.

,,   gentleman tennent, Cragcullie, Dumbennan; Anna Smith, his spouse, George, their son. II. 417

,,   cottar and tradesman, Craigcullie, Dumbennan, and Elspet Adamson, his spouse. II. 416

,,   herd, Nether Creichnalaid, Fyvie. II. 298.

,,   *See* **Patrick,** elder, of Cults.

,,   servant, Cushney. I. 436

,,   tennent, Over Drumbulg, Gartly. II. 447.

,,   servant, Over Drumfoal, Botarie. II. 437

,,   tennent, Ferrar, Aboyne, and his wife. I. 62.

,,   son of Margrat Wilson, tennent, Ferrar, Aboyne. I. 64.

,,   Litle Finersie, Echt, and his wife. I 213.

,,   sub-tennent, Fornat, Skeen, and his wife. II. 488

,,   servant, Foverane, Foverane. II 149.

,,   tennent, Kirktoune of Glenbucket, Glenbucket. I. 521.

William, *See* **John,** of Hallhead.

  ,,   *See* **Patrick,** of Harlaw, Aberdeen.

  ,,   tennent, Hattown, Skeen, and his wife. II 498

  ,,   Mr., minister, Kintore. I. 395

  ,,   Mr , younger, Kintore. I. 395.

  ,,   servant *See* **James** *or* **John,** Knockespock

  ,,   Leyheade, Tullich, and his wife. I. 159

  ,,   *See* Sir **James,** of Lesmoir.

[,,] Sir [seventh] of Lesmoir, deceast. *See* [**Margaret** Learmont], Lady duager of Lessmore, Daach of Essie

  ,,   servant, Drumblate II. 266.

  ,,   tennent, Melgum, Coldstone, and his wife. I 18, 24.

  ,,   *See* **John,** Littel Milne.

  ,,   tennent, Netherfulzement, Auchindore, no trade, and his wife; no child. I. 507, 509

  ,,   *See* **Patrick,** of Nethermoor

  ,,   Elizabeth Cruickshank, relict of William, Old Aberdeen. II. 588

  ,,   of Old Gowell, New Machar, Old Aberdeen, and his wife and five children II 545, 594.

  ,,   chapman, Overboddom, Insch I. 252

  ,,   herd, New Rayne, Rayne. I. 280

  ,,   *See* **George,** of Rothnie

  ,,   *See* **Hugh,** Scotshall

  ,,   servant, Mill of Shives, Tarves II. 204

  ,,   Session Clerk and teacher, Clerk and Collector appointed for the Parish of Streichen, Streichen I. 599, 610.

  ,,   tennent, Torrenbui, Invernochtie, and his wife I. 540

  ,,   gentleman tennent, Toloch, Ruthen; James and Isobell, his servants. II 430.

  ,,   cottar, Toloch, Ruthen, and his wife. II. 430.

  ,,   merchant tennent, Turriffe, and wife and daughters. II 341, 346

  ,,   tennent, Wardheade, Glenmuick, and his wife. I. 176.

  ,,   of Westseat, clerk and collector, appointed for the parishes of Cabrach, I. 522; Dumbennan, II. 413; Kinnoir, II. 424; Ruthen and Botarie, II. 429, Gartly, II. 442; Rhynie and Essie, II. 448; Glass, II. 455

  ,,   servant, Whythill, Ruthen II 430

Wiolet, servant. *See* **John,** Borland

APPENDIX III.

GORDONS AT SCOTTISH UNIVERSITIES.

(1)[1] UNIVERSITY AND KING'S COLLEGE, ABERDEEN, 1601 TO 1860

1773 **Abercromby,** s. of Henry G., min Ardersier; M A. 1777; stud. div
       1777-80. Min Banff 1793-1821.

1817   ,,   **Lockhart,** s of Abercromby G , min. Banff , stud
       div. 1822-25. Min. Greyfriars, Aberd 1828-43

1621. **Adam.**

1627.   ,,   M A. 1631. S. of William G , baillie of Banff, Prof. of Greek
      at Mell

1664.   ,,   Aberdeensh , M.A 1668. S. of James G., min. Kinkell; min.
      New Monkland, Glasgow

1817.   ,,   *See* Mar Coll. 1817.

1826.   ,,   Moray.

1830.   ,,   Sutherland.

1832   ,,   **Annand,** Craig; M.A 1846   [*See* Edinburgh, 1845, *infra.*]

1601   **Alexander.**

1609   ,,   M.A. 1613   Min Glenmuick, Logie Coldstone.

1620.   ,,

1623.   ,,

1628.   ,,

1631.   ,,

- 1633   ,,

1654   ,,   M A 1657.

[1] In the entries under (1) King's College, and (2) Marischal College, the plan has been followed of making the information taken from the University Records end with the first sentence. The next sentence comprises identifications from other sources, and when such differ from identifications given in one or other of Mr. P. J. Anderson's *Officers and Graduates of King's College, Roll of Alumni of King's College,* or *Fasti Academiae Mariscallanae,* they are placed in square brackets

1655   **Alexander,** major, Moray; M.A. 1659

     ,, bajan at Mar. Coll. 1655; minor, Aberdeensh.; M.A 1695.

1660 . ,, Aberdeensh., M.A. 1664.

1664 ,, s. of Pitlurg.

1669. ,, Sutherland.

1670 ,, jr. of Birkenburn.

1672. ,, s. of James G., from Terrisoul.

     ,, s. of Patrick G., at Loath in Sutherland.

1678. ,, Strathbogie, M.A. 1682 (Moray).

1679 ,, M.A. 1683.   S. of Patrick G., Humanist; Humanist, 1695-
        1738.

[1688 ,, pays spoon money.]

1721. ,, major, Foveran; M.A 1725.

     ,, minor, of Garlie, grandson of Kilgower, Sutherland.

1731 ,, s. of Prof. George G.; M A. 1735.   Min.·Kintore 1742-66.

1734. ,, **Henry,** Dublin.

1736 ,, Moray. [Advocate 1752]

1737. ,, Banffsh.

1738. ,, Aberdeensh.

1749. ,, Aberdeensh.

1763. ,, Aberdeensh.

1765. ,, Moray.

1768. ,, Banffsh., M.A. 1772.

1769. ,, s. of Henry G., min Ardersier; M.A 1773; stud. div.
        1773-77. [Tobago.]

1775 ,, Aberdeensh.

1817. ,, Aberdeensh., M.A. 1829. [S. of Alexander G., Huntly;
        B.A. Oxon. 1842 ; M.A. 1847 ; Hackney, Dalston.]

1832. ,, Cabrach; M.A. 1846 [LL.D. 1853; min Congr. Church,
        Londonderry, Walsall, Leyton, London.]

1837. ,, Old Machar; M.A. 1841; stud. div. 1841-42. Sch. Old
        Aberdeen.

1839. ,, Forres.

1846. ,, Fordoun.

1854 ,, Rothiemay; M.A. 1858.   Min. F.C., Lethendry.

1738.   **Archibald,** Banffsh.

1641.   **Arthur,** M A , 1648. [Advocate 1661.]

1820. ,, **Forbes,** originally Arthur Forbes. [Of Rayne, W.S. *infra.*]

1647.   **Charles,** Moray; M.A. 1651.

1655 ,,

1668.	**Charles,** Aberdeensh
1672.	„	Aberdeensh.; M.A. 1676 Min. Campvere 1686-90, Dalmeny 1691-95, Ashkirk 1695-1711 ; prof. div. 1698, declined
1673.	„	s. of Straloch ; M.A 1682.
1676.	„	Keith.
1723.	„	Buchan ; M.A. 1727.
1729.	„	[**Hamilton**], Ross. [Advocate 1735, *infra*.]
1735.	„	Aberdeensh.
1752.	„	*See* Mar. Coll. 1751.
1756	„	Aberdeensh. [M.A. Harvard 1762.]
1799	„	Aberdeensh M D Edin. 1810
1806	„	Sutherland.
1815.	„	Sutherland , (*see* Edinb. 1819); stud div 1821-22. [S of George G., min. Loth.; min. Assynt 1825-43; F.C.]
1822.	„	Aberdeensh.
1831.	„	Midlothian.
1851.	„	**R. H. D.,** Glass; M.A. 1855, stud. div. 1855-57. [Sch. Cullen]; min. Seafield, St. Andrews-Lhanbryd
17—.	**Cuthbert,** M.D. 1785.
1641.	**David,** M.A. 1645.
1655.	„	Banffsh.; M.A. 1659.
1814.	**Donald,** Sutherland ; M.A 1819; stud. div. 1819-21 [Sch Farr, Tongue]; min. Stoer 1829-36, Edderton 1836-43 , F.C.
1826.	„	Midlothian.
1680.	**Francis,** M.A. 1684.
1837.	**Fraser.** [S. of Alex. G., Aberdeen ; advocate's apprentice there 1839.]
1613	**George,** M.A 1617. [Brother to laird of Cluny.]
1615	„
1618	„	M.A. 1622.
1630.	„	of Huntly.
1635.	„
	„	yr. of Gieth
1643.	„	M.A. 1647.
1647	„
1648.	„	of Southerland.
1649.	„
1651.	„
1652.	„	s. of Park.
1655	„	M.A 1659. S of Sir John G. of Haddo ; Regent 1659-63 , 1st Earl of Aberdeen 1682.

1665. **George**, Strathbogie.
1667.   ,,   Rothiemay.
1668.   ,,   from Terpersie.
1670.   ,,   yr. of Badinscoth.
1674.   ,,   Aberdeensh
1689.   ,,   M.A. 1693. S. of Prof. Patrick G., 1693-1730.
1696.   ,,   M.D. 1702 [?]. S. of James G., min Banchory-Devenick.
1701.   ,,
1704.   ,,   at Bursary Competition.
1718   ,,   Bogie.
1725.   ,,   M.A. 1730. S. of Prof. George G , Prof. of Hebrew 1730-67
1732.   ,,   **James**, London; M.D. 1758.
1736.   ,,   Aberdeensh.
1739.   ,,   Aberdeensh.
1749.   ,,   **William Algernon**, s. of Theodore G., min. Kinethmont; M.A. 1753; stud. div. 1754-58. Min. Tullynessle 1759-71, Keith 1771-94
1757.   ,,   Farr, Sutherland; M.A. 1761; stud. div. 1761-63. [Min. Clyne, 1764-70.]
1762.   ,,   Sutherland.
1766.   ,,   Strathbogie; M.A. 1770; D.D. 1795. Min. Mortlach 1781-93, Aberdeen 1793-1811.
1770.   ,,   s. of Henry G., min. Ardersier; M.A. 1774.
1772.   ,,   of Hallhead; M.A. 1776. [Advocate 1782, *infra.*]
1805.   ,,   Aberdeensh.; M.A. 1809.
1806.   ,,   Aberdeensh.; M.A. 1810.
1807   ,,   **Huntly**, Banffsh.; M.A. 1812; stud. div. 1812. Sir W. Scott's amanuensis.
1820.   ,,   Caithness.
1823.   ,,   **Henry**, Banffsh.
1835.   ,,   Evie.
1841.   ,,   Assynt.
1854.   ,,   St. Vigeans; M.A. 1858. LL.B. Lond. 1865; asst. prof. Nat. Phil. 1862; teacher, Manchester.
1840. **Gregory**, Inverallen.
1664. **Henry.**
1801.   ,,   Banffsh.; M.A. 1805.
1816.   ,,   **George**, Banffsh. [S. of Abercromby G., min. Banff; Oriental Bank, London.]
1845.   ,,   Durris.
1639. **Hugh**, M.A 1643. Min. Fortingal, Comrie, Row, Cardross, 1654-87.

1784. **Hugh,** Sutherland.
1794.   „   Aberdeensh.; M.A. 1798.
1605. **James.**
1625.   „   major.
       „   minor.
1626.   „   M.A. 1630. Min Kearn [Kinore].
1630.   „   brother of George of Huntly.
1632   „   M.A. 1636. Fifth son of Sir Robert G. of Straloch; min. Rothiemay 1641-86.
1635   „   M.A. 1640. Min. Tough, Alford.
1639.   „
1641.   „
1647.   „   Aberdeensh.; M.A. 1651. S. of John G. of Overhall; min. Knockando 1670-82, Urquhart (Elgin) 1682-89.
1657.   „   (from Mar. Coll.); M.A. 1661. S. of William G., mediciner; min. Banchory-Devenick [?]
1659   „   Strathbogie; M.A. 1663. Min. Glass.
1660.   „   Aberdeensh.
1661.   „   yr. of Rothiemay.
1662.   „   Aberdeensh.; M.A. 1666. Min. Coull.
1663.   „   Strathbogie.
1664.   „   s. of Pitlurg.
1666.   „   major.
       „   Strathbogie, bro. of John G. in same class; M.A. 1670. Min. Rhynie 1680-1716.
1668.   „   Strathbogie.
1676.   „   Enzie.
1677.   „   yr. of Birkenburn.
1679.   „   bro. of Badinscoth.
1680.   „
[1687.   „   pays spoon money.]
1726.   „   Banffsh.
1743.   „   Gartly, 1st burs.; M.A. 1747. [Min Fetlar 1754-1803]
1746.   „   Aberdeensh.
1780.   „   Aberdeensh. [Advocate 1790, *infra.*]
1794.   „   Aberdeensh.
1796.   „   Banffsh.; M.A. 1800.
1798.   „   Angus; M.A. 1802.
1805.   „   Aberdeensh.
1808.   „   Aberdeensh.; M.A. 1812.

1808. **James,** Moray; M A 1812.
1811.   ,,   Aberdeensh.
1825   ,,   Aberdeensh.; M.A. 1829.   M.D. Edin. 1833 ; Old Aberdeen.
1831.   ,,   Elgin.
1851.   ,,   Glass; M.A. 1855.
1614. **John,** major ; M.A. 1618.   D.D. 1635; min. Kirkmichael, Kinedar,
            .   Elgin.
          ,,   minor.
1622.   ,,
1628.   ,,
1640.   ,,   M.A. 1644.
1642.   ,,   M.A. 1646.
1645.   ,,   of Haddo.
1651.   ,,
1652.   ,,   major.
          ,,   minor.
          ,,   yr. of Park.
1654.   ,,   Ross, M.A. 1658   Min Kiltearn 1664-90.
1656.   ,,   s. of Straloch.   From Mar. Coll.   M.A. 1664 ; M.D. 1673 ;
                F.R.C.P. Lond. 1687 ; Kt.
          ,,   Strathbogie.   From Mar. Coll.
1657.   ,,
1660   ,,   Fechil.[1]
          ,,   Aberdeensh.[1]
1665.   ,,   Ross ; M.A. 1669.   From Mar. Coll.
1666.   ,,   major, Strathbogie ; M.A. 1670.
          ,,   minor, Aberdeensh , M A 1670
1668   ,,   major, from Coclarachie.
          ,,   minor, s. of Gordonstone.   [Advocate 1681, *infra*]
1670   ,,   Strathbogie.
1672   ,,   s of Patrick G. at Loath ; M A. 1676.
          ,,   from Seatoun ; M A 1676.   [Hon. burgess, Old Aberdeen, 1682.]
          ,,   Ireland , M.A. 1676.
1674.   ,,   bro. of Patrick G in same class
1678.   ,,   Aberdeensh.
1690.   ,,   [of Glenbucket.]
1697.   ,,
1702   ,,   at Bursary Competition

[1] There is a " John Gordon, Aberdeensh ," among the graduates of 1664, and another among
   those of 1669

17—.   **John,** s. of Dr. John G. of Collystoun; M.D. 1712. *See* Mar Coll.
                1691.

1708.   „
1713.   „
1716.   „   Mar; M.A. 1720.
1730   „   Aberdeensh.; M.A. 1734
1733.   „   Aberdeensh.
1741.   „   Angus; M.A. 1745.
         „   Moray. [Surgeon, army.]
1744.   „   Banffsh.
1745.   „   Aberdeensh.
1763   „   Banffsh.
1766.   „   Ross, M A 1770. Min. Alvie 1788-1805
1787.   „   *See* Mar. Coll. 1787
1788.   „   s. of George W. A G., min. Keith; M A 1792. M D. Edin.
                1805.
1793   „   Banffsh., 1st burs.
1796.   „   Aberdeensh.
1800   „
1802   „   Aberdeensh., M A 1806⎫ [?] ⎧Army surgeon.
         „   „   M.A 1807⎭   ⎩Min. Bolton
1805.   „   Angus, M.A. 1809.
1815   „   Banffsh.
1817   „   Kincardine O'Neil.
1819   „   Aberdeensh.
1822.   „   Banffsh.
1833.   „   Old Machar.
1842   „   major, Forres.
         „   minor, Thurso; M.A 1848. Min. F.C. Edderton
1856.   „   Clatt. [Cong. min England.]
1691. **Kenneth.** [Advocate 1703, *infra.*]
1638. **Lewis,** of Huntly. [3rd Marquis]
1645   „   M A. 1649.
1665.   „   major, Strathbogie; M.A. 1669. Min Aboyne
         „   minor, Strathbogie, M.A. 1669   S of James G., min Rothie-
                may; min. Rothiemay, Kirkcaldy, Kinore 1680-1716
1668.   „   s. of Gordonstoun.
1721.   „   Buchan, M.A. 1725 (Banff).
1740.   „   Aberdeensh
1813. **Mackay,** of Swiney, Caithness. [*See* Edin. Univ. 1817]

1604. **Patrick.**

1606.   ,,

1628.   ',,

1629.   ,,   M.A. 1633   S. of Thomas G. of Kethock's Mill; regent,
                civilist, humanist, prof. of Hebrew 1640-95.

1635.   ,,

1645.   ,,   M.A. 1649.

1648.   ,,

1652.   ,,   Sutherland; M.A. 1659   Sch. Maryculter; min. Coull.

1674.   ,,   yr. of Nethermoor.

1677.   ,,   Aberdeensh.; M.A. 1681.

1682.   ,,   Mearns; M.A. 1686.

1693.   ,,   at Bursary Competition.

1696.   ,,   at Bursary Competition.

[1697.   ,,   pays spoon money.]

1720.   ,,   Strathspey. [Sch. Aberlour, Bellie; min. Enzie, Rhynie,
                Bellie 1731-69.]

1733.   ,,   Aberdeensh

1738.   ,,   Aberdeensh.

1739.   ,,   s. of Prof. George G.; M.A. 1744.   Librarian 1744-47.

1749.   ,,   Aberdeensh.

1773.   ,,   Pennsylvania, s. of Knockespock.

1782.   ,,   s. of George W. A. G , min. Keith.

1797.   ,,   Angus. [Min. St. John's, New Brunswick.]

1829.   ,,   Aberdeensh.

1813.   ,,   *See* Mar. Coll.

1842.   ,,   Cromdale; M.A. 1846; stud. div. 1846-52. [Sch. Advie,
                Tomintoul]; min. Duncansburgh, Cumlodden.

1776. **Pryce,** s. of Henry G., min. Ardersier.   Major in the army.

1711. **Richard,** Aberdeensh.; M.A. 1715. S. of John G., M.A. [not identi-
                fied above]; civilist 1696-1717; Regent, deposed 1717.

1643. **Robert,** M.A. 1647. Sch. Rothiemay; min. Botarie.

1656.   ,,   appt. of Strathloch.

1661.   ,,   Buchan.

1663.   ,,   Strathbogie.

1670.   ,,   s. of Avachie.

1672.   ,,   from Thornibank.

1674.   ,,   Moray.

1675.   ,,   Mar.

1706.   ,,

1718. **Robert,** Banffsh.; M.A. 1722.

1738.   ,,   Aberdeensh.

1742.   ,,   Dornoch; M.A. 1746.

1817.   ,,   Aberdeensh.

1834.   ,,   Keith.

1856. **Samuel,** Clatt; M.A. 1860; B.D. 1869. Cong. mn. Rochester.

1797. **Silvester,** s. of Wardhouse.

1718. **Theodore,** s. of William G. of Drumbuilg; M.A. 1722. Sch. [Mortlach], Cairnie; mn. Cabrach, Kennethmont.

1782.   ,,   s. of George W. A. G , mn. Keith, M.D. 1796. Inspector of military hospitals, Jamaica.

1798.   ,,   Aberdeensh.; M.A 1802; M D. 1814. L R.C.P. 1815; F.R.C.P. 1838 ; surgeon to the Forces.

1610. **Thomas.**

1611.   ,,

1613.   ,,   M.A. 1617. [Brother to laird of Cluny.]

1617.   ,,   M.A. 1621.

1621.   ,,   M.A. 1625.

1665.   ,,   Buchan.

1670.   ,,   s. of Strathloch.

1713.   ,,

1727.   ,,   s. of Prof. George G.; M.A. 1731. Librarian, regent, humanist, prof. of Greek.

1736.   ,,   s. of Thomas G., mn. Lonmay; M.A 1740 [Min. Dundurcos 1747-58, Speymouth 1758-84.]

1770   ,,   s. of Thomas G., min. Speymouth. *See* Mar. Coll. 1770.

1834.   ,,   Old Machar.

1601. **William,** M.A. 1605. Mediciner 1632-40.

1608.   ,,   major.

  ,,   minor.

1638.   ,,

1639.   ,,   of Newton.

1647.   ,,

  ,,   M.A. 1651. [Sch. Monymusk, mn. Bourtie, Edinburgh, Kintore.]

1649.   ,,   M.A. 1661.

1670.   ,,   Strathbogie

1675.   ,,   major, Aberdeensh.

  ,,   minor, Aberdeensh.

1678.   ,,   Moray.

1682.	**William,** M.A 1686	
1689	· ,,	nephew to Gordon of Seaton
1693	,,	
1696.	,,	at Bursary Competition.
1701.	,,	
1713.	,,	
1715	,,	M.A. 1719
1720	,,	Banffsh.
1728.	,,	of Park.
1738	,,	Aberdeensh
1740	,,	major, Aberdeensh.
	,,	minor, Aberlour; M.A. 1744.
1742	,,	Banffsh.
1759.	,,	Sutherlandsh
1764.	,,	Ross.
1767.	,,	Moray; M A. 1771 , stud. div. 1771-74. Min. Elgin 1784-1837.
1778	,,	s of Hallhead; M.A. 1782.
1787	,,	Moray, M D. 1806. [L.R.C.P 1807]; surg. 93rd Foot.
1789	,,	Banffsh
1793	,,	Sutherland.
1795	,,	Aberdeensh.; M A. 1799
1808.	,,	Aberdeensh.
1820	,,	Inverness-sh., stud div. 1824-30.
1823	,,	**Grant,** Moray, M.A 1827 ; stud. div. 1828-30. [S. of William G., min. Elgin.]
1828	,,	Farr.
1832.	,,	Santeren, Portugal
1843	,,	Cabrach; M A. 1847 ; stud div. 1847-51. Min. Glenbucket 1854-63, Glenbervie 1863.
1848.	,,	Speymouth. [S. of min. Speymouth; M.D. Edin. 1854; staff asst. surg. army]
1853.	,,	Cromdale

(2) MARISCHAL COLLEGE AND UNIVERSITY, ABERDEEN, 1601 TO 1860.

1670.	**Adam,** Glenbucket	
1744.	,,	
1786.	,,	s of John G. of Cairnfield. [W.S. 1776, *infra.*]

1813. **Adam**, s. of Alexander, 4th Duke of Gordon [and Jane Christie]. Of Newtongarrie.

1817.   ,,   (bajan at King's Coll.), s. of James G., Craigton, Kincardine O'Neil; M.A. 1821.

1834.   ,,   s. of James G. of Littlefolla.

1619. **Alexander**. S. of William G., burgess, Aberdeen, and nephew of James Cargill.

1628.   ,,

1631.   ,,   [not Lord Auchintoul as in *Fasti Acad. Marisc.*, II. 207 : *supra*, p. (134), *infra*, p. (528)].

    ,,

1633.   ,,   M.A. 1637. Sch. Rothiemay, min Inveraven.

1640.   ,,   S. of John G, burgess, Aberdeen; Sch Rothiemay, min. Kirkmichael.

1650.   ,,   M.A. 1654.

1655.   ,,   *See* King's Coll. 1655.

1677.   ,,

1688.   ,,   Min. Logie Buchan.

1693.   ,,

1698.   ,,   M.A. 1702.

1699.   ,,   M.A. 1703.

1700.   ,,   M.A. 1704, King William Divinity bursar 1706-10. Min. Foveran 1712-26.

1704.   ,,   M.A. 1708. [Author of *Itinerarium Septentrionale*.]

1706.   ,,   of Abergeldie; M.A. 1710. Adv. in Aberd. 1718.

1711   ,,   of Glengerrach.

1720.   ,,   of Hilton; M.A. 1724.

1728.   ,,

1732.   ,,

17—.   ,,   London; M.D. 1737.

1738.   ,,

1748.   ,,   S of Alex. G., Blairtown, min. Kirktown (Jedburgh) 1775-85.

1763.   ,,   of Logie, M.D. 1788. M. Corp. Surg. 1796 ; R.N.

1768.   ,,   M.A. 1772. Min. Daviot and Dunlichity 1781-1801.

1771.   ,,   s. of John G., Birse.

1774.   ,,

1787.   ,,   s. of James G., min. Bellie ; stud. div. 1791-95. [Chaplain, Fort George.]

1798.   ,,

1799. **Alexander,** s. of James G., writer, Peterhead.

1800.   „   s. of George G., min Aberdeen. Surg. H.E.I.C.S.

1805.   „   s of Charles G , adv. in Aberdeen , M A. 1809. Adv. in Aberdeen ; commissary clerk.

1807.   „   s. of Alexander G., merchant, Peterhead.

1809.   „   s. of William G. of Aberdour.

1814.   „   s. of Samuel G., soldier, Aberdeen ; 1st bursar ; M.A. 1818. [Sch. Auchterless] ; min. Forglen 1845.

1818.   „   s. of Alexander G. of Newton

1820   „   . s. of Lewis G., merchant, Aberdeen   Druggist, Aberdeen.

1827   „   s. of Alexander G., captain in East Indies.

1831.   „   s of James G. of Littlefolla

1847.   „   **Herman Adam,** s of Alexander G., sheriff-substitute, Dornoch. [Officer in the army.]

1848.   „   s. of Alexander G , min Forglen. Merchant, Calcutta.

1858.   „   s of Alexander G., bookkeeper, Dublin.

1745. **Andrew,** M.D. 1761. S. of Francis G., surgeon, Fochabers. Chief surg. in one of the hospitals in the W. Indies.

1708. **Arthur,** of Law.

1711   „   of Carnousie

1733 **Benjamin,** from Balbithan.

1668 **Charles,** M.A. 1672.

1680.   „   M.A. 1684   S. of John G. of Comrie ; vicar of Little Baddow, Essex.

1694.   „   of Buthlaw ; M.A 1698   Adv. in Aberdeen 1703.

1719.   „

1725.   „   M.A. 1729.

1739.   „   of Abergeldie ; M.A 1743.

1749.   „

1751.   „   (at King's Coll. 1752-54) ; M.A. 1755 ; stud. div. 1755-58. S. of Peter G , Banff, min. Cortachy 1774-95.

1764.   „   of Buthlaw ; M A. 1768.

1766.   „

1774.   „   s of Patrick G., Aberdeen   Adv. in Aberd. 1783, commissary clerk.

1796.   „   s. of John G. of Edintore, Forres.

1806.   „   s. of George G. of Auchleuchries, M.A. 1810.

1814.   „   s. of Charles G., adv. in Aberdeen. W.S. 1824.

1822.   „   s. of George G. of S Kelpick, Sutherland.

1837. **Charles,** s. of James G. of Littlefolla.
1846.   ,,   s. of James G , Glenmuick. M.D. King's Coll. 1850 ;
        Brazil, Natal.
1831.   ,,   **William,** s. of William G., mercht., Fordoun.
1749. **Cosmo,** of Clunie [Advocate 1758, *infra ;* Lord Rector 1827,
        etc]
1772.   ,, s. of John G., Gartly , stud. div. 1775-80.
1842. **Daniel,** s. of John, farmer, Blair Athole. Min. F C., Montreal.
1702. **David.**
1705.   ,, Adv. in Aberd. 1724.
1738.   ,,
1768.   ,,
1813. **Edward.**
1653. **Francis,** M.A. 1657. S of George G., burgess.
1664.   ,,
1758.   ,, S. of Francis G , shoemaker, Aberd.
1787.   ,, s. of John G. of Craig. Adv. in Aberd 1796. [Ensign
        68th Foot 1784, and Ensign on half pay of 16th Foot, from
        1785 till his death in 1857, aged 84]
1615. **George.**
1616.   ,, medius.
        ,, minor.
1620.   ,,
1670.   ,,
1672.   ,,
1673.   ,,
1676.   ,, s. of Mark G.
1678.   ,,
1679.   ,, of Aradoul.
1681   ,, M A. 1685.
1685.   ,, M.A. 1689.
1688.   ,, M.A. 1692. Min. Rosemarkie 1700-06, Cromarty 1707-49.
1696   ,,
1701.   ,,
1709.   ,, major.
        ,, minor.
1711.   ,,
[*c.* 1716 ,, King William divinity bursar 1721. Min. Bourtie 1723-43,
        Drumblade 1743-63.]

1727.	**George.**
1736.	,,	of Carnucie.
1743.	,,
1750.	,,	M A. 1754. [S. of John G., Huntly.]
1756.	,,
1757.	,,	S. of George G., Gartly.
1761.	,,
1765.	,,	Min. Sorn 1789-1805 ; D.D. Glasg. 1804.
1767.	,,	M.A. 1771.
1775.	,,	s. of William G., Aberdeen ; M.A. 1779.
1782.	,,	s. of Alexander G. of Aberdour.
1784	,,	s. of Adam G., Sutherland ; stud. div. 1787-91. Min. Loth 1802-22.
1801.	,,	s. of George G., min. Aberdeen ; M.A. 1805. [Supng. surg. H.E.I.C.S.]
1803.	,,	s. of Robert G., min. Drumblade ; M.A. 1807. Captain, 42nd Highlanders.
1815	,,	s. of William G., min. Urquhart (Elgin) ; M.A. 1819 ; stud. div. 1819-21. Min. Birnie 1832-93 ; LL.D. 1859
1820.	,,	s of Alexander G. of Newton ; M A. 1824.
1822.	,,	s. of Hugh, merchant, London ; [not M.A.]. (*See* Edinb. 1827) ; min. Knockando 1834-39
1824.	,,	s. of John, farmer, Rhynie , M.A. 1828 ; stud. div. 1833-36. Min. Glenrinnes 1843-63.
1826.	,,	s. of William, M.D Jamaica.
1843.	,,	**Robertson**, s. of Maxwell G , min. Foveran.
1855.	,,	**Huntly**, s. of Charles G., N. of Scot. Bank inspector, Aberd. L.R.C.P. and S. Ed.
1615.	**Gilbert.**
1619.	,,	Burgess 1624.
1674.	,,	S. of Walter G , burgess
1634.	**Henry.**
1641.	,,
1740	,,	Min. Ardersier 1757-64.
1797.	,,	s. of Henry G of Knockespock , M.A. 1801. Indian army.
1619.	**Hugh,** M.A. 1623 Regent 1630.
1821.	,,	s of Robert G., merchant, Lond
1829	,,	s of John G., farmer, Rhynie ; M.A. 1833.
1831.	,,	s. of Hugh G. of Manar.

1639. **J.**
1617. **James.** Dep. keeper of the signet 1631.
1628.   „
1630.   „   M.A. 1634.
1633.   „   M.A. King's Coll. 1636.
1634.   „   Min Drumblade 1659-1662, Kinkell 1662- .
1657.   „   *See* King's Coll. 1657.
[1665.] „   M.A. 1669.
1668.   „   (1).
        „   (2).
1670.   „
1677,   „   major.
        „   minor.
1685.   „
1687.   „   S. of Thomas, bro. to late Laird of Lesmoir; min. Kinloss
            1699-1750
1695   „   M.A 1699. Min Premnay, Bourtie, Alford, Alloa 1706-49.
1696.   „   M.A. 1700. Min Knockando 1712-26
1697.   „
1708.   „   from Daoch.
        „   from Knockespock.
1718.   „   **Brebner,** of Knockespock   Chief judge of Grenada.
1720.   „   major; M.A. 1724   S. of Dr. John G., physician, Aberd.;
            M.D., Professor of Medicine 1734-55.
        „   minor.
1723.   „   guild bursar.
1728.   „
1734.   „   M A. 1738. [Sch. Rhynie 1740-47]; min Cabrach 1747-95.
1738.   „
1741.   „   Dundorcas, min. Bellie 1770-1809.
1767.   „   S. of Thomas G., Crathie.
1771.   „   s. of James G. (now Macgregor), Mortlach; M.A. 1775.
1778   „   s. of Henry G. of Knockespock.
1783.   „   s. of James G., Keith.
1790   „   s. of James G., Kirnemuir; M.A 1794.
1796.   „   s. of William G., Dundee; M.A. 1817.
1804.   „   s of William G., Buchromb; M.A. 1807; stud. div. 1808-11.
1809   „   s. of George G., min. Aberdeen. Surg. H E I.C S.
1819   „   s. of Alexander G., baker, Aberdeen; M.A. 1823. Min.
            Cabrach 1827-49

1821	**James,** s. of Alexander G., capt. Aberdeen militia.
1824.	,,	s. of Francis G., advocate, Aberdeen. M.D Edin. 1830.
1827.	,,	s. of Hugh G. of Manar.
1830.	,,	s of George G., capt. 42nd regt., Drumblade.
1831	,,	s of William G., capt. 92nd regt. [W.S 1852.]
1604.	**John.**
1609.	,,	Regent c. 1616-19.
1613.	,,
1619.	,,
1626.	,,
1630.	,,
1631.	,,
1636.	,,
1637.	,,
1653.	,,	(1).
	,,	(2).
1654.	,,	M A 1658. Regent c. 1664-65.
1656.	,,	See King's Coll. 1656
1660.	,,	See King's Coll. 1660.
1665.	,,	See King's Coll. 1665
1670.	,,	major.
	,,
1671.	,,
1672.	,,	of Embow. [M P. infra.]
1673	,,
	,,	minor, Moray.
1674.	,,	of Brachlie
1677.	,,	major.
	,,	minor.
1678.	,,	of Edenglassie
	,,
1679	,,	Hallhead.
1681.	,,
1686	,,	major.
	,,	minor.
1688.	,,
1691.	,,	S of Dr. John G of Collystoun; M D. King's Coll. 1712; surgeon apothecary, Aberdeen.
1696.	,,	s of Achoynonie.

1697. **John,** M.A. 1701. S. of John G., Newmill of Foveran.

1700.   „   M.A. 1704. Min Glenbucket 1709-17, Gamrie 1717-31.

1702.   „   M.A. 1706. S. of Provost John G., Aberdeen ; min. Deer 1711-18

1710.   „

1714   „   Achanachy.

1717.   „   M.A. 1721.

1718.   „   M.A. 1722.

1720.   „   from Craig; M.A. 1724.

1728.   „

1732.   „   M.A. 1737; D.D. 1764. S. of John G. of Hilton (M D. King's Coll. 1712); min. of St. Paul's Episcopal Church, Aberdeen 1741-89.

1738.   „   of Craig, M.A. 1743. Adv. in Aberd. 1753 ; sheriff clerk.

1741.   „

1747.   „   M.D. 1755. Afterwards John Gordon Cumming of Pitlurg.

1749.   „   of Cairnfield.

1751.   „

1757.   „   S. of James G , Mortlach.

1759.   „   S. of John G., Cairnie.

1760.   „

1761.   „   of Craigmile.

        „   S. of Geo G., late Dean of Guild.

1772.   „   s. of James G of Coclarachie.

        „   s. of William G , Glass ; M.A. 1776 ; stud. div. 1775-79. Min. Strathdon 1782-1803, Duffus 1803-27.

1773   „   s. of George G., Westfolds ; M.A. 1777.

1775.   „   s. of John G. of Pitlurg. Aftds. J. Gordon Cumming Skene of Pitlurg and Dyce ; Lieut.-gen.

1777.   „   s. of James G. in Strathaven.

1779   „   s. of John G of Cairnfield   [Advocate 1789.]

1781.   „   s. of Robert G., Milltown of Noth, Rhynie.

1783.   „   s. of James G., min. Cabrach ; stud. div. 1787-92. Min. Cabrach 1795-1816.

1784   „   s. of Francis G., Oldmeldrum. Adv. in Aberd. 1792.

1785.   „   s. of Patrick G. of Avochie   W.S. 1794

1786.   „   s. of Robert G., Upper Banchory.

1787.   „   major, s. of Charles G., of Wardhouse.

        „   minor, s. of William, mercht , Aberdeen.

1787.   **John,** s. of Lewis G , min. Drainy (from Kıng's Coll. in 1789). Surgeon,
         H.E.I.C.S

1795.   ,,   s. of Thomas G., min. Aboyne ; M A. 1799. Jamaica.

1797.   ,,   s. of John G., Aberdour ; M.A. 1801.   Sch Strichen.

1799.   ,,

1801.   ,,   s. of John G , major, 92nd Foot.

1802.   ,,   major, s of John G., min. Strathdon.   *See* King's Coll. 1802.

           ,,   minor, s. of George G., mın. Aberdeen ; M.A. 1806.   Lıeut.
                Bombay Artillery.

1806.   ,,   s. of James G , M.D. Keith.   L.R.C.S. Ed., Keith.

1810   ,,

1816.   ,,   major, s. of Alexander G. of Newton ; M A. 1820.

           ,,   minor, s. of John G., min. Cabrach , M.A. 1822.

1824.   ,,   s. of Wıllıam G., M.D. Jamaica.

1829.   ,,   s. of Willıam G. of Aberdour.

1831.   ,,   s. of Robert G., farmer, Kirkmichael, Banffsh.

1832.   ,,   s. of Robert G. of Nairn Lodge.

1838   ,,   **Salmon,** s. of William G., M.D. Jamaica.

1844   ,,   s. of Wıllıam G., mercht., Rothiemay ; M.A. 1848.   Min. Eng.
                Presb. Ch., Wharton.

1641.   **Lewıs.** S. of Pitlurg.   M.D.   Dean of Faculty 1664.

1726.   ,,

1755.   ,,

1761.   ,,   M A. 1765; D D Kıng's Coll. 1815.   Min. Drainie 1768-1815,
                   Elgın 1815-24.

1794   ,,   s. of Lewıs G., mın. Draınıe.   Lieut. H.E.I.C.S.

1805.   **Maxwell,** s. of George G., min. Aberdeen ; M.A. 1812 ; stud. dıv.
                   1811-14 Min. Foveran 1815-40   [Not M.A. King's Coll.
                   as in Scott's *Fasti Eccl. Scot.,* iii. 608.]

1830.   **Morison,** s. of Wıllıam G , Elgın.

1606.   **Patrick.** [Burgess 1620, agent to the King of Poland.]

1658.   ,,   S. of Alex. G., weaver burgess.

1664.   ,,

1669.   ,,

1681   ,,   S. of John G., yr., merchant burgess.

1683.   ,,   M A. 1687.

1693.   ,,

1698.   ,,   M.A. 1702.

1699.   ,,   major.

1699. **Patrick,** minor; M.A. 1703. S. of Patrick G , min. Coull; min.
Cushnie 1711-17, Lumphanan 1717-32, Fintray 1733-44.
1706.   „   of Abergeldie.
1729.   „
1732.   „
1735   „
1750.   „
1762   „
1813.   „   s. of John G. of Avochie, W.S.
1652. **R.**
1622. **Richard.**
1593 [?]. **Robert,** of Straloch, M.A. 1597. [? The first M.A. of the College,
Cat. Scot Writers.]
1609.   „
1625.   „
1650.   „   M.A. 1654. Min Dunkeld.
1651.   „
1660.   „   Gordonston. [M.P. *infra.*]
1680.   „
[1682.   „   M A. 1686. *See S. N. & Q*, 2nd ser. ii. 41].
1685   „   M A. 1689. Founder of Gordon's Hospital [?]
1702.   „   M.A. 1706. S of George G., master of Trades' Hospital.
1704.   „   M.A. 1708. Min. Rathven 1715-20.
1752.   „
1753.   „
1754.   „   M.A. 1758.
1765.   „   M.A. 1769; stud div. 1769-73. [Sch. Rhynie 1771-79];
min Drumblade 1795-1820.
1789.   „   s. of John G. of Greeshop, Elgin [W.S. 1798.]
1799.   „   s. of Lewis G., min. Drainie. [Capt., H.E.I.C.S.]
1813   „   s. of John G., min. Cabrach; M.A. 1817.
1818.   „   s. of George G., min. Aberdeen; M.A. 1822; stud. div.
1822-26. Sch. Foveran.
1819.   „   s. of Col. [?] John G., Aberdeen.
1604. **Thomas.**
1631   „
1640.   „
1657.   „
1666   „

1671.	**Thomas.**	
1672.	,,	
1678.	,,	of Lonmay; M.D.
16—	,,	M.A. 1685.
1687	,,	s. of John G., elder, burgess
1688.	,,	Rolland bursar.
1699	,,	M.A. 1703. S. of Lewis G., min Aboyne; min. Lonmay 1709-43.
1722.	,,	M.A. 1726. S. of James G., min. Kinloss; min Cabrach 1740-46, Auldearn 1747-93.
1723	,,	
1757.	,,	of Crathenaird; M.A. 1761; stud div. 1761-63. Min. Aboyne 1784-1826.
1761.	,,	of Licklyhead.
1770	,,	s. of Lewis G , Mortlach; M.A. 1774
	,,	s. of Thomas, min. Speymouth. (From King's Coll. 1770); of Whitburn, W.S. 1782
1775.	,,	s. of John in Pitlurg; M.A. 1779 of Harperfield.
1803.	,,	s. of Charles G. of Cairness. Major-General; historian.
1667.	**Walter.**	S. of Walter G., burgess.
1606.	**William.**	
1618.	,,	
1626	,,	
1627.	,,	
1636.	,,	
1660	,,	
1662-82	,,	Porter of the College.
1666.	,,	M A. 1671.
1677.	,,	[Sch. Auchindoir.]
	,,	minor.
1681.	,,	
1694	,,	The family historian.
1696	,,	unus, s. of Lesmore; M.A. 1700.
	,,	alter; M.A. 1700. S of Alex. G., Mill of Straloch.
1701.	,,	M.A. 1705.
1706	,,	unus; M.A 1710. Sch. Kingussie; min. Urquhart and Glenmoriston 1730-39, Alvie 1739-87.
	,,	alter.
1708	,,	M.A. 1712.

1728 **William,** from Newtile.
1732.   ,,   M.A. 1736. Author.
1743.   ,,   of Fetter Angus, M.A. 1747.
1747.   ,,   M.A. 1751. S. of Thomas G., min Lonmay
1750.   ,,   M.A. 1754.
17—.   ,,   M.A. 1755.
1753.   ,,   S. of John G., Wardhouse
1755.   ,,
1757.   ,,   M.A. 1761. S. of James G., Mortlach; min. Urquhart (Elgin) 1769-1810.
17—.   ,,   LL D. 1765; solicitor at law, Edinburgh
1764.   ,,
1765.   ,,   stud. div. 1769-73. Min. Clatt 1797-1820
1767.   ,,
1775.   ,,   s. of Robert G., Sutherland
1776.   ,,   s. of Charles G. of Abergeldie.
1777.   ,,   s. of George G. of Rothnay. W.S. 1789.
1788   ,,   s. of Alexander G. of Aberdour.
1796.   ,,   s. of William G. of Blelack.
1799.   ,,   major, s. of William G., innkeeper, Aberdeen
      ,,   minor, s. of John G., major, 92nd Foot.
      ,,   minimus.
1809.   ,,   s. of George G , min , Aberdeen   Adv in Aberd. 1825.
1817.   ,,   s. of William G , min. Urquhart (Elgin); M.A. 1821   M.D. Edinb. 1827 ; surg H.E.I.C.S.
1822,   ,,   s. of William G , M.D. Jamaica. Surg H.E.I.C.S , aftds. Jamaica.
1825   ,,   **Robert,** s. of John G., mercht., Gibraltar. Solicitor, Keith.
1828   ,,   s. of William G. [?]. General in the army.
1854   ,,   s. of William G., sharebroker, Aberdeen. Adv. in Aberd. 1864, city chamberlain, town clerk. [LL D , 1903]
1857   ,,   **Forbes Sharp,** s of George G , carter, New Pitsligo ; M.A. 1861. Sch. Auchmedden, Aberdour.

(3) UNIVERSITY OF ST ANDREWS, 1429 TO 1896

14—. **Adam,** B.A. 1457; M.A 1459
14—.   ,,   B.A. 1479, M.A 1481.
1533.   ,,   S Salvator's College; B.A. 1535; M.A 1536 (non comparuit)

14—. **Alexander** de Gordoun, B.A. 1430 [He and 8 others " non tum fuerunt expediti ad gradum Baccallariatus propter pestem nec solverunt totam debitam rectori "] ; M.A. 1433.

[1600.   ,,   *See Earldom of Sutherland*, pp. 239, 314.]

1706.   ,,   S. Leonard's College [" e classe Mri Thomae Tailziour Baccalaureorum Regentis "] ; M.A. 1707.

1781.   .,,   United College.

1839 **Andrew**, Unit. Coll. Min. Logie Buchan 1850.

1823. **Charles**, Unit. Coll.

1840.   ,,   **Alexander**, M.D 1840. K C.B 1897.

1869.   ,,   Newlands, Peeblesshire, Unit. Coll

1891   ,,   Tobago [? M A.], Unit. Coll.

1718. '**Daniel**, S. Salv. Coll ; M.A. 1721.

1827. **Francis**, Unit. Coll.

1867   ,,   Unit. Coll., M.A 1873

1633. **G[eorge]**, " Comitis Sutherlandiae frater germanus," S Salv Coll

1680.   ,,   S. Salv. Coll.

1769.   ,,   Unit. Coll.

1834.   ,, **Hume**, Unit. Coll.

1850   ,,   **R.**, Unit. Coll.

1862.   ,,   Lord Haddo, Unit. Coll. Afterwards sixth Earl of Aberdeen.

1866.   ,,   Monifieth, Unit. Coll.

1867   ,,   **More**, Edinburgh, Unit Coll

1875.   ,,   St. Andrews, M.A 1879.

1896   ,,   Lord Haddo.

1616. **Gilbert**, S. Salv. Coll. , M.A. 1619.

1870. **Henry**, Monifieth, Unit. Coll.

1647. **Hugh**, S. Mary's College

     James, B.A 1437.

1551.   ,,   S. Mary's Coll., " nominatus et electus successor venerabili patri domino Galtero abbati Vallis Lucide. Natio Britan."

1661.   ,,   de Lismor, S. Salv. Coll

1782.   ,,   Unit. Coll

1784.   ,,   Unit. Coll

1839.   ,,   **Fred. Skinner**, Unit. Coll. Min. of Scottish Episc. Ch., D.D

1863.   ,,   Unit. Coll.

1559. **John**, S. Leon. Coll. ; B.A 1562 , M.A. 1563.

1586.   ,,   S. Leon. Coll.

1615.   ,,   S. Leon. Coll.

1627. **John,** " Comes Sutherlandiae," S Salv. Coll

1765.   ,,   Unit. Coll.

1773.   ,,   Unit. Coll

1781.   ,,   Unit. Coll.

1862.   ,,   Unit. Coll.

1863.   ,,   **A.,** St. Andrews

1563. **Patrick,** S. Mary's Coll.

1613.   ,,   S. Mary's Coll

1688.   ,,   [" Reverendus vir Magister Patricius Gordon presbiter receptus est in Album, Jun 1 "] ; B.D. 1690

1545. **Robert,** S. Leon. Coll.·

[1600.   ,,   *Earldom of Sutherland,* pp. 239, 314]

1780.   ,,   Unit Coll.

1827.   ,,   Unit. Coll.

1889.   ,,   **S.,** London, Unit. Coll.

1829. **Thomas,** Unit. Coll.

     William, B.A. 1429

1766.   ,,   S. Mary's Coll

1827.   ,,   Unit. Coll.

1861.   ,,   Unit. Coll.

1886.   ,,   London, Unit. Coll.

(4) UNIVERSITY OF GLASGOW, 1640 TO 1891.

1682. **Adam,** Dean of Faculty 1682.

1640. **Alexander,** M.A. 1644   Min. Inveraray, Largs, Greenock, 1650-1700

1672.   ,,   M.A. 1676.   Min. Kirkcowan, Sorbie 1689-92

1763   ,,   eldest s of John G. of Beldorny.

1749.   ,,   4th s. of William, Earl of Aberdeen   Senator Coll Just., as Lord Rockville.

1776   ,,   ·   2nd s. of Alexander G., mercht., Glasgow

1849.   ,,   eldest s. of Alexander G., villicus, Kilmodan ; M D. 1858   .   Spalding, etc

1882.   ,,   s of William G., insurance agent, Glasgow , M.A 1887 Baptist min. Egremont.

1821. **Allan Maconochie,** 4th s. of Maxwell G., writer, Edinburgh

1676 **Archibald.**

1818   ,,   **Campbell,** 2nd s. of George G., min. Sorn; M.D., C.M. 1826.

1882. **Charles James Mackay,** s. of Robert G., Tobago , M.A. 1887 ; B.A. Oxon. 1892.

1749.	**Cosmo,** 3rd s. of William, Earl of Aberdeen Colonel in the army
1859	**Daniel Miner,** s. of William G., mercht., Pictou, N.S.; M.A. 1863, B.D. 1866, D.D. 1895. Presb. min. Canada; prof. Syst. Theol., Presb. Coll., Halifax
17—	**David,** Hibernus; M.A. 1773
1849.	,, youngest s. of Alexander G , villicus, Kilmodan.
1823.	**Edward,** only s of Charles G., mercht., India.
1836.	**Francis Wright,** youngest s. of William G., mercht., Glasgow
1776	**Gabriel,** 2nd s. of William G., teacher, Glasgow.
17—.	**Gardiner,** Hibernus , M.A., M.D 1775.
1739.	**George,** s of George G., gent. in Newry.
1770	,, eldest s. of Alexander G., mercht , Boston in New England.
1781	,, eldest s. of James G., mercht., Glasgow.
1805	,, 2nd s. of David G., mercht., Edinb
1815	,, eldest s. of George G., min. Sorn
1818	,, **A.,** 3rd s. of Maxwell G., writer, Edinburgh.
1829.	,, **Henry,** eldest s. of John G. of Cairnbulg; M D. 1833.
1884	,, s. of Paul G., Helmsdale; M.B. 1889. Helmsdale, etc.
1843	**Gilbert,** eldest s. of John G., farmer, Ayrsh.
18—	**Hans,** Hibernus; C.M. 1827.
1840	**Henry,** 2nd s. of William G., writer, Dumfries.
1790.	**Hugh,** only s. of Rev. John G., Linlithgowsh.
1855.	,, **Alexander,** b in New Brunswick; M.D. 1859. Prof. Anat. and Med , Dalhousie Coll., Halifax.
1664.	**James,** s. of Craigland.
1669.	,, s. of Hugh G., min Row; M.A. 1673. Min. Rosneath 1682-94.
1722.	,, s. of Robert G. of Langmore.
	,, Ireland.
1729.	,,
1770.	,, eldest s. of William G., Stirling.
1782.	,, b. in India, only s. of John G., nauclerus.
1785	,, 3rd s of James G , mercht , Glasgow.
1822.	,, 3rd s. of Alexander G., Liverpool.
1838.	,, eldest s of William G., writer, Dumfries.
1855.	,, 2nd s. of John G., min. Twynholm. Min. Stobhill, Twynholm.
1859.	,, **Henry,** s. of James G , vet. surg., Whithorn; M.D. 1863. C.M. 1865. Carstairs, etc.
1866	,, s. of Andrew G., mercht., Lanarksh; M.B 1878. Coatbridge, etc.

1629   **John.**
1658.   „
1724.   „   s. of John of Kirkconnel.
         „   M.D. 1750. Surgeon, Glasgow; the "Potion" of *Roderick Random.*
1777.   „   eldest s of John G. of Pitlurg.
1762.   „   eldest s. of James G., mercht, Glasgow.
1764   „   eldest s. of James G, mercht, Glasgow.
1770.   „   eldest s. of George G., M.D. St Christopher; M.A., M.D. 1775
1771.   „   eldest s of Hugh G., farmer, Co. Down.
1785.   „   2nd s. of James G., mercht., Glasgow.
1818   „   T., 2nd s. of Maxwell G., writer, Edinburgh. W.S 1825.
1821.   „   eldest s. of John G, mercht., Glasgow.
1837.   „   only s. of Henry G, mercht, Liverpool.   Advocate 1846.
1847   „   3rd s. of John G., farmer, Ayrsh.
1856.   „   eldest s. of John G., mercht, Glasgow.
1880.   „   **Dyce,** s. of John G., mercht., Garmouth, M.B. 1887. Easdale, etc
1891.   „   s. of Alex. G., cashier, Glasgow, M.B, C.M 1896. High Blantyre.
1744.   **Lockhart,** 3rd s of John, 3rd Earl of Aboyne, LL.D 1752 Judge adv. gen of Bengal 1787.
1800.   **Patrick,** 5th s of James G., mercht., Glasgow
1822.   **Peter,** youngest s. of James G., mercht., Glasgow
1662.   **Robert.**
1693   „   Min. Crossmichael 1702-22.
1702.   „   Ireland
1741.   „   3rd s. of William G, chiliarcha, Jamaica.
1787   „   youngest s. of John G., farmer, Dunscore
1817   „   eldest s of Robert G., mercht., Richmond, Va.
18—   „   C.M. 1827.
1845.   „   6th s of William G, writer, Dumfries.
18—.   „   Hibernus, M.D. 1831.
1878   „   **Pope Ross,** s. of John G, Edderton, M.A. 1882; M B., C.M (Edin.) 1886. Dingwall, Montana.
1822.   **Samuel,** 2nd s of Robert G, farmer, Closeburn.
1682.   **Thomas,** admitted regent; s of Patrick G., regent, King's College
1746   „   **Knox,** 2nd s. of John G., merchant, Belfast.
1809.   „   only s. of William G., artifex, Ireland   O S min. Falkirk.

1815. **Thomas**, 2nd s. of James G., Glasgow.
1843.   ,,   **A.**, youngest s. of Samuel G., farmer, Armagh
1858.   ,,   s. of John G., min. Twynholm; M.A. 1864, B D. 1879.
               Min. Edgerston 1892.
1658 **William.**
1691.   ,,   min. Barr 1699-1724.
1713.   ,,
1739   ,,   s. of William G., mercht., Jamaica.
1748.   ,,   of Fyvie, 2nd s. of William, Earl of Aberdeen.
17—.   ,,   Scotus; M.A. 1766.
1815.   ,,   eldest s of Maxwell G., Edinburgh.
1829   ,,   s. of William G , mercht , Aberdeensh
1860.   ,,   **Leslie**, s. of Adam G., min. at Bervie, M.D 1862. Glasgow,
               Australia.
1864   ,,   **Ireland**, s. of Robert G., bank agent, Kirkcudbright ; M.A.
               1869 ; B D., Edin. 1872. Min. Walkerburn, Tongland.
1877.   ,,   s. of Paul G., Helmsdale ; M.B , C M. 1883. Govan, Helms-
               dale, etc.

(5) UNIVERSITY OF EDINBURGH, 1594 TO 1860

1845 **A.,** Edinburgh.
1735. **Adam.**
1838.   ,,   Aberdeensh. (Med.).
1845.   ,,   **A.,** Craig.
1833 **Aeneas B.,** Kirkcudbright.
1669 **Alexander.**
1689.   ,,   M.A. 1692
1709   ,,
1713.   ,,
1726.   ,,
1728.   ,,
1739   ,,
1762.   ,,
1765.   ,,   (Law).
1775.   ,,   (Med.).
1779   ,,   (Med).
1784.   ,,   (Med.).
1785   ,,

1790.	**Alexander.**	
1792	,,	(Med.)
1799	,,	
	,,	(Med.).
1804	,,	(Med.).
1811.	,,	Montrose.
1813.	,,	Aberdeen.
1813	,,	*Sir*, Galloway.
1816.	,,	Galloway
	,,	Aberdeensh (Med).
	,,	Forfarsh.
1817.	,,	Edinburgh (Med).
1820.	,,	Aberdeensh.
1820	,,	Kirkcudbright (Law).
1823.	,,	**L.**, Banff (Div).
1826	,,	Elginsh. (Law). Writer, Elgin , sheriff subst., Sutherland
1831	,,	Kirkcudbright.
	,,	junr , Edinb. (Law).
1832.	,,	**Thomas,** Belfast
1836	,,	Kirkcudbright.
1838	,,	Co. Down (Med.) ; M.D. 1841.
1841	,,	**M.,** Edinburgh.
1849	,,	Edinburgh.
1854	,,	Sutherlandsh. (Law).
1856	,,	Coventry.
1860.	,,	Keith (Law).
1699	**All.** •	
1822	**Allan M.,** Edinburghsh.	
1823.	,, Edinburgh (Law).	
1839.	**Andrew,** Edinburgh	
1842.	,, do. (Div.)	
1779.	**Archibald.**	
1783.	,,	(Law)
1800.	,,	(Med.)
1814	,,	Lochmaben.
1822.	,,	**C.,** Ayrsh. (Med).
1827.	,,	Edinburgh , 1828 (Med.) , M.D 1834 C B. 1856
1729	**Charles.**	
1768.	,,	(Med.).

1768. **Charles.** (Law).

1769.   ,,

1798.   ,,

1806   ,,   (Med.) ; M.D. 1810.

1811   ,,   Banffsh. (Law).

          ,,

1818.   ,,   Sutherlandsh.

1819.   ,,   Loth (Div. *See* King's Coll. 1815)

1820   ,,   Edinburgh (Law).

1823.   ,,   Aberdeen (Law). W.S. 1824.

1824.   ,,   Sutherlandsh. (Div.).

1831.   ,,   Edinburgh, 1832 (Med).

1838.   ,,   **Alex.,** Banffsh. (Med.)   M.D. St And. 1840.

1851.   ,,   Perthsh.

1790. **Cosmo.**

1851.   ,,   **Reid,** Edinburgh.

16—. **David.** M.A. 1693.

1762.   ,,

1771.   ,,   (Med.).

1787.   ,,

1798   ,,

1803   ,,   (Med.).

1826.   ,,   Edinburgh.

1828   ,,   **H.,** Kirkcudbrightsh. ; 1832 (Law).   W.S. 1837, *infra.*

1838.   ,,   Nova Scotia (Med.) ; M.D 1841.

1850   ,,   Northumberland.

1860.   ,,   Forfar.

          ,,   **Jenoway,** Edinburgh.

1800 **Donald.**

1841.   ,,   **C.**

1753. **Duke,** assistant librarian 1763-1800 , M.A. 1800'(*Scots Mag.* 1802, p.
          18).

1824. **Edward,** Berwicksh

1825   ,,   Yorks. (Med.).

1828   ,,   **Strathearn,** Inverness , 1831 (Med.) , 1832 (Law).   M.P.
          etc., *infra,* pp. (522), (528).

1813. **Evelyn M.,** Edinburgh.

1846. **Evan,** Inverness-sh.

1800. **Francis.**

1829.   **Francis,** Edinburgh (Med).
1831.   „   **Hastings,** B.A. Cantab. (Med.).
1834.   „   **Wight,** Edinburgh (Law).
1836.   „   **W. L.,** Edinburgh.
1839.   „   **David** of Abergeldie (Law).
1824.   **G. C.,** Edinburgh.
1681.   **Gabriel,** M.A. 1684.
1773.   **Gardiner** (Med.).
1659.   **George,** M.A. 1663
1702.   „
1706.   „
1719.   „
1730.   „
1735.   „
1763.   „
        „   (Med.)
1773   „   (Law)
1776   „
1778.   „   Aberdeen (Med.)
1779.   „   (Law).   Advocate 1782.
1782.   „   (Med).
1800.   „
1803.   „   **James** (Med).
1813.   „   Mortlach (Law).
1820.   „   **Alexander,** Edinburgh (Med) ; M.D. 1826.
1821.   „   Elgin.
1822.   „   **C.,** Kirkcudbright.
1827.   „   Aberdeen (Div.   *See* Mar. Coll. 1822)
1828.   „   Elginsh.
1829.   „   **John Robert,** Kincardinesh.
1830.   „   **D.,** Edinburgh.
1832.   „   **Dalrymple,** Edinburgh (Med.) , M.D 1837.
1838.   „   **Murray,** Orkney (Med.).
1840.   „   Edinburgh (Med.).
1845.   „   **James,** Sutherland (Med.).
1857.   „   **James,** Banffsh.
1859   „   Edinburgh (Law)
1813.   **Gilbert,** Lochmaben.
1835.   **Gordon Clunes,** Edinburgh , 1837 (Law).   W.S. 1842.

1838. **Hamilton D.,** Lanarksh.
1809. **Henry.**
1816. „ Edinburgh (Law). W.S. 1825, *infra*
1819. „ Edinburgh.
1820. „ **P. M.,** Glasgow.
1846. „ Dumfries (Law). Sheriff clerk of Dumfriesshire
1859 „ Perthsh.
1859. „ Perthsh. (Law).
16—. **Hugh,** M.A. 1645
1774 „ min. Anwoth 1790-1808.
1786. „ (Med.).
1811. „ s. of Hugh G , min. Anwoth. Min. Monquhitter 1829.
1858. „ **W. M.,** Sutherlandsh.
1814 **Hunter,** Edinburgh , 1820 (Law). W.S. 1824
1838. **Huntly George,** Glasgow (Med.) ; M.D. 1841 Surg.-General, Army.
1648 **James.**
1661. „
1677 „ M.A 1677.
1681. „ M.A 1684
1701. „
17—. „ M A 1724.
1738 „
1751. „
1763 „ Scotus (Med)
1770. „ (Med.).
1786 „
1787. „ (Med.)
1788. „ (Law). Advocate 1790
1790 „ **Far.;** 1791 (Law).
1791. „ (Law) Advocate 1793.
1797. „ (Med.).
1800 „ (Med.)
1802 „
1808 „ Min. Borgne
1810. „ Co Down (Med.) ; M.D. 1815
1811. „ **A.,** London (Med) ; M D. 1814
1812. „ Galloway.
1813. „ London.
1813 „ Canongate

1813. **James,** Dumfries.
1814.   „   Berwicksh.
1815.   „   Caithness.
1819.   „   Edinburgh.
        „   Edinburgh (Med).
1821.   „   Banffsh.
1822   „   Edinburgh
1823   „   Liverpool (Med.)
        „   Dumfries.
        „   Edinburgh (Law)
1825   „   **Corbett,** Edinburgh (Med.) , M D. 1830.
1828.   „   Dumfries (Law).
1829   „   Aberdeensh. (Law).
        „   **M.,** U Canada ; 1830 (Med.).
1830.   „   Aberdeen (Med.) ; M.D. 1833.
        „   Aberdeensh.
1832.   „   Aberdeensh. (Law).
1833.   „   **F.,** Edinburgh
1834.   „   **Fraser,** Banffsh. (Law).
1835.   „   Edinburgh (Med.)
1837.   „   Edinburgh ; 1841 (Law). W S. 1845.
1838.   „   Elgin (Law)
1839   „   Edinburgh.
        „   Dumfriessh ; 1840 (Div).
1840.   „   **B.,** Charleston, U.S.A (Med.).
        „   **C.,** Perth (Law).
        „   Edinburgh.
1841.   „   **L.,** Forfarsh ; 1843 (Law). Union Bank, Brechin
1850.   „   **Fraser,** Edinb. (Law) W.S 1852
1853.   „   Banff (Law). Solicitor, Keith
1856.   „   Perthsh.
1857.   „   Whithorn.
1859.   „   **John,** Banff (Law).
15— **John,** 2nd s of Alexander G. of Lesmoir , M.A 1594   Min Crimond.
1641.   „
1646.   „
1706.   „
1756   „
1762.   „

1764. **John,** primus (Med.)
           „   secundus (Med.).
1767.   „   (Law).
1768.   „
1771.   „
1773.   „   (Med).
1776.   „   (Med.).
1784   „   (Law).
1791.   „   (Med.).
1792.   „   (Law)
1793   „
1793.   „   (Med.).
1796.   „   Sir, Bart.
1799   „   Moraysh.
1800   „   Dumfriessh.
           „   (Med.) ; M.D. 1805.
1804.   „   (Law).
           „   (Med.).
1809.   „   Edinb.
           „   Edinb.
1810.   „   Banffsh. (Med.).
1812.   „   Armagh (Med.) , M.D. 1813
1813.   „   S. Leith.   Min Speymouth.
           „   Dumfriessh.
1814.   „   Elgin (Med.).
1817.   „   Galloway, 1824 (Div.)   Min. Twynholm.
1818.   „   Galloway (Law).
1821.   „   C., Inverness (Law).   Solicitor Inverness
           „   T., Edinburgh (Law).   W S. 1824.
           „   Aberdeensh. (Med.).
1822.   „   Edinburgh.
1823.   „   Perth.
1826.   „   Edinburgh.
1828.   „   **Thomson,** Edinburgh , 1831 (Law).   Advocate 1835.
1829.   „   Kirkcudbrightsh.   M.A. 1832 [?]
1831.   „   Prestonpans (Med.).
1839.   „   Liverpool ; 1841 (Law).   Advocate 1846.
1843.   „   Edinburgh (Law).
1850   „   Edinburgh.

1852. **John,** Sutherlandsh.
1857.   „   Edinb.
1859.   „   **Wilson,** Edinb.; 1860 (Law).
1793. **Joseph.**
1800.   „   (Law). W.S. 1804
1717. **Lewis.**
1767.   „
1831.   „   **D. B.,** Edinb.
1776. **Lockhart** (Med.).
1817. **Mackay,** Caithness (Med.).
1789. **Maxwell.** W.S. 1793.
1806.   „
1810.   „   (Med.).
1812.   „   Edinb. (Law).
1832. **Morison,** Elgin.
1831. **P. B.,** Ayrsh.
1711   **Patrick,** M.A. 1714
1738.   „
1763.   „   (Law).
1783.   „   **Alexander** (Med.)
1798. · **Peter.**
1815.   „   Aberdeensh. (Med)
1819. **Richard,** Edinb. , 1823 (Law).
[1601. **Robert.** *Earldom of Sutherland,* pp 239, 249, 314-5]
1669.   „
1672.   „
1681.   „   M A. 1683.
1691.   „
1704.   „
1710.   „
1767.   „
1770.   „   (Med.).
1783.   „
1785   „   (Med.).
1791.   „
1792.   „   (Law).
1796.   „   (Law).
1797.   „   (Med).
1804.   „   Min. Kinfauns, Edinburgh.   D.D. Mar. Coll. 1823.

1820. **Robert, M.,** Richmond Va.
1823.   ,,   Dumfries; 1827 (Law)   W.S. 1830
1824.   ,,   **H.,** Galloway.
1829   ,,   Edinburgh (Med.).
1829.   ,,   **Macartney,** Kirkcudbright (Law)
1829.   ,,   Haddington (Law).
1833.   ,,   **Haldane,** Edinburgh , 1835 (Law)
1834.   ,,   Belfast (Med.).
1837.   ,,   Edinburgh , 1841 (Div.)
1794. **Samuel.**
1823.   ,,   Galloway.
1724. **Simon,** M A 1727
1826. **Stewart,** Edinburgh.
1787 **Theodore** (Med.)
1813   ,,   Aberdeen (Med.).   *See* King's Coll. 1798
1705. **Thomas.**
1728.   ,,
1764.   ,,   (Law).
1803.   ,,
1813.   ,,   Edinburgh (Med.).
1832   ,,   Kirkcudbright , 1836 (Div.)   Min Newbattle, D D. .
1832.   ,,   London.
1833.   ,,   Kirkcudbright (Med.) ; M.D 1837
1836   ,,   (Law).
1856.   ,,   Forfar (Law)
16—. **Walter,** M.A 1689
1634. **William,** M.A. 1637.
1662.   ,,
1681.   ,,   (1), M.A. 1683
    ,,   (2).
1688   ,,
1699.   ,,   M A 1700
1711.   ,,
1723.   ,,
1726   ,,
1758   ,,
1761.   ,,
1763.   ,,   (Law)
1766   ,,   (Law).

1775. **William.**
1778   ,,   (Med.).
1782.   ,,
1783.   ,,   (Law).
1786.   ,,
1791.   ,,   (Med.).
1796.   ,,   (Med.)
1797   ,,
1804   ,,   (Law)   .
1810.   ,,   Madras.
1813.   ,,   Forfar (Law).
1813.   ,,   Edinb (Med); M.D. 1818.
1815   ,,   Kirkcudbright.
         ,,   Captain R N., London.
1818.   ,,   Edinburgh (Law).
1819.   ,,   **B. J.**, Galloway (Law).   Proc. fiscal, Kirkcudbright.
1821.   ,,   Banffshire.
1822.   ,,   Dundee (Med)   '
1823   ,,   Murrayshire (Med.)   M.D. 1827.
         ,,   Yorks. (Med)
1826.   ,,   Kincardineshire (Med.).
1827.   ,,   **Grant**, Moraysh. (Div.); M.A, King's Coll. 1827.
1829.   ,,   Edinb.
         ,,   **Francis**, Ayrsh.
1832   ,,   Edinburgh (Med.).
1838.   ,,   Strabane (Med) ; M.D. 1842.
1838.   ,,   Hull (Med.) , M.D 1840.
1842.   ,,   **Loudon**, Forfar (Med.) ; M.D. 1846.
·1846.   ,,   Orkney (Med.).
1848.   ,,   Dumfries; 1852 (Div.).   Min Kirkwall, Ruthwell, Abernethy.
1848.   ,,   Orkney ; 1852 (Div.).
1850.   ,,   Morayshire (Med) , M.D. 1854.
1855·   ,,   Edinburgh (Med.) , M.D. 1862.
1853·   ,,   **G.**, Nairn.   '
1856   ,,   Bervie (Med.).

(6) IN HEW SCOTT'S *FASTI ECCL. SCOT.*, AND NOT IDENTIFIED IN
THE UNIVERSITY LISTS

1560.   **Alexander,** bishop of Galloway.   I. 775.
1574.   „   min. Inveraven.   III 236.
1586.   „   min. Botriphnie.   III. 193.
1745.   „   min. Glasserton   I. 732.
1577   **Andrew,** min. Dalry.   I. 710.
1807.   **David William,** min. Morebattle, Gordon, Earlston.   I. 465, 524, 527.
1585.   **George,** min Tongland.   I. 723.
1586.   „   bishop of Galloway,   I. 776.
1695.   „   ord. in London, min. Leuchars till 1706, when he accepted a
                    congregation in London.   II. 450.
[1583.   **James,** parson of Clatt   *S. N. & Q*, 2 iv. 171.]
1690   „   from Presb. congregation, Glendermot, min. Cardross.   II.
                    350.
1692.   „   (s. of James G.; M.A., K.C. 1661); min. Foveran.   III. 608
1567   **John,** bishop of Galloway.   I. 776.
1574.   „   min. Petty.   III. 270.
1594.   „   min. Clatt.   III. 552
1781.   „   min. Dolphinton.   I. 221
1677.   **Robert,** min. Dunkeld, Caputh, Abercorn, Clunie.   II 787, 795, 799;
                    I. 165.
1793.   „   min. Carsphairn, Girthon.   I. 707, 714.
1585   **Roger,** min. Whithorn, etc.   I. 733, 747, 776.

APPENDIX IV.

GORDONS, MEMBERS OF PARLIAMENT, SCOTLAND.

1605. —— **Gordon,** laird of Badenscoth, sat as a minor baron in convention 1605.

1689. **Adam,** *Sir,* of Dalfolly.—Sutherlandshire 1689 conv., 1689 until his death *s.b.*[1] 25 Oct. 1700.   Knighted 1695-6.   S. of William G. of Dalpholly, by a dau. of John Cor of Mitchel Elphinstone. He *m.*   dau. of Urquhard of New Hall, and *d.* 21 Sept 1700, leaving with other issue a son, Sir Wm. G , of Dalpholly, afterwards of Invergordon, M.P, cr. a bart. 8 Feb. 1704.

1754. ,, *Lt.-genl. Lord,* of Cuttieshillock and Woodtoun.—Aberdeenshire 1754-61, 1761-8, Kincardineshire 1774-80 (then major-gen.), 1780-4 (lt.-genl.) 1784, until he acc. the Chiltern Hundreds *s.b.* 19 June 1788.   4th s. of Alexander, 2nd Duke of Gordon, genl. in the army, col. 1st regt of foot 1782, gov. of Edinburgh Castle 1796, of Tynemouth Castle 1778, col 66th regt. 1763, 26th regt. of Cameronians 1775, served in Gen Bligh's expedition to the court of France 1758, held a command in America 1765, commander-in-chief of the forces in Scotland 1789-98 , *d.s.p.* 13 Aug. 1801, having *m.* 2 Sept. 1767, Jane, dau. of John Drummond, of Megginch, co Perth, dowager of James, Duke of Athole ; she *d.* 22 Feb. 1795.

1612. **Alexander,** of Cluny.—Aberdeenshire 1612.   Sir Alexander G., of Cluny, cr. a bart. 31 Aug. 1625,? *m.* 1st Elizabeth, dau. of Sir William Douglas, 9th Earl of Angus ; he *m.* also Violet, dau. of John Urquhart, of Cromarty ; and lastly, 22 June 1641, Elizabeth, widow of Sir John Leslie, of Wardes, and dau. of John Gordon, of Newton ; she *d.* at Durham 2 Dec. 1642.

[1] [Shortly before]

1641. **Alexander,** of Erlestoane.—Kirkcudbright stewartry 1641. Son of John G., of Earlston, by his 2nd wife, served heir to his father 23 Oct. 1628 ; a stanch royalist, said to have declined a baron-etcy on 4 Jan. 1612 ; *m.* Elizabeth, dau. of John Gordon, of Pennynghame (grandfather of Alexander, 5th Vict. Kenmure), and *d.* Nov. 1653 ; his grandson, Sir William, was cr a baronet 9 July 1706 See Foster's *Baronetage.*

1661.   ,,   · Dornock 1661, ? of the Embo family.

1689.   ,,   provost.—Aberdeen 1689 conv., 1689 until his death *s.b.* 15 April 1693. [*See* Mr. A. M. Munro's *Memorials,* p. 185].

1700.   ,,   of Gairthrie.—Sutherlandshire 1700-2, 1702-5.

1702   ,,   of Pitlurg.—Aberdeenshire 1702-7. Son of Robert G., of Pitlurg, by his wife Jean, dau of Sir Richard Maitland, Lord Pitrichie. He *m.* Jean, dau. of James G., of Ellon, and had a s. and dau.

1722.   ,,   of Ardoch.—Inverness burghs 1722, 13 April until un-seated 19 Oct. following.

1875.   ,,   *Lt.-genl. Sir,* of London, K.C.B.—East Aberdeenshire 1875-80, and since 1880 general in the army K.L.H. and M. (2nd s of George, 4th Earl of Aberdeen), hon. equerry to the Queen since 1862, D.Q.M.G. Crimea and 1855-60, comd. a division in India 1867-70, also the Eastern district England 1871-2, col. 100th regt.; *b.* 11 Dec, 1817, *m.* and has issue. *See* Foster's *Peerage.*

1774. **Cosmo,** advocate, of Cluny.—Nairnshire 1774, until appointed a baron of the exchequer in Scotland 1777. Admitted advocate 29 July 1758, baron of the exchequer 1777, until he *d.* 19 Nov. 1800 (his younger brother, Alexander of Belmont, Tobago, died at Bath 11 Jan 1801).

1875 **Douglas William Cope,** *Lord,* of London, lieut. Coldstream Guards.— West Aberdeenshire 1876-80, Huntingdonshire since 1880. 3rd s. of Charles, 10th Marquis of Huntly, and heir-pre-sumptive to the titles, lieut. and capt. Coldstream Guards 1874-80 ; contested Hunts 1874 ; *b.* 11 Oct. 1851.

1869. **Edward Strathearn,** Q.C. LL.D. Glasgow, Dean of the Faculty of Advocates.—Glasgow and Aberdeen Universities 1869-74, 1874 (Queen's advocate for Scotland, March 1874), until ap-pointed a lord of appeal in ordinary 17 Oct. 1876. Advocate

1835, sheriff of Perthshire 1858-66, solict.-genl. Scotland 1866-7, lord advocate Scotland 1867-8, 1874-6, M.P. Thetford 1867-8, lord of appeal 17 Oct. 1876, P.C. (eldest s. of John Gordon, major 2nd regt, by his wife Catherine, dau. of Alexander Smith); *d.* 21 Aug. 1879, aged 65, having *m.* 1845, Agnes, only dau of John McInnes, esq., of Auchenreoch, co. Stirling, and had issue. *Infra*, p. 528.

1586   **George.**—Aberdeen 1588 conv.

1669   ,,   *Sir*, of Haddo, knt. and bart.—Aberdeenshire 1669-74, 1678 conv. 1681-2, then a senator of the college of justice. Sir George G., 3rd baronet (on the death 1665 of his brother, Sir John, to whom his father's estates had been restored in 1661), advocate 1668, P.C 1678, a lord of session 8 June 1680, and raised to the president's chair 14 Oct 1681, lord high chancellor of Scotland 1682-4, and on 30 Nov. 1682 was elevated to the peerage, etc, as Earl of Aberdeen, Viscount of Formartine, Lord Haddo, Methlick, Tarves, and Kellie, by letters patent dated at Whitehall, setting forth the services of his ancestors, the suffering and death of his father in the royal cause, and his own splendid abilities and faithful discharge of his official duties (s of Sir John G of Haddo, 1st bart.); *b.* 3 Oct. 1637; *d.* at Kelly 20 April 1720; having *m.* Anne eldest dau. of George Lockhart, of Torbrecks, heiress of her brother William. His s and heir, William, 2nd Earl, M.P

1685   ,,   s of Sir Robert G, of Embo (1689).—Dornock 1685-6, 1689 conv, 1689 parlt. ("George brother of John Gordon, of Embo"), until his death *s.b.* 21 Dec. 1692, when he is styled "Capt George Gordon, s. of the deceased Sir Robert Gordon, of Embo". Brother of John G., M P, sons of Robert G, M P.

1681.   ,,   *Sir*, of Edinglassie.—Banffshire 1681-2, 1685-6.

1854.   ,,   **John James,** Lord Haddo.—Aberdeenshire 1854-7, 1857-9, 1859, until he succeeded as 5th Earl of Aberdeen 14 Dec. 1860, *b.* 28 Sept 1816, *d.* 22 March 1864, having issue. *See* Foster's *Peerage.*

1625.   **James,** laird of Lesmoir, younger.—Aberdeenshire 1625 conv. Son of Sir James G., of Lesmoir, cr. a bart 1 Sept. 1625. He *m.* [Helen] dau. of Sir Thomas Urquhart, of Cromarty, and *d.* in his father's lifetime, leaving 2 daus.

1689. **James,** younger of Creachlee.—New Galloway 1689 conv., 1689 until his death *s.b.* 27 Aug. 1690.

1594. **John,** *Sir,* laird of Lochinvar.—Sat as a minor baron in the conventions 1594, 1597. Son of Sir James G., of Lochinvar; justiciary of the lordship of Galloway 1555, 1587; *d.* 23 Aug. 1604, *m.* 1st Juliana Home, of Wedderburn, and 2nd, in 1563, Elizabeth, dau. of John, Lord Herries, father of Sir Robert, M.P., and had issue.

1617.   ,, the goodman of Buckie.—Inverness-shire 1617 conv., 1617 parlt., including Caithness and Ross

1628.   ,, of Innermarkie.—Banffshire 1628-33.

1643.   ,, of Cardines.—Kirkcudbright stewartry 1643 conv., 1645, the laird.

1681.   ,, *Sir.*—Sutherlandshire 1681-2 (then John, eldest s., heir-apparent of Sir Robert G., of Embo, knt. and bart.), 1689 conv. (younger), 1689 parlt. (his name is included in the act of 25 April 1693 " concerning members who have not signed the assurance") until his death as Sir John G., of Embo, *s.b.* 10 May 1700. 3rd bart. of Embo, married and had issue.

1685.   ,, *Sir,* of Doall.—Sutherlandshire 1685-6.

1700.   ,, *Mr.,* younger, of Carrell.—Sutherlandshire 1700-2.

1708   ,, provost of Aberdeen —Aberdeen (now Montrose) burghs 1708-10. Probably 3rd and youngest s. of Charles 1st Earl of Aboyne; died 22 July 1762. [*See* Mr. A. M. Munro's *Memorials,* p. 200].

1742.   ,, *Sir,* of Invergordon, bart.—Cromartyshire 1742-7, 1754-61. 2nd bart. (s. of William G, M.P.); registered arms in the Lyon office 1756, *d.s.p.* 25 May 1783. *See* Milne's list of Nova Scotia baronets, Foster's *Baronetage,* p. xiv.

1781   ,, of Kenmure.—Kirkcudbright stewartry 1781, until declared unduly elected, 6 Feb. 1782. Vice-lieut. Kirkcudbright stewartry, capt. 17th regt. of foot (2nd s. of John, eldest surviving son of William, 6th and attainted Viscount Kenmure), restored by act of parlt. 17 June 1824; *d.s.p.* 21 Sept. 1840, aged 90, having *m.* Miss Morgan

1841.   ,, **Frederick G. C. H.,** *Lord.*—Forfarshire 1841-7, 1847-52. Admiral R N. (3rd son of George, 9th Marquis of Huntly), assumed the additl. surname of Hallyburton 1843; *b.* 15 Aug. 1799; *d.s.p.* 29 Sept. 1878, having *m.* 24 Aug. 1836, Lady

Augusta Fitzclarence (proceeding patent 24 May 1831), sister of George 1st Earl of Munster and widow of Hon John Kennedy-Erskine (M Ailsa); she *d* 8 Dec. 1865.

1649. **Ludovick,** *Sir,* of Gordonstown.—Elgin and Forres-shire 1649. 2nd bart. (on the death of his father Sir Robert Gordon, 1656), *b.* 15 Oct. 1624; *d.* 1686, having *m.* 1st, 1 Jan. 1644, Elizabeth, dau and heir of Sir Robert Farquhar, of Menie, and had with other issue a son, Sir Robert, M P.; he *m* 2ndly (contract 6 March 1669) Jean, dau. of John Stewart, of Ladywell, widow.

1586. **Robert.**—Inverness 1586 conv.

1612.   ,,   *Sir,* of Lochinvar, knt —Kirkcudbright stewartry 1612. Entered as a bart., 1 May 1626, in Milne's list, *see* Foster's *Baronetage,* which states that " he was made Governour of Nova Scotia, bot his patent does not invest him tytle baronet, bot he has power to create Judges, Generalls, Archbishops, Bishops, etc." (s. of Sir John, M.P.); *m.* Isobel, dau. of William Ruthven, 1st Earl of Gowrie; *d.* Nov. 1628, having had with other issue a son Robert, probably M.P.

1628   ,,   —New Galloway 1628-33, 1639-41 (of Knockbrax), 1643-4 conv. Possibly son of Sir Robert, M P., last named.

1630.   ,,   *Sir,* knt. and bart.—Inverness-shire 1630 conv Hon. Sir Robert G., of Gordonstoun, the historian of his family (2nd s. of Alexander, 11th Earl of Sutherland), gentleman of the bedchamber to King James 1606, knighted 1609, gentleman of the bedchamber to Charles I., who created him a baronet of Nova Scotia, with remainder to his heir male whatsoever, 28 May 1625, being the first of that order, sheriff-principal of Inverness-shire 1629, vice-chamberlain 1630, P C. Scotland 1634; *b* 14 May 1580, *d.* 1656, having *m.* 16 Feb. 1613 Louisa, only child and sole heir of John Gordon, Lord of Glenluce, dean of Salisbury, brother of George, 4th Earl of Huntly, and had issue.

1649.   ,,   *Sir,* of Embo.—Sutherlandshire 1649-50, 1661. 2nd bart. (on the death of his father, Sir John); *d* 16 Oct 1697; father of Sir John, M.P 1681.

1663.   ,,   *Sir,* of Langdale.—Sutherlandshire 1663 (? identical with Sir Robert of Embo)

1661. **Robert**, of Lumsdeall (Rumsdeall) —Sutherlandshire 1661-2, 1678 (then described as of Rogart)

1672.   ,,   *Sir*, 1673, of Gordonstoun, younger (1672).—Sutherlandshire 1672-4, 1678 conv. (younger), 1681-2 (younger), 1685-6 (a knight, younger). 3rd bart. (s. of Sir Ludovick, M.P.); *b.* 7 March 1647 ; *d* 1701, having *m.* 1st Margaret, eldest dau. of William, 11th Lord Forbes, and relict of Alexander, 1st Lord Duffus ; he *m.* 2ndly, Elizabeth, only dau. of Sir Wm. Dunbar, of Hempriggs, bart., and had with other issue a son, Sir Robert, M P.

1715.   ,,   *Sir*, of Gordonstown, knt. and bart.—Caithness-shire 1715-22. 4th bart. (son of Sir Robert, M.P), claimed the earldom of Sutherland ; *d* 8 Jan 1772, aged nearly 80, having *m.* 26 May 1734, Anne, only dau. of Sir William Maxwell, of Calderwood, bart. ; she *d.* 11 March 1808, aged 89

1690. **William**, *Lt.-col.*, of Craig.—Kirkcudbright stewartry 1690 until his death *s b.* 12 April 1693.

1708.   ,,   Lord Haddo.—Aberdeenshire 1 June 1708 until *s.b.* 18 Jan. following, he being incapable of taking his seat, being the eldest s. of a peer of Scotland 2nd Earl, K.T., a representative peer 1721-46 ; *d.* 30 March 1746, aged 70 leaving issue. *See* Forbes's *Peerage* ; s. of Sir George G., bart., M.P., cr. Earl of Aberdeen.

1708.   ,,   *Sir*, of Dalfolly, knt. and bart.—Sutherlandshire 1708-10, 1710-13, 1714-15, 1715-22, 1722-7 (then of Invergordon) ; Cromartyshire 1741 until his death *s.b* 30 Dec. 1742. Of London, banker, cr. a bart. 8 Feb. 1704, purchased Inverbreakie and called it Invergordon ; a commissioner for stating debts due to army (s of Sir Adam, M.P. 1689) ; *m.* Isabel, dau and heir of Sir John Hamilton, of Halcraig, Lanark, and *d.* at Chelsea 9 June 1742, having had with 2 daus. a son, Sir John, who succeeded as M.P.

1776   ,,   *Lord*, brother-german to Alexander, Duke of Gordon.— Elginshire 1779-80, 1780-4 (vice-admiral of Scotland 1782), Inverness-shire 1784-90. Son of Cosmo George, 3rd Duke of Gordon, K.T., served in 89th foot and 37th foot, depy. ranger St. James's Park and Hyde Park, 1778, and lt -col. north fencible regt. same year, vice-admiral of Scotland 1782-95, recr-genrl. duchy of Cornwall, M.P. Horsham 1792-6 ;

b. 15 Aug. 1744, *d.* 1 May 1823, having *m.* 1 March 1781, Hon. Frances Ingram-Shepherd, and dau. and co-heir of Charles, 9th Viscount Irvine; she *d.* 29th Sept. 1841, aged 80.

1820.   **William,** *Rear-admiral R.N.*—Aberdeenshire 1820-6 (of Minories), 1826-30, 1830-1, 1831-2, 1833-4, (capt R.N.) 1835-7, 1837-41, 1841-7 (a lord of the Admiralty) 1847-52, (then rear-admiral) 1852 until he accepted the Chiltern Hundreds *s b.* 22 Aug. 1854. Brother of George, 4th Earl of Aberdeen, entered the navy 1794, com.-in-chief at the Nore; *d.* unm. 3 Feb. 1858, aged 73.

APPENDIX V.

(1) MEMBERS OF THE FACULTY OF ADVOCATES

1683. **Alexander,** 2nd s. of George G., IV. of Coclarachie [" s. to Straloch," *Mylne's MS.*[1]]. Raised to bench as Lord Auchintoul, 1688.

1752.   „   s of Charles G., merchant, Elgin. Of Whitley; sheriff of Elgin 1757 ; *d.* 1783.

1759.   „   3rd s. of William, 2nd Earl of Aberdeen ; *b* 1739. Sheriff-depute of Kirkcudbright 1764 , raised to bench as Lord Rockville 1784 , *d.* 1792.

1771.   „   eldest s. of William G. of Culvennan, W.S., *b.* 1748. Sheriff of Wigton and of Kirkcudbright ; kt. 1800 ; *d* 1830.

1774.   „   **Spalding,** eldest s. of Alexander Spalding of Holm, and Jean only d. and heiress of Robert G. of Shirmirz ; *b.* 1750. Assumed name of Gordon ; sheriff-depute of Wigton ; *d.* 1794.

1661. **Arthur,** 9th s. of Robert G. of Straloch. " Admitted under the usurpers," *Mylne* ; readmitted 1661 ; *d.* c. 1680.

1735. **Charles Hamilton,** s. of Sir William G. of Invergordon. Entered King's Coll., Aberdeen 1730 (*see* also *Fasti Acad. Marisc.,* 1., 70-1) , *d.* c. 1761.

1885.   „   **Thomas,** eldest s of James Wilkinson G. of Cairness.

1758. **Cosmo,** of Cluny. M.P. for Nairnshire 1774-77 ; Baron of Exchequer 1777 ; *d.* 1800

1835. **Edward Strathearn,** 2nd s. of Major John G , late of the Queen's Royals , *b.* 1814. Entered Edinburgh Univ. 1828 ; adv. depute 1852 ; sheriff of Perth 1858 ; solicitor gen. 1866 ; Lord adv. 1867-68, and 1874-76 ; P.C. 1874 ; M.P. for Thetford 1867-68, for Glasgow and Aberdeen Universities 1869-76 ; Created, 1876, Baron Gordon of Drumearn, co Stirling, in

---

[1] " Chronological list of the Lords of Session from 1532 to 1718 and Advocates admitted during that period," by Robert Mylne (*see* D N B), MS in Edinb. Univ. Library.

the Peerage of the United Kingdom for life, and appointed a
Lord of Appeal in Ordinary; *d.* 1879 *Supra*, pp. (512), (522).

1668. **George,** 2nd s. of Sir John G. of Haddo; *b.* 1637 M A. King's Coll,
Aberd. 1659. "He took not the oaths to K. William"
(*Mylne*). *See supra*, p. (487)

1707.   ,,   2nd s. of Sir James G., 5th bart. of Lesmore; *d.* before 1756.

1713.   ,,   yr. of Neathermuir (*Mylne*). Of the Middle Temple; *d.* 1768.

1782.   ,,   yr. of Hallhead, *d* c 1833.

1874. **Henry Erskine,** 2nd s. of John G. of Aikenhead, Glasgow.

1893. **Huntly Douglas,** youngest s. of late Baron G. of Drumearn; *b.* 1866.

1790. **James,** eldest s. of John G. of Craig; *b.* 1767; *d* 1852

1793.   ,,   eldest s. of Alexander G. of Culvinan; *b.* 1771. D.L. Kirkcudbright; *d.* 1843.

1681. **John,** s. of Sir Ludovick G of Gordonstoun.

1737.   ,,   s. of   G. of Buthlaw; *d.* c. 1775.

1789.   ,,   yr. of Cairnfield; *d.* 1793

1801.   ,,   3rd s. of late John G, clerk to the Signet. Entered the army
1808; *d.* at Barbados 1816.

1824.   ,,   of Cairnbulg; *b* 1787 D.L Aberdeensh.; *d.* 1861.

1835.   ,,   **Thomson,** s of late John G., M.D. Adv dep. 1840 and 1846;
sheriff of Aberdeensh. 1847, of Midlothian 1849; rector of
Marischal College 1849 and 1850, *d.* 1865.

1846.   ,,   s of late Harry G., Liverpool; *d.* 1862.

1703 **Kenneth,** s of the Laird of Cluny. " Suspended from Bench before
the Lords 17 Dec., but reponed 30 Dec. 1708; " *d.* c. 1760.

1712 **Robert,** s of Cluny; *d* 1729.

1760.   ,,   s. of Sir Robert G. of Gordonstoun. Succ. to baronetcy 1772;
d. unm. 1776.

1716. **Thomas;** *d.* before 1756.

1527 **William.**

1586.   ,,

1642.   ,,   s of Robert G. of Straloch.

1681.   ,,   2nd s. of Sir William G. 4th bart. of Lesmoir. "In a Bill:
he qualified himself 29 June 1708" (*Mylne*) Assumed his
mother's name of Learmonth, and succeeded to Balcomie,
King's advocate to K. James II.

1683.   ,,   s. of Sheilagreen (*Mylne*).

1755.   ,,   yr of Carryl, *d.* c. 1759.

1768   ,,   s. of late Charles Hamilton G., *d.* c. 1778.

(2) WRITERS TO H.M. SIGNET.

1796. **Adam,** of Arradoul and Cairnfield.　Apprentice to Craufurd Tait; W:S. 16th June 1796.　2nd s. of John G. of Cairnfield, Banffshire, *b* 13th Feb 1773; *d.* 17th March 1847, *m.* 4th March 1799, Elizabeth, dau. of Patrick Cruickshank of Stracathro, Forfarshire.

1827.　　„　**Hay,** of Avochie.　Apprentice to John Gordon; W.S. 15th Nov 1827.　2nd s. of Major Adam Hay, of the 35th Regiment; *b.* 18th Sept 1803; *d.* 8th April 1872, *m.* 13th April 1841, Anne M'Kerrel, eldest dau. of James Brown, chartered accountant, Edinburgh.　Assumed name of Gordon.

1723. **Alexander,** of Cairnfield.　Apprentice to George Kennedy; W.S. 25th Nov. 1723.　S. of Robert G. of Lunan; *d.* 21st Feb. 1775, aged 87, *m.* (1) Elizabeth, dau. of Gordon of Cairnfield; and (2) Jane, dau. of Gordon of Shillagreens.

1890.　　„　**Shand.**　Apprentice to Henry Tod, W.S. 17th March 1890. S. of Alexander G., S.S.C., Edinburgh; *b.* 17th July 1867.

1830. **Arthur Forbes,** of Rayne.　Apprentice to John Gordon, junr.; W.S. 9th Dec 1830.　S. of Colonel Arthur Forbes of the 32d Regiment; *b* 2d June 1806, *d.* 27th Aug. 1873; *m.* 20th April 1843, Charlotte, eldest dau. of Colonel William Balfour of Trenaby, Orkney. [Assumed name of Gordon.]

1763 **Charles,** of Cluny.　Apprentice to William Fraser of Ford; W.S. 15th July 1763.　2nd s. of John G. of Cluny, Aberdeenshire; *d.* 8th May 1814; *m.* 8th Nov. 1775, Joanna, dau. of Thomas Trotter of Mortonhall, Mid-Lothian.

1824.　　„　Apprentice to John Ker; W.S. 7th July 1824.　S. of Charles G, advocate in Aberdeen; *d.* 12th Oct. 1848, aged 47. *unm.*

1831. **David Hutchison,** of Larglanglee.　Apprentice to Andrew Stone; W.S. 15th June 1837.　Fourth s. of Robert G. writer in Kirkcudbright, *b.* 10th Aug. 1813; *d.* 16th March 1878, *unm.* Procurator-fiscal of Kirkcudbright, 1839-78.

1720. **George.**　Apprentice to Ronald Campbell; W.S. 15th March 1720; *d.* 21st March 1747; *m.* 2d Aug. 1727, Katherine, dau. of James Cleland, merchant, Edinburgh.

1740. **George.** Apprentice to James Craig; W.S Jan. 1740. Eldest s. of George G., writer in Edinburgh; *b.* 1715, *d* 16th Oct. 1783; *m.* Feb. 1747, Joan Mary, dau. of Captain James Muirhead of Lauchope, Lanarkshire.

1838.   ,,   **More,** of Charleton. Apprentice to Adam Gib and Robert Ellis; W.S. 29th June 1838. S. of John Shank More, advocate; *b.* 21st March 1816, *m.* 10th Aug 1848, Janet, dau of Harry Gordon, Liverpool. [Assumed name of Gordon.]

1842. **Gordon Clunes.** Apprentice to, and 2nd s. of, Joseph G., W.S. W.S. 19th July, 1842; *b* 29th May 1811; *d.* 25th Nov 1843, *unm.*

1825. **Henry,** *Rev.* Apprentice to, and eldest s. of Thomas G , W.S. W.S. 1st July 1825; *d.* 12th Dec. 1880, *unm.* Licensed 1835; called to Presbyterian Church, Gananoque, Canada, 1837, Moderator of Presbyterian Church of Canada, 1854

1824. **Hunter.** Apprentice to, and eldest s. of, James Farquhar G., W.S. W.S 3d June 1824; *d.* 1855, aged 54, *unm* ; latterly a barrister in London.

1631. **James.** Deputy-keeper of the Signet, 1631.

1829.   ,,   Apprentice to James Mackenzie and William Innes; W.S. 12th Nov 1829. S. of William G. of Hallmyre, Peeblesshire, *d.* 11th March 1870; *m.* 18th July, 1844, Harriet, eldest dau. of J. Davis, Seatown.

1845.   ,,   Apprentice to Andrew Storie and William R. Baillie , W.S. 20th Nov 1845. Eldest s. of the Rev. Robert G , D.D., one of the ministers of Edinburgh; *b.* 24th July 1821; *m* 18th June 1852, Agnes Webster, 2nd dau. of J. H. Miller, merchant, Glasgow; sheriff-substitute at Banff, 1853-77.

1794.   ,,   **Farquhar.** Apprentice to (1) John Gordon, and (2) Adam Rolland , W.S. 19th Dec. 1794. Eldest s. of John G. of Balmoor, W.S.; *d.* 23d Dec. 1843, *m.* (1) 13th Nov 1797, Lilias, dau of Charles Hunter of Burnside, Forfarshire; and (2) 1805, Margaret, only child of Robert Haldane of Airthrey, Stirlingshire.

1852.   ,,   **Fraser.** Apprentice to Robert Mackay , W.S. 15th July 1852. S. of William G , residing at Minmore, Banffshire; *b.* 7th Sept 1816, *d.* 1861, *m.* 27th July 1851, Eleanor Sinclair, dau. of Archibald Leslie of Balnageith, Elginshire.

1763. **John,** of Balmoor. Apprentice to Leonard Urquhart; W.S. 8th July 1763. S of Alexander G. of Auchenlachries, Aberdeenshire; *d*. 24th Oct. 1789, *m*. 16th Oct. 1770, Margaret, dau. of James Stuart, of Binend, Lord Provost of Edinburgh.

1774   ,,   Apprentice to James Gartshore; W S 24th June 1774. Eldest s. of Thomas G , surgeon in Dumfries, *b*. 1748; *d*. 27th Oct. 1832; *m*. 21st July 1786, Jane, eldest dau. of Thomas Shairp of Houston, Linlithgowshire.

1789.   ,,   of Carleton Apprentice to John Tait, W.S. 26th June 1789. S. of Alexander G of Carleton, Ayrshire, *d*. 13th March 1817, *m*. 24th June 1793, Margaret, only dau. of Dr. Jasper Tough of Hillhead, Ayrshire.

1794.   ,,   of Avochie. Apprentice to Andrew Steuart, junr., W.S. 19th Dec. 1794. Eldest s. of John [? Patrick] G. of Avochie; *b*. 1771; *d*. 11th July 1842, *unm*. Deputy Receiver-General.

1825.   ,,   **Taylor,** of Nethermuir. Apprentice to James Heriot; W.S. 18th Nov. 1825. 2nd s. of Maxwell G., W.S.; *b*. 1801; *d*. 24th June 1884; *m* Dec 1855, Margaret Grant, dau. of Robert Watson.

1804. **Joseph,** of Carroll. Apprentice to Charles M'Intosh; W.S. 16th Feb. 1804. Eldest s of Captain John G. of Carroll, Sutherlandshire, *b*. 1777; *d*. 7th March 1855; *m*. 30th July 1808, Ann, youngest dau of Gordon Clunes of Crakaig, Sutherlandshire; clerk to admission of Notaries-Public, 1839-55.

1769. **Lachlan Duff,** of Park. Apprentice to Alexander Stuart, W.S. 26th June 1769 4th s. of John Duff of Culben, Morayshire; *d*. 14th May 1808; *m* 14th Sept. 1781, Rachel, 2nd dau. of Roger Hog of Newliston, West-Lothian.

1793. **Maxwell,** of Nethermuir. Apprentice to (1) Colquhoun Grant, and (2) John Taylor; W S. 28th June 1793. S. of William G. of Nethermuir; *d*. 24th Dec. 1809, *m*. 30th March 1799, Jane, dau. of John Taylor of Blackhouse, Ayrshire, W.S.

1731. **Robert.** Apprentice to James Budge; W.S. 18th August 1731; *d*. June 1740.

1798.   ,,   of Edintore. Apprentice to John Innes; W.S. 17th Aug. 1798. Eldest s. of John G. of Grieshop and Edintore, Elginshire; *d*. 1st Aug. 1815; *m*. 30th Aug. 1806, the widow of Archibald Burnett, Bengal.

1830.   ,,   of Bardarroch. Apprentice to Alexander Blair, W.S. 18th Nov. 1830. S. of William G., senr., writer in Dumfries;

b. 1807; *d.* 2d Dec 1883; *m* 23d April 1840, Sarah, 2nd dau. of Wilson Fisher, Whitehaven.

1672. **Thomas.** Apprentice to Alexander Hamilton; W.S. 24th July 1672. Eldest s. of James G of Buthlay, Aberdeenshire; clerk of Justiciary, 6th Nov. 1682; *d* about 1697; *m.* 9th Sept. 1673, Janet Fletcher.

1782.   ,,   of Whitburn Apprentice to Andrew Stuart; W S 5th July 1782. Only s of the Rev. Thomas G, minister of Speymouth; *d.* 6th March 1845; *m.* 6th April 1785, Letitia, dau. of Hugh M'Veagh, manufacturer in Huntly

1840.   ,,   Apprentice to James Macallan; W.S. 12th Nov. 1840. Fourth s. of William G. of Campbelton, Kirkcudbright; *b.* 14th Feb. 1817, *d.* 9th Oct. 1876, *m.* 6th July 1847, Eliza Cecilia, 3rd dau. of George Shaw Brooke, Jaffna, Ceylon.

1868.   ,,   **Jarron.** Apprentice to James Hope and Robert Mackay; W.S. 22d July 1868. S. of James G., merchant in Forfar; *b.* 15th Oct. 1837; *m.* 22d Aug. 1871, Caroline Elizabeth, only dau. of Henry Churton of West Mount, Cheshire.

1664. **William.** Apprentice to John Bayne, W.S. 14th Nov. 1664, *d.* March 1680; *m.* 25th Jan 1666, Helen Anderson.

1742   ,,   of Greenlaw and Culvennan Apprentice to Thomas Goldie, W.S. 25th Jan. 1742 Only s. of Sir Alexander G. G. of Earlstoun, bart.; *b.* 1706; *d.* Oct. 1757; *m.* 1740, Isabella, dau. of John M'Culloch of Barholm and Jean Gordon of Culvennan, his wife.

1742.   ,,   Apprentice to (1) Hugh Somerville, and (2) Archibald Stuart, W.S. 5th July 1742. S of Dr John G. of Hilton, physician in Aberdeen; *d.* 1788 Latterly a solicitor in London.

1789.   ,,   of Rothney. Apprentice to Samuel Mitchelson; W.S. 9th July 1789. Only s. of George G. of Rothney, Aberdeenshire; *d.* 10th Feb 1824.

1824.   ,,   of Culvennan. Apprentice to Alexander Blair; W.S. 12th Feb. 1824. Eldest s. of David G, captain in the Dumfriesshire militia; *b.* 17th Aug. 1800, *d.* 27th Jan. 1858; *m.* 17th Aug. 1825, Agnes Marian, 3rd dau. of John Hyslop, London.

1882.   ,,   **John.** Apprentice to Robert Strathern; W.S. 27th Oct. 1882. S. of John G., merchant in Dundee; *b.* 2d Dec 1857.